Bibliography

Jefferson Davis (1808-1889)
President of the Confederate States
in the American Civil War was
Adjutant of the 1st U.S. Dragoons
in 1833-34. Serving with Kearney.
Robert E. Lee. General in the
Confederate States Army was Colonel
of the same Regiment in 1861.
J. E. B. Stuart the great cavalry
leader of the American Civil
War, also of the Confederate Army
joined the 1st U.S. Dragoons in
1854 -

PERSONAL AND MILITARY HISTORY

OF Philip Kearny.

BY

J. WATTS DE PEYSTER.

PERSONAL

AND

MILITARY HISTORY

OF

PHILIP KEARNY,

1st U.S. Dragoons

MAJOR-GENERAL UNITED STATES VOLUNTEERS.

March 4th 1837.

"*Dulce et decorum est pro patriâ mori.*"

KEARNY BADGE MOTTO.

"THE BRAVEST MAN I EVER KNEW AND THE MOST PERFECT SOLDIER."

LIEUTENANT-GENERAL WINFIELD SCOTT.

„Ein Mann voll stiller Größe,"

Schmalz's Denkwürdigkeiten des Grafen Wilhelms zu Schaumburg-Lippe.

BY JOHN WATTS DE PEYSTER,

NEW YORK:
RICE AND GAGE, PUBLISHERS.
BLISS & CO., NEWARK, N. J.
1869.

WEED, PARSONS AND COMPANY,
PRINTERS AND STEREOTYPERS.
ALBANY, NEW YORK.

TO THE

VOLUNTEER ARMY OF THE UNITED STATES,

AS

INDIVIDUALS AND AS A WHOLE,

THE NOBLEST EXAMPLE

OF

PATRIOTISM

PRESENTED IN ANCIENT OR MODERN HISTORY,

WHOSE MORAL COURAGE AND INTELLIGENT DISCIPLINE,

WHOSE DEVOTION, PATIENCE AND PERSEVERANCE

CONQUERED AND CRUSHED THE GREATEST REBELLION

EVER RECORDED IN HISTORY,

OR EVER UNDERTAKEN

AGAINST THE

RIGHTS OF A PEOPLE AND HUMANITY;

TO

OUR VOLUNTEER SOLDIERS AND SOLDIER-CITIZENS,

WHO OVERCAME, NOT ONLY

THE ENEMY IN ARMS IN THE FIELD,

BUT

FOES AS DANGEROUS, BECAUSE INSIDIOUS AT HOME.

THIS BIOGRAPHICAL SKETCH OF A

VOLUNTEER GENERAL,

A

GLORIOUS TYPE OF THE AMERICAN SOLDIER,

IS DEDICATED

WITH THE

RESPECT, ADMIRATION AND GRATITUDE

DUE

FOR HIS COUNTRY SAVED AND ITS CONSTITUTION PRESERVED,

BY THE

AUTHOR.

CONTENTS.

Preface .... v to vii
Introductory Remarks .... ix to xii

CHAPTER I. .... 13 to 26

A glorious Retrospect; Origin of the KEARNY Family; Their Relations and Connections in this Country, and their Military Affiliations.

CHAPTER II. .... 27 to 35

The KEARNY and WATTS Families and their Connections; their Civil and Military services.

CHAPTER III. .... 36 to 46

The Springtide of Youth; Childhood, boyhood, youth and education of PHILIP KEARNY. The child Father to the Man.

CHAPTER IV. .... 47 to 51

In the Saddle at last—Lieutenant PHILIP KEARNY's first military service at the Far West in 1837—1839, with Notices of the frontier Settlements about that period.

CHAPTER V. .... 53 to 92

A representative American—Lieutenant KEARNY at the French Military School of Saumur. The Feast of Kings; Twelfth Night Festivities—A Ball given by an American Officer in France worthy of commemoration.

CHAPTER VI. .... 63 to 74

El Tell and El Sersous; France in Africa—A description of the theatre of hostilities between the French and Natives in Algiers; its climate, physical appearance, and a consideration of the principal historical events which preceded Lieutenant KEARNY's service in that region.

CHAPTER VII. .... 75 to 86

Through El Bibau—The passage of the Atlas Mountains, through the Gates of Iron, by Marshal VALÉE and the Duke of Orleans, one of the most remarkable military excursions on record.

CHAPTER VIII. .... 87 to 110

Over the Mousaia to Medeah and Milianah—The African Battle above the Clouds; Campaign of 1839, and Campaign of 1840; Lieutenant PHILIP KEARNY's "Baptism of Fire" on the Plains of Metidjah and of the Cheliff, at the Siege of Milianah and Passage of the Mousaia.

CHAPTER IX. .... 111 to 122

From the Mississippi to the Rocky Mountains—The Expedition of 1845, from Fort Leavenworth, along the "Oregon Trace," to the South Pass, thence to Bent's Fort, and homewards along the "Santa Fe Trace" to the starting place; with beautiful notices of remarkable natural objects from the Correspondence of a distinguished Army Officer.

CHAPTER X.............................. 123 to 135

The Mexican War — Captain PHILIP KEARNY in Mexico and his famous company, mounted on Iron Greys; his service along the Rio Grande in 1846; selection of his company as the body-guard of Major-General SCOTT at Vera-Cruz; the Dinner at Puebla; " An arm for a brevet;" the pursuit to Rio Frio; the first Americans in arms on the Rim of the Basin of Mexico; the Crossing of the Pedregal.

CHAPTER XI.............................. 136 to 151

he Gurita San Antonio: Charge of the One Hundred — The battle of Churubusco; KEARNY's famous charge of two miles with 100 American dragoons, through 5,000 Mexican Infantry and Cavalry — Captain PHILIP KEARNY the first man, sword in hand, to enter Mexico — one of the most audacious feats recorded in military history, which " has no parallel in modern warfare."

CHAPTER XII.............................. 152 to 153

Home, sweet home — Sword presentation to Brevet-Major PHILIP KEARNY.

CHAPTER XIII.............................. 154 to 157

The Golden Gate and Victory of the Rogue River — One of the most brilliant feats of Indian fighting performed by our old Army.

CHAPTER XIV.............................. 158 to 166

KEARNY a Wanderer: "Round the world" — "KEARNY, in Paris, rendered important service to the Loyal North, in 1859—'60."

CHAPTER XV.............................. 167 to 183

The Italian Campaign of 1859; KEARNY, a Volunteer at Solferino; decorated with the Cross of the Legion of Honor.

CHAPTER XVI.............................. 184 to 200

"The Type Volunteer General of the War:" KEARNY's return to America in search of a military command; Bull Run; a Sufficiency of Parallels from European History.

CHAPTER XVII.............................. 201 to 218

A Model Brigadier and Pattern Brigade Commander, PHILIP KEARNY, " the 12th Brigadier U. S. V., on the Original List of Generals of that Rank," at work, making his famous 1st New Jersey Brigade; KEARNY's Views in regard to carrying on War.

CHAPTER XVIII.............................. 219 to 227

Plans and Correspondence; KEARNY foretells the Greatness of GRANT.

CHAPTER XIX.............................. 228 to 251

The Second Advance to Manasses, occupation of the Rebel camps and works; HIDDEN's glorious charge and death; KEARNY's brilliant initiative of active operations; Reports with Lists of those who distinguished themselves.

CHAPTER XX.............................. 252 to 256

Irritants and Assuasives; Poison and Antidote; KEARNY thanked by the New Jersey Legislature.

CHAPTER XXI.............................. 257 to 262

From Alexandria through Yorktown to Williamsburg; KEARNY in command of the 3d (afterwards 1st) Division, 3d Corps, Army of the Potomac, Composition of KEARNY's Fighting Division.

CHAPTER XXII.. . . . . 263 to 298

The Battle of Williamsburg, Monday, May 5, 1862; "KEARNY, the last to leave Yorktown, the first up to save HOOKER;" KEARNY's first magnificent appearance on the battle field; Repulse converted into victory; His glorious aspect and influence in a fight; Anecdotes, Incidents, Correspondence and Reports.

CHAPTER XXIII .... 299 to 307

EXEMPLI GRATIA, Exemplary Volunteer Generals.

CHAPTER XXIV .... 308 to 329

The Peninsula Campaign No. 1; Seven Pines and Fair Oaks; KEARNY a prophet as well as a General and a Soldier; Letters, Anecdotes, Incidents, and Reports.

CHAPTER XXV .... 330 to 359

Peninsula Campaign No. 2; Fair Oaks to Oak Grove to Malvern Hill; The Seven Days' Battles: Oak Grove, Mechanicsville, Gaines' Mills, Savage Station, White Oak Swamp, Glendale, Malvern Hill; Correspondence, Parallels, Remarkable Occurrences and Reports.

CHAPTER XXVI .... 360 to 371

Companion and Supplementary, a partial review of the Peninsula Operations on the Left: Popular proneness to exaggeration; KEARNY's practical foresight and ability; The KEARNY Patch, Diamond and Cross, and Badge or Medal.

CHAPTER XXVII..... .... 372 to 385

Harrison's Landing, Chafing on the Bit—Interesting Correspondence and Revelations of the Truth.

CHAPTER XXVIII........................ 386 to 403

Pope and the "Army of Virginia;" From the Rapidan to Warrenton; KEARNY again in the field; KEARNY's division the first, of the Army of the Potomac, up, in line, for the relief of Pope; Pope vindicated.

CHAPTER XXIX .... 404 to 406

Pope and the "Army of Virginia;" Something on the ever ready, fighting, 3d Corps; KEARNY's final Correspondence and last Report; KEARNY's little Bugler.

CHAPTER XXX .... 407 to 433

Chantilly—A striking example of a second-class decisive battle; STONEWALL JACKSON defeated; The Army of Virginia saved; Redeeming Victory of the Union Troops, and startling Death of KEARNY.

CHAPTER XXXI .... 434 to 481

Death and Burial of "the bravest man I (SCOTT) ever knew, and the most perfect soldier;" Charming Reminiscences from KEARNY's Comrades in arms.

CHAPTER XXXII .... 482 to 512

The Epilogue—A summing up of the characteristics of Major-General PHILIP KEARNY, with interesting anecdotes throughout his career.

PREFACE.

"That elegant force in history, which characterized TACITUS and PLUTARCH, seems to have disappeared in our time; certainly in biographies. * * * When I compare the present Sketch with the Ideal which I had conceived, it is with actual timidity that I venture to publish it. A perfect biography I cannot indeed prepare, since the Count (SCHAUMBURG-LIPPE) carefully kept secret the majority of his greatest deeds. * * * It was my simple intention to portray even his character as a commander and a ruler (organizer) from the stand-point of his magnanimity, and establish every trait of this picture with anecdotes. Yet even such a sketch, at least with my powers, can be nothing more than a fragment. Perhaps I may claim that no one at a previous time could have produced comparatively as complete a history of the Count's career as this one. Lest any one should find fault, or occasion for it should appear, I did not embody much information which I actually possessed. I do not urge this as a satisfactory excuse for the faults of my work, but simply as a reason why they merit pardon, and on that account I pray the indulgence of the public."

THEODOR SCHMALZ'S "*Denkwürdigkeiten des Grafen.*
WILHELMS *zu* SCHAUMBURG-LIPPE." 1783.

THE preparation of this Biography, or rather Biographical Sketch of the Military Career of Major-General PHILIP KEARNY has been looked forward to for six years, not only as a sincere pleasure, but as a solemn duty. Almost all the notices of this distinguished General, which have appeared in the different papers and periodicals, were little more than the amplifications of the sketch of him prepared by the writer for the New York *Times* in 1861. This sketch grew into one more worthy of the subject in the columns of the New York *Citizen* of January 25th, 1867, and February 1st and 8th, 1868. On the 17th of January, 1868, CORTLANDT PARKER, Esq., counsel, and intimate friend of the deceased General, delivered an Address before the New Jersey Historical Society. This noble tribute of friendship was afterwards furnished to the editors of the *Northern Monthly Magazine*, and appeared in the three numbers of that periodical for November and December, 1867, and February, 1868. It was subsequently published, by request, as a pamphlet of forty-nine pages. Mr. PARKER had free access to all the papers in the possession of the immediate family of the General, and the results of his labors are equally interesting as a charming composition and as a valuable contribution to history. To it the writer of the present work is indebted for much connected with the last year of the hero's life, especially extracts from letters, etc. Otherwise the facts herein presented are altogether new, and the views of General KEARNY are derived from personal and confidential intercourse from boyhood to middle-age.

The writer hesitated for a long time before resuming the pen, feeling that nothing could be done which deserved the name of a biography until certain letters, documents, and books could be obtained and examined. Manuscripts, etc., etc., are known to have existed which have eluded the anxious search of the historian. The kindness of friends, and an examination of correspondence, has filled some of the minor gaps, but others still exist, one of which is General KEARNY's Algerian experience, as glorious to himself as interesting to the public. On his return to the United States he wrote an account of his African campaign, which was "privately printed." Not a copy of this, however, is to be found, although diligent search has been made in every quarter, where an exemplar ought to have been preserved. Most of his correspondence was, doubtless, among the papers of an aged relative, his mother's sister, one of the most loyal, noble, and generous of women, deceased in June, 1866. This was either committed to the flames by her, or burned after her decease as a sacred trust not to be violated when the grave had closed over both, the one who wrote as a son to a mother, and the other to whom the confidential letters were addressed. A valuable letter, which was in hand last fall, has likewise disappeared, whether destroyed or stolen for the autograph, since it possessed a signature in full, a very rare thing with KEARNY's letters, who generally signed "PHIL," or "K."

The author of these pages was the only cousin of General KEARNY, on his mother's side, brought up with him in the house of their maternal grandfather, Hon. JOHN WATTS. This excellent man, General KEARNY's grandfather, was ennobled by his benevolence. His best memorial is a grand charitable institution which he endowed in the city of New York. Mr. WATTS was a monument of affliction, in that he had seen his wife, six handsome, gifted, and gallant sons, and four daughters precede him to the grave. One childless daughter survived him and three grandchildren, General KEARNY, his sister, Mrs. MACOMB, who died in Europe 30th April, 1852, and the writer.

Peculiar associations intensified the ties which united the survivors, sole representatives of a race which had occupied so prominent a position in the annals of their native State for nearly a century "in troublous, times." In youth the pursuits of General KEARNY and the writer of these pages were identical, and it was to the house of the latter that the former returned from time to time to talk over the strange adventures experienced in a remarkably checkered career. Together in 1834 they visited Europe, and the majority of the opinions expressed herein are founded on personal recollections. If affection, admiration, studies, in common, interchange of thoughts, intercourse without reserve, and a memory remarkable for its tenacity can enable any one to produce a reliable biography, the following may be considered authentic. As a patriot, as a public officer, and as a soldier, PHILIP KEARNY was a grand example, worthy of study, imitation, and commemoration. As an officer in the service of our country, his glory belongs, particularly, to his native State, from which he was appointed to the United States Army. As a General, unsurpassed, wherever and whenever he was tried for courage, fidelity, self-sacrificing, energy, and ability, his glory is equally the property of the whole country. As West Point had nothing to do with his achievements, as he owed nothing to its training, to its cast influence, to its academic line of thought, or to its terrible prejudices, he may be considered a magnificent type of a Volunteer soldier, for from private life was he appointed to his first commission; from private life it might be said he again sprang into the saddle in 1846—since he recalled his resignation to partake in the glories of the Mexican war—and from private life abroad he returned home to reassume his uniform and assist in saving his country. As a Volunteer, he participated in the dangers and fatigues of a campaign in Africa which carried the tricolor through the "Gates of Iron" and over the Atlas into the strongholds of Abd-el-Kader. He partook in the operations of that campaign which laid the basis of the present Kingdom of Italy, and a Major-General of American volunteers, he died on the field of battle. Therefore to the Volunteer Armies of the United States, and more particularly to the officers and soldiers of his immediate commands—especially that nonpareil New Jersey Brigade which he created, and that glorious First Division of the Third Corps of the Army of the Potomac at whose head he fell—are these pages dedicated, with the deepest and warmest gratitude of the author.

INTRODUCTORY REMARKS.

"Truth is to History what Eyes are to animals; if their eyes are torn out, they become useless. Just so deprive History of Truth, and it is no longer of any value or utility."—POLYBIUS.

"STA VIATOR, HEROEM CALCAS!"

Field-Marshal MERCY's epitaph on the battle-field of Nordlingen, where he fell, 1645.

A WONDERFUL epoch has closed. This generation stands like spectators around the upheaved ruins—not yet settled—of an unparalleled moral as well as physical earthquake. Even as at the period of the great French Revolution of 1789 (1793), humanity has made one of its gigantic strides, in advance, which compensate for the inaction of ages. Not that human progress ever stands still, but at times it almost seems to do so, groping its way along like one still half asleep, or like one just awakened from a lethargic or drugged slumber. Happy he who has enjoyed the advantages of occupying a stand-point whence to observe, with a philosophic view, the phases and the marvels of the convulsions; more fortunate he who has associated with the heroes, the martyrs, or the victims of the catastrophe, and has the ability and leisure to collect and prepare for grander histories the details of the tempest he has witnessed, and the words, the gestures, the deeds of those who towered, like peaks irradiated with the sun of glory, amid the colliding storm-clouds, freighted with thunder and devastation.

In a retired quarter of the metropolis of the "Babylonish Captivity of the Papacy" stood an old building, once the convent of St. Marcel, since the first Empire transmuted into a "Succursale" of the "Grand Hotel" at Paris, devoted to the reception of the invalids of that army which had borne the tricolor, the emblem of popular triumph, through conquered capitals, east and south, to the remotest bounds of civilization. In its cool garden and along its corridors had grouped and walked, fighting their battles over again in interchange of recollections, heroes who had marched and combatted over the fiery sands of Egypt, the classic soil of Italy, the castle-crowned mountains of Germany, the dreary bogs reclaimed by Teutonic feudalism, the rugged ranges of the Iberian sierras, and the snowy steppes of Russia. Around this garden, shutting them in from the industry of social life, whose blessings and comforts they had renounced for the fascinating career of arms, rose high walls, which formerly closed in the members of the church militant, the monkdom of the cloister, scarcely greater strangers than the monkdom of the flag to the busy and comparatively happier world of every-day life. But unlike the dispossessed friars, the vision of these invalids was not bounded by bare walls, suggestive of no thoughts save those connected with the dull monotony of monastic life. Thickly strung together, like a zone of jewels, from the rich mine of the military annals of France, close side by side, a series of MURAL TABLETS extended around the garden, devoted to the immortalization of glorious deeds and of heroic souls, that recalled the triumphs in which the veterans had participated—triumphs whose narration had made their watch-fires the centres of epopees as grand as the strophes of Ossian. What a glorious seclusion, redolent with the perfume of patriotic devotion, brilliant with the lustre of military achievements, musical with the eulogies of the heroic dead!

What a contrast to these tablets, those tablets set in the walls of the old ducal palace which commemorate the ARNOLDS, the DAVISES, the STEPHENSES of that Republic which once contested the empire of the Mediterranean with the twin sister of the Adriatic, and left memorials of its commercial daring in lands which are scarcely now accessible to European enterprise.

Yet both these classes of monuments should be preserved with equal care, for they establish the truths of History, and maintain them against the flattery of sycophants, the changes of political opinion, or the venial pens of prejudiced or political writers, changing, as one we have seen, with the hour and with personal interest.

This little book seeks to erect a memorial to one of the most striking figures in the great AMERICAN CONFLICT to crush the "SLAVEHOLDERS' REBELLION." Its pages present a sketch of the career of one of the men most prominent for their ability, their influence, their prowess, and their genius for war.

The student of American History, in his quiet library, surrounded by such works, whether rude or polished in their language, still careful in their presentation of truths, is like the visitor in the garden of the "Succursale" (at Avignon), of the "Hotel des Invalides" at Paris. He can abandon himself to the reflections engendered by the stories of the Rebellion, and as he turns from shelf to shelf, and saunters through the historic pages, the eyes of his mind can contemplate COMMEMORATIVE TABLETS, set up on the walls of his imagination, some, like those of KEARNY and of LYON, presenting examples of patriotism and self-sacrifice; others, such as those of LEE and DAVIS, recalling evil men, prominent in the leadership of treason and of sin, but none the less remarkable or worthy of consideration as beacons on that reef of crime on which a confiding section went to wreck and ruin.

Contemplating and reflecting, before him will pass a panoramic series of the actions of the Rebellion. Each Biographical Sketch will serve as a portrait in the gallery of word-pictures, and ever and anon a prominent figure will start into life, if the pen of the biographer is equal in its power to the part played by his hero in the magnificent procession of the war pageant.

To future students of history such biographies, however imperfectly written or faulty in their style, will prove of incalculable interest; to future writers of history, of inestimable value. To every one who contemplates, like a philosopher, the changes which our national organization underwent in five years (1860–'65), every work connected with the cataclysm will be of value, as a record and a memento of what human will, single or combined, erring but energetic, can accomplish to injure or to preserve; while the general story and its results will serve and operate as a warning against the misdirection of human efforts in the future to deface or destroy a national structure, faulty in some of its details, but sublime in its general conception; an edifice purified from the stains of slavery, and renovated through the patriotism of the loyal men of all sections, destined to stand, with open doors, a refuge and an asylum to the oppressed and suffering throughout the world.

The history of the "SLAVEHOLDERS' REBELLION" is the record of a treason without a parallel in its criminality: a treason against God's best gifts, against Free thought, Free action, a Free land—

a treason against the PEOPLE—whose voice, when it utters its will with determination, but *without violence*, is the voice of God. Those who, like KEARNY, led the van for the PEOPLE; who, without ambitious purposes, laid down their lives for the People; who bore the burden and heat of the day, and "paid the last full measure of devotion" that their country might live; soldiers, patriots, martyrs—such indeed were champions of Liberty. One of the grandest of these was KEARNY, and this book is a MEMORIAL of him. He deserves the best monument of which the pen, pencil, or chisel is susceptible. But the hero will not despise any memento, however humble, which is the result of the best efforts of the author and a tribute of his affection.

MAJOR-GENERAL PHILIP KEARNY, U. S. V.

From the original grand equestrian portrait in the possession of the Author. Indorsed as the best likeness by the General's family.

PERSONAL AND MILITARY HISTORY

OF

MAJOR-GENERAL PHILIP KEARNY.

CHAPTER I.

A GLORIOUS RETROSPECT.

"Through the shadowy past,
Like a tomb-searcher, memory ran,
Lifting each shroud." MOORE.

"The hand of the reaper
Takes the years that are hoary,
But the voice of the weeper
Wails manhood in glory."

"This chivalric figure looks as though it had just leaped from the centre of a medieval battle-piece."

Though living in these modern and prosaic days, his bearing is essentially romantic; he looks the knight-errant. Such a rider on such a steed takes the mind back to the days when the badge of nobility was skill with the sword and grace in horsemanship; when to be a gentleman was to follow the profession of arms; when the joust and the tournament assembled all the beauty and all the valor of feudal monarchies; when

"Nine and twenty knights of fame
Hung their shields in Branksome Hall,
And quitted not their harness bright,
Neither by day, nor yet by night;
But carved at the meal
With gloves of steel,
And drank the red wine through the helmet barred."

These words are full of truth, suggestive.

There is scarcely an individual endowed with the power of observation, who, while examining a collection of modern or recent portraits, has not been struck with the peculiar face and bearing of some one or other of the individuals presented, who, notwithstanding the costumes and accessories, seems out of place among the pictures of cotemporaries. Certain striking peculiarities of feature or expression, suggest the idea that a mistake has occurred; that the likeness of one distinguished in the days of chivalry has fallen into the hands of a Vandal, to whose purse or whim the painter has sacrificed his art, as well as the truth, and concealed the armor, dinted by cimeter or falchion, beneath the stiff and ungraceful costume of this century. No one who has has ever studied the lineaments and expression of PHILIP KEARNY, his carriage, his bearing on foot or seat in the saddle, but must appreciate this, and acknowledge in their hearts that his soldierly face and knightly person would look more appropriate under the morion and the mail of FRA MOREALE, of DU GUESCLIN, or of BAYARD, or in the plumed hat lined with steel, and polished breastplate of a RUPERT, a MONTROSE, or a DUNDEE; nor deem him in the saddle unworthy of Sir RICHARD VERNON's glowing description of that "Imp of Fame," who, on the field of Agincourt, so glorious to his manhood, declared:

"And be it death proclaimed throughout our host
To boast of this, or take that praise from God
Which is His only"——

Thus spake Sir RICHARD:

"I saw young Harry—with his beaver on,
His cuisses on his thighs, gallantly arm'd,—
Rise from the ground like feathered Mercury,
And vaulted with such ease into his seat
As if an angel dropp'd down from the clouds,
To turn and wind a fiery Pegasus,
And witch the world with noble horsemanship."

Wandering through the galleries of Europe, the writer has more than once been startled at recognizing in a grand equestrian picture, or an exquisite military portrait, something which recalled a friend or relative distinguished for those qualities which indicate the natural soldier. Any one who was intimately acquainted with Major-General PHILIP KEARNY, and the race from which he sprang, or with which he was connected, can understand this feeling.

In the Palazzo Spinola, in Genoa, there is a magnificent painting by VAN DYKE, hung on hinges, which, when swung out from the wall in order to present its beauties in the most advantageous light, both horse and rider, nearly natural size, seem to stand out from the canvass and become instinct with life. It is one of those incomparable equestrian portraits, regarded as almost priceless gems of art, in which the rival of RUBENS and of TITIAN peculiarly excelled. Such a portrait, in fact, to one who knew him well, would at once recall General KEARNY. In him, mounted on his favorite gray charger, Moscow, the great painter would have welcomed a subject worthy of his genius, and have handed him down to posterity in all the brilliancy of his design and coloring; and fiction would have seized upon him as its hero, and have commemorated his career in verse like the "Max Piccolomini" of SCHILLER, or in romance like the Claverhouse of "Old Mortality."

This is no over-drawn picture. On some public occasion, at a ball in the Grand-Ducal (Pitti) Palace, in Florence, KEARNY appeared as a Knight Templar, clothed from head to foot in chain armor. To dance gracefully—and gracefully he did dance—under such a weight of steel, proved what immense physical power he possessed. The writer has a sleeve of chain mail, taken from one of the catacombs of Egypt, which belonged to a Crusader. Each link is rivetted separately, and the whole suit was worth a prince's ransom. This sleeve weighs four and a half pounds. The whole tunic must have weighed over eighteen pounds; the entire suit over four times that number. Under this weight KEARNY waltzed as lightly as if clad in silk, and wore it so aptly that the illusion was perfect. To the company it seemed as if one of those haughty chevaliers had risen from his tomb to grace the festival, or as if one of their effigies had started into life.

Again, at a fancy ball—unequalled ever in the city of New York—given by Commodore JOHN C. STEVENS, KEARNY was conspicuous as a Kabyle chieftain, in a perfect costume, which he had probably captured in Algiers. So correct was it in every detail, that from his belt swung a severed head imitated to the life, or rather death, in sugar, but nevertheless so corpse-like that he was compelled to lay it aside from the horror it excited. On this occasion likewise, had one of Abd-el-Kader's kalifas or beys appeared in the ball-room, he could not have looked and played his part with greater grace and tact than did the American Volunteer, who may have crossed steel with the original under the shadow of the Atlas.

"Though an American by birth, and intensely American in his sympathies, General PHILIP KEARNY carried in his veins blood that distinguishes the leading nations of Europe.

"On his father's side he was Irish, and thence he derived his impulsive, roving, danger-courting blood, the temper that never stops to count odds nor calculate chances.

"On his mother's side there were two diverse elements not often combined in one person—the strong native sense, and the shrewd common sense of the canny Scot, and the fiery nature, the love of pomp, splendor and beauty, the ardent soul and the chivalric bearing of the Gaul."

Close investigation, however, would lead to the conviction that the KEARNYS are Scotch-Irish, for the name is certainly Gælic. The cousin and executor of our hero has a family tree, showing all the marriages as far back as 1506, and traces back the family long anterior to that date, to two brothers who first settled in Ireland. The name was originally O'CLEARMAN, which, he says, meant "soldier." KEARNY, in its original spelling, CEARNACH, in Gælic or Celtic, does signify "soldier."* The name must have been derived from some deed of note in war, for all private names are in one sense derivatives. KEARNY was thus not only a soldier by name but by nature, and a true inheritor not only of the designation but of the spirit of his race.

It is seldom that a man born to command, and imbued with all the peculiar characteristics of a military leader—that is, one who would be selected from the crowd as a soldier-born—who has not sprung from a race of soldiers, or been brought up amid military associations, or who has not in his veins the blood of those races which instinctively produce soldiers, for such races do undeniably exist. Prominent among them is the Celtic race, which has been tempered by the Frank (pure Saxon), or Gothic blood in France, and by the Gothic in Spain.

This is peculiarly the case with the French Huguenots, whose strongholds and recruiting grounds were in those parts of France which were originally the seats of Norman, Burgundian, or Visogothic power. From the former stock came the DE LANCEYS. If any family of this State ever shone in arms, in times which tried men's souls, and proved their loyalty in every way it was possible to do so, it was these same DE LANCEYS, who, either through its own scions or connections, saw almost every male in the field from Brigadier-General down to Cornet; a family, whose descendant

* "KEARNS is a term signifying soldiers in Irish History. As for the term O'CLEARMAN KEARNY, the inquisitive reader is referred to Dr. KEATING'S History of Ireland, where the genealogy of the O'KEARNYS is to be found." In Gælic "CLIAR" means "*gallant*" or "*brave*," and "MAN," "*hand.*" Consequently KEARNY O'CLIAR-MAN doubtless signified "the soldier of, or with, the brave hand." "CEARNACH" is likewise translated "*victorious.*"

died upon the field of Waterloo, Colonel and Quartermaster-General on WELLINGTON'S staff, evincing with his dying breath an unselfish solicitude for the life of his commander, more precious to his country and the world than his own, dying a death which was worthy of the purest days of chivalry—that is, of that chivalry which romance has invested with such a glorious halo, and which did actually exist in certain individuals, of whom, perhaps, the most genuine, or rather the best known examples, were BAYARD and MONTROSE.

PHILIP KEARNY was indeed a Huguenot*—not a Puritan. Glory was the breath of his nostrils.

Although no one will deny that the Irish blood has fight enough in it, it is very questionable if the WATTS' blood and all its affiliations and connections—among these the KEARNYS—did not get the greater part of their military instincts, their *war-motor* power, from the DE LANCEYS. The spirit of these latter was the yeast to make everything tending to soldiership ferment in the different families into which it was infused. This DE LANCEY blood was a grand one. From the moment the first of the name arrived in New York it made itself felt. As statesmen, as they would justly be termed in the Old World, or as politicians in this country—before the term "politician" implied something derogatory—or as soldiers, they exerted the most astonishing influence in the Province or Colony of New York. No one who has examined into its records will pretend to deny this. Exiled for opinion's sake, the English government acknowledged their worth by giving them high employment, which their services, their zeal, courage and fidelity, even to the death, proved that they deserved.

---

* "There was a great difference, however, to be remarked between them (the Huguenot soldier) and the religious insurgents of more northern countries; for though both the sterner fanaticism which characterized Scotland and England not long before, and the wilder imaginations and fanciful enthusiasms of the far south, were occasionally to be found in individuals, the great mass were entirely and decidedly French, possessing the character of light and somewhat thoughtless gayety, so peculiar to that indifferent and laughter-loving nation.

"Thus, though they had prayed earnestly, after having fought with determination in the cause which to them was the cause of conscience, they were now quite ready to forget both prayer and strife, till some other cause should reproduce the enthusiasm which gave vigor to either.

"They sat in groups, then, round fires of an old apple-tree or two which they had pulled down, and drank the wine, procured, it must be acknowledged, by various different means; but though they sang not, as perhaps they might have done under other circumstances, nothing else distinguished them from any other party of gay French Soldiers carousing after a laborious day."—JAMES' "HUGUENOT."

John Watts, the second of that name—for his father, by the addition of an "s," changed his name Watt to Watts; while his mother's family simultaneously by dropping an "s" from Nicolls became Nicoll—was the first of the family born in this country. By position, property, marriage, and ability, he became one of the most influential citizens of his native city and of the colony previous to the Revolution, and occupied a place in the first rank of the provincial leaders. He was a prominent member of the General Colonial Assembly, Chairman of several of the most important Committees, Member of the King's Council from 1756 until 1782, when the connections between the Thirteen Colonies and the mother country was dissolved. Had the party with which he linked his fortunes been successful, he was destined to fill the gubernatorial chair, which had been occupied by his brother-in-law, the eminent James de Lancey, and by the no less extraordinary Cadwallader Colden (grandfather of the wife of his son, John Watts, Junior), one of the "celebrities" of this State, especially notable as a physician, philosopher, inventor, historian, and magistrate.

Although a consistent Loyalist—for which he suffered the confiscation of his property and died in exile in Wales—he distinguished himself while in office by upholding the popular rights, and when neither Governor, Lieutenant-Governor, nor any other Member of the Council dared, or would do so, he withstood the arbitrary demands of the Earl of Loudon, in regard to billeting troops upon the citizens of New York, and "spoke his mind in favor of the people." He was one of the original Founders and Trustees, in 1754, of the New York Society Library; in 1760 he presented its first clock to the public Exchange of his native city; and in 1770 he became the first President of the New York City Hospital.

He was a coadjutor in all the political triumphs of his brother-in-law, Lieutenant-Governor James de Lancey, "an ornament to his country," one of the most remarkable men the State has ever produced, "whose biography is the history of our Colony, from the period he reached man's estate to the day of his death." Throughout his long career, John Watts afforded him the cordial and active support of his energy and influence, and when a sudden death deprived the Colony of de Lancey's capacity for government, he continued for thirteen years to act in accordance with his principles and carry out his sagacious views.

Hon. JOHN WATTS, Senior, married ANNE, the second daughter of STEPHEN DE LANCEY, who immigrated to New York in 1686. They were the grandparents of Brevet Major-General STEPHEN WATTS KEARNY, U. S. Army, and great-grandparents of Major-General PHILIP KEARNY, U. S. Volunteers.

ROBERT WATTS, the eldest son of the preceding, married LADY MARY, daughter of WILLIAM ALEXANDER, Earl of Sterling, Major-General in our Revolutionary Army. Their daughter, again, married her cousin-german, JOHN WATTS KEARNY. The son of this latter, PHILIP JOHN KEARNY, born and bred in the State of New York, was mortally wounded at Gettysburg, Major of the 11th New Jersey Volunteers, having proved himself a brave and able officer. His commission of Lieutenant-Colonel had been made out and was ready for the signature of the Governor of New Jersey, to be issued to him in case he survived. Unhappily, he could not rally from the amputation of his leg, and died in New York city, aged twenty-one years, 9th August, 1863. His career proved that he was a worthy scion of that race and name which had already given two Major-Generals to their country.

STEPHEN, the second son of the JOHN WATTS, first named, was a brilliant officer in the Anglo-American Army. Already at the age of twenty-two he was the Major of the intrepid batallion of Loyalists, known as the "Royal New Yorkers," or "Johnson Greens," raised by his brother-in-law, Sir JOHN JOHNSON, son of the famed Sir WILLIAM JOHNSON, who was knighted and created Major-General for resplendent service, more particularly for his victory over DIESKAU, at the head of Lake George, in 1755. He afterwards captured Fort Niagara in 1759. Sir JOHN JOHNSON by his conscientious loyalty probably hazarded more in the cause of the Crown than any other American. His domains, which were confiscated, were the fairest and most extensive of any colonist, except the estate of Lord FAIRFAX, in Virginia. After the Revolution he held the position of Superintendent General and Inspector General of Indian Affairs in British North America, likewise other high trusts. His wife, MARY WATTS, daughter of the first JOHN WATTS, of the city of New York, was made a prisoner and confined at Albany as a hostage for the good conduct of her husband. She was one of the most remarkable women of her day, as conspicuous for the power of her mind as for those other qualities which most adorn her sex, and to such an extent had she won the affection and respect of her husband's "faithful Mohawks," that they threatened the most terrible reprisals in case that she suffered the least injury. Her daughter, CATHERINE MARIA, married Major-General BOWES, who was killed at the storming of Salamanca. Before the breach was rendered practicable, Lord WELLINGTON determined on an attempt at escalade. "In this unfortunate attack Major-General BOWES and one hundred and twenty men fell. The conduct of this gallant officer had been on all occasion conspicuous. In leading on the storming party he received a wound, which was no sooner dressed than he returned to the post of honor, and died gloriously in the service of his country. The monument of a soldier can bear no prouder epitaph than the record of such facts."

Her eldest son, WILLIAM JOHNSON, was Lieutenant-Colonel of the 28th Regiment of Foot, B. A. Another son, JAMES, fell on the same occasion with his brother-in-law, Major-General BOWES, and gallantly supporting him, by his side.

In 1777, when ST. LEDGER entered the Mohawk Valley to co-operate with BURGOYNE, STEPHEN WATTS commanded the sixty picked marksmen who constituted the British advance-guard, and cleared the way for the invading column. He was second in command at the battle of Oriskany, fought 6th August, 1777, near the mouth of the creek bearing that name, between Rome and Utica, in this State. It is a mooted question, even not yet determined, whether Sir JOHN JOHNSON was General-in-Chief in this action; but if he had been so, and if his conduct had equalled the terrible resoluteness of his young brother-in-law, the result of the conflict would have been still more disastrous to the colonists, who lost their General and half their troops engaged. The two most distinguished officers on the field, Major-General HARKEIMER and Major WATTS, were both shot through the leg. The wound of the former terminated fatally. The latter, left for dead upon the field, recovered from his faintness, crawled to a brook or creek to slake the thirst occasioned by his dangerous wound, and was actually found two or three days afterward with his leg in a shocking condition by some Indian scouts, and conveyed to the British camp. He lost his limb, but long survived the operation and his exile in England.

This battle of Oriskany, celebrated in history and romance, in prose and poetry, was the most bloody, for the numbers engaged, and the most obstinately contested at the North during the Revolution. It was as momentous in its effects as a side issue can be, and with its twin-combat styled, in error, Bennington, on the Walloomscoick, an affluent of the Hudson, *in the State of New York*, decided the fate of BURGOYNE.

ANNE, the eldest daughter of this Major STEPHEN WATTS, married Major JOHNSON, of the British Army, cousin of Lord PALMERSTON, late Premier of England, and his eldest son, JOHN, was a Captain in the same service. This Captain JOHN WATTS was present at the battle of Bladensburg, at the capture of Washington, and at New Orleans. He was also Vice-Governor, or Deputy Warden of Walmer Castle, one of the Cinque Ports, of which the Duke of WELLINGTON was Warden. The "Iron Duke" having died at Walmer Castle, Captain JOHN WATTS had charge of the remains of the "world's conqueror's conqueror," and accompanied the body to its last resting-place, in St. Paul's Cathedral, London. These facts, as well as those similar ones which follow, are interesting to show how the WATTS and DE LANCEY blood had an affinity with the army. Many more curious connections of the family of WATTS could be noted, but for fear of tiring the reader's patience we will return to the consideration of the DE LANCEY line, proper, which, in itself, is almost sufficient to occupy the space which was originally assigned to this branch of the subject.

In France there were two distinct species of nobility, the nobility of the Sword and the nobility of the Robe. The former occupied a much higher rank in society than the latter. The events of the last century have corrected this prejudice, and except in times of a great war, like our civil war, the sword yields to the robe or toga. In Europe it is not even yet so. The DE LANCEYS belonged to the ancient nobility of France. They were hereditary soldiers, and their property "fief was probably holden by the feudal service of the banner or lance, hence their surname DE LANCEY." A cion in this gallant race died as a Mestre de Camp (*i. e.* Colonel, according to the old French title, of a cavalry regiment) of the Life Guards or Household troops of Louis XIV, at the battle of Malplaquet, so glorious to the French army, although compelled to abandon the field to MARLBOROUGH. From this race sprang STEPHEN DE LANCEY, father of ANNE, wife of Hon. JOHN WATTS, Senior, hereinbefore referred to. Her sister married Admiral Sir PETER WARREN, K. B., who commanded the expedition that took Louisburg, the key of the French insular possessions in North

America. Her brother, JAMES DE LANCEY, was a Captain, B. A., and her nephew was JAMES DE LANCEY, Lieutenant-Colonel of the 1st Dragoon Guards, B. A. Her brother, the great-uncle of Major-General STEPHEN WATTS KEARNY, was Brigadier-General OLIVER DE LANCEY, of the British Army, who, from his entrance into military life, was pre-eminent for gallantry. He commanded the New York Colonial troops almost throughout his life. In the French war of 1756 he was a Colonel, and led the New York Provincials in ABERCROMBIE's campaign, and received for his services in this war the thanks of the Colonial Assembly, equivalent to our Legislature.

His daughter, SUSAN, married Lieutenant-General Sir WILLIAM DRAPER, K. B., Knight of the Bath, of the British Army. Another daughter, CHARLOTTE, married Field-Marshal Sir DAVID DUNDAS, K. B., Commander-in-Chief of the British Army. Another daughter, ANNA, married Colonel JOHN HARRIS CRUGER, commandant of his father's-in-law, General DE LANCEY's, 1st Battalion. He was the gallant defender of Fort 96 in South Carolina. No Loyalist officer performed more responsible or arduous duty with greater credit. The General's son and namesake, OLIVER DE LANCEY, Jr., rose to be Lieutenant-General in the British Army. The famous Prime-Minister, PITT, the younger, appointed him Barrack-Master General of the British Empire. Be was also Colonel of the 17th Light Dragoons, a very high honor in England, and in 1796 Member of Parliament. With him ended one branch of this glorious family.

STEPHEN, the youngest son of General DE LANCEY, Senior, commanded the 1st Battalion of New York Volunteers during the Revolution, held that rank in the British Army, and in 1797 was Governor of the British Island of Tobago and its dependencies. The two daughters of the latter married: SUSAN, first, Colonel WILLIAM JOHNSON; second, Lieutenant-General SIR HUDSON LOWE, Knight Commander of the Bath, the Governor of St. Helena during BONAPARTE's captivity there—the faithful servitor of his country, calumniated by prejudiced writers, who would not sift out the truth, so nobly vindicated in WILLIAM FORSYTH's History of the Captivity of NAPOLEON at St. Helena. (New York: Harper Bros., 1863);—CHARLOTTE, Colonel ——— CHILD, British Army. Their brother was Colonel SIR WILLIAM HOWE DE LANCEY, "the excellent Quarter-Master-General," on the staff of WELLINGTON at the battle of Waterloo, in which he was mortally wounded "in the middle of the action." He died the death of a hero. The following is too interesting to be omitted in the life of Major-General PHILIP KEARNY, as it regards a near kinsman whom he greatly resembled in magnanimous characteristics. "The Duke's personal staff, who had shared so many glories and dangers by the side of their commander, fell around him in rapid succession. The Prince of Nassau, one of his aids-de-camp, received two balls. The gallant General DE LANCEY was struck with a spent cannon-ball while animating and leading back to the charge a battalion of Hanoverians who had got into confusion."

Here permit the writer—who is of Hollandish or Dutch descent, and right proud of a race which has produced the best soldiers and sailors on record, from the days of JULIUS CÆSAR and PHARSALIN, through nineteen centuries of unsurpassed patriotism and renown, down to HASSELT and ANTWERP in 1831–2—to make a remark in justice to his people, and put the saddle on the right horse. Prejudiced authors have stated that the Dutch and Belgian troops (then united under one crown, that of Holland) behaved the worst at Waterloo. The exact contrary was the fact. As a general thing they displayed remarkable tenacity. It was some of the German contingents who behaved so badly in this campaign, and none so shamefully as a regiment of Hanoverian cavalry, the "Cumberland Hussars," whose "dastardly conduct" caused them to be subsequently disbanded and their Colonel cashiered. The Dutch, under CHASSEE, "the bayonet General,' who won immortal honor in 1832 for his defence of Antwerp against overwhelming numbers of French and Belgians, faced the music, like the Dutch infantry at Fleurus, 1700, and at Almanza, 1707, and did as well as any English, not only at Quatre-Bras—a fight in its relation to our Gettysburg, equivalent to BUFORD's magnificent stand on Oak Ridge, 1st July, 1863, but in that—

> ———"first and last of fields! king-making victory!"
> ———"Immortal Waterloo!"

But to return to General DE LANCEY "He exclaimed as he fell, 'Leave me to die; my wound is mortal; attend (or look) to the Duke, and do not waste that time on me which may be usefully employed in assisting others.' These orders were too promptly obeyed, and, when on the following morning, the bloody field was traversed, he was found yet living, and to the satisfaction and joy of his friends, hopes—fallacious ones, alas!—were entertained of his recovery. He was removed to the village of Waterloo, and Lady DE LANCEY, who had arrived at Brussels a week before the battle, had the sad consolation to attend her dying husband, who expired six days after the battle—a martyr probably to his generous disinterestedness."

His fate is enshrined in the verse of Sir WALTER SCOTT, ¶ XXI. of his poem, "The Field of Waterloo:"

"Period of honor as of woes,
What bright careers 'twas thine to close!—
Marked on thy roll of blood what names
To Britain's memory, and to Fame's,
Laid there, their last immortal claims!
Thou saw'st in seas of gore expire
Redoubted Picton's soul of fire—
* * * * *
DE LANCEY *change Love's bridal wreath*
For laurels from the hand of death—
* * * * *
Ah! though her guardian angel's shield
Fenced Britain's hero through the field,
Fate not the less her power made known
Through his friend's hearts to pierce his own!"

The second son of STEPHEN DE LANCEY, PETER of the Mills, likewise filled a conspicuous place in the early annals of New York. He married ELIZABETH, daughter of the distinguished Colonial Governor, CADWALLADER COLDEN, and settled upon a large estate known as the "Mills," on the Bronx River, at West Farms, Westchester County, State of New York. He became the ancestor of that branch of the family known as the "Westchester DE LANCEYS." PETER DE LANCEY of the Mills, like all the rest of his Loyal family, suffered through his fidelity to principle.

The following beautiful lines were written by a stranger, an Englishman, who visited the old DE LANCEY Manor, in Westchester County, State of New York, about fourteen miles from the city of New York, expecting to find some memorials of that gallant, courtly, and eminent race still existing. But alas! in the same manner that war, exile, confiscation and death, had smitten and scattered the proud owners, so had flood fire, and improvement (?) laid waste or altered their once ornate possessions. A pine, towering in its native majesty, alone survived to mark the spot where once a flourishing Loyal family exhibited its stately hospitalities or enjoyed the sweets of a home, the abode of prosperity and ability. A contrast so marked, between the past and present, moved even an alien, and in poetic numbers he recorded his sympathy and chronicled the desolation:"

"Where gentle Bronx, clear winding, flows
His shadowing banks between;
Where blossom'd bell and wilding rose
Adorn the brightest green;
Memorial of the fallen great,
The rich and honor'd line,
Stands high in solitary state
De Lancey's ancient pine.

"There, once at early dawn arrayed,
The rural sports to lead,
The gallant master of the glade
Bedeck'd his eager steed;
And once the light-foot maiden came,
In loveliness divine,
To sculpture with the dearest name
De Lancey's ancient pine.

"And now the stranger's foot explores
De Lancey's wide domain,
And scarce one kindred heart restores
His memory to the plain;
And just like one in age alone,
The last of all his line
Bends sadly where the waters moan—
De Lancey's ancient pine.

"Oh greatness! o'er thy final fall,
The feeling heart should mourn,
Nor from De Lancey's ancient Hall
With cold rejoicing turn:
No! no! the gen'rous stranger stays
When eve's calm glories shine,
To weep—as tells of other days
De Lancey's ancient pine."

Peter de Lancey's eldest daughter, Alice, married Ralph Izard, of South Carolina, who shone as a patriot and a statesman in our Revolutionary struggle. Their son, George, (set down as Ralph, Junior, in the family tree) Izard, rose in 1814 to the rank of Major-General in the United States Army, which he entered as Lieutenant of the regiment of Artillerists and Engineers in 1794. This gallant officer experienced the same fate in 1814, which was intended for TAYLOR in 1846–'7, and was experienced by HOOKER before Gettysburgh in 1863. He had just completed all the preparations to which is due the defeat of the British at Plattsburg, in 1814, when he was superseded by MACOMB, just as HOOKER was superseded by MEADE.

PETER'S daughter, SUSANNA, married Colonel THOMAS BARCLAY, B. A. His son, JAMES, was colonel of a regiment of Loyalists, and died in exile. Another son, WARREN, displayed such gallantry when only fifteen years old, in the battle of White Plains, 1776, that he was made a Cornet of the 17th British Light Dragoons at that early age.

JANE, fourth daughter of PETER DE LANCEY of the Mills, married Hon. JOHN WATTS, Junior, then Recorder of New York, afterwards founder of the LEAKE and WATTS Orphan House. The bridal festivities at Union Hill, in the borough of Westchester, on the evening of 2d October, 1775, were sufficiently gay to receive a conspicuous notice in the "Gazetteer" of the day. These were the grand-parents of Major-General PHILIP KEARNY. This JOHN WATTS will be referred to more at length hereafter.

Many others of the family distinguished themselves in official positions, and even some of those who chose a military career may have been omitted in this notice. Not a few of their descendants served with honor in th Union ranks during the last civil war. Three great-grandchildren of this pair, brothers, came out of the struggle with the U. S. brevets of Colonel for services, at the age of twenty-one, Lieutenant-Colonel, at eighteen, and Major, at nineteen.

That the men of the race whose blood flowed in the veins of Major-Generals STEPHEN WATTS KEARNY and PHILIP KEARNY rose to such high commands, speaks sufficiently for their ability and fitness for the profession which they selected and in which they shone. That the women of that same race chose soldiers for their partners, testifies in what direction their predilections ran. Their children were worthy of their mothers; those mothers "worthy to bear men."

Major-General PHILIP KEARNY had a double portion of this blood, through his grandmother and great-grandmother.

Will any one deny that his career was worthy of the most glorious of his ancestry?

CHAPTER II.

THE KEARNY AND WATTS FAMILIES AND THEIR CONNECTIONS.

"An affectionate regard for the memory of our forefathers is natural to the heart; it is an emotion totally distinct from pride. * * * They are denied, it is true, to our personal acquaintance, but the light they shed during their lives survives within their tombs, and will reward our search, if we explore them. If the virtues of strangers be so attractive to us, how infinitely more so should be those of our own kindred; and with what additional energy should the precepts of our parents influence us, when we trace the transmission of those precepts from father to son through successive generations, each bearing testimony of a virtuous, useful, and honorable life to their truth and influence."

LINDSAY.

As EARLY as 1716 we find a KEARNY settled in Monmouth county, New Jersey. He came from Ireland, and was a man of note. His son, PHILIP KEARNY, was an eminent lawyer, who died 25th of July, 1775, a little less than a year before the Declaration of Independence. One of his sons, FRANCIS, entered the Royal service, and was a captain in the corps of Colonel BEVERLY ROBINSON, known as the Loyal American Regiment of New York. In 1782 he appears as a Major in ALLEN's Corps of Pennsylvania Royalists. He rose to a Lieutenant-Colonelcy, went to Ireland after the war, married, and would seem to have settled and died there. This family were very particular about the spelling of their name, and if such a thing were possible, the General would turn in his grave with indignation if he knew that his name was written and printed with two E's, *K e a r n* E *y*, instead of *K e a r n y*.

PHILIP KEARNY, the son of the first PHILIP, "removed to Newark, and left children, whose descendants are set down as living in New

York." He was the grandfather of Brevet Major-General Stephen Watts Kearny, U. S. Army, and of Philip, the father of Major-General Philip Kearny, Jr., U. S. Volunteers, the patriot, martyr, and subject of this biography.

Stephen Watts Kearny was a student of Columbia College, in the city of New York, in 1812, and would have graduated in the summer of that year. As soon, however, as it became a certainty that war must ensue between the United States and Great Britain, he applied for and obtained a commission in the U. S. Army. On the 12th of March, 1812, while still in his eighteenth year, he was appointed *from New York* 1st Lieutenant in the 13th U. S. Infantry. He distinguished himself particularly in storming a British battery, and throughout the assault on Queenstown Heights, 13th October, 1812. Lieutenant-Colonel Christie, commanding his regiment, himself wounded in this action, presented young Kearny with his sword on the field of battle for the cool and determined manner with which he executed the command which devolved upon him. A companion in arms states that as "1st Lieutenant of Captain Ogilvie's company, he (S. W. K.) enjoyed, at an early age, the character of high promise his after years developed. He was made prisoner on this occasion, and sent to Quebec," and was long detained in captivity. He became Captain in April, 1813, Brevet-Major in April, 1823, and Major in May, 1829. Upon the organization of the 1st U. S. Dragoons, he was appointed their Lieutenant-Colonel, 4th March, 1833, and Colonel, 4th July, 1836. On the 30th June, 1846, he was commissioned Brigadier-General, was placed in command of the Army of the West, and made the conquest of the Province of New Mexico. He received the Brevet of Major-General, United States Army, for gallant and meritorious conduct in New Mexico and California, to date from the battle of San Pascual, 6th December, 1846, in which he was twice wounded. He commanded the combined force, consisting of detachments of sailors and of marines and of dragoons, in the battles of San Gabriel and Plains of Mesa, 8th and 9th of January, 1847, and was Governor of California from the date of his proclamation, 1st March, 1847, down to June of the same year. On the 31st October, 1848, he fell a victim at Vera Cruz to illness contracted in the course of his arduous service during the Mexican war. Like his nephew, Major-General Philip Kearny, he died for his country.

The General's brother, Archibald Kennedy Kearny, who died

MAJOR GENERAL PHILIP KEARNY'S BIRTH PLACE, No. 3 BROADWAY, NEW YORK CITY.

1st July, 1868, in New York city, aged 83, was a Lieutenant in the U. S. Navy during the war of 1812, '15. He commanded a division of gunboats stationed in the Lower Bay for the protection of New York harbor.

Commodore LAWRENCE KEARNY, U. S. Navy, was a second cousin of the preceding and third cousin of his nephew, Major-General PHILIP KEARNY.

PHILIP KEARNY, the subject of this biographical sketch, who fell a Division Commander at Chantilly, 1st September, 1862, was born, according to the majority of accounts, the 2d of June, 1815—his brother-in-law, whose wife, SUSAN KEARNY, had the Family Bible, says the 1st June, 1814, which collateral circumstances would go to prove was the correct date—at No. 3 Broadway, in the First Ward of the city of New York, which, together with the adjoining building, No. 1, was formerly owned by his great uncle, Hon. ARCHIBALD KENNEDY, then Captain, B. N., who married Miss ANNE WATTS, eldest sister of Hon JOHN WATTS, Jr., who purchased, in 1792, subsequently lived and died in No. 3.

No. 1 Broadway was *built* by this Captain KENNEDY, and stood next to the glacis of Fort George. It was an elegant mansion, and only rivaled by one other in the city, that of Hon. WILLIAM WALTON, Esq., in Queen Street, now Franklin Square, who married MARIA DE LANCEY, niece of the first JOHN WATTS and cousin of the second. Mr. WALTON's affluence, and generous entertainment of the British officers, led to the taxation of the colonies, and eventually to the Revolution. While the British held New York, the first story of No. 3 served as a Post Office, the slits remaining evident in the doors down to 1836. The company-rooms, lofty and spacious, were in the second story. When public entertainments were given, these latter were connected with the grand apartments in No. 1 by a staircase and bridge. These two buildings were among the very few that escaped the great fires of 1776 and 1778.

Hon. JOHN WATTS, Junior, maternal grandfather of Major-General PHILIP KEARNY, was a man more ennobled by his generosity and benevolence than he could have been by any hereditary titles or honors. He founded and endowed the LEAKE and WATTS' Orphan House, in the city of New York, one of the noblest and purest acts of benevolence, taking into consideration all the facts connected with its endowment, in the whole list of our country's elemosynary institutions. In regard to this, a reader will pardon the quotation from a speech, at one of the Anniversary Meetings : " There is yet another whose name we are accustomed to associate with that of JOHN G. LEAKE, and who deserves no less our admiration and our gratitude. Had he been less magnanimous, less generous than he was, this happy home, these invaluable privileges, would not have been ours. Through an informality in the will, the money devoted to the erection and support of this institution might have become the property of JOHN WATTS. His it was by inheritance and undisputed right. But he was one of those men whose heart extent of riches cannot narrow or degrade—who retain, amid the luxuries and opulence of fashionable life, noble and generous influences. He knew that his claim to this property was uncontested; yet without reluctance, he yielded it to fulfil the benevolent intentions of its donor. LEAKE and WATTS—their names are fitly associated, and worthy of being transmitted to the latest posterity. The rare benevolence of the one, the stern integrity of the other, are qualities which the Philanthropist and Christian will delight to contemplate, and which all will unite to admire. They stand out in prominent relief, in a depraved and sordid age, in evidence that there are always spirits which delight to bless and improve their race."

This Orphan House is at once a magnificent monument to JOHN WATTS, the actual donor of its funds, and—through the designation he modestly and honorably gave it, sharing the honor by placing his own name second to that of anothers in the title—a memorial of his bosom friend and connection, from whom the money was originally derived. It is also a witness of Mr. WATTS' sorrows, since the property came to him through his finest son, ROBERT, who scarcely lived long enough to acquire legal possession of it, and died before he had the opportunity of enjoying this magnificent bequest of the brother-in-law of his great-aunt, MARGARET WATTS (married to Major ROBERT WILLIAM LEAKE* of the British Army), and the friend and fellow student of his father.

This Mr. WATTS was a man as remarkable for his manly character as for his generosity. He was full of "saving, common-sense," "that most uncommon kind of sense." In his famous "Thoughts,"

* ROBERT LEAKE, the father of Major ROBERT WILLIAM LEAKE, was an officer who had seen much and varied service. He was wounded and maimed in the battle of Dettingen, in 1743, where his horse was shot under him, and he was engaged at Culloden, on the Royal side, in 1746. His loyalty was rewarded with the post of Commissary-General to the forces in North America, and in 1757 he was acting as Commissary General to the army commanded by the ill-fated Braddock.

PASCAL, the deepest of thinkers, and acutest of mathematical reasoners, whose scientific development of the proofs of Christianity, or rather the demonstration of its truths, is marvelous in its clearness and resultiveness, declares "common sense is superior to genius." Besides being possessed of such admirable judgment, he was a man of iron will, and, with his keen activity of mind and body, out of place under the new order of things, since he could not stoop to court popularity, as public men are compelled to cringe and bow to obtain it in these days. Nevertheless, although he shrunk from office, he was called upon to fill several positions of dignity and importance.

He was the last Royal Recorder of the city of New York; was a Member of Congress in 1793–'5; was thrice unanimously elected Speaker of the 14th, 15th, and 16th Sessions of the New York Legislature—January, 1791, January, 1792, and November, 1792—and was Judge of Westchester county, 1802–'8, etc. Disgusted at the measures resorted to by his political opponents—measures founded on hereditary antagonism which has outlived the competitors—he withdrew from public life, as he deemed no position worthy an honest man's efforts which compelled him to pander to the meanest prejudices of the mob to win their votes. Thenceforward his attention was devoted to the care of his large estate and the vast interests confided to him.

Young PHILIP KEARNY inherited a great many of the peculiarities of his grandfather, his generosity, energy, determination, love of horses, and wonderful horsemanship, for at the age of eighty-seven, when most old men are incapable of any exertion, Hon. JOHN WATTS was not only a splendid, but a venturesome, rider. Upon one occasion a horse-dealer brought him an animal to try, which turned out to be a violent and unbroken colt, which sprang into the air, rearing and plunging as soon as Mr. WATTS was in the saddle. Through all its struggles he sat unmoved, and when the animal had become quiet, dismounted as calmly as if nothing had occurred.

When a boy, young PHIL KEARNY was a reckless rider and a perfect horse-killer. He rode just as fearlessly over the worst as over the best roads. Upon one occasion, often adverted to in the family, while quite a little chap, eight or nine years old, he frightened his father almost to death, galloping his horse furiously for miles over an old corduroy road full of holes and inequalities. It must have been an extraordinary feat and escape, since it was often referred to by men who were too bold riders themselves to dwell upon anything which was not something astonishing in its display of daring.

Neither PHILIP KEARNY, father nor son, were residents or citizens of New Jersey, in the strict sense of the word. The father inherited a country house near Newark, but his home was in New York. About the year 1820 he had a house at Greenwich, on the North River, about the foot of the present West Twentieth street. General KEARNY's mother, SUSAN WATTS, at that time, was in very delicate health. She was a lovely character, and a charming, handsome woman. She died while the General was still quite young. About 1827, PHILIP KEARNY, Senior, lived on the east side of Broadway, nearly opposite to Morris street, then called Little Beaver Street or Beaver Lane. His nephew, who furnishes the facts, thinks that Mrs. KEARNY died here, but she must have died long before this, for the writer, who can recall facts and faces farther back than that date, has no recollection of her.*

At one time it is likely the KEARNY family lived in Greenwich street, just in the rear of No. 3 Broadway, doubtless on made lots, part of the river front belonging to the WATTS' property, whose garden extended originally to the river. In fact, the waves at high tide and during a storm broke over an extension of the back piazza, thrust out to the west like the stem of a ⊥, about midway the present block, between Broadway and Greenwich streets.

While PHIL KEARNY was still in college, his grandfather, seeing his inclination for the army, offered to secure to him $1,500 a year, a very handsome allowance in those days for a young man, if he would study for the ministry. "Mr. WATTS thought the ministers had a good, safe time," and as he had lost all his sons, he did not wish the eldest of his only two grandsons to be exposed to the vicissitudes of a career which had cost him the most brilliant of his own sons, GEORGE. PHIL KEARNY declined his grandfather's liberal offer, and as he was compelled to choose a civil profession, selected, much against his will, the Law, and fulfilled the usual course in the office of the Hon. PETER AUGUSTUS JAY.

Thus, it will be seen, that one of the most dashing officers that ever lived came very near being made a clergyman. The same

---

* "She died in March 1823." G. H. K. for E. K. July 11, 1868.

BREVET FIRST LIEUTENANT GEORGE WATTS,

1st U. S. Light Dragoons.

Aid de Camp to Brig. Gen. Winfield Scott, at Chippewa, etc., 1814–'15.

thing occurred with regard to HOOKER, who was destined by his father for the Church. A strange coincidence that "Fighting Joe" and "Fighting PHIL" soldiers born, generals by instinct, commanders of rival divisions in the same corps, narrowly escaped an exchange of the uniform of the army for the robes of the Church-militant. HOOKER often alludes with humor to the overthrow of his father's cherished plans, when he received his appointment as a Cadet to prepare himself for the saddle instead of the pulpit.

Having alluded to GEORGE WATTS, this would seem to be an appropriate place for presenting a sketch of this distinguished officer, who was a perfect type in everything, form, feature, disposition, mind and service, of his nephew, General PHILIP KEARNY, like him destined a generation afterwards to fill his place as Aid to General SCOTT, and serve with him in another war equally glorious to both.

On the 18th March, 1813, he was appointed from New York Third Lieutenant of the 1st U. S. Light Dragoons, and promoted to a Second Lieutenancy 13th August, the same year. Shortly afterwards General SCOTT selected him as an aid-de-camp, and as such he acted in the campaign of 1814. He was breveted First Lieutenant for "gallantry and distinguished service in the battle of Chippewa, 5th July, 1814, and for distinguished service in BROWN's Sortie from Fort Erie." When the cavalry was reduced after the war, he was retained, May, 1815, in the 1st United States Infantry, but being a "horseback-man" by nature, he could not stand the pedestrian service, and resigned the 15th January, 1816.

The following conversation, had with Lieutenant-General SCOTT 15th April, 1865, taken down at the time, afterwards submitted to and approved by him, is all-sufficient testimony of that distinguished General's estimate of his two aids-de-camp, uncle and nephew, who not only looked alike, but were alike in every quality which makes and adorns a soldier:

"Lieutenant GEORGE WATTS, of the United States Dragoons, Major, by courtesy, was my aid-de-camp during the campaign of 1814. He was of a very affectionate nature, and a very brave man—it might be said the bravest of the brave. He looked very like PHILIP KEARNY, his nephew, likewise, subsequently, my aid-de-camp. If one man is more brave than another, PHILIP KEARNY was that man. He was the bravest man I ever knew, and a perfect soldier.

"Lieutenant GEORGE WATTS, my Aid, saved my life on the morning before the battle of Chippewa. The circumstances are as follows: At the mouth of Street's Creek, which empties into the Niagara River, immediately adjacent to the battle-field of July 5th, stood a house occupied by a Mrs. STREET. As there were no males belonging to her family, she had applied to me for protection, and I had given her a safe-guard, which was perfectly respected, and she made money by selling milk and different articles to the American troops. She invited me to breakfast with her, and I accepted the invitation. I had just prepared my first cup of coffee, and was about to raise it to my mouth, when I experienced the truth of the proverb, that 'There is many a slip 'twixt the cup and the lip.' My Aid, GEORGE WATTS, perspiring very freely, had risen from the table and stepped across the room to another table, near the window, to get his pocket-handkerchief out of his dragoon helmet, or casque, which he had previously placed there. My cocked-hat lay upon the same table, and I lost it in consequence. Looking out of the window, he turned to me and said, quietly but significantly, 'In three minutes the house will be surrounded by Indians.' I set down my untasted coffee, rushed from the room, cleared the piazza and steps with one bound, and ran 'like a man' for the bridge which communicated with our own side of the stream. Thus, GEORGE WATTS, by his promptness, saved my life, for the whole thing had been arranged by Mrs. STREET with the intention of murdering and scalping me. She had given the signal by waving something from the house as soon as we had sat down to breakfast.

"The same night after my victory at Chippewa, I made Mrs. STREET's house our hospital, and its rooms and the court-yard, in which I had caused tents to be pitched, were filled with our wounded. When I visited the house I found the treacherous woman and her daughter, a very pretty person, engaged in attending to the wants of the wounded British officers in the second story. I saw the latter carrying refreshments to a wounded British officer to whom she was engaged to be married. As she had been moving through the rooms filled with blood from injuries and amputations, her dress was completely drenched to the knee. Both mother and daughter avoided catching my eye, and I avoided any attempt to make them catch mine; for they were women, and, as such, I could not feel vengeance, although they had attempted to compass my death. As I said before, upon this occasion I owed my life to Lieutenant WATTS."

That affectionate remembrance of his aids had not warped his judgment in after years is proved by the extract of a letter from him to General BROWN, dated Queenstown, Upper Canada, 15th July, 1814.

"I cannot close this account of meritorious conduct without mentioning the great services rendered me by those two gallant young soldiers, Lieutenants WORTH and WATTS, my aids. There was no danger they did not cheerfully encounter in communicating my orders, and by their zeal and intrepidity won the admiration, as they had before the esteem, of the whole brigade. They both rendered essential services at critical moments by assisting the commandants of corps in forming the troops under circumstances which precluded the voice from being heard. Their conduct has been handsomely acknowledged by the officers of the line, who have joined in requesting that it might be particularly noticed.

(Signed) W. SCOTT."

His opinion of KEARNY has been too often expressed in official reports, conversation and letters, to need any repetition here.

ROBERT WATTS, the eldest brother, living, of GEORGE, the dragoon, entered the United States Army 31st July, 1813, as Captain in the 41st Regiment of Infantry; but none of the family seem to have taken kindly to foot service, and he resigned in the same year. He was afterwards a Major of Volunteer Cavalry during the war of 1812–15. Thrown from his horse in the execution of a rapid movement, his whole command in column rode over him at speed, yet, strange to say, when picked up not a horse's hoof had touched him. General SCOTT spoke of him as a remarkably handsome man. He is still remembered by his cotemporaries as the handsomest man of his day in the city of New York; and one who had the opportunity to know him by long experience, declared that he possessed a perfect temper, like his aunt, Lady MARY (WATTS) JOHNSON, whose playful humor exhilarated the whole household."

CHAPTER III.

THE SPRINGTIDE OF YOUTH.

"Sometimes forgotten things, long cast behind,
Rush forward on the brain and come to mind."—DRYDEN.

"He was a lovely youth,—I guess
The panther in the wilderness
Was not so fair as he!"—WORDSWORTH.

"When a younker up I grew,
Saw one day a grand review,
Colors flying, set me dying
To embark in life so new."—OLD SONG.

WHILE the KEARNY family lived in Broadway opposite Morris street, young PHIL KEARNY was a pupil at UFFORD's school, on the west side of Broadway, on the corner of Cedar street. At that time he was very fond of drawing pictures of soldiers and designs of armies on his slate. Sometimes he condescended to caricatures of Mr. UFFORD and his school-fellows. He always had a great talent for drawing, and sometimes he drew well, that is, whatever was connected with military matters or horses. Some of his sketches of soldiers possessed considerable merit. If memory serves, he produced equestrian groups which were spirited.

PHILIP KEARNY was never a very strong or robust boy, nor given to any violent exercise, except riding on horseback. In the saddle he made up for his ordinary quietness of demeanor. Whenever he could get a horse he rode furiously, in fact he was a regular horse-killer.

What he was in early years is clearly depicted in a letter of the Rev. Dr. OGILBY, who officiated with so much eloquence and feeling at the floral decoration of his grave, in Trinity churchyard, New York city, by the members of Post PHIL KEARNY, No. 8, G. A. R., of the Department of New York, on Sunday, 1st June, 1868:

"In my boyhood we were neighbors, and, at times, playmates. My recollection of him is that of a mild and gentle boy, whose dark eye was distinguished rather for softness than for that fire which kindled it in later life. I remember, when I heard of his conspicuous gallantry in the Mexican war, I was astonished, and said to myself, 'Can this be the gentle boy of my early remembrance?' I never met him afterwards until we were brought together by the hand of death. In the midst of the war he came from the thickest of the fight to bury a child who had been stricken down in the apparent security of a peaceful home. Such is our mortal life! I officiated at the funeral of the child, over the same grave upon which the flowers were so soon strewn upon the dust and ashes of the father."

At a later date he was sent to Round Hill School, at Northampton, Mass., the noted institution kept by Dr. JOSEPH G. COGSWELL, afterwards the world-wide known Superintendent and Organizer of the Astor Library, and Mr. GEORGE BANCROFT, now Minister from the United States to the North German Confederation, the American historical writer. Dr. COGSWELL seems to recollect him well while under his charge. "In answer to your inquiries about Major-General PHILIP KEARNY, while a youth at Round Hill School," he replies, "I can only say that he then evinced none of the military spirit which in after life marked his career with such a halo of glory. He was remarkable for his gentle and amiable character, his great docility, faithful observance of the school regulations and for his devotion to his studies. He took high rank as a scholar, and was greatly beloved as a pupil. When the school was opened at Cold Spring by Dr. BECK and Mr. WATSON, and he left Round Hill and became a pupil of it, it may be that a military spirit was already stirring within him, and on that account he wished to be near West Point;* or that, being so near that great nursery of military heroes, he there caught the spirit which became his passion and made him one of the bravest and greatest of our grand captains."

At the suggestion of Dr. JOSEPH G. COGSWELL, certain questions were addressed to the Reverend JOHN LEE WATSON in regard to the school-boy career of General KEARNY after he left Round Hill, Northampton, Mass. To the kindness of that gentleman is due the following statement, which is very interesting, although Mr. WATSON falls into a general error in regard to KEARNY'S

* This opinion of the excellent Doctor is mere surmise; West Point had nothing to do with PHILIP KEARNY or his merits.

ever having been a cadet.* KEARNY was placed at the Philipstown school in May, 1830. He entered Columbia College as a Sophomore, in the fall of that year.

It is reasonable to suppose the latent military element in KEARNY'S structure was kindled by the "blare of bugle and roll of drum" from across the river, just as the same martial notes rouse up the Cadets to their daily routine of drill and study. Doubtless his martial instincts responded to the clarion's call, just as ARTHUR'S "war-horse neighed as at a friend's voice," when

"Far off a solitary trumpet blew."

This and no more. Thus much justice must concede, and truth then refuses to allow any more. It is much more reasonable to believe that General SCOTT and the other officers visiting the Philipstown school, attracted by his family resemblance, spoke to KEARNY of those gallant spirits of his race who had shone or still were shining in arms, whereupon feelings kindred to theirs awoke to life in the boy's mind, feelings like germs buried in the earth, which only required accident and light to germinate, grow, flower, and fruit in great deeds.

PHILIP KEARNY came to our school at Philipstown, in the Highlands, in May, 1830, with the intention of preparing himself for admission to Columbia College, New York, in conformity with the wishes of his friends. For a time he pursued his classical studies with great diligence, and gave much encouragement as to his future progress. But it soon became evident that all his own inclinations tended towards a military education. The Academy at West Point, with all its animating sights and sounds, was constantly before his eyes; several of his school-fellows were preparing for examination as Cadets; an officer of the Academy came over every day to instruct our pupils in Mathematics; there was considerable intercourse between the officers of the Academy and ourselves, and also between the pupils who had relatives on either side; and, besides that, Colonel THAYER and General SCOTT, both of whom had relatives under our care, visited our school at stated periods. All these circumstances combined to fill the mind of KEARNY with a strong desire, or rather with a perfect passion for a military education; and at last he came and told us that "he could not see his way to study for College any longer; that he never should be good for anything unless he went to West Point, and that he would thank us very much if we would inform his friends of the state of the case." Accordingly we advised his friends that it would not be wise or prudent to thwart his inclinations.

During the short time that KEARNY was with us we became very much attached to him. In his conduct and character as a boy, the often-quoted line of WORDSWORTH seems peculiarly to apply to him, "The boy was father to the man." Such as he was with us and among his schoolmates, he continued to be in after life in his brilliant career as an officer of our gallant army. He was bold and daring even to recklessness; fond of all manly sports; the best gymnast in the school; an excellent horseman, and an indefatigable pedestrian. He was

* "WEST POINT, July 29th, 1863—General KEARNY never was at West Point as a cadet. I have had the record of those who have reported here examined. This is a complete record. I am positive he never was here." A. S. W., *Brev. Maj.-Gen., U. S. A.*

always obedient and respectful to his instructors, and entirely submissive to authority. As to the state of his moral or religious character, at that time, I do not now feel myself competent to express any opinion. * * *

* * * * * * *

I believe that this comprises all my recollections of "the boyhood of PHILIP KEARNY." While I was Rector of Grace Church, Newark, New Jersey, (from about 1846 to 1854,) I frequently met him, and he often took occasion to say how much he was indebted to Dr. BECK and myself for the excellent training that he received during the time that he was at the "Highland School,"—as he expressed it—"the most critical period of his life;" he said that "it made a man of him." I have only to add that I took much interest in KEARNY'S life as a soldier, and during the war of the rebellion I followed his course through all his military operations, up to the time of his last battle; and when I read the account of his death I could not but call to mind the words, which, in his school-boy days, were so frequently on his lips,

"DULCE ET DECORUM EST PRO PATRIA MORI."

KEARNY was seven or eight years older than the writer, and as he was always kept away at boarding-school, it was not until he had reached the age of fifteen that the latter's reminiscences of him commence. About the year 1830 he came to reside with his grandfather, Hon. JOHN WATTS, in whose house the writer was born and brought up. Thenceforward they were constantly together for six or seven years. Even at that time KEARNY was very peculiar, proud and shy, and averse to those associations which youths of his age generally form from impulse rather than from judgment. His companions were selected, with all the coolness of maturer age, for qualities which suited his prejudices—and these extended to everything. In the choice of friends, he was regulated by his own arbitrary rules of what they should be, rather than what they were. He was fond of dress, and exceedingly neat and careful of his person, and always affected a sort of military carriage or touch of something military in his costume, so that any observer would have said, "There goes a soldier in civil clothes, or one intended by nature for a soldier." In corroboration of this, the following quotation from a letter to the writer is apposite: "When we were on our way home, at West Point (the boats never landed at Cold Spring, where KEARNY was at school) we saw a young gentleman step on board with a Mediterranean cap on (you remember that cap): I thought that that cap could only cover PHILLY'S head, so up I jumped, and the young gentleman turned his head, and much to our mutual delight, it proved to be good Phil, on his way to town to spend a week; so we joined company, and I had the satisfaction of having him with me for a week. He is coming to town in about two weeks to be examined before he enters college."

One of the first remarks of Kearny's, which the writer remembers was, that whenever he owned a pair of horses, they should be named *Tilly* and *Count Lippe.* Although so much younger, he was sufficiently read in history to be astonished at Kearny's partiality for two generals, the most marked, perhaps, in military history for qualities not only directly opposite each other, but differing from those of the vast majority of leaders of armies. Subsequently, however, when military reading became a passion, it was no longer difficult to understand why Kearny selected these men as his favorites. The youth was father to the man. Kearny was already thinking. When close after-study made their characters known, the predilection was no longer surprising. Tilly, whom his great antagonist, Gustavus Adolphus, styled the "Old Devil," on account of his cruelty, and the "Old Corporal" from his strict attention to drilling, was a thorough soldier. As an organizer and as an administrator he had no superior in his era, the first fourteen years of the "Thirty Years' War." As a general he was unconquered, until new tactics, new material, new men, grown great in their experience under a new order of things, appeared in Germany. His command-in-chief, for nearly a quarter of a century, was a career of victory, until Gustavus shattered and ruined the magnificent army which Tilly had created, at Leipsic, in 1632, and finished the work by putting an end to his antagonist's fame and life at the Lech. A persecuting priest (it has been stated that he was an affiliated Jesuit), in his intolerant bigotry, perfectly chaste as regarded women, sober, uncompromising, in his self and general discipline he was in many respects a consummate commander. With him originated the expression, "a ragged soldier and a bright musket." Doubtless Kearny liked him because he was a stern and sagacious disciplinarian, one who knew how to knead a discordant personnel into that fanaticized unity which makes an army a machine, irrisistible to everything but another army inspired with ideas more potent in their influence than mere fanaticism, and sufficiently disciplined to execute simple manœuvres and maintain cohesion.

As to his second favorite, Kearny had, much in common with Count Lippe, a quick temper, a rough tongue, an open hand, a compassionate heart, an acute, active mind. To their sick and wounded both were equally attentive, and their supervision of their camps and hospitals was only limited by their other pressing duties. Those who will study the life of Count Lippe, after they have read these pages, will find that Kearny had not studied the German in vain. They will perceive that he understood what was needed in a general, when he left the beaten track of popular opinion—always fonder of "shams," or "would-be's," or "butchers," than real generals—to pick out and appreciate a man so great in his influence on his times, and greater in the parts he was called upon to play than most of those to whom such prominent positions have been intrusted. A soldier who won, enjoyed, and retained the esteem and confidence of Frederick the Great, king and hero, and of Pombal, the great Portuguese minister, the Richelieu of his century, must have been one far above his fellows, at least in some grand properties, if not in the startling magnitude of a Ferdinand of Brunswick (under whom he served for some time as general of artillery) in the capacity of handling a huge host to advantage; or of a Ziethen or a Seydlitz, marvelous in their specialty, and unsurpassed in the world's history as creators and leaders of cavalry—still equal to either, if not superior, in a combination of qualities, which made him shine in the high and difficult posts to which he was called by public opinion as the person best fitted to fill them.

Count William of Schaumburg-Lippe, sometimes styled Count Lippe-Buckeburg, was a general of an entirely different type from Tilly; but as a disciplinarian, as a tactician, as an artillerist, and as a commander, in his sphere, he is chargeable with scarcely a single error of judgment. The officer who could convert "Westphalian peasants into Prussian soldiers," and "fifteen hundred ragged, ill-paid Portuguese vagabonds, commanded by officers as poor, idle and beggarly as themselves, into ordinary soldiers," worthy the name and capable of beating good troops, must have understood his business thoroughly.

Two anecdotes of him attest his coolness and self-confidence: During the year 1758–'9, he greatly distinguished himself as a general of the Hanoverian artillery (to whose command he had been appointed by George II.), under Prince Ferdinand of Brunswick. One day he invited a number of Hanoverian officers to dinner, and while the company were in the full enjoyment of the entertainment, cannon-shots were heard, and several balls flew about the tent. The company started to their feet, exclaiming that the French were at hand. The Count pacified them as far as regarded the enemy, although it is doubtful if his explanation left his guests with undiminished appetites. "Do not be alarmed, gentlemen," said he, "I wished to convince you how well I can rely upon the officers of my artillery. Accordingly I ordered them, while we were at dinner, to practice at the flag-staff over my tent." Whether the guests did feel at ease after this explanation is questionable. But the cannon-balls continued to fly about, and, if memory serves, one story runs that a final shot, by hitting the main support of the pavilion, brought the whole structure down upon the company and put an end to the frolic. Had one of our generals indulged in such dangerous sport, he would have been considered a lunatic, and Mr. STANTON would have been down on him in a trice for waste of ammunition and material. The Count, however, was not crazy. There was a perfect method in his madness, and he won the respect and admiration of every sovereign and commander under whom he served—so much so, that JOSEPH, King of Portugal, one of the most bigoted of Roman Catholics, was willing to purchase the services of a rough, uncompromising Protestant by concessions and gratuities rarely made even to the most transcendant genius—concessions, in the case of Count LIPPE, which circumstances rendered a necessity. When he quitted Portugal, the king conferred upon him extraordinary honors, and gave him magnificent presents: six golden cannon, each weighing 32 pounds, mounted on ebony carriages, heavily ornamented with silver, a button and aigrette of diamonds for his hat, and the royal portrait set with the same precious stones. To these the King of England added a sword mounted with diamonds.

By "Practical Strategy,"—a term used by an expert in the military art, which drew down upon the writer, in 1862, the thunder of the oldest West Point Professor,—by Practical Strategy afterwards carried out in so masterly a manner by ROSECRANS and SHERMAN—Count LIPPE, in 1762, gained for himself immortal renown, without even venturing to bring his badly organized Portuguese troops into direct collision with the Spaniards. Merely by skilful manœuvring, the selection of positions and encampments by the English and Portuguese, the admirable Spanish army was checked, and prevented from making an attack with advantage, till, at length, weakened by sickness and want, it was obliged in autumn to retire from the kingdom.

In 1776, when a new war seemed imminent between Spain and Portugal, the Queen Regnant of the latter kingdom desired that he should reassume the command of her army. Feeble health, the greatest drawback to a general—Marshal Count SAXE, says, "a general *must* possess robust health"—would not permit him again to take the field.

Fear was something unknown to Count LIPPE.* A second anecdote proves this. A similar one is told of General SEVES, better known as Soliman-Pacha, a French convert to Islamism, and right hand to Ibrahim-Pacha, in making that Egyptian army which conquered the Turks so gloriously at Homs and at Beylan in 1831, at Konieh in 1832, and again at Nezib in 1839.

One day, while Count LIPPE was strolling through his camp, a Portuguese soldier, incited by insane religious fanaticism, or, perhaps, instigated by a bigoted priesthood, fired at him with an air-gun. The ball passed through the Protestant general's hat. Without quitting the spot he called several officers about him. His officers begged him to withdraw. No; he determined to maintain his position until he could discover the rascal, At length he spied him out just as he was taking aim a third time, from his tent. Count LIPPE ordered him to be hung upon the spot. The Regimental Chaplain insisted upon being allowed to administer extreme unction to the culprit before he was executed. The Count refused, and the intended assassin was run up instanter, unshriven—a fearful fate for one of his faith.

That PHILIP KEARNY, at the age of fifteen, selected two such characters as his heroes, proves that he had already read and thought discreetly upon military matters, since both TILLY and Count LIPPE were distinguished rather for scientific and solid properties than for dash and brilliant qualities.

Nevertheless, by a strange contradiction, although KEARNY thus selected men of thought for his favorites, he always wished to be a Hussar, particularly, as he admitted, on account of the jaunty dress

* "Furcht kannte er gar nicht."

The writer has heard it stated, or else some one wrote out to one of the family, that KEARNY was sent out of Italy, in 1859, for his too rash self-exposure. As will be shown from his own letter, he came very near experiencing at Solferino the same fate that he met at Chantilly.

and attractive service of that corps. Moreover, in youth, the tactics he affected were reckless cavalry charges, although convinced by theoretical experiment that they were made in vain against the resistance of a steadfast infantry and the fire of a capable artillery. In after life, when he aspired to a general's command, he had lost all his predilections for cavalry. "An officer who commands a cavalry regiment"—was about the amount of what he said—" has to perform double duty. He has in fact to drill two regiments instead of one, the one of bipeds and the other of quadrupeds; and I don't know but that the latter is the easiest to make and manage."

While General KEARNY and the writer lived together in the house of their grandfather, from 1829 to 1834, almost all the leisure time of both was spent in mimic campaigns, with armies composed of from four to six thousand leaden soldiers with perfect trains of artillery, and even other adjuncts of a well-provided host. Battles were fought according to a digested system, which even regulated what proportion of those knocked down by the mimic fire of musketry or artillery should be considered as dead or too severely wounded to take part in the rest of the campaign, and how many as slightly wounded, and how long the latter should be looked upon as remaining in the hospital before they were again available. The firing was done with small spring-guns, one shot for each cannon, one for each regiment or separate detachment of infantry and so many for each line of sharp-shooters. When the firing, alternating, had gone through both lines of battle, the different bodies were moved a shorter or longer determined distance, according as they belonged to the different arms, over spaces dictated by the real relative speed of the different services, whether light or heavy cavalry, light or line infantry, field or reserve artillery. This was not left to hazard, but according to a written or stipulated code. Field works and permanent fortifications were constructed of pasteboard, and the irregularities of ground represented by piles of books and similar objects, built up in accordance with agreement before operations commenced. One siege lasted a number of weeks, and the tidy, dearly-beloved, and respected old house-keeper, wife* of a

* Mrs. F—— T——. This admirable woman deserves more than a passing notice. A sad and eventful life was hers. A debt of gratitude is due to her, for an affection and fidelity, motherly, as great as rare, of nearly thirty-five years, to the WATTS family. Such was General KEARNY's appreciation of her devotion to his grandfather and race, that he united in presenting her with an annuity which, together with her own property, enabled her to live consistently with the position in life which she was entitled to fill.

former sword-master at West Point, was driven almost wild by the accumulation of dust, and the appropriation of huge dining-tables of solid mahogany, the pride of her heart, whose oiling and polishing absorbed the greater part of her time. Every other kind of table or flat piece of furniture was impressed, which could be dragged out of its place and made available to eke out the theatre of action. She could scarcely be pacified at the subsequent disorder of the spacious rooms and the prohibition, strictly enforced, against sweeping and dusting, lest the bustle should knock down or disarrange the soldiers. Fleets of paste-board were even attempted, but maritime operations could not be made to work, since many a pellet which hit the sides of a vessel would level all on board, and then a quarrel would ensue as to how many were killed and how many wounded, which often ended in a fight, and put an end to *mimic* hostilities until the actual hostilities, between the leaders, were settled and the wounded honor of either or both was appeased. A very forcible shot from one of the spring-guns, close at hand, against a paste board ship, had the same effect as the impact of one of FARRAGUT's vessels, when they butted the iron-clad "Tennessee" in the Bay of Mobile. All the poor little leaden soldiers were knocked off their feet and a number overboard. As the question of how many knew how to swim and how many ought to be drowned was never taken into consideration, when the code of procedure was drawn up, it led to so much argument, that the belligerents came to the conclusion of NAPOLEON, that it was as useless for them as for him to attempt the empire of the sea. KEARNY continued to enjoy this amusement even while he was in college, and perhaps still longer. When he began to go into society, he took so much pains with his dress, and spent so much of his time out of the house, that he gradually relinquished a game which had given him such great delight and occupation for years.

He used to sleep under an old but very fine engraving of NAPOLEON BUONAPARTE, tri-color in hand, at the bridge of Lodi, perhaps for the purpose of deriving inspiration from the picture in his dreams. Strange to say, throughout all the military talk which occurred, the writer has no remembrance of his discussing NAPOLEON or his Marshals, with the exception, perhaps, of one, SUCHET. His favorite generals, at that time, were almost all those who figured in wars prior to the rise of NAPOLEON. One reason may have been, there was such a total disagreement as to their excellence that no satisfactory result could be arrived at by any discussion; whereas, the achievements of those who had flourished at previous dates were themes which could be canvassed without degenerating into open ruptures—ruptures which, in after years, grew out of differences hardly more important, and yet occasioning long estrangements that were only healed by temporary absence. In such cases, mutual respect, affection and still higher sentiments of esteem, brought the cousins together again, and everything went on as pleasantly as if no unkind feeling had ever arisen.

After passing through Columbia College, in New York, and studying Law in that city, he accompanied the writer to Europe in 1834. There his only idea seemed to be looking at soldiers and their manœuvres. He would be out of bed with first dawn, to wander forth and watch the exercises of a regiment of cavalry. Artillery he never had any eye or taste for, and then but very little for infantry.

CHAPTER IV.

IN THE SADDLE AT LAST!

"Arouse ye, my comrades, to horse! to horse!
To the field and to freedom we guide!
For there a man feels the pride of his force,
And there is the heart of him tried.
No help to him there by another is shown,
He stands for himself and himself alone."
SCHILLER'S "WALLENSTEIN'S LAGER."

"Faugh-a-ballagh—clear the way, boys!
Never did our gallant corps
Yield an inch of ground behind them,
Give an inch of ground before."
NUGENT TAILLEFER.

ON the 3d September, 1836, the death of his grandfather, Hon. JOHN WATTS, set young PHILIP KEARNY free, at last. For several years he had been chafing under the restraints of civil life, like a caged eagle or panther. At once he exerted all his interest to obtain a commission in the United States Cavalry, and on the 4th (8th) March, 1837, was appointed Second Lieutenant of the 1st U. S. Dragoons, commanded by his uncle, STEPHEN WATTS KEARNY.

This able and gallant officer had only been commissioned Colonel of this "model regiment" on the 4th of July of the previous year, but he may be said to have commanded it from the first. Yes, to him is due the organization of the first real cavalry which the country possessed since the general disarmament after the war of 1812–'15. It is true that HENRY DODGE, a sagacious frontiersman, an experienced ranger, and a gallant man, was its first Colonel, and STEPHEN WATTS KEARNY only its first Lieutenant-Colonel, but the latter was the creator and soul of that magnificent little body of cavalry, whose superior or equal has never been seen on this continent.

"If ever there was a soldier by nature," are the words of one of his classmates in Columbia College and fellow officers in the war, an uncle of the writer, who commanded a company in the regular service, during the war of 1812–'15, before he was of age, "if ever there was a man whom I considered really chivalrous, in fact, a MAN in all that that noble term conveys, that natural soldier and gentleman was STEPHEN WATTS KEARNY."

Upon the receipt of his commission, PHILIP KEARNY immediately abandoned the enjoyment of all the luxuries placed at his command by the inheritance of a splendid fortune—equal at this time to $1,000,000—and started for the West to join his command at Jefferson Barracks, on the Mississippi, 12 miles below St. Louis, in Missouri.

It has been more than once stated in print, in this connection, that JEFFERSON DAVIS was Captain in the regiment at the time PHIL KEARNY was Lieutenant. This is an error. DAVIS became 1st Lieutenant, 4th March, 1833, and was Adjutant in 1833–'4, but resigned in 1835. Still, the moral to be deduced is the same as if they had met or simultaneously served. Well might PARKER exclaim, "How widely divergent their subsequent paths of life and thought!" COLONEL BRACKETT in his history of the U. S. Cavalry, says, "It would, no doubt, have been much better for the country had he (DAVIS) been killed during that period; but it was designed otherwise, and he resigned on the 30th June, 1835. DAVIS, as a cadet, manifested a proud, haughty, and cold disposition, which he seems to have retained through life. He is eminently selfish, and has no friends aside from those who can be of use to him. Nevertheless, it must be admitted that he was a good officer, and gained the respect of those with whom he was thrown in contact."

What a contrast, the histories of KEARNY and of DAVIS. KEARNY after an honorable life—a life of patriotic duty, fulfilled to the uttermost—and a heroic death, was buried in the tomb of his fathers, amid the tears and lamentations of a people and its army, both of whom loved and admired him, and appreciated the great loss which they had sustained. DAVIS, after rising to the bad eminence which he sought to attain, fell, like Lucifer, from his height of pride, and continues to exist, like the arch-spirit of evil, the object of scorn to every good and honest man throughout the universe. He presents an example of great gifts perverted for the perpetration of the greatest crime of which a man is capable—treason: in his case a double treason, not only against his country, but against God's most precious gift, Liberty; treason, for the establishment of slavery, and the substitution of slavery, with all its evils, for freedom; treason against the country that educated and made him, which his great gifts, with nobler aims, might have illustrated and glorified, as did the dead KEARNY; a country which the misapplied intellectual powers of himself and party persistently labored to betray and to destroy.

From 10th June, 1837, to 21st May, 1839, while KEARNY remained West of the Mississippi, he devoted himself with great ardor to mastering the details of his profession. During a portion of this time, 22d August, 1838, to 10th April, 1839, he was aid-de-camp on the staff of Brigadier-General HENRY ATKINSON, who commanded in that region, and had his headquarters at St. Louis.

Active service in the line, as well as on the staff, gave KEARNY an opportunity of a course of double instruction, similar to that of young staff officers in the French army, who, after being educated in their own peculiar duties, serve for a stated period with the different arms to acquire a practical knowledge of each. KEARNY'S after life proved that he profited by his opportunities. Thus he became proficient in details which can never be acquired for subordinate positions (line or field) by theory, or any amount of study. A general, born with the genius for command, may so fit himself by study for a high station, that a very little practice, good subordinates, and an efficient staff will enable "his genius to compensate for the want of experience," as in the cases of LUCULLUS, SPINOLA, GUSTAVUS ADOLPHUS, TORSTENSON, CONDE, FREDERIC, and NAPOLEON. But this never can be the case with a line or field officer.

Let us see what one of his comrades says of KEARNY at that time: "I recollect him only as an active, energetic subaltern of cavalry, discharging efficiently all professional obligations, and in personal bearing observing the most gentlemanly courtesy towards his peers; always brave, and generous to a degree that won for him the admiration and esteem of all who knew him."

What changes have taken place since KEARNY joined his first command on the banks of the Mississippi! At that time the Jefferson Barracks were as far out of town, as regarded St. Louis, as one of the southern tier of Westchester villages was to New York in the beginning of the century. Then, the population of St. Louis did not exceed, if it equalled, 10,000 souls; and it is doubtful if the whole State of Missouri contained as many people in 1837 as St. Louis and its suburbs do at the present day.

"The City of St. Louis," to quote a letter of an officer, a friend of KEARNY, written a few years afterwards, "extends over a large space—large enough for twice as many inhabitants as it contains. Many of the shops are small wooden structures; not a few lots are still unoccupied, and about them, as about the whole town, there is an air of dirtiness, as if the city had grown up rapidly from the soil, and was not yet free from much adhering mud. And such a busy stir as there was in the streets, and in the hotels! The people that thronged the latter appeared to be generally intelligent, genteel-looking persons, who had come West probably for making investments."

The same officer, a very distinguished loyal general during the late war, makes the following remarks, worthy of preservation, in a letter dated June 6th, 1857, while on his way to join the army, ostensibly sent out to subject the Mormons to our institutions, which it did not do. The army was only used in the interests of slavery. The writer of the letter resigned in disgust; but even then he prophesied that triumph which God has vouchsafed to Freedom. One of the first prominent victims of the late struggle was the commander of those troops, that able ALBERT SYDNEY JOHNSTON, the hope of the Slavocrats, who did not do their work negligently in 1858–'9, or whenever he had an opportunity to do it.

"Chicago—with its 109,260 inhabitants in 1860—250 miles to the northeast of St. Louis, where KEARNY was stationed in 1837–'9, was still little more than a settlement, grouped around Fort Dearborn, and the house of the Indian agent. These were the only edifices to be seen there in 1832," the year when the writer quoted entered West Point, and the Black Hawk War broke out. "In 1840, Fort Dearborn had entirely disappeared, and Chicago contained 4,853 inhabitants."

In 1837, the "Father of Waters" had still a population peculiar to itself. Arks, broad-horns and flat-boats, of more or less primitive construction, barges and keel-boats, drifting with the current, or navigated by a class of men rough and rude, but intellectually strong as they were physically powerful—a class which produced Abraham Lincoln—had not yet been superseded by steamboats for the general transportation of merchandise.

KEARNY lived to see changes, which to predict would have been set down as madness. Fort Leavenworth, on the border line between Missouri and Kansas, was then far, far out in the wilderness. When

KEARNY returned from Europe and his Algerian campaign, it was a sort of nucleus, around which border progress—the pen came near writing civilization, of which, in its true sense, it is very doubtful if there is very much on the border—had just begun to aggregate itself. All beyond was wilderness, in the true sense of the word. Then the one regiment of dragoons, which superseded DODGE'S "Border Rangers," sufficed to keep the Indians in awe. Now thanks to civilization and its inevitable whiskey and contracts for the benefit of political favorites at Washington, their control, in the slightest degree, tasks the brains of a Lieutenant-General and an army almost as numerous as that which fought four grand battles in the valley, and captured the capital of Mexico.

When KEARNY next appeared upon the frontier, in 1845, Fort Leavenworth had become a great frontier depot. St. Louis had over 50,000 inhabitants, Missouri over 500,000. Before he died, those sparsely populated regions, whose protection constituted his first chief duty, had become thickly peopled States. Missouri alone could boast of 1,182,012. Beyond these a tier of new States had grown up, and carried civilization 500 to 900 miles farther on to the plains, which, in 1837, were the domain of the Indian, the Buffalo, and the Trapper.

CHAPTER V.

A REPRESENTATIVE AMERICAN.

"Dreaded in battle and loved in hall."

"Bold as thou in the fight,
Blithe as thou in the hall,
Shone the noon of my might." —St. Olave.

"Prepare a banquet, and, costly let it be,
And in magnificence bespeak my mind;
Whate'er the East of delicacy yields,
* * * Let the commanders,
Worthy companions in the well-fought field,
Be summon'd to partake. The cheerful goblet
Shall raise our souls." * * *.—Frowd.

"The banquet waits our presence; festal joy
Laughs in the mantling goblet, and the night,
Illumined by the tapers' dazzling beams,
Rivals departed day." —Brown.

"There was a sound of revelry by night,
And "Saumur's" capital had gather'd then
Her beauty and her chivalry, and bright
The lamps shone o'er fair women and brave men;
A thousand hearts beat happily; and when
Music arose with its voluptuous swell,
Soft eyes look'd love to eyes which spake again,
And all went merry as a marriage bell.—Childe Harold.

As mentioned in the preceding chapter, "the First Regiment U. S. Dragoons was the first corps of the cavalry arm established by the government, after the general disarmament subsequent to the war of 1812–'15. Consequently, at the time of its organization, and for several years afterwards, no complete system of cavalry tactics had been provided." Joel Roberts Poinsett—Secretary of War under Martin Van Buren, 1837–1841—conceived the idea, in the first year of his term, of sending out to France three of our dragoon officers, "for the purpose of going through the regular course at the "Royal School of Cavalry," at Saumur; who, on their return to this country, were to compile a work on Cavalry Tactics, moulded on that of the French system, but so modified as "to suit the wants of our own service." The three officers selected were, 1st Lieutenant, WILLIAM EUSTIS; 1st Lieutenant, HENRY S. TURNER, and 1st Lieutenant, PHILIP KEARNY, Jr. The result of their labors was the Cavalry Tactics, printed by order of the War Department, at Washington, and bearing date 10th February, 1841,—three weeks before the close of Mr. POINSETT's term of office. Colonel BRACKETT, in his History of the U. S. Cavalry, remarks: "The system of Cavalry Tactics adapted to the organization of the Dragoon Regiments, was authorized by Hon. J. R. POINSETT, Secretary of War, on 10th February, 1841. It is mainly a translation of the tactics of the French service, and has not been yet improved upon, though several attempts have been made, which have all proved failures. I believe almost every cavalry officer of experience considers the tactics of 1841 as far superior to anything which has yet been introduced into our service."

Pursuant to orders, PHILIP KEARNY left his regiment to proceed to Washington, D. C., 21st May, 1839, and there received farther orders, dated 9th August, 1839, to proceed to France on special duty.

"The Three" sailed from New York in August, and "arrived at Fontainbleau October 1st, 1839, where they found the U. S. Minister, Mr. CASS, on a visit to the royal family, then residing at the Chateau, in the midst of one of the finest forests in France, 37 miles S.S.E. of Paris. They were presented at Court by Mr. CASS, and had every reason to be satisfied with their reception. They dined twice at the Chateau, and accompanied the king to a review of troops at the Camp of Instruction." On the 8th October "the Three" were at Saumur, but KEARNY, after remaining there a short time, "obtained a leave of absence, and accompanied the Duke of Orleans, eldest son of LOUIS PHILIPPE, on one," if not two, "of his campaigns in Africa." The incidents of that campaign—which will be treated of in full in subsequent chapters—were given "in a full and most interesting report," made at the time to Major-General SCOTT, commander-in-chief of the U. S. Army, by Lieutenant KEARNY, who, after his return from Europe, was attached to the staff of that General as aid-de-camp, thus succeeding, in regular order of generations, as it were, to a position of honor held by his uncle, GEORGE WATTS, of the 1st U. S. Light Dragoons, during the campaign of 1814.

But the reader may say, Where is Saumur? and what of the Military Academy? The question is a just one.

Saumur, about one hundred and seventy miles southwest of Paris, is a cheerful place, gleaming from afar with its white buildings, and one of the most picturesque towns, in its quaint structures, towers, pinnacles, and spires, on the Loire. It stands on the left bank of that river, and prior to the "Revocation of the Edict of Nantes," 24th October, 1685, was one of the strongholds of the Huguenots, or Protestants of France, who were driven forth from their native country, or worse, by that iniquitous decree. Two centuries ago it was the capital of a district in the province of Anjou—known as the "Saumurois." The confines of this petty government presented exactly the outline of one of those delicious pears for which France is so celebrated, and Saumur was situated at the apex or root of the stem. Its capture by the Vendeans, 10th June, 1793, was one of the grandest exploits of that marvellous effort of loyalty and honor.

The Royal Cavalry School, transferred to this city from Angers towards the close of the preceding century, is located to the southwest of Saumur, and covers quite a large space with its buildings, riding-schools, and grounds for exercise and drill. It is destined to receive officers, non-commissioned officers (from three hundred to four hundred of this grade), and even picked riders (*cavaliers*). They are instructed in every branch of information appropriate to their Arm, and, after a complete course, are distributed through all the cavalry regiments in the army, to diffuse a complete knowledge of the horse and horsemanship and the best method of imparting instruction according to a uniform system.

It is somewhat curious, just as our three young American officers were sent to complete their military education at the Royal School of Cavalry, at Saumur, so Pitt and Wellington took a course of lessons at its predecessor, the "Academy of Equitation," at Angers; the latter, in 1785–1787. Thus the bitterest and the most successful enemy of France laid the foundation in a French Military School of that knowledge of war which led the latter—"the Iron Duke" of after years—through Vimiera, Vittoria, and Waterloo, to Paris.

While at the Cavalry School at Saumur, Lieutenant KEARNY determined to give an entertainment which would not only do honor to himself but to his country. He was incited to doing this by the generous sentiment which he felt for the attentions he had received and in order to make some adequate return for the civilities shown by the civil and military authorities of the place to the three American officers resident among them.

The story of this ball is as follows:

On "Twelfth Night," (1840)—an anniversary kept in Europe with almost as much exactitude as Christmas—General DE BRACK, in command at Saumur, gave a party at his residence.

Formerly "Twelfth Night," or the "Eve of the Festival of the Three Kings," was one of those periodical seasons which have always been consecrated by European nations to amusement and festivity. Thus, we find BARENTZ and HEEMSKERCK imprisoned amid the Artic ice, on the coast of Nova Zembla, during that terrible winter of 1596–'7, expending their last little supply of wine in pigmy bumpers to the king of the festival, and with a courage and spirit without example, indulging in all the customary merriment of home, which they seemed destined, in all human probability, never to revisit, and when they were, to all appearances, *within* the jaws of destruction.

The Twelfth Night king was a potentate, with authority and functions somewhat similar to those exercised by the King of Misrule in Old English Christmas revels. Among the more elevated and refined classes of society, this festival assumed a stately character, and became susceptible of very great display. The selection of King and Queen was generally left to chance and determined by a bean, which was placed in a cake, cut and distributed in pieces before the supper. The drawer of the slice containing the bean became King or Queen, and was privileged to select a partner to share his or her temporary regal honors. All drank to his or her majesty, who reigned and received homage from every one during the evening. In this custom originated the French title of the festival, The Feast of Kings ("La Fete de Rois), for which the revolutionary government of 1793 substituted, "The Merrymaking of those without breeches, *i. e.* Radical Democrats" ("*La Fete des Sans Culottes*"), through their hatred of anything savoring of royalty. Before the disastrous close of the reign of LOUIS XVI., the French monarch and his nobles waited on the Twelfth Night king. This proves the importance given to the occasion in former days.

KEARNY was "prevented by indisposition from attending the party at the house of General DE BRACK on Twelfth Night," wrote the first of "the Three," who kept a sort of journal of what transpired, "When the cake was cut, some of the ladies sent him a piece with the bean in it, and from that the ball originated. He first intended to give a party at the assembly rooms, but the idea gradually expanded, and when he was offered the grand rooms of the school, he put the whole thing in the hands of some French officers, with 'carte blanche' as to expense. The result was a ball which eclipsed even the grand ball given by the city, some years before, to the Duchesse DE BERRI, and which seemed to be the only notable event on record when we arrived there. The rooms were beautifully decorated under the superintendence of General DE BRACK, who was an artist. The supper was sent from Paris by one of the most celebrated restaurateurs; flowers in profusion came from Angers and other places," "each lady on entering received a bouquet of the choicest flowers in an elegant silver holder," "and with the music of the fine brass band of the school, and an excellent string-band from the city, nothing was wanting to make the whole affair a perfect success. Applications were constantly received for invitations, many from a great distance, and if it had been delayed much longer, the rooms would not have held the crowd. KEARNY employed an artist who was present to make a picture of the ball, a copy of which he presented to General DE BRACK."

KEARNY's ball "was gotten up in a style of magnificence that was wholly unprecedented in that part of the country"—these are the words of another eye-witness, the second of "the Three." It was "given 11th February, 1840, and presided over by the Commandant of the School, General DE BRACK," whose wife KEARNY selected as the Queen of this substitute Twelfth Night merry-making celebration, and it was attended by all the prominent people of that particular section, and by many from Paris and elsewhere. It was in every respect a brilliant affair, and procured for General KEARNY, from the inhabitants, the most enthusiastic acknowledgments, for the liberality he had displayed in thus contributing to their enjoyment. An artist was engaged to make a picture of the scene on canvas. In this he was very successful in giving admirable likenesses of several prominent individuals."

The only discrepancy, in the recollections of those who participated in the festivities, is as to whether the town or the giver of the *fete* employed the artist who executed the picture which commemorated this graceful evidence of KEARNY's patriotism and grateful appreciation of the courtesies of the French government and officials, but more particularly the attention of the officer in command. At all events, by whomsoever commanded, the original picture, or a copy of it, was a prominent object, at the time of the General's death, among the paintings which adorned his spacious and elegant mansion, at Belle Grove, on an elevation opposite Newark. This building stands on the site of a country residence which, prior to the Revolution, belonged to his grand-aunt, whose husband built and dwelt in No. 1 Broadway, a very fine building for its date and the young city of New York, and originally owned the adjoining No. 3, in which KEARNY was born.

This painting is on too small a scale to do full justice to the occasion, but it affords some idea of its splendor, attributable in a great measure to the variety, grace, and elegance of the numerous uniforms of the Turkish, Polish, American, and French officers belonging to the different arms and services, which filled the room—uniforms, of whose richness and contrast, our people, accustomed to the universal sameness of our present blue, tame and simple, can have no idea whatever. At that time the Turkish and Polish military costumes were still, if not the most serviceable, the most striking in Europe. They were susceptible of any amount of decoration, almost as much so as the Hungarian, with its plumes, embroidery, jewels, lace, buttons, jacket and dolman. All that is most attractive in the dress of the Chasseurs d'Afrique—to which KEARNY was afterwards attached—was borrowed from the Polish; everything which looked well and yet was serviceable, just as the Zouaves, was modeled on the Turkish military costume. All that was rejected was those details which were in reality unmilitary and unfitted for active service. All that was good and good-looking was retained. And, yet, KEARNY told the writer that his own uniform, that of the American Light Dragoons of thirty years ago, was as effective and imposing as any in the room. Doubtless he made it so, although it was very jaunty in itself. The coatee, blue, double-breasted, was not a frock, but cut in a much more graceful fashion; the collar, cuff and turn-backs, bordered with lace and ornamented and trimmed with gold, pantaloons, blue-gray mixture, known as light army-blue, with two stripes of orange cloth up each outward seam; the cap, such as the French term "shako," with drooping, white horse-hair pompon, or rather plume, silver and gold ornaments, and gold foraging cords and tassels. The latter could be detached and worn over the coat and around the neck, producing the effect of an aiguilette. The sash was silk net, of a deep orange color, which, if made in France, as the writer has seen them made, shone in the glancing lights like a waving zone of gold. Thus KEARNY described it, and thus our officers did not make a bad show among the dazzling dresses whirling in the waltz, or polka, or promenading about.

When KEARNY resigned, in 1851, the same striking and elegant uniform was still worn by our Dragoons; and the writer will never forget his expression and manner, when he came back in 1861, and saw some of his own regiment again, in Washington, after the lapse of ten years. "I left them," said he, "a set of elegant gentlemen, and now I come back and find them a set of dirty blackguards." The Dragoons at the National Capital certainly did not present an attractive appearance in May, 1861: especially in the horrid felt hat of an "Italian bandit,"—as some one styled it—which JEFFERSON DAVIS, while Secretary of War, had clapped on their heads.

That this ball must have been something extraordinary, there can be no doubt, from the glowing accounts given of it by those who were present, and KEARNY's lavish expenditure, doubtless, did make a strong impression on a people so susceptible to display as the French, particularly at that period, when extravagance had not attained the vast proportions it has reached under LOUIS NAPOLEON. That it must have cost a very large sum, is certain, from the horror-stricken expression of KEARNY's agent, when called upon to remit the necessary moneys. He threw up his hands, as if the young representative of American munificence had lost his senses.

DOCUMENTS.

The following letters, received from the U. S. War Department, Washington, D. C., arrived too late for incorporation, and are therefore printed and added entire. The author hereby acknowledges the assistance of Brevet Major-General E. D. TOWNSEND, Assistant and Acting Adjutant-General U. S. A.

SAUMUR, October 12, 1839.

MONSIEUR LIEUTENANT-COMMANDER MICHAUD:

SIR:—Let me take the liberty of consulting with you, (as you are the officer to whose charge the General has entrusted us), on the course that I had best pursue whilst at Saumur, to answer the end that government has in view in sending me abroad. And to do so let me first explain the organization and the origin of our regiment.

At the close of our late war with Great Britain, in 1815, our cavalry regiments were disbanded. In 1833, after one of our Indian wars had proved the necessity of having cavalry on the frontiers, ours, the First Regiment of Light Dragoons, was raised. It was organized, not by squadrons, but by companies, each company having a captain and a first lieutenant and a second lieutenant. It was officered principally by officers taken from the infantry. Everything was new to them. The cavalry regulations for the manœuvres were taken from the French, almost literally translated. But as for police and the internal administration of the regiment, and everthing else of that kind, there was no other precedent than as far as the experience our officers had had whilst in the infantry—some had been in for many years; the present Colonel for more than twenty years, having served during the war.

Through the zeal of our officers, and from our being kept constantly actively employed in sending detachments through the Indian country, our system and discipline has been rendered nearly complete. But as in cavalry, which, like the French, has been kept progressing in perfection ever since the great wars of Europe, everything useless has been rejected, and everything requisite is practiced in the best manner. It is for the purpose of making a statement of the differences that exist between our own and the French cavalry, that I have been sent abroad.

My object is to remain at Saumur for six months, for the purpose of acquiring the French language, becoming instructed in the use of the sword, and of arms pertaining to cavalry; to follow a course of riding, but rather the "pratique" than the theory, and more especially for gaining ideas generally, to assist me in the more thoroughly visiting and making observations on the regiments themselves. Secondly, to visit some of the best dragoon and light cavalry regiments; proposing also, should it be advisable and meet with the approval of our Secretary of War, to visit the regiments in active service in Africa.

The result of these observations is intended to make known to our government, and more particularly to the Colonel of our regiment, the differences that exist in the organization, in the manœuvres, in the police, in the administration, and in all the internal regulations of the French cavalry and our own. Also, to inform myself of the course pursued with the soldier from his joining as a recruit till admitted to the squadron.

Your advice as to the consideration of the above points will be esteemed a great favor and kindness by

Your obedient servant,

P. KEARNY,

Second Lieutenant First Dragoons.

Lieutenant-Commander MICHAUD,

Instructor of the School of Cavalry.

SAUMUR, October 16th, 1839.

HONORABLE J. R. POINSETT:

SIR:—We arrived here last Monday a week, and reported to general BRACK, the commandant of the school, on the following day.

I have not written to you before, from my not having had anything satisfactory to communicate. I am now happy to say that, at least as far as I am concerned, I will be enabled to accomplish at Saumur the objects proposed. As I understood from you in our first interview at Washington, it was your intention, in sending Lieutenants EUSTIS and TURNER, that they should remain one year, and accomplish in that one year, as far as they were able, the studies pursued by the students in the course of two years—the usual term at Saumur.

For myself, I had the highly gratifying honor to have been selected originally with the same intent, but finding myself situated in a manner that rendered my stay in the army uncertain, I considered myself in honor bound to explain to you the circumstances. I had the satisfaction to find that my motives were understood, and the honor of being sent abroad on a leave of absence, having military subjects for its purpose.

I have repeatedly regretted that your being obliged to leave Saratoga so immediately after your arrival (which I had not been aware was your intention) prevented my seeing you to converse with you in a more particular manner as to the precise disposition of my time whilst abroad.

At Washington, you spoke of my entering Saumur under the sanction of our government, and remaining there with the others for a few months, and then, by traveling, to make myself acquainted with the interior economy, and all that was connected with the French cavalry, by observing, as an eye-witness, what was actually practiced in the best regiments—communicating the same to you unofficially, by letters, or by a private report on my return—though, as I understood it, rather by accumulating facts, by which yourself and our Colonel would be enabled to institute comparisons between the utility of the practices of our own and the French regiments.

I think that in our conversation you did not fix a precise time for my stay at Saumur, but rather left it to myself to remain a few months. Had I had a second interview with you on this subject, I would have requested you to name the precise time. But as that did not occur, and to fix on a precise time in advance was necessary for regulating my studies here, I determined it at six months, that being about the time you would have recommended, and decidedly the period best adapted for the objects for which I have come abroad. For six months could not be more serviceably spent than in mastering the French language, availing myself of the riding-school, and becoming instructed in the sword exercise, and in the use of arms proper to cavalry, and more particularly the gaining ideas to enable me to study most advantageously the regiments that I shall afterwards visit.

The *élèves* of St. Cyr, and all foreign officers (there are at present here two of the *cidevant* Polish and Turkish services), are put under the immediate directions of one of the Instructors. We have been placed under the charge of Lieutenant-Commander MICHAUD, an officer who stands high in his profession, and who, even in this short time, has evinced a degree of polite attention that merits our sincere thanks.

Finding that our situation generally, and more particularly my own, was not fully understood, I wrote, as to a friend, to this Mr. MICHAUD, explaining, in a few lines, the nature of my mission. This was translated into the French by our Professor of that language, an Englishman, but one who had been recommended to us as being thoroughly master of the French from a fifteen years' residence. A copy of the same accompanies this communication. It was handed to General BRACK; he approved of it, and under his authority Mr. MICHAUD told me that he understood and entered fully into my views, and would, through his instructions, enable me to attain the objects I proposed. Let me take the liberty of assuring you that there could not be rendered a greater favor, both individually and as from the Institution, than this permitting me to pursue an unusual course at a school where, as at West Point, there are none but regular classes. The course is two years, and each year and part of a year has its particular branches of study; and on my part, let me assure you that, if assiduity and zeal for my profession will avail anything, an opportunity like this shall be improved to the uttermost.

In my letter to Mr. MICHAUD, you will perceive an allusion to my visiting some of the French regiments serving in Africa. Should you have no positive objections, I think that this and the particular regiments that I visit had better be left to the advices that I may gain in conversation with General BRACK—an officer who distinguished himself whilst in the Imperial Cavalry, and also with other officers here.

In the course of a few days, Messrs. EUSTIS, TURNER or myself will give you a more concise account of the school; as a cursory remark, I inform you that there are two classes of officers among the students here. The class to which we shall be attached, though their course does not commence till January, is that composed of the *elèves* of St. Cyr—St. Cyr being a preparatory school for the Infantry and Cavalry officers. Those who are intended for the Cavalry, after finishing their course here, are sent to Saumur to learn Cavalry duties. The other class of students are called the "Officers from the Regiments," that is, they are officers who, before coming here, have already served for some years with their regiments.

Besides the department of Instruction are three other military branches connected with the Institution: one is the School for Non-Commissioned Officers—the best and most capable of the privates being selected and sent here to be prepared as non-commissioned officers for their regiments. The second branch is for the instruction of their cavalry bands—boys—the sons of *Gendarmes* and old soldiers being sent here, to be rendered musicians previous to being admitted into the regimental bands. The effect of it is plainly visible; and I doubt if the English bands, though sustained at enormous expense by the officers, can equal the French. The third branch is the School for Farriers. It may be added, though not appertaining so immediately to the military, that there is connected with the school a very large Government Haras, numbering some as beautiful animals as I have ever seen, many of them Arabs, many, too, of English blood, all being destined for the use of the Institution.

Sir, again let me apologize for thus addressing you unofficially, but such I believe is your desire, and is the only mode for an officer communicating direct with the War Department.

Sir, with all respect, &c.,

Your most obedient servant,

P. KEARNY,
Second Lieutenant First Dragoons.

The Honorable
J. R. POINSETT,
Secretary of War, Washington.

CHAPTER VI.

EL TELL AND EL SERSOUS.

FRANCE IN AFRICA.

"I speak of Africa."

SHAKSPEARE'S "HENRY IV."

"Behold the African,
That traverses the vast Numidian deserts
In quest of prey, and lives upon his bow.—

ADDISON'S "CATO."

"COMBATTRE ET SOUFFRIR."

"*Journal de l'Expedition et de la Retraite de Constantine en* 1836 *; par un Voluntaire, Officier de l'Armee Afrique.*"

KEARNY IN ALGIERS.

SICILY was considered the training ground of the Roman and Carthaginian armies, contending for the Empire of the Mediterranean. Algiers has been the training ground of the French Army —dreaming of another European career of conquest and spoliation like that which they enjoyed under the First NAPOLEON. The present French ruler seems never to have forgotten a remark made by FREDERICK THE GREAT: "That if he were King of France, not a shot would be fired in Europe without his permission." It is a very hard school; it forged and tempered the steel-heads of those columns which did the fighting in the Crimea; who stormed the heights at Alma; brought succor at Inkerman; captured the Malakoff, and wrested victory from the Austrians in 1859, from Monte Bello to Solferino.

Although a tropical land, the vicissitudes of the temperature are as fearful as those which convert iron into steel. In the mountain regions, only a short distance from the coast, the changes are almost incredible. In the retreat of the first expedition against Constantine—23d November to 11th December, 1836—the French suffered as much from snow and cold as they did in other years from heat.

This retreat, in many of its hardships and perils, was a repetition in miniature of the retreat from Moscow, 1812. Indeed, some of the old officers declared that during this campaign of seventeen days they had encountered in Africa the icy cold of Moscow and the bottomless mud of Warsaw. No wonder KEARNY did not contemplate the mire of the sacred soil with a dread equal to that of McCLELLAN, after floundering through that of Barbary, roadless, and soaked with the continual and severe rains of that zone.

During the second siege of Constantine, which was successful, one French regiment was exposed "for fifty hours, without rest or sustenance, to a pelting storm of snow and rain."

Lieutenant RAASLOFF, of the Danish Artillery, a very prominent officer, who, like KEARNY, participated, as a volunteer, in the campaigns of 1840–41, relates a very interesting anecdote of this retreat, from commencement to end a series of the most fearful sufferings, labors, and privations. One of his friends, who was present, told him that after twenty-four hours of almost insupportable miseries, he mustered his energies to enable him to live through the coming night, which promised no alleviation of them, standing, leaning against his horse and holding him by the bridle. Two private soldiers, wrapped in their cloaks, had lain themselves down in the deep mud at his feet. After they had remained quiet in this uncomfortable position for some time, one of them suddenly roused himself into a sitting position and exclaimed: "Well, I declare, I wonder what they are playing at the Varieties Theatre (in Paris) to-night," after which he sank down again into the sleety slush and slumber of exhaustion. When the day broke, RAASLOFF's friend sought to awaken the two sleepers, but in vain. They both slept the sleep which knows no waking. What an illustration of the careless disposition of French soldiers, and under such circumstances!

Then again, during the operations in summer, the heat almost surpasses belief. In some of his letters, KEARNY spoke of men and horses falling dead around him from the heat under a burning sky, like the heaven of brass prophesied to the Israelites as a curse. Notwithstanding, the French troops were called upon to undergo marches and privations—such as it is almost impossible to conceive that men can survive, especially during the season of the Simoon, or wind from the desert. Life at times becomes a burthen to them, and the exclamation is quoted as made by more than one: "I wish that the Bedouins would grow out of the ground by millions and put an end to us all." All this, however, realizes the truth of the proverb, "Fatigue and privation render the soldier careless of danger," and, or yet make the best soldiers.

The writer can speak, to some extent from personal experience, in regard to the climate in the fall. Suffering from a disease of the chest, he made a trip to Algiers in 1851, in the latter part of the month of November, which CASTELLAE, an old African campaigner, styles "the Father of Tempests" (*le pere des tempetes*). The party experienced the truth of this remark. They looked forward to a trip over summer seas of not over forty-eight hours' duration. Vain hope! Worse weather and more wicked seas were never encountered on the ocean. It was not only tempestuous, but the wind was intensely cold and penetrating, one of those terrible piercing northwesters, descending from the snow-clad Cevennes and Pyrenees, which share dominion with the Mistral, whose cradle is the everlasting snows and glaciers of the Alps. These are the winds which render the south of France so dangerous to persons affected with weak lungs, and make the navigation of the "Gulf of the Lion"—not "of Lyons," as it is now written—so perilous during the late fall, winter, and early spring.

The Merovée left Marseilles, 15th November, at 2 P. M., in one of these gales so fierce that the steamer, instead of putting forth on its direct course, crept along the French coast not five miles from the land until off Cape Creux, one hundred and eighty-five miles, where the mountains are thrust forth just north of the Gulf of Rosas. Thence the vessel was steered for the straits between Majorca and Minorca, passing in sight of the former and of Cabrera—a den of horrors for the French prisoners taken by the Spaniards during the Napoleonic wars—and then directly south for Algiers, where it arrived on the 18th, about 11 P. M., having consumed eighty-three hours in accomplishing what the passengers were assured would take only forty-eight. Amid all the discomforts of this passage, there are incidents which linger on the memory like glimpses of fairy land. On the 17th the passengers had a magnificent view of the Spanish coast, with the Pyrenees rising in all their grandeur, one sheet of glistening snow, like a vast succession of pyramids of polished Pentelican marble, and on the night of the 17th, in perfect contrast, the shores of Majorca—where the best oranges eaten in France are grown—were plainly visible, all bathed in lovely moonlight.

Finding Algiers anything but a suitable place for an invalid, and the temperature entirely dependent upon the sun, which did not shine auspiciously, since it poured almost the whole time, the party determined to seek a more propitious climate. While the sky is clouded and the rains fall, fires are indispensable for those who do not enjoy good health and are accustomed to such a comfort; then when the sun does come out, the contrast makes the heat almost insupportable. While in Algiers, the party saw all that was to be seen; ascended the mountain Sahel, in the rear of the city, looking down upon the plain of the Metidjah, where PHIL KEARNY fought in 1840, the last time that the Arabs ventured a descent into the fertile lowlands, between the Sahel and the Lesser Atlas, an intervale varying from fifteen to twenty-five miles in width—many remembered an American officer who distinguished himself the last time the Arabs descended into the plain—drove in and out the different gates through the new and stupendous fortifications, and along the splendid military roads; climbed to the ramparts of the Emperor's Fort; visited the son of the last Mufti, himself an old man, at his villa a few miles outside the walls, who did not think much of the French, but seemed to have the highest respect for the broadsides —which he had heard—of England and America; threaded the lanes, and roamed through the Cazbah, the former palace of the expatriated Deys; in fact viewed everything except the interior of a mosque—and that no one cared to enter for fear of cold, or adding to it, from walking on damp floors with bare feet—a sacrifice visitors must make to their curiosity, since everyone had to take off his boots or shoes.

The return passage occupied nearly five days, in consequence of a succession of fierce blows. The Merovée sailed from Algiers on the 20th, at 1 P. M., in the height of a strong Libecchio or southwester, and, with a heavy sea running, steered toward the Islands of Majorca and Ivica, passing so close to the former that the city of Palma—its capital—was distinctly seen. On the 22d, 2 P. M., when off the Gulf of Rosas, the Mistral burst from the N. E. like a thunderbolt upon the steamer, with the fury which makes it a terror at this season to those who navigate these waters. The tempest and the sea leaped into existence simultaneously, as if they had been evoked by the wand of an enchanter, and the vessel was struck down and deluged with water in an instant. No description can do justice to a veritable Mistral, or give a just idea of its powers. A very ugly heavy sea rose like magic. Almost the first filled the whole deck, crowded with soldiers, well, sick, and wounded. The captain hoisted jib, put the helm up, wore ship, and ran for the port of Palamos, as the nearest safe harbor, Rosas not being sufficiently good holding ground. While rounding to, the light iron boat was almost rolled over, the gunwale went under, decks flooded, wind howling; but once before the gale, all right, although the sea, bright green, foam-crested and streaked, followed like a wall, threatening to poop the steamer—that is, break over the stern—and sweep the decks, and reared like a wall before. All the time the sky was as serene and beautiful as possible, and the sun shone in all its brilliancy; meanwhile the wind raging like fury. With the first gust the captain remarked: "The Mistrao"—so they call it in their patois—"was a good broom; it swept the sky clean." And so it did, and visibly, driving before it the dense masses of clouds like vast flocks of sheep hunted by dogs, and in a very few minutes the vault above was one vast expanse of blue, undefiled by a single stain.

Palamos seemed quite a pretty place, or rather a series of villages than one continuous town—with houses and churches constructed of stone—picturesquely disposed around a circular bay, well protected from the prevailing winds. Some of the houses were on the beach almost at the water's edge, the others a little back in the gorges of the hills—apparently well cultivated and handsomely wooded—which surrounded the harbor like the wall of an amphitheatre, while the main town at the Eastern extremity of the bay has a mole and breakwater sheltering quite a commodious although small port. There were a number of vessels at anchor here, one a bark, the rest large-sized coasters. On Sunday, 22d, 6 P. M., after twenty-four hours' detention, the wind having subsided, the Merovée put to sea, but, at the same spot as the day before, off Cape Creux, was assailed by a second and severer edition of the Mistral, and driven back to Palamos. On Monday morning, 23d, 2 A. M., anchor was weighed a second time, and at 11 P. M. on the 24th the party landed in Marseilles in another rain storm. This is a worse climate than America. When it don't rain, oh, how it blows, so cold, so bitter cold! A calm, quiet, joyous day, and clear sunshine, seem incompatible. Rain and lowering skies and murggy, warm, damp weather, with pouring or soaking rain, always go together. On board the steamer there were said to be five hundred soldiers, mostly invalids, many with constitutions prostrated with African fever. Whether drenched from the waves, which broke over the vessel, or the rain, which fell in floods, succeeded in the Gulf of Perpignan by the Mistral, which—while it broomed the sky of clouds and unveiled the sun—brought with it the piercing cold of the Alpine snows and glaciers, these soldiers had no shelter whatever, for five days, but a sail stretched across the bow, simply to break the force of the icy gale.

Allusion has been made to the condition of the five hundred invalids on board the Merovée, during the return trip. This was nothing to the crowd on the passage to Algiers: it seemed as if there was scarcely an inch of the deck but was occupied with soldiers, colonists and their wives, children, and all those who could not afford to pay for better accommodations. The tempestuous weather was bad enough for those unaccustomed to it, but it was the intense cold that made it so terrible to these exposed human beings. The wind, descending from the snow-clad Alps, Cevennes, and Pyrenees, penetrated like "gimlets of ice;" and it was stated in Algiers that on board a naval transport, the "Pluton," from Toulon, loaded with troops, which put into Minorca, one or two men died from the effects of the cold, and a number of others—"a dozen" was the word used—were so severely frost-bitten as to become, comparatively speaking, invalids for life. These troops were not either sick or wounded, returning from Algiers with broken constitutions—who make the transit, whatever may be the state of the weather, without shelter on the open deck—but healthy reinforcements from the mother country.

Lamping, a German officer, who served in Africa in the "Foreign Legion," who spoke from experience, testifies, that "a pickled herring has more space allotted to it in the barrel than a soldier on board a French (Mediterranean) steamboat."

"During the summer the surface of the Mediterranean is almost as smooth as a mirror. The blue transparent water looks so gentle and harmless that one can scarcely believe in the terrific powers which slumber in its bosom. In the later autumn it entirely alters its character: storms, and frequently even hurricanes, render the African coasts the most dangerous in the world."

The changes of temperature in the province of Algiers itself, present contrasts just as startling as the sea which bathes its shore. In mid-summer the thermometer rises to 100°, and in the winter in the mountain regions, snow storms rage with violence. As a rule, in the spring and early fall, and always during the summer, the extreme heat is constant in the plains and valleys. Amid the mountains, however, sudden storms occur when the thermometer falls, to such a degree that the soldiers suffer as much from the cold and wet as they had previously from the heat and drought. In the fall, winter, and spring the rains are very cold, and often of long continuance. The author of "A Summer in the Sahara," writing from Medeah, 22d May, 1853, records that even at that late period "Winter still kept his foot planted on the white summits of the Mouzaia," and on the 28th October, 1840, the summit of the Djebel Mouzaia, or else the Beni Sala, visible from the north through the Pass of Tenyah, is represented like a glistening pyramid of frosted silver. This must be the mountain, Nador, alluded to by CASTELLANE, 19th November, 1840, which rises to the north of Medeah. He says, "the last platoons of the rear-guard disappeared behind Mount Nador. The last image, the remembrance of France, seems to have withdrawn." These, however, may be exceptional cases, although it would seem not, since a deserter related the following curious anecdote of the Emir's troops, who occupied that pass in October, 1840. "The Arab Regulars in order to protect themselves against the cold, stuck each one his leg into the wide pantaloons of his next neighbor, and thus lay down to sleep, chained or trowsered together, as it were, in one mass." Had the alarm been sudden, "The Philistines are upon thee," they must either have been all captured or slaughtered. Fortunately, they had time to disengage themselves before they were attacked by the French troops. This proves, however, that it must have been exceedingly cold to compel acclimated men to resort to such an expedient to keep themselves warm in the presence of the enemy.

RAASLOFF, at another place, furnishes statements which prove what a fearful mortality attends the campaigns in this fitful climate. In 1840—the year when KEARNY won his spurs, and first saw fire—during the months of July, August, and September, there was a monthly average of 14,000 sick, and during the last five months of that year 7,000 died in the military hospitals in Algiers. This does not include those who were sent back to France to die or recover there.

In the year 1841, the number of days during which patients were on the sick list amounted to 2,269,588. These, divided by 75,000 men, give 31 days in the hospital for every military man in

Algiers. During this same year, the mortality in the hospitals in Africa was 7,812, to which must be added 484, who died on their passage back to France, or in the hospitals there. Total, 8,296, or over 11 1-2 per cent. of the effective force of the army.

As to the mortality and suffering among the beasts of burthen, it was almost incredible. Not a single expedition took place which, when it terminated, might not have been justly termed disorganized in a far greater degree than our own dear Army of the Potomac, on the 2d September, 1862, when, to elevate the rehabilitating powers of McClellan and his favorites, it was represented to be in such a shocking condition. If any officer wishes to appreciate the hardships of a soldier's life, he has only to make one campaign in Africa, to comprehend all its labors, privations, hardships, and dangers—the worst, since the climate engenders diseases which assail the body through the mind as well as through the ordinary channels. One of these is nostalgia, or home-sickness, to which Raasloff and Lamping both feelingly allude. The other is that inexplicable depression of spirits—very similar in its effects to the preceding, but yet not altogether the same, which too often converts a slight or curable wound into a dangerous one, or mortal, such as neither surgeon, medicine, nor any amount of care can alleviate.

To show of what indomitable stuff Phil Kearny was made, when he left Saumur to proceed to Algiers he was so ill that he had to be carried to his carriage, and one of his comrades wrote out to the United States that "he would not be at all surprised if Kearny left his bones in Africa." Whether it was that intense mental excitement overcame any physical weakness, there was something astonishing in the manner in which the climate of Algiers, so trying or fatal to the majority, agreed with him. One of his relatives refers to this at the time, quoting from one of his letters, that while he was dashing about and fighting for the love of the thing under the burning skies of Africa, when men and horses were falling around him from the effects of the intense heat, he was breathing in health and strength, and returned home in robust health.

Having thus endeavored to present a clear idea of the climate of that region in which France forms the nerves and sinews of her army, as bad, if not worse, than the majority of the weather which our armies had to encounter, the reader may desire to know something in regard to the French conquests and wars in Northern Africa.

In May–July, 1830, General BOURMONT landed a French army, and captured Algiers. By this conquest the French obtained a colony, fertile and accessible, which they had long coveted, and considerable plunder. It is questionable whether they have ever derived any other benefit from it than the formation of an army, which, as far as it goes, shows it has no superior. Down to 1845, the conquest was hardly more than nominal, although the campaign in 1840, in which KEARNY participated, gave some very rude shocks to the native powers of resistence. In 1836 occurred the first expedition against Constantine which ended in disaster.

Up to this time ABD-EL-KADER, although a powerful chief, had not become the supreme leader of the Arabs, although he had opposed the French with ability and intrepidity, especially in the west, for several years. There, in 1832, before Oran, he experienced a Gettysburg defeat in a conflict which lasted three days, like our own great battle for national existence. In 1835 he seemed to have established a regular government, and even to have reconstructed the Arab nationality. During the succeeding years he gained great desultory successes over the French. These, on the 3d May, 1837, concluded with him the Treaty of the *Tafna*, which, while it conceded great advantages to the Arab Chief, and afforded him the amplest opportunities to consolidate his power, left them free to turn their arms against Constantine and restore their military credit by the capture of that place, 13th October, 1837. This was a happy stroke, both of arms and of policy, for the French, since their influence had suffered greatly by their failure under its walls.

The subsequent campaigns of 1840 and 1841 may be said to have broken the confederated power which ABD-EL-KADER had consolidated. Then the campaigns of 1842 and 1843 were directed against the individual tribes, and soon brought them to reason.

When DAMREMONT, the French Governor and Commander-in-Chief, was killed before Constantine, 12th October, 1837, at the moment when his plans for the capture of the city were on the point of being crowned with success, the command devolved upon VALEE by the unanimous voice of those highest in rank, as well as by right of seniority. He realized the truth of the dying words of the heroic Colonel COMBES, who fell in the triumphant storming. Pierced with two balls, this officer of the old Roman type reported the success of the movement, which he had directed and led, and closed the account with these words: "Happy," said he, to the Royal Duke of

Nemours, "happy are they who are not wounded to the death (or mortally); they will live to enjoy the triumph—*i. e.*, or reap the rewards." Then he withdrew to his tent, and the next day the army had to deplore his decease. VALEE received the prize due to DAMREMONT, just as too many in our late civil war assumed the laurels which ought to have been hung on the tombstones of the dead.

For the capture of this African stronghold—the prize of so much blood and suffering—VALEE was raised to the dignity of Marshal of France, and made Governor-General of Algiers. His power was despotic, and his disposition did not move him to use his authority with gentleness. W. VON RAASLOFF, a distinguished representative of the Danish Artillery, afterwards Minister or Political Agent from Denmark to this country, hereinbefore quoted, who made the campaign in 1840 under him, and another under BUGEAUD, would seem to represent him as one of the most severe and most unfeeling of men. If his character is not overdrawn by this writer, he might almost be styled pitiless.

RAASLOFF relates two anecdotes of VALEE, the first of which occurred while he was serving in Spain during the time of NAPOLEON; of the second of these the Danish Volunteer was an eye-witness. The one proves that VALEE had no generous appreciation of the nobility of manhood, the other that he had no sympathy for the grandeur of that fortitude which NAPOLEON declared to be the first of military virtues. KEARNY himself related another incident, which shows such a hard heart, that it is to be hoped that memory has been treacherous. Upon one occasion an hospital had been established in a position which the Marshal had selected for his headquarters, or else the cries of the wounded disturbed him. He at once ordered them to be removed out of earshot; and that night the Arabs made a dash, or stole within the lines, and cut off all their heads. This, however, was about the substance of the story. Whether this be true or not, the old Marshal was a pitiless disciplinarian. His Napoleonic contempt for human life, as RAASLOFF styles it, would not be tolerated by our soldiers in this country.

Yet it was, perhaps, well that KEARNY saw his first real service under such a man, who, with all his faults, was a commander of very great ability, and the "creator of the French Artillery" of his day. It taught him the difference between the true and the sham, the "Man of Iron" from the want of appreciation of men, and the "Man of Iron" from the inexorable demand of the hour, the latter the man for the crisis of a nation. He could apprehend all that was great in VALEE and lay it to heart as an example to be followed, and appreciate all that was unworthy of imitation, as exemplified by his speech to the DUKE OF ORLEANS, when the young Prince bade adieu to his troops after the expedition through the "Iron Gates." Amid the profound and general emotion, VALEE was heard to exclaim: "Now it is time to die. After having counted three sons of the King in my army, and having seen two under fire, nothing is left for me but to quit (*dechoir*)."

ABD-EL-KADER, which signifies "Servant of the Almighty," and refers to his saintly extraction and religious education and claims, a true representative of Arab ability, was a politician of no mean capacity, and a General well adapted to develop and direct the warlike and fanatic tribes which acknowledged his authority. His personal appearance was alone sufficient to inspire respect. The writer had ample opportunities of judging of this. He was introduced to him in 1851, had rooms adjacent to him in the same hotel in Marseilles, and saw him again in 1852 at Avignon. At this time he was about forty-seven years of age. No portrait begins to do justice to his beauty—if such a term can be applied to a man; although it is just in his case, for very few women could surpass him in the delicacy and regularity of his features. Select the handsomest portrait ever exhibited of this Arab Chieftain, and it falls far short of the original in the prime of manhood, since no painting could give any idea of the gentle expression of his eyes and countenance in repose, nor of its fire when aroused.

As KEARNY's report of his experiences in Algiers, made to Major-General SCOTT, on his return in the fall of 1840—although diligent search has been made in former years, and even after this was partly written—is not to be found among the archives of the War Department nor elsewhere, and as all documents, letters, and memoranda relating to his service in Africa appear to have been destroyed, therefore a tenacious memory, the narratives of cotemporaries, and a series of first-class works on Algerian affairs, are the sources from which the following chapters or narratives have been compiled. That KEARNY went to Algiers with the DUKE OF ORLEANS was always understood; that he passed the Gates of Iron with that Prince is stated by a military historian; that he was at the storming of the

Pass at Mouzaia is testified by the Prince DE JOINVILLE, brother of the DUKE OF ORLEANS that he displayed great gallantry and fortitude is borne witness to by his immediate commander and comrades. Many of the incidents can be corroborated from the reminiscences of the writer, who had them from KEARNY himself, from references in letters, and from conversations in Europe and Africa with participants in the campaign of 1840. The descriptions of the operations themselves, and of the localities are from the best historical works upon the subject, or from the narratives of volunteers who took part in the events which they describe. The operations in the fall of 1839, and of the spring and summer of 1840, were among the most glorious for the French arms in Africa. In October, the Duke of Orleans achieved a moral military triumph which will ever be coupled with his name—the passage of the "Iron Gates of the Atlas." The marvelous cleft threaded by the French column was justly considered impracticable for an army, much more so for one carrying with it any kind of artillery or material. The natives were almost justified in believing that no armed opposition was necessary to render it unfortunate, since nature itself had done all that was requisite to make it dreadful and perilous, and a single shower could not only render the bold adventure impossible, but utterly destructive. The belief that the Roman Legionaries—those universal and irresistible conquerors, who have left traces of their iron-handed occupation throughout Northern Africa, in whatever quarter the French have penetrated—had never achieved the passage of these "Iron Gates," must have been a great incentive to the Duke and to his troops. To accomplish what the Romans had not, was indeed a superlative honor. At all events, the fact was well established, that if the Roman Eagles, at some unknown date, had gone through the "Iron Gates," no other military ensign had passed through except the Gallic Cock, eleven years afterwards, to be superseded by the Imperial Eagle.

In the ensuing year the same young, gallant Prince achieved even greater fame by a purely military triumph at the Pass of the Mouzaia, since the Gates of Iron were not defended; whereas the Col de Mouzaia, scarcely less strong by nature, was held by a strong force of ABD-EL-KADER's best regular troops, likewise an army of irregulars, admirable sharpshooters, all inspired with the courage of fanaticism, which, in such a natural fortress, could not have been overcome but by the discipline of picked veterans win-

CHAPTER VII.

THROUGH EL BIBAN!

"Il visita ensuite l'Algérie ou il obtint d'occompagner le Duc d'Orleans, comme aide-de-camp honoraire, pendant la campagne des Portes dé Fer."

DE TROBRIAND, 1, 290.

"To traverse the Black Mountains from Neustadt to Freyburg, it is necessary, for the space of two hours, to travel along a narrow valley between perpendicular rocks. This valley, or rather this crevice, at the end of which runs a torrent, is only a few paces wide, and is named the 'Valley of Hell.' By this terrible defile the greater part of the French army (under Moreau, in 1796,) traversed the Black Forest, with an enemy (the Austrian army) on its front, on its flanks, and in its rear. It was of this valley that Marshal Villars, in 1700, wrote the following concise note to the Elector of Bavaria, who pressed Villars to cross the Black Forest and join him: 'This Valley of Neustadt, which you propose to me' is the road which the people call the 'Valley of Hell.' Well, if your Highness will pardon me the expression, I am not devil enough to pass through it."—*Campagnes de Moreau ; Cust's* "*Annals of the Wars,*" § 43, 1, 5, 56. Compare Murray's "*Handbook for Southern Germany,*" 397.

——"behold black Acheron!
Once consecrated to the sepulchre."

—Childe Harold.

"Come on, we'll quickly find a surer footing,
And something like a pathway, which the torrent
Hath wash'd since winter."

—Manfred.

In the summer and early fall of 1839, the despatches from the Generals in Algiers to the Home Government plainly demonstrated that hostilities, sooner or later, were inevitable. Abd-el Kader seemed to look forward to a renewal of the war as the only method of maintaining his authority over the Confederation of Tribes, which he had labored so long to bring about and consolidate. Marshal Valee, Governor-General of the French possessions, was perfectly willing to accept the gage of defiance, and was even willing to provoke the Emir to throw it down that he might take it up.

This state of affairs soon became known in the army, and thus, at an early date, Kearny became apprised of what was going on in Africa. He at once applied to the French Government for permission to accompany an expedition into the interior, and make a campaign under generals who had already won a reputation where-ever a soldier's name was known and respected. His request was acceded to, and whether as an honorary aid on the staff of the DUKE OF ORLEANS, or as a supernumerary officer attached to the finest light cavalry regiment in the service, he had an opportunity to acquire, under the best conditions, a practical military knowledge, and learn the utmost which a soldier is called upon to endure. These gratifying appointments gave him a delightful position and protected him against the prejudices entertained by the aged commander-in-chief against foreign officers, whose presence in his camp was extremely distasteful to him. They annoyed and bored him. Such, at all events, was KEARNY's opinion. And armed with despotic power, and gifted with an unamiable disposition, it is not likely that he would have made the American volunteer's service particularly agreeable to him, had the young transatlantic dragoon been forced to come in direct contact with him, or without the intermediation of powerful and willing protectors.

In the fall of 1839 an expeditionary corps was assembled in the province of Constantine, whose constituents were brought thither partly in transports, direct from France, and partly from Algiers.

The command-in-chief was assumed by Marshal VALEE. Under him the DUKE OF ORLEANS had a fine division. To the staff of the latter Lieutenant PHILIP KEARNY was attached as an honorary aid-de-camp.* The Marshal and Royal Duke privately resolved to undertake with this corps the somewhat adventurous march from Constantine, along the Akkaba precipices, through the Jujura (*Djordjora*) to Algiers—adventurous, indeed, for if ABD-EL-KADER, or any of his dependents (which latter, at that time, the French had no longer any right to trust), with a mere handful of their people, had undertaken to bar the way, at certain defensible points, the French column, totally destitute of any resources except those which it carried with it, would have been placed in a most desperate position; nay, more, if only a few days of rain had occurred, the principal defile would have become totally impassable. When all these risks are taken into consideration, this march seems like a bravado, since no real advantages could be obtained through it, while, on the contrary, as long as ABD-EL-KADER had not ratified the Convention of Tafna, which regulated the boundaries of the French and his own jurisdiction, and had not publicly acknowledged

* DE TROBRIAND'S "Quatre ans de Campagnes, etc,' '1, 290.

it, this march could only serve still more to excite the inimical feelings of the Arabs who adhered to the Emir. This march has been represented by the French as an act of taking possession of the country ceded to them; but "such an interpretation of it can only excite a smile," for the reason that at times the French troops advanced with such celerity that they appeared more like a body of fugitives than an army of conquerors, and because they scarcely left any more traces of their passage through the greater part of the country traversed than a ship of its course through the ocean.

Until the French army had actually marched through the district, which they were about to attempt, the most wonderful representations and the most fabulous descriptions of its defiles were received with most implicit faith in France. The following relation is compiled from various authentic sources, but particularly from the journal of an officer who participated in whatever glory accrued to the expedition, which, in many respects, was truly glorious, since almost every human success is dependent upon fortune, and it required a concurrence of the most fortunate accidents, the favorable co-operation, not of men alone, but of nature also, not merely to make it successful, but to prevent it from being disastrous.

This description will show what extreme difficulties the expedition had to overcome, and how well it was adapted to exalt the impressionable minds of the French, so easily excited and affected by elevated and extraordinary ideas.

The renown of this exploit will be forever connected with the name of the Duke of Orleans, the pet of the nation, but especially of the Army of Africa, whose dangers and privations he had so often shared in 1835, 1839, 1840—an army which not only looked up to him as an able and courageous leader, but confided in him as the true and acknowledged friend of the soldier.

On the 24th October, 1839, the expedition was at Setif, seventy-nine miles west-south-west of Constantine, directly south of the Gulf of Bougia. The troops believed that they were destined to open the communication between Setif and Bougia, through the most important Kabyle tribes, which dwelt in the mountains around the latter port; an operation of the greatest consequence as regarded the affairs of the province of Constantine. The Kabyles, with whom the feint of negotiations was initiated, did not show themselves so much opposed to laying out a road through their land as the French authorities had expected.

On the 25th October the column marched in a direction which still kept up the idea that the objective was Bougia. On the 26th, early in the morning, the course was changed, and after a march of two hours a joyful murmur suddenly arose throughout the column, for the soldiers of the advance guard had discovered that they were not on the road to Zamourah—a small town northwardly and westwardly of Setif, occupied by Turks, which had submitted to the French—but were "going it loose" in a more southerly direction towards El Biban, that awful pass renowned for ages. In a moment the cries, "Algiers!" "El Biban!" "Les Portes de Fer!" "the Iron Gates!" were in every mouth. Without orders the soldiers quickened their pace; from front to rear the music of its favorite song resounded in each regiment. There was no more fever in the column. The brave French felt no more sickness, no more fatigue; no one considered the countless difficulties which they had to encounter, or the weakness of the column, or the mountain brooks, which a single shower could swell into torrents, and thus render advance and retreat equally impossible. The wildest enthusiasm took possession of the troops, in which the leaders perceived a sure token of a brilliant result.

Now that the secret was out, the most important affair was to secure, by the rapidity of the march, those advantages which had already been won through the astute and scrupulous silence of Marshal Valee, and make the most of them. In two days, 26th and 27th October, the expedition had accomplished over sixty miles, and already on the evening of the latter day, the peaks of El Biban were visible. On the 28th, the divisions, commanded respectively by the Duke of Orleans and General Galbois, separated, the former inclining to the left and south, while the latter wheeled off to the right into the plain of Medjanah, in order to secure the good will of the Turks of Zamourah for the French, and to finish the necessary preparations for establishing the great military camp at Setif, first occupied by the French, under the same General Galbois, in 1838. It had rained on the morning of the 28th, and the column did not move again until this rain had ceased, since its continuance would have rendered the defile of El Biban impracticable. The column consisting of a single division, that of the Duke of Orleans, comprised 2,551 foot, of the 22d of the Line and of the famous 2d and 17th Light Infantry, 248 cavalry detachments, from the 1st and 3d Chasseurs d'Afrique—to the former of these Kear-

NY was attached—and Spahis; and 250 men of the more scientific corps, engineer troops (Sappers and Miners), one company, and artillerists with four 12 pounder mountain-howitzers, on the pack-saddle system. Each soldier carried provisions for six days, and sixty cartridges; 800 head of cattle and sheep followed the division. The Administration (Field Commissariat) had the precaution to add a reserve supply of provisions for seven days more. Proud and exalted at the very idea that they were about to solve a military problem which the Roman legions had never dared to undertake, the troops advanced with alacrity.

After a difficult march—severe upon the troops on account of the obstructions encountered, rather than the distance traversed—in the bed of the Oued-Boukheteun, the mountain valley all at once began to contract, and grow more and more narrow; gigantic, savage-looking masses of rock, heaped the one upon another, rose up before the troops and restricted the sphere of vision in the most peculiar manner. Next the column had to labor along a rough foot-path, up ascents almost perpendicular, succeeded by descents almost as precipitous. The spade and the pickaxe of the Sappers and Miners were continually called into action to render these practicable for the cavalry and pack-mules, especially those of the artillery. Each time that the column had attained the plateau which crowned the wild summit of one of these ridges, they hoped that the barrier was surmounted, but on arriving at the crest, the soldiers beheld new peaks present themselves like an immense sea of rocky waves, clothed with wild woods and crowned with cactus and aloes.

At length they plunged into a deep defile, and all at once found themselves hemmed in on every side by gigantic walls of limestone, which, a few moments before, they had not been able to discover, piled up in isolated and detached fragments, several hundred feet in altitude, their outlines sharply drawn against the blue sky in strange and fantastic shapes. Farther away, towards the east and west, all these isolated peaks arrayed themselves into parallel ranges of gray or swarthy limestone, leaning, as it were, against abrupt granite supports,* the latter shooting up perpendicularly to the

* No one need be surprised at these limestone walls, being propped up by still more stupendous walls of granite, since primary limestone, associated with granite, is of the same age and has the same origin. They are Plutonic. There is a remarkable instance of this in the Highlands, on the Hudson River, near Sing Sing, and at Cruger's Station.

height, in some places, of 800 or 900 feet, in others, of more than 1,000 feet, whose crest line, broken by long intervals, illuminated by the light of the sun, presented the aspect of an immense rampart with colossal embrasures. These walls, which seemed to realize the fable of Atlas, and support the azure vault, were not more than from 40 to 100 feet apart, and had the effect of appearing to close in upon each other in order to frustrate any attempt to advance.

After a rough and almost scarped descent, the troops found themselves in the wildest position it is possible to conceive, in a little patch of green, shaped like a pointed egg, or rather the orbit of a comet, cut off at the butt by angular rocks, most savage in their aspect, while the whole contour was surrounded, except where the rifts afforded entrance and exit, by almost unappreciable walls of limestone, whose summits, at an immense height, overhung their bases, craning over as if to see what was passing beneath them, and along the narrow track, which, again and again, crossed the thread of water known as the Oued-Boukheteun. This streamlet, after it leaves the mountains, receives the name of the Oued-Biban. A feeble brook in the dry season, after heavy rains it becomes a wild torrent, which fills the whole defile.

The ellipse of verdure, just described, constitutes a sort of vestibule or entrance-court to the "Gates," and can be compared to nothing but a narrow trap or deep kettle, in which an enemy could have overwhelmed the column with the greatest ease, shooting down the troops from the surrounding cliffs, slaughtering them like poultry—"tame ducks" is the word in the journal generally followed, in a coop, without their being able to inflict the slightest injury in return. The exit is a split, not over eight feet broad, cleft vertically through the beetling Titanic cliffs—the loftiest, of reddish granite, the lowest of gray or dark-hued limestone.

This split was the FIRST IRON GATE.

After passing through this opening, the column had to string out along a narrow path formed by the disintegration of the marly portions of the rock, and clamber over huge blocks of chalk, almost filling the gigantic furrow between the parallel walls, which seemed to spring up to meet the sky. The SECOND IRON GATE was soon reached, and, twenty paces farther on, the THIRD; both of these, like the FIRST, cleft as perpendicularly as if cut with a plumb-line, but so narrow that there was scarcely room for the passage of a loaded pack-mule. Fifty paces farther on, again, the FOURTH IRON GATE was encountered, a little less narrow than the three previous ones. Three hundred paces farther on, the defile proper ceases, and opens into a beautiful and gracious valley.

How many centuries must have elapsed before the waters of a little brook could have worn down this abyss,* whose wonders are not susceptible of a description which can afford, to any one who has not seen them, a just idea of the reality—an abyss which in all time has received the title of the IRON GATES OF THE ATLAS, and whose passage has been regarded with awe! The domination of the country would almost seem to appertain to the master of an army which dared to attempt, and succeeded in passing them, in the attitude of a conqueror.

Through these Iron Gates the van-guard hurried on, the Marshal and DUKE OF ORLEANS with their staffs (including KEARNY) leading, amid the triumphant clangor of military music and the jubilant shouts of the soldiery, which seemed to make the very rocks tremble. The only trace of this interesting expedition which remained behind upon its stage was the simple inscription, engraved by the sappers upon the natural walls of the pass:

"ARMEE FRANCAISE, 1839."

About seven or eight hundred feet beyond the fourth Iron Gate, the defile enlarges, and opens into such a smiling and peaceful valley that nature seems to have placed it at this point for the express purpose of cheering up the soul rendered extremely melancholy by the gloomy depths of the preceding gulf, so unearthly and so savage as must abate the courage of the manliest with an irresistible sensation of awe.

That he accompanied the column which forced its passage through those famous Gates of Iron must have been a never-ending source of congratulation to KEARNY; for while it was received in

* "It appears to me that one of the best proofs of the youth of our globe, or of its population, at all events, is that its surface gold has not been exhausted. Gold is such an essential to civilization that if the world were as old as some believe, it would have been exhausted long ago. These are the words of Brigadier-General J. W. P., one of the acutest of observers and a very scientific man. After visiting that strange passage on the route from Fort Leavenworth, through Fort Laramie, to the South Pass of the Rocky Mountains, known as the 'Devils's Gate,' he writes: 'It looks, at first view, as if that gentle, pellucid stream (the "Sweet Water") had worn a passage through the hard granite— * * but on a closer examination I was confirmed in a previous opinion, that the channels of rivers are formed for them oftener than they are by them."

France as a glorious achievement of her armies, it had a most beneficial effect upon the tribes of Algiers, who looked upon the French as something more than human for having dared to attempt it.

As soon as the soldiers—carrying in their hands leafy branches, torn from the scattered palms, which counted their growth by centuries, and grew here and there among the rocks—issued forth into this lonely dell, they saluted with shouts of joy and welcome, that sun which they had completely lost sight of in the previous abyss, whose rays now almost blinded them. Here they halted for a space to rest, and under the influence of recollections, fresh and vivid, of the awful scenery which they had traversed, these brave men soon forgot all their fatigues in communicating to each other impressions made upon them by the wonders they had witnessed.

Militarily, to occupy or bar the Biban Pass would be impossible, since it can be turned, but for the light infantry to do so, would have required some days, when every minute was precious. The DUKE OF ORLEANS did everything that the military art teaches to get possession as soon as possible of the farther end of the defile, and thus, in a measure, to insure the safe passage of the column. Fortunately, all the measures which foresight indicated were superfluous. Not a single enemy showed himself. The expedition was favored with the finest weather, and nothing surpassed the joyous sense of relief in which the army passed the first evening out of this Brobdinagian trap.

The next day, the 29th October, the division which had bivouacked on the bank of the river Makalou, six miles north of El Biban, traversed an immense forest, and finally reached another beautiful valley, bordered by the chain of the Jurjura. Here Marshal VALEE derived intelligence, from letters seized upon captured messengers of ABD-EL KADER, that the Kalifa (Lieutenant) of the Emir had established himself on the plateau of the Fort of Hamza, in order to bar the road to Algiers against the advancing division.

To frustrate this movement, the division made a forced march on the 30th, through a country so destitute of drinkable water, and so abundant in salty, that the natives styled it the "Thirsty Way."

Meanwhile, the DUKE OF ORLEANS pushed ahead, with two or three companies of picked infantry, the whole of the cavalry, and two mountain howitzers, in the direction of Hamza. This fort occupies a position selected with judgment. During the period of the Turkish domination it was a place of such importance that the

Deys always maintained a strong garrison within its walls. This was by no means due to any military perceptions of their engineers, for the Romans, unsurpassed in their occupation of keypoints, built a fort there, named Auzea, coeval with their first invasion of the country, which was confided to a garrison of veterans. Tradition ascribes, however, the foundation of Hamza to a king of Tyre, who flourished nine centuries before the Christian era. The last account belongs to fable rather than history; but the French were only following the footsteps of the Romans, who won more than one signal victory under its ancient walls, which dominate a vast plain at the intersection of three valleys, the first leading towards Algiers, about fifty-five miles to the northwest; the second towards Bougia, from seventy to eighty miles to the northeast, and the third to the Gates of Iron (El Biban), from forty to fifty miles to the eastward. To the westward again, a road crosses through a depression, or "Col," of the Jurjurah to Medeah, fifty-five miles to the west by south on an air line.*

When the French column arrived on the heights of the Oued (Stream) Hamza, the hills on the opposite side were covered with mounted Arabs, who broke and fled without firing a shot as soon as they were charged by the French cavalry. This must be the action which serves as the basis for the anecdote of Count St. Marie, for it does not appear that the Arabs had any artillery with them in the other actions in the open field in which the Duke was present, nor is there any account of warlike opposition at any previous time during the advance of the expedition: "One day, at sunrise, the rocks called the Iron Gates in the Bibans were covered with Arabs, defending the passage of the defile. The Duke of Orleans, enveloped in a brown *burnous*, appeared on horseback at the head of the first attacking column. In the midst of a shower of grapeshot, ordering the charge to be sounded, he was the first to reach the guns of the Arabs, which he compelled them to abandon in disorder."

The fort of Hamza was found deserted; 150 Arab regulars, thrown into it as a garrison, had abandoned it. The fort, which had been a square, with bastions at the corners—the French ex-

* It is extremely difficult to locate places on the maps, for the reason that the different accounts not only disagree with each other, but with any map, and the maps themselves, English and French, and French and semi-official French, are not only discordant as to names, but as to locations.

pression is a "starry-square," (*carré etoilé*)—was little better than a mass of ruins. The revetments had either fallen or were in a miserable condition, so as scarcely to hold together or sustain themselves. The interior constructions were nothing better than heaps of rubbish. Five cannon were found here, three of which were spiked.

Having completed the destruction of this once important stronghold, the French resumed their march, expecting to be attacked at any moment by the tribes which acknowledged the authority of ABD-EL-KADER, whose territories they had now entered. They did not meet with any resistance of the slightest consequence until, on reaching a plateau along one of the affluents of the Issen, they found themselves in face of a body of cavalry and quite a numerous array of infantry. The DUKE OF ORLEANS, having placed some companies in ambush, turned the Arabs with his cavalry, and drove them against the companies in reserve. These did not fire until the Arabs almost ran against the muzzles of their muskets. Then the French poured upon them such a slaughtering volley as put them to flight with quite a severe loss; a few shells from the mountain howitzers cleaned them out entirely. RAASLOFF calls this a brilliant affair, and adds, as if they constituted more formidable obstructions, that the column crossed a number of mountain streams, which in less favorable weather might have proved impassable. Some of these traverse the Biban Pass itself. One is an affluent of the Adousse, which empties into the Gulf of Bougia. All are capable of being transformed by a single heavy shower into raging torrents.

The same difficulties attended the march of the next day, 1st November, and it was late in the evening before the column, worn out by the terrible fatigues which they had undergone, reached the camp of Fondouck, where the division RULHIERE, sent out from Algiers to escort them in, awaited their arrival. Thus ended an excursion—which deserves the title of a "military promenade" rather than any more serious term—of seven days, through a country bristling with perils, inhabited by a population which had always inspired the previous rulers of Algiers with the greatest dread and caused them the liveliest disquietude for the stability of their power. The distance accomplished was not in itself so very great, ranging from 150 to 200 miles, but the natural difficulties overcome made it more trying and laborious than an ordinary march of double the distance. The news of the successful arrival of the column in Algiers occasioned, not only in the colony but throughout France, the liveliest joy and enthusiasm, which, to comprehend, a man must appreciate the dangers which actually impended over it, verily, like the sword of Democles.

The route followed by this comparatively "little band" led through warlike and inimical tribes, from whom no assistance, in the shape of the necessaries of life, could be expected; but on the contrary, open hostilities at any moment. The whole of the country traversed was in the highest degree difficult, and the unforeseen occupation of the "Iron Gates," or even a few heavy showers, might have proved the ruin of the division. The country itself, and its resources, were only known by report through the accounts of the Arab guides, who were little to be depended on. Such critical circumstances constitute the greatest charm, however, of war, and elevate the soldier, not only in his own eyes, but in those of his comrades and countrymen.

When the column arrived at Algiers, the enthusiasm was indescribable. The Duke of Orleans gave a grand banquet to the whole division in the square of Bab Azum. Thus, in the beginning of November, 1837, joy reigned in Algiers, and the future was forgotten — while the storm-clouds were gathering over the Colony, which burst with a suddenness and fury as terrible as unexpected. No one surmised that this apparent triumph was the forerunner of the greatest disaster. It is impossible, in such a work as this, to go further into anything like a historic consideration of the causes which led to the ensuing campaign, in which Kearny was conspicuous, and made the American name glorious through his fortitude and his valor. Abd-el-Kader — who knew that every action which tended to elevate the French in the opinion of the natives depreciated his own influence in an equal degree — had been waiting for a pretext, and was glad that an excuse was now given him for the resumption of hostilities, by this expedition through the "Gates of Iron." He held his forces all ready in the leash, and now he let them loose in all the fury of fire and sword upon that beautiful plain of the Metidjah, which embraces Algiers in its arc of luxuriant fertility, whose either extremity bathes its verdure in the sea. No declaration of war preceded the inburst of devastation. Up to the very gates of Algiers swept the Arabian cavalry in the prosecution of what they deemed a "Holy War." The Emir's fury fell, not only upon the scattered garrisons beyond the reach of succor; upon the colonists who saw the fruits of years of patient toil disappear in a moment in flame; but also upon the native tribes who had submitted to the French and had refused to arm against them. Years afterwards, the sad mementoes of this erruption were still visible in the Metidjah, and the colonists had not yet recovered their confidence in the protection of the French government, for the political horizon could scarcely have seemed more serene, on the evening of the 30th November, 1839, and yet with the dawn of the next day the hordes of ABD-EL-KADER poured down from the Lesser Atlas, and, except within the lines of Algiers, left nothing behind them but corpses, ruins and ashes. All who survived were dragged into captivity. It is said that Marshal VALEE was not disappointed at this turn in events; and if those who treat of the French Dominion in Algiers are correct in their judgment of his character, it was very likely that he was pleased at the opportunity of adding to his military renown by a successful campaign at the close of his life. The idea expressed by RAASLOFF, the Danish eye-witness, is equivalent to this: "The Emir precipitated the hostilities which Marshal VALEE had invited." RAASLOFF's exact words are: "VALEE and ABD-EL-KADER wished to bring on the war."*

* This chapter is the only one in the whole book which is not founded on original documents, or well-known works. There is only one definite authority for it, quoted at the head of the Chapter, which is to be found at Page 290, Vol. 1: "*Quatre Aus de Campagnes a l'Armee du Potomac*, par REGIS DE TROBRIAND, Ex-Major-General au Service Volontaire, et Colonel au Service Regulaire des Etats Unis d'Amerique," Paris, 1868; which seemed sufficiently corroborated by rumor, intimations and references in letters. The subject-matter of the residue of this biography is either founded on personal knowledge, publications, or information derived from actors in the events treated of. *In almost every case*, where practicable, the language of the original has been incorporated. Whether or no KEARNY accompanied the Duke of Orleans to Africa in the Fall of 1839, this chapter is nevertheless valuable, inasmuch as it serves as an introduction to the subsequent campaign, and more particularly as it presents an accurate account of one of the most brilliant expeditions of the French Army in Algiers. Although scarcely attended with any bloodshed, it is a notable example of what may be accomplished by audacious energy in an art or science in which success depends on what the Romans verified two thousand years ago, and Marshal SAXE formulized as a rule or principle of war, that victory depends more upon the legs than upon the arms of the soldiers. This all *great* Captains demonstrated to be the fact since we have any reliable accounts of military progress.

CHAPTER VIII.

OVER THE MOUZAIA TO MEDEAH AND MILIANAH.

"THE AFRICAN BATTLE ABOVE THE CLOUDS."

"Major-General P. KEARNY, * * * at the age of twenty-two, accepted the commission of Second Lieutenant First Dragoons, and soon after was sent to Europe by the government, to study and report upon the French cavalry tactics.

"To accomplish this object he entered the military school at Saumur, France, and from thence went to Africa, where he joined the First Chasseurs d'Afrique, as a volunteer. By his daring exploits he attracted the attention of the French army, and was presented with the Cross of the Legion of Honor."—"*Military and Naval History of the Rebellion in the United States*;" *by* W. J. TENNEY."

"A trois heures du matin le canon douna le signal. '*Allons, enfants*,' s'écrie le DUC D'ORLEANS, '*les Arabes nous attendent et la France nous regarde!*' Et les troupes gravissant les rochers s'emparent du premier plateau où elles font une halte.——Ensuite commence l'escalade du piton. La résistance fut terrible, la premiere colonne seule était engagée, un nuage épais dérobait à la rue les combattants. Bieutôt une *fanfare* annonça la prise d'un des mamelosn. A ce momens le soleil, se dégageant de son voile de ténèbres, èclaire les flancs de la montagns, et l'on peut admirer d'une part les efforts presque surhumaines de nos soldats, qui ne se laissent arrêter par aucune crainte; d'autre part, le calme et le sang-froid des Arabes, qui penchés sur l' abîme l'œil attentif, le doigt sur la détente du fusil, attendent, immobiles, le moment de viser juste et bien. Le 2d Léger, encouragè par la voix si puissante du général CHANGARNIER, redouble d' ardeur, et le drapeau français est arboré sur la crête la plus élevée."—*La Comtesse* DROROJOWSKA'S "*Histoire de l'Algerie*."

"The Federals fought not less firmly [at Williamsburg], encouraged by their chiefs, HOOKER, HEINTZELMAN, and KEARNY. KEARNY *in especial*, who lost an arm in Mexico, and *fought with the French at the Mouzaia, and at Solferino, had displayed the finest courage*."—"*The Army of the Potomac*," by the PRINCE DE JOINVILLE.

CAMPAIGN OF 1839 AND CAMPAIGN OF 1840.

IN December, 1839, VALEE, having received strong reinforcements from France, gladly accepted the defiance of ABD-EL KADER, and recommenced hostilities. He divided his troops into different columns, and launched these forth against the enemy in every direction. Everywhere the French resumed the offensive gloriously.

As the First Chasseurs d'Afrique played a distinguished part in several of the first engagements which followed, it is but fair to suppose that, as PHILIP KEARNY was attached to this regiment, the young American volunteer, with the daring and dash which was always conceded as peculiarly his own, had a share in its dangers and honors.

It was a fortunate thing for PHILIP KEARNY that, although he had an honorary position on the staff of the DUKE OF ORLEANS, for actual service, his place was with the First Chasseurs d'Afrique; and still more fortunate that their commander was Colonel LE PAYS DE BOURJOLLY—afterwards Lieutenant-General and Senator of France. This chivalrous officer, directly the reverse of his superior in disposition, was a perfect gentleman. He was a grand specimen of the French colonel of romance. Through his family, position, and personal character, he stood equally high. Intimate associations with him, demonstrated at once what a French gentleman should be to fill the character ascribed to the grand and true nobility of the "old school," and also what a gentleman actually was. To his inferiors in rank he was as kind, generous, and forbearing as he was independent, fierce, and resolute towards his superiors, maintaining his own rights and those of his subordinates against the presumption of higher rank with a dignified determination which would not yield an inch to the encroachments of authority. KEARNY always spoke in the highest terms of Colonel LE PAYS DE BOURJOLLY, and the latter—to whom the writer carried a letter of introduction, in 1851, from his cousin—remembered his volunteer companion-in-arms as a valued friend, testifying the warmest feelings towards him, and an affectionate pride in the fame and success of his subsequent career. The writer has heard him translate to his aid and company the historical eulogies of his former pupil.

It was of inestimable advantage to KEARNY to be attached to the First Chasseurs d'Afrique, which "had always been a favorite regiment, brave and triumphant in the field;" "indefatigable, enterprising—a model light cavalry." The DUKE OF NEMOURS, second son of LOUIS PHILIPPE, generally wore its uniform; the DUKE OF AUMALE, a still younger son, shared all its dangers. This shews how highly this corps was esteemed. ST. MARIE, a reliable authority, testifies that "the Colonels who have had the command of the First Chasseurs have always been men of family, fortune, and education. The consequence is, that the officers are received into the best society, wherever they go." This proves that Colonel LE PAYS DE BOURJOLLY could not have held the position he occupied had he not been the "elegant gentleman" and thorough soldier he was.

The first collision of a year—which numbered twenty successful engagements—took place in the early part of December between the camp of the Arba and the course of the Arrouch (Harrach), about eighteen miles southeast of Algiers, where a force of 1,200 Hadjouts—audacious robbers, practicing the tactics of the ancient Numidians—were encountered by a column, consisting of detachments of the Fifty-second Line Infantry and of the 1st Chasseurs, charged, completely beaten, and scattered.

About the same time, towards the end of December, 1839, the regular batallions of the Emir made an attack upon a convoy between Boufarick—a fortified camp and small village on the Harrach, in the middle of the plain of the Metidjah—and Blidah, at the foot of the Little Atlas, twenty-nine miles south by west of Algiers, on the direct road to Medeah. These Arabs were likewise charged home by the French and driven into a ravine, where they experienced a considerable loss. Let no one undervalue these sons of Northern Africa—descendants of the ancients Vandals, who, in A.D. 697 drove the Romans out of Africa—of whom it has been said "the very men partake of the nature of the lion."

A few days afterwards, on the last day of the year 1839, the united forces of the KALIFAS, of Medeah, and of Milianah, Lieutenants of the "Modern Jugurtha,"—as ABD-EL-KADER has been appropriately styled—suffered a complete rout. This was the first time that the Emir's newly-created regular infantry had an opportunity to measure themselves with the French invaders in the open field. They occupied a position chosen with no small degree of military capacity, between Blidah and the Chiffa. The ravine of the Oued (river, bed of a river, or defile) El-Kebir was occupied by ABD-EL-KADER's regular infantry, supported by from four thousand to five thousand cavalry. The ground was very favorable for defence, and the Arabs were well posted. The inequalities of the ground served as intrenchments for the Kabyles, who are excellent marksmen, and do terrible execution with their long guns or rifles, which will carry almost as far as European wall-pieces. Their position enabled them to deliver a plunging fire upon the French, whose counter volleys proved almost ineffectual. Marshal VALEE, who commanded the French column in person, soon became satisfied that the only way to decide the affair was at once to resort to cold steel. He accordingly launched the Twenty-third Line Infantry, and Second Light Infantry—a famous regiment, commanded by the no less famous CHANGARNIER, surnamed by his troops the "Iron Head"—also the First Chasseurs d'Afrique, against the enemy. The ravine itself, which covered their front like a vast dry ditch, and the steep acclivity beyond, was overcome with impetuosity, and the assailants soon found themselves face to face with the Emir's regulars, who had contracted their line to meet the French fairly and squarely. Fortunately for the latter, the Arabs, like the *Wahabees*, dread the "long nail" at the end of a musket; and the French charge, with that weapon, which tests the solidity of a line, overthrew that infantry which ABD-EL-KADER had taken so much pains to organize, and hurled it back upon the cavalry, to whom it communicated the disorder. In a few minutes there was no more resistance; every Arab was seeking safety in flight. The enthusiastic intrepidity of the French horse and foot rendered any further attempt to make a stand unavailing. The field of battle was covered with the corpses of the Arab infantry and cavalry; over four hundred dead were counted. Three flags, or military ensigns, five hundred muskets, and a piece of artillery, were the trophies of the day. Colonel LE PAYS DE BOURJOLLY led the charge which captured this gun, a present from the French Government to ABD-EL-KADER on the conclusion of the last truce. With a short-sightedness about equal to that of our Washington authorities in regard to the Indians, as a rule, and towards the South in 1860–'61, the Home Government at Paris, although they knew that the Emir would not long keep quiet, made him a present of a section of field-artillery. As BOURJOLLY said with an ironical smile: "They gave him guns to shoot down their own troops with."

RAASLOFF calls this again a "brilliant affair," and AL ISON says: "This success, though not on a great scale, was very important as restoring the spirits of the troops, and giving the turn to a long train of disasters." CASTELLANE calls Oued-el-Aleg "the tomb of one of the regular batallions of the Emir."

Colonel LE PAYS DE BOURJOLLY was very proud of his share in a conflict which was better known in France as the affair of Oued-el-Aleg. In this officer's cheerful study or reception-room, ornamented with trophies of his Algerian campaigns, glistening in the sunlight which floods the apartment through the broad expanse of windows opening to the sunny east, in Paris—where the writer met several officers who had served in Africa with KEARNY, and had many pleasant things to say of him—hung, in 1851, a grand painting of the capture of ABD-EL-KADER's cannon. In this, BOURJOLLY, in the uniform of his regiment and splendidly mounted, leads the charge, spurring his white barb to cut down the artillery men at the gun. CHANGARNIER, who led the infantry, claimed a lion's share of the honor of the day, and a duel was considered imminent; but VALEE—flattered in BOURJOLLY's report as having accompanied the cavalry—conceded the glory to the First Chasseurs d'Afrique. In the painting, however, the infantry are seen in the back ground with Marshal VALEE at their head, following up the success in another quarter.

From the admirable sketch of the life of KEARNY, by a distinguished New Jerseyman, it would appear as if one Colonel GUIÉ, and not LE PAYS DE BOURJOLLY, commanded the First Chasseurs d'Afrique while KEARNY was attached to them. This is an error. BOURJOLLY continued Colonel of the First Chasseurs d'Afrique until 21st June, 1840, when he was made Marechal-de-Camp—synonymous with General of Brigade. By that time all the hard fighting was over, as the second engagement at the Col de Mouzaia was on 15th June, 1840, when the army was retracing its steps.

If BOURJOLLY had not been in command, and actually with his regiment, at this time, he never could have made such a display in a picture, since an hundred witnesses would have started up to disprove his claim to the honor.

In November, 1851, the writer was standing on the ramparts of the Emperor's Fort—built by CHARLES V.—which dominates the city of Algiers, and commands a partial view of the rich plain which spreads itself, clothed in all the luxuriance of tropical vegetation, from the shores of the deep blue Mediterranean to the dark blue ranges of the Atlas; while standing there and looking down upon the plain of the Metidjah, most interesting to the native of a Northern clime in its palms and natural features peculiar to this land of story, a stranger approached him and prefacing his words with a military salute, remarked: "Monsieur," pointing to the south, "has been there." "No; this is my first visit to Africa." "Are you not an American? Did you not serve in the Chasseurs d'Afrique?" "No; I only arrived in Algiers yesterday." "This is strange; I thought you were an American officer who served with that regiment, to which I belonged." This mistake of identity led to an explanation, and the soldier then went on to express his admiration for KEARNY for his dash and his daring. "He was a very brave man," said he; "I have often seen him charging the Arabs with his sword in one hand, his pistol in the other, and his reins in his teeth." Such testimony from an old African trooper tells the whole story, and it was corroborated by others. Several officers who had served with him, who were encountered on the passage between Algiers and Marseilles, were loud in his praise. One, who was a *Marechal-de-Logis* (Quartermaster's Sergeant of Cavalry) in one of the companies of the First Chasseurs d'Afrique, which made the campaigns of 1839–40 (in 1851 a Lieutenant in the same regiment) spoke of him in about the same terms as the old soldier who thought that he recognized KEARNY on the summit of the Chateau de l'Empereur. It would require too much space to follow KEARNY through all the details of his Algerian experiences, it will be sufficient to note the most remarkable. The best proof that he profited by all that he saw is the development of ability disclosed in the last year of his life, when he had attained a position to show how great he really was, and how much greater he might have become had he survived.

In Algiers he learned the enormous capabilities of a well-trained infantry. He never could speak in terms of sufficient commendation of the French Light Infantry. He said that their conduct was something magnificent, their coolness combined with enthusiasm; their orderly disorder; accommodating discipline to the terribly broken and difficult ground on which they had to operate; their individual intelligence and combined action. He was justified in his eulogies, for no country ever possessed a more perfect light infantry than that which so often scaled the Atlas and cleared the way for the columns and trains. Fine as the cavalry was with which he served, noble its deeds, and wonderful its endurance, it was ever the light infantry for which he reserved his enthusiasm. This was just, for if ever there was a difficult country to gain ground in against an intrepid foe—which only needed scientific training and good weapons to secure their independence—that country was the Atlas.

To restrain the natives the French were obliged to maintain an army of 100,000 men. PULSZKY, who bases his statements on authentic documents, sets down this number, and adds that the colony costs France $20,000,000 a year. The biographer of Marshal VALEE admits that he had an army of 57,000 strong, excellent troops, no one can deny. He had girdled that portion of the plain of the Metidjah, which had been colonized and brought under cultivation, with a chain of camps, forts and block-houses; and yet in

November-December, 1839, "all the Province of Algiers was involved in a general blaze." In 1840 the natives were driven back apparently across the Lesser Atlas, defeated and disorganized. Notwithstanding, in May, 1841, they were back again in the Metidjah, and slaughtered a whole company—49 men lost their heads, and one hid in the bushes, severely wounded—the garrison of a block-house, not more than nine miles from Algiers, nor three from Delhi-Ibrahim, a considerable military post, not more than three or four miles W. by S. of that city. Well might LAMPING exclaim: "So you may judge tolerably well of what is meant by the French territory." A people who could defend their independence with such indomitable pertinacity were antagonists worthy of any troops in the world. Where would the South be now if they had evinced a like unconquerable spirit under disadvantages as disproportioned and odds as overwhelming.

The combats already described, as well as minor collisions, taught the Emir that it would not do to risk the troops, which had cost him so much labor to organize, in any more pitched battles. Many times his banner was descried in the plain floating over his scarlet batallions and squadrons in the distance, but on all occasions the combat which the French sought diligently was refused by their leader.

On 25th April, 1840, Marshal VALEE determined to carry the war into the interior, and on the 27th marched from Blidah upon Medeah. Between these two places rose the mountain of the Mouzaia, 5,117 feet high. To afford some idea of the difficulties which the invader had to encounter, the new military road from Blidah to Medeah, laid out in the most scientific manner, crosses the Chiffa no less than sixty-two times. Nevertheless, this road, a marvel of engineering, becomes impassable at times in winter, and its maintenance requires constant repairs. Like the Khyber Pass, in Afghanistan, it might be the grave of an invading army in the hands of an enemy which knew how to combine their efforts and avail themselves of the natural difficulties. The road by which VALEE advanced was doubtless that followed by the Roman legions. It is longer and even more difficult than the new one constructed by the French. It crosses the Col de Tenyah, or rather Col de Mouzaia, for Tenyah simply signifies "Peak of the Mountain." The defile Tenyah begins about nine miles west of the Haouch (farm) of Mouzaia, which again is about fifteen miles from

Blidah, and twenty-five from Algiers. It requires a peaceable march of two hours to reach the neck or cleft of the mountain through which the road crosses. LAMPING, who climbed it more than once in the course of the various campaigns in which he was engaged, says that from the foot of the Col de Mouzaia up to its highest point, is full seven hours' march when no resistance is encountered. In May, 1840, that ascent which required seven hours in peaceful times, was to be made under a constant fire of sharpshooters, each of whom selected his man. On both sides, the defile is partially cultivated, but the greater portion of the narrow path, traversed by many rivulets, leads through a rough thicket, sometimes interrupted by bold lime cliffs. Towards the crest of the range it becomes continually narrower; the cliffs from both sides approaching each other so closely that scarcely four men can march abreast; finally two conical rocks form a kind of natural gate. Besides all this, the road clings in many places to the sides of a precipitous mountain. In the depths below, to the right, so far down that its murmur can scarcely be heard in the dry season, in summer trickles a thread of water, in winter roars an irresistible torrent; while to the left hand soar the rocky cliffs. In the distance—as seen through the pass—soars the snow-capped peak of Nador, beneath which nestles the objective of Marshal VALEE, Medeah, embosomed in the luxuriant groves of fruit-trees, the fragrance of whose flowers, in their season, are said to be sickening to those who seek their cool shelter to sleep over night. RAASLOFF, the distinguished Danish officer who, like KEARNY, served as a volunteer under VALEE, in his interesting work, published at "Altona" in 1845, furnishes a view of this defile at the instant when the French troops were forcing it, in October, 1840, climbing the serpentine track which clings, mid-air, to the precipice, with the Kabyles, conspicuous in their white "bournous" or cloaks, firing upon them from every covert afforded by the overhanging or projecting rocks. At first sight a soldier would agree with PULSZKY that fifty resolute men might, here, detain an army for several days. Facts, however, have demonstrated the truth of Marshal BUGEAUD's address to his officers at Orleansville that "an army which knows how to obey, an army which knows how to suffer, is the hope and strength of the country; the time will never come when it will be found wanting to France." Accordingly, in 1830, Maréchal-de-Camp (Brigadier-General) ACHARD, with a single batallion of the 37th

Infantry of the Line, carried the Pass of the Mouzaia, although it was defended by 2,000 Turks, Kabyles, and Arabs. The foremost of the French rushed with fixed bayonets into what seemed the very jaws of death; but, says LAMPING, the Arab or Bedouin, the Kabyle, who is great and admirable at the hour of death, who never begs his life or utters an unmanly complaint, has "a holy horror of the bayonet." ACHARD's Infantry burst through the African ranks with a heroism which had its parallel in that of the four Hungarian batallions, which under General GUYON, carried the Branyiszko Pass, 5th February, 1849.

KEARNY was now to witness and have a share in an exploit similar to that of GUYON's, which was almost dramatic in its effects, if death had not made it sublime. The PRINCE DE JOINVILLE, in his "Army of the Potomac," refers to KEARNY's participatiou in this severe fight on the Mouzaia, which he couples with Solferino, as if to have *been there* was indeed something to speak of.

From the 1st May, starting from the "Tomb of the Christian"—a ruined monument, so styled, in reality an ancient burial-place of the Mauritanian kings,—till the 12th of the same month, when the army reached the foot of the northern range, proper, of the Atlas, every mile of the advance had been won by a combat. The march was one continual skirmish. The column might almost have been said to have cleaved its way onward as a ship ploughs through a head sea, only the waves were not impassive adversaries, but surges of irregular cavalry, which made incessant and harrassing attacks on the French flanks, front, and rear, and returned shot for shot, and cut of yataghan for slash of sabre. In repelling these assaults, the First Chasseurs, to which KEARNY was attached, were invariably successful, executing a number of brilliant charges. In one of these, the DUKE OF AUMALE, the youngest son of the king, made a dash with a single company of this regiment and achieved a brilliant success, by the rapidity and hardihood of his manœuvre.

The manner in which the Arab horse are accustomed to fight accounts for the old soldier's description of KEARNY's conduct on such occasions, "charging with his sabre in one hand, his pistol in the other, and his reins in his teeth." The Bedouin, or Arab horse, hover round a column all day with wild yells of "Lu-Lu," galloping up without order, within 80 or 100 yards of the French sharpshooters, "and discharging their rifles, at full speed. The horse then turns off of his own accord, and the rider loads his piece as he retreats; and this is repeated again and again all the day long."

"The Bedouins never wait for a close encounter hand to hand when charged by our cavalry; they disperse in all directions, but instantly return. The only difference between them and the Numidians, of whom SALLUST says, 'They fight flying, and retreat, only to return more numerous than before,' is, that the Numidians of old fought with bows, and the Bedouins with rifles."

"This kind of fighting is equally dangerous and fatiguing to us. It is no joke to be firing in all directions, from sunrise to sunset, and to march at the same time, for we seldom halt to fight at our ease. The general only orders a halt when the rear-guard is so fiercely attacked as to require reinforcements. Any soldier of the rear-guard who is wounded or fatigued has the pleasant prospect of falling into the hands of the Bedouins, and having his head cut off by them. One comfort is, that this operation is speedily performed: two or three strokes of the yataghan are a lasting cure for all pains and sorrows."

ABD-EL KADER had neglected nothing which could render the defence of the Col de Mouzaia successful. To the natural bulwarks of this formidable pass, he had added abattis, entrenchments armed with batteries, and a strong redoubt, on the very culminating point or principal peak. To man these works he had drawn together large numbers of troops, and especially all the sub-clans of the great and valiant tribe of the Mouzaia. These last had always shown themselves the most intrepid of the Arab infantry whenever the French had forced the passage of the Col. The very geographical position of this tribe of the Kabyles had won for it the highest consideration from the Turks, while they governed Algiers. It depended directly on the Agaa of the Capital; it had received large concessions of fine land in the plain; it was exempted from tribute of all kinds; and was charged with a sort of supervision over the other mountain tribes.

On the 12th May, at 3 o'clock in the morning, the DUKE OF ORLEANS, pointing to the crest of the Mouzaia—seven hours' march from the foot of the mountain—and the entrenchments which crowned it, crowded with defenders, whose white garments glistened like silver in the rising sun—addressed these words to the French soldiers, impatient to begin; "My boys, the Arabs are expecting us, and France is looking on." Then he gave the signal for the attack.

In an instant the scarped flank of the rocky heights was covered with French soldiers, leaping, climbing, mounting almost at a run. The drums beat, the clarions sounded the charge; the officers animated the men with their voices and by their examples. The first column gained the lowest plateau without much difficulty. There they found themselves before three lofty swells, or rounded elevations, disposed in echelon, each crowned with a formidable redoubt. At this point the resistance was terribly resolute. From the ramparts of these natural forts, strengthened artificially, the Arabs delivered a plunging and murderous fire upon the assailants. Between these, three masses of rock thrust themselves forth at intermediate points, which afforded covers to the enemy, armed with "long rifles, which carry almost as far as wall pieces." Thus sheltered, the Arabs kept up a continual and lively direct and cross-fire upon the French, who, to overcome the ascent of the abrupt rocky steep, were obliged to cling to every projecting rock, to every bush, and consequently were unable to reply. Soon a thick smoke enveloped the mountain like a cloud, and nothing more was visible to the rest of the army below. This state of affairs lasted several hours. During this time nothing was heard but an almost continual roll of musketry, to which the artillery added their reports like single and severe claps in a thunder storm, and ever and anon, as the fire slackened, the progress of the attack could be distinctly measured, by the responses of the drums and bugles of the Second Light Infantry, higher and higher, amid the cloud which enveloped the mountain. At length, about mid-day, a peculiar flourish of clarions or bugles announced a decided success. The Second Light Infantry had carried the second and commanding peak.

Then the two other columns moved in turn, and began to ascend the heights under the fire of the enemy. The column LAMORICIERE having made itself master of a wooded ridge which extended to the right of the peak, the Arabs, who were dislodged by this success, came together again in his rear, and posted themselves in a ravine. By this disposition they were enabled to stop the march of the column D'HOUDETOT, with which the DUKE OF ORLEANS advanced. At once the young general ordered the soldiers to unsling their knapsacks and make a bayonet charge. To this the Arabs opposed such a vigorous resistance that all the troops in succession became engaged. The very staff was obliged to cut in and defend themselves. General SCHRAMM, Chief of the Duke's staff, fell wounded at the side of the DUKE OF ORLEANS, and other officers were hit. Fortunately a battalion of the Twenty-third succeeded, in a measure, in turning the ravine. They rushed with the bayonet upon the Arabs, who, taken in flank by this unexpected attack, disbanded and fled.

Meanwhile, the first column DUVIVIERS had arrived at the foot of the main redoubt. There they were received with such terrific discharges of musketry that even these veterans recoiled. It was now three o'clock in the afternoon. For twelve hours these brave men had not ceased to march, to climb, and to fight. On all sides the men were falling, overcome with heat, fatigue, and thirst. A last effort remained to be made, the most important of all, and the least indecision would have compromised the success of a day so heroically begun. General CHANGARNIER comprehended this critical moment, and turning towards the Second Light Infantry, he placed his sword under his arm as coolly as if on the exercise ground, and gave the order, "Forward." At the sound of his voice, so reassuring in its calmness, the drums beat and bugles sounded the charge, the ranks reformed, the soldiers rushed upon the redoubt, some succeeded in making a lodgment within the entrenchments. The Arabs, thus vigorously assailed, defended themselves no less resolutely, but at length, attacked on all sides, they began to waver, then to yield ground, and finally fled before the French, who swept everything before them. Then the tricolored flag, planted on the very summit of the Atlas, was saluted by the roll of all the drums, the flourishes of trumpets, and the enthusiastic shouts of the army.

The Col de Mouzaia was gallantly carried, (after a desperate fight like that of HOOKER's at Lookout Mountain "above the clouds,")*

* BATTLES ABOVE THE CLOUDS are not so rare as many think. In 1692, there was not only a battle fought, but a campaign carried on, on a level with the limit of perpetual snow. Marshal CATINAT, "*Pêre le Pensée*," a term applied a century afterwards to NAPOLEON, established his camp on the summit of the Cottian Alps, near Fenestrelles, a spot still renowned in military annals as the "*Prê de Catinet.*" The remnants of the French and Sardinian entrenchments are still to be discerned amid the snow. In the previous century the same nations encountered in as elevated regions, and pitched their tents amid the clouds, under the famous LESDIGUIERES and PRINCE THOMAS OF SAVOY, grandfather of the great PRINCE EUGENIO VON SAVOY, as he wrote his name in the languages of the three nations from which he derived his blood.

In 1797, on the 22d March, MASSÉNA defeated the Austrians on the summit of the Julian Alps, when cavalry charged and artillery manœuvred on fields of ice, while the infantry waded to the attack through deep snow drifts. Some of the fortresses which constituted the "Armour of Piedmont" are on peaks so lofty that their garrisons often basked in the sunshine, when the lower world was entirely shut out from them by strata of clouds.

and Medeah occupied. This Algerian "battle above the clouds" was as much more romantic in its incidents than our own, as the Atlas Mountains exceed in altitude the Lookout range, but not more glorious. The disposition of the ground simply made the effect finer.

So much space has been given to the consideration of the details of this battle of the Col de Mouzaia, because it very much resembled our own battle of the South Mountain, 14th September, 1862, which the writer looks upon as the most brilliant feat of arms in the long list of glories which the Army of the Potomac can claim as their own. The success in the Tenyah Pass, as in that sunny Sunday fight in Turner's Gap, depended on the possession of a peak to the right of the road: only the Algerian Peak was 960 metres, 3,200 feet in height, and the Maryland, 1,000 feet. LAMORICIERE and CHANGARNIER had noble representatives in MEADE and DOUBLEDAY, and DUVIVIER in poor RENO. The DUKE OF ORLEANS, the hero of the day, might have been proud of such a substitute as HOOKER; but in McCLELLAN, VALEE had a very poor proxy. It would have been well for the former if he had possessed a little of the latter's iron will and severity.

There is a great parity of circumstances between the advance of McCLELLAN, from Washington, through Frederick, to Antietam, and of VALEE from Blidah to Medeah, besides the mere fact that in both, a mountain range, vigorously defended, had to be overcome. It took McCLELLAN twelve days to advance forty-five miles, over excellent roads, and through an open and friendly country, without opposition—VALEE, the same length of time to fight his way fifteen miles through an extremely difficult country, against the opposition of every soul in that country who could bear arms; when every hour brought a skirmish, and every day a bloody conflict. McCLELLAN had ample supplies, and troops double the number of his adversary. VALEE could depend upon nothing except what he could carry with him, and the Arabs outnumbered him at least two to one, fighting on their own soil, every inch of which was well known to every man, with a virulence and courage which the rebels might equal, but could not surpass. When VALEE did come in contact with the enemy entrenched and admirably posted in his mountain fortress, he inflicted such a defeat upon him as needed no second battle, no indecisive Antietam, to effect his object, the capture of Medeah. KEARNY might have told all this to Mc-

CLELLAN, and have afforded him the benefits of his experience, had he been permitted to have access to him, or had his counsels been listened to, even if they were not accepted. It is needless to go farther, although McCLELLAN is chargeable with a total want of strategy at South Mountain, for he could have turned the rebel positions there through Braddock's Gap, a course that would have obviated a hard day's fight, and have produced far greater results, with a much less sacrifice of life. But, VALEE, if not a man of genius, was a capable and experienced soldier. No wonder that KEARNY, when he looked upon McCLELLAN, looked back, as he wrote, with deep regret upon the absence or want of such brilliant commanders as those under whom he had seen the great African chain conquered and crowned with the ensigns of France.

ABD-EL KADER's troops, thus driven from their position—selected with so much address, fortified with so much care, and defended with so much resolution—fell back into the "Wood of Olives," another strong post. This is a narrow tongue of land, separating the water of the Chiffa from those of Oued-el-Djer, or Djels, midway between the Col de Mouzaia and Medeah. Here another short, but severe combat ensued, in which CHANGARNIER again distinguished himself, and dislodged the Arabs with some loss inflicted upon them, and impressed them with still stronger convictions of the futility of further resistance to such troops as he commanded. On the 17th May, the French army advanced down the Southern slope of the mountain and occupied Medeah, one of the objectives of the French operations. The other was Milianah next to be assailed. These keypoints occupy the same position, relative to Algiers, towards the south-west, as Constantine, towards the east by south, and constituted ABD-EL-KADER's chief strongholds in this direction.

Medeah is situated on a plateau on the summit of the Lesser Atlas, surrounded by a belt of gardens and enormous groves of fruit trees, particularly oranges, almonds, and olives; all the tropical fruits, however, are produced in abundance. It is one of the oldest cities in Africa, of Roman origin; and an immense aqueduct, of Roman construction, clothed with creepers, winding like a serpent and following the levels, still conveys to the town the water of the mountain springs, and feeds its numerous fountains. It was once very populous; and this aqueduct and other Roman remains attest its former importance.

The plateau upon which it is built has a rapid descent towards the valleys of the sea-coast, while it slopes more gently down in the direction of the desert, so that the town may be said to look into the Sahara. Its altitude above the sea is 3,018 feet. This plateau sinks sheer down on two sides, and these precipices make it susceptible of easy defence. A rather high stone wall, one mile in circumference, encompasses the town, pierced by five gates, two to the north, and three respectively to the south, east, and west. These gates, in 1840, were weakly defended by a few loopholes. Above the south gate two old 8-pounder Spanish culverins were mounted, which were captured by the French, and preserved as trophies. Like Algiers, Medeah has a Casbah and a very pretty palace, the residence of the former Bey of Titteri.

Such was the first purely Arab town which KEARNY saw, and thence he could look down into the great desert, of which such wonderful stories had been told. Here he had an opportunity to note the marked differences in the climate of Algiers. In winter the weather is very cold, and in summer the heat is excessive. But when does the summer commence? The military author of a "Summer in Sahara" speaks, 22d May, 1853, of "winter still having one foot planted on the white summits of the Mouzaia, eight miles N.N.W. of the town;" and PULSZKY alludes to the snow capped mountains, which cool the hot and dry winds of the desert. The mountain Ouanseris, 5,904 feet high, easily seen from Medeah, sixty-five miles to the southeast, in January, 1842, was all white with snow; and some sharp needles of the Jurjura, or Djordjora, about the same distance to the eastward, are covered with snow the whole year round.

CASTELLANE, in describing Mascara, still farther to the south, but on the same range, says, "the climate is frightful during the winter in this part of the country; snow, rain—rain which beats upon the tent like strokes of a stick—hail, winds, and every irregularity of climate."

At Medeah, three mountain ranges seem to come together; one from the west, one from the north, and one from the east. Towards the south, had the human vision sufficient range, KEARNY might have beheld the Great Desert—not altogether so in reality, since French military exploration has proved it to be an ocean of sand, thickly dotted with islands of verdure and fertility, with abundant water, at no very great depth, responding to artesian wells—for, as before stated, Medeah, from the elevation of its site, overlooks all intervening objects in that direction.

LAMPING, who campaigned in this country in 1840–'1, remarks that the tract of country must have been thickly peopled at some former time, judging from the cemeteries which he and his comrades saw in their marches in the district of Medeah.

"These are generally near the tomb of a marabout, and of enormous extent: they might truly be called cities of the dead. The graves are all exactly alike; no distinction seems to exist among the dead. All are carefully covered with masonry, to keep the jackals from scratching up the bodies; and indeed no one can wonder that the Bedouins should wish to rest undisturbed in death after such restless, wandering lives. Each grave was marked by a large upright stone, but no date told the dying day of him who lay beneath it, no escutcheon proclaimed his birth and descent."

On the 20th of May, VALEE—having left behind him in Medeah a garrison of two thousand four hundred men—retraced his steps across the Atlas to the farm of the Mouzaia, at the foot of the mountain, on the Northern side. The indefatigable Emir did not permit the peaceful prosecution of this march. A very severe attack upon the rear-guard occurred on the 20th, in the "Wood of Olives," in which that picked body of men, the Riflemen, (*Chasseurs d' Orleans, or de Vincennes*) suffered such terrible losses that it might have been looked upon as destroyed as a battalion, and as such it took no further part in this campaign. The first period of the great spring operations was ended. The DUKE OF ORLEANS and the DUKE OF AUMALE, both of whom had evinced the highest distinction in the discharge of their functions, bade adieu to the army to return to France. All the disposable troops were now brought together, and every possible preparation made for the next move.

While the French were straining every nerve to reorganize their columns, ABD-EL-KADER was not idle, and sought by able dispositions to render his numerous but scattered forces available for a protracted defensive. One body remained in the neighborhood of Algiers to harass the territory around this city; a second maintained the blockade of Medeah; a third was posted in the lowlands along the River Cheliff to observe and obstruct the advance of a French column upon Milianah; while a fourth was posted at the bridge of El Cantara, which spanned this river to the west of Milianah, on the route to Mascara and the province of Oran.

On the 5th June, the French column, ten thousand strong, started afresh from Blidah; pressed forward from the west end of the plain of the Metidjah into the Atlas; on the 7th passed the Cap or Col de Gontas—about fifteen miles east of Milianah, and about eighteen miles west of Medeah—and on the 8th captured Milianah after a short but brisk engagement, fortunately in time to arrest the conflagration, kindled by order of ABD-EL-KADER. This, but for the efforts of the French, would shortly have laid the whole place in ashes. Like ROTOPSCHIN, ABD-EL-KADER resolved to destroy his Moscow with fire rather than leave it in a condition to tempt the return of its own population, which he had driven forth to settle in a more inaccessible place, or to serve as a permanent shelter to the invader. An immense convoy of ammunition and provisions had accompanied the march of his troops, partly to serve as a supply for a garrison of three thousand men, which VALEE established in Milianah, and partly to re-victual Medeah, and thus enable its garrison to hold out through the winter.

Milianah, situated about eighty miles west-south-west of Algiers, nestles in the bosom of the mountains, surrounded on all sides by an abundance of water, the greatest of blessings in this torrid clime. Towards the north and west the ground is flat, with a gentle descent to the plain of Cheliff. Towards the east and south it sinks precipitously from the wall of the city down into a very deep valley, which, full of the most beautiful gardens, presents a prospect from the town which can scarcely be exceeded in beauty. This valley of the Cheliff was to Milianah—the Richmond of ABD-EL-KADER—what the Shenandoah Valley was to the rebel capital. It was his granary; the soil scarcely needed the hand of industry to produce the richest crops. Magnificent harvests rewarded the rude Arab irrigation. On these two last mentioned sides (eastward and southward) Milianah, like Medeah and Constantine, is not susceptible of attack.

Milianah, the ancient Maniana, is another evidence of the strategical engineering of the Romans. Its site, like every other selected by that wonderful military nation—of whom it was said: "A God must have instructed them in the art of war"—rendered it a military post of the highest importance. When ABD-EL-KADER consigned it to the flames, it was indeed the Emir's Moscow. It was his chosen city, which he had destined to become the center of Arab industry. There he had constructed his forges; and all his grand establishments, since situated on a detached mountain plateau, even as if on a cornice, ("*en corniche*,") its position was admirably calculated against any attack, except that of European discipline and artillery. Handsome houses, flagged with marble, with galleries in the second story, supported by graceful columns and magnificent Moorish sculptures, attested the opulence of the ancient inhabitants. Four miles to the northeast, the mountain Zakkar towers to the height of five thousand and thirty-one feet, the sixth peak of the Atlas in altitude. From its flank bursts forth abundant fountains of the purest water, not only sufficient to supply the town below—built on a spur of the lofty source—but susceptible of furnishing motive power to a large number of manufactories. When the French entered by the Gate of Zakkar, all that remained of this comparative magnificence was the palace of the Emir and a few other buildings.

Lamping speaks of Milianah as *besieged* and taken by the French on this occasion:

"One half of the besiegers assailed the town from below, while the rest, having planted some cannon on a height commanding the town, poured their shot down upon it. When Abd-el-Kader saw he could hold the place no longer, he determined to retreat by the only gate which was left still free, and first rode, sword in hand, through the streets, cutting down every one who would not follow him. Nearly all effected their retreat in safety, and most of the families settled on the northern slope of the Lesser Atlas."

This bears out the writer's recollections of Kearny's account of these operations; he always spoke of this capture as the *siege* of Milianah, and referred to the cemeteries—such as excited theast onishment of Lamping—in connection with this service. He said that one of these old Turkish graves made a capital place to sleep in during the investment. The head, foot, and side stones at once afforded shelter from the wind, and kept a man from rolling out. Wrapped in his cloak, or burnous, he often slept soundly and comfortably over one of the former inhabitants, sleeping still more soundly underneath him. Castellane refers to a "cemetery which received, in 1840, an entire garrison." It is situated at the foot of the walls, and as this is one point from which the town was assailed, it is very likely that this is the spot to which Kearny referred.

Having left a garrison of three thousand men in Milianah, Valee marched thence, 12th June, through the Djendel—the district of

FRENCH TROOPS FORCING THE PASS OR TONYAH OF THE MONSAIA, ALGIERS, 1840.

country between that town and Medeah. Down to 1841 these towns had been, as it were, advanced posts of French-African occupation. After that time they became the basis of French occupation in Algeria. This movement was for the purpose of supplying Medeah, and in order to do so, it was necessary to cross a spur of the Col de Mouzaia, the third time this spring, but now from south to north, and not, as previously, from north to south.

On this occasion the Zouaves—imitation Arabs—moved with more celerity than the real natives, and were beforehand in the occupation of the pass. By a manœuvre which proved that Abd-el-Kader was an intuitive General, the Emir surpassed the experienced leaders of the French in their own profession, and came near involving the whole column in destruction. Finding that he could not anticipate the French Light Infantry, he hurried forward his Arabs, parallel to the French, in perfect silence, under the blind of a rocky ridge. Simultaneously, 15th June, both reached the summit of the mountain. The van and main body were permitted to pass unmolested, but the rear-guard was saluted with an unexpected volley from an invisible enemy. This fire covered the ground with dead and wounded. Profiting by the surprise, the Arabs threw themselves upon the French, and a hand to hand combat ensued, in which the Arabs, four times repulsed, returned as often to the attack. Bayonets, modeled after the yataghan, were crossed with the original weapon, swords with the long and keen, but rude and home-made dagger of the Arabs, and the discharges of the rifles and muskets were answered by pistol-shots, muzzle to muzzle. Of the 800 Zouaves and Chasseurs de Vincennes, on whom as usual the brunt of the combat fell, 120 were killed, and 300 wounded. Raasloff says 32 dead, 290 wounded; and adds that it required a lively fire of Artillery to bring off the remains of the rear-guard. While any soldier must admire the disciplined courage of the French troops, he cannot refuse the highest meed of admiration to Abd-el-Kader and the regulars he had formed. Again and again the Emir led these regulars to the charge, and, judging from results, it would have gone very hard with the French if the Arab chief had had a competent artillery, with which to answer that of the French Marshal. Valee having supplied Medeah, again dispatched Changarnier back to Milianah with 5,000 men, to escort a convoy of provisions. He was again attacked by Abd-el-Kader, and only repulsed the Emir after another severe engagement. It was now the end of June, and the heat had become so intense that farther operations were impossible, and on the 5th July the army was placed in summer quarters, men and animals pretty well used up. The cavalry sent over from France was so thoroughly disorganized, that of the ten squadrons there was no longer any trace; and even the Chasseurs d'Afrique, mounted on Moorish barbs, the artillery and train, could only parade a very few horses which were in serviceable condition. Of the men, 7,000 died from disease between August and December—a mortality of about one-eighth, without counting those who fell in battle, or had already succumbed from sickness during the three previous months.

Nevertheless, the return of the hot season brought with it no repose for the troops—is the remark of the Duke of Aumale. The summer and autumn passed in supplying the posts which the French had occupied in the spring, an operation as difficult and as murderous as their conquest had proved. The bullets of the foe, the climate, and incessant fatigue, thinned the ranks of the soldiery, and as a just compensation, carried off very many of the officers.

The Duke of Aumale, in his historical sketches of the Zouaves and Foot Chasseurs or Riflemen—their real title might be translated African Foot Cavalry—Paris, 1855, says it would be impossible, in a succinct narrative, to describe all the combats which took place during this bloody campaign on the plain of the Metidjah; at the Col (pass) of Mouzaia; at the foot of the Chenouan; in the valley of the Cheliff; on the Ouamri; at the Gontas. Every day was marked by an engagement, every inch of ground was disputed. The cavalry of all the tribes of the provinces of Algiers and of Oran, supported and kept in hand by the Emir's "*Reds*"—the name given by the French soldiers to Abd-el-Kader's regular cavalry, clad entirely in red or scarlet—inundated the plain; every passage of the mountain was defended by the Emir's regular infantry, and by thousands of Kabyles.

This insures the fact that Kearny learned his business in a very hard but thorough school, for the lightest of the French trooper's duties in Africa is less like a military promenade than many deemed the worst in European soldiering. For fortitude, as well as for gallantry, he won equal consideration, and in one of the marches (when, under a torrid sun, water was so scarce and thirst so burning that the men threw themselves down to lick up a puddle) Kearny marched on foot to add his example to those afforded by his regular comrades. Moreover, on this occasion, when many had to be brought in on ambulances or vehicles, he came in among the foremost on foot, high in spirit, however exhausted in strength. It is a great pity that his journal of these trials is lost, for this expedition, although "illustrated by so many deeds of glory," was attended with no results adequate to its harassing labors, inasmuch as the French columns on their return to the coast were followed by the Arabs of ABD-EL KADER, who swept with fire and sabre the plains between the Atlas and the capital of Algiers. Nevertheless, it taught KEARNY many a lesson, turned to account in his after years; in his Mexican campaigns; his expedition against the Indians of Oregon; and that year of service against the rebels—lessons which bore fruit in the admirable discipline and police of his First New Jersey Brigade, and in the example he set to the officers and men of the army; an example imitated so honorably by BERRY, who followed his type to glory at Chancellorsville, and BIRNEY, who, up to the end of the war, helped to make the reputations of others, and win successes of which the rewards were reaped by immediate superiors.

PARIS, April 20th, 1840.

SIR:—I have the honor to inform you, that I left Saumur on the 25th of March, since which time ill health has obliged me to remain at this place. In accordance with my letter to you of October 16th, 1839, after remaining attached to the Cavalry School at Saumur for six months, for the purposes therein mentioned, I have left it to carry out the objects proposed when I came abroad: that is, to, by personal examination, make myself acquainted with the practices of cavalry regiments in the French and other services. In that same letter I mentioned that I thought it would be profitable to visit the regiments serving in Africa, as there alone would I have the opportunity of observing troops in active service in the field. This present spring's campaign, under the DUC D'ORLEANS and Marshal VALEE, has presented an occasion which I am anxious to improve. It is true that you have not signified your opinion to me since receiving my communication, but as you had laid out no system of travels for me in particular, when I left America, I presumed that had it not met with your approbation, you would have signified the same to me. Indirectly and unofficially, however, I have heard that in respect to the plans in my letter, you made no objections; though, indeed, so unofficially has it reached me that I would not be justified in an ordinary case in considering it an authority, but in my peculiar situation it is a circumstance to aid me in making up my determination. Were the campaign a thing I could see some months later, I would be far better satisfied in waiting till I heard from you explicitly, and till my health, which has been extremely delicate, was in a greater measure restored to me. But that cannot be, as after the middle of June all active operations cease, and do not recommence till late in fall, or the ensuing year; and that this is a subject more worthy of my attention than aught else, I am fully persuaded of from what service I have had in the Dragoons, and more especially from our Colonel's high opinion of the ends to be obtained by an examination of what a theatre of war must constantly present.

It is, sir, with extreme regret that I find myself without written intructions for myself, and directions to our Minister at this Court, to exercise his influence in my behalf, for I am thus obliged to go as a mere private officer traveling, instead of an accredited agent of the public, which throws in my path obstacles, where there otherwise would be none. Might I then ask for instructions, it would be more satisfactory, as assuring me of your approval of such plans as I may have laid down, or giving me orders to pursue another course. I should think it most advisable for me, in the course of the ensuing summer, after my return, to be present at the Camp of Instruction at Lunéville, where, annually, five to six thousand cavalry are assembled; and, also, to visit the German and English Cavalry. As the system of schools varies always essentially from the practices in regiments, I have refrained from sending communications to the Department which might be incorrect in their conclusions, as applied to the French Army generally, and wait until I have studied regiments in detail. Still I have seen sufficient to be convinced that though the French theory of tactics is the most perfect, and though (as they are allowed by all nations) their manner of going through a campaign is the least harrassing and destructive of soldiers, that here the study of their army stops. For their grooming and the state of their horses, their stables, and everything that refers to them, their quarters, and everything pertaining to high discipline in garrison and military neatness, are everywhere here wretched in the extreme—to a degree that would not be tolerated nor dreamt of in the most slovenly company of our whole regiment. These points must be studied in England, where, perhaps, they are carried to an excess, and in Germany where, both in the Prussian and Austrian cavalry, I believe it must be perfect.

Sir, I leave Paris to-morrow. The campaign was to have opened on the 20th April (to-day), and I indulge the hope of, by rapid traveling, not being more than a week behind hand.

I have the honor to be,

With high consideration,

Your obedient servant,

(Signed) P. KEARNY,

First Lieutenant First Dragoons.

The Honorable J. R. POINSETT,

Secretary of War.

ALGIERS, 7th May, 1840.

MON. GENERAL VISCOUNT DE SCHRAMM.

GENERAL:—I take the liberty of sending you this letter at the same time that I transmit to you the letters of General CASS, Ambassador of the United States near His Majesty the King of the French, addressed, the one to yourself, the other to General Viscount DE RUMIGNY, in the hope that you will have the kindness to obtain for me an authorization from His Highness the DUKE OF ORLEANS, or from Marshal VALEE to join the first expedition which can take place during the time I can remain in Algiers.

I would not have taken the liberty to make this request if I was not an officer sent out by the Government of the United States, with the object of studying my profession in Europe in order to introduce improvements into our Cavalry. With this intention I have been attached for the last seven months to the Royal Cavalry School at Saumur; and I am one of the three officers admitted by the Government in last October. At present I have the permission of my Government to travel during the rest of the year, to observe the practicable working of the regiments themselves. In doing so, I am entirely free to dispose of my time as seems most advantageous to myself. Still as our ambassador has no positive instructions from our Government to prefer this request to the French Government, he considered that the letters addressed to you and to General RUMIGNY (with whom he had the honor of being acquainted) would be sufficient to obtain this authorization, if such a request was a proper one to be granted. A severe sickness prevented me from arriving in Africa before the departure of this expedition, but if it should last some time longer I would be happy to join it immediately. In any event, I request your intermediation to obtain for me an authorization to join the next, even if it consists of only a single regiment.

This request is not made with the intention of annoying you by joining the General's staff, which must always be sufficiently numerous, but to attach myself to some regiment of Cavalry which belongs to an Army Corps.

I have the honor to be, with the highest consideration,

Your very humble and very obedient servant,

P. KEARNY,

Lieutenant Dragoons, United States Army.

ALGIERS, May 8th, 1840.

THE HONORABLE J. R. POINSETT:

SIR:—I have the honor to inform you that I arrived here yesterday, the 7th of May.

I was unable to leave on the 21st, as I had expected, General CASS changing his intention as to applying for me for an authorization from the French Minister of War to join the intended expedition; moreover, I was detained two more days, till the 24th of May [April], in waiting for the private letters he had offered me to Generals SCHRAMM and RUMIGNY, and which were necessary as introduction to their notice. This made me too late for the packet from Toulon of the 27th, and it only leaves weekly.

Our Consul here, Mr. JACROUS, has, since my arrival, exercised in my behalf the influence he has; but, as I had not an authorization from the Minister of War, the commandant of the place, Colonel DE MARENGO, did not feel himself entitled, though anxious to serve me, to grant me a pass to join the army, but forwards by to-day's express, my letters for me. As I find that the army left on the 26th, from Blida, and the communications are impracticable but for large convoys and escorts, I have little reason to be flattered with the hopes of an answer being in time to be of the service I had hoped. As the letters General CASS favored me with to General SCHRAMM and to General RUMIGNY did not enter at all into the details of my having been sent abroad by Government, and the objects of my travels, I felt necessitated to accompany them by one from myself, applying to General SCHRAMM, who is Chief of the Staff of the Army of Africa, to obtain for me from the Marshal VALEE or the DUC D'ORLEANS (though he is here only acting as a subordinate General) an authorization to join any expedition that might take place whilst I remained in Africa—in fine, a permission to be at liberty to pass wherever I might please in Africa. I herewith send you a copy of the same.

Successful or not in this or any other endeavor I may make whilst abroad to obtain those ends for which Government has sent me, believe me, Sir, as always actuated by the truest zeal for the service, and it is in this that I rest the hope, in some degree, to make up the deficiencies of knowledge and the want of experience.

I have the honor to be, Sir,

With the highest sense of respect,

Your obedient servant,

(Signed) P. KEARNY,

Lieutenant First Dragoons.

The Honorable J. R. POINSETT,

Secretary of War, United States.

ALGIERS, July 1st, 1840.

SIR:—I have the honor to report myself as just returned from the late expedition in the province of Algiers, Africa, under the orders of Marshal VALEE, and at the same time transmit, to be forwarded to the Secretary of War, a letter —[letter and report both lost]—detailing some observations made whilst with the French troops.

I have the honor to be,

Your most obedient servant,

(Signed) P. KEARNY, JR.,

Lieutenant First Regiment Dragoons.

General R. JONES,

Adjutant General United States Army, Washington, D. C.

CHAPTER IX.

FROM THE MISSISSIPPI TO THE ROCKY MOUNTAINS.

THE SOUTH PASS.

"Well pleased, could we pursue
The Arno, from his birth-place in the clouds,
So near the yellow Tiber's—springing up
From his four fountains on the Apennine,
That mountain-ridge, a sea-mark to the ships
Sailing on either sea." ROGERS' "ITALY."

IN the fall of 1840, Lieutenant PHILIP KEARNY returned from his European mission, having done honor to Mr. POINSETT's selection of him as well as to the American name. He was almost immediately appointed aid-de-camp to Major-General ALEXANDER MACOMB, Commander-in-Chief of the United States Army. This distinguished officer is best known to the American people for his decisive victory at Plattsburgh, 11th September, 1814, when, with one thousand five hundred Regulars, aided by a body of three thousand militia and volunteers—under Generals MOERS, a soldier of the Revolution, and STRONG—from New York and Vermont, he repulsed and defeated an army of from fourteen thousand to fifteen thousand British veterans, fresh from triumphs over the troops who had conquered Europe, under the leading of NAPOLEON and his chosen Lieutenants. KEARNY retained this position until the death of General MACOMB, which took place, at the Headquarters of the Army and Capital of the nation, 25th June, 1841. From October to December of that year he was on duty at the United States Cavalry Barracks at Carlisle, Pennsylvania. Thence he returned to Washington as aid-de-camp to Major-General WINFIELD SCOTT, next Commander-in-Chief of the United States Army. With him KEARNY remained—"dispensing elegant hospitality"—from December, 1841, to April, 1844, when he was relieved and ordered to join his company. On 12th May, 1844, he was with his regiment at Fort Leavenworth, and was enabled by his experience in Africa to prepare his immediate command for efficient service against the Indians, and the projected display of our military strength upon the plains.

In May, 1845, Colonel STEPHEN WATTS KEARNY, with five companies of his regiment, the First United States Dragoons, made a march to the South Pass at the summit of the Rocky Mountains. This was the first military expedition which struck out so far from the settlements into the Indian country. Its object was to awe the savages and thus afford protection to the emigrants who were crossing the plains in great numbers on their way to settle in Oregon. The writer is indebted for some particulars of it to Major ALEXANDER SARANAC MACOMB, brother-in-law to General, then Lieutenant, PHILIP KEARNY, whose tent-mate he was on this occasion.

The incidents of this military promenade are the more familiar to his mind, and afforded the Major greater pleasure, since he found himself once more among old friends and associates, having served three years with the First Dragoons before he was transferred to the Second Regiment, and thence as aid-de-camp to the staff of his father, Major-General MACOMB. The many agreeable reminiscences connected with the novelty of the trip, the jokes among comrades on the march and by the camp-fire, would naturally make all who survive look back with pleasure to the period when they were still young and fresh enough to enjoy an excursion which was accompanied with just enough danger to season it.

The staff of this expeditionary column consisted of:

Lieutenant HENRY S. TURNER, Adjutant and Acting Assistant Adjutant-General of the Third Military Department on the expedition through the Rocky Mountains, and at the headquarters in St. Louis, Missouri, 1845; Captain First Dragoons, April 2d, 1846; in the war with Mexico, 1846–'47, as Acting Assistant Adjutant-General of the Army of the West, participating in the combat of San Pascual, California, 6th December, 1846, where he was wounded by a lance; Skirmish of San Bernardo, California, 7th December, 1846; Passage of the San Gabriel River, California, 8th January, 1847; and Skirmish on the Plains of Mesa, 9th January, 1847. He resigned, 21st July, 1848. This gentleman is (1868) President of the Union National Bank of St. Louis, Missouri, and the author has to thank him for much interesting information.

He was Acting Assistant Adjutant-General on the Staff of Briga dier-General Atkinson at the same time that Philip Kearny was attached to the same military family as Aid, in 1839.

Lieutenant James Henry Carleton, Quartermaster, afterwards Brigadier-General.

Lieutenant William Benjamin Franklin, Topographical Engineer. This very able, scientific man, afterwards rose to the rank of Major-General of Volunteers, and commanded, first a Corps, and then a Grand Division in the Army of the Potomac, afterwards the Expedition to the Sabine Pass. * * * * * *

* * * * * * * * * * *

His division comprised the famous New Jersey Brigade, made and commanded, from 14th August, 1861, to 2d May, 1862, by General Kearny.

G. J. De Camp, Surgeon, since dead.

The five companies of Dragoons were commanded respectively by:

Captain Philip St. George Cooke, now Brigadier General and Brevet Major General U. S. Army; author in 1862, of a new book of Cavalry Tactics.

Captain Benjamin D. Moore, killed 6th December, 1846, in a charge upon the Mexican Lancers at the battle of San Pascual.

* * * * * * *

Lieutenant William Eustis, afterwards, 1845, Captain of 1st Dragoons, resigned 1849. He was the son of Brevet Brigadier General Abram Eustis, who served in the war of 1812-'15, who died Colonel of 1st U. S. Artillery, at Portland, Maine, 1843. He was a very fine officer, and Hooker says he owed a great deal to his training. Captain Eustis is still living, a prominent civil engineer at Natchez, Mississippi, and has shown great kindness in assisting the writer in the preparation of chapter on the Ball at Saumur.

1st Lieutenant Philip Kearny. Kearny, Eustis and Turner while in France, and at the cavalry school of Saumur, translated the French Cavalry Tactics, which in 1841 was adopted for the U. S. Dragoons, and published by order of J. R. Poinsett, Secretary of War.

Lieutenant Philip Kearny's command was a fine company, under good discipline, and evinced in every respect the influence of its commander, who always had the power of infusing a high military spirit into his men.

This command, 1st U. S. Dragoons, took up its line of March from Fort Leavenworth about the middle of May, as soon as the grass was sufficiently grown to afford good grazing for the animals. Fifty head of sheep and twenty-five head of oxen were driven with the column under charge of the commissary, by order of Colonel KEARNY, "always a provident officer, so that the officers and men were furnished with fresh beef and mutton, every now and then, until they got into the buffalo country." It is more than likely, however, that this foresight was due to the lessons learned by Lieutenant KEARNY in his Algerian campaign, for, according to Lieutenant LAMPING, (Oldenburgh Service, author of the "French in Algiers," who served as a private for some time in the Foreign Legion, and participated in a great number of severe expeditions,) "besides what rations were loaded on mules, each soldier carried nine days' provisions, consisting of ship biscuit, rice, coffee, and sugar. Bread and wine are not given on a campaign, owing to the very limited means of transport, for it would be impossible to use wagons and the number of mules and donkeys required to carry the provisions, for a march of five weeks is great enough as it is. Cattle are driven, and during an expedition each soldier is allowed double rations —that, is one pound of meat daily."

The tactics adopted by the French generals in Africa afford capital lessons for the warfare on our plains, nor are the habits and usages of the semi-barbarous tribes of Africa, or those of the Turcos, which won such a name in the Solferino campaign—a corps organized by the French—very unlike the American savages, even in the treatment of the dead. Both as a rule torture the living captive, and the Kabyle carries off, as a pendant at his saddle bow, the whole head of a fallen enemy; whereas the Indian strips off the scalps to ornament his person or accoutrements. The Indian is the most sensible, for the scalp is easily preserved, and more merciful, as far as life is concerned, for, if rescued in time, a scalped man may survive; a man with his head wholly or even half severed off, certainly not. Moreover a dead-head is a ghastly object at best, and soon becomes unpleasant unless salted or smoked, as practiced by the Dyaks of Borneo, who set as great a value on the heads of their enemies as the Kabyle, and take as much pains to secure them and more to preserve them longer as cherished ornaments of their homes.

"The bivouac of a French column in Africa usually forms a perfect square, modified, of course, by the ground; the infantry, who are outside, lie in double file behind their piled arms. Each battalion sends out one company as an advance post, and another company remains within the lines as a picket. The baggage, artillery, and cavalry are placed in the middle. The cavalry do not furnish any outposts as horsemen, especially in broken ground, as they are too much exposed to the fire of the Bedouins and Kabyles, who steal singly towards us. The infantry, on the contrary, can more easily hide themselves, and by laying their faces close to the ground can hear the slightest sound. This is essential, as the Bedouins and Kabyles, upon all fours, like wild beasts, fall upon single outposts, or shoot them from a distance when they can see them; for which reason the outposts change their ground after dark, to deceive the enemy. They generally draw back a little, leaving their watch fires burning, which enables them to see whatever passes between them and the fire."

The line of march followed was that which is called the "Oregon Trace," along the North Fork of the Platte River. At Fort Laramie, what live stock remained were left to fatten, as bison were now at hand. At this Fort commences the ascent of the mountains; it is very gradual, and quite practicable for wagons. Along the valley of the Sweet River, fat buffaloes were met in abundance. About the 1st July, the command reached the summit of the South Pass, and the troops were mustered at the head waters of the rivers which flow thence into the Pacific. The return march was by the same route as far as Laramie; thence along the base of the mountains to Bent's Fort, under Pike's Peak, a considerable trading post near New Mexico, and thence again along the Sante Fé Trace, to Fort Leavenworth. The troops arrived in splendid condition, having accomplished a distance of about two thousand three hundred miles in ninety-nine days, without the loss of a man by accident or sickness, and with the expenditure of but a few horses.

General Stephen Watts Kearny held a council with a large delegation of Sioux warriors at Fort Laramie, and this display of troops, at this date, so far out from the settlements, had the desired effect, and for some time to come the emigrants were not molested by the Indians.

The following notices of prominent objects encountered along this march westwards, although not compiled from the correspondence of Kearny or officers attached to the expedition of 1845, are, nevertheless, pertinent. The reader will find them graphic and interesting from the peculiar manner in which things seen are presented and commented on. They are from the pen of a common friend—an officer who distinguished himself in the Mexican war —who traversed, a few years afterwards, the same route followed by the expeditionary column, while things remained in about the same condition, and long before those great changes occurred which made such a stride in advance, in ten years, as would have cost half a century for their accomplishment in the Old World.

About one hundred miles west of Fort Leavenworth, that fertile soil, which attracted into Kansas such vast numbers of immigrants with its prolific yield, changes its character and becomes less and less prolific.

FORT LEAVENWORTH.

"The land is pretty nearly occupied at last—that is, the good land; for, from about a hundred miles westward of this point to the Rocky Mountains—a distance of some five or six hundred miles—the soil is said to be very poor and not worth occupying. There is probably more waste arable land in the Continent of Asia now than there is in North America.

"The prairie is a heaving, swelling ocean of grass, mingling mistily with the sky, like the unbounded sea. In the ravines—or rather troughs of this sea—are occasional streams, or perhaps series of water-holes, bordered with a thin skirt of trees. All else is grass. A strange absence of animated life is observed. A solitary wolf now and then; one antelope; a few doves and larks; two or three crows; a few other birds, one toad, one lizard, and some cat-fish, are almost the only living things, except grasshoppers and flies, that we have seen in the entire distance traversed. Not until two or three days since did we begin to see even the wreck of a buffalo, their bleaching, decaying skulls and bones then beginning to appear scattered here and there upon this their vast and ancient pasture ground. Their carcasses, as we advanced, became more numerous, until at length, yesterday, we saw pieces of their furry skins, recently torn off, scattered about the deserted lodges of the Pawnees."

[Some eighty miles east of Fort Kearny, about midway between that post and Fort Leavenworth, upon the left or north bank of the "Little Blue," a branch of the Republican River.]

"After a soaking day's march, the rain-clouds of the day are retiring in the distance, with low-muttered thunder; the lightning flashes out, as of a summer's eve, at various points of the horizon; and small masses of clouds move slowly over the twilight sky of the west, as if surveying the field of battle of the day. The air is mild and warm, and the cricket is filling the stillness of the night with its pleasant song.

"Not the least pleasant part of the march, to my ear, is the harvest hymn of the insects, which raise a constant strain of thanksgiving—a joyous fritinancy of song—

for the ripe weed-seeds that grow along the road, for the road is bordered with weeds. As if in fulfilment of the curse pronounced upon man, they spring up, not only where he tills the land, but even where his wagon-wheels have plowed.

"The column as seen in the distance, moving across the prairie, presents the appearance of a small blackish head, (for the regiment looks small in such unbounded space,) followed by a very long whitish tail. This tail is the baggage-train, for the wagons, drawn by six mules each, are roofed with white cotton covers.

"The Platte River, upon the right bank of which we are encamped, is by far the greatest curiosity that we have seen. It seems to be nearly a mile wide, and yet it is so shallow that one may wade across it. Its current is all filled with sand-flats and little islets. It is but very little below the general level of the country. Right along the edge of the stream is a little ridge of sand, and then several miles back is a larger ridge. The land between these ridges is very level and is all sand, except a little covering of black vegetable mould. The horses lick this soil in a way that shows that there is something saline in it; and it is here, perhaps, that the buffalo finds salt, or its substitute. It is said that if holes be dug in this soil for water, the water is cool and pleasanter to the taste than the river water, but that it is certain death to drink it. The country is very level, and the Great Pacific Railroad, if ever built, may run along the Platte, from its mouth, above Fort Leavenworth, to where it takes its rise in the Rocky Mountains. There is not so much timber, however, but that even ties, as well as rails, would have to be brought from a distance.

"Our road still leads up the right bank of the Platte, which still remains as great a curiosity as ever. Imagine an immense ditch dug through the rolling, undulating prairie from west to east—from the Rocky Mountains to the Missouri River—some several miles in width, and two or three hundred feet in depth, and you can form some idea of the valley through which the Platte runs. The river itself is in the middle of this valley, and consists of a mile or more in width of shallow threads of water running among sand flats and small islands. The banks of the river are but a little above the water, while those of the valley are deeply seamed and gullied, and look like chains of rugged mountains. On the precipitous slopes of some of the deep gullies there are clumps of cedar, reminding one of the belts of fir trees that are lifted up into the cold, thin air by the loftiest mountains. Nowhere else is this cedar seen here. The smooth, wide, and nearly level bottom valley is verdant with rich pasture, and along the course of the river, on either side, numerous herds of buffalo are seen grazing.

"At one of our encampments a buffalo was noticed wading across the river towards us, and some of the men couched in the grass to lie in wait for him. On he came, boldly and determinedly, though occasionally stopping to look at our camp. Numerous mules and horses were feeding peacefully there, and this seemed to reassure him. Presently, reaching the shore and mounting the bank, he stopped a while in half surprise to gaze upon the novelty of the scene before him. There he stood, with his shaggy front lifted up high, in a boldness of relief and an untamed spiritedness of attitude that gave him, I assure you, a most magnificent appearance. Pang! went a rifle: and the noble brute but barely blinked. Whang! went another; and now he starts on the run for the inland priarie. But whang! whang!! whang!!! go the fire-arms—pistols, musketoons, and rifles of all sorts.

Pierced with numerous balls, the amazed animal stops again to gaze; and so do his pursuers stop, half-frightened at the blood and fierceness of his look. Again he starts to run, and again his pursuers renew their fire, until at length, exhausted by his efforts to escape, and from the loss of blood from his many wounds, he falls, tumbles down upon the plain, and out the butcher sallies with steel and knife to cut him up."

[Camp near Court House Rock, two hundred and forty miles west of Fort Kearny, on the North Platte.]

"Court House Rock is a castle-like mass of limestone, which probably received its name from those with whom a court-house was considered as the grandest of all edifices. Near by it are two other masses, which from this point look like pyramids. There is a solidity, repose, durability, and a gradual ascending of the thoughts towards heaven in the pyramid, that doubtless gave that monument a great retroactive effect upon the character and manners of the Egyptians. How serene is the expression of the face of all their ancient statues!

"'Chimney Rock,' a little to the west of the preceding freak of nature, ought to be called 'Monumental Rock,' for it is perfectly like a monument. The valley of the river opened out there, and this monument, as it stands on the slope of the right bank of the valley, overlooks an immense level region of country, and can be seen from a great distance. As we struck our camp and marched by it early in the morning, we entered, among numerous other resemblances to works of art, such as temples, palaces, pyramids, domes, towers, turrets, and buttresses; and finally, after a march of some twenty miles, an immense wall, not unlike a city's wall, extended across the way, rising to the height of five hundred to one thousand feet above the river, and through which there is a lofty gate-way.* Through this gate-way we passed, while a hawk was hovering around its summit, as if around a mountain's crag. So like the ruins of a Babylon or a Karnac, or some such city, was the entire scene of this day's march, that when, at an early hour, the cry of the wolf, like that of the jackall, resounded through the stillness, the illusion was almost perfect. And then the reflection arose—where's the difference between this, nature's mockery of art, and art itself, since, some once-mighty Thebes, where myriads of human beings have swarmed, and where human art has run its course, what now remains but exactly such shapes as these? The primeval stillness that rests upon the one could hardly be distinguished from the pall of oblivion that has settled over the other.

"From the gateway on, our route has not presented much of interest; being almost void of animal life, and scorched with drouth.

"We have passed through the lofty gateway of Scott's Bluffs, and encamped among the *mock* ruins. These when the morning dawned, shewed to a beautiful effect, dome, pyramid, turret, tower, monument and battlement, rising in calm repose amidst the grey light. And when two Indians came riding over the scene, like any two Arabs over the ruins of a Karnac or a Nineveh, the illusion for a moment was complete. There was a charm in this apparent playful effort of in-

* This is almost the same *lusus naturæ* as the "Iron Gates" of the Atlas, only this is single and those are quadruple.

telligence on the part of nature that was quite captivating. Here, before the human race was created—before man was born—Nature had mimicked beforehand his proudest seats of empire. From the lofty walls in the west to the monument in the east (which needed only the figure of a man upon it with folded arms, in a pensive mood, to be complete), the distance was more than twenty miles; giving a grand idea of the vastness of this irony of nature at the grandeur of man. It is in a wilderness which will probably never become much peopled, and the sandy, shallow Platte flows away in mock commercial importance in the distance. Our good mother, Nature, seems to be in a very kindly, amiable mood, when she can be thus so seriously facetious at our expense.

"If you have been in Canada again this summer, you may probably have fallen in with some Sioux Indians; for, if I am not mistaken, they used to reside about the great lakes, and have gradually retired from these before the advance of the white man. They extend now along the Platte far up into the Rocky Mountains. A party of these which met us as we were coming away fom Laramie, furnished the column considerable amusement. It consisted of an Indian and his wife and two small children. The man was mounted on a horse, with a boy astride behind him. He wore a soldier's cap with a feather stuck in it, and by his side hung a large dragoon's sabre. He looked pretty fierce and warlike, but behind him was another horse which he led by a lariat. Two lodge-poles were attached to both sides of this horse, at one end, while at the other they trailed upon the ground; and upon a staging, fixed upon these poles, rode his wife and a small girl. It was as odd a compromise between savage and civilized life as ever was seen. The addition of an axle-tree and two wheels to the poles would have been an effort at civilization absolutely beyond the Indian's capacity; yet he seemed to be, naturally, as much of a man in every respect as we are. * *

"We have passed several large collections of lodges, and there is now one just above me, and another below; for the Indians still come here, as has been their wont, to intercept the buffalo when they come down from the prairie to drink in the Platte and roll their huge carcasses in the sand and mud. * * * But their white conical lodges, the original of SIBLEY'S tent, seen amidst the green margin of the Platte, look pretty. Near them, always, are tripods, formed of three poles tied together at the tops, from which are suspended quivers and a white shield. In time of war, however, the shield is red. It is a tasty, picturesque sight, and I suspect that it originated with the Canadian French, who, from marital alliances with the Sioux, seem to follow them westward into the mountains.

"This Point (Fort Laramie) appears to be the center of the buffalo-robe trade—not that the buffalo are numerous here, but that the trade naturally finds this as one of its centers.

"I am told that the robes are prepared by the Indian women, and that a great deal of patient labor is bestowed upon them. To tan the robe they put upon the hairless side a preparation made of the brains, liver, and marrow of the animal; and the skin is made supple by being drawn repeatedly athwart a rope.

"Already these robes have become comfortable, for, though the days are very warm, the nights are cold. We are at an elevation of four thousand two hundred and fifty feet above the level of the sea—an elevation at this latitude which ought to render it pretty cool the year round.

"Fort Laramie, for an outpost, is a pretty place. It is situated in a large basin through which a clear large stream, called Laramie Forks, flows, skirted with cotton-wood trees. A bridge across this stream; the white edifices of the post; the numerous men and animals of the military corps now assembled here; the blue peaks of mountains seen in the west--all these form a scene which, come upon in so wild and desert a region, looks odd, interesting, and beautiful.

"The westernmost of the Rocky Mountains, 'Laramie Peak,' will soon be peering at us over the intervening hills."

[Camp two hundred and fifty miles west of Fort Laramie.]

"At length we have left the Platte, which we had followed so long, and struck across to one of its tributaries, which we are still on, and which is called the Sweet Water. It is a fine, large mountain brook, clean, sweet, musical in its bubble, and stocked with fish; but not a tree or shrub is seen along its course. Its course is from the S.W., and it is one of the remotest tributaries of the Mississippi. We shall still follow it several days up the South Pass, where its head source is not far from that of other brooks which flow westward into the Pacific.

"A few hours before arriving upon the banks of this stream, we passed through a region where potash occurred in the greatest abundance. There were several ponds lying along our route that had become dried up, and the potash that was left in them looked like that which is seen in the potash kettle after the lye has been evaporated. It lay in large clots, so that hundreds of tons might have been shoveled up.

"We are at length among the Rocky Mountains indeed, and if you were to see them you would admit that they merited their name. Such nude, bold masses of granite I have never before seen. They rise as abruptly from the sandy soil around them as if from the waters of the sea—no debris lie scattered down their sides, only a few stunted cedar or pine dot them here and there, and small patches of grass among the rifts invite the mountain sheep—all else is cold, bare, massive granite. But what is remarkable, such only is the case with these mountains, that for the last four days have appeared on our right—those on our left have been covered with soil, and seemed black with fir forests from their crests half way down their flanks—the rest of their height being brown with grass.

"To-day we have been in sight, almost all the time, of Fremont's Peak. It is a range of mountains, rather than a peak, and is covered with snow; a garland of beautiful cumulus clouds has hung round its brow all day."

[Camp at "Red Buttes," about fifty miles N. W. of Laramie Peak.]

"The Sweet-Water is rather an interesting stream. For some thirty or forty miles of its course it runs along the base of a chain of granitic hills. At last it runs through them in a chasm about one hundred feet wide and two or three hundred in depth. It looks, at first view, as if that gentle, pellucid stream had worn a passage through the hard granite—that after dallying along their base for a while, as might a young girl with an old bald pated man, it finally bolted right through them, and went laughing away in freedom into the open country beyond;

but on a closer examination I was confirmed in a previous opinion, that the channels of rivers are formed *for* them oftener than they are *by* them. This strange passage through the rock is called 'The Devil's Gate.'"

[Summit of "South Pass," East slope.]

"I write you from the banks of a hyaline stream skirted with golden willows. The pure crystalline Sweet-Water runs away in romping glee towards the distant Gulf of Mexico. * * * * * The Wind River Mountains, from whose flanks it pours, are looking down upon us seriously from the northwest. There is something sublime in being at a point among mountains, so far inland, from near which go forth to such widely distant mouths, three such large rivers as the Columbia, the Mississippi, and the Colorado. It is like being in the immediate scene where Nature is carrying on one of her grandest operations.

"We left the Pacific Springs at sunrise this morning, and by ten o'clock we were drinking your health in a cup of water from this fine stream. From Green River to this point the country seems like one huge swell, as of the sea, the ascent and descent being very gradual and forming an easy roadway. The road for a part of the distance to-day was strewn with cornelians; but the country is the same dreary desert as ever. Does it not seem strange that such large rivers should head on a region so dry and barren.

"The country, otherwise, is uninteresting; it is a lifeless waste, glaring in barrenness and aridity to an unpitying sky. The stunted sage bushes look like the stray poils of beard on a witch's chin, making the barrenness look doubly barren."

[Ford on Green River, 110, West Longitude.]

"We encamped for two nights upon the Sweet Water, finding considerable grazing for our lean and hungry animals; but finally, at about ten o'clock A. M., on the 25th, we crossed the dividing line to the Pacific Spring, which flows away in a small, clear thread of water to find its way at last into the distant Gulf of California. As we looked back there was a ridge of high land which separated us from our eastern homes."

"The height above the sea at that point of the ridge over which the road leads is about 7,500 feet, considerably over a mile, and yet so gradually had we attained this elevation that we never should have suspected; and, indeed, we should never have known that we were among mountains at all, were it not for the snowy summits of the Wind River Range, which rose immediately on our right; for the abrupt rocky heights, which I mentioned to you in my last, we had left behind and out of sight.

"And thus we came through what is called the South Pass. After a long, gradual ascent, we then commenced the descent, which is a little more rapid than the ascent, but still pretty gradual. And our road has been descending most of the way since, a distance of some sixty (60) miles, but through such barrenness and desolation as you could hardly conceive. The land is but a waste of sand, sparsely dotted with wild sage and grease wood, both small shrubs. Hardly a tree is anywhere to be seen, and only once in a mile or two along the road."

[Summit of the "South Pass," West Slope, one thousand miles from Fort Leavenworth.]

"We are on a deeply furrowed stream, the Big Sandy, which winds through, without fertilizing, the soil. The rabbit, the sage hen, and the raven, or a large species of crow, are all the animals met with. Behind us rose the Wind River Mountains, and how beautifully did they look one morning when the sun first shone upon them! Their lofty summits, shrouded with clouds and snow, and yet lit up by the sun, gave forth a warm but benevolent smile, well befitting such a benefactor of mankind as poured from its flank: the three great streams, the Oregon, the Colorado, and the Missouri. Before us, as we advanced towards the north, arose the chain called the *Uintah* Mountains. Running east and west, they presented their northern slopes to us, and they were covered with far more snow than are the southern slopes of the Wind River Range, though the former are more than one hundred miles to the southward of the latter—the difference arising from a difference in exposure—the one being to the north and the other to the south.

"The solemn, serious beauty of the Uintah mountains, their summits covered with snow, standing like a vast hydrant pouring forth rivers of water, again arrest my gaze.

"At length, at about 11 o'clock, A.M., to-day, we reached the verge of the right bank of Green River. The valley through which it runs is pretty wide, and the enclosing banks are steep and precipitous. The view below burst upon us all at once; and after such barrenness, how beautiful it appeared!

"There is a solemn joy in these mountains that lifts up the heart as in a temple of worship, where the winds and the streams are the music of the choir, and the hoar peak seems preaching holy Sabbath to the land."

CHAPTER X.

THE MEXICAN WAR—KEARNY IN MEXICO.

"In process of time, when your Western territories are perfectly settled from the Ohio to the Mississippi, which in time cannot fail to be perfected; and when your Western and Southern colonies become in population as numerous as the sands of the sea—then will the riches of Potosi attract the attention of the Americans to the conquest of Mexico and Peru. This is an object which, from the magnitude of its wealth, is certain in time to take place; but as that cannot happen for at least fifty or an hundred years, I think, gentlemen, we should not postpone taking a part of the wealth of that country immediately; therefore I freely offer my services to the Congress on such an expedition; and on my honor, I will serve them as faithfully as I have my king and country, "for I am a soldier of fortune." So, taking the bottle, I filled a glass, and drank to an expedition against the *Golden Spaniard*. My toast was productive of much laughter, mirth, and good humor, together with many observations on the situation and wealth of the Spanish colonies so contiguous to them; and I am inclined to believe, that at that time even the company did not think that the possession of the wealth of Mexico was quite so difficult, or required so many years' application and study, as to arrive at the knowledge of the Philosopher's stone."—"*Life, Adventures, and Opinions*" *of and by* Colonel GEORGE HANGER. *London*, 1801.

LIEUTENANT PHILIP KEARNY was too much of a real soldier to be able, after having tasted the excitement of actual service, to submit to the constraints, the indolence, and monotony of garrison life. After his return from Algiers he chafed under the restraints of inactivity for nearly five years, hoping all the time for something to occur which would give him new opportunities for distinction in active service.

Notwithstanding war seemed imminent with the Mexican Confederation, in 1845, it was scarcely conceivable that a power like Mexico, which had been utterly foiled in its invasion of Texas, in 1835–'6, which had suffered a miniature Waterloo at San Jacinto, 21st April, 1836, at the hands of a thousand undisciplined frontiersmen, would dare to rush into a war with such a gigantic power as the United States, upon a mere question of national honor—for the possession of Texas had become a mere question of honor.

Whether from the same reasons which actuated WORTH, or because his promotion had not corresponded with his hopes or merit, or from the persuasion that his services were undervalued, KEARNY on the 2d April, 1846, tendered his resignation, which was accepted as of the 6th of that month. Had he dreamed that a war was upon us, he would never have done so.

No sooner, however, had the clash of arms resounded from the Rio Grande, and the national banner been unfurled amidst the blaze of battle, than KEARNY, like WORTH, sought to recall his resignation, and applied to the government to be restored to his former rank and position.

On the recommendation of Major-General SCOTT, Commander-in-Chief, and Brevet Brigadier-General ROGER JONES, Adjutant-General U. S. Army, he was reinstated in the army on the 15th April, 1846. It was not until the 9th July, that he was enabled to join his regiment, having been employed in the meantime in recruiting his company up to the war-footing. He was determined that it should be a model troop in every respect, not only in men, but in horses, and he repaired to the West, where he knew he could find such material as he wanted—material which he had seen put to the test of a march of two thousand three hundred miles, and come out of the trial first proof. With a liberality which distinguished every prominent action of his life, he determined to augment the government bounty out of his own private purse, in order to obtain not only first-class men, but first-class animals. His principal recruiting ground was Illinois, and at the State Capital, Springfield, he fell in by accident with a resident lawyer, who was looked upon as a rather eccentric, but earnestly patriotic man, by name ABRAHAM LINCOLN, who was touched by the enthusiasm of the young dragoon officer, and zealously assisted him in carrying out his plans. This eccentric man, as he was styled, was afterwards, "HONEST ABE," President of the United States, and the Lieutenant KEARNY, whom he assisted in raising that model company of dragoons, was HIS appointment as a Brigadier-General, one whom he always styled "HIS GENERAL;" one whom he destined for the highest command, when an untimely shot put an end to the life of the man of his choice, as unexpectedly as the shot of the assassin, BOOTH, put an end to his own, so precious to his country.

When KEARNY reached New Orleans, on his way to Mexico, the appearance of his command attracted the attention of the whole city, who were in a condition to judge of the relative value of troops, since the majority of those destined to earn such distinction in Mexico, passed through the streets of the "Crescent City."

The New Orleans *Tropic* devoted quite a space in its columns to KEARNY and his dragoons, from which the following is an extract. The rest of the article is even more complimentary, but needs no quotation here, as it is altogether personal and refers to events in the life of KEARNY, with which the reader is already acquainted.

"Lieutenant PHILIP KEARNY, nephew of General STEPHEN WATTS KEARNY, arrived here day before yesterday with as fine a company of cavalry as was ever seen in New Orleans; the horses, ninety in number, are all greys, and beautiful in the extreme. The men are picked and noble-looking fellows. The trappings of the horses and the accoutrements of the riders are all that the most fastidious commander could wish."

KEARNY was not despatched into Mexican territory until October, 1846, when the fighting for the year was over.

His first service was along the Rio Grande, where he did not come in contact with the enemy. What struck him most, while in the neighborhood of Camargo—and he often referred to it as something marvelous—was the vast extent of the burial-grounds devoted to the interment of the American soldiers. His investigations led him to believe that the same influence which produced such fatal effects in the French army in Africa, was the cause of the mortality among our troops—that is, nostalgia, or home-sickness, which was attributable, however, to a different origin. French soldiers, as a general thing, have few ties which bind them to their homes, and it is rather the deprivation of those gay distractions and familiar scenes that brings on, in Africa, where there is scarcely any alleviation of their labors and sufferings, that awful depression of spirits which proves so fatal to life. In the case of our Western volunteers, who were mostly men of family, and accustomed to comforts of which an European soldier would never dream, it was actualy home-sickness. This moral miasma took a strong hold upon our Western volunteers, and populated vast cities of the dead, similar to those around Medeah and Milianah, which have attracted the attention of others besides KEARNY, who have campaigned in the Atlas. This nostalgia seemed to exercise comparatively no effect upon the regulars.

KEARNY, with his company, did not join TAYLOR until after the capture of Monterey, and the advance of the army of occupation to Saltillo.

Major-General SCOTT having completed his plan of operations, based upon the capture of Vera Cruz, and the advance from that port directly upon the Mexican capital, a large portion of the troops under General TAYLOR were withdrawn from the line of the Rio Grande and marched to the coast, to be embarked for the new point of concentration.

The general public, who have not participated in military operations, suppose that it is a light task to follow and relate the every day action of an officer and make it interesting. To furnish a mere diary would be easy, but such a narrative would be almost devoid of interest. The soldier and line-officer are almost indistinguishable parts of a grand machine, from which the killed and wounded fall off like chips or filings, unnoticed, except by those who are immediately interested in each individual. An able General compared those who fell to the parings of a man's nails, so little were they missed, and of so little account were they among the casualties of a great army and a protracted compaign. It is only when fortune accords to a man the opportunity to achieve a deed of high emprise that the historian can linger upon the picture, and make him a prominent object in the vast and crowded panorama of a war. We shall see KEARNY enjoying one of the fortunate occasions, and profiting by the opportunity to its utmost extent. Meanwhile, it is all sufficient to say that in the ordinary routine of duty, he did his share of it thoroughly, and in every position and on every occasion won the approbation, as he had always enjoyed the respect, of his superiors, as well as of his comrades.

On TAYLOR's line of operations KEARNY had no chance to shine, but he was neither unnoticed nor forgotten. In the latter part of November, when SCOTT determined to withdraw about five thousand troops from TAYLOR, his first selection was couched in the following words:

"You will * * put in movement for the mouth of the Rio Grande the following troops:

About five hundred regular cavalry of the First and Second Regiments of Dragoons, including Lieutenant KEARNY's troop."

* * * * * * * * *

These four words from such a man as SCOTT were in themselves no small meed of praise. The very fact that SCOTT thus designated him by name was a high encomium. Such a man and such a troop he wanted for himself. KEARNY had previously served under his immediate eye. He knew the young soldier thoroughly; knew that in him he had a weapon of approved temper, appropriate for a crisis, and in his troop a select body of soldiers, for, disciplined by KEARNY and inspired by his example, they could not be otherwise than *good* SOLDIERS.

"*Including Lieutenant* KEARNY's *troop*;" four words, but significant as an oration. We shall see that whenever SCOTT did let them loose they did their duty better than well—that when KEARNY was left to himself, the young Captain wreathed his brow with laurels as immortal as those due to the conquest of a country by ten thousand men, which has elevated SCOTT to the first rank as a General—a conquest which will be remembered in the military history of our country as one of its marvels, when subsequent battles, attended by a slaughter of as many men as constituted the whole force under WINFIELD SCOTT's command, are unnoticed or forgotten. Results dignify actions. In Europe, SCOTT would have been overwhelmed with dignities and rewards, whereas he was repaid for an achievement, which added new lustre to our national escutcheon, with an ingratitude which disgraced a Democratic administration in the eyes of the whole world.

Before his connection was severed with the "army of occupation," KEARNY was entrusted with a duty which very nearly cut short his career and nearly added his name to the list of victims of the assassin tactics of the Mexicans.

About the 11th January, 1847, Lieutenant JOHN A. RICHEY, Fifth United States Infantry, bearer of despatches for General TAYLOR, started from Saltillo towards Victoria. Having passed through Monterey, he arrived, the 13th January, at the small town of Villa Gran. Here he separated himself from his escort—consisting of ten Dragoons—and entered the town for the purpose of purchasing provisions. Alone and unsuspicious of danger, he was lassoed and murdered under the most atrocious and cowardly circumstances. The despatches which he bore were taken from his person and at once transmitted to SANTA ANNA. From the information derived from these, the Mexican commander-in-chief became possessed of SCOTT's plans, and learned to what an extent TAYLOR's army had been depleted to complete that collecting on a new line under General SCOTT. The result was, he struck at TAYLOR. Thus, had it not been for the murder of RICHEY, the battle of Buena Vista—on which it might be said the subsequent operations of the whole Mexican war pivoted or depended—would never have been fought. Buena Vista was one of the decisive battles of the world, as events turned out, for in many respects it was THE battle of the Mexican war which gave us auriferous California, and determined the whole future of this continent.

The reader may ask what has this to do with KEARNY? This much: he narrowly escaped at this time the fate which befell the unfortunate RICHEY; and had a similar and impending cast of the lasso encircled his throat with the same successful aim, there would have been an end of this biography and of one destined to fill a prominent place in the gallery of American Generals, Patriots, and Heroes.

On his arrival at Vera Cruz, the splendid condition of KEARNY's company—he was promoted to a Captaincy in December, 1846—coupled with the fact that its commander had formerly been his aid-de-camp, induced the general-in-chief to constitute it his body-guard. This connection with headquarters prevented KEARNY from participating in any of the cavalry engagements which occurred between our Dragoons and the Mexican horse, which attempted to harass our army and hinder the progress of the siege.

When the city surrendered, KEARNY escorted his victorious chief on his triumphal entry, and he used to dwell with exultation on the superb appéarance of his men and horses in that ovation, due to the scientific generalship of SCOTT. He said that his men felt as much pride in the matter as himself, and were up the greater part of the previous night furbishing their arms and accoutrements and cleaning their horses, so that the latter "shone like glass bottles" when paraded the next morning. KEARNY was always exceedingly partial to iron greys, and no horses in the world look better than those of this color when in high condition and properly groomed.

On the advance from Vera Cruz, KEARNY was always with General SCOTT, and saw little or no fighting. That he profited by the lessons in strategy taught by that superlative commander, at the expense of the enemy, the future proved. NAPOLEON held TURENNE in the highest esteem as a finished general, and this campaign was carried on in the highest style of TURENNE. After the battle of Cerro Gordo he was detached in pursuit, and it was reported at the time that he came near capturing SANTA ANNA.

The writer recollects perfectly KEARNY's account of one chase and its incidents; but it may have occurred on one or another

BREVET MAJOR PHILIP KEARNY,
Captain 1st U. S. Dragoons, Mexico, 1847.
From portrait in possession of Author.

occasion (at Tepeahualco? or after Puebla), when KEARNY was sent out with a flag of truce in order to try and open communications with the defeated army.

The following letter from an officer, an eye-witness of the incident, a friend of KEARNY, refers to the pursuit after Cerro Gordo, which occurred about this time. It also alludes to an interesting fact, which has been related, to show that KEARNY, like a great many other soldiers of his stamp, was, to a certain extent, a fatalist, and put implicit faith in his star:

"In Mexico he (KEARNY) commanded a company of horse of the First Dragoons, which accompanied General SCOTT'S movements in his march from Vera Cruz to the Capital. At the battle of Cerro Gordo he followed up in advance the pursuit of the retreating enemy. I remember seeing him in full career after them. His horses were all white (grey), and showed that they had received the care and attention for which the First Dragoons, his uncle's regiment, were honorably distinguished; but for the want of proper forage in the barren strip of *tierra caliente* through which the army had been marching and operating for several days, they had become very much reduced in condition; and consequently, in the rapidity of the pursuit, not a few of them tumbled down headlong upon the road, never to rise again. It was a sad sight to see animals dying in that way in those days, but the service during the late war got quite beyond these scruples, whole squadrons of horse being wasted with as much dash and recklessness as though the destruction of property were a great merit.

"The next incident that I remember in the career of General, then Captain KEARNY, occurred among a party of officers at a hotel in Puebla. These officers were dining together a short time previous to the continuance of the march of the American army upon the city of Mexico; and the conversation turned upon the approaching conflict. Captain KEARNY spoke with a great deal of feeling, with an earnest unaffected thirst for glory, and said he would give his left arm for a brevet. The army moved not long afterwards, and in the very first day's battles in the valley of Mexico, Captain KEARNY pursued the routed enemy again, up to the very gates of the city, and there lost his left arm, by a shot from the enemy within the walls. It is needless to add, that he received a brevet.

"My pen has dwelt thus long upon the theme, because of the particular pleasure which I have derived from the intercourse which

I have happened to have with him. Take him altogether, I have seldom met with a more agreeable gentleman, or a more chivalric soldier."

It is said that KEARNY remarked, before he went to Mexico, that he felt sure that he would not lose his life, that he would return alive, but that he felt equally assured that he would lose his left arm. NAPOLEON had implicit faith in his star, and actually pointed out, on more than one occasion, the very star which, according to his belief, presided over his destiny. Presentiments are very common among military men, and a great many instances are related in which they are known to have come true, without affecting their conduct, however. DESAIX is a curious instance of this. When he joined the army of Italy, in 1800, on his return from Egypt, he remarked that he was afraid the bullets in Europe would not know him again, and he fell at Marengo, a few days subsequently, the very first battle in which he was engaged and almost immediately after he came under fire.

In the advance from Jalapa, KEARNY had few opportunities of displaying his superior soldiership, but it was only from lack of opportunity. As a common friend recently remarked of him:—"High soldiership, as in his case, exhibited itself often, in attention to a multitude of minute details, which inspire confidence and tell in the hour of action. This enabled him with his troops to penetrate to the very gates of the city of Mexico, where he lost his arm. While the army lay in Puebla he performed several daring reconnoissances, by which he procured much valuable information; but, as the enemy avoided combats, there was no special opportunity to add to his laurels."

Shortly after the dinner alluded to, at which KEARNY expressed his willingness to purchase a brevet at the price of the very arm he actually expended in obtaining one, he was entrusted with a mission of some danger and importance, over whose remembrance he was accustomed to laugh heartily when he recalled the details of the "Run."

While our army was at Puebla drilling and organizing into that irresistible machine which, like the beast "with great iron teeth" in the vision of DANIEL, "brake in pieces," and trampled in the bloody-mire every antagonistic armament, SCOTT, on the 11th July, 1847, resolved to take some action in behalf of the American prisoners held by the Mexican authorities. These were Majors GAINES and BORLAND, Captain CASSIUS M. CLAY, and their associates, captured at Incarnacion, near Buena Vista, in the preceding January, likewise passed midshipman ROGERS, taken in December, 1846, near Vera Cruz, and since then imprisoned as a spy.

To Captain PHILIP KEARNY was entrusted the proposals for an exchange, and he was sent forward with two companies of dragoons, under a flag of truce, to endeavor to communicate with the Mexican military authorities.

At seven A. M., 12th July, KEARNY started out, accompanied by the SEMMES who afterwards became a traitor to his flag, and made his name notorious as a burner of merchantmen, until his career in the Alabama was closed by the destruction of that Corsair by the Kearsage, commanded by the glorious WINSLOW.

KEARNY expected at this time to be able to continue on, and enter the city of Mexico, and trotted on rapidly, filled with the glad hopes of carrying good news to his imprisoned countrymen, while enjoying the glorious scenery, for which the journey to the Aztec Capital is almost without a rival. As he proceeded, to his right soared the Malinche, "the storm-gatherer of Puebla," whose rugged peak served as a barometer to the inhabitants of that city, and, beneath it, stretched away the plains of Tlascala, while to his left the picturesque pyramid of Cholula stood out against the clear blue sky; while over all towered the eternal snow-crowns of Popocatapetl and Iztaccihuatl, which look down, at the same time, into both the valleys of Puebla and Mexico.

What thoughts must have passed through the "Knightly" mind of KEARNY, thus pressing onward in the track of CORTES.

Ten miles from Puebla, the Black River (*Rio Prieto*) was crossed, and as much farther on again the dragoons dashed into the village or town of San Martin. As they approached this small but populous place, there was an awful stir, and forth fluttered a body of Mexican Lancers about equal in number to the American detachment, who "vamosed the ranch" in such a hurry as to leave behind their baggage, and even some of their party, who broke off and took to the bushes. Among these were CANALIZO's son, a Lieutenant-Colonel of cavalry, and two or three of his men. The youth was eventually looked up by two of his papa's aids, subsequent to the termination of the chase, and conducted back in safety to the parental wing. These aids, with half a dozen blanketed lanceros, returned, under escort of KEARNY's dragoons, to San Martin, to recover their general's baggage and to hunt around for the missing youngster.

Away went the Mexicans, consisting of about seventy lancers, led by Generals CANALIZO (formerly President *ad interim* of Mexico) and PORTILLO (who had disgraced himself by his prominent action in the FANNING massacre (FANNIN ?) in Texas in March 1836. The Mexicans left in such haste, and spurred so furiously, that KEARNY described the road over which they traveled as resembling one on which a flurry of early wet snow had fallen, so whitened was it with the froth flakes which fell from the horses, urged to the uttermost by the merciless Spanish spur.

As KEARNY did not care if the chase lasted to the gates of the capital, as that was *his* objective, he held in after he found that fear had lent wings to the enemy, and contented himself with keeping them in sight. It was AINSWORTH'S DICK TURPIN'S ride to York over again in the plural. KEARNY caught a glimpse of them at the Puente (bridge) de Tezmolucan, eleven miles from San Martin; and at Rio Frio, about eleven further on—making forty miles accomplished since mounting—came in full sight of the two generals pursued, then winding away up the heights beyond the Cold River (*Rio Frio*). By this time the Mexicans had somewhat recovered their senses, or felt that their horses had the heels of the pursuers, for they halted, as if to investigate the white flag conspicuously displayed; then, seemingly, not liking the appearance of the escort, resumed their flight. This inspection, through glasses, doubtless, was repeated several times, till discretion seemed the better part of valor, and away they went, as if convinced of the truth of the old saying, "the devil (American) take the hindermost" if he can catch him. As KEARNY'S men had been in the saddle for ten hours, and all chances of overhauling the red pennons had passed away, the Captain halted at an inn at the bridge across the Rio Frio, and sent forward a Mexican on a fresh horse to catch the fugitives.

In an hour or two this native intermediary returned, accompanied by an aid of General PORTILLO, who protested against KEARNY'S further advance, but entered into an arrangement, in behalf of his superior, for a meeting on the following morning, when KEARNY was to ride forward, accompanied by SEMMES, as an improvised aid, and five dragoons. So, amid good cheer and much merriment, evoked by the rapid "change of base" effected by the Aztec chiefs, the night passed very pleasantly, clouded by only one drawback, that the protest of the Mexican officer precluded a glimpse of the Valley of Mexico, which, in all its glorious beauty, was visible from a range not more than ten or eleven miles beyond their place of repose.

The next morning, 13th July, KEARNY, with SEMMES, the latter's servant, and one dragoon to carry the white flag, rode forward to meet General PORTILLO, who was encountered just beyond the Hill of Sleep, (*Cuesta del Sueno*) with five lancers, who, with his two aids, made his party eight, when seven was the stipulated number. PORTILLO—like LOUIS XI. of France at his interview with EDWARD IV. of England, on the Bridge of Picquigny, across the Somme, 29th August, 1478—had no idea of giving his adversaries a chance of "gobbling" him, if a little addition of force could prevent it, even though *contra mores.* PORTILLO, after mutual salutes and explanations, refused permission for KEARNY either to continue on to Mexico, or even to proceed any farther, although the glorious vision of the basin of the capital could be witnessed from a crest only seven or eight miles in advance. He feelingly reproved KEARNY for the "unchivalric" manner in which the latter had hunted him out of his comfortable quarters in San Martin, and gently protested against such an obliviousness of the amenities of war, then kindly offered to take charge of the despatches of which KEARNY was the bearer. As there was nothing else to be done, this was agreed to, and KEARNY, not to be outdone in politeness, escorted the general as far as PORTILLO would permit him: half-way back to his detachment, whom, it appeared, had been originally left or stationed in San Martin as a picket of observation to watch the movements of General SCOTT and his troops, or more likely to collect the reports of spies in Puebla and forward them to SANTA ANNA.

KEARNY described PORTILLO as SEMMES does in his "*Service Afloat and Ashore,*" only somewhat more mirthfully, or less respectfully. SEMMES says, "he was a good-looking man, rather stout (it is to be feared dashing PHIL rendered this 'punchy'), of about fifty years of age, and quite dignified and gentlemanlike in his manners." The effect of the latter part of this description is marred by the additional remarks that the stout and genteel general "not being well dressed," "being mounted on a small pony," having "a somewhat villainous expression of countenance,"—which, adds SEMMES, "I did not wonder at so much when I was informed by our guide that he had been a prominent actor in the massacre of

FANNIN")—disadvantages which must have required an awful amount of dignity to compensate for them, and KEARNY's recollections of PORTILLO, if memory serves, were very much akin to Mr. Pickwick's idea of bulky Mr. Tupman's putting "himself into a green velvet jacket with a two-inch tail" to attend Mrs. Leo Hunter's fancy ball. Indeed the meeting of KEARNY, on his sixteen hand horse, (he always rode a very large horse, and SEMMES was mounted on an elephantine animal,) and PORTILLO, on his pony, recalls that of CHARLES THE BOLD, on his noble charger, with LOUIS XI., on his little ambling palfrey, when the effect was almost grotesque. The reader who does not recognize the simile cannot have read "Quentin Durward," by SIR WALTER SCOTT. If he has not, he will thank this allusion if it leads to a perusal of that charming novel.

Thus KEARNY just came short of being the first of our gallant "Boys in Blue," to visit pacifically, but "in arms and under banner," the Mexican Capital, into whose gate he was destined to cut his way only four weeks later (20th August), as a conqueror, inside of which his comrade, Major MILLS, was actually killed.

No reader, however intelligent, can comprehend military operations without *good* maps. Even with *good* maps it is difficult to comprehend details without some acquaintance with tactics and terms. Consequently, there is no attempt made in this chapter to follow the movements of the army, and readers are referred to MANSFIELD's generalized and RIPLEY's detailed but partial, or prejudiced, "History of the Mexican War;" likewise SEMMES "Service Afloat and Ashore," very interesting and instructive, as well as other works, not so accessible, but worthy of examination as the records of a conquest as memorable as that of CORTEZ.

When SCOTT had abandoned the idea of making a direct attack on Mexico from the east, and accomplished his remarkable movement, *favored by Providence*, the direction of his renewed operations was from the south. Two battles were fought on this line prior to the Tacubuya Armistice. The first at Contreras, August 19th and 20th; the second at Churubusco, August 20th, 1847.

Between these two villages, to the west and north, about nine miles apart by the road and the villages of San Antonio and San Augustin Hapan—the latter about six miles east of Contreras—lay the volcanic region called the "Pedregal."

This Pedregal was thrown up in sharp rocks and broken pieces, in such a manner that the Mexican officers supposed it to be impassable.

"South of the Capital the great thoroughfare is the Acapulco road, which enters the city along the causeway and at the Garita of the San Antonio. A line of entrenchments had been commenced, connecting the fortified hacienda of San Antonio, six miles south of the city, with the position of the Mexicalcingo. From the immediate vicinity of the hacienda, the Pedregal extended west to the mountains. The Pedregal was an obstacle of no ordinary nature to military operations. A vast field of lava, interspersed with a few patches of arable land, it was practicable for the passage of any troops at but few points, and entirely impracticable for cavalry or artillery, except by a single mule-path."

This lava field was rent by chasms, which intersected it with their rifts in such a manner that to worm a way across it, even in the day time, was a work of time, difficulty, and peril; and yet it was absolutely necessary to reconnoitre it, as it lay between the wings, or grand divisions, of the army. The credit of this difficult operation has always been given to the arch-rebel LEE, when an officer of the United States Engineers, and he is said to have been the only officer who made his way across the Pedregal; but the writer understood at the time that KEARNY was the one who first traversed this extremely difficult and perilous track on horseback, and was the first thus to link the combinations of our separated divisions through the information which he carried across. KEARNY, on his return from Mexico, dwelt upon this exploit as one of the most difficult he had ever achieved. KEARNY, if not the first, was certainly one of the first who succeeded in doing so. It was wonderful how he succeeded in accomplishing the feat, as he made his way over at night—moonlight, however, it is true—leaping his horse over the clefts, which nobody but a fearless rider like himself would ever have dreamed of attempting.

CHAPTER XI.

THE GARITA SAN ANTONIO.

'THE CHARGE OF THE 'ONE' HUNDRED."

"Half a league, half a league,
  Half a league onward,
All in the Valley of Death
  Rode the 'one' hundred.
'Charge,' was the captain's cry;
  Theirs not to reason why,
Theirs not to make reply,
  Theirs but to do and die,
Into the Valley of Death
  Rode the 'one' hundred.

* * * *

" Cannon to right of them,
  Cannon to left of them,
Cannon 'before' them
  Volley'd and thundered;
Stormed at with shot and shell,
  They that had struck so well,
Rode thro' the jaws of Death,
  Half a league back again,
Up from the mouth of Hell,
  All that was left of them,
Left of 'one' hundred.

"Honor the brave and bold!
Long shall the tale be told,
Yea, when our babes are old—
  How they rode onward."

TENNYSON.

"While CLAVERHOUSE, who, like a hawk perched on a rock and eyeing the time to pounce on its prey, had watched the event of the action from the opposite bank, now passed the bridge at the head of his cavalry at full trot, and, leading them in squadrons through the intervals and round the flanks of the Royal infantry, formed them on the moor, and led them to the charge, * * * their broken spirits and disheartened courage were unable to endure the charge of the cavalry, attended with all its terrible accompaniments of sight and sound;—the rush of the horses at full speed, the shaking of the earth under their feet, the glancing of the swords, and waving of the plumes, and the fierce shouts of the cavaliers. The front ranks hardly attempted one ill-directed and disorderly fire, and their rear was broken and flying in confusion ere the charge had been completed; and in less than five minutes the horsemen were mixed with them, cutting and hewing without mercy. * * * Their swords drank deep of slaughter among the unresisting fugitives. Screams for quarter were only answered by the shouts with which the pursuers accompanied their blows, and the whole field presented one general scene of confused slaughter, flight, and pursuit."

SCOTT'S "*Old Mortality.*"

"The eagle eye of CORTES lighted up with triumph. Turning quickly around to the cavaliers at his side, among whom were SANDOVAL, OLID, ALVARADO, and AVILA, he pointed out the chief, exclaiming: 'There is our mark! Follow and support me!' Then crying his war-cry, and striking his iron heel into his weary steed, he plunged headlong into the thickest of the press. His enemies fell back, taken by surprise, and daunted by the ferocity of the attack. Those who did not were pierced through with his lance, or borne down by the weight of his charger. The cavaliers followed close in the rear. On they swept with the fury of a thunderbolt, cleaving the solid ranks asunder, strewing their path with the dying and the dead, and bounding over every obstacle in the way." * * * "The guard, overpowered by the suddenness of the onset, made little resistance, but, flying, communicated their own panic to their comrades. The tidings of the loss soon spread over the field. The Indians, filled with consternation, now thought only of escape. In their blind terror, their numbers augmented their confusion. They trampled on one another, fancying it was the enemy in their rear."

PRESCOTT'S "*Conquest of Mexico.*"

KEARNY'S CHARGE.

HOWEVER honorable and pleasant a position it may be to command the body-guard at headquarters, in the society of men pre-eminent in ability and position, it is not the place for a young officer to win fame. In foreign countries and in royalties—where favors *drop* into hands not entitled to receive them, to the prejudice of those who have borne the burthen and heat of the day, who have deserved and not obtained—a post around headquarters, is a capital place to get a decoration or an advance step in rank. Unfortunately, it is too much so in this country, but not in anything to the same degree as abroad, since the army at large see clearly and judge honestly, and only acknowledge that soldiership as of the true ring and genuine stamp which has undergone the baptism of blood and the purification of the fire of battle. The reputation which is sought at the cannon's mouth is the true glory of the soldier. KEARNY knew this. He had yearned to shine in his proper sphere, the front of battle. The man who could offer his left arm as the price of a brevet, as he had done among his fellow-officers at Puebla, was the man to court danger as a coy mistress. Like KORNER, when he indited that "Sword Song," which will live forever, he must have often toyed with the "iron bride" which hung at his thigh, and prayed to see her shining face blush with the blood of the enemy.

"Thou sword at my left side,
What means thy flash of pride?
Thou smilest so on me,
I take delight in thee,
Hurrah!

"The clanging trumps betray
The blushing bridal day;
When cannons far and wide
Shall roar, I'll fetch my bride.
Hurrah!

"Yes, in my sheath I clash;
I long to gleam and flash
In battle, wild and proud,
'Tis why I clash so loud.
Hurrah!"

Throughout the advance from Vera Cruz to this moment, when his ardent wishes were to be gratified, his heart must have leaped whenever the signal to charge was blown and beaten, with the strong desire to answer it with the spur and the appropriate order.

On the 18th August, a reconnoissance was made by four of the engineer corps—three of whom afterwards became notorious rebel generals—with a support of cavalry and infantry. An engagement or skirmish ensued, in which KEARNY distinguished himself, and enabled the engineers to perform their duties with success and results. This service was of sufficient consequence to deserve a special mention in SCOTT's official report.

It is surprising how irresponsive to the deeds of our own soldiers are the lyres of our poets. The world has read with admiration the "Charge of the Six Hundred" at Balaklava; but how few would have ever heard of that feat of "derring do" had it not been sung by the poet laureate of England. And yet the charge of Captain PHILIP KEARNY, at the battle of Churubusco, was as worthy the genius of TENNYSON as the charge of the Light Brigade "into the jaws of death" in that Crimean valley, with three armies as spectators.

To appreciate the marvel of dash and bravery, it is necessary to understand the theatre in which it was displayed. Our little army less than nine thousand men all told—it has been set down at six thousand fighting men, as the Rebels counted their forces—small indeed in its numbers in comparison to the magnitude of its exploits, but great indeed in the successes it achieved—awoke from their bivouacs on the morning of the 20th August, 1847, with the assurance of victory; that whatever their General willed them to do, would grandly by them be done.

In front of them, in the heart of the enemy's country, occupying the village of Churubusco, and in a chain of fortified positions—strong in the natural dispositions of the ground, still stronger in the art with which it had been fortified, and even stonger yet in the outnumbering forces—were disposed twenty-seven thousand to thirty thousand Mexican troops, backed by the population of the city of Mexico, who could turn out, if they willed, fifty thousand males capable of bearing arms. These forces, outnumbering ours four to one, or at least three to one, held the village, of solid construction; and scattered buildings of stone, along their line of battle, lined the dykes, and almost impervious hedges of thorny maguey or cactus lurked in the extensive plantations of tall maize, and filled the field-works with their small arms and artillery. The flat land was broken and difficult, and rendered more so by the enclosures, morasses, and canals or ditches which covered it with a network of obstacles.

"The ground on which the troops operated"—is the language of the gallant WORTH—"off the high-road, is remarkably intersected; loose soil, growing grain, and, at brief intervals, deep ditches, for the purpose of drainage and irrigation. These ditches vary from six to eight feet in depth, about the same in width, with from three to four feet of water—the reverse banks lined with the enemy's light troops.

"When I recur to the nature of the ground, and the fact that the division (two thousand six hundred strong, of all arms) was engaged from two to two and a half hours in a hand-to-hand conflict with from seven thousand to nine thousand of the enemy, having the advantage of position, and occupying regular works—which our engineers will say were most skillfully constructed—the mind is filled with wonder and the heart with gratitude to the brave officers and soldiers whose steady and indomitable valor has, under such circumstances, aided in achieving results so honorable to our country—results not accomplished, however, without the sacrifice of many valuable lives."

Through this ground, and the Mexican line-of-battle, ran several causeways. One of these passed through the village of Churubusco.

All of these united with the causeway of San Antonio, which bisected the field-of-battle in a direct line, almost north and south, and terminated five and a half miles distant in the Grand Plaza of Mexico, upon which front the National Palace and Cathedral. At the junction referred to, and the apex of the right and acute angled-triangles formed by them, was the bastioned bridge-head (*Tete de Pont*) on the Churubusco River. This was held by a strong garrison with three pieces of heavy artillery.

It has been the fashion to decry the Mexicans as soldiers, although the Spaniards and French found them foes which proved worthy of their steel. Like the Turks, and their cognates, the Arabs, Kabyles, and Moors, every people of Spanish blood have proved themselves most tenacious in the defense of fortifications and walled towns—witness Sarragossa.

This the French experienced before Puebla in 1863, and the capture of this city was considered of sufficient importance to justify the elevation of General Forey, its captor, to the dignity of Marshal.

The Mexican engineers understood their business thoroughly, and it is admitted that the works which they threw up for the defense of their capital were of exceeding strength, and "admirable both in their construction and locality." The bridge-head was a beautiful work, solidly and scientifically constructed, with wet ditches and embrasures and platforms for a large armament. Moreover, it was flanked by a massive stone church or convent, surrounded by strong field-works mounted with heavy guns.

Previous to the battle of Churubusco, Captain Kearny could restrain himself no longer, and had requested permission to participate in the impending action. This was granted, and with his command, Company F, First United States Dragoons, was detached for general service, and he was attached to the division of General Pillow. He was now watching the course of events, and, like Dundee at "Bothwell Brig," biding his time and opportunity.

Meanwhile the roar of Mexican musketry—"more than twenty thousand muskets were continually discharged with a rapidity which showed the stern determination of the enemy"—"was the greatest noise of all the din of battle; it was continued and terrific, drowning the noise of the artillery, the shouts of the combatants, and the groans of the wounded."

Despite the severity of such a fire, and the fearful play of the artillery, our troops forced their way across the river. At the same time a vigorous assault was made upon the bridge-head. The garrison, so to speak, finding their position turned and in danger of being taken in reverse, thus cutting off their retreat, slackened the "particularly spiteful" fire to which RIPLEY feelingly alludes, and after a short conflict, abandoned the work, and fled over the bridge in the rear towards the city.

Previous to this time KEARNY had been able to effect nothing. He had accompanied PILLOW in his advance from Coyacan, a village farther to the east or left on the Rio (River) Churubusco. He had experienced a "great difficulty" in getting his horses across the broken country, partially inundated, and the deep and intervening ditches, to the causeway, but had succeeded in doing so. There he was joined by a troop of the Third Dragoons, commanded by Captain A. T. MCREYNOLDS. During the course of the action, a gallant attempt was made to turn the Mexicans with this small body of horse, and with them assail the left flank of the enemy. The deep ditches which traversed the "wide and marshy fields" prevented the carrying out of this manœuvre, and the cavalry, after ineffectual endeavors to execute it, were compelled to return to the causeway, and there await the development of events. As soon as the bridge-head had been carried, PILLOW says: "I then let him loose. Furious was his charge upon the retreating foe, dealing death with the unerring sabre."

Before KEARNY, however, could bring the "unerring sabre" into play some time elapsed. The Dragoons had to make their way through the mass of obstacles which encumbered the causeway before they could operate or even form. To the left of the bridge-head the huge wagons, which composed the Mexican ammunition train, were crowded together in the road leading from Churubusco, which entered the work from the west, or its right, immediately along the bank of the river. Every draught animal attached to these had been killed, and the passage was almost blocked up by the mass of wagons, war material, and dead men and animals, shattered and thrown together by the answering fires of assailants and defenders. To heighten the confusion, one of the powder wagons took fire, and threatened an immediate explosion. This would have been most disastrous in the narrow space completely jammed with the bloody wreck and rubbish of war, through which our advancing cavalry had to pick and force their way. With a reckless daring some of the soldiers on the road devoted themselves to the preservation of their comrades. They climbed into the burning wagons, tore out the ammunition chests already kindled into flame, and tumbled them into the ditch before the fire could reach their contents.*

A path thus frayed for him by this exertion of heroism, KEARNY was now enabled to extricate his dragoons, and get them forward on the causeway, where it was partially clear. The retreating Mexicans had meanwhile made good use of their respite, and had already placed a distance of over a mile and a half between themselves and their pursuers. As soon as he had space, KEARNY formed his troop,

---

* "More of the New York Boys. We most gladly give place to the following additional leaf in the chaplet of glory worn by New York, for that her sons have proved themselves worthy of such a mother:

"We hardly know how we could have omitted the name of the gallant KEARNY, for it has often been on our lips with words of admiration and praise, but we can hardly lament it, since it affords us this opportunity to lay before our readers such details as the following interesting communication furnishes:

To the Editor of the Courier and Enquirer:

"Allow me to add a sixth to the names of the gallant 'New Yorkers,' whom you so justly mention with admiration, as having, under the folds of the American flag, soaked with their blood the soil before the city of Mexico.

"I know the omission was accidental, and therefore recall it to your recollection: I allude to Lieutenant (now Captain) PHILIP KEARNY, of the First Dragoons, as chivalrous an officer as ever wore spur or belted sabre.

"Having served ten years in the far West with his regiment, with the exception of two passed in France, under the requisition of Government, during which he served a campaign with the army in Africa, he was about to resign his commission and retire to his estates, when the country was startled by the battle of Palo Alto.

"Hastening to Washington, he arrived in time to withdraw his resignation, and was empowered to raise his own troops. He immediately applied himself with all his energies to the task, and by lavish expenditures of his own means, in addition to the bounty offered by Government, he was soon at the head of a body of picked men superbly mounted.

"Joining General SCOTT at Vera Cruz, his troops were made his body-guard, and participated at the battle of Cerro Gordo, enduring, in common with the rest of the army, the fatigues and exposures up to the city of Puebla.

"At the battle of Churubusco his Dragoons (it is unnecessary to say that he was at their head) were in the thickest of the fight.

"Charging upon the retreating masses of the enemy, and exposed to the murderous discharge of four batteries, belching cross-fires of ball and grape-shot, besides an incessant torrent of musketry from all sides, his arm suddenly fell helpless at his side, shattered by a ball a little below the shoulder. Although suffering intense pain, and bleeding profusely, he still retained his position and command, till, becoming faint, he reeled in his saddle, and was only prevented from falling by the hold of one of his dragoons.

"From exhaustion and loss of blood he soon swooned entirely away, and being placed in a blanket, was carried to the rear of his men.

"The next day his arm was amputated, and at the last accounts he was doing well.

"My acquaintance is slight with Captain K., much more so than with Lieutenant SCHUYLER HAMILTON, the only other of the gentlemen that you mention whom I have the pleasure of knowing, but whose elegance and modesty in the drawing-room fully prepared me for his gallantry in the field of battle; but, slight as it is, I felt bound to call your attention to what I doubt not was an accidental omission." S.

and galloped furiously after. His original force, small as it was, had only been augmented by a single platoon, under Captain KERR, who was accompanied by Colonel HARNEY without a command. The column overtook the Mexicans about a half a mile outside the Garita (Barrier or Gate) of San Antonio Abad, through which the causeway enters the city. Beyond this commenced the suburbs of Mexico.

Into the dense mass of thousands of the enemy—SANTA ANNA and several other generals were involved in the tumult—KEARNY plunged his command. It is not probable that it exceeded 100 horsemen. It could not have comprised over a hundred and fifty horsemen, volunteers included, had his ranks been full, after deducting casualties and sick—victims to the enemy, campaigning and climate. It plunged into the Mexican armed crowd, just as one of the Brigantines of Cortes crushed its way onwards through the midst of the enormous fleet of Aztec war canoes on a like sunny May-day (1521), 326 years previously; or just as CORTES himself, with his devoted band, charged home, and wrested victory out of defeat.

> "Out of this nettle danger we plucked the flower safety,"

at the famous battle of Otompan, or of Otumba, on the 8th July, 1520. Or perhaps, even more like the charge of CLAVERHOUSE, at Bothwell Bridge, after the gate and barricade had been battered down by the artillery and cleared by the infantry; when that model trooper of the day followed up the Covenanters until his "Life-Guard's swords were blunted and their horses blown."

The sabres of the dragoons scattered death and dismay through the Mexican *soldatesca*, and hewed their way onwards with as fatal effect as the light broadsides of the vessel of the Conquistador through the fleet of their Aztec forefathers. Those of the crowd who were not cut down or ridden over, either threw themselves into the ditches on either side of the causeway, and dispersed over the fields, or else jammed themselves, in a confused mass, into the entrance of the barrier.

A battery or lunette, mounting two guns, defended the Garita.* The garrison—either bewildered and terror-stricken at the wild

* There was a regular line of defences from the Nino Perdido Gate to that of San Antonio. There the line stopped. To the left or east of it was a lunette connected, a quarter of a mile farther on, a priest's cap or swallow-tail, detached, and about a quarter of a mile to the left of this again a simple redan or fleche.—"*Map attached to Official Report.*"

tumult, which surged upon them in all the panic of a rout, instead of the assured victory they had been promised, or determined to make good their position regardless of their own people—now opened their fire upon friend and foe, dealing death promiscuously amid the crowd.

Unfortunately, while this charge was progressing with so much success, General SCOTT—unaware of its success or opportunities—had despatched an order to arrest the pursuit, fearful that it might be carried too far, and compromise what had been gained. As soon as this order reached Colonel HARNEY "he caused the recall to be sounded from the rear." Amid the thunder of artillery and the shouts and cries and uproar of the flight, the notes of the bugle were either unheard or unheeded by those in advance. Those in the rear, however, gradually obeyed the signal, and small parties continually dropped off, from time to time, as the trumpet notes which conveyed the order made themselves heard. Thus, those who held on their adventurous way were soon reduced to "three or four sets of fours." With this hand-full, KEARNY kept on as undauntedly—

> "Into the jaws of Death,
> Into the mouth of Hell,"

as if he had been followed by the whole force with which he launched out upon the enemy. In this he was accompanied by Major MILLS, of the Fifteenth Infantry, who had joined his squadron as a volunteer after participating in the fierce struggle in which his own regiment had its Colonel wounded and one-third of its force cut down.

Just in front of the Garita a ditch had been dug nearly across the causeway. Although numbers of the Mexicans had been precipitated into this cut by the pressure of the mass behind, it was yet impassable for men on horseback. Perceiving that the Mexican mounted officers—mingled with the flying crowd—abandoned their animals to make their way across this obstruction on foot, KEARNY threw himself from his saddle, called upon his men to follow, dashed across the ditch, and threw himself into the midst of the Mexicans, to enter the battery with them. He was nobly supported by two officers and about a dozen dragoons. It is a sorrow and a shame that American History has not preserved the names of all these men. From the context it would appear that the officers were Captain ANDREW F. MCREYNOLDS, Third U. S. Dragoons, from Michigan, who was severely wounded on this occasion, and Lieutenant JOHN LORIMER GRAHAM, Tenth U. S. Infantry, like Major MILLS, serving with Captain KEARNY, and "attached" to his command, also severely wounded. It is a very curious fact that KEARNY, MCREYNOLDS and GRAHAM, were all three injured on this occasion, in the left arm. Major MILLS fell, slain at, or, as claimed, inside, the very gates.

KEARNY always had a confused idea of what occurred at this juncture, and yet he preserved a distinct recollection of many interesting incidents. He said that when he threw himself into the press, hewing his way over the rampart and into the battery, he distinctly saw one Mexican officer pointing him out to the infantry in the work, and by his gestures, urging the men to take good aim and shoot him down. The features of this officer seemed to have been impressed upon his mind with such vivid force that he could have recognized him subsequently. The jam soon prevented KEARNY from using his weapons, and it appeared as if a hundred hands had hold of him at once; otherwise, the pressure itself rendered his sword arm powerless. How he extricated himself he never could tell. When he found himself free, his leather baldrick or cross-belt—to which his officers' cartridge-box was attached—was gone, likewise his pistol. It had been torn off in the struggle to get free, likewise his waist-belt; yet he could not remember how or when. This may be readily conceived, when the reader calls to mind that a cannon had been belching forth death almost in the face of KEARNY and his little band, striking down Americans and Mexicans on either hand. Thus fell the gallant Major MILLS; thus the staunch MCREYNOLDS and GRAHAM were disabled.

Nothing saved KEARNY and the survivers of his party but the panic, inspired by his audacity. Terror-stricken, the Mexicans at the moment when he was in their power seemed to have shrunk back appalled. They either abandoned their guns or ceased to charge and discharge them; and even the musketry discontinued its fire. It was the very churm of battle, a whirlpool of human life. But the thunder of the tempest had a pause. Had KEARNY been followed by the number with which he commenced this charge, or had no signal of recall been blown, and had he been supported by a force of infantry, he could have made his way into the city, and Mexico, most probably, would have been captured that day. From the Garita of San Antonio to the Grand Plaza is less than a mile and three-quarters, and within the barrier there was not a single defensive work, and no organized defenders had there been any. All was indiscriminate panic, consequent confusion and flight.

The following extract from the "other side," or Mexican History of this war, is too complimentary to justify its omission. The reader will pardon its inaccuracies, since the Mexicans, from their own showing, were in no condition to see things clearly or relate them accurately:—

"General SANTA ANNA, with his staff and General ALCORTA, retired also from this place"—the Villa or Village of Portales, about three-quarters of a mile in the rear of the bridge-head, "which still was contested." "He mixed himself with the cavalry, and, desperate, gave the whip to some of the officers, who fled. On the causeway a horrible disorder was seen; all were confounded, and pushed one another, and trampled one another under foot.

"The American dragoons, mounted on fleet horses, coming up to our rear-guard, increased the fright, by crushing those whom they met in their way. General SANTA ANNA reached the Garita of San Antonio, and after him, the rest of ours, cut to pieces, mixed up with some of the enemy's dragoons, intoxicated with blood. The men at the guns discharged some grape-shot among these, and the infantry, feeling that their entrance was now covered, opened a thick fire along the causeway, animated by the presence of Generals SANTA ANNA, ALCORTA and GAONA, who personally commanded them. At this moment an American officer, in an uniform of blue, penetrated *through* the low earthen rampart, mounted on his horse, sword in hand, dealing sabre-blows, and falling wounded on the esplanade." [Mark this: *inside* the San Antonio Gate must be inferred from the Mexican account.] "Many swords were drawn to kill him; but the others also hastened to defend him on seeing him fall. He rose crippled, radiant with valor, and smiling at the felicity of being at the Gates of the Capital."

This officer was PHILIP KEARNY!*

* "It is not often that we prodigalize eulogium. We do not consider every officer who comes back wounded a hero. That epithet must be won by more than mere bravery—it belongs only to bravery in the excess; patience under fatigue; unmurmuring endurance of pain, and an ardent thirst for glory. Of all the officers who have fought under our banners, no man has shown all those characteristics more fully than Captain KEARNY. Yet no voice here has been loud in his praise, no city newspaper has invited public attention to his gallantry, and called upon the citizens of his native place to do him honor. If the story of his charge at Churubusco be not exaggerated, certainly there is no cause to be shown why he should receive two brevets, as did Captain MAY. Captain KEARNY is in

Finding himself alone, but free, KEARNY comprehended his situation at once, that nothing was to be done but get out of the scrape as soon as possible. He accordingly retraced his steps along the causeway on foot. It would have been fortunate for him had he continued to do so, for he had scarcely withdrawn when the Mexicans remanned their guns, and commenced firing grape down the road. Unluckily, KEARNY encountered one of our dragoon horses, whose rider had been killed, sprang into the saddle, and attempted to spur him into a gallop. But the animal was done up, and whether from exhaustion or wounds, could scarcely hobble along. Another discharge of grape now tore down the causeway. While on foot, the first missiles passed over his head. Firing too high was a common fault of the Mexicans. They seem to have often aimed along the line of metal, without allowing for the dispart. Being elevated in the saddle, a single ball took effect and completely shat-

---

fine health, but we regret to learn that Lieutenant GRAHAM, who accompanied the charge and shared in his misfortune, has not recovered from the effect of his wound, for the want of attention, but has just passed through a dangerous illness. We hope they may both be shortly again in the saddle. To show that we have not exaggerated the merit of Captain KEARNY, we subjoin a description of his and his troop's share at the battle of Churubusco:

"The charge of KEARNY'S dragoons upon the flying masses of the Mexicans in the battle of Churubusco is one of the most brilliant and decisive feats which have occurred in the war. As soon as our troops had carried the formidable *tête de pont* by which the avenue leading to the city was laid open to cavalry, Captain KEARNY'S dragoons rushed upon the flying masses of the Mexicans with an impetuosity and fury which made amends for the scantiness of their numbers, and bore them back in confusion upon the town. The enemy had upon the causeway a force of cavalry fourfold that of our own, but the narrowness of the avenue prevented him from availing himself of this superiority, and reduced the conflict to those single-handed issues in which the Mexicans must ever yield to our prowess. The audacity of the onset of KEARNY'S troops struck dismay to the host which fled before them. The retreat became a confused rout, and the causeway was blocked up by the entangled masses of the enemy. But even through this obstacle the triumphant dragoons forced their way, trampling down those who escaped their relentless sabres. Scattering their foe before them, the dragoons came at last within reach of the formidable batteries which defended the gates of the city, and a murderous fire was opened upon them, which was even more terrible to the fugitive Mexicans than to the dragoons. The latter continued their pursuit up to the gates of the city, and were shot down or made prisoners upon the very parapets of its defences. This was the moment, if ever, that Gen. SCOTT might have entered the city, had the instant possession of it conformed to his preconceived designs. Already had the inhabitants of the town set up the cry that the Americans were upon them, and the whole population was stricken defenceless by panic terrors. But the dragoons were recalled from the pursuit, and the survivors of that desperate charge withdrew, covered with wounds and with honors.

"In every narration of the events of Churubusco we have seen this charge and pursuit of KEARNY'S dragoons commemorated and applauded, but it appears to have impressed the Mexicans far more than the popular mind of our own countrymen. In various letters which we have seen written by them from the capital, they speak of the audacity of the dragoons as terrible and almost supernatural."—*New Orleans Picayune, Nov. 21st*, 1847.

tered the bone of KEARNY's left arm, between his elbow and shoulder. He described the pain as excruciating, but still was able to keep the saddle. The flow of blood, however, soon brought on such exhaustion, that he was about to fall when he came across a group of our soldiers. They staunched the blood as well as they were able, placed him in a blanket, and carried him to the hospital. He suffered terribly until an operation was performed; and he often said no words could express his sense of relief as soon as the arm was amputated. While Surgeon DE LEON was at work, General PIERCE, of New Hampshire, held his head. KEARNY often spoke with gratitude of the feeling displayed on this occasion by the future President.

Thus had his presentiment been realized. He had saved his life, but lost his left arm as he foretold. Nor had the words, lightly spoken at the dinner in Puebla, fallen unheeded to the ground. He had won his brevet, and paid the price with his left arm.

This was the end of KEARNY's service in Mexico; brief, but how glorious! He was not at that time the robust man he afterwards developed into, nor was his wound an ordinary one. Scarcely any of the arm was left, it was taken off so near the shoulder. Before the stump was healed, SCOTT was in Mexico, reveling—if the consciousness of a triumphant issue due to his superior generalship is not thus correctly construed, what is?—in the halls of the Montezumas.

On the 13th September, Mexico was virtually captured; on the 14th, "Old Glory" waved over the National Palace, and SCOTT entered the city amid the acclamations of his soldiers.

Captain J. W. P——, Fourth U. S. Artillery, serving as Infantry, stood with the remains of his regiment, drawn up in the Grand Plaza when SCOTT entered. The old General, the hero of two wars, was in full and splendid uniform. Conspicuous above all the rest towered the grand Commander-in-Chief, as magnificent a specimen of an American as he was an illustrious example of a general. Behind followed an escort of dragoons, grand men on tall horses. As the honored Chief entered the open square, a loud hurrah, a shout such as can issue from none other than Anglo-Saxon throats, burst from the troops already drawn up there. Brandishing their sabres high in air, the dragoons responded with a like manly hurrah; and the old walls and buildings echoed, until they seemed to shake, to such victorious cheers as no Latin or Hybrid race can utter.

But the first man who had entered, sword in hand, the gate of that captured capital, was Captain Philip Kearny.

DOCUMENTS.

EXTRACTS FROM OFFICIAL REPORTS.

"Arriving here, the 18th (August), Worth's division and Harney's cavalry were pushed forward a league to reconnoitre, and to carry or to mask San Antonio, on the direct road to the capital. This village was found strongly defended by field works, heavy guns, and a numerous garrison. It could only be turned by infantry to the left over a field of volcanic rocks and lava; for, to our right, the ground was too boggy. It was soon ascertained, by the daring engineers, Captain Mason, and Lieutenants Stevens and Tower, that the point could only be approached by the front, over a narrow causeway, flanked with wet ditches of great depth. Worth was ordered not to attack, but to threaten, and to mask the place.

"The first shot fired from San Antonio (the 18th) killed Captain S. Thornton, Second Dragoons, a gallant officer, who was covering the operations with his company.

"The same day a reconnoissance was commenced to the left of San Augustin, first over difficult mounds, and farther on over the same field of volcanic rocks and lava which extend to the mountains, some five miles from San Antonio towards Magdalena. This reconnoissance was continued to-day by Captain Lee, assisted by Lieutenants Beauregard and Tower, all of the engineers, who were joined in the afternoon by Major Smith, of the same corps. Other divisions coming up, Pillow's was advanced to make a practicable road for heavy artillery, and Twiggs' thrown farther in front to cover that operation; for, by the partial reconnoissance of yesterday, Captain Lee discovered a large corps of observation in that direction, with a detachment of which his supports of cavalry and foot, under Captain Kearny and Lieutenant-Colonel Graham, respectively, had a successful skirmish." (Compare Semmes' "Service Afloat and Ashore," pages 378–384.)

Major-General Scott's *Official Report, No.* 5, *of the* "*Battles of Contreras and Churubusco,*" *Executive Documents, No.* 1, *page* 304.

"Arriving at Coyoacan, two miles by a cross-road from the rear of San Antonio, I first detached Captain Lee, engineer, with Captain Kearny's troop, First Dragoons, supported by the rifle regiment, under Major Loring, to reconnoitre that strong point; and next despatched Major-General Pillow, with one of the brigades, (Cadwallader's,) to make the attack upon it, in concert with Major-General Worth on the opposite side."

Major-General Scott's *Official Report, Ibid., No.* 32, *page* 309.

"As soon as the *tete de pont* was carried, the greater part of Worth's and Pillow's forces passed that bridge in rapid pursuit of the flying enemy. These distinguished Generals coming up with Brigadier-General Shields, now also victorious, the three continued to press upon the fugitives to within a mile and a half of the capital. Here Colonel HARNEY, with a small part of his brigade of cavalry, rapidly passed to the front, and charged the enemy up to the nearest gate.

"The cavalry charge was headed by Captain KEARNY, of the First Dragoons, having, in squadron, with his own troop, that of Captain McREYNOLDS, of the Third—making the usual escort to general headquarters; but, being early in the day attached to general service, was now under Colonel HARNEY'S orders. The gallant Captain, not hearing the *recall* that had been sounded, dashed up to the San Antonio gate, sabring in his way all who resisted. Of the seven officers of the squadron, KEARNY lost his left arm, McREYNOLDS and Lieutenant LORIMER GRAHAM were both severely wounded, and Lieutenant R. S. EWELL, who succeeded to the command of the escort, had two horses killed under him. Major F. D. MILLS, of the Fifth Infantry, a volunteer in this charge, was killed at the gate."

Major-General SCOTT'S *Official Report, Ibid., No.* 32, *page* 315.

"Captain KEARNY, of the First Dragoons, commanding a squadron composed of his own and Captain McREYNOLDS' companies, was on duty with my division during the action, and made his way with great difficulty across the wide and marshy fields and deep ditches. Seeing no field for the action of his fine squadron until the *tete de pont* was carried, I had held him in reserve. I then let him loose. Furious was his charge upon the retreating foe, dealing death with the unerring sabre, until he reached the very suburbs of the city, and drew from the enemy's batteries at the garita a heavy and destructive fire, by which the gallant Captain lost his left arm; and Captain McREYNOLDS, Third Dragoons, who nobly sustained the daring movements of his squadron commander, was also wounded in the left arm. Both of these fine companies sustained severe losses in their rank and file also."

Major-General PILLOW'S *Official Report, Ibid., page* 340–'1.

"The reports of Major SUMNER, commanding First Battalion, and Lieutenant-Colonel MOORE, commanding Second Battalion, which I have the honor to forward herewith, will show in what manner the other troops and squadrons of my command were employed. The three troops of horse, brought by me on the field, being ordered away in different directions, Major SUMNER and myself soon found ourselves without commands. I then employed myself with my staff in rallying fugitives and encouraging our troops on the left of the main road. Major SUMNER, towards the close of the engagement, was placed by the general-in-chief in charge of the last reserve, consisting of the rifle regiment and one company of horse, and was ordered to support the left. This force was moving rapidly to take its position in line-of-battle, when the enemy broke and fled to the city. At this moment, perceiving that the enemy were retreating in disorder on one of the main causeways leading to the city of Mexico, I collected all the cavalry in my reach, consisting of parts of Captain KERR'S company, Second Dragoons, Captain KEARNY'S company, First Dragoons, and pursued them vigorously until we were halted by the discharge of the batteries at their gate. Many of the enemy were overtaken in the pursuit and cut down by our sabres. I cannot speak in terms too complimentary of the manner in which the charge was executed. My only difficulty was in restraining the impetuosity of my men and officers, who seemed to vie with each other who should be foremost in the pursuit. Captain KEARNY gallantly led his squadron into the very intrenchments of the enemy, and had the misfortune to lose an arm from a grape-shot fired from a gun at one of the main gates of the capital. Captain McREYNOLDS and Lieutenant GRAHAM were also wounded, and Lieutenant EWELL had two horses shot under him."

Colonel WILLIAM S. HARNEY'S *Official Report, Ibid, page* 347.

"Return of killed, wounded, and missing of the army under the immediate command of Major-General WINFIELD SCOTT on the 19th and 20th August, 1847.

HARNEY'S BRIGADE.

Killed:

"First Dragoons, Company F (KEARNY'S)—Privates PATRICK HART, JAMES McDONALD, ——— McBROPHY, JOHN RITTER.

* * * * * * *

"Third Dragoons, Company K (McREYNOLDS')—Privates EDWARD CURTIS, AUGUSTUS DESSOLL, GEORGE DUVER.

Wounded:

"First Dragoons, Company F (KEARNY'S)—*Captain* PHILIP KEARNY, *severely, lost left arm;* Lieutenant LORIMER GRAHAM, (Tenth Infantry,) *attached,* severely.

"Third Dragoons, Company K (McREYNOLDS')—*Captain* A. T. McREYNOLDS, severely; private ——— COWDEN."

Senate Executive Document, No. 1, *December* 7, 1847, *page* 431.

CHAPTER XII.

HOME, SWEET HOME.

* * * "Behold my success in your service," and the Abbe produced a long leather case, richly inlaid with gold.

"Faith, Abbe," said I, "am I to understand that this is a present for your eldest pupil?"

"You are," said Montreuil, opening the case, and producing a sword; the light fell upon the hilt, and I drew back dazzled with its lustre; it was covered with stones, apparently of the most costly value. Attached to the hilt was a lable of purple velvet, on which, in letters of gold, was inscribed, * * *

Devereux.

'Tis a sword of Spain" * * *
"Behold! I have a weapon:
A better never did itself sustain
Upon a soldier's thigh: * * *

Othello.

After his return from Mexico, in December, 1847, decorated with the loss of his left arm, and honored with a brevet—which he had won as justly as ever a brevet was earned—for distinguished gallantry in action—for which, alone, such a distinction should be conferred—Major Kearny was on recruiting service in the city of New York from May, 1848, to July, 1851. During this period, for the first time in many years, he was settled down in the midst of his few surviving relatives and many friends, and happy in his own home, built on a portion of the country seat of his great-grandfather on his mother's side, Honorable John Watts, senior. He used to speak with delight of this period, when he was "master of his own establishment, his nice garden, and pretty play-ground for his children," in his native city.

During his sojourn in New York, a compliment was paid him which he always seemed to regard as the most welcome token of his fellow citizens' appreciation of his military services. A great many persons at the time, especially New Yorkers, did not think that the government had taken sufficient notice of Kearny's gallantry at the Gates of Mexico. Many officers had received two brevets for far less conspicuous merit. In fact, such was the injustice shown that one of the finest officers in the service returned his brevet in disgust. PHILIP KEARNY was a member of the Union Club, a body of gentlemen, which comprised numbers of the first men of the city, both as to position and intelligence. This body of representative citizens determined to present a "costly and superb testimonial" of their feelings towards their fellow-member "for gallantry during the Mexican War, but especially at Churubusco." This testimonial was a "magnificent sword," which was indeed magnificent for the time when it was made. As a rich and chaste specimen of art it has never been exceeded, although more money has been lavished upon similar presentation gifts in recent years. "The guard was formed by a large spread eagle in gold, holding in its beak the head of a serpent, the folds of which constituted the guard, which was studded with agates. The handle itself was solid silver, richly chased, and it was fastened to the blade of "the ice-brook's temper," arabesqued and polished in perfect taste.

"The scabbard, which was also of sold silver, was relieved with ornaments in gold and etchings. In a long oval was a sketch of the battle of Churubusco, where Captain KEARNY lost his left arm, and within a circle, the word "CHURUBUSCO." Upon one of the bands was a representation of Hercules crushing the Serpent, and on another a military device, admirably arranged. The following inscription shows the purpose of the gift:—"Presented to Captain PHILIP KEARNY, Jr., First Regiment U. S. Dragoons, by his Friends and Associates, members of the UNION CLUB, New York, 1848."

The sword was enclosed in a curiously contrived case of black walnut, which was worthy of the weapon it contained.

When his body lay in state, prior to his interment, in the parlor of his mansion at Belle Grove, this sword was clasped in the arms of the dead soldier, closely pressed to that bosom which had twice been decorated by the hands of foreign sovereigns, for the same pre-eminent soldiership that won the exquisite weapon for the fallen warrior—a weapon his patriotic right arm never again could wield for the country he loved so dearly, the country for which he died.

CHAPTER XIII.

THE GOLDEN GATE; AND VICTORY ON THE ROGUE RIVER.

"TAUSEND TEUFLEN! that I should say so, and so like to be near my latter end," ejaculated the Captain; but under his breath, "what will become of us, now they have brought musketry to encounter our archers?"

SIR WALTER SCOTT'S "*Legend of Montrose.*"

IN midsummer, 1851, KEARNY received orders to join his company in California, and sailed for San Francisco in August of that year.

Thither he was not unwilling to proceed, as he wished to look after some very large investments made for him by an agent, but without his knowledge. These turned out very unfortunately, and swallowed up a fortune. Nevertheless, as lucky in his daring speculations as in his military dashes, he more than retrieved the loss while at the "Golden Gate."

The writer has reason to be well acquainted with all these circumstances, for to him, as to a brother, in preference to all others in the world, PHIL KEARNY came for assistance in difficulties for which he was in no way responsible in honor nor called upon to remedy, except through that high sense of chivalry and regard for his name which always distinguished his actions. Prostrate from typhoid fever and almost powerless, the writer was still happy to be able to accomplish all that was necessary, and this fact is mentioned simply to demonstrate the mutual confidence and affection at crises which existed between his cousin and himself.

It was during this period of KEARNY's residence in New York that he experienced that attack of varioloid—taken in the discharge of his duty—which was almost as severe as the worst form of small-pox. He was very deeply scarred in consequence of this disease, and through it a complete alteration was wrought in his appearance. Not only were his features affected, but a complete physical change occurred. From this time forward he began to spread and develop into that magnificent figure of a trooper which attracted the attention of every one who saw him as he lay upon the embalming table. From this time, also, that resemblance between the cousins, which had so often attracted notice, terminated, and was no longer remarked.

Major PHILIP KEARNY had scarcely been transferred from the Atlantic to the Pacific coast when he demonstrated the truth of what has so often been claimed for him, that he seemed destined to shine in whatever he undertook. His summer campaign of 1851, against the Rogue River Indians, was one of the most telling blows ever delivered by our army in this harassing warfare. These savages at that period were the most wicked, most warlike, and most difficult to subdue of all the tribes on our Pacific coast. What rendered them more formidable was the fact that they occupied a district which intercepted all intercourse between Oregon and California; scattered along and across the direct road, north and south, on the banks of the Rogue River, which drains a rugged, mountainous wilderness, and flows as a general thing west and perpendicular to the coast, emptying into the Pacific, twenty miles south of Port Orford, and fifty miles north of Crescent City.

Much information in regard to this expedition is derived from Major-General RUFUS INGALLS, Chief Quartermaster for so many campaigns of the Army of the Potomac. At that time he was stationed at Fort Vancouver, on the Washington shore of the Columbia River, where he fitted out Major KEARNY. To use his language, "this handsome campaign opened that country." It has often been commented upon with surprise how KEARNY, one-armed as he was, kept his saddle on all occasions, even when the march lay along mountain tracks most dangerous, and often seemingly impracticable for a soldier on horseback; tracks difficult enough for the sure footed mules. The principal engagement was that of the Table Rock, laid down on the maps as Fort Lane, about midway between Roseburg, north, and Crescent City, south. The former (Roseburg) is the residence of JOE LANE, as he was familiarly styled, then Governor of the Territory, who wrote to KEARNY one of the most flattering letters which can reward an officer who has succeeded in solving a difficult and dangerous problem. He gave him the greatest credit for the ability with which he had planned, and the resolution with which he had executed his operations. The fight at the Table Rock was a complete triumph. It awed the savages, pacified the district, and accomplished the great object in view, making the route safe between our farthest north-western territory and California. On this occasion a very gallant officer fell—Captain STEWART, who passed through the whole Mexican war with distinction, unscathed, to die at the hands of a miserable Indian, shot through the body with an arrow by that savage whom he had rushed forward to save from the just fury of our troops. The torture which preceded his decease must have been terrific, as was testified by his reply to Major KEARNY's question, "STEWART, are you suffering much?" "Suffering! I feel as if a red hot bar of iron was thrust through my bowels."

Major KEARNY took the greatest pride in the letter which he received from Governor LANE of Oregon in relation to these engagements and their happy results. This letter he exhibited to the writer when next they met with an honest exultation, such as he seldom displayed, as an acknowledgment of his able and brilliant soldiership. This letter, like all the rest of the testimonials which KEARNY received from time to time, is no longer to be found. As soon as the present work was projected, a letter was addressed to Governor LANE in the hope that a copy of it might have been preserved by him. The following is the Governor's reply, but it cannot approach the concise elegance with which he expressed his commendation in the original document:

ROSEBURG, Oregon, April 27th, 1868.

GENERAL DE PEYSTER:

SIR:—I regret my inability to furnish you a copy of the letter you mention in yours of the 21st January,* but it affords me pleasure to supply, as well as I can from memory, a brief statement of the conduct, in Oregon, of the late General

---

* NEW YORK, No. 59 EAST 21ST STREET, January 21st, 1868.

Governor JOSEPH LANE, *formerly, about* 1851, *Governor of Oregon:*

SIR:—The person who addresses you is the cousin, co-heir, and biographer of Major-General PHILIP KEARNY. About the year 1852, or 1853, my counsin, General KEARNY, then Major United States Dragoons, came to my house on the Hudson, having just returned from the Pacific coast and his campaign against the Rogue River Indians, which gave peace to that Territory. He showed me a letter from you, in which he seemed to take great pride. In this you gave him the highest credit for the ability with which he had planned the expedition, and for the vigor and intrepidity with which he had carried it out.

If I recollect aright, you stated in that letter that the chastisement which he had inflicted on those particularly lawless tribes had given peace to the State or Territory of which you were the Executive. What has become of this valuable testimonial, I know not. If you could give me a duplicate of it you would oblige me exceedingly. If you cannot give me a copy, can you not give me a paraphrase, or a certificate of equal force, to embody in the General's biography.

Your early attention to this will exceedingly oblige me, and assist me to present to the world properly a peculiar phase in the life of my cousin.

Very respectfully,

Your obedient servant,

J. WATTS DE PEYSTER.

KEARNY, the important results of which induced from myself the merited compliment to which you allude.

During the summer of 1851 Major PHIL KEARNY received orders to proceed with two companies of United States Dragoons, Captains STEWART and WALKER, from Oregon to some point in California. En route, he was informed of a recent attack of the Rogue River Indians, in which they succeeded in killing quite a number of miners, and doing other mischief.

These Indians were at that time the most warlike and formidable tribe on the Pacific coast. Never having known defeat, they were exceedingly bold in their depredations upon the miners and settlers, and were the terror of all. Major KEARNY determined, if possible, to give them battle, and finally found them, three hundred braves strong, in the occupation of an excellent position. He ordered an attack, and, after a sharp engagement, succeeded in dislodging them, killing, wounding, and capturing fifty or more. It was here that the lamented, brave, and brilliant STEWART fell. The Indians retreated across Rogue River, and feeling that they had not been sufficiently chastised, the Major concluded to pursue them, and, whilst in the prosecution of this purpose, I joined him. He followed until the Indians made a stand quite favorable to themselves on Evans Creek, about thirty miles distant from the scene of their late disaster. Here he again attacked them, killed and wounded a few, and captured about forty, among the latter a very important prisoner in the person of the Great Chief's favorite wife. By means of this capture, and these successes an advantageous peace was obtained. Being an eye-witness, in part, of KEARNY'S movements and action, I can, with great truth, and do with no less pleasure, bear testimony to his gallantry as a soldier and his ability as an officer. I was then, and still am, sensible of the great good secured to Oregon by his achievements at that particular time.

Very respectfully, your obedient servant,

(Signed) JOSEPH LANE.

CHAPTER XIV.

KEARNY A WANDERER.

"And from his native land resolv'd to go,
And visit scorching climes beyond the sea."
BYRON'S "*Childe Harold.*"

"Yon sun that sets upon the sea,
We follow in his flight;
Farewell awhile to him and thee,
My native land—Good Night!"
BYRON'S "*Childe Harold.*"

"Sir, to a wise man all the world's a foil:
It is not Italy, nor France, nor Europe
That must bound me, if my fates call me forth;
Yet, I protest, it is no salt desire
Of seeing countries, shifting for a religion,
Nor any disaffection to the state
Where I was bred, and unto which I owe
My dearest plots, hath brought me out."
B. JOHNSON'S "*Volpone.*"

KEARNY A WANDERER.

AFTER that gloriously successful campaign against the Rogue River Indians, in which Governor LANE bears such explicit testimony to his enterprise, gallantry, and efficiency, KEARNY was stationed in different parts of California. All his own letters, which were exceedingly able and interesting, have been either lost, mislaid, or destroyed; but the writer has been able to find a series of intimations from the only surviving relative on his mother's side, his aunt, in which his movements are constantly referred to.

In one, written out to Europe on the 7th October, 1851: "I received a letter from Major PHIL this morning, he desires remembrance to you; he is at his quarters in the beautiful Valley of Sonoma (in Northwestern California), well contented with the balmy breezes and the society of some right pleasant officers—is going to take a look at Southern California; expects to receive the acceptance of his resignation about the middle of this month, and then comes home. I am sorry for this; I had set my heart upon your meeting him on the top of the Pyramids; now you must not go until next year, when you and PHIL can take a fresh start from New York. I think that will be delightful. We can all think seriously about it when the Major comes to New York."

On the 14th November, the same correspondent wrote: "I have received another letter from the Major; still enjoying himself to the full, expecting now daily to hear that his resignation is accepted, and be off to France by way of China, India, and Egypt; a snug way to get to Paris. He has a great deal of military parade, guard-mounting at nine and a half in the morning, dress foot parade at retreat, with trumpets sounding, sometimes with full band (military doings), from day-break until nine at night, tattoo. His advice to have a post established at a certain point has been approved by General HITCHCOCK (Fort Lane, on the Rogue River scene of his victory?) on his visit to Oregon."

KEARNY's next letter, dated 14th November, 1851, spoke of sailing the next day in the United States ship-of-war Vincennes, as a guest of the Commander, Captain HUDSON, to the Sandwich Islands, from thence to proceed to China, Calcutta, Bombay, where he expected to arrive in April, 1852.

As intended, he sailed in the Vincennes, for China, stopping on the way at the Sandwich Islands. On the 7th December, 1851, he was at Honolulu. "He had the upper and second story in a new cottage with a piazza running around; the native family (a chief's) occupied the lower. He breakfasted with them, or in his own apartments, and dined at a French restaurant. The Vincennes, a noble ship, struck the trade winds in four days, then went on dashingly, making, for hours at a time, twelve knots."

Hence, KEARNY went round the whole world, and met with a great many strange and interesting adventures. He visited a great many places, whither Americans very seldom go, except in the pursuit of gain. He appears to have stopped at Ceylon, and on his return was full of his stories of strange lands, but always declared that he had seen no such scenery—which united all those beauties, which afforded him the most pleasure,—as the banks of the North River immediately opposite the glorious Catskills.

Again and again, while at Tivoli, and standing on our pine-clothed shore, with our magnificent mountains before his eyes, our majestic river at his feet, and the murmur of air, of trees, and of waves whispering music in his ears, he was wont to exclaim: "I have been throughout the world, and, after all, when I get back here and look around me, I feel I have seen nothing more beautiful, nothing so beautiful elsewhere." Or, as he remarked at another time, "The more I gaze upon this scenery, the more it satisfies. One can dwell in its midst, or return to it again and again, without its tiring. It is satisfyingly lovely. Always the same in its features and effects, yet ever changing in its expression, and ever presenting some new or hitherto unnoted charm."

In the spring of 1853, KEARNY was in Paris, where the writer met him in the full enjoyment of the society of the distinguished officers with whom he had served under the torrid sun of Africa, and with whom he was destined to serve again under the scarcely less burning sky of Italy—soldiers in the highest sense of the word, who appreciated him as a glorious type of an American soldier. One of these was that cavalry General MORRIS so often mentioned in orders for brilliant feats of arms. When KEARNY first knew him he was Major of the Chasseurs d'Afrique. Since that time he had risen to the rank of General of Division in the Cavalry of the Imperial Guard. Between 1840 and 1853 he had distinguished himself on numerous occasions, particularly at the capture of the Smalah (camp) of ABD-EL-KADER, at the battle of Isly, and in the Crimea. KEARNY was attached to his staff, as volunteer aid, at the battle of Solferino.

Although decorated by the loss of his arm, and by universal acclaim a brilliant cavalryman, few men bore their honors with more diffidence. For a man who had done and seen so much as KEARNY, his deportment was entirely devoid of ostentation. It was at this time that he introduced the writer to one of the best artillery officers in our service, a man of rare gifts, an able and fluent writer, whose correspondence is well worthy of preservation, for the beauty of its descriptions of scenery as well as the elegance of its style. This officer also published an admirable translation of a French political work which, if the ordinary class of our miserable politicians ever read, might have served as indications to enable them to avoid the shoals on which our country was nearly wrecked in 1860–'61. When the writer began to collect notes for this work, a letter was received from the party immediately before alluded to, an extract from which is extremely interesting, as it refers particularly to the time when all three met in Paris:

"Yours * * * requesting to be informed of any incidents in the life of General KEARNY * * has just been received. I regret that I am not able to furnish you with any that would probably be possessed with any general interest. My intercourse with him, though not infrequent during our period of military service, was always of a casual nature; yet I saw him in many traits of character that won my esteem and kind regard. He was marked by a generous disposition, exhibiting itself at times in an affecting mood of self abandonment, and even desolateness, which was calculated to give one a deep and attractive interest in him. He had some of the very best traits of the soldier: he was gallant, ambitious, devoted, enterprising, decided, and embued with a thorough love for his profession. Though possessed, in many respects, of sound sense and good judgment, yet there are some incidents of his life, known to me only in vague, general outline, that seem to border on the romantic. * * *

It was in the spring of 1853, I think, that he, Lieutenant BANKHEAD, of the Navy, and myself, were at a reception of English and Americans given by the Emperor NAPOLEON III., at the Tuilleries. I was much struck at the bearing of Major KEARNY. He had then left the service, but still bore the title, and for the occasion, wore the uniform. He was introduced to the emperor by our own minister, Mr. RIVES; and when his name and services were being mentioned, he shrank as if from modesty and bashfulness, although a lost arm showed that he had not shrunk in the face of the enemy." * * *

KEARNY subsequently returned to the United States, and devoted considerable time to embellishing his country-seat, Belle Grove, which he had recently purchased. It is on the Passaic, immediately opposite to Newark, and on its commanding site he afterwards constructed his elegant mansion, which he gradually filled with the finest statuary and choicest paintings. For his means, KEARNY was a munificent patron of American art, and his collection contained several masterpieces of native chisels and pencils. Their aggregate display he never lived to enjoy, for he had scarcely brought them together in his New Jersey home, when he resumed his uniform; and it is very doubtful if, living, he ever had an opportunity to admire all his gems of art together, although the body of the hero lay in state surrounded by them.

An enthusiast in everything he undertook, it was about this time that he turned his attention to the finest wool-bearing sheep. In the selection of his animals he spared no expense, and it is doubtful if there was a finer flock for its size in the United States.

He also paid some attention to cattle, but it would seem that his investments in this line were not fortunate. One certainly was not, and he very soon relinquished the idea of forming and maintaining a herd. He visited the writer's neighborhood several times to examine the magnificent Devons at "The Meadows," owned by the brothers WAINWRIGHT, both of whom, like KEARNY, relinquished the sweets of happy homes to serve and save their country. The elder, WILLIAM P. WAINWRIGHT, a Christian gentleman, commanded the Seventy-sixth New York Volunteers, a very fine regiment, with great distinction. The younger, CHARLES S. WAINWRIGHT, a very able, practical man, commanded the First New York Artillery, a corps surpassed by none in the service. Both breveted Brigadier-Generals for gallant and conspicuous service, survived the friend whom they admired. We shall see the younger, referred to by KEARNY, as displaying unusual gallantry and capacity at the battle of Williamsburgh.

KEARNY always and earnestly desired to settle on the banks of the North River. Several of the sites which were the objects of his choice are for natural positions and peculiar charms unexceeded by any in the most beautiful district of the Hudson, between Hyde Park and the boundary line between Duchess and Columbia Counties. One of these sites is the prominent Turkey Point on the west bank of the River, about three miles below Saugerties. KEARNY never desired to settle in New Jersey, and he did not actually begin to build on the Passaic until he found himself unable to purchase any one of the places which suited his taste on the Hudson. Concerning this the writer can speak with certainty, for his own agent, at the request of KEARNY, was employed to negotiate and attempt the purchase of one magnificent site in Red Hook and another in Hyde Park. Besides these, a number of others were examined, and in two cases, KEARNY offered higher prices than were actually realized for the same property afterwards, when sold.

It has often been the occasion of remark that KEARNY did not visit the Crimea to witness the siege of Sebastopol 1853–'5. This is easily explained. His business required his attention after his return home in 1853 in consequence of his frequent and protracted absences, and he was detained for a long time in consequence in this country. Subsequently accident—severe injuries from the fall of his horse through a bridge—and circumstances beyond his control prolonged his stay on this side of the Atlantic. Nothing but insurmountable obstacles would have kept him from witnessing and participating in the grand drama of suffering and peril in the trenches, and on the blood-stained heights before Sebastopol. The atmosphere of such a charge as that of Balaklava would have been as congenial to his instincts as fire to the fabled Salamander, or to the actual "Salamander," the nickname applied to the British General CUTTS, of KING WILLIAM'S Wars, whose elements seemed to be danger and the exchanging fires of opposing batteries and lines.

KEARNY, however, was one of those restless dispositions which cannot brook any repose, however charming, provided it afforded none of that excitement which, to him, was the very breath of his nostrils. He suddenly started off, in 1856, to be present at the coronation of the Emperor ALEXANDER at Moscow, and nothing could exceed his graphic description of the *fêtes* which attended the ceremony. He seemed to experience a vivid satisfaction in his recollection of the military displays in which he participated and the pomp of which he was a spectator. He also made a tour through Spain, and, previously, to prepare himself for it, applied his energy to mastering the Spanish language. This was characteristic of the man, and although the writer cannot speak with certainty as to all the foreign tongues which he understood, he was certainly proficient in French, and was acquainted with the Italian and Spanish—very likely, the German also, in a less degree, since he took a great deal of interest in the military matters of Germany, and visited Prague, to be present at some grand reviews which were held near that city. It is very curious, but when, in 1852, the writer reported in favor of the gray uniform and system for the designation of rank, which in many respects was identical with that adopted by the Rebels, this color and system received the full endorsement of KEARNY, who dwelt with emphasis on the superior advantages of grey,*

---

* * * "BLUE is now (1854) the national military color of nearly the whole civilized world. The United States, France, Belgium, Holland, Sweden, Prussia, Greece, Switzerland, several of the minor German States, Spain and Great Britain, in many branches of their services, Naples, States of the Church, Piedmont, Tuscany, Turkey, and even Tunis, have adopted the dark blue coat, with some little difference of ornament. What objection can there be to the assumption of the well-known IRON-GREY as the uniform of the State of New York? None is more beautiful or striking than the old national GREY, faced and trimmed with bright yellow somewhat similar to the dress of the Voltigeurs, or Foot-Riflemen (See ¶ 1004, U. S. Army Regulations 1847). The Tyrolese and Austrian Riflemen, likewise the Modenese, wear a similar grey with a shade of blue, which makes a very simple and handsome suit. Likewise the Noble Guard of Tuscany. With their gold embroidery and splendid appointments, the latter's was the richest uniform * * * abroad. A light bluish-grey tunic, and darker pantaloons, constitute the undress uniform of Austrian General Officers. But a month since, and the English War-Ministry adopted a grey uniform for their Light Infantry and Rifles, very similar to that of the Austrian Cacciatori, or Sharpshooters.

Iron-grey, the coat lighter than the trousers, would make a very handsome uniform for our generals and staff-officers, and at once distinguish them from the regulars of equal grades. As it is abroad, accustomed constantly to see the uniform of the United States Army and Navy, it is impossible for foreign officers to appreciate the trifling changes

founded on what he had observed at the grand Austrian reviews. He laid particular stress upon the rapidity with which the powder smoke swallowed up lines in grey, and rendered them invisible to an antagonistic force. That this was the fact had previously been shown by experience and statistics.

In 1859 and 1860, KEARNY resided in Europe, and in the latter year EDWIN DE LEON, "late confidential agent of the Confederate Department of State in Europe," in his "Secret History of Confederate Diplomacy Abroad," admits that KEARNY rendered important service to the Loyal North while in Paris. This is his language: "While the interregnum in the diplomatic representations lasted, by the lagging on the stage of the reluctant veterans of Mr. BUCHANAN's Ministers, before the new ones had arrived to represent the views and wishes of Mr. LINCOLN's administration, one Minister made himself wonderfully active, at both the English and French foreign offices; and in other places where public opinion was to be influenced. This was Mr. SANFORD, then, as now, Minister to Bel-

---

which designate the State service This often places a State officer in an unpleasant position, and renders a long and embarrassing explanation necessary, unless he wishes to practice deception and sail under false colors.

Over and above the many cogent reasons urged, * * the following additional recommendations may not be without weight. At morning and evening twilight; in foggy, muggy, and rainy weather, a body of men thus clothed would be undistinguishable at a very short distance, and amid the smoke of battle they would be swallowed up at once in the clouds of kindred hue. Grey and yellow, or gold, form the richest dress in the world; without bullion, it is the cheapest, taking into consideration its serviceability, it is national to a great degree, and last, not least certainly, *it is the least fatal to its wearer*. Grey, it is stated, was the uniform of the English troops in the reign of WILLIAM III., and is now again adopted by the Light Infantry on account of its suitableness for corps exposed to practiced marksmen, and, themselves, assigned to the dangerous duty of sharpshooters. It is now worn by the Austrian riflemen, and good reasons must have dictated the choice, for it was not appropriate to any province of the Empire.

"It would appear, from numerous observations, that soldiers are hit, during battle, according to the color of their dress, in the following order: *Red, the most fatal;* ("*our scarlet is more distinguishable than any other color* (BATTY's "*Campaign of* 1815, *page* 160)*; the least fatal, Austrian grey. The proportions are: red,* 12*; rifle-green* 7*; brown* 6*; Austrian bluish-grey,* 5." (JAMESON's *Journal, No.* 105.)

General PHILIP KEARNY stated that, during a sham fight he saw at Prague, in Bohemia, in 1851, in which seventeen thousand men, with thirty-four pieces of artillery and a rocket brigade were engaged, he was particularly struck with the admirable fitness of the GREY DRESS of the Austrian riflemen, of which a full battalion, about one thousand, were acting as skirmishers; at times invisible, when the powder-smoke rolled over the field, disappearing in its curling clouds on account of the similarity of their uniform, and again appearing when least expected like phantoms, as the breeze, aided by the movements of the combatants, drove aside the sulphurous canopy. He added, he was astonished at the facility with which they were lost to view, and that uniforms of grey cloth, for riflemen, had not been maintained in this as well as in every other country where military propriety or appropriateness of dress is the object of constant and scrupulous attention." *Brigadier General* DE PEYSTER's *Report of* 1852; ECLAIREUR 11, *page* 31.

gium, but who gave himself a roving commission, and worked indefatigably, some said obtrusively, on the Northern side. So omnipresent and so brisk was he in his movements, that some wicked wag dubbed him—the 'Diplomatic Flea;' and though perhaps open to the charge of over-zeal, or officiousness, he certainly was one of, if not *the* most efficient advocate of the Northern cause in Europe.
* * *

"GENERAL FREMONT, who was then in Europe, also threw the whole weight of his name and influence on the Northern side, *as did also Gen.* PHIL KEARNY, *whose social qualities had given him influence in certain circles in France.* The great horde of Americans resident abroad possessed but little weight or influence, either from intelligence, culture or distinction of any kind. They were chiefly people of good incomes, who left home because they found themselves—or imagined themselves (GOOD)—of more consequence abroad; and at the commencement of the war it was rather their style (!) to affect sympathy with the Southerners, as representing the more aristocratic side" (BETTER).

It is very curious, but equally true, that in whatever character, KEARNY undertook to shine, he always played his part well; his hospitality was princely, his equipages and horses inferior to none in style, beauty, and qualities. His taste was chaste and elegant, and in his appreciation of the beauties of nature, nothing could exceed his delight in them or his judgment in the selection of points of view. Since his resignation in 1851, his wanderings were worthy of a more lengthy notice, for he reveled in perils, in the gratification of his instincts, from which the majority of even the boldest men would have shrunk, or at all events, have but rarely indulged their fancies. It is very unfortunate, as noted more than once before, that his correspondence between 1851 and 1861 seems to have entirely perished, since KEARNY wrote well, and described what he saw concisely but with a peculiar force, which rendered his descriptions "word-pictures." Had he ever written a book, it would have been a gallery of word-pictures, for, as he often declared, the people of our day demand and will not be satisfied with any other style of writing.

Thus, all the pains possible have been taken, to follow the hero of this sketch throughout all his various wanderings, and it is to be regretted, for the sake of the reader, that so few data from the hand of KEARNY have rewarded the diligent search made for them.

Judging from what has been preserved, or what still lingers on the memory, they would have amply repaid perusal, and his letters alone, edited with care and judgment, would have constituted in themselves not only an agreeable and instructive book, but, like MICHELET'S "Life of LUTHER"—constructed almost entirely from his correspondence—would have presented the best word-portrait of KEARNY, and the most attractive and satisfactory history of his remarkable career.

CHAPTER XV.

ITALIAN CAMPAIGN OF 1859.

KEARNY AT SOLFERINO.

"In thy faint slumbers I by thee have watched,
And heard thee murmur tales of iron war;
Speak terms of manage to thy bounding steed;
Cry, courage! to the field! and thou hast talk'd
Of sallies and retires; of trenches, tents,
Of pallisadoes, frontiers, parapets;
Of basilisks, of cannon, culverin,
Of prisoners ransomed, and of soldiers slain,
And all the current of a heady fight."

SHAKSPEARE'S "HENRY IV."

"The shining images of war are fled,
The fainting trumpets languish in my ear,
The banners furl'd, and all the springtly blaze
Of burnish'd armor, like the setting sun,
Insensibly it vanished from my thought."

YOUNG'S "BUSIRIS."

PARIS, 14th July, 1859.

"MY two months' absence has been all that a military man could have desired—a school of such grandeur as rarely occurs, even here in the Old World—and the drama has been complete.

"Leaving Paris the day after" (10th June) "the emperor, I arrived just two days before him (14th July).

"I have roamed about everywhere, and *in the day of Solferino, I was not only present with the line of our cavalry skirmishers, (but) as well in every charge that took place.* That day I was mounted from six in the morning till eleven at night—scarcely off my horse even for a few minutes—depend on it, he was a good one. The cavalry of the guard came up some sixteen miles in full trot and rapid gallop to take our places, under fire; for there was a gap we had to stop. I remained until I saw the Mincio passed and Peschiera invested, and the whole Austrian army demoralized and broken up.

"The night before the battle I had a miraculous escape, having been inveigled by false guides into the midst of the Austrian masses.*

"There are seven American officers following the Piedmontese army. I am going to the baths of Homburgh for awhile. Paris is very warm, more so than I have ever known it. My health has been excellent until I arrived home. When at Turin I had a *coup de soleil.*

"The peace has taken us by surprise—it is in consequence of some underhand and revolutionary moves of Count CAVOUR, which the emperor had to put a stop to.

"Very truly, yours, "PHILL."

When General KEARNY returned from Italy, while in conversation with the writer, he expressed the utmost admiration for the French army, and their doings at Solferino, he seemed to feel that the Austrians might have won the battle, or maintained their position, had they held out with greater tenacity or been aware of the condition and dislocation of the Allies. The reader may remember that quite a stampede was reported, just as occurred at Wagram in 1809, and according to the journals some of the French troops did not stop until they reached Brescia. The presence of NAPOLEON III. in front of Solferino, at the crisis, electrified the French, and a renewed attack, fed with fresh troops, carried the keypoint of the Austrian position. Then, the scale long poised, declined, deciding the victory against FRANCIS JOSEPH.

The letter with which this chapter opens, written within three weeks after the great battle to which it refers—a battle in which General KEARNY so distinguished himself as to win (a second time) the cross of the Legion of Honor—covers the whole ground; tells the whole story.

KEARNY, like others of his race, was a very unequal man in his conversation. At times he was particularly reticent, and seldom prone to narrative. In referring to his military service, he usually alluded to it incidentally and as a means of illustrating a question under discussion, or to give point to an argument, rather than directly as a matter in which he was personally interested.

---

* General KEARNY had just such another hair-breadth escape after Glendale, 30th June, 1862, and at Chantilly, 1st September, 1862, a similar plunge into the skirmish line or lines of the Rebels cost him his life. *Doubtless*, it was his previous immunity made KEARNY feel that he bore a charmed life.

It is very doubtful if he himself ever kept much, if any, record of his service.* When it pleased him to shine in conversation, he shone, but unless he chose to talk upon the subject of his own selection, under the spur of some immediately occurring excitement, he retired within himself or chatted on indifferent subjects. This may have been real modesty, because he did not wish to seem to boast of what he had passed through. In this he very much resembled the Count LIPPE, so often referred to as his foil. This is the principal reason, perhaps, why so little is known of the details, as far as regarded himself, of the great events in which he participated.

To those who watched the course of operations in Northern Italy in 1859 with any interest, or remember what occurred in that momentous campaign of about two months and a half, it will be apparent that the Austrians in the initiative collisions—like the army of the Potomac in too many cases—were defeated rather through the demerits of their own leaders; through the meddling of the central government; through the unusual wet-weather, and from the fact—which told so often against our forces in the South—that, as a rule,—certainly as long as they were west of Milan, and always as regarded the inhabitants of cities, towns, and large villages—they (the Austrians) were fighting in the midst of a population hostile to them, and friendly to the Allies—a population which did all they could to deceive the one, and assist the other with reliable information.

General—then Major—KEARNY was fully able to judge of the difficulties which attended the preliminary movements of the Austrians. The spring of 1859 was one of flooding rains and freshets, in a country more susceptible than almost any other to inundations. The Austrians were greatly blamed by those who pretended to be judges, as well as by the majority of quidnuncs, for not advancing at once to Turin and dictating terms to the King of Sardinia. This opinion is such as might be expected from parties not acquainted with the theatre of war.† Doubtless the Austrians might have

* One of his friends, who served with him in Mexico, and afterwards associated with him in Paris, remarked in a letter—"Of his service in Algiers, I know but little; simply that he served as an officer in the French cavalry, I believe, and that is all. I doubt even whether he himself ever kept much record of it." The same observation holds good to his whole career.

† Had the Sardinians fallen back on Genoa, and the French reinforcements landed at that port, the Allies could have taken the Austrians in the rear, and the result would have been another Marengo.

moved with more energy, but that energy would have been inconsistent with a methodical method of carrying on war according to principles and rules of strategy, with the disposition of the people, and with the constitutional characteristics and traditions of their army. Had they plunged forward into a country intersected by rivers and streams, which in very rainy seasons overpass their bounds and convert whole districts into vast shallow lakes, the whole army might have been caught in a trap and so entirely ruined that the Allies could have blockaded their fortresses and taken possession of whatever they deemed expedient, or that the German Confederation would have permitted.

The theatre of war on which the French and Sardinians first encountered the Austrians is said to be one which was seldom traversed by tourists, but was visited by General KEARNY in 1834, in just such a wet season as in 1859. The following remarks, compiled from a journal kept at that time, may be interesting to show the obstacles which impeded the movements and operations of the Austrians without hampering the counter-operations of the Allies, whose lines of supply—railroads and capital highways—both resting on secure bases, were not affected by the same extraordinary difficulties as those of their enemy.

KEARNY could thus judge from personal observations of the terrible impediments to military movements which result from long continued and excessive rain in the greater part of the basin or lowlands between Turin and Milan.*

In August, 1834, KEARNY started from Genoa for Milan, intending to cross the Simplon into Switzerland, but was compelled, on reading the *Lago Maggiòre*, to turn back upon Turin, by way of Novara—where RADETSZKY defeated the Sardinians in 1849. Heavy rains preceded and accompanied this journey. It is needless here to dwell upon the loveliness of the scenery through which he climbed to the summit of the Apennines, since the interest of the matter on hand begins with his arrival upon the monotonous plains of Lombardy, when the intervening summit shut out the last glimpses of the azure Mediterranean. Soon afterwards the party looked upon a turbid flood, or lagune, into which the overflowings of the rivers had converted the level country as far as they could see.

* Readers should bear in mind that the bed of the Po is much above the level of the surrounding country, and that this river like our Mississippi, is kept within bounds by dikes or, as we term them, levees.

While amid the mountains they had echoed each other's admiration of the effects of a heavy thunder-storm—whose beneficial results in tempering the air rendered their ride the more delightful, while the reverberations rolling through the gorges seemed like answering roars of parks of artillery—little dreaming that the consequences of storms, such as had broken upon them and varied the attractions of the journey, would render its prosecution impossible. As soon as the party came in sight of the Scrivia, they found that instead of an insignificant, fordable stream, it was rushing furiously towards the Po, and had been converted into a Mississippi, covering the country for one league on either side of its usual channel; the neighboring villages rising up in the midst like so many miniatures of Venice. Some distance beyond Novi, where the more elevated grounds subside into the level, on the spot where JOUBERT was defeated by SUWARROW and slain, in 1799, KEARNY's carriage met postilions who had just traversed the ground with the King of Wurtemberg. They informed him that many of the bridges were under water, and that they had been compelled to pass one at full gallop, fearing it would give way before they could get over. In many places the road was hub-deep; the fertile fields were hidden beneath a tawny flood, and where it had subsided from an even still greater previous rise, slime and sand, brought down from the mountains, disfigured their cultivation. Turning aside towards Alexandria, the driver sought to avoid the inundation by a more elevated detour and by a country road, but found that he had not bettered his condition, so directed his horses again towards Tortona, where the bridge was still practicable. The situation was by no means satisfactory, and KEARNY's party were actually stunned by the exaggerated accounts of the freshet. Arrived at the Bridge of Tortona it was with difficulty the travellers were permitted to pass. Theirs was the last carriage over, and prints in the writer's possession at this day are stained with the muddy water which invaded the trunks on the rack behind and under the box in front. Engineers in charge of the long bridge across the Scrivia—about one thousand feet in length—were in doubt if it had not already yielded somewhat to the violence of the stream, which, as the tourists hurried across, roared against the abutments, and wet them with its foam. It was no agreeable promenade, for at intervals the structure, which must have been very strong to resist the current, trembled beneath the shock of trees and timber, brought down against it, as if they had been so many battering rams. Beyond the river, the causeway was knee-deep with water, running so violently that it was difficult at times to keep straight ahead. The bed of the Scrivia at low water is a vast waste of gravel over 1,200 feet wide; the stream itself being ordinarily from 300 to 400 feet in width."

The night KEARNY arrived at Tortona the waters subsided, and thence to Milan the route was uninterrupted. This shows how suddenly the affluents of the Po swell, overflow, and subside. As regards the Po itself, a Piedmontese soldier, engaged as a servant, related that while encamped with several battalions upon the upper part of that river, it rose so suddenly in one afternoon, that had not the commanding-general received notice of its menacing aspect from a peasant, the whole force must have been overtaken in the night and many drowned.

From Tortona the road continued through a low country, intersected by many torrents, whose passage always presents dangers in rainy seasons. The trees and crops were ever present proofs of the wetness of the rank, although fecund, soil, which is scarcely drained by a network of canals. At the willow-grown, marsh-bordered Po, the travelers found the country people repairing a bridge of boats, four of which, together with a mill, had been carried away by the freshet. Both the Po and Ticino were so swollen at this time that they seemed almost impassable barriers to the movements of any large body of troops.

Continuing the journey on northwards from Milan, along the Olona and Ticino, KEARNY and his friends arrived at Arona, only to find the town so invaded by the *Lago Maggiore* that they were forced to go ashore from the carriage as from a boat, by means of a plank resting upon a sill of the Hotel della Posta. Here they learned that the passage of the Simplon was impossible; that rains had occasioned such destruction that bridges and whole villages had been swept away; and the party were actually compelled to retrace their steps towards Turin, to get across the Alps by Mount Cenis.

KEARNY was now about to traverse the very ground fought over by the present belligerents, which had been the arena of the world since HANNIBAL halted under the immense cypress of Somma, said to be two thousand five hundred years of age, under which KEARNY had stood a day previous. This wonderful tree, one of the largest of its species known, stands on the field on which (B.C. 217) that great strategist of the world defeated the drenched and half-frozen legions of Scipio, for the contest took place in winter. Twenty-three feet in girth, it rises to the height of one hundred and twenty-one. Hannibal reposed under it, Julius Cæsar visited it, and Napoleon respected it, altering his road to spare such a living monument of the past.

From Arona, Kearny traveled through Oleggio to Novara, whose fortifications, once so important, were, in 1834, partially dismantled. Between this place and Oleggio, the road was bordered by rice fields and swamps, which render the country cold and unhealthy to its population, and mortal to strangers. Thence to Turin the country changed its character, and became at times woody, varied, and attractive.

Having thus traversed the western portion of the fighting ground of 1859, Kearny knew from actual survey that it was not wonderful that so little had been accomplished by the Austrians. The best proof of the admirable engineering of the invaders was, that they did move their hundred thousand troops and maintain them in a country which, in a rainy season, resembles the bottomless lands of the Netherlands, and is often converted into a district as much the dominion of water as of solid ground.

Such were the difficulties which the Austrians had to encounter when hostilities commenced, or rather, at the only time when a forward movement could have placed them in the heart of the Sardinian territory, and made them, with energy and generalship, masters of the situation. As American readers, however, will doubtless take but little interest in a campaign which, grand as it was, was dwarfed by our own great civil war of four years, and by the "Seven Weeks' War," in which Prussia inflicted a much more overwhelming defeat, at Sadowa, in 1866, upon Austria, than that of Solferino, in 1859, the following remarks will be confined to the principal collisions along the route upon which the Emperor, the Imperial Guard, and, consequently, Kearny operated.

The following table of comparative chronology of the events of the two campaigns in Italy, 1800 and 1859, conducted by the two Emperors, Napoleon I. (while First Consul) and Napoleon III., may be of interest, although there is no comparison between them as to the ability shown. The campaign of 1800 was a stroke of genius, based upon a plan, to which three, if not four of the finest military minds in Europe, Carnot, Moreau, Marescot, and

BUONAPARTE, contributed their ideas. Several generals of great ability co-operated with the suggestion of their especial experiences; among these latter, MARMONT, to whom was due the successful transportation of the artillery across the Alps. The campaign of 1859 displayed no genius, but a great amount of brilliant and desperate fighting, in which the talents of experienced officers could be brought to bear with combined power under the direction of a supreme authority, endowed with uncommon common-sense,* or the faculty of profiting to the utmost by the peculiar gifts of counsellors and subordinates.

KEARNY joined the French army at Alexandria, and there, with his usual liberality, gave a grand dinner to the officers with whom he was associated—what the medieval war-hero might have termed a "festival of swords," but those of the present era must more appropriately style the "festival of missiles." As KEARNY was attached to the Cavalry of the Guard, he took no personal part in the subordinate engagements, although he was an eye-witness of all that opportunity permitted, and a keen observer of the events of the compaign. An American gentleman who accompanied him to Italy, writes that even "in Paris, he (KEARNY) was much distinguished for the accuracy of his knowledge of military affairs, and his acquaintance with the strategy of the modern wars." With these facts established, what a pity it is that his correspondence from Italy in 1859, has disappeared beyond recovery, in an equal degree with the report of his experiences under the same flag in Algiers in 1840.

* "Sound sense is better than abilities."—WELLINGTON, 8th August, 1813. "Common sense is superior to genius."—PASCAL.

1800.

May 6th.—NAPOLEON I.—First Consul left Paris for Geneva.
" 14th-20th.—French Army crossed Mount St. Bernard.
" 20th.—NAPOLEON I. crossed Mount St. Bernard.
" 31st.—Sixty thousand French in Lombardy.
June 2d.—NAPOLEON I. entered Milan.
" 9th.—Battle of Montebello, in the Pass of the Stradella.
" 14th.—Battle of Marengo. Death of DESAIX.
" 15th.—Convention of Alexandria, having reconquered Italy in forty days.
July 2d-3d.—NAPOLEON I. back in Paris.

1859.

May 10th.—NAPOLEON left Paris.
" 12th.—His arrival at Genoa.
" 15th.—NAPOLEON III. at Alexandria with his army. One hundred and fifty thousand French in Italy.
" 20th.—Battle of Montebello.
" 31st. } June 1st. } Engagements at Palestro.
" 4th.—Battle of Magenta.
" 7th.—NAPOLEON III. entered Milan.
" 9th.—Combat of Melegnano, having conquered Lombardy in forty days, dating from the day he joined the army.
" 24th.—Battle of Solferino.
July 10th.—Peace of Villa Franca.
" 16th.—NAPOLEON III. back in Paris.

Notwithstanding the discipline of the opposing armies, which ought to have been perfect if mere drill could ensure perfection, the fact is worthy of note, that the Austrians, two hundred and fifty thousand strong, appeared to have no settled plan, and in almost every case the antagonists *happened* to meet "when no general battle was expected," just as the Federals and Rebels ran into each other at Gettysburg. Montebello resulted from a reconnoissance on the part of the Austrians; Magenta grew out of a combination of accidental circumstances, as far as its magnitude was concerned; and Solferino likewise. This is the view of one who followed the armies, who constantly refers to the "strange tactics of the Allies," "the slackness of pursuit;" remarks that they "did what they had done all along—advanced in the track of the Austrians," and compares this "advance," which ought to have been a sharp following-up of a worsted enemy, to "a military promenade in a rich country, by easy stages, not yet too hot," and in another place, "to an agreeable promenade in the park." The strategical movements, as regarded time, might be set down as "perfect failures."

Throwing aside the skirmishes and actions, which actually had little or no effect upon the main campaign, there were only three battles fought.

In the first, Montebello—20th May—the Allies had every reason to plume themselves on the result. It was a fair stricken field, and the Austrians were worsted in their trials, with every arm, and in every position.

This first action occurred upon a theatre whose glorious recollections must have inspired a people much less alive to such impressions than the French with almost invincible courage. It was upon the same field of Montebello that LANNES and VICTOR, on the 9th June, 1800, defended the Pass of Stradella, a strategic key-point, against the Austrians, and enabled the French forces to concentrate for the battle of Marengo, fought five days afterwards. This victory was due more to DESAIX—who purchased it with his life—and in a lesser degree to KELLERMAN, the younger, and MARMONT, than to NAPOLEON I. The latter could not agree for many years, either upon what took place or even what he wanted to appear should have taken place. The defeat of the Austrians, however, whether due to DESAIX or to NAPOLEON, gave the whole of Piedmont, Lombardy, and the Milanese into the hands of the

French, and as KELLERMAN said upon the field, of his charge, it placed the Imperial Crown upon the head of the first NAPOLEON, whose nephew and successor was awaiting the issue of the conflict of Montebello at almost the same distance from the immediate field of action as his uncle fifty-nine years previously.

The credit of this victory, won 20th May, 1859, although it must be shared with the Sardinian cavalry, whose charges were brilliant, was due in a great measure to General FOREY, who had fallen, in some degree, under the displeasure of LOUIS NAPOLEON in the Crimean campaign. This General amply redeemed himself. Americans will remember him for his capture of Puebla in Mexico, 16th–19th May, 1863, for which he was raised to the dignity of Marshal.

Montebello was a battle of charges and counter-charges—very much of the same stamp as Ligny, 1815, which was won by hard fighting. This contest is, moreover, remarkable from the fact that the French reinforcements—like those of the Rebels under KIRBY SMITH, whose arrival decided the first battle of Bull Run, 21st July, 1861, in their favor—were brought to the very field in railroad trains, and that the troops actually commenced a desultory fire upon the enemy from the windows of the cars.

The battle of Palestro, although creditable to the Sardinians and their King, and to the Zouaves, was comparatively a side issue.

At Magenta the grapple was long and doubtful. As at Torgau, in 1760, as at Marengo in 1800, the Austrian commander-in-chief telegraphed in mid-battle the gain of a victory. Everything turned upon the profitable employment of time. As at Aspern in 1809, the question was purely one of capacity to follow up a success. The slow Austrian was again no match for the quick Frenchman, who profited by the respite. Moreover, the Austrians lacked such men as our INGALLS to supply them. They displayed great intrepidity, but they fought on empty stomachs. The French brought up fresh troops on decisive points, and hurled them upon troops physically and morally exhausted, and so, throughout the history of the two nations, immense battle-fields were decided at particular points by mere fractions of the hosts engaged. For a long time the result was very doubtful, General McMAHON, created Marshal and Duke of Magenta, "saved the French army," and decided the victory, which was scarcely a victory, if the Austrians, according to custom, had not abandoned the field before the question was wholly fought out. The moment they commenced to retire the effect was the same as though they had been thoroughly defeated.

At Solferino—24th June—at one time affairs went very much as at our first Bull Run, while the hard fighting lasted, and the slightest inclination in the scales of fortune, either one way or the other, might have decided the result differently. As at Wagram, in 1809, a panic was reported in the rear of the French. General KEARNY always said, while he exalted to the skies the courage and conduct of the French, that it was a "touch and go" matter, and that if the advantages enjoyed by the Austrians had been duly employed as they should have been, the victory must have remained with them. It was very much like Gettysburg, with a different result. The Austrians occupied a fine position, and if the hearts of their men had been in their work, as those of the Army of the Potomac were, four years afterwards, in *their* work, Italy would not now be a United Kingdom.

The French were altogether as confident and determined as the Rebels; their heart was in the business before them, and they triumphed. Had our troops held the heights of Solferino, the superiority of the men would have compensated for the inferiority of their leaders. Solferino realized the remark of Major-General BECKWITH, B. A., a Waterloo veteran: "That every battle comes down to the last ten minutes, and that army wins which has ten minutes the most fight in it." KEARNY, throughout life, always seemed to have not only the decisive ten minutes fight in him, but ten minutes more to spare. Had the Austrians fought at Solferino as the English at Inkerman, "a soldier's fight," as the English commander admits, the French would not have had the ghost of a chance.

This, the decisive battle of the campaign, in many respects resembled our third day's fight of Gettysburg, provided the ridge we occupied had formed a comparatively staight line of ten or twelve miles, instead of a fish-hook of not over five miles in the extent of its curve. The Sardinians occupied the same relative position as the corps of the rebel EWELL; BENEDECK's corps representing our extreme right on Culp's Hill.

BENEDECK was posted not far from Lonato, where the first BONAPARTE, on the 3d August, 1796, signalized himself by frightening four thousand Austrians into laying down their arms to a detachment of about twelve hundred French. The knowledge of this exploit must have steeled the nerves of the Sardinians—many of whose forefathers served under NAPOLEON I—to an intrepidity akin to such high-souled determination. Castiglione, a little to the northwest of Solferino, was the scene of one of the French Republican victories of the same date as the preceding. This is credited to NAPOLEON, but in reality was due to AUGEREAU. When BONAPARTE "spoke only of retiring across the Po, it was on the earnest remonstrance of AUGEREAU that the resolution of marching against the enemy was adopted." AUGEREAU's resolution led to the victories of Lonato and Castiglione, and when that General was made a Marshal and a Duke, his title was derived from the latter, the field of his victory. Here again the Austrians threw up the game before it was decided, and their subsequent retreat proclaimed the triumph of the French.

The Heights of Solferino were to the Austrians what the prolongation of Cemetery Ridge—where WEBB met the shock and fury of the top high-tide wave of the "Slaveholder's Rebellion"—was to the Army of the Potomac.

PICKETT's charge was a repitition of the onset of the Foot Chasseurs and Volunteers of the Imperial Guard, which succeeded, captured the key-point, pierced the Austrian center, and decided the battle. PICKETT failed for the very reason that MANESQUE succeeded. The Army of the Potomac saved itself. Intuitively the Union troops streamed to the menaced point to feed the fight. On the contrary, the Austrians did not reinforce or replace the exhausted defenders of Solferino. Their army went to ruin in consequence, just as the Army of Northern Virginia would have gone to ruin then and there on that 3d July afternoon, had PICKETTS' repulse been followed up with energy; fully justifying the remark of the rebel sympathizer, the British Colonel FREEMANTLE:

"It is difficult to exaggerate the critical state of affairs as they appeared about this time. If the enemy, or their general, had shown any enterprise, there is no saying what might have happened. General LEE and his officers were evidently fully impressed with a sense of the situation."

In this battle the Austrian cavalry played the same part as BUFORD in the disastrous fight of Oak Ridge, 1st July, 1863. JOHN BUFORD, to your honor let it ever be remembered, that with your cavalry division of 2200 men (A. B. J. 152) you held at bay one-third of LEE's army until the First Corps came up; fought in support of the infantry all through that sultry summer day; and when all seemed to have gone to wreck, you presented such an imposing front to the successful enemy, as enabled the beaten troops to establish themselves on Cemetery Ridge! "The steadfast front of BUFORD's cavalry in the flat to the left of our position, deterred the enemy from pursuing."

The Austrian cavalry exhibited the same self-sacrificing devotion. The Brigade MENSDORFF* boldly advanced into the plain of Medole, on the Austrian left, to draw the fire of the French artillery upon it, and thus to extricate the Austrian artillery—subjected to a front and flank fire—from the awkward position in which it found itself. The cavalry succeeded in this act of noble devotion, and accomplished its object, although at a heavy loss.

About 2 P. M. the cavalry of the Imperial Guard, under MORRIS, to whose staff KEARNY was attached, came up to relieve the Second Corps, McMAHON, fill the gap left by the advance of that corps, and connect the Fourth Corps, under Marshal NIEL, with the Third, under CANROBERT. This advance of this magnificent body of horse was represented in a spirited sketch from the pencil of M. R. DE LA GIRONNERRIE, Lieutenant in the Dragoons of the Empress EUGENIE, published in the Paris "*Illustration.*" They came up, Chasseurs, Dragoons, Lancers, Cuirassiers, in column of squadrons, having accomplished six leagues† at full trot or gallop, in the midst of horrible clouds of dust, across a country very "impracticable" for cavalry, and assumed a position in front of the Austrian infantry. These last attempted to make a break when the Light Brigade of Chasseurs d'Afrique and Guides were let loose upon them. At

---

* (See RŒMER, page 22) There was an Austrian Colonel, MENSDORFF, who, in September, 1813, distinguished himself at the head of a body of cavalry, hovering upon all the French communications between Dresden, Leipsic, and Torgau."—CUSTS' WARS, 2, 4, 107. Could this be the same man, still a bold dragoon, and, like RADETZKY, an enterprising leader, in a green old age,

† This was nothing to the exploits of the Mounted Troops of the "inimitable TORSTENSON." (STUART's *History of Infantry, page* 85.) "Will the cavalry of the present day march fifteen miles" (German; sixty to seventy-five English) "and fight a battle, as did the cavalry of TORSTENSON in 1645 (23d November, 1644,) at Iuterbok." ("STEINMETZ's *Musketry Instruction for the Cavalry Carbine and Pistol*, page 14). For this battle of Iuterbok, see J. W. de P's TORSTENSON, page 111. What made the achievement of the Swedish Cavalry the more wonderful, they performed this march "on one fodder" (TORSTENSON to WRANGEL, 24th November, 1644), and nothing saved even the remnant of the Imperialists, which escaped, but the complete exhaustion of the victor's animals. Near Juterbok (ALISON, iv. 152, I.), the Prussian Landwehr, many armed with pikes (SCHERR's BLUCHER, iii. 138-40), gave the "bravest of the brave," NEY, a thorough beating, and placed the name of BULOW OF DENNEWITZ in the rank of Prussia's greatest heroes.

the same time General MORRIS supported this movement with his Lancers, Dragoons, and Cuirassiers. The Austrian infantry were completely overthrown, as well as the Dragoons of the Austrian Imperial Guard and the Hungarian Hussars, reputed the finest cavalry in Europe, who attempted to save their comrades on foot.

When the order was despatched to the Chasseurs d'Afrique to make their brilliant onset above referred to—likewise depicted by the Chevalier GIACCOMELLI in the "*Illustration*"—KEARNY requested permission from General MORRIS to go forward and witness this charge of his old comrades of Africa. KEARNY had beheld how they charged the Kabyles and Arabs; he wanted to see if they could scatter and slaughter the Austrians in a like peculiar way.* "*When the charge took place he* (KEARNY) *participated in it, holding his bridle in his teeth, with his characteristic impetuosity.*" "Among the officers in this charge I can only remember" —continues the letter of a Boston gentleman who accompanied KEARNY to Italy—"JEROME BONAPARTE PATTERSON," a West Point graduate, and American, from Baltimore. "Twenty-seven officers and non-commissioned officers were among the killed and wounded" of the Chasseurs. A relative, formerly an officer United States Dragoons, adds, that "General MORRIS slightly reproved KEARNY" for thus allowing his ardor to carry him away, but, as KEARNY says in his own letter that he "was not only present with the line of our (French) cavalry skirmishers, but as well in *every* charge that took place," the reproof was doubtless that of a fond father, who, fearing the loss of a daring boy, reproves the act in such an evident tone of admiration as to nerve and stimulate to greater deeds of daring gallantry. This brief reference to KEARNY, filled out by his own sententious avowal, constitutes him a grand figure in the glorious participation of the Cavalry of the French Imperial Guards in the tremendous conflict of Solferino. It shows that an American Volunteer played his part with sufficient distinction and audacity to attract the attention and win the applause of an army of which it was remarked, in one of their previous invasions of Italy, that they marched to death with as gay a disregard of life as if they had the assurance of rising again from the dead to renew the struggle the

* The French Cavalry "did little or nothing on that occasion" (the Italian War of 1859). The French Cavalry was positively wasted on the march, rendered unfit for action, and reduced to insignificant dimensions. (STEINMETZ, 21-2, "Miscellanées Militaires, by General Grand, President of the Cavalry Commission at the French War Office, p. 20.")

next day, or like the ancient British who "made their boast that they exposed their bare bosoms and white tunics to the lances and swords of the men at arms with as much confidence as if they had been born invulnerable."

It is very curious that the Austrians contemplated the very movement which MEADE, according to WARREN, had in view on the 2d July at Gettysburg, to turn the rebel flank, and that the rebels actually attempted, 2d July, P. M., when so signally checked by SICKLES. In both cases, Gettysburg and Solferino, the idea of turning was abandoned, and the affair came down to a parallel fight, culminating in an attempt to pierce the center, which in the former case failed, and in the latter case succeeded.

Thus General KEARNY, who had commenced his education for a general's command in Africa, with the study of a war with light troops, and took his next lessons in the Mexican war in grand tactics and strategy—most beautifully carried out in TURENNE style, although on a small scale as regarded numbers—completed his course of instruction in a campaign on the grandest scale, since the Allies and the Austrians brought on the battle-field at Solferino almost, if not altogether, double the numbers engaged on our side or the Rebels' in any battle during the "Slaveholders' Rebellion." It is true that the numbers we had on paper at Chancellorsville and at the Wilderness approached somewhat those of the opposing armies at Solferino. A great proportion of these could be as little counted as actually engaged, as the corps of 20,000 men under JEROME NAPOLEON, which was on the march towards the scene of conflict on the Mincio (1859), or the army of the ARCHDUKE JOHN at the epoch of Wagram, 1809.* Had the latter brought his forces into action, as he could have done with ease had he intended so to do, their co-operation would have settled the fate of the First NAPOLEON, and obviated all the horrors of 1812, especially at Borodino and the Beresina; of 1813, particularly at Leipsic; of 1814, and of 1815, at Waterloo.

RŒMER in his charming book "On Cavalry" says, that all the actions of the campaign of 1859 were decided by bayonet charges.† This would have been totally impossible in our war, for the charging

* "An Austrian army, to the end of time, will never cease to be procrastinating." (CUSTS' WARS, *2d Series*, iv., 83.

† RŒMER'S "*Cavalry; its History, Management, and Uses in War.*" Chap. iii. 113-115, etc.

column, if of any extent of front, would have been annihilated at a distance by the artillery or musketry fire. This is proved by the (our) medical returns. HANCOCK's charge at Williamsburgh, of which so much was said at the time, was a myth.* McCLELLAN reported it as he reported everything. His system of laudation was nothing more than a part and parcel of his system of self-deception, an exuberance of kind-heartedness. In his injustice (charged in KEARNY's letters in 1861–'2, and from the Peninsula), if nothing else, he did resemble NAPOLEON. HANCOCK should not object to having the truth told about Williamsburgh. He is a brilliant soldier, and can afford to discard laurels not actually won, since he is entitled to so many which he did win fairly and magnificently.

KEARNY's military education was now complete. He had prepared himself thoroughly for a general's command. How he discharged the duties of that position when called upon, the country well knows.

For his brilliant soldiership in the campaign of Solferino, KEARNY received the Cross of the "Legion of Honor"† from the French Emperor. He was very proud of *this* distinction, because he was the *first* American who had ever been thus honored for *military* service.

Little did KEARNY dream when he saw one hundred and forty thousand to one hundred and fifty thousand French and Sardinians, marshalled along a front of ten to twelve miles, that he would live to see within three years one million five hundred thousand free

* His first laurels were gained at Williamsburg; but the story of a celebrated charge that gave him the day's applause and McClellan's encomium of the "superb HANCOCK,' was altogether fictitious. The musket, not the bayonet, gave him the victory." "*Campaigns of a Non-combatant*," by GEO. ALFRED TOWNSEND, 1866, page 73.) Compare DE TROBRIAND, I. 201; Capt. BLAKE, 84, &c.

† It has been stated, and the statement has been repeated by American writers, and a French military author, also, who ought to have known whether the fact was so or not, that PHILIP KEARNY received the *Cross of the Legion Honor* from LOUIS PHILIPPE, for his gallantry in Algiers in (1839?) 1840. The writer is of opinion that this is partly a fact and partly an error. KEARNY was at that time an officer in the military service of the United States, and consequently *could not* accept any foreign decoration. That the story is current, and has been repeated by a gentleman who had ample opportunities of knowing the truth, renders it very probable that LOUIS PHILIPPE, on the recommendation of his sons, the DUKE OF ORLEANS, who commanded a division and corps, with whom KEARNY served in Africa, and the DUKE D'AUMALE, who served with the very regiment to which KEARNY was attached, offered KEARNY the cross, which his military obligations to the United States compelled him to refuse. KEARNY was too modest a man to mention such a fact himself, but doubtless this is a true explanation of the case. Although he was the first American who ever received the Cross of Honor for *military service*, was he the first who received it for *gallantry in action?*

Americans of the North, marshalled along a line of fifteen hundred miles against from five hundred thousand to one million supporters of slavery and their savage allies. Much less did he dream when he *saw* the confusion which reigned at times in the vast trains accompanying the French army and sometimes precluded the advance of troops, when rapid movements were indispensable to decisive success, that he would see armies, as great as ours, fed with the regularity of a family; and that same RUFUS INGALLS—who fitted out his little expedition against the Rogue River Indians in 1851—in 1861–'5 feeding the Army of the Potomac, and moving trains more numerous than those of the Allies, over roads so bad that no European quartermaster could conceive their badness, with almost the certainty of a well regulated machine. KEARNY could appreciate and exemplify the nobility and extent of American courage. He was yet to learn the scope and grandeur of American intelligence as applied to logistics or military intendancy, in which the French were hitherto supposed to excel all other nations.

CHAPTER XVI.

"THE TYPE VOLUNTEER GENERAL OF THE WAR."

"Denn Blitze Gottes spruhte dein Blick! dein Ruf
War Donner! Siegeszeichen dein Federbusch!
Dein Arm War Sturm! Dein Schwert den Deutschen
Leitender, tilgender Strahl dem Feinde!"

STOLBERG'S "*Ode to* BLUCHER."

"A Governor not too *im*-perfect would have recognized this GUSTAVUS, what his purposes and likelihoods were; the feeling would have been, checked by due circumspectness, '*Up, my men! let us follow this man; let us live and die in the cause this man goes for. Live otherwise with honor, or die otherwise with honor, we cannot, in the pass things have come to.*'"

CARYLE'S FREDERIC THE GREAT, I., 249.

"And 'mid this tumult KUBLA heard from far
Ancestral voices prophecying war." COLERIDGE.

"In native swords and native ranks
The only hope of safety dwells." BYRON.

"The trade of war demands no saints."

SIR WALTER SCOTT'S "*Abbot.*"

"This WALPOT—a citizen of Bremen, first Grand Master of the Knights Hospitalers—was not by birth a nobleman, but his deeds were noble."

CARLYLE'S "FREDERIC THE GREAT," I., 84.

WAR is a difficult science, which cannot be mastered by experience alone; its principles and rules require *careful study* and *reflection.* Lessons picked up at random are generally uncertain or erroneous, often costly to him who receives them, and almost always fatal to the State. "Whatever argument," says WASHINGTON, "may be drawn from particular examples, superficially viewed, a thorough examination of the subject will evince that the art of war is both comprehensive and complicated; that it demands much previous study, and that the possession of it in its most improved and perfect state is always of great moment to a nation." NAPOLEON I. admitted, after fourteen campaigns and unparalleled successes, that *experience in war, familiarity with the combat, and the best developed war-like virtues, were insufficient to form good officers; and regretted that most of his generals had not had opportunities to acquire the theoretical knowledge they were so much in need of.* FREDERIC II. thought in like manner, and in a characteristic letter, which he wrote to General FOUQUET, he remarked: "*Of what use is* EXPERIENCE *if it is not guided by* REFLECTION?"

RŒMER'S "*Cavalry; Its Uses,*" &c.

"Reading and Discourse are requisite to make a soldier perfect in the Art Military, *how great soever his practical knowledge may be.*"

MONK, *Duke of Albermarle.*

"By the Portuguese law" (when Portugal was a country whose influence was felt) "every person was bound to serve in this force" (militia, called Ordonenzas) "for the defence of the country, from eighteen to sixty years of age. They were organized in battalions of two hundred and fifty men each, under the command of the chief landed proprietors of the district, and, *invariably*, whether against the Moors or Spaniards, *rendered more important services to their country than the regular army.*" STUART'S "*History of Infantry.*"

"No regular army, but every citizen a soldier."

Motto of the Swiss Confederacy

"Militare nihil est, sed sapere necesse est."

Roman axiom, from "*Les Evolutions de Ligne,*" *by*
Colonel LAVELAINE DE MAUBEUGE.

On the 18th June, 1816, the Prussian visitors at Carlsbad got up a festival in honor of the anniversary of *Belle Alliance* (Waterloo), but, already, among certain classes, had 1813 (the uprising of the German PEOPLE) been so completely forgotten that the aristocracy wished to celebrate the *occasion entirely* distinct from the citizens. "Nonsense!" with an oath, said BLUCHER, and attended the banquet of the Citizens, although their invitation was subsequent to that of the Caste, to which he *seemed* to belong. "Badges of honor, titles, dignities, rewards, precious and various, have fallen to my lot," spoke BLUCHER, in answer to the toast in his name, "but I find the most gratifying recompense in the love of my fellow-citizens, in the respect of my associates, and in the consciousness of having done my duty." Then he repaired to the entertainment of the YUNKERS (equivalent as a rule, *with glorious*—is it profane to say *god-like—exceptions*, to the caste of Federal officials), and expressed himself with BLUCHER-like clearness: "The sons of citizens and nobles"* (parallels in their own conceit, are to be found in plenty in this country), "have fought out this conflict (Germany's War of Liberation), side by side, with equal bravery; and, therefore, should they now dance, and associate, and rejoice over the victory together, like brothers."

JOHANN SCHERR'S "BLUCHER," III., 419.

Several of the greatest generals noted in history were born great captains, developed their immense powers by study, and stepped from civil life or authority into military commands on the grandest scale. LUCULLUS, in antiquity, is the ex-

* Was there no exhibition of this exclusiveness of caste exhibited during our great war? The reader will find in TOWNSEND'S "*Campaigns of a* "*Non-combatant*" the following sentence, at page 269: "Not the least among the causes of the North's inefficiency will be found the ill-feeling between the professional and civil soldiery; a Regular contemns a Volunteer; a Volunteer hates a Regular." The writer has heard similar expressions of opinion and feeling from Volunteer officers who served with marked distinction. But there were god-like exceptions to any assumption of superiority among the Regulars; among these Major-Generals HOOKER, HUMPHREYS, PLEASANTON, and many others, friends, whom every patriot delights to cherish and honor.

ample quoted by FREDERIC THE GREAT. But it is needless to refer to such distant times. SPINOLA, CROMWELL, BLAKE, the GREAT CONDE, are well known examples; but the most remarkable, perhaps, is LORD CLIVE. "The fame of those who subdued ANTIOCHUS and TIGRANES grows dim when compared with the splendor of the exploits which the YOUNG ENGLISH ADVENTURER achieved at the head of an army not equal in numbers to one-half a Roman Legion. His name stands high on the roll of conquerors," "but it is found in a better list, on the list of those who have done and suffered much for the happiness of mankind." "It is hard to say whether he appears with more lustre as the hero whose single exploits laid the foundation of a mighty empire, or as the governor whose resolution and integrity stamped the characters which have given stability and permanence to its power." "LORD CLIVE'S *genius for war was intuitive; he had little instruction, and no counsellors, for he was one of the few men whose conduct was always directed by the dictates of his own mind*, and whose decisions were, therefore, secret. Like all great men, he took counsel only of himself; and like the first of the CÆSARS, the talents of other men could add little to his genius. *He was born a leader;* and the great LORD CHATHAM *pronounced him to be a heaven-born general;* for without experience, or being much versed in military affairs, he had surpassed all the officers of his time. *He was*, in truth, *compelled to form himself as well as his officers and his army;* and it is said that, *of the eight officers who commanded under him at the defence of Arcot, only two had ever been in action, and four out of the eight were mere factors of the* (East India) *Company*, induced by CLIVE'S example to volunteer their services. But although nothing is known of the steps he took to prepare himself for military life in youth, he was early remarkable for a bold and adventurous spirit. An aversion to control marked his boyhood and his maturity. . . . . He certainly devoted much of his time, on his arrival at Madras, and for the first five years of his residence there, to reading, during which period he must have acquired a considerable amount of knowledge. It would be unreasonable, therefore, to suppose that he was wholly indebted to his genius—nor are, indeed, men ever so—yet, doubtless, like all great minds, he could not only devise and decide, but he could communicate his ardent spirit to his followers, and awaken a devotion which can alone be acquired in war by great natural qualities. The East India Company never had a more zealous, upright, and efficient servant; and it is without question that Great Britain mainly owes her Eastern Empire to LORD CLIVE."

ALISON, MACAULAY and LIEUT.-GEN. HON. SIR EDWARD CUST.

MAJOR PHILIP KEARNY, decorated for resplendent soldiership abroad, brevetted for gallant and meritorious service at home, whose empty sleeve was a continual reminder which rendered words superfluous to tell that he had won his honors in "the fore-front of the heady fight"—had finished his most thorough course of preparation for a General's command. Having reached the age of forty-six years, he was now about to prove that the time devoted to perfecting himself in his profession had not been thrown away. His quickness of eye and peculiar faculty of acquiring at a glance a complete knowledge of the topography of any field of action—his unerring military sagacity—had as much to do with winning the Cross of the Legion of Honor, as his dash and intrepidity. In that short, sharp, and decisive Italian campaign of 1859, he had developed as much mind as action.

In the fall of 1860, and during the ensuing winter, startling events, treading upon the heels of events no less momentuous and unexpected, revealed the mournful fact that the peace which had blessed our country with half a century of prosperous development without a parallel, was about to terminate. The crisis towards which all the great events of American history had been tending, from the formation of the Government to the election of ABRAHAM LINCOLN, was at hand. The blackness which portended the tempest hung over the land. All hopes that the clouds would disperse had given way to an almost awful awaiting of the bursting of the storm It broke in the roar of the cannon which opened on Fort Sumter; but the menace of the preceding ominous thunder had been heard long before that artillery flashed forth the signal that "peace had ascended to Heaven."

No sooner had the tocsin of alarm resounded across the Atlantic, than KEARNY's patriotism responded to the appeal. There needed no fiery cross to summon him to arms. His own ardent spirit answered the invocation of his menaced Fatherland as instantly as the explosion of a gun follows the application of the match—as instantly as beacon was wont to answer beacon when the English coast or Scottish border was menaced by the foe.

KEARNY had always looked forward to an opportunity of shining in war under the flag of his country. But his wildest dreams had never pictured that he was to loom up the grandest military figure of a civil war in the United States, in whose presence all previous civil wars were to sink into insignificance.

Alas, the stage on which KEARNY was so greatly to deport himself, the theatre in which he was to display so admirably the results of his natural gifts when matured by experience, was no longer the Tell and the Atlas, the Alps and the Milanese, Africa and Italy, but his own dear country, convulsed by a Rebellion begotten of the "Barbarism of Slavery;" more barbarous in the spirit it had engendered that the savageness of the Kabyles, strangers to Christianity, against whom he had first flashed his sabre.

He was now about to draw his sword, not against the Mexican, the enemy of the United States; nor the Indian, the opponent of civilization; nor the Austrian, the foe of liberal ideas; but against traitors as criminal as those who linked their fortunes to the impious CATALINE; against patricides, who aimed their murderous steel against the Constitution and the laws—the integrity and the very existence of their native land.

His patriotism was all aflame; a patriotism which ordinary minds can scarcely conceive; a patriotism which very few men have sufficient magnanimity to appreciate. To him the word "Fatherland," or "native country" were not mere expressions or empty words. His associates had hitherto been chosen from that class of men—many of these Southerners, and their affiliations or connections, who were looked upon in Europe as the finest, nay, the only types of American gentlemen—for few men, however independent in their line of thought, can reason with BURNS:

> "The rank is but the guineas *stamp*,
> The man's the gold for a' that;"

Or with WYCHERLY:

> "I weigh the MAN, not his title;
> 'Tis not the king's stamp can make the metal better."

The majority of the ablest officers who betrayed their country, and broke their oaths of allegiance, had been his companions in arms. The reader will remember that three, who rose to high commands in the rebel army, one to the highest, were with him upon the first occasion in which he distinguished himself in Mexico, that reconnoisance which SCOTT styled the greatest of the campaign; and STONEWALL JACKSON's chosen successor in command, was with our hero in his charge into the very gate of the Aztec capital. His style of life, his taste for art and display, yes, it may as well be admitted, his strong inclination for luxurious and elegant ease, were more consistent with the habitudes of Southern than Northern life and manner of living.

But there is often a depth of feeling in individuals of this type which falsifies the judgment of ordinary men. CAVOUR was an example of this. In the bosom of the man of the world and the "lion of society" beat the heart of a patriot; of a statesman, as alive to the interests of his country, as a FRANKLIN or an ADAMS or a WASHINGTON. The flame may not have been as pure, according to the superficial judgment of the world—because the world judges simply by the outside—but it was as ardent and unselfish. *Self* disappeared before the question of COUNTRY. "*What am I,*" exclaimed KEARNY, "*if no longer an American?*" This exclamation summed up the whole argument. He, the soldier, who had served all over this Continent, had learned what a magnificent empire acknowledged our sway; he, the wanderer, who had traversed land and sea, had learned what nationality meant. "CIVES ROMANUS SUM" had been the watchword which carried a citizen of the greatest Republic of antiquity safe and respected throughout the then known world. It enabled him to brave the despot on his throne, and daunt the savage in his wild. Years after that grand old Republic had lapsed into a centralized absolutism—God grant that such be not the fate of ours. ST. PAUL, the true exemplar of a Christian gentleman, the greatest examplar of manhood, owed his safety to his declaration to the Centurion and Chief Captain that he was a *free-born* Roman citizen. Even so KEARNY felt with regard to his birthright: "*I am an American citizen, was his boast, his defence, and his pride.*" "He loved his country, its grand present, its almost infinitely grander future. He saw the crumbling of foreign empires, the worthless trial of foreign greatness. He saw clearly how all that was old was destined to sure decay, and how much the world was to owe to the freedom, the education, the civilization of the American Republic. And then, too, America was his country. To her he had sworn allegiance. For her he had lost his arm; for her he had braved death on every battle-field from Vera Cruz to Mexico, and at the hands of the treacherous savage. And so to save the nation, to do his part to secure her existence, and to put down villainy and insanity, which threatened her life, *though dissuaded by all his military friends in Paris,* he hastened to give all the energies of his nature to the cause of his dear country. Those who conversed with him and knew the thoughts of his heart, those alone can know how firm and unalloyed was the patriotism which brought him home."

"We parted in Paris, in 1860,—" are the words of a letter from an officer who served, in 1859, with the Sardinians, as KEARNY did with the French—"and I returned home, and I remember his last request was to let him know the state of affairs in the United States. As soon as the secession of the Southern States appeared inevitable I informed him to that effect, and received for answer that he would immediately return home to offer his services to the Administration in the war; concluding by saying that he had no trust or confidence in the Southern men or measures from the start, and that they were unfit to govern themselves, even if they should succeed in establishing their independence, as there was nothing practical about them." General MUFFLING, in his "*Passages from My Life*," has (page 267–'8) an apposite remark in this connection: "The great mass of the French people are very intelligent, but there are many vain, egotistical, and quarrelsome individuals amongst them, *who must be summarily dealt with.* One who yields appears to them weak; he who changes his measures, inconsistent and trifling." KEARNY saw through the Southerners as MUFFLING did the French. It is a pity that our government did not act in 1865 as BLUCHER and MUFFLING did in 1815. The matter would have been settled, if blows became absolutely necessary, at the cost of a score or two of lives! This would have established tranquility and secured its continuance. There would have been no more talking of renewing the struggle, but peaceable if not cheerful obedience to the inevitable.

"I suppose you are already familiar with the cool treatment he received from the government on his application for service, and he seemed on more than one occasion to me to think seriously of giving up all hope of employment by the action of the Administration, but *persevered until his claims were acknowledged.*"

At that time it was not thought necessary to have trained soldiers to command our raw levies, and their merits were never fully acknowledged throughout the war, or KEARNY's "splendid *coup d'œil;* his quiet judgment, *sang-froid,* and prompt decision; his electric influence, with his soldiers and splendid valor, would have been sooner acknowledged.

Early in the spring of 1861, on receiving the first reliable intelligence of his country's imminent peril, KEARNY broke up his luxurious establishment in Paris, took ship for the United States, and without the loss of an hour, as soon as he arrived in New York, proceeded on to Washington to offer his services to the President.

Well may his eulogist declare, that he was not welcomed as he should have been. It was with KEARNY as it had been with many an able man before him. He was rejected because the mine of untold preciousness was concealed beneath the modest demeanor inseparable from true gentility and heroism. Even so, FERDINAND II., Emperor of Austria, rejected KONIGSMARCK, a man very much akin to KEARNY in his military qualifications. Even so, LOUIS XIV. refused with scorn the services of PRINCE EUGENE, the greatest general ever thus vouchsafed for the salvation of Austria. Even so, FREDERIC THE GREAT turned his back upon LAUDON, because he did not like his books; and learned by sad experience that he had driven into the enemy's ranks the most dangerous adversary and the ablest general the King encountered in his whole subsequent career. Each of these monarchs were akin to him.

——" whose hand,
Like the base Judean, threw a pearl away,
Richer than all his tribe."

But although KEARNY was like to KONIGSMARCK, and to Prince EUGENE, and to LAUDON in his eminent ability, his spirit was none of theirs. Undeserved mis-appreciation and rejection could not arm his hand against the authority which would not recognize his merit, nor glue his sword to its scabbard. From the President of the United States he turned to the Governor of his native State. The reader will remember that, when the Federal Government first called upon the loyal Executives to furnish their appropriate quotas of troops, it was generally understood that the different Governors were to be permitted to appoint a number of general officers, in proportion to the numerical force organized within their jurisdictions. Thus it was—through local political influence—that John A. Dix obtained his Major-General's commission.

Up to this time, KEARNY had never claimed to be otherwise than a citizen of the "Empire State." He was a New Yorker, born and bred. Like his uncle—Major-General STEPHEN WATTS KEARNY—before him, he had been appointed to the United States army from New York. The majority of his interests lay in his native city, derived from ancestors who never had any connection with another State. Consequently, on the advice of Lieutenant General SCOTT, he hastened back from the Capital of the nation to the Capital of his native State, there to prefer his claims for appointment as a General—due to him as a citizen of acknowledged talent, of experienced ability, of tried valor, who had proved himself under his own and foreign ensigns, always, everywhere, "every inch a soldier."

His life-long career, his very record of service, ought to have been sufficient to have obtained for him one of the four Major or Brigadier-Generalships to which the State of New York was entitled. That his arrival was not unnoticed, and that the man himself was well-known, is demonstrated by the following article, of which a copy was furnished for this work as soon as its preparation was made known.

"Among the late arrivals, we notice the name of that distinguished officer, Major KEARNY, late of the army.

"Major KEARNY, after an absence of two or three years, returns home to offer his services in the support of our Government and the flag under which he has so nobly battled. He is now at Albany, urging upon the Governor his *claims* to a high position *in the Volunteer force of the State.* In this connection, it will not be amiss to state what have been Major KEARNY'S services and military experience.

"He entered our army in 1836 as Lieutenant of Dragoons, and for years served on our Western frontier, under that able and distinguished officer, STEPHEN WATTS KEARNY, then Colonel of First Dragoons, and afterwards in connection with Commodore STOCKTON, the Conqueror and Military Governor of California. Major KEARNY afterwards served in the war with Mexico, and lost an arm in a gallant charge at the City of Mexico. General SCOTT mentions him as among 'the bravest of the brave.'

"In addition to his almost constant military duty in this country, he had the glory of serving a campaign in Africa, under the DUKE d'ORLEANS, and still later he served with the French Cavalry at *Solferino*, and received from the Emperor public acknowledgment of his service and bravery, and a decoration of the Legion of Honor.

"Few men have seen more active service, and still fewer of our countrymen have ever witnessed the movements of such large and splendid armies.

"His valuable experience should not be refused at this time, when *we are so sadly in want of experienced commanders* WITHOUT A TAINT OF TREASON. Such is Major KEARNY. His time, his fortune, his great experience, are freely offered, and should be accepted by *his native State.*"

KEARNY bore with him to Albany a certificate from Lieutenant-General SCOTT, Commander-in-Chief of the United States army, of which the following is a copy:

HEADQUARTERS OF THE ARMY,
WASHINGTON, May 1, 1861.

To His Excellency Governor MORGAN, *of New York:*

SIR:—I beg leave to suggest *Major* PHILIP KEARNY, *of New York*, late a distinguished officer of the army, for a high commission in the *New York Volunteers.* Major KEARNY'S long and valuable experience in actual military service seems to commend him as a useful as well as a valuable commander and disciplinarian. He is among the bravest of the brave, and of the highest military spirit and bearing.

With the highest respect,
Your Excellency's
Most obedient servant,
(Signed) WINFIELD SCOTT.

It would scarcely be believed that the claims of such a man were ignored in favor of individuals who had scarcely more to recommend them than the presumption with which they preferred their applications, and the want of principle with which those applications were pressed and backed by ignorant politicians, and worse. The letters of many of our influential citizens, men of acknowledged judgment and worth, received no more attention than the testimonial of General SCOTT, of which KEARNY himself justly wrote, 8th May, 1864: "General SCOTT'S letter to Governor MORGAN is certainly very strong, and I presume it is the only testimony of the kind that he has ever extended to any individual." KEARNY chafed terribly under the treatment to which he was subjected.

But why linger on this theme, so disgraceful to that body of men who had the power to put the "right man in the right place," to do their duties by their State and country, and did it not. They were politicians; that stamps their action. Sufficient to say, Governor MORGAN was not to blame—a gentleman, an able man, an upright Governor, whose talent for organization was felt throughout the whole war.

Rejected by his native State—would that the fact did not blemish its record—KEARNY returned to Washington. To the eternal honor of New Jersey and her citizens, they could appreciate him. Let him who doubts this read the eloquence of one of her sons and compare it with the feeling language of that Memorial Address from the pen of another—one to whom his appointment was subsequently due—one who prepared and delivered a noble tribute to KEARNY'S memory, which the writer will freely quote with grateful acknowledgments—CORTLANDT PARKER, Esq., of Newark,* the counsel and friend of the patriot soldier, whom he knew how to appreciate and commemorate:

"More nearly than any other, he (KEARNY) represented in his views and theory the popular conception as to the method upon which the war should be fought. He reflected, moreover, more truly than any other high commander, the exalted, unselfish, uncalculating patriotism which glowed in the hearts of the people. His fiery nature took affront at every attempt to dwarf the grand conquest into anything else than a struggle for the sublime principle of nationality. He had no confidence in politicians, but little respect for dignitaries, no love for anything but the cause. Intriguers, cowards, martinets, small men essay-

* Nor let his coadjutors in this patriotic work be forgotten.—PET. HALSTEAD, Esq., and H. N. CONGER, Esq., of Newark, New Jersey.

ings to crowd down great ones, he detested with implacable detestation. But to courage and upright manliness, he lifted his hat with instinctive reverence. For the soldier, whether officer or private, who cherished a genuine pride in his profession, and labored, only for duty's sake, to excel in every requirement of the service, he had esteem unbounded—not always exhibited, indeed, by outward act, but none the less genuine and profound. In battle, fierce as a lion, on parade sometimes stern and impetuous, almost to injustice; in the hospital, by the bedside of the wounded and dying, his heart grew tender, his voice as soft as a woman's; even his touch had healing in it. Men who only saw him with the hood of pride upon his face, judged him incapable of emotion. They did not know how, under all the hard crust, there lurked the tenderest thoughtfulness for the health, comfort, and lives of his command; how, out of his own purse, he ministered to their wants; how, even in the heat of battle, thoughts of home and kindred, like flashes of sunshine, illumined the stony, stoical nature; how, in the battle-pauses, he was wont to pen messages of remembrance from the ghastliest field to those who, afar off, watched his plume with solicitude and affection. It is no wonder, indeed, that men misjudged him; he had no mirror set in his breast that all the world might see and know his thoughts; rather, he was reticent, reserved, surrounded by a hauteur which few men cared to penetrate; and so, in the estimation of all but a few intimates, he suffered a sort of martyrdom, when he should have been crowned a king of men."

"And so PHILIP KEARNY, after weeks of waiting at the doors of the New York Executive, jostled by political intriguers, turned away in perfect disgust, absolutely unable, since he could not be a private with one arm, to find a place where he could serve the country he had come three thousand miles to fight for.

"Accident placed a Jersey friend in possession of the fact that he was in America.

"The noble first brigade of three year's troops was then gathering for the field, from which so few of them returned. It was evident at a glance that all such men needed was a leader who could appreciate their merits. Without Major KEARNY's knowledge, this friend hastened to urge his appointment to command them. It was a matter of much more difficulty than he imagined.

Looking back, it seems inconceivable how it could have cost so much exertion to secure the appointment of such a man to such a place. It took nearly three months to accomplish it. Not till Bull Run had illustrated our need of educated, experienced soldiers was it done. And how, in the meantime, did the restless spirit of the patriot hero chafe at the delay—for he knew his own capacity and appreciated the character of the war. Sure that the nation would

* FOSTER's "New Jersey and the Rebellion." Chapter XLV. 804–'5.

eventually triumph, he knew, then, nevertheless, that it was all which experience has found it to be."

Then the NEWS of BULL RUN came.

The writer cannot close this chapter without making a few remarks in regard to Bull Run. Never was a battle more misrepresented or misunderstood. The panic which occurred neither originated with the troops who were engaged, nor those who did the hard fighting, nor did it assume its disgraceful proportions through them. The whole matter was more or less intentionally misrepresented by such as Mr. RUSSELL, who ought to have known better, and HIS story not THE story was read all over the world in the columns of a paper enjoying the most extensive circulation, a paper the most hostile to the North, and the most deliberate detractor of its people and of its armies.

Had Mr. RUSSELL been as well read in military matters as he assumed to be, and was believed to have been, he would have refrained from using his pen so freely, since foreign history contains more disgraceful panics among her regular troops than occurred at Bull Run among our militia. Major-General BARNARD, United States Engineers, refers to a number of instances of these unaccountable panics, dissolutions of armies, or "*debacles*," as the French say, in his work: "The C. S. A. and the Battle of Bull Run." The writer, also, immediately after the occurrence and before the general had taken up his pen, wrote several articles in vindication of our men and collected a number—which might easily be increased tenfold—of instances of panics in regular armies far exceeding that of the 21st July, 1861, in our aggregation of raw troops, for that could scarcely be termed an army in which the regiments had only been brigaded for the first time on their march towards the enemy, and had never been manœuvered together as brigades or divisions. "Passing over without comment or consideration the plans and action of General McDOWELL, critical examination will disclose the truth that it was no want of courage and conduct on the part of our privates that lost the battle; the fault lay with their immediate officers and with men who have strangely escaped the blame, and risen to high commands." Moreover, had our rear-guard or reserve division been brought into the field, or even a part of it, to counteract the effects of the arrival of KIRBY SMITH, Bull Run, instead of a defeat, would have been a victory, had not God for the welfare of the country willed it otherwise.

On 28th August, 1640, the Scotch forded the Tyne at Newburn, and attacked the English army, 6,000 strong, "which fled with a speed and disorder unworthy of their national reputation."

At Tippermuir, 1st September, 1644, the defeated Lowlanders, volunteers, fighting for the House of Hanover, accustomed to the use of arms and bred in a warlike age, fled so precipitately that "many broke their wind, and died in consequence."

At Philiphaugh, 13th September, 1645, the army of Montrose, after five resplendent victories, won against great odds, was annihilated in an equal degree to that of DE GUEBRIANT, at Tuttlingen.

At the Pass of Killecrankie, 17th June, 1689, CLAVERHOUSE, with an army of undisciplined Highlanders, dissipated a regular army of Anglo-Scotch troops, under a tried and reliable general, MACKAY. The flying regulars abandoned cannon and everything else; two regiments alone stood fast (like our reserve), while all the rest were routed.

On Sunday, 13th November, 1715, an engagement took place at Sheriffmuir, between the loyal Anglo-Scottish army under the DUKE OF ARGYLE, and the rebel under the EARL OF MAR, which was the counterpart of Bull Run in many particulars. The EARL, victorious on the left, nevertheless drew off to Ardoch; while the DUKE, equally successful on the right, withdrew to Dumblane. On both sides the left fled, while the right maintained their ground. The English General WHITHAM "fled almost to Stirling Bridge."

At Preston, 20th September, 1745, the English troops either laid down their arms, or ran; and the witty Lord KERR observed of their commander, SIR JOHN COPE, "that he believed he was the first general in Europe who had brought the first tidings of his own defeat."

About the same remark was addressed to the COUNT OF CLERMONT, Commander-in-Chief of the French, routed at Crevelt, 23d June, 1758, when spurring into Neuss, he demanded, "if many of his runaways had passed that way." "No, my lord; you are the first—far ahead."

Two or three more British achievements in this line may not be unacceptable to American readers. When RUSSELL touched up his account of Bull Run in colors borrowed from the privilege of romantic narrative, had he forgotten the stern facts of the "Race of Castlebar," or the "Castlebar Races," where 1,150 French and "some few of the malcontent peasantry," (CUST), or 800 French and about 1,000 peasants, with two light guns, (GORDON), attacked, 27th August, 1798, 2,000 or 3,000 English regulars (CUST), with 14 pieces of artillery in a good position. The English broke and ran; some to Tuam, 38 miles from the field of battle, that same night, and an officer with 60 riflemen, in 27 hours made good his race to Athlone, 80 miles from Castlebar. None of our men beat that.

Take Plattsburg, 11th September, 1814, as another nice example, where MACOMB, with 1,500 regulars and about 1,500 militia and volunteers, defeated or drove back 12,000 British regulars, "with a most excellent train of artillery" (these are the British General CUST'S figures), the veterans of many wars, and the conquerors of NAPOLEON'S best generals and troops in Spain. General SMITH, B. A., on page 186 of his "Precis of the Wars of Canada," says: "Several very efficient and excellent brigades were forwarded from Bordeaux, from the Duke of Wellington, to Canada." So that these, the veteran conquerors of veteran conquerors, were soon to be repulsed by raw American troops of the line, volunteers and militia, defending the line of the Saranac, a stream which, if in the same condition, as stated, that it was when the writer saw it, ought to have been forded in line of battle, like the Tagliamento by the French, 16 March, 1797. The result of this action was the precipitate retreat of the British army, leaving behind them their sick and wounded to the humanity of the Americans. Gen. CUST admits that a panic occurred among the British troops in the attack on Fort Erie. But scarcely anything equals the results of WHITELOCK'S operations in Buenos Ayres, when the British general not only capitulated and abandoned his own field, but, to save his beaten army—beaten through the incapacity of their own commander—yielded the previous glorious conquest of Sir SAMUEL AUCHMUTY, which was not endangered.

All fought-out, mis-handled troops are liable to panics; and shame to him who, on that account, charges cowardice on the Anglo-Saxon race.

Such reference to the past is only justifiable to meet the aspersions and unmerited sarcasms of a people who egged us on to the Great American Conflict, and then wickedly abandoned us; a government "Perfide Albion," which, when our nation, in its agony asked for a cup of cold water for the sake of common lineage, and language, and liberty, took a sponge, dipped it in vinegar, and thrust it upon our lips at the point of the spear, as an American poet phrases it, wounding, as well as outraging humanity, in the Northern People.

There is no braver people on the face of the earth than the English nation, and were there no other proof on record, their conduct during the great India Rebellion, and their prompt suppression of it, would exalt them to the pinnacle of human fame as Christian soldiers, the truest types of purest chivalry. But we, Americans, are not behind them, and therefore RUSSELL'S reproach deserves a ROLAND for his OLIVER.

The preceding are English catastrophies; but let not Continental nations forget that their records teem with equally sorrowful disasters, which an invidious consideration would assign to the deficiencies of race, whereas they are chargeable to the inexplicable, and, in most instances, temporary feebleness of humanity.

Without dwelling on Agincourt, 25th October, 1415, where the chivalry of France and sixty thousand men at arms melted away before two thousand English horse and thirteen thousand English infantry, like a loose snow wreath in a warm spring rain, whose drops, in this case, were English cloth-yard arrows; or referring to medieval panics, review the many parallels in war since the introduction of gunpowder, which revolutionized the military art.

At Montlhery, 15th July, 1465, LOUIS XI. met CHARLES THE BOLD. The former with his French triumphed on the left wing; the latter with his Burgundians on the centre, and on the right. LOUIS XI. abandoned the field, but nothing more, and saved Paris, his capital, as the Unionists did in July, 1861. What makes this parallel to Bull Run more apposite, "the roads were thronged with fugitives, flying from those who had fled with equal precipitation in other directions." One Royal officer never drew rein till he reached Lusignan, one hundred and seventy-five miles, in Poitou, and a Ducal cavalier never spared spur till he was at home one hundred miles to the northward, in Hainault.

At Tuttlingen, Thirty Years' War, 24th November, 1643, an army of eighteen thousand veterans, French and Franco-German, was just wiped out by twenty thousand Germans. The former lost a marshal, four thousand killed and wounded, seven thousand prisoners, and pretty much all their material. Night alone stopped the pursuit, and saved a remnant.

In 1702, 14th October, at Friedlingen, VILLARS had great difficulty in rallying the conquerers (his own French) running away from the beaten Imperialists.

In 1704, the rout after Blenheim, and in 1706 those after Turin and Ramillies were not more terrible than the flight after Bull Run, and these three occurred among troops accustomed to conquer, and veterans formed in long and constant wars.

At Leuthen, or Lissa, 5th December, 1757, thirty-three thousand Prussians attacked ninety thousand Austrians in a fortified position, of whom twenty-three thousand five hundred were taken prisoners, six thousand five hundred were killed or wounded, and not over thirty-seven thousand came together again of the remainder, who fled across the mountains. On the 19th, the Prussians captured seventeen thousand six hundred and thirty-five more Austrians in Breslau, so that FREDERIC, in three weeks, used up or took nearly twice as many of the enemy as he had numbers to achieve this marvel. A month to a day before Lissa, 5th November, 1757, FREDERIC, with twenty-two thousand Prussians dispersed, like chaff before the wind, sixty three thousand French and Franco Germans, "his cavalry sweeping SOUBISE and HILDBURGHAUSEN (their generals) from the face of the earth." It was not near so bad as this at Bull Run—let our calumniators make all the misrepresentations of which the incidents are susceptible in regard to our loyal army—yet the allied army was composed of trained soldiers, and ours of militia, or their equivalent.

What will our depreciators say of the panic among the victorious French after Wagram, 1809; among their veterans at Albuera, 1811, or again after Solferino, 1859; or of the routs of Winkowo* in 1812, or of the catastrophy of the Katsbach, or of Dennewitz, or of Leipsic, 1813, or Vittoria, in the same year; or of MARMONT'S corps after Laon, in 1814, or of that "*sauve qui peut!*" the worst of all, after Waterloo.

Did space permit, page after page might be filled with such reference, from Narva, fought 30th November, 1700, in a Russian snow storm, down to that famous "day of the Pass of Cambrills, 15th June, 1813," under the torrid sun of Spain, of which General CUST says (2, IV. 54): "The best of the story was, that all (three) parties ran away (Gen.) MAURICE MATHIEU (French) ran away, (Gen.)

---

* CUST'S *Wars*, 2d Series, IV., 304; GRAHAM'S *Military Ends and Moral Means*, 307.

Sir John Murray (English) ran away, and so did (Marshal) Suchet, (French). He (Suchet) was afraid to strike at Murray, knew nothing of Maurice Mathieu, and had not even been able to communicate with Tarrajona," (besieged, which he came out to relieve.).

CHAPTER XVII.

A MODEL BRIGADE, AND A PATTERN BRIGADE COMMANDER.

"O vous, jeunes guerriers, qui brulant de valeur,
Prets a vous signaler dans les champs de l'honneur,
Vous arraches aux bras d'une plaintive mere
N'allez point vous flatter, novices a' la guerre;
Que vous debutterez par d'immoetels exploits:
Commencez sans rougir par les derniers emplois:
Durement exerces dans un travail penible,
Du fusil menacant portez le poids terrible;
Rendez, votre corps souple a tous les mouvements
Que le dieu des guerriers' enseigne a ses enfants;
Tous fermes dans vos rangs en silence immobiles,
L'oeil fixe sur le chef, a ses ordres dociles,
Attentifs a sa voix, s'il commande, agissez;
En mouvements egaux a l'instant exerces,
Apprenez a charger vos tubes homicides;
Avancez flerment a grands pas intrepides,
Sans flotter, sans ouvrir et sans rompre vos rangs;
Tirez par pelotons en observant vos temps;
Prompts sans inquietude et pleins de vigilance
Aux postes dout sur vous doit rouler la defense,
Attendez le signal et marchez sans tarder
Qui ne sait obeir ne saura commander."

"*L'Art de la Guerre*," *par* FREDERIC LE GRAND.

"After the glorious cavalry stroke at Haynau, 26th May, 1813, the king of Prussia said, grumblingwise, to BLUCHER in Strehlen, "You had quite a favorable, handsome fight at Haynau, but as a drawback suffered quite a loss of *my Guards.*" "Your Majesty," answered BLUCHER, "I am heartily sorry for the loss of so many gallant fellows, but under such circumstances, the head of a Guardsman (regular) is of no more consequence than that of a Landwehrman (volunteer)."

BIESKE'S "BLUCHER," 9.

"The Rhine alone the armies stayed.
'Shall we or not, now France invade?'
Some argued 'yes,' some argued 'no'—
Old BLUCHER cut them short, with 'Go,
Bring staff-maps here. To enter France
Presents no obstacle; advance.
Where stands the foe?' 'The foe, just here'—
Point out the spot; thrash him, that's clear;
Where's Paris?' 'Paris? there it is.'
'The finger on't; we'll take Paris.'
Now throw the bridges 'cross the Rhine,
I'm sure champagne has greater zest,
And where it grows must taste the best."

KOPISCH'S "BLUCHER *on the Rhine.*"

Now that New York had rejected Phil. Kearny, had rejected the "Type Volunteer General of the War," New Jersey adopted him. Henceforward, Philip Kearny belongs to New Jersey. New Yorkers have no claim to his pre-eminent honors, except through his blood, birth and burial. The laurels which Kearny won in 1861–2 must be hung on the trophy of the State which was proud to number him among her representative men, and extend to him the rights of a son and a citizen. God bless her for it! The only error she committed was when she gave up his remains for interment in this, his native State, which had disowned him, instead of retaining them for deposit among her own dead heroes and in her own soil.

On the 21st July, 1861, the North lost the battle of Bull Run; but the rebels did not win any thing but the possession of the field, for the gain was altogether with the North. It cemented the free States; it awakened the people to the necessity of organizing a proper army; it taught the government that they could no longer trifle with events.

The reverse which Kearny's prescience had foreseen, only stimulated his patriotism. He no longer stood upon rank or right. He proclaimed his willingness to lead a regiment or even to take a subordinate line-command in any which should be raised. But the hour had come and the man.

Lincoln, who had by this time recognized in the one-armed applicant for a generalship that Captain K e r n y whom he had assisted in raising his famous troop for the Mexican war, determined to pay no more attention to the suggestions of any one in this regard, but act in accordance with his own sound common sense. Accordingly, on the 25th July, 1861, the commission was dated 7th August, 1861, he appointed Major Philip Kearny Brigadier-General, with rank from 17th May previous, which placed Kearny "twelfth on the original list" of officers of that grade, and assigned him to the command of the First New Jersey Brigade, in Franklin's Division of the embryo Army of the Potomac.

It has always been an interesting question whether volunteer troops would fight better if organized into brigades and divisions by States, or if distributed, without regard to their origin, by regiments into brigades comprising troops from different sections. It has ever been the writer's opinion that the massing together of the troops from each State, in a State uniform and under a State flag, would be the wisest course, since it would develop the highest feelings of State pride, and thus make the troops from one State anxious to surpass those from another, creating a generous rivalry, which must inevitably be productive of the most beneficial results.

These arguments in favor of a thorough State organization were urged upon Governor HUNT in 1850, and doubtless New York would have had a simple but elegant uniform of her own had it not been for officers who wished to maintain one identical with that of the United States. This view of keeping the troops of each State distinct was a favorite one with PHILIP KEARNY. Fortunately, to enable him to carry out his idea, the first four regiments furnished by New Jersey had not been distributed to different commands; consequently, KEARNY was enabled to set to work at once, with all his energy and experience, to make this homogeneous body of Jerseymen soldiers worthy of himself and of their State, and an example to the country of into what superlative troops a grand officer can transmute willing, patriotic, and brave citizens.

KEARNY'S New Jersey Brigade was composed of the First, Second and Third regiments from this State, which had reported to General SCOTT at Washington, on the 29th of June, 1861. These three were joined by the Fourth Regiment N. J. V. — the latter accompanied by a New Jersey battery of six pieces, under Captain WILLIAM HEXAMER — which reached Washington on the 21st August.

"Within twenty-four hours after receiving notice of his appointment,* he (KEARNY) joined the troops at Alexandria.

"The Jersey brigade happened to be lying together. Therefore, in spite of a strong desire, on the part of the then Secretary of War, to separate them, in

* "On Saturday the decision of the Government was taken; on Sunday we obtained the sanction of his Majesty; on Monday we came down to Parliament, and at this very hour, while I have now the honor of addressing this House, *British troops are on their way to Portugal.*" EXAMPLE OF PROMPTNESS. *Prime Minister* CANNING, *12th December*, 1826.

order to abolish State pride even in such a matter, he was able to procure himself to be assigned to their command, and entered upon his duties with constitutional alacrity.

"Those who had most strongly urged the appointment of General KEARNY had no expectation that he would possess such excellence as he immediately displayed; his dash, his chivalric bravery, his generosity and lavish expenditure of his large wealth to make his troops compare favorably with others.

* * * * * * * * *

"There was no idea of his talents as an organizer; his fervid enthusiasm for his profession; his close study of the art of war, and intimate acquaintance with its history; his magnetic influence over men; his intuitive perception of character; his strategic genius, and his almost more than conscientious devotion to his military duty.

"But a single month revealed all those qualities for which circumstances would present the exhibition. Personally and intimately acquainted myself with the leading officers of his finest regiment, I was astonished to find that his first letter, written a week after knowing them, photographed their characters as if he had always been their companion.

"And he addressed himself with such energy to the improvement of his brigade, that, in three months, it was confessedly the best disciplined around Washington.

"His severity, sometimes brusque, often eccentric, at first made him unpopular. But the men soon saw he was less indulgent to the shortcomings of officers * than to theirs; that he studied their comfort and aimed at their improvement. But officers and men soon found that there was but one path to his good will; one way of escaping severity—the full and punctilious discharge of duty, and that, if they were equal to its requisitions, they were not

---

* "When the troops occupied Madison Square," after the riots in 1863, "I often walked up there and talked with the soldiers. In reply to my question, to one of them, if he had served under General KEARNY, he replied: 'Yes, and a splendid General he was; bold as a lion and full of fight.' 'Was he liked by the men?' 'And sure he was, by all.' 'Was he not very strict?' '*And he was hard on the men*, or my own name's not KEARNEY, *but then, he was a d—d deal harder on his officers, and never spared himself in camp or in fight, day or night.*' Letter of R. W——, a cousin, both of PHIL. KEARNY and the writer, to whom the latter is indebted for several new facts and papers."

"MARSHAL SAXE, he was a strict disciplinarian, and had, as he himself related, been brought up in a strict school. A French general having attempted to excuse some disorders in his corps, on the grounds of not wishing to exercise severity towards the *officers*, MAURICE said: 'You are a young soldier, *Monsieur le General*, and do not *yet know that forbearance towards the* OFFICERS *may sometimes be severity towards the* SOLDIERS, by rendering punishments necessary that attention on their part might have averted. Even I, when colonel of cavalry, was ordered by old General SECKENDORF, to follow for three days on foot, in rear of my own regiment, in consequence of some disorders committed by the men; and yet I was the son of a king, and a favorite son, too. This was, no doubt, sharp practice." Major-Gen. MITCHELL's Biographies of Celebrated Soldiers, 285.

only appreciated, but most generously applauded; while any thing like shunning duty met with most terrible rebuke. And they saw that he required nothing but what he himself did; that days and nights were spent fitting himself for greater duties, or carefully attending to their best interests.

"And so soon they came to love him, worship him. They would go with him any where, reposing without question on his judgment."

The language of a friend, whose admiration and affection has survived the death of its object, has already been quoted. Let the reader now compare the opinion of a stranger, one who only knew KEARNY through his record of service, and the opinions of those who served with and under him:

"As the Army of the Potomac gradually assumed the form of an orderly, systematic body of troops, with admirable appointments and thorough discipline, in the fall of 1861, when General KEARNY was only a Brigadier, there were not wanting those, even then, who saw in the one-armed Jerseyman qualities that fitted him, rather than the cautious, unready MCCLELLAN, to command the magnificent army of nearly two hundred thousand men, and hurl it against Richmond.

"Looking back, now, as we can historically, upon the leaders of that host, we are justified in saying that he was the wisest, the most experienced, the best read, the most sagacious, as well as the bravest and most dashing officer in all that army. For twenty-six years he had followed the profession of arms, in the spirit and with the chivalry of a knight of the middle ages. Had he lived a few centuries earlier, he would have ridden by the side of LOUIS the Ninth, or fought the Saracen, shoulder to shoulder, with RICHARD CŒUR DE LION. At Marignano, he would have mingled his blood with that of the Chevalier BAYARD, "the bravest and the most worthy." At Rocroy, at Freiburg, and at Nordlingen, the great CONDE would have found in him a brother hero, as intrepid and fierce in the onset, as skillful in tactics, as gay and as gallant as himself, when the festivities of victory succeeded the toils of war.

"Those whose attention was caught by his dashing horsemanship, his martial figure," "the jaunty Piedmontese cloak, trimmed with Astrackan lamb's wool, and loaded with Brandenburgs and cord," "and the gold lace with which his uniform was all aglow, were not aware how firm, cool, systematic and thoroughbred a soldier was to be found in General KEARNY. In this respect he resembled the 'BAYARD of the Army of Northern Virginia,' STONEWALL JACKSON, who won so much repute for swift marching and fierce onset, that few gave him, as he deserved to have, credit for as much ability and strategy as Lee, or any other of the generals."

Lest the world should suppose that such encomiums were the offsprings of a vivid imagination, inflamed by passion, filled with the knightly figure of PHIL. KEARNY, and ringing with the reverberating praises of men dazzled with his gallantry—with the "galantuomo" of America—the following private letter written by a very intelligent sergeant in the First New Jersey Brigade (after KEARNY had been in command of it several weeks, and while it lay near Alexandria) is a convincing proof that the reality was equal to the ideal in this case. Yes, indeed, that the reality which so seldom equals the ideal, in the case of the "American BAYARD," actually surpassed, far surpassed it:

"As regards our General, I will endeavor to give you some of the traits of his character in connection with his command. 1st. He is untiring in his efforts to promote the comfort and well-being of his men. For instance: I was standing the other day engaged in conversation with Dr. SUCKLEY, the Brigade-Surgeon, who, by the way, is a first-rate man, having been in the United States service for the past fifteen years, when one of Gen. KEARNY'S orderlies rode up and placed a small packet in his hand with the General's compliments. The doctor opened it, and found wrapped up in a note twenty-five dollars in gold, the note saying it came from General KEARNY for Dr. SUCKLEY to use for luxuries for the patients in the hospital under his (Dr. SUCKLEY'S) charge. 'There,' said the doctor, 'that is fifty dollars he has sent me for that purpose since we have been here, some two months.'

"2d. His discipline is of the strictest kind; though there is never any thing like domineering or arrogance about him, yet he will have his rules and regulations carried out, as to drill, etc., to the very letter.

"The brigade is fast approaching what I should judge to be its legitimate and proper standard of military perfection, under his unceasing endeavors to make it what he says it shall be, if the officers and men will only bear a helping hand, namely, the most useful and efficient in the service.

"3d. When we came over into Virginia, the officers cared little, and of course the men cared less, about doing things by system, even that while we were stationed at Camp Olden, Trenton; but under his guidance no person would believe that this was the same body of troops; perfect order about every thing, men look neater, and appear to better advantage on parades or reviews, and drill better. In fact, there has been a complete revolution of every thing appertaining to the whole brigade.

"4th. I can compare his popularity with the men to nothing else but to the French army in the days of NAPOLEON I; they almost worship him, and would follow wherever—follow, did I say? no, they would *go* wherever he points as the path of duty.

"5th. Their confidence in his military skill is unparalleled in the history of *this* country since the days of WASHINGTON. He seems to have every little item of military education and stratagem, necessary to be used in such a campaign as this, at his finger's ends, and, no matter what he may be doing, should any officer ask his opinion on this point, or his advice on that particular, he will give either just as if he had been thinking of nothing else than the subject suggested by the question; in a word, he is a military man in the strictest sense of that term. His perception of the capabilities of a man for any work he may be wanted for is as quick as lightning, and he only needs a glance. He is also very strict about members of other brigades coming inside our lines without passes, and we have had orders to arrest any such found on the roads, or in any of the camps, while we may be on patrol duty; also, any of our own men found outside *our* lines, without passes from their colonels. You can judge, by these instances, somewhat of his character as a disciplinarian.

"I think I have written quite enough to convince any person of his fitness for the responsible post he now occupies. The question used to be asked, before he came, 'Who shall lead us on?' but now it is, 'When shall we be led to meet our enemies?' There are no fears of the result of such a meeting for an instant crossing our minds. Our final success is sure. Perhaps many will fall before it is attained. I may be of the number; but if I should, I wish all my friends to know that I fell at my post of duty, trusting in Him who alone is able to save from sin, who is on our side, aiding in putting down the most black-hearted and damnable rebellion the world ever knew. But I fear I shall weary you with this long dry letter. I am well and hearty as ever, and can still lift my eyes to the hills whence cometh our salvation. May God prosper our arms and nerve our arms for the great work before us."

Within twenty-four hours — as stated — after receiving the notice of his appointment, KEARNY joined his troops in front of Alexandria, and established his headquarters in the Episcopal Seminary, about three miles to the south of that venerable but intensely rebel city. At this time the rebel commander-in-chief, JOSEPH E. JOHNSTON, had his headquarters in Centerville, but his advance occupied positions from which not only were the spires of the capital and the dome of the capitol visible, but Arlington Heights were actually within cannon shot of his outposts. One of the points held by the rebels was on Munson's Hill, not more than six miles north-west of Alexandria, and KEARNY was urged to withdraw from the position he assumed as too dangerous to be maintained. Well might KEARNY declare that he held the very outworks of the Union lines, and made his brigade in the very presence of the enemy. "Do they forget," * * are KEARNY's own indignant words, "that I, on the heels of Bull Run, faced the enemy with a

Jersey brigade in advance of all the others, against all, McClellan * * *et id omne genus*, nearly forcing me back to the Seminary. Do they forget me at Manassas? My Jersey brigade that inflicted with panic the retiring enemy?" His Third regiment was among the first of our troops to come into direct collision with the pickets of the enemy and to suffer loss in its ranks from rebel bullets.

"While thus promoting the efficiency of his brigade in drill, comfort, and health, in which he succeeded wonderfully, he kept them all alive to the fact that they were soon to fight. General McClellan had given orders to withdraw their outposts to a line near Washington; General Kearny expostulated successfully, and kept his troops constantly on the watch. They were the vanguard of the army. His object was to generate military vigilance."

"The experience of the brigade during the fall and winter months was marked by but few incidents of importance, the time being mainly occupied in drill and the ordinary camp duties. There were now and then occasions, however, when the *tedium* was relieved by movements which served to test the mettle of the troops and prepare them for the dangers and hardships of future campaigns. The Third Regiment was among the first to come into direct collision with the pickets of the enemy and to suffer loss in its ranks from rebel bullets. On the 29th August, this regiment, while reconnoitering near Cloud's Mill, fell into an ambuscade, and lost two men killed and four wounded. On the same day a company of the Second Regiment had a skirmish with a body of the enemy, in which one man was wounded, the rebel loss being twelve in killed and injured. On the 29th of September, General Kearny made the first important demonstration which had had been since Bull Run in the nature of reconnoissance in force, the troops consisting of the First Brigade, Hexamer's battery, and a company of Colonel Young's Kentucky Cavalry. The object of the movement being to ascertain the character of the enemy's works on Munson's Hill, some distance from our lines, where he was supposed to be strongly fortifying, the expedition was conducted with the greatest caution, and, the troops behaving with the greatest steadiness, though within shelling distance of the enemy, it was eminently successful, General Kearny obtaining precisely the information he wanted, and information, too, which proved of the greatest value as a guide in future operations. On the 15th of October, a detachment of the First Regiment fell in with the enemy, mainly cavalry, and after a brisk skirmish, in which they emptied a number of saddles, retired with the loss of three or four killed. These skirmishes were only important in so far as they trained the men to vigilance and celerity of movements, though they undoubtedly gave a spice to the otherwise dull and monotonous life of the camps."

While thus kept in enforced inaction, KEARNY's active mind was continually dwelling upon the best plan of operations, although that military sagacity and acquaintance with military lore, which had excited the surprise and admiration of the French Generals, was neither invited nor suffered to participate in the councils of McCLELLAN. It is a curious fact, which the writer heard remarked in the fall of 1861, that McCLELLAN seemed to put more confidence in his German division than any other in his army, and no one had more access to him than its commander, except some especial favorites, not one of whom maintained his relative position in the Army of the Potomac longer than a few months after McCLELLAN lost his own.

As it may interest the reader to know what KEARNY's views were in regard to the prosecution of the campaign in Virginia, the following may be considered as a sort of epitome of his opinions. It is founded on conversations, letters, in which military considerations were too much intermingled with private matters to permit their insertion, from remarks repeated by common friends, and his own indorsement of suggestions laid before him from time to time. To sum the whole matter up, KEARNY was very much of the same opinion as LORD NAPIER — the one who has just acquired so much celebrity by his successful Abyssinian campaign — that "the way to defeat an Asiatic army is by going straight to their heads, on every occasion." Upon which a critic remarks: "We suspect this remark contains the first principle of successful war everywhere.'

This is undoubtedly so, provided the "forwards," or "have-at-them" is subordinated to the immutable laws of Strategy and Tactics, and to the rules of PRACTICAL STRATEGY,* which always involve the hardest kind of fighting, when the favorable opportun.ty presents itself. This was invariably the case with every general who has left a great name behind him, and nothing hurled the first NAPOLEON from his throne but that persistent hammering — feints and blows — inaugurated by BLUCHER, which made him the idol of his Prussians, of all the soldiers he commanded, of the whole allied army, and a greater favorite with the English nation than even their own greatest man, the "Iron Duke" himself.

During the fall and winter, while the Army of the Potomac in a surfeit of plethoric incapacity, was lying in the mud around Washington, while McCLELLAN was weaving those airy fabrics of ambition which resulted in the sacrifice of as fine an armament as ever obeyed the orders of one man, and in his own ultimate difficulties and removal, KEARNY was engaged in making that famous New Jersey Brigade which was the admiration of the army, a brigade of which Brigadier-General C. S. W—— wrote, on the 21st April, 1862, from the camp before Yorktown: "I am much inclined to think that KEARNY's brigade is the best in the whole army; also that New Jersey has in all respects fitted out her troops better than any other State. We have one brigade of Jersey troops in our (HOOKER's) division, so I can judge somewhat."

The following note is evidence that the State of New Jersey itself was not backward in doing its peculiar duty. Would that all the other States had emulated such a noble example:

HEADQUARTERS NEW JERSEY VOLUNTEERS,
SEMINARY, October 7, 1861.

His Excellency, Governor Olden (of New Jersey): SIR: * * * * * * I take this occasion, your Excellency, to express to you the great admiration from all, military and civil, who observe us, of the most liberal judicious, and enduring nature of all our equipments and other army supplies. As a General Officer, commanding troops of the State (New Jersey), I feel it as an additional incentive to us all.

I have the honor to be, your Excellency's obedient servant,

P. KEARNY, Brigadier-General Commanding.

---

* PRACTICAL STRATEGY.—"I readily accept from you this expression. It comprises all that can be said or written upon skill in war, and I agree with you that this is best evinced by sparing the lives of its instruments as much as possible. "*Lives of the Warriors*," by General HON. SIR EDWARD CUST, B. A., 1868; "Letter Dedicatory," III. [COMPARE "*Practical Strategy*," as illustrated by the Achievements of Field Marshal TRAUN, by J. W. DE P., 1863.]

The greater part of the time before the Army of the Potomac moved to commit that fatal error, the march up the Peninsula, which had its origin in mistaken judgment, its unsuccessful execution through incompetent handling, and its results in a series of disasters, half-fought-out battles, or unimproved victories, little better than defeats, except that so many thousands of the best rebel troops were swept from the board by the valor of our soldiers, not the generalship of their chief—General KEARNY was engaged in a correspondence in regard to the best plan of operation to be adopted. KEARNY was always in favor of a direct advance upon Richmond on the line afterwards followed by GRANT. This, as we enjoyed the command of the Chesapeake and its tributaries, would have enabled the fleet to supply the army as it moved onward through the various estuaries which penetrate so far as to almost obviate the necessity of any line of supply by land, or which, at all events, by constantly affording new bases of supply, necessitated only very short and easy wagoning transportation.

Three plans were discussed in a correspondence with KEARNY. The first was to mask Manassas with a sufficient force to ensure the safety of Washington and hold the enemy in that quarter in complete check; and, promptly, with the balance of the Army of the Potomac thrown forward in echelon, fall upon and capture the rebel forces along the Potomac, engaged in blockading that river or in support. This was very much in the spirit of CARNOT's plan of operations in the year 1793,* when he restored confidence to the Republican armies, and converted defeat into victory.

---

* CARNOT.—One of the most remarkable and successful of the combinations of the wars of the French Revolution, executed in 1793, and due to CARNOT, may be taken as the first example of the manner of applying the Principle 1 of Strategy, viz.: "To have, as the object of all operations and manœuvres, the bringing the mass of the forces successively into collision with fractions of the enemy." CARNOT involved the Principle (1) alone in his combination, and sent the entire unoccupied French army to Dunkirk, with orders that, as soon as the marked numerical superiority thus given on that point should have decided the victory, to proceed to the next of the seven points" (and armies), "and when the mass of the French again brought into collision with a fraction of the enemy, should have again given victory, to proceed to the next, and so on. (CUST. 1, 4, 1793, 152–'3.)

By this means the mass of the French was brought into collision with fractions of the enemy, in the following manner:

The second way sketched out was to divide the army of the Potomac into two bodies, the smaller to move down or rather up the Shenandoah Valley, cleaning out the enemy as it advanced; the other and larger body to follow the line of the Orange and Alexandria railroad, the left wing on the line through Fredericksburg, both operating simultaneously and dependently. A junction was to be made through Gordonsville or Charlottesville, and thence a combined blow delivered from the North and West upon Richmond. This was said to have been GRANT's original idea in 1864. Such was very much the system on which ROSECRANS acted, which carried him from Murfreesboro' into Chattanooga, and closely resembled the plan which carried SHERMAN from Chattanooga to Atlanta. Such was a course parallel to that of GRANT — SHERIDAN taking care

---

1 The DUKE OF YORK and FREYTAG were beaten — the former embarked, the latter retired.

2. The army passed to Menin, and the PRINCE OF ORANGE was beaten.

3. The army arrived at Maubeuge, and CLAIRFAYT experienced a defeat in return.

4. The army proceeded to the Vosges, and the DUKE OF BRUNSWICK, being in a minority, was likewise defeated.

5. The army having joined that of the Rhine, chased WURMSER from the neighborhood of Strasburg.

Hence, one of the most remarkable and best manœuvres in the wars of the French Revolution is nothing more than a simple deduction from Principle 1. The object CARNOT had, when forming the combination, appears to have been nothing else than to bring the mass of the French into collision with successive fractions of the Coalitionists. This combination was good, because it was in accordance with one of the principles of strategy; had it been in accordance with two, it would have been much better; if with the three first principles, as far as possible under the circumstances, perfect.

The five victories produced an imperfect though a great result; because the enemy, being attacked in front, he was driven back on his natural and prepared lines of retreat.

It appears that the Principle 1 might have been involved to the same extent, and the Principle 2 involved with it in addition, in the formation of a combination upon the same data, in the following manner: After the victory of Dunkirk, the French army, instead of attacking all the while in front, and thus losing the best part of the fruits of victory, should take the Meuse, with its five fortified towns, as the base of manœuvres, and thus intercepting BENJOWSKI, CLAIRFAYT, and the PRINCE OF ORANGE from their communications, attack them in *reverse*, or even *in rear*, defeat them (which would be an easier task than to defeat them in front), and drive them as vigorously as possible away from their lines of retreat.

CARNOT has received, generally, great honor for his combination, and merits it; for, from the ordinary proceedings of the great majority of generals of his day, it is greatly to be feared, that, in almost any other hands than his, the additional army might have been divided into seven parts, and sent to reinforce the seven armies." —"*Elementary Treatise on Strategy*," by EDWIN YATES, B.A., London, 1855. (Second edition, pp. 14–17.)

of the rebels in the Shenandoah Valley — after he had worked through the "Wilderness" and struck home at the Army of Northern Virginia, in Petersburg-Richmond.

The third plan was to make Norfolk the base of operations, and march on Richmond through Petersburg. In the last two cases a sufficient force was to be left to cover Washington, which was to co-operate with the main body at the proper time and opportunity.

The Shenandoah Valley was never to be left open, but a sufficient force was to be stationed therein to close it against any such attempts as were made from time to time by JACKSON and his successors. ROSECRANS was sent into the Shenandoah Valley to gather together, in 1862, the forces sprinkled about at random, and provide for the safety of the capital and the purging of that channel of disaster, which was a constant scene of disgrace, until fiery PHIL. SHERIDAN swept through it with the besom of destruction, with the steel to the bosom of the rebel army, and the "torch to the roof" for the rebel supplies, which latter course the French critic on our war, ROUSSILLON, declared "should have been applied at the outset," and which was withheld only too long for the safety of our troops and of Washington, and for the honor of our arms. This Shenandoah Valley, was, indeed, one of disaster and disgrace to the North, through utter want of that "practical strategy" which distinguishes key points and eliminates the useless while conserving the beneficial. Whether correctly or not, it has been stated that, "Winchester was taken and retaken seventy-six times;" whereas it should have been taken by PATTERSON, or rather by his motor, in July, 1861, and never afterward suffered to relapse into the power of the enemy.

During the winter and early spring, a correspondent, stimulated by the questions and approbation of General KEARNY, was continually studying out the feasibility, the details and parallels of his first two propositions. In August, 1861, a detailed account was published of the campaign of the Austrians against EUGENE BEAUHARNAIS, in 1813–'14, which was almost analogous throughout to KEARNY's second plan; and likewise the winter campaign of GŒRGEY, which was similar in its effects. This system was exactly the one followed by NAPOLEON in 1797, when he with his main army advanced directly through Friuli, while JOUBERT turned the Austrian right through the Tyrol; precisely as KEARNY'S secondary army should have operated in the Shenandoah Valley.

The same combined and simultaneous action, although not immediately subordinate, as in 1797, occurred in the campaign in which NAPOLEON operated in Germany, and MASSENA, in Italy, in 1805, and again in 1809, under the Viceroy EUGENE, in Italy; NEY, working in together to the same ends on the Tyrol, and MARMONT from Dalmatia. In 1813 the game was reversed, and the French plan was put in execution against themselves with like successful results.

The campaign of 1813 was a perfect reproduction of the campaign of 1797, only in 1813, the Austrians from the east, under Hiller, were pressing westward on the direct line followed by NAPOLEON, sixteen years previous, with FENNER, flanking through the Tyrol, retracing the steps of JOUBERT down the Adige. Had our armies operated simultaneously through the Wilderness and up the Shenandoah, the rebels could not have maintained themselves at Manassas or at any intermediate point on the line of the Orange and Alexandria railroad. Had they attempted to do so, they would have found themselves in the same predicament as the Russians in their retrenched camp at Drissa, on the Dwina in 1812.

After the conflagration of Moscow when KUTUSOFF operated upon the French flank along the Toluga road, the game was reversed, and the combined operations which should have culminated on the Beresina, to the utter destruction of the French, only failed through the tardiness of Admiral TSCHITCHAGOFF and General WITTGENSTEIN.

JOMINI remarks, " without doubt, the fault of Admiral TSCHITCHAGOFF in a very great degree contributed toward their extricating themselves from the scrape. * * * It is a question which should be most admired, the plan of operations which brought the Russian armies from the extremity of Moldavia, from Moscow and from Polotsk to the Beresina, as to a rendezvous in time of peace, which only just fell short of effecting the capture of their redoubtable adversary, or the admirable constancy of the hero thus pursued, which succeeded in forcing a passage."

A similar result to the one proposed was indicated by the simple occupation of Gallicia by SCHWARTZENBERG in 1813. (Charras, *Guerre de*, 1813, iv. 100, etc.) The French had to abandon Poland at once and fall back behind the Elbe. Then, had Prussia been ready to move, the French would certainly have been thrown back, with ease, beyond the Rhine.

A French army could have lived off the Shenandoah Valley, which would have obviated transport; the Union army ought to have done so.

In 1814, BLUCHER's line of advance of the Army of Silesia was equivalent to the "forwards" of an army up the Shenandoah, the main army of the Allies representing ours under GRANT in the Wilderness.

MASSENA, as admitted by NAPIER, need never to have fought the battle of Busaco, 1810, which he lost, had he turned WELLINGTON at the first, through the Valley of the Mondego, to the right, or as he afterward attempted to do, when too late, through Boyalva, to the left.* As an example of this course, take GRANT's campaign of the spring of 1862. ALBERT SYDNEY JOHNSTON was at Bowling Green; the capture of Forts Henry and Donelson threw him back two hundred miles, beyond the Tennessee.

In fact, the grand tactics, whose successful carrying out General KEARNY witnessed at the Col de Mousaia, in 1840, was an exact type of the stragetical plan McCLELLAN should have followed, only on a grander scale, and more extensive, but not more difficult theatre of action. NAPOLEON III conceived similar moves in 1859. Why they failed is incomprehensible, considering the generals and troops he had under his control. At a later date, writing upon the same subject, GENERAL KEARNY says: "It would have been so beautiful to have pushed after the enemy, and in doing so, *isolate* Fredericksburgh, *carry* it easy, occupy that road, and thus turn those river batteries;

* HARPERS' ALISON, III, LIX. 349-'50, especially 350, Col: 2.

all the while near enough to Washington in case of any attempt upon it."

Then as to reconnoissances in force, KEARNY exactly agreed with GUROWSKI (recall NAPOLEON'S demonstration the night before Waterloo to discover if the English were retreating or determined to stand the hazard of the morrow's die):

"McCLELLAN acts as if he had taken the oath to some hidden and veiled deity or combination, by all means not to ascertain any thing about the condition of the enemy.

"Any European, if not American old woman—in pants, long ago would have pierced the veil by a strong reconnoissance on Centreville. Here 'All quiet on the Potomac.'"

"And I hear generals, WEST POINTERS, justifying this colossal offense against common sense, and against the rudiments of military tactics, and even science. 'Oh noble, but awfully dealt with American people!'"*

Had McCLELLAN ever read the extraordinary military career of JOHN CAVALIER, with which KEARNY was well acquainted, and of which he often spoke, he would have understood the enormous advantages enjoyed by LEE, occupying a central position in a mountainous country, well known to him and his subordinates, and have provided against them, as GRANT eventually did, or any GENERAL would have done. CAVALIER, it is true, was a marvel of genius, a heaven-born general. A peasant by birth, and bred a baker's apprentice, before the age of twenty he became general-in-chief of the Protestants of Languedoc, with no other knowledge of tactics but what he had picked up by watching the manœuvres of troops in the streets of Anduze, or acquaintance with strategy except through the inspiration of common sense. He never had over three thousand men in hand and actually engaged in a body under his command, and never wanted more, but he kept that number always complete, every one of which was a picked and tried soldier. Like STONEWALL JACKSON, he was a fanatic, and his troops were thoroughly fanaticised, fighting with the halter around their necks, and worse.

---

* GUROWSKI'S *Diary*, 1, 157. Compare 97, 127, 133, etc., with LANGEL'S "United States during the War," 208, 234-'6, 240, etc., etc.

This, together with a discipline of iron, quadrupled their strength. Even all this, however, without the genius of CAVALIER, would have accomplished nothing. To and fro, like FREDERIC THE GREAT in the Seven Years' War, he shot like a shuttle, and either paralyzed, held at bay, or beat sixty thousand Royal troops, of whom twenty thousand were veterans, cavalry as well as infantry, well supplied with artillery, commanded by one Marshal of France, three able Lieutenant-Generals, three *Marechaux-de-Camp*, and three Brigadiers, no less distinguished. Marshal MONTREVEL estimated CAVALIER'S numbers at twenty thousand, although they never exceeded three thousand, "forged in the fire of battle and tempered in the sweat of marches." CAVALIER was constantly victorious in isolated encounters, until a simultaneous concentrated movement nearly destroyed his column at Nages, when he descended from his mountain fastnesses into the lowlands, cutting loose from his base. Nevertheless he did not succumb to any force of arms, although he must have finally been worn out by constant hammering. He fell a victim to a diplomacy, which, in its deceit, resembled that which put an end to the Algerian war by the seizure of ABD-EL-KADER—and terminated the Seminole war by a similar treacherous capture of OSCEOLA. As it was, the necessity of crushing him promptly and matching his genius, forced LOUIS XIV to send into the south of France the finest soldiers and best officers at the disposal of the French Minister of War. The English critic speculates with horror upon the effect of the presence of those generals and troops in Germany, but especially at Blenheim, both of which CAVALIER kept fully employed in distant Languedoc. Had CAVALIER never risen or been less than he was, the sun of LOUIS XIV would not have set in disgrace, and his motto of "NEC PLURIBUS IMPAR," "not an unequal match for numbers," might have been realized in an empire as extensive as that of NAPOLEON; and, as it was based on religion, more durable.

Indeed, the failure of the English fleet, under Sir CLOUDESLEY SHOVEL, to co-operate with CAVALIER frustrated the grandest plan of the Camisard leader and his adherents. Had the English captains succeeded in establishing a communication with the Cevenol leaders, and furnishing them with the needed supplies, it is almost impossible to calculate the enormous results which might have followed.

But the reader may say, what has this to do with our war? Everything. The plan of operations which finished CAVALIER was the plan of KEARNY who was worthy to be named with VILLARS, who ended CAVALIER's career as GRANT ended LEE's. Incessant activity, simultaneous attacks of converging columns, allowing no respite, high-souled magnanimity blended with soldierly decision — no "pottering, half-heartedness," but BLUCHER-like "FORWARDS," everywhere, when the tide had turned, and was on the rise; and it was on the rise in the winter and spring of 1862.

KEARNY knew all this well. He was thoroughly posted in military history. His information in this regard surprised generals of the highest rank and ability abroad. Nevertheless, he could take advice from outsiders, and thankfully avail himself of the industry and ability of others, even if they did not bear the trade-mark of the National Military Academy — that Academy, the glory of our country in its grand men, whose natural greatness it so greatly develops; the damage to our people in the caste-influence, and prejudices it has engendered; a curse almost, in particular cases, in its little men, by permitting them to claim weight for their opinions on exhibiting the original stamp of its mint. Sending a man to West Point who has not soldierly instincts in him, does not make him a soldier, any more than the mode of officering the English church makes good Christian ministers. It creates a caste like the Egyptian priesthood, whose members claim for every one within the pale all the dignities and emoluments of the office; in which individuals may possess the spirit, but it would not be natural to believe that the whole did.

Alas! were not all of KEARNY's forebodings, founded on the apathy and mismanagement of that fall, winter and spring, fully realized in the sacrifices and incapacity of the ensuing summer and autumn?

CHAPTER XVIII.

PLANS AND CORRESPONDENCE.

ULYSSES. They tax our policy and call it cowardice;
Count Wisdom as no member of the war;
Forestall prescience, and esteem no act
But that of hand. The still and mental parts,
That do contrive how many hands shall strike,
When fitness calls them on, and know, by measure
Of their observant toil, the enemies' weight,—
Why, this hath not a finger's dignity:
They call this bed-work, mappery, closet-war;
So that the ram, that batters down the wall,
For the great swing and rudeness of his poise,
They place before his hand that made the engine,
Or those that with the fineness of their souls
By reason guide his execution.

SHAKSPEARE'S *Troilus and Cressida.*

"All the time which subsequently elapsed" on the morning of Waterloo, after his dispositions were made, "was time squandered, absolutely lost (by NAPOLEON); and often in war, losses of this kind can never be repaired."

CHARRAS' "*Histoire de la Campagne de* 1815, *Waterloo.*"

"In this the King of France [LINCOLN] established his own headquarters [*Washington*]. He did not himself pretend to be a soldier, further than a natural indifference to danger, and much sagacity qualified him to be called such; but he was always careful to employ the most skillful in that profession, and reposed in them the confidence they merited." LINCOLN, it is stated, used to call K-E-R-N-Y "his general."—*Quentin Durward.*

MANY persons have supposed that KEARNY'S unfavorable opinion of McCLELLAN was subsequent to those displays of inability — that is, inability to adjust, direct and fight so vast a force as the country confided to him;* in fact, to fill commensurately the immense role to which circumstances, to retard and ripen events, assigned him — an inability which paralyzed

* "The first, most important, and prominent step in the prosecution of the war, and one whose consequences were felt to the end, was the defective and injurious organization given to the Army of the Potomac in the winter of 1861–'2. It was most unfortunate, that, *with the finest* MEN *and material ever furnished to any army* of the world, that army should have been organized with so little reference to the rules of war governing the organization of armies," &c., &c. Major-General A. PLEASANTON'S Supplementary Report. Examine carefully pages 3 to 6.

our army at the best season of the year for active operations. This surmise is not correct. Already, in the fall of 1861, KEARNY appears to have lost all confidence in him, from the fact that McCLELLAN seemed to have lost all confidence in his troops. Writing from his, the headquarters of the New Jersey Volunteers, at the Episcopal Seminary, near Alexandria, December 8, 1861, he observed:

> "I am in favor of sending for one of them" [referring to some experienced French general], "because I find that General McCLELLAN is too distrustful of his forces since Baker's affair (Ball's Bluff) to adopt the true keypoint in strategy."

April 16, 1862, he sums up the matter:

> "Indeed, I have been deadly opposed to the river plan, as uncovering Washington, without a single advantage. Besides, McCLELLAN is too slow to manœuvre out of a scrape."

KEARNY's soldiership was always too prompt and energetic, not only for McCLELLAN, but for those immediately over him in command. Had KEARNY's advice been followed, KEARNY's "practical strategy" would have manœuvred the rebels out of their insulting positions in front of Washington the fall before the spring they did evacuate them, and almost as soon as they showed themselves there. His subsequent occupation of Manassas was, perhaps, taking the times and all the other attending circumstances into consideration, one of his most brilliant acts. It was not appreciated, because never properly brought before the people, and because the people, as a rule, appreciate no result of soldiership which is not purchased with lavish profusion of blood.

When BURNSIDE went to Albermarle Sound, he supposed the blow was aimed at Norfolk. "If Burnside takes Norfolk," he said, in effect, "he has the key of Richmond in his hand, and can go in through Petersburg, if he only knows how to turn it."

Nevertheless, KEARNY was anxious to give McCLELLAN every possible chance, as is shown by the following communication, which has not yet been published.

It was written 15th December, 1861, at his headquarters in the Seminary, near Alexandria.

"As I have * * * animadverted on General McCLELLAN, and stated my disappointment as to his military conduct of the campaign, I lose no time to guard you and, through you, others as to the danger of interfering with his plans, whatever they may be. Such a course, in precipitating him from one policy to another, would be disastrous. The administration was wrong in expelling SCOTT — the only one fitted by his *habit of victory* and undaunted temperament for handling masses. His mind was strong as ever, although it may have turned too much to detail, which he performed badly and slowly. These minor deficiencies should have been cared for for him. His high moral, military and political standing were such that he should have been preserved by the administration as an ægis in case of mishap. And with volunteers as *invaders*,* no military calculations from *past* history permit you to be assured against it. Believe me, with a great admiration for the pure character of Mr. LINCOLN, which all believe in, I do not think that his administration would survive a second Bull's Run. I am convinced that McCLELLAN feels this, and is rendered over-cautious by it. But all allow him consummate abilities — that is, talents.† I certainly admit it myself. I deny him one spark of military genius, and yet an undaunted, sober courage.

"He has been wofully wrong, politically; for, in the eyes of foreign governments, our inaction can only pass for pusillanimity. He was equally wrong as to the temperament of his troops. They have less discipline to-day (mine additionally, from injudicious interference, in taking from me artillery and cavalry merely to leave them an uncontrolled bad example in our midst) from useless reviews, which their good sense tells them is nonsense, and out of place for an army that has a stain to wipe out, and from the continuous *qui vive* in which we kept, until after BAKER's affair, and which has subsided into the idleness of winter quarters without the boldness of avowing it. Equally in an ill-judged delay, as a matter of season in October the roads were firm (and in this country the mere wood roads, out of season, are impassable), the days were long, the temperature genial, nor was there an excuse on the plea of material — our batteries were completed, our cavalry more than sufficient. As to numbers the enemy increases his force even more rapidly than we do.

---

* Prussian "Seven Weeks War," in 1866, subsequent to the Slaveholders Rebellion, closed 1865, certainly disproved this if our Great Civil War had not already done so.

† "I entertain a very high opinion of ——'s talents; but he always appeared to me to want what is better than abilities, viz.: sound sense. There is always some mistaken principle in what he does. 8th August, 1813, and again, 10th June, 1814, * * "if he had less pride and more common sense, and could have carried his measure into execution as he ought to have done, it would have succeeded" WELLINGTON, "rich in saving common sense." This bears out the old adage, "common sense is genius in its working dress." "To act with common sense, according to the moment, is the best wisdom I know," HORACE WALPOLE. "Fine sense and exalted sense are not half so useful as common sense." AUSWAHLER. PASCAL has some very curious and apposite remarks on geometrical minds, Chap. IX. § III., worthy of consideration in this connection.

And here was a false elementary computation by the general. And *it was* McCLELLAN'S plan to have opened the game at that time. The mishap of BAKER unnerved him. He did not dare to trust his troops if they failed at their first step. The trifling details as to a move detailed at length in army orders to the command (only the last care, when all else has been arranged), proved incontestably that such was the case. In forty-eight hours after, I asserted that the day of the campaign was *indefinitely* postponed.

"However, General McCLELLAN is not such a man of universally allowed talents not to have his own determined line of policy. It is that I deprecate interfering with him now that I write, lest I may have been previously misunderstood.

"SCOTT is gone, and none more likely than McCLELLAN remains. All are equally untried. Military habit of mind and practice of necessary military elements may have become instinct. Energy, militarily directed, may be second nature. The logic of military comprehension may surpass all other analysis — all of which make good subaltern generals — but genius alone can suffice for operations of hundreds of thousands, over a space of near a continent; and that man is yet to prove himself.

"I have finished all my paper, and I fear have bored you with a very long letter. My health has a regular break-down, but I will soon be up. With best regard," etc.

It is seen that in closing his letter KEARNY alludes to his health. It is a great mistake to suppose that KEARNY enjoyed robust health. The only time that he ever seemed to be free from the most distressing attacks was while he was in Africa, and engaged in active service in the presence of the enemy, feeling, as it were, the grating of his blade. While at Saumur, in 1839–'40, he was often confined to his bed; when in Italy, in 1834, he was dangerously sick.

He used to remark that it might be said he had lived upon calomel; or again, that he had taken calomel enough to kill a horse. People were often deceived in regard to his condition, from the fact that his energy rose superior to his bodily ailments the moment that duty called him into the saddle. Days of constant exposure and activity were often succeeded by sleepless suffering, when nature most demanded the recuperation of repose. He aged terribly during the short period of his generalship, and was very grey when he fell.

Again he wrote, still from the same spot seven weeks afterward.

HEADQUARTERS NEW JERSEY BRIGADE,
CAMP SEMINARY, VA., February 8, 1862.

"Yours * * * have been received. It was a truly military treat, and evinced what I claim for you as a *specialite* in talents, a wonderful command of facts from the past, with a genius in their adaptation to evolve particular theories for a future.

"You have placed GŒRGEY'S campaign in a most impressive light before me. I had read the same book, and had almost forgotten it. I read it, although an American officer, more as a *political* theme; at best only in a tactical light, and without particular reference to the map.

"After one general glance at it, for main points, you prove that you studied it in the light of strategy. One thing is certain; it was a *Winter's Campaign* and each battle was fought with as much artillery as we possess. * * *

"Still, there is much that is different, if you adduce it as a *Strategy*, that is applicable to ourselves. I do not regard it as such, further than as a proof of the power of overcoming obstacles.

"GŒRGEY'S army was never more than what would be two to three or four of our divisions, the Austrians small in proportion; whereas the theatre of war was boundless.

"Our armies are about 400.000 to 500.000 of a side, and although extending across 1,000 miles, being intersected by mountains, are both separate and united, at least admit of no manœuvring around our enemy.

"There are but two plans open to us.

"To manœuvre against Richmond or New Orleans. As to the value of these two *objective* points of strategy, I maintain that, whilst New Orleans is the easiest, and yields the greatest extent of country for a capture, that Richmond, from its *moral* importance, is the point which will prove the most decisive, and would carry with it the Valley of the Mississippi, and would isolate the war to almost only South Carolina; at all events to the extreme Secession States.

"General SCOTT, partly as a very great tactician (I believe that the war would have been finished by this time had he remained in command), and principally as a Virginian, decided for the Kentucky theatre of war.

"It is very certain that this is also MCCLELLAN'S. One is led to suppose so from the agglomeration of forces there. They are nearly two-thirds in excess of the enemy, besides the flotilla.

"That the enemy must fall back, beaten or otherwise, and Tennessee be overrun (provided, as would be the case, we detach some 50,000 picked men from this army to the West, MCCLELLAN going in person), and New Orleans taken, is a certainty.

"The only question which would arise are, in the first place: BEAUREGARD would occupy the Alleghanies, and prevent any entrance into Virginia, with far more facility than he ever does at Manassas. In the second place, if BEAUREGARD is gifted with genius (and those who know him intimately, with a life-long experience, although they deny it, in their hearts accord it to him), he may, when our armies are launched well South, operate himself in our rear, and with a last effort in Tennessee jeopardize, if not destroy, our previously victorious career.*

"I maintain, therefore, that, although the river courses and its commercial importance point out the Valley of the Mississippi for us to adopt as our line of operations, that Richmond, though at present the more difficult and apparently physically, '*materiellement*,' the less important, is, in fact, the object we should strive for; '*materiellement*,' also, because, that taken, Virginia would be found full of Unionists.

"North Carolina would declare itself so, without a blow. We then have the *debouches* of the Alleghanies in our favor, since their population is with us, and form the key-point of the corners of the Middle States and Southern States, we palsy all, overrun the still rebellious, demand New Orleans and the Mississippi banks to reassume against factionists, their comforts, their commerce, their welfare, and their peace.

"So much for my reasoning. The problem I consider nearly reduced to the tactical, and I would like you to consider this, and tell me how best to dislodge the people from Manassas.

"For myself I say, that it is even now to be done as it would have been much better done in September, in October, even in November, viz., rapidly to *mask* Manassas, and simultaneously with troops from all quarters, even Baltimore, fall on JOHNSTON. He and all beyond him would be cut off, or get back most rapidly into Manassas. We could take and hold Winchester,† and then commence a turning move, cutting the rebels from the Rappahannock; all this while offering them a pitched battle. If they themselves disposed (they would be forced) to come out of their intrenchments at Manassas to get it. We are superior to them, and I do not see why, in *masses*, we should not fight as well, and if we are to be beaten, then the oftener we are beaten the sooner we will learn to fight. It is the history of all beaten people, who have *men* and *money* in superabundance.

"Another plan seems to me to mask Manassas towards their right, and then with forty thousand men, destroy their thirty thousand men south of us from Occoquan Creek to Aquia, &c. This, also, would most probably force them to fight in the open field, and then to seize Fredericksburg and thus communicate with expeditions up the York river, or James and (although it has some fearful difficulties) thus attack Richmond almost from the rear (from the north and north-west).

---

* The reader will see herein foreshadowed BRAGG'S Kentucky campaign of 1862, but more particularly HOOD'S desperate venture, which was checked before Nashville, December 15th and 16th, 1864.

† Winchester was considered an important stragetic point before the Revolution, and was fortified at the earliest date of the Anglo-Colonial-French Wars. "Memoir of Gen. GRAHAM," Edinburg, 1862.

"Now I am very anxious to have you give me your views *pro* and *con*, and as to feasibilities. In the idleness of our camps, we the poor generals, discuss *ad libitum*, all these plans, inasmuch as General McCLELLAN'S policy is to exclude every one from his presence. At first there were a few generals admitted to see him (about the time of his reviews). Latterly there is nobody. Some generals, as HEINTZELMAN, &c., &c., have not seen him at all, except at these reviews, and the others almost not at all. This quality of reticence and secrecy are valuable qualities in a man like LOUIS NAPOLEON, or in one of genius—a quality other than mere talents—but I consider it most unfortunate in McCLELLAN. Talents he has; genius he has not. The trifles in the army, which in results, swell to essentials from their utter mismanagement, prove that McCLELLAN (even if from our great resources he succeeds) is at the antipodes of that genius, which, like the first NAPOLEON, could dispense, if he pleased, with all aid, since in the midst of a campaign, he could regulate the smallest supplies of a newly organizing regiment. So far * * * from your not being able to advise for large bodies of men, none that know you will disclaim it. If there exists a preventive, it is that you take the world a little bit too much by force instead of receiving it in practical working order, such as human nature constitutes it. But I have not the slightest doubt, but that your friends will gradually be able to bring your utility more into notice."

Again, KEARNY wrote from Alexandria, on the 19th February, 1682:

"Saturday evening I received a telegraph notice of the serious illness of 'ARCHIE' (his idolized son). I took forty-eight hours' leave, arrived home Sunday at dawn, comforted AGNES, I believe witnessed a favorable change in the disease" (typhoid fever) "of my boy, and left on Monday at 11 P. M. Arrived yesterday in time to take my place, at 10 A. M. on the Board, I had been detailed to (clothing and uniform), and at night went to my brigade. * *

"I have to thank you for four interesting letters, although not meeting fully my hopes. I had hoped that as to passing pieces in the mud that you would have been able to have remembered to have joined in your extensive reading positive facts as to what had been used.

"The printed matter you sent me was most interesting. You have a wonderful faculty of introducing and printing for the public, subjects that are *apropos*.

"The notions are good; as to certain points; as to masking Manassas, it may have been originally yours, but it also belongs to General McDOWELL and others.

"It spoke for itself; the moment you could not force them. As to the idea of Albemarle Sound, I know that it was yours a long while since. I am quite ready to suppose, that you were treated thus * * * precisely because you had given to him, or others (his staff) ideas which struck him as feasible; that he intended to adopt them, (or they might have coincided with his actual plans,) and feared lest by an interview, he might betray the importance he attached to them; or it might truly be, that he is necessarily so overworked, that he could not find time to see you.

"There is so much indiscretion, even treachery, that McC——— has made a rule to see few officers.

"HEINTZELMAN and most of the generals never see him; I think that he is wrong, for much escapes him that ought to be done, and especially since he is an engineer; and since he has brought so many other engineers, and put them in high places, who are as ignorant as himself. I sometimes think, that C. F. SMITH, and GRANT, and BUELL will cut him out, although I am quite ready to believe that no person surpassed McC——— as a man of gre t talents, as a mathematician and calculator. He is also a man of real courage, although I find in many occasions that he has been guilty of '*tatonnement*.' But all allow that McC——— is a superior man. I am sorry to say, that I think, that he wants first what General SCOTT excelled all military men in, his *genius* for command (the innate knowledge of handling men), and yet you are of the opinion that SCOTT was overrated.

"I refer you to the French School of Generals, where *élan* and tactical powers of mind elevate the officer, and are regarded as procuring success far more than strategic subtlety. For myself, I know of no one short of NAPOLEON, in this century that has equalled SCOTT; and it is to be remembered that he led his men to the bayonet charge, at a period when all had been in the habit of running."

Before closing this chapter, a couple of paragraphs from the Address of CORTLANDT PARKER, Esq., are too apposite to be omitted — even although they embrace what may seem to be a repetition of ideas already presented—since they contain extracts from PHIL. KEARNY's letters, reflecting on passing events:

"And so the autumn of 1861 rolled on; KEARNY, and a few like him, impatiently longing for the order to advance; Ball's Bluff checking and delaying it, and carrying sorrow and almost dismay to the hearts of the Northern patriots; Dranesville, partially reassuring them, the victories south and west invigorating the resolution of the Nation; General MCCLELLAN bustling hither and thither, reputed busy and successful in organization; the Cabinet, the President and the Nation, waiting long, at first with full, then with scarce half confidence in the commanding General, for the moment when, with the advance of the Army of the Potomac, the haughty Confederacy should disappear.

"It was not long, however, before the lynx-like perception of General KEARNY saw the truth as to his commanding General, and he expressed it, not insubordinately, but confidentially, and with many cautious and generous hopes that he might be mistaken. In October, 1861, he writes: 'I see a vacillation in his great objects, allowing small objects to intrude.' 'That General McClellan,' he writes, in February, 1862, 'has had full sway for his great *specialité* — talents of calculation and long-headedness — is most fortunate for him and the country. But the United States alone, of all countries, could have supplied by her wonderful virgin resources for a want of genius of command which would, early in September have decided, by *timely fighting* and *maneuvering, what we were doing now by dead momentum.* Fifty thousand more troops on the Potomac would have maneuvered the enemy, with sure success, out of Manassas in September last; England would not have insulted us; foreign powers not been doubtful of us; *the greatness of the American name been more immediately vindicated*, and the terrific expenses been saved by a speedy termination of the war.' March 4th, 1862, he speaks more decidedly: 'Although there is no one exactly to replace McClellan, I now proclaim distinctly that, unless a chief, a LINE officer not an engineer, of military *prestige* (success under fire with troops), is put in command of the Army of the Potomac (leaving McClellan the *minor* duties of General-in-Chief), we will come in for some *awful* disaster; the only person to take his place is General C. F. Smith, in the Army of Kentucky.'

"Up to this time he and General McClellan had never clashed. These opinions were the result of his observation, and very much of his conviction that Ball's Bluff was really an advance from which McClellan shrunk back and threw the blame on General Stone unjustly — scared by the first disaster. Not long after he saw himself what he deemed evidence of the inferiority of McClellan's genius, and thenceforward he was decided in his depreciation of him.'"

CHAPTER XIX.

THE SECOND ADVANCE TO MANASSAS.

"NEW JERSEY BLUES, the bold and true,
Though small the State, the men though few,
They prov'd, in eighteen sixty-two,
They'd deeds of seventy-six outdo;
New Jersey Blues, ye bold and true,
Were worthy KEARNY, KEARNY you!"

"Like all the troops from this State (New Jersey), their gallant conduct during the years that the command existed, rendered invaluable aid to the National cause."

CAPT. BLAKE'S "*Three Years in the Army.*"

"DORSET is fled to RICHMOND."

RICHARD III.

"'Charge, CHESTER, charge! On, STANLEY, on!
Were the last words of MARMION."

SCOTT'S "*Marmion.*"

"No man shed tears for noble MUTIUS;
He lives in Fame that died in Virtue's cause.

TITUS ANDRONICUS.

GLOSTER. "Now is the winter of our discontent
Made glorious summer by this 'son' of York."

RICHARD III.

"HOS EGO GLORIOSOS FECI TULIT ALTER HONORES."

VIRGIL.

"And now he writes * * for his redress:
Sweet scrolls to fly about the streets of Rome!
What's this, but libelling against the Senate,
And blazoning our injustice everywhere?"

TITUS ANDRONICUS.

THE fall of 1861 had been wasted. It was a season admirably adapted to military movements. This is admitted by all the generals who testified before the Committee on the Conduct of the War. The winter also had drifted away in inaction. MCCLELLAN, "from his comfortable house in Washington, issued orders to all the military forces of our country," while, throughout, the rebels continued to flaunt their insulting ensigns within sight, not only of our camps, but almost of our Capital.

This they may be said to have blockaded (in the same degree that Sebastopol was besieged), since their batteries commanded the Potomac, and menaced any foraging parties — sorties, in fact — which ventured beyond our lines. Even Drainsville, so highly honorable to our arms, had been a mere sporadic effort, altogether without results, except the glory acquired by the troops engaged. That which had made KEARNY most indignant at the outset was the rebel occupation of Munson's Hill,* and a friend, in constant communication with him, recorded that, if his suggestions had been attended to, or his proposition had been accepted, the enemy would have been driven out at once, ignominiously, if not actually captured. As on so many other occasions, KEARNY's proposition to move out against them was made known to the rebels by some traitor within our lines almost as soon as it was suggested; and they availed themselves of this, so as to render the contemplated manœuvre as unnecessary as unadvisable.†

The spring at length arrived. The general-in-chief now talked of moving, in the worst season for military movements, after having wasted the best, since it is indisputable that, as a

---

* "CAMP SHERMAN," Washington, *Sept.* 27, 1861.

"The rebel flag is now waving in sight of the President's house. I, myself, saw it, though unable to distinguish the colors. The place is Munson's Hill, three and a half or four miles from the city. Daily skirmishes take place in hearing of the city; even now I hear the report of musketry in the distance, and perhaps some good soldier has fallen in defense of his country, while I have been writing these three lines."—*Soldier's Letter*, by LYDIA MINTURN POST.

† That we made no reconnoissances in force at this time is most astonishing, utterly inexplicable. GUROWSKI, in his Diary from March, 1861, to March, 1862, refers to this at page 157: "McCLELLAN acts as if he had taken the oath to some hidden and veiled deity or combination, by all means not to ascertain any thing about the condition of the enemy. Any European, * * long ago would have pierced the veil by a strong reconnoissance on Centreville. Here 'All quiet on the Potomac.' And I hear Generals * * justifying this colossal offense against common sense, and against the rudiments of military tactics, and even science. Oh, noble, but awfully dealt with American people."

On the subject of reconnoissances the military reader is referred to "Theorie Generale des Reconnaissances Militaires, mise en Concordance avec le Reglement sur le Service des Armees en Campagne et deduite des Pratiques les plus usitees dans les Guerres Modernes; ouvrage compose pour S. A. R. le Duc de Brabant, et offert a ce Prince en manuscrit illustre; par VICTOR-SEVERIN SOBIESKI DE JANINA, Capitaine commandant la 5e batterie montee, au 2e Regiment d'Artillerie Belge, ex-premier Eleve de l'Ecole, d'application de Varsovie. Librarie Militaire, de J. DUMAINE (Ancienne Maison Anselin), Rue et Passage Dauphine, 30, Paris, France."

rule, our finest weather is in the fall, especially that lovely period "Indian Summer," when the balmy atmosphere of the spring is tempered by the bracing coolness of the autumn.

In the second week, "the Ides of March," the rebels evacuated Manassas, but not altogether, as they still held their immense works with a rear guard and made a display of maintaining the post.* According to their own accounts, their determination to do so was not influenced by any action on our part. To those who place implicit faith in official reports, there is no benefit to be derived from the discussion of their motives. It is not likely, however, that they abandoned such scientific and extensive works as they had erected at Centreville and Manassas, if they had not been kept thoroughly advised of the contemplated movements of the Army of the Potomac. JOE JOHNSTON, who had succeeded BEAUREGARD in the chief command in front of Washington, at the close of January, 1862, was not the man to abandon an inch of ground which could be contested with advantage.† As KEARNY'S report, in regard to his participation in that admirably executed advance which drove their rear guard out of their immense works was "suppressed" * * by McCLELLAN,§ it is very likely that he had accomplished much more and deserved far more credit than his superior, prejudiced and partial, was willing to bestow upon an independent

---

* According to TOWNSEND'S Cyclopedia, vol. Ṙ, 21, 62: quoting Herald, 12th March, 1862, etc.: The rebels advanced to Vienna to cover preparations for retreat. KEARNY was sent to guard the party rebuilding the bridge at Beck's (Burke's) Station, March 10th. Vienna, according to the map at hand, is only 12 miles due west of Washington.

† See "*Battle Fields of the South*," chap. xix, page 161 and 163–'4.

§ CORTLANDT PARKER, General KEARNY'S particular friend and counsel, at page 13, of "PHILIP KEARNY, SOLDIER AND PATRIOT," uses these words: * * "General McCLELLAN suppressed his report, as if not entirely pleased with the occurrence." The writer applied to the War Department through influential friends (to whom he tenders his warmest thanks for their assistance), and all the replies agreed as to there being no such report to be found. In McCLELLAN'S own report, at the place where the evacuation is referred to (pages 122, "*Enemy's Works at and near Manassas*," etc., to page 132, where the subject of Manassas is dismissed) General KEARNY'S name is not mentioned, neither the services of his brigade; nor is there any reference to General KEARNY'S own especial report, which is not to be found, nor those of his subordinates, of which copies are annexed to this chapter.

Since this was written, an officer of the United States Army, holding a Major-General's command at that time, remarked that he had heard the KEARNY report (referred to) spoken of and discussed.

thinker, out-spoken, and filled with ideas antagonistic to his policy.

In the preparation of that portion of this biography which relates to the occurrences of 1862, it was determined that KEARNY himself, eye-witnesses and disinterested narrators should be permitted, as far as possible, to tell the whole story.

"In March, 1862, the rebels evacuated Manassas, hastened thence by the enterprise and dash of General KEARNY. It is but justice to notice this, for his reports never saw the light. Indeed, that affair, instead of helping his advancement, evidently and most wrongfully retarded it. We will tell the story in his own words, under date of March 12, 1862: 'I was on the Uniform Board;* dined with the Prince DE JOINVILLE on Thursday; the next day leisurely got up and went to the ferry to go to camp. I was just going on board the steamer when General SUMNER got off, and said quite excitedly and flurried to me, 'Why, your brigade is off; ordered to Burke's Station to relieve General HOWARD in guarding a railroad party.' I hurried to camp; found the brigade still there; went to FRANKLIN'S headquarters; he was in W——, and, by telegraph, sent us varying orders from moment to moment, as if all in W—— were undecided. Finally, late in the day, orders came to take forty-eight hours' rations, and be prepared to remain two days at Burke's. It was three o'clock; the troops looked elegantly, and although the march was awful

---

* The following letter in connection with this Uniform Board has interest, inasmuch as it refers to a common friend, whose appointment from civil life proves that the Militia can produce officers of the highest capacity as well as West Point. It is not well to forget that the Militia, in the famous defence of Lille, rivalled the Regulars led by the famous BOUFFLERS; and this has been the case often elsewhere, even in our own war.

HEADQUARTERS NEW JERSEY BRIGADE,
CAMP SEMINARY, *January* 21, 1862.

"Your most interesting letter still affords me subject of reflection, and, strange to say, the BURNSIDE expedition seems to be about to realize your project as to Albemarle Sound" (the advance on Richmond, through Petersburg, from the base of Norfolk).

"I think that I thanked you for the interesting extracts you forwarded me from the useful translations made by you from the German. * * * It was a noble pearl before conceited * * * * * I have recently been thrown into contact, most agreeably, with General BUTTERFIELD. He seems a charming gentleman and of the right material. I give you credit for your discernment to him. He has been brought forward entirely by regular officers, * * * and therefore solely on his merits. I have ever said that his Twelfth regiment was one of the most superbly set up regiments that I have ever seen in any quarter of the globe, and principally composed of raw men (so much the better for him with his good discipline). * * * The South must crack and crash." * * *

Again he speaks delightfully of the same General, 28th April, 1862: "I saw our noble friend BUTTERFIELD yesterday; he was General in the Trenches. He is bound to be a very distinguished officer; he has a peculiar gift of administration, and great military spirit, and is a noble-hearted fellow."

owing to the roads, they kept up their spirits. It was four o'clock, daybreak, when I arrived at Burke's. I slept an hour, mounted a fresh horse, and galloped about until twelve with General HOWARD and others, studying my position. I was then gallopping about, except a nap for two hours, on other fresh horses, till nine at night. The next day I ascertained by negroes that the enemy were preparing to leave. I immediately pushed on with my troops and manœuvered in all directions, all which resulted in my driving them back everywhere. I kept applying for orders, which were not sent me, but still I kept on. General MCCLELLAN'S whole movement has been thus brought about.

"'I was the first to enter the stronghold at the Junction. My Third New Jersey planted their flag, and I was returning to Centreville when I met General MCCLELLAN and all his staff, and some two thousand horse, approaching with skirmishers, as if we were Secessionists.* They had done the same thing in advancing to Fairfax Court House, which I had taken some twenty-four hours previously."

According to a Philadelphia correspondent: "The smoke was still rising from the black ruins of the numerous quarters and storehouses recently fired. Some of the quarters, which had not been fired, were filled with articles of value, which time had not permitted their owners to carry away. There were provisions enough to last the regiment for a week, and of good quality. The men were not slow to appropriate what lay before them. Among other things found were barrels of eggs, already cooked by the fire. General KEARNY was with the advance all day, and gave the men free access to everything left behind. As he rode into the works, after their occupation, and drew up in front of our line, lifting his cap under the Stars and Stripes, three rounds of applause welcomed the hero of Cherubusco and the San Antonio Gate.

"In approaching Manassas on this occasion, General KEARNY expanded his brigade over the country, so as to make the enemy think him the van of the whole army. Hence they made a precipitate retreat, leaving the very meal they were about to make untasted, for the use of their adversaries. It was a bold, skillful, and energetic movement, and deserved a commendation which it

* "General MCCLELLAN, advancing in consequence of information received from General KEARNY, accompanied by his staff and two thousand horse, was met by General KEARNY as he was returning to Centreville. The advancing party had skirmishers in front, and were altogether unprepared, but of course greatly delighted, to find that they had encountered, not Secessionists, but their own troops."—*Newark Daily Advertiser March 17th*, 1862.

"I am glad enough to hear that the Jersey Volunteers under General KEARNY'S command were the first to occupy Manassas. They were eleven miles in advance of any other part of the army in that direction; and when General MCCLELLAN and his staff were on their way, they met General KEARNY *returning*, and when General MCDOWELL reached the village he found it in possession of part of General KEARNY'S brigade, as before stated.

"I am so glad that this was a fact."—E. W. L., *14th March*, 1862.

did not receive. His Division commander, he thought, evidently disliked it, and General McClellan suppressed his Report, as if not entirely pleased with the occurrence."

Compare with the foregoing the account of a war-correspondent, who accompanied this advance:

"The occupation of the three successive points — Fairfax Court-House, Centreville and Manassas — has neither been fully nor accurately stated. They were all taken possession of without bloodshed; but not without danger and daring.

"The 2d New Jersey regiment reached Sangster's Rail Road Station on Sunday (9th March), between three and four P. M., over eleven miles in advance of any other part of the army in that direction, and by the boldness of the movement led the rebel forces in that neighborhood to believe that a large national force was at its back, and both rebel cavalry and infantry were seen by the regiment to fly at its approach.

"In the meantime the New Jersey troops, under Captain Van Sickle and Lieutenant Holt, advanced by the Cross Roads upon this village, and took possession of it about 5½ P. M. Sunday, the bulk of the rebel cavalry retreating before them.

"Troops were left at the junction of the Cross Road with the old Braddock Road, with orders to advance cautiously towards Centreville.

"The next morning an advance guard of the 1st regiment, consisting of Company B, entered Centreville, followed by the remainder of the regiment about 11 A. M.

"The same day (Monday) the 3d New Jersey scouted the country in front of Sangster's Station, and at 7½ Tuesday morning entered Manassas.

"Cooking fires were found still burning, and even coffee pots on them boiling, food spread out on tables, &c., with other evidences of hasty leave-taking, and, for once, of a movement on our part being made without the rebel's previous knowledge. A large quantity of subsistence stores, small arms scattered about, tents, &c., were also left behind. The cannon had all been removed, and some of them replaced by logs of wood painted in imitation of their predecessors. The rebel's cars were heard by our advanced troops running all day Sunday — now supposed to be engaged in withdrawing their artillery. Col. Averill, acting Brigadier, made a reconnoisance on Manassas Plains on Monday night, but did not enter the fortifications at the junction."

There was just enough fighting to show what might have been done had Kearny been let loose on the 7th, instead of being pulled to and fro by see-saw orders.

One of the most brilliant cavalry exploits of the Great American Civil War occurred during these brushes with the enemy's

30

rear-guard. This was the charge of First Lieutenant HARRY B. HIDDEN, of New York city, with a sergeant and twelve men of the 1st N. Y. (Lincoln) Cavalry. KEARNY had "ordered him to move forward cautiously and feel the enemy's position."

On Sunday, 9th March, he fell in with the pickets of the enemy, a score in number, and drove them in, till finally he was suddenly surrounded by a hundred and fifty of the enemy. The alternative was to cut his way out, or to surrender at discretion. "Will you follow me?" said the unshrinking officer, "To the death!" was the unanimous reply; and through the rebel ranks they hewed their way, turning not to the right or left till they emerged from the forest at Sangster's station, the enemy either fleeing or laying down their arms before them. After this daring action, and while making their way to the camp, with thirteen prisoners, one to each man, one of the skulking assasins, who had laid down his arms, seized his musket and shot the retiring officer dead upon the spot.

The ball entered the back, near the top of the shoulder, and passed out through the neck under the chin, severing numerous blood vessels, whose profuse bleeding soon closed the career of one of the most promising men in our army.

Lieutenant HIDDEN was possessed of the most manly beauty, beloved by all who knew him, and by none more than his companions in arms.

General KEARNY has stated that this charge has not been surpassed in gallantry by any during the war, and it is the general theme of conversation among those cognizant of it in Washington and Alexandria.

According to another account, "KEARNY, who saw the whole movement, declared it to be one of the most brilliant he had ever seen, and took each man by the hand on his return and complimented him for his bravery."

With a praiseworthy liberality, which, had it been imitated, would have filled our country with the most interesting memorials of the war, HIDDEN's family had a large picture painted of this little affair, which sparkles like a gem of the first water amid so much paste. The picture is a study in itself, from the attention paid by the artist to costume and accessories. It hangs on the staircase of the New York Historical Society, and in itself is a valuable piece of history.

As this advance and occupation of Centreville and Manassas was a very important incident in KEARNY'S career, and one almost unknown to his countrymen, too much evidence cannot be brought together in establishing the fact beyond doubt or cavil. JOHN S. FOSTER, in his "New Jersey in the Rebellion," presents the following statement:

"Meanwhile the torpor which had characterized the War Department, and operated as a check upon all movements in the field, had been dissipated by the selection of EDWIN M. STANTON, a man of rough but inexhaustible energy, as Secretary, in place of SIMON CAMERON, and a vast army having been accumulated on the south of the Potomac, on the 27th of January, 1862, an order was issued by the President, directing General McCLELLAN to 'impel all the disposable force of the army,' on or before February the 22d, for the seizure and occupation of a point upon the railroad north-westward of Manassas Junction. The Commander-in-Chief, however, by inducing the President to consent to an advance upon Richmond, by way of the Peninsula, obtained a practical suspension of this order, and no advance, consequently, was made at the time designated by the Executive. All this time, however, General KEARNY, restive under constrained inaction, was watching with sleepless vigilence for opportunity to show the folly of inactivity, and at length he realized his desire. On the 7th of March his Brigade was ordered to Burke's Station, on the Orange and Alexandria railroad, for the purpose of guarding a party of laborers, and reaching there, on the following day, made an extended reconnoissance of the country for several miles around. Subsequently, he was informed by some negroes, that the enemy was preparing to leave Manassas.* *He was not slow to act upon this hint.*

"Apprising General FRANKLIN of the information received, but without awaiting orders, he at once pushed on with his troops, throwing out skirmishers over a wide extent of country, and driving steadily before him the scattered pickets of the enemy. On the 9th the Second and Third Regiments, with a squadron of the Lincoln Cavalry, occupied Sangster Station, a point on the Alexandria railroad, about five miles from Bull Run and nine from Manassas Junction; the Fourth Regiment acting as support to the advance. Here they surprised a detachment of Rebel cavalry, killing three, and capturing a lieutenant and eleven men, and losing one officer of the cavalry, killed at the first fire. The First Regiment had, meanwhile, advanced to Fairfax Court House, whence, on the morning of the 10th, a detachment under Major HAT-

* "Rebel reports show that their (rebel) evacuation of their winter camps was completed on this very day," 8th March, 1862.—FOSTER, page 71 to text pages 70–72. "The rebels advanced to Vienna to cover their preparations for retreat."—TOWNSEND'S (gigantic) Cyclopedia of the War, R. 21, 62, March 10th. *Herald*, March 12th, 1862.

FIELD and Captain VAN SICKLE was sent forward to Centreville, which place was entered about noon — the remainder of the regiment coming up shortly after, under Lieutenant-Colonel McALLISTER. On the same day, the remainder of the brigade, pushing cautiously forward, reached, and at ten o'clock in the morning, entered the abandoned works at Manassas Junction — eight companies of the Third Regiment being the first to take possession, and hoist the regimental flag. The withdrawal of the enemy at this point had evidently been precipitate, and an immense amount of hospital and commissary stores was found, together with eighty baggage-wagons, several locomotives, four or five cars, two hundred tents, and other property of value. Among the trophies were also seven flags, one of white silk, with the motto, 'Carolinians in the Field — Traitors, Beware,' and another bordered with heavy silver fringe, with the inscription, 'State Rights: Sic Semper Tyrannis.' "

Any one who is familiar with the grand operations of war, will perceive that KEARNY's advance on this occasion, very much resembled one, with which every one who pretends to be acquainted with military history, ought to be aware, that of SEYDLITZ on Gotha, in 1757.

At the same time, the sudden abandonment of their hutted camp by the rebels, calculated to have been capacious enough for 60,000 men, and presenting certain evidence to a soldier's eye, that it had recently sheltered 30,000, resembled the flight of the Syrians, in the days of King Joram. These had been investing Samaria, and reduced it to great straits, when they became impressed with the idea that they were about to be attacked by overwhelming numbers, and fled for their lives, leaving their camp even as it was.

About two thousand two hundred and fifty years after this occurrence, during the Italian war of 1848, something similar took place, when that obstinate octogenarian, RADETSKY, ate up CHARLES ALBERT's dinner at Codogno.

Neither of these are the case in point referred to. The example of SEYDLITZ, however, is apposite almost to the letter.

In October, 1757, the French and Franco-Germans advanced with the expectation of getting possession of Torgau, Wittenberg, Leipsic, and especially Dresden, depots as important to Prussia at that period, as Washington* to us at all times.

* General MITCHELL, in his "Biographies of Eminent Soldiers," FREDERIC THE GREAT, page 306, says the delay of Marshal SOUBISE at Halberstadt saved Magdeburg, whose loss to Prussia would have been equivalent to that of Washington in our case.

On the 13th (19th) October, SEYDLITZ, an officer most famous as a leader of cavalry, was detached by FREDERIC THE GREAT, to watch the enemy. Remarkable as he was in the conduct of his own proper arm, SEYDLITZ displayed equal capacity in the direction of every other, and of all the arms combined.

It is more than likely that several of the victories credited to FREDERIC were due to the generalship of SEYDLITZ, his eye, head and hand; Freyberg, in 1762, certainly was in this union of qualities. KEARNY closely resembled this Prussian. Both, bred cavalry officers, were as sagacious strategists and as perfect tacticians as they were hard fighters. It is more than probable that FREDERIC's greatest defeat at Cunersdorf might have been averted, or greatly lessened in degree, had not SEYDLITZ been stricken down, severely wounded, even as KEARNY was killed, at a crisis.

In advance of the main Prussian army, the dispositions of SEYDLITZ, which cleared the French out of Gotha, were elegant. FREDERIC cannot repress his admiration.*

Just as KEARNY, in approaching Manassas, expanded his brigade over the country, so as to make the rebels imagine he was the van of the whole Union army, even so SEYDLITZ disposed of his cavalry force on the 13th (19th) October, 1757. It would seem that he spread his hussars over an extensive front, vast in proportion to his numbers, with his dragoons — who skirmished on foot as well as mounted — in the second line, so as to give the idea that he was followed by a large body of infantry, deployed in line of battle.† Meanwhile, his supports were posted so as to be able to protect his retreat, in case the enemy discovered his strategem. The French and their Ger-

* "Any other general," says FREDERIC, " except SEYDLITZ would have applauded himself to have escaped, in such a situation. without loss. SEYDLITZ would not have been satisfied with himself, had he not derived gain. The example proves that the capacity and fortitude of the general, are, in war, more decisive than the number of his troops. A man of mediocrity, who should perceive himself under such circumstances, discouraged by the awful appearance of the foe, would have retired as he approached, with the loss of half his men, in a skirmish of the rear guard, which the superior cavalry of the enemy would have been in haste to engage. The artful use made of the regiment of dragoons, extended and shown to the enemy at a distance, was highly glorious to General SEYDLITZ in so difficult a situation."

† Compare pages 44-48—General SEYDLITZ, a Military Biography, by Captain ROBERT NEVILLE LAWLEY, 2d Life Guards: London, W. Clowes & Sons, 14 Charing Cross, For private circulation only, 1852.

man allies were convinced that no less than the whole Prussian army was upon them. They abandoned Gotha precipitately, leaving behind them, prisoners, booty, and the very dinner of their Commander-in-Chief.

The exalted opinion of FREDERIC himself, in regard to this achievement, is fully borne out by NAPOLEON in his "observations" on this campaign. "SOUBISE at once transferred his head-quarters to Gotha, and occupied the town with eight thousand grenadiers and a division of cavalry. He had scarcely installed himself therein, when SEYDLITZ disposing his fifteen squadrons in a single rank (or line), marched boldly upon the head-quarters, which hastened to save itself as quickly as possible, in the direction of Eisenach. The eight thousand grenadiers retreated, after firing a few shots; the head-quarters baggage, and prisoners fell into the hands of the Prussians. This shameful event was the prelude to ROSBACH." Even as this dash of SEYDLITZ into Gotha, was the prologue to ROSBACH, even so KEARNY's stoop on Manassas, might and should have been the prelude to a grand victory and a decisive campaign, had McCLELLAN permitted him to follow it up. As he said on another occasion, "If you once whip, you must always whip. It becomes a way of doing the thing." In the same manner that SEYDLITZ swept down like an eagle with wide extended wings, upon Gotha, even so KEARNY made his bold, skillful, and energetic movement on Manassas, and gobbled tents, small arms, stores, prisoners, booty, and trophies; among these seven flags, one of white silk, belonging to a South Carolinian corps, and, according to a private account, another, the flag of a Georgia regiment.

A cotemporaneous letter states, that KEARNY's brigade was eleven miles in advance of any other troops.

According to a Major-General, who followed in the track of KEARNY, and wrote on the 11th March, from Fairfax Court House—

"The enemy has abandoned his works at Centreville and Manassas, and fled, leaving tents and barracks standing, many tools, spades, etc., and considerable provisions. Whiskey in all the tents and barracks, pretty much."

This energetic and successful movement of KEARNY invites and will reward reflection. Reader, soldier or civilian, is it probable that a general like JOE JOHNSTON would have abandoned commissary's stores, war materials, some of which were articles difficult to replace, and left behind him flags, and even his unburied dead* in the hospitals, unless the evacuation of his works had been hurried by a sharp aggressive? That general who conducted his retreat, during the Atlanta campaign, so as to rival that of the Allies after LUTZEN and BAUTZEN, in 1813, and left not a linchpin behind for SHERMAN, was not the man to yield any booty or trophies except under compulsion.†

In the first place, it is useless for the rebels to deny what follows, because it is the sworn evidence of unbiassed witnesses, and what McCLELLAN himself admits, must be conceded by his friends. "I should judge," swears I. S. POTTER, "as far as I am able to do so, that the troops had left there in great haste. Several hundred barrels of flour, that they had attempted to destroy by burning, lay there in a pile partly consumed. There was also a part of a train of cars there, partially destroyed. Among other things, I found a very complete printing office, with press, types, forms standing, an imposing stone, army blanks, etc., and I should think a little newspaper had been printed there. They left tents standing, both at Manassas and Centreville."

BAYARD TAYLOR testifies that the last of the rebels left Centreville on Sunday morning, and there were a few left at Manassas Junction on Monday as late as 2 P. M.

JOHN T. HILL, a resident at Centreville, swore that General JOHNSTON returned to that place on Saturday evening, staid all night, and left on Sunday morning, 9th March, by the way of Stone Bridge, which was then blown up. He had with him 2,000 Infantry and 2,000 Cavalry. They moved off in a hurry,

---

* *See Report Col.* SIMPSON, *3d N. J. V., attached.*

† To the reader who may not be familiar with the operations in 1813, it is due to state that the Allies withdrew so defiantly that NAPOLEON could gain no advantage over them. In an ebullition of indignation, or ill temper, he sacrificed some of his best troops in a reckless charge upon their rear-guard, near Reichenbach, and exposed himself and staff so recklessly that his favorite, DUROC, and General KIRGENER were killed by a cannon ball, following on just behind him. The noble conduct of the Prussians and Russians drew forth, then, the bitter exclamation, "What! after such a butchery, no result? No prisoners? Those fellows will not leave us a nail; they rise from their ashes. When will this be done?"

and if our troops had been quicker, and had continued their march, they would have caught this rebel rear-guard. Manassas was not burnt till Monday, 10th of March.

McCLELLAN (11th March) corroborates all this: "Their movement from here (Fairfax Court-House) was very sudden. They left many wagons, some caissons, clothing, ammunition, personal baggage, etc. Their winter-quarters were admirably constructed, many not yet quite finished."

What a pretty little fight swift-footed KEARNY might have had with deliberate JOHNSTON had the former been allowed to move just one day sooner. Both had about the same numbers, and the superiority possessed by KEARNY in artillery and infantry, would just have made up for the advantage of position enjoyed by JOHNSTON. Had Schicksal (Fate) so decreed, it might have furnished the handsomest episode of the war, and if KEARNY had won would have been the entering wedge to great results. If, as usual, on the one hand, the rebels had reinforced their rear-guard, KEARNY would likewise soon speedily have been reinforced, for there were plenty of troops — good men and true — within supporting distance, burning for a fight. Here, as so often, Time was against us. Had it favored, the decisive battle might have been fought in 1862, just where we suffered such a physical reverse in 1861.

McCLELLAN's own language demonstrates the correctness of KEARNY's views, as expressed in his letter — that the true plan was to mask Manassas with a sufficient portion of our grand army, and then pivoting on Alexandria sweep round to the left and gobble or destroy all the dispersed divisions of the rebel army* occupied in maintaining the blockade of the Potomac, and cantoned all along the right bank of that river and occupying Fredericksburg. Thus, one by one, as events developed themselves, they equally and simultaneously proved not only the correctness of KEARNY's views and predictions, but showed

* "He, General KIRBY SMITH, told me that McCLELLAN might probably have destroyed the Southern army with the greatest ease during the first winter, and without running much risk to himself, as the Southerners were so much over-elated by their easy triumph at Manassas, and their army had dwindled away."—*Three Months in the Southern States, April—June*, 1863, by Lieut.-Col. FREEMANTLE, Coldstream Guards.

that he was a great strategist, in whose mind the map of the theatre of war was displayed. He was not only capable of estimating the intrinsic value of positions, but their relative bearing to each other. Then, when the fighting actually commenced, his perfect comprehension of tactics, and their practical application was equally shown, even as his plan (detailed in a letter — destroyed among others, by a relative since dead) for the capture of the rebel force on Munson's Hill was superciliously whistled down the wind, to his great chagrin. Even so were his plans for the capture of Manassas, and the rebel force in that position, regarded as the vain imaginings of a military dreamer, if they were even listened to with consideration. Had KEARNY been allowed to advance on the 7th March, according to NAPOLEON's method of formulating chances, the odds were ten to one in favor of his trapping JOE JOHNSTON; a capture in itself equivalent to a victory.

As it was, even with his celerity and boldness, he reaped no benefit before the public, and his report, whose publication would have been a partial act of justice, was not only suppressed but must have been kept back, or subsequently destroyed, since no copy is reported as to be found in the archives of the war office, nor in any publication by authority examined, although the reports of his subordinates are on file at Washington and were kindly furnished to assist in the preparation of this work.

To say that KEARNY bore these slights and wrongs with philosophical equinamity would be doing injustice to the high spirit of the man, and, considering all the reports which were spread abroad prior to his appointment, the only wonder is, that instead of writing as bitterly as he did, he did not write more so and more.*

---

* Persons who blame KEARNY for the freedom with which he wrote home, should recollect that only those who fear scrutiny and criticism object to letter-writing. WELLINGTON experienced the difficulty in a greater degree, but how did the "Iron Duke" meet it? Read No. 510, "Selections from the Dispatches and General Orders of Field Marshal the Duke of Wellington," page 453:

LOUZAN, 16*th March*, 1811.

To the Earl of Liverpool:

* * * * * * * * * * * * *

"I am sure your Lordship does not expect that I or any other officer in command of a British army, can pretend to prevent the correspondence of the officers with their

The great error that KEARNY committed was in not confining his criticisms to those by whom they were deserved, but in going out of his direct course to reflect upon those who felt kindness and admiration for him. Still, as he doubtless never intended that these letters — "epistolary soliloquies" — should come before the public, success would have modified his views; and if he had risen to the high command for which he was destined, when death struck him down on the threshold of fortune, he was too loftily magnanimous not to have forgotten the injuries done to the brigade and division commander. Had he lived, the very letters, for which he has been so much blamed by many would have passed through the fire into thin air like many of his bitter speeches, sarcasms, which, although in a measure deserved by those at whom they were aimed, were the expressions of a wounded spirit, rendered extremely irritable by sickness, suffering, over-work and calculated misappreciation. Thus one wrong begets another, and McCLELLAN's injustice to KEARNY, evinced by the suppression of his report (if Mr. PARKER is correct as to the fact), in regard to the operations of his brigade and their occupation of Manassas, was the source of all that was temporarily unloveable and unlovely in a generous nature.

---

friends. It could not be done if attempted, and the attempt would be considered an endeavor by an individual to deprive the British public of intelligence, of which the Government and Parliament do not choose to deprive them. I have done every thing in my power, by way of remonstrance, and have been very handsomely abused for it; but I cannot think of preventing officers from writing to their friends. This intelligence must certainly have gone from some officer of this army, by whom it was confidentially communicated to his friends in England; and I have heard that it was circulated from one of the officers, with a plan."

CAMP KEARNY, VIRGINIA, March 15, 1862.

BRIGADIER-GENERAL KEARNY:

SIR — I hasten to lay before you a report of the movements of the squadron (Companies A and H) of the First New York (Lincoln) Cavalry, while attached to your brigade during your advance to Centreville and Manassas.

Leaving our camp at three P. M., Thursday, the 6th instant, I joined your column on the Little River Turnpike, furnishing the advance guard, commanded by myself, and the rear guard, in charge of Lieutenant THOMSON. On the march that day and evening, my command was constantly employed in scouting, bearing orders, etc. At four o'clock A. M., of Friday I reached Burk's Station, and was assigned my camping ground. Shortly after daylight my entire squadron was drafted away in squads of from five to twenty men each, to act as videttes and scouts in the vicinity of Burk's Station, and to operate with the various infantry regiments of your brigade, being subject to the orders of their several colonels. On Saturday, Captain JONES, with fifteen men, accompanied yourself on an extended visit to all the pickets and sentries of your command. This detachment, accompanied by yourself, also made an extended reconnoissance along the line of railroad toward Fairfax Station. The remainder of my command, in charge of myself, Lieutenants HIDDEN, ALEXANDER and THOMSON, was detached in small parties, reconnoitering and acting with the different regiments of your brigade. On Sunday morning the usual number of pickets and orderlies was furnished by me, and duly posted. At ten o'clock, Lieutenant ALEXANDER, with twenty men, was dispatched on scouting service towards the Occoquan; his report is forwarded herewith. At the same time, Captain JONES, myself, Lieutenants HIDDEN and THOMSON reported, with twenty men, to yourself. Lieutenants HIDDEN and THOMSON were dispatched to the different picket stations to obtain more mounted men, and shortly after reported to you at Fairfax Station with an additional force of thirty men. At this point Lieutenant ALEXANDER also reported from his scouting expedition, thus increasing my command to seventy men. While awaiting the arrival of the infantry, my young officers were dispatched with men in every direction to look for the enemy, who was known to be near us. When the infantry came up, myself, Captain JONES and Lieutenant THOMSON were sent with twenty-five men to scour the woods around Payne's Church, as far as the Old Braddock road. Lieutenants HIDDEN and ALEXANDER accompanied you to Sangster's Station, as detailed in Lieutenant ALEXANDER's report. From Payne's Church I dispatched Lieutenant THOMPSON to you with a report of my movements. I subsequently received orders from you to advance to Fairfax Court House, in company with a detachment of infantry, and soon arrived at that place, approaching it cautiously, to find that it had been evacuated by the enemy but a short time before. Shortly afterwards I returned to Fairfax Station, arriving there at dark, and received orders to occupy Payne's Church for the night. I was here joined by Lieutenants ALEXANDER and THOMPSON, and their detachments. I here learned of the glorious death of Lieutenant HIDDEN, of my company. He was a splendid officer and a courteous gentleman, whose loss is deeply felt by all who knew him, but by none more than myself.

On Monday morning I was forced to return to Burk's Station with my entire command for the purpose of obtaining forage for my jaded horses. In the afternoon I was dispatched to Headquarters with orders. Lieutenant ALEXANDER with fifteen men was ordered to accompany you to Centreville, which he did, entering that strongly fortified place with you in advance of any other Union troops. Subsequently Captain JONES received orders to follow you with the remainder of the squadron and did so without loss of time. An extended reconnoissance was then made towards Bull Run by Lieutenant ALEXANDER, who learned that the rebel forces were but a few hours in advance. That night the squadron returned to Payne's Church to await further orders. On Tuesday morning I received orders from you to take a position beyond Sangster's Station for the purpose of holding the railroad to that point. At four P. M., I returned to Payne's Church, and before my men could dismount, was ordered to march to Manassas and occupy that point, relieving the Third New Jersey Regiment. After a tedious march of five hours, without forage for the tired and hungry horses, I arrived at Manassas at nine P. M., to find myself with one hundred men far in advance of the army, occupying the rebel stronghold, while on every side was found evidence showing that the enemy had taken a hasty departure but a few hours previously. Our camp was alarmed once during the night by the approach of several horsemen, who fled at the fire of the sentry. We were surprised shortly after daylight on Wednesday by the arrival within our lines of several contrabands, and when we left at four P. M., to return, thirty negroes had sought our protection—some of them having walked twenty-five miles the previous night. On Wednesday afternoon I reported to you at Fairfax Court House, and was again quartered at Payne's Church. On Thursday you kindly permitted my command to rest, a relaxation from duty being absolutely required by the horses in the squadron.

On Friday I was ordered to report with my squadron to my regiment at Fairfax Court House, and was thus relieved from duty with your brigade.

In concluding this report I beg to return you my sincere thanks for the kindness and attention which my command universally received at your hands, and beg to assure you that it is a matter of deep regret with both officers and men of the squadron that they were not permitted to serve longer under your immediate command. In conclusion, I take this opportunity to return my thanks to the officers and men of the squadron for the energy and alacrity displayed in performing the arduous duties required of them.

I also forward herewith, at your request, the names of the men who so nobly sustained Lieutenant Hidden in his brilliant charge at Sangster's Station on the 9th instant:

Corporal E. LEWIS,
Company H, since promoted to be Sergeant.
Private CHARLES P. IVES,
Company H, since promoted to be Corporal.
Private ROBERT C. CLARK,
Company H, since promoted to be Corporal.
Private ALBERT H. VAN SAUN,
Company A, since promoted to be Corporal.

Private	MICHAEL O'NEAL,	Company	H.
"	JAMES LYNCH,	"	"
"	CORNELIUS RILEY,	"	"
"	HUGH McSAULEY,	"	"
'	HERMANN CAMERON,	"	"
"	JOHN CAMERON,	"	"
"	MARTIN MURRAY,	"	"
"	JOHN BOGERT,	"	"
"	WILLIAM SIMONSON,	"	A.
"	CHESTER C. CLARK,	"	"
"	JOHN NUGENT,	"	"
"	JOHN R. WILSON,	"	"
"	HENRY HIGGINS,	"	"

Private Wilson alone captured three prisoners, compelling them to lay down their rms, and accompany him from the field.

I have the honor to be, sir,
Your obedient servant,
(Signed) J. K. STEARNS,
Captain Commanding Squadron.

HEADQUARTERS, SECOND REGIMENT, NEW JERSEY VOLUNTEERS,
CAMP SEMINARY, VA., March 16, 1862.

SIR: I proceed to furnish to the Headquarters of the First Brigade, General FRANKLIN'S Division, a detailed account of the movements of this regiment during the past week, while upon its march towards Manassas and vicinity.

Pursuant to Brigade orders (excepting Captain TAY'S Company, doing picket duty at the time), repaired to the Brigade parade, on Friday, the 7th instant, at one o'clock P. M., where General KEARNY'S command was formed. The regiment was provided with the shelter tent, six days' rations, forty rounds of ball cartridge issued to each man, and in the cartridge boxes, together with thirty extra rounds to each man, transported by the quartermaster. With the knapsacks packed, and thus provided, the regiment, in company with the rest of the brigade, proceeded on its march to Burk's Station, on the Orange and Alexandria railroad, by way of the Little River turnpike and the Old Braddock road, reaching its destination about midnight, after a long and tedious march, the road after leaving the turnpike, being considerably obstructed with mud.

On the march, the flank companies, commanded by Captains CLOSE and WILDRICK, were detached and placed under the command of Lieut. Colonel BROWN of the Third Regiment, constituting with similar companies from other regiments, a light battalion in advance of the brigade. The remaining seven companies under my command encamped at the station that night, and remained there till the morning, Sunday, the 9th instant, when by order of General KEARNY, we proceeded up the railroad to Fairfax Station, leaving two companies, under Captains WIEBECKE and STOLL, at the rifle-pits, constructed by the enemy in rear of the station. From this point a scout of twenty men, under Lieutenant VREELAND, accompanied by two mounted dragoons, proceeded in the direction of Fairfax Court House, while the balance of Lieutenant VREELAND'S company, under Lieutenant BLEWETT, skirted the dense wood adjoining the station on the north. Communication was at once opened with Colonel TAYLOR in command of the Third Regiment, in advance at Sangster's Station, and with Colonel SIMPSON, in command of the Fourth Regiment, in the rear. While occupying this position, two companies, Captains BISHOP and HOPWOOD, under command of Major RYERSON, were sent forward to act as flankers for Colonel TAYLOR'S command.

About eleven o'clock A. M., I received information that the enemy's pickets had been driven back by a detachment of cavalry just in front of Colonel TAYLOR'S Regiment, and at the same time was ordered to withdraw the companies acting as flankers, also Lieutenant BLEWETT'S command, skirting the adjoining wood, and proceed with my battalion to the support of Colonel TAYLOR, which order was promptly executed. About two P. M., I was ordered with my command, consisting of five companies, to take position in line of battle on a commanding hill just in advance of Colonel TAYLOR'S regiment, and hold it until the darkness of the evening would enable me to withdraw without being observed. This hill was the picket-station occupied by the enemy, and from which our cavalry had just driven them, and was but little more than five miles from Manassas Junction.

About seven P. M., I left this position (the companies retiring behind the hill separately), and proceeded back to Fairfax Station, where we encamped in company with the Third Regiment, and where we remained until the morning of Tuesday, the 11th instant, when, pursuant to orders (the flank companies and the picket company having now rejoined us), we took up our line of march to Fairfax Court House, and entered the town with band playing. Here we encamped upon the ground selected by Colonel SIMPSON for this regiment, and remained in camp there until Friday, the 14th instant, when, in company with the whole brigade, at seven P. M., we struck our tents and took up our line of march, back to this camp, arriving there about midnight. The men returned in good health and full of enthusiasm, created by the movements of this brigade during its absence from camp.

A single casualty occurred during our absence; Captain DUFFY'S company was detailed by Colonel TAYLOR, commanding the post at Fairfax Station, on Monday, the 10th instant, as a guard for the erection of the telegraph from the Station to the Court House. A private of this company, THOMAS W. SPRIGGS, was accidentally shot through the head while removing his musket from the stack, and expired in a few moments.

Your obedient servant,

(Signed), J. M. TUCKER,

Colonel Second Regiment New Jersey Volunteers.

To Captain J. M. WILSON,

Assistant Adjutant-General.

CAMP NEAR FORT WORTH,
VIRGINIA, March 16, 1862.

SIR: In pursuance of order this moment received, I have the honor to report the following as an account of the movements of the Third Regiment New Jersey Volunteers, during the march of the last week towards Manassas.

Left Camp Fort Worth, Friday, March 7, 1862, about four o'clock P. M., with the First Brigade (General KEARNY'S); that night marched to Burk's, twelve miles, and bivouacked. The 8th, Third Regiment marched to camp near railroad, one mile east of Fairfax Station, and relieved the picket of the Sixty-fourth New York State Volunteers. Left camp on the 9th, on a reconnoissance with twenty cavalry of the First New York Regiment, towards Occoquan; returned to Fairfax Station about noon. Soon after, received orders from yourself in person to take some five companies, or parts thereof (balance of our regiment being picketed to guard our left flank and Fairfax), and proceed by railroad and march upon Sangster's Station, three miles east of Bull Run. About half a mile this side of Sangster's the enemy appeared, in reconnoitering parties of cavalry and some infantry, on the right and left of the railroad. They fell back as our flankers advanced. The regiment marched steadily until the advance reached Sangster's; there, in your presence and by your orders, they occupied a commanding position, in line of battle, on the crest of a hill to the right of the railroad. I had under my orders, of the First New York Cavalry, sixteen men and one corporal, under First Lieutenant HIDDEN. Just before leaving the railroad, I ordered this officer to advance in the open fields and reconnoitre, and if the force was not greatly superior to his own, he might charge them. He went off at a brisk trot, nor did he check his horses until he charged into the midst of their pickets. The enemy being greatly superior in numbers, and having the advantage of cover of pines, he lost his life in the gallant charge, but drove the enemy into a rapid retreat, leaving arms and many knapsacks and blankets. Thirteen prisoners were taken, with a lieutenant and non-commissioned officer. They proved to be the First Maryland Regiment. Very soon after, the Second Regiment of KEARNY'S Brigade came up and joined us; they occupied the ground of the enemy's picketing regiment until night, when a small company was left to guard Sangster's Station until next day. That day—10th instant—by your orders, eight companies of the Third Regiment marched upon Union Mills late in the day, and bivouacked the same night beyond Sangster's Station. At four A. M., the 11th instant, contined the march; arrived at Bull Run and found the bridge partially burned—it took about one hour to repair it. Crossed, and continued a rapid march to Manassas Junction. Arrived at half-past nine A. M., previously having deployed into line of battle and sent Captain GIBSON, with a flank company of skirmishers, into the place. We found it deserted, except by a few citizens, with two or three wagons, loading the spoils left by the rebels. The flag of the Union was instantly hoisted upon the flag-staff of one of the enemy's works; about which time you joined our regiment, upon which, by your order, had been conferred the honor and great satisfaction of hoisting the American ensign upon the notorious hold of the rebels. The regiment, by your orders, marched the same day to Centreville, where they arrived at sunset. The following morning, 12th instant, returned to Fairfax Station, and the same day to Fairfax Court House. Remained at Fairfax Court House until the 14th instant, at six P. M., at which time the regiment marched with the brigade under your orders to our present camp at Fort Worth, arriving at half-past one A. M., 15th instant, having been detained nearly one hour in crossing Cameron Run.

The regiment stood the march remarkably well.

I have the honor to be,

Very respectfully, etc.,

(Signed), G. W. TAYLOR,

Colonel Third New Jersey Volunteers.

To Brigadier-General P. KEARNY,

Commanding First Brigade, Franklin's Division.

HEADQUARTERS FOURTH NEW JERSEY VOLUNTEERS,
CAMP SEMINARY, VA., March 16, 1862.

Brigadier-General P. KEARNY,

Commanding First Brigade, Franklin's Division, Army of the Potomac:

GENERAL—I have the honor to make the following report of the movements of the Fourth Regiment of New Jersey Volunteers, since the 7th instant. On that day it received orders to march with the other regiments of the brigade to Burk's Station, on the Alexandria and Orange railroad, fourteen miles from this camp. The regiment left at three P. M., and in consequence of its being the rear guard of the whole brigade, including the wagons, and the very bad state of the cross-road from Anandale, it did not reach its destination till four o'clock the next morning (8th); everything, however, having been brought up in good order. The regiment was immediately put in position by your orders, as a movable force, to attack the enemy at any point he might present himself; the three other regiments occupying eligible positions on the approaches to the station from the south, west and north. In the afternoon, by your direction, I accompanied you in a reconnoissance of the country about the place for several miles; the object being to become thoroughly acquainted with the roads, so as to be ready to meet the enemy at any point; and in parting with me you gave me my orders for the night.

The next morning, about sunrise, eight contraband slaves came in from Manassas and reported to you that the rebels were sending away their guns and other property, and were about leaving their fortifications. You thought their representations such as to cause a more thorough questioning, and directed me to conduct it. I did so; putting down the result in a letter to you, which you dispatched immediately to General FRANKLIN. Directly after this, you ordered the brigade to move forward towards Sangster's Station, seven miles up the railroad, and within three miles of Bull Run. The Third New Jersey was directed to take the advance along the railroad; the Second New Jersey, in echelon, at proper distance, to support the Third; the Fourth New Jersey similarly disposed to support the Second; two companies of the First New Jersey to flank the railroad by the Braddock road to the north, and the remaining companies of the First to hold Burk's Station. In this way the advance was cautiously made as far as Fairfax Station, a distance of four miles. Reaching this place, the brigade, by your direction, was again advanced farther forward cautiously; the different regiments occupying the same relative position, but the Third moving more directly on Sangster's Station; the Second taking position on the right of the railroad, about a mile beyond Fairfax Station, at the lead-colored house on eminence; the Fourth at the little church at Fairfax, to guard the road leading to Fairfax; the First regiment remaining as before at Burk's Station, and the Braddock corners. At this time the rebel cavalry could be very plainly seen with my glass at about one and a-half miles off to the north-west, posted behind a fence in front of a wood. Up to this period I had, by your direction, accompanied you in the field. Leaving me to go forward to join the Third in the advance, you directed me to take command of the Second and Fourth, and give orders according to the exigencies as they might occur. Soon after, I heard the advance engaged with the enemy, and receiving an order from you through Assistant Adjutant-General WILSON to push forward the Second to the burnt railroad bridge to sustain the Third, the Fourth to take the place of the Second, and the First that of the Fourth—the two companies of the First still remaining at the Braddock Corners — I made the changes accordingly, and then rode forward to report to you at Sangster's Station. Here I found you writing a dispatch to General FRANKLIN, informing him of the brilliant charge which had just been made by a small detachment of Captain STEARNS' company of Lincoln Cavalry, which formed your escort, against a large body of the rebels, said to be one hundred and fifty strong, by which they were totally routed, and fourteen made prisoners, among them a Lieutenant STEWART, late from West Point. You immediately ordered me to join my regiment, and with it, two companies of the First New Jersey under Major HATFIELD, which had been posted at the Braddock road, midway between Fairfax Station and Fairfax Court House, and a company of the Lincoln Cavalry, under Captain STEARNS, to take Fairfax Court House. I promptly returned to my command, found it eager for the work, and ordering, at the Braddock road, Major HATFIELD and command of two companies of the First, and Captain STEARNS, to join me, I dispatched Lieutenant-Colonel HATCH, Fourth New Jersey Volunteers, with two companies of the Fourth New Jersey, and Captain STEARNS' company of cavalry, to make a detour to the left, to cut off the enemy in his retreat from Fairfax Court House by the Centreville road. The enemy's pickets were seen between us and the town, and it was supposed they were backed up by a large force in the neighborhood. Waiting till the proper time to make the dispositions come out simultaneously at Fairfax Court House, I took immediate command of the balance of my forces, and had the pleasure of seeing Lieutenant-Colonel HATCH just in position to cut off the retreat of the enemy while I was ready to press him in front. Skirmishers were thrown out to the front and on either flank on an advance, and just before entering the town, when the opportunity admitted, the main body was deployed into line of battle. Unfortunately for the real test of our troops, we found to our surprise, no enemy, the great body having left, as I learned from the inhabitants, some time in October, and only the scouts and pickets, who had been seen in the morning, having occupied it since. This fact, however, does not at all militate against the spirit and determination of my command, which was all that might be expected from the inheritors of the military fame of Jerseymen, and who only await a standing foe to show their real mettle.

I would be derelict did I not also report that you joined me before entering the place, and with your usual spirit and good judgment, led the troops into the town, which we entered at about five P. M.

By your direction, I immediately wrote a dispatch to General FRANKLIN, reporting our occupation of Fairfax Court House, and you then left me with instructions to hold possession of the town with the Fourth New Jersey. This I did till the next morning, March 10th, when the Federal troops pouring in (the advance under Colonel AVERILL), and receiving an order to march to the Braddock Corners to support the advance of the First regiment by that road to Centreville, I left the town with my regiment, took position at the "Corners," remained there all night, and next morning returned, by your direction, to the vicinity of Fairfax Court House, where I selected the camping-ground for the brigade. Here we remained till the afternoon of the 14th instant, when receiving an order at five o'clock from General Headquarters to return to this post, the whole brigade moved at six, and reached our destination after midnight.

I think it proper to state, that when at Fairfax Court House, on the 13th instant, with Assistant Adjutant-General PURDY, and Assistant Adjutant-General WILSON and other officers, and a squadron of dragoons, I visited the battle-ground at Manassas, of 21st July last, and at the recent headquarters of the Confederate Army of the Potomac, a building said to belong to a Mr. WEIR, I found a large number of official documents, among them the original order of General BEAUREGARD, dated July 20th, promulgating "confidentially" to the commanders of brigades his plan of battle for the next day. Accompanying this was the order of General JOSEPH E. JOHNSTON, approving the plan and *directing it to be carried into execution.* I also found the original report of Lieutenant ALEXANDER, Engineer Corps, General Staff, giving a statement of the prisoners and wounded, and of the property found after the battle. The leaving these important documents, like the other property which I saw scattered around, shows with what haste the rebels must have retreated before our forces; but what discovers the perfect panic which must have ensued, is the fact, which *I witnessed,* of their having left four dead bodies, laid out in their hospital dead-house ready for interment, but which they had forgotten or neglected to bury.

Very respectfully submitted,

(Signed), J. H. SIMPSON,
Colonel Fourth New Jersey Volunteers.

HEADQUARTERS FIRST NEW YORK CAVALRY,
CAMP KEARNY, March 17, 1862.

Captain J. K. STEARNS,
Commanding Company "H" Second Squadron:

SIR—I have the honor to report that in obedience to orders received from Bragadier-General KEARNY, I marched from Burk's Station on the morning of the 9th instant, with twenty men. My orders were to proceed to the Pohick road, and scour the country right and left, which I did as far as Brimstone Hill, I then returned to Ely's, where I learned from the officer commanding the pickets of the Third New Jersey, that a squad of rebel cavalry had just driven in two of his pickets. I immediately started in pursuit, and having followed them about three miles, returned to Fairfax Station, and reported the circumstance to the commanding General. I was then ordered by the General to accompany him to Sangster's Station, and on arriving there to occupy a road leading to the right, going into a large wood; my orders being to intercept a large body of rebel infantry from getting in there. It was about this time that the brilliant charge was made by Lieutenant HIDDEN of our regiment. General KEARNY then rode up and informed me that Lieutenant HIDDEN had fallen, and was perhaps only wounded, and ordered me to charge with my party and drive the enemy into the woods, and procure the body, if possible; we did so, Lieutenant THOMPSON and myself, and recovered the body. I then returned to Fairfax Station and reported to you.

I am, sir, very respectfully,
Your obedient servant,

(Signed), WM. ALEXANDER,
Second Lieutenant and Adjutant First Battalion.

HEADQUARTERS, FIRST REGIMENT, FIRST BRIGADE, FRANKLIN'S DIVISION,
CAMP SEMINARY, VA., March 17, 1862.

To Captain JAMES M. WILSON,
Assistant Adjutant-General, First Brigade:

SIR—I have the honor to forward the inclosed reports concerning the First Regiment, First Brigade, Franklin's Division, under the immediate command of Lieutenant-Colonel MCALLISTER—being myself at the time unable to ride on horseback on account of rheumatism, but was in the field during the time making myself as useful as possible under the circumstances.

Very respectfully,
Your obedient servant,

(Signed), A. T. A. TORBERT,
Colonel First Regiment New Jersey Volunteers.

FIRST REGIMENT NEW JERSEY VOLUNTEERS,
CAMP SEMINARY, VA., March 17, 1862.

To A. T. A. TORBERT,

Colonel First Regiment New Jersey Volunteers:

SIR—In accordance with your request I herewith transmit to you a report of the movements of our regiment after leaving this place for Burk's Station, on Friday, March 7th.

We left our brigade drill-ground and marched across to the Little river turnpike, on this side of Anandale. I was ordered to send forward our two flank companies, leaving *seven companies* (one company being on picket). We reached Burk's Station about one o'clock A. M., on the 8th; our regiment was then stationed along the edge of the woods near BURK's house.

After General HOWARD's brigade left, we were ordered to take a position along the woods north of the railroad, which order I executed immediately. I then examined all the roads leading to the camp grounds, placed pickets, and rested for the night. On the morning of the 9th I received an order to send three companies to BURK's house. We started at once. Then came another order to send two companies, under the command of Major HATFIELD, to the old Braddock road. I detailed companies B and E; they started without delay, leaving me but two companies. After two o'clock P. M., I received an order to bring in the three companies at BURK's house, and march up the railroad to support Colonel SIMPSON at the church near Fairfax Station. On reaching that, I did not see Colonel SIMPSON, but met General KEARNY, who ordered me to march up to Farr's Cross-roads, leaving one company—company K—at Paine's Church; with the remaining four companies I arrived at Farr's cross-roads about five o'clock P. M. (9th), and formed line of battle, and remained in that position until our General arrived from Fairfax Court House, when he told me to encamp there for the night; to be on the alert; that it was an important point; that the enemy were in the neighborhood; and if attacked, hold it until reinforcements came to my aid. I put out pickets up the Centreville road one and a half miles; also down the Fairfax road towards Paine's Church, and also, towards Fairfax. We were vigilant that night, but were unmolested. About eight o'clock next morning (10th) received a verbal order from General KEARNY, by his aid-de-camp, Lieutenant BARNARD, to throw forward scouts in rear of Centreville, and am happy to say, I soon found a corporal and three men ready and willing to undertake this apparently dangerous enterprise. In about an hour afterward I received an order to send forward towards Centreville one company. I immediately ordered company B, Captain VAN SICKELL, to push forward; and, in accordance with our General's instructions, had a communication kept up with me, and through me, with General KEARNY, by Captain VAN SICKELL, sending back a man every three-quarters of a mile that he advanced. Between twelve and one o'clock the General ordered me to advance with our regiment to Centreville, which I did—Captain VAN SICKELL and Lieutenant TANTUM, with company B, having reached that place before we did, and some hours ahead of any other troops.

Permit me to say here, that our regiment was the last to leave Centreville, at the Bull Run retreat, and a part of it the first to enter it on the retreat of the enemy. We staid all night, and the next morning were ordered to return to Fairfax Court House.

In conclusion permit me to say, that General KEARNY deserves a great deal of credit by this bold push towards the enemy's lines; and by the *energy* and *bravery* thus displayed, caused the enemy to leave in great haste, leaving many valuables behind them.

Respectfully, your obedient servant,

(Signed), R. McALLISTER,

Lieutenant-Colonel First Regiment New Jersey Volunteers.

FIRST REGIMENT NEW JERSEY VOLUNTEERS,
CAMP SEMINARY, VA., March 17, 1862.

To A. T. A. TORBERT,

Colonel First Regiment New Jersey Volunteers:

SIR—On Sunday morning, March 9th, I was ordered by General KEARNY to take two companies and proceed to Farr's Cross-roads, by the Old Braddock road, and there wait for reinforcements from Fairfax Station. I arrived at the Cross-roads about noon. My command consisted of companies B and E. At the Cross-roads we discerned the enemy's cavalry on a hill near the Court House; but, having positive orders to remain at the Cross-roads, I did not feel at liberty to pursue them. However, I sent out a small detachment, under command of Lieutenant TANTUM, in order to get as near the enemy as possible, under cover of the pines, so as to watch their movements. By so doing we found that the enemy was moving back and forth from the Court House to the old Braddock road, a distance of about one mile.

At four o'clock the Fourth New Jersey, under Colonel SIMPSON, came up, when we marched to the Court House—the two companies under my command were deployed as skirmishers. When near the Court House, by order of General KEARNY, we marched on at *double-quick*, and I may also add that the enemy did the same, only in an opposite direction. I then received orders from General KEARNY to march back to the Cross-roads and join my regiment, and there bivouacked for the night.

Very respectfully, your obedient servant,

(Signed), DAVID HATFIELD,

Major First Regiment New Jersey Volunteers.

FIRST REGIMENT NEW JERSEY VOLUNTEERS,
CAMP SEMINARY, VA., March 17, 1862.

To A. T. A. TORBERT,

Colonel First Regiment New Jersey Volunteers:

SIR—I have the honor to report that I was ordered by Lieutenant-Colonel MCALLISTER, on Monday morning, 10th instant, at half-past eight A. M., while stationed at Farr's Cross-roads, to take my command and proceed cautiously up the Braddock road towards Centreville, and after passing our pickets, to send out an advance guard; which I did, sending Lieutenant WILLIAM H. TANTUM on with fourteen men. I was also furnished with four cavalrymen, to act as a patrol, and to report to him at intervals, as we proceeded. I received the first communication from Lieutenant TANTUM when at Cedar Run, which I forwarded to Lieutenant-Colonel MCALLISTER, saying that he had possession of five contrabands, and had caught up with the four scouts sent in advance. Lieutenant TANTUM halted with his guard until I brought up my reserve; he then advanced about a mile, when I received word that appearances were favorable, to come on with all possible dispatch, as he would be in Centreville in an hour. The message I immediately sent to Lieutenant-Colonel MCALLISTER, and proceeded on. Lieutenant TANTUM arrived at Centreville about half-past eleven A. M., where he immediately posted four sentries in different places in the village—one at each of three forts.

I arrived there at fifteen minutes after twelve o'clock, noon, and took possession of General JOHNSTON'S headquarters, and there awaited the arrival of the First Regiment, which came in about four o'clock P. M.

The New York Forty-fourth Regiment arrived at about half-past three o'clock P. M.

Very respectfully, your obedient servant,

(Signed), S. VAN SICKELL,

Captain Company B, First Regiment New Jersey Volunteers.

CHAPTER XX.

IRRITANTS AND ASSUASIVES.

POISON AND ANTIDOTE.

"My death and life,
My bane and antidote, are both before me."
ADDISON'S "*Cato.*"

THE neglect of MCCLELLAN to take advantage of this success (detailed in the preceding chapter) by immediately following up the retiring and, to all appearance, surprised enemy completely satisfied General KEARNY of his (MCCLELLAN'S) incompetency. From thenceforward his opinion of him was fixed.

"The stupid fact is (he writes March 17th, 1862), that, not content with letting me and others push on after the panic-stricken enemy, fighting him a big battle, and ending the war — for his panic promised us sure success — MCCLELLAN, so powerful with figures, but so weak with men, has brought us all back. It is so like our good old nursery story—

'The King of France, with twice ten thousand men,
Marched up the hill, and then marched down again.'

The result will be, that, in Southern character, they will more than recuperate, more than think us afraid of a real stand-up fight, meet us at the prepared points, possibly play ugly tricks at the capital, and nonplus or force us to fight with the worst of chances against us; and all this, because when MCCLELLAN, out of confidence since his failure at Ball's Bluff, despairing of a direct attack on Manassas, invented, with the aid of engineers (men who are ignorant of soldiers), the plan of turning the enemy by a sea-route, instead of availing himself of the good luck of the enemy's retreat, thinks that he must still adhere to his sea-plan, like the over-stuffed glutton who thinks he must cram because he has in hand an '*embarras des richesses*.' "

March 31st he writes, sketching a campaign* for the enemy, which was not attempted till POPE'S time:

* "The war of 1806 broke out; and the Prussians, proud of their former fame, took the field against NAPOLEON. MASSENBACH, then a colonel, was Quartermaster-General to Prince HOHENLOHE'S army, and, as the storm-clouds of battle drew on towards each other, foretold, with wonderful clearness, accuracy and precision, the ruin which the measures in progress were certain to bring upon the army and the country! Looking back to these terrible times, trying the avowed and registered predictions delivered

"Our present affair is a terrific blunder. Instead of following up, overtaking and whipping the enemy as they retired panic-stricken, he is attempting an affair of rivers. I do not know his full means of action; but I do know that, if opposed with enterprise, the Southern army, recuperated under the plea of our evading a real fight, will seize Centreville and Manassas, just in rear of forces left on the Rappahannock, cut them off, restore the uninjured railroad, steam via Harper's Ferry to Baltimore and Washington, and be back in time to meet us before Richmond;* because the batteries on the York and James rivers, if as formidable as the captured resources of Norfolk should have made them in guns, will oblige us (if we have no iron-armored gunboats) to land our heavy pieces and take them piecemeal (besides expending thus gratuitously much blood†), all which takes time. I can only account for this absurd movement from General McClellan and his advisers not having sufficient simplicity of character. It would have been so beautiful to have pushed after the enemy, and, in doing so, isolate Fredericksburg, carry it easily, occupy that road, and thus turn those river batteries, all the while near enough to Washington in case of any attempt on it. They will tell you that it was a want of subsistence, etc. This only proves how unpractical McClellan and his advisers are. And it is precisely from a mismanagement of these simple details in our own camps on the Potomac that I have the more and more learned to distrust him entirely. However, Johnston is a very slow man, and our resources are enormous, so we must win, and McClellan will, no doubt, pass down in history as a great general. What annoys me the most is, that he has stupidly blundered in carrying out his own plans. We should, at least, have kept the enemy impressed with the idea of our direct advance, and withdrawn division after division in the stealthiness of night, and under the curtain of strong corps."

This was an early day for such criticism. They meant what Grant afterwards painfully executed. Some 200,000 men lay 'round Washington then. The rebel force was barely 40,000.

---

day after day by Massenbach, in the Prussian council of war, by the subsequent events, we are, in profane languages, bound to confess that no man ever spoke before in a more perfect spirit of prophecy. All that he foretold came to pass to the letter." In the same way Von Bulow.—Gen. Mitchell's "Biographies of Eminent Soldiers," 319.

* "Massena," he (Souvaroff) says, in a memorandum on the subject, "has no object in waiting for us when he can beat us in detail. He will first throw himself upon Korsakoff, who is nearest to him, and then upon Condé, and that will probably be enough for him." How just was the prophecy.—Gen. Mitchell's "Biographies of Eminent Soldiers," 157.

† "The celebrated Souvaroff was accused of cruelty, because he always at once stormed fortresses instead of investing them and starving out the inhabitants and the garrisons. The old hero showed, by arithmetical calculations, that his bloodiest assaults never occasioned so much loss of human life as did, on both sides, any long seige, digging and approaches, and the starving out of those shut up in a fortress. This for McClellan."—Gurowski's Diary, Vol. I, page 164; February, 1862.

The direct advance would have been necessarily overwhelming; no manœuvers could have resisted it. Looking back, and with the knowledge we now possess, we know that, undertaken then, the direct advance must have been speedily successful, economizing rivers of blood and thousands of lives. Says POLLARD in his *Lost Cause*, page 262:

> "On March 1st, 1862, the number of Federal troops in and about Washington had increased to 193,142 fit for duty, with a grand aggregate of 221,987. Let us see what was in front of it on the Confederate line of defense. General JOHNSTON had in the camps of Centreville and Manassas less than 30,000 men; STONEWALL JACKSON had been detached with eleven skeleton regiments to amuse the enemy in the Shenandoah Valley. Such was the force that stood in McCLELLAN'S path, and deterred him from a blow that, at that time, might have been fatal to the Southern Confederacy."

We have said that McCLELLAN seemed but ill satisfied with the sudden and skillful movement of KEARNY upon Manassas. Perhaps it was in consequence of this; but, whatever the reason, in a few days after he tendered him a command (to which, as numbered fourteen on the list of brigadiers, he was long entitled) of a division, vacated by the promotion of General SUMNER to a corps. General KEARNY was more than glad to accept, only desiring that, inasmuch as his FIRST JERSEY BRIGADE had been perfected by such toil, expense and zeal, he should be at liberty to carry it with him, exchanging it for one of SUMNER'S, which lay close by FRANKLIN, and the consent of whose brigadier was obtained. General McCLELLAN did not discourage the project, but General FRANKLIN at once rejected it, upon which General KEARNY, feeling his JERSEY BLUES to be a trust especially confided to him, and realizing their adoration of him, most generously declined the proposition, and, ranking many division generals, remained with his brigade. This conduct was rewarded, as might readily be expected. As soon as it was known, in spite of orders to avoid all demonstrations, the enthusiasm of his brave boys could not be restrained. His appearance was the signal for irrepressible cheering. His men would have followed him, or gone at his bidding anywhere, against any odds; "nor did a Jersey soldier ever forget it."

Another writer thus expresses the same idea, but in such elegant language that it will bear insertion, even at the risk of repetition:

"Just about the time the overland advance was thus abandoned for 'an affair of rivers,' General KEARNY was offered the command of a division. He was more than glad to accept the honor, on one condition: that the 'Jersey Blues' should be embraced in his command. McCLELLAN was not unwilling, but FRANKLIN rejected the proposition, and KEARNY determined to remain brigadier and command his own brave boys. The effect of this decision on his brigade can be imagined. It gave him boundless control over their sympathies and their conduct. He could not ride down the line on parade without arousing cheers from every company. They would have followed him (as his Dragoons did follow him up to the gate of Mexico, and as his men did always everywhere until he fell at their head) into the charge at Balaklava,

'Into the jaws of death,
Into the mouth of hell,'

Though

'Cannon to right of them,
Cannon to left of them,
Cannon behind them
Volleyed and thundered.'"

With all this, the step caused General KEARNY much regret. His subordination to men of much less military experience than his own perpetually annoyed him. He had strong reliance upon his own powers, a reliance which was by no means conceited, and which was afterward strongly justified. Feeling himself equal to almost any task, he could not help longing to take the place of some one of those whom, in his confidential correspondence, he styled his "inferior superiors."

It was some alleviation to his disappointment, and the state of harassed feeling which his inferior position occasioned, to find himself valued as he was by NEW JERSEY and its LEGISLATURE. How much its patriotic Executive regarded him he was not then aware, and his correspondence betrayed an unjust opinion upon that subject.

But the Press, the People and the Legislature of NEW JERSEY, all exhibited their admiration and attachment for him in such a manner as could not be otherwise than gratifying.

On the 20th of March, 1862, the LEGISLATURE passed a RESOLUTION, declaring—

"*That* NEW JERSEY *highly appreciates the disinterested fidelity of General* PHILIP KEARNY, *in declining proffered promotion rather than separate himself from the command of* JERSEYMEN *intrusted to him.*"

On the 28th of the same month, a SET OF RESOLUTIONS was passed, in the following terms:

"RESOLVED, *That to the* NEW JERSEY VOLUNTEERS *belongs the praise not only of checking the retreat of the Federal Forces retiring from Bull Run, and greatly aiding in the preservation of the National Capital from capture, but also of advancing, unsupported, on the Rebel stronghold at Manassas, and compelling its precipitate abandonment; and that General* KEARNY *deserves the warm approval and thanks of the Nation for his boldness in making this advance, and this skillful strategy he displayed in its execution.*

"RESOLVED, *Thut having already testified our high appreciation of the self-sacrifice and fidelity to his trust, which led General* KEARNY *to decline promotion rather than leave his Brigade, we now express our regret at the existence of any such necessity, and respectfully suggest to those in authority the propriety (unless it be inconsistent with the public interest) of combining all the* NEW JERSEY TROOPS *on the Potomac into one Division, and placing the same under the command of General* KEARNY, *whose devotion to his soldiers, care for their comfort and discipline, and brilliant qualities as an officer, entitle the country to his services in a higher position than the one he now occupies.*

"RESOLVED, *That a Copy of these Resolutions be forwarded to the* HONORABLE THE SECRETARY OF WAR."

The idea contained in the second of these resolutions was a favorite one with General KEARNY, who believed our troops would fight better if brigaded by States; but the fear that State pride might occasion dissension made the plan unpalatable at Washington.*

* This chapter is quoted entire (with the exception of the notes and of one paragraph from the pen of JOSEPH B. LYMAN, Esq.), from the ADDRESS of CORTLANDT PARKER, Esq., entitled: "PHILIP KEARNY, THE SOLDIER AND PATRIOT." Newark, New Jersey, March, 1868.

CHAPTER XXI.

FROM ALEXANDRIA, THROUGH YORKTOWN, TO WILLIAMSBURG.

"My ships are ready, and
My people did expect my hence departure
Two days ago."
WINTER'S TALE.

"When, in 1707, the DUKE OF SAVOY desired * * to conceal his retreat, he commenced to 'withdraw' his heavy artillery. * * Then he ordered that some light field pieces should be left in the lines, which should keep up a fire * * to amuse the enemy and prevent them from suspecting his retreat. * * All things being thus disposed, he decamped secretly in the night."—RUSES DE GUERRE.

"Are you content to be our general?"
TWO GENTLEMEN OF VERONA.

THE "Affair of Rivers" was decided on in March. It was not until April that it was carried into execution. So much has been said and written by war-correspondents, pamphleteers, military critics, sensational and historical penmen, that it is needless to discuss or enter into details, except as to KEARNY.

This expedition, conceived in weakness, was a cripple from its birth. Misbegotten, its lot was misfortune and its end humiliation. Nevertheless, from its commencement to its termination, it was a glorious climacteric in the life of the Army of the Potomac, and in the career of the majority of the subordinate commanders.

On the 17th April, KEARNY embarked on board of the splendid steamer "Elm City," and on the 23d April found himself in the estuary of the Pocosin, or Poquosin river, which opens into the Chesapeake, just below the mouth of the York river.*

* "When I first went to General KEARNY he was near Alexandria, expecting every hour and minute to receive an order to go down the river; at last came an order to go forward the other way, viz., by the Alexandria and Orange railroad, and that way to reach Richmond. We got as far as Catlett's — there waited three or four days, expecting orders to go forward — at last orders came to return to Alexandria, and there take shipping for Yorktown. We returned, expecting to embark the same day — but had to wait a week. We sailed, expecting to land under fire the day we reached the York river. Well, after some delay, we reached the York river, passed it, and anchored in Pocosin, or Poquosin Bay, where we are still, and probably will be laying for another week, and then we may go to Fortress Monroe or somewhere else."—*Private Letter from one of* KEARNY'S *Staff, Pocosin Bay, 25th April*, 1862.

Here he was "kept waiting to land, and fretting himself over the want of practical skill which, as he said, sickened his soldiers by cooping them on the transports, because they dared not hazard a landing under fire."

It was not until 30th April that he was permitted to disembark.

While "cribbed, cabined and confined" on ship-board, a vacancy occurred in the command of the 3d Division (formerly C. S. HAMILTON'S) of the 3d Army Corps, HEINTZELMAN'S. KEARNY now deemed it due to himself, his friends, the army and the country, to accept this step. Amid grief, ill-concealed and heartfelt on his own part, and amid the tears and lamentations of the troops he had made his pride and his worshippers,* he was relieved of his old and assumed his new position 2d May, 1862, at the head of the 3d Division, whose title was changed to that of 1st Division on the 3d August following. Its position was alongside of that commanded by HOOKER. Both of these were encamped in close vicinity to the ground, one and a half miles S. S. E. of Yorktown, where the tents of Generals LINCOLN and LA FAYETTE were pitched and the park of American Artillery was established during the memorable seige of Yorktown in 1781, which affixed the seal to the liberties of our country. KEYES' Corps lay in advance of the headquarters of WASHINGTON and ROCHAMBEAU; these latter in rear of the park of French Artillery, about two miles south by east of the beleaguered town.†

---

* "In battle, the voice of the man whom the soldier loves nerves his heart, and, rather than forfeit his esteem by flight, he will remain at his post and die. * * * * And this was the secret of KEARNY'S popularity in his division; and among the thousand camp traditions of that singular and gifted man, there is not one of needless insult or cruelty to soldiers in the ranks. For them he had always the looks and language of cheer; while for his officers he had often such words of biting, bitter scorn as only General KEARNY could utter — falling on them like angry flashes of lightning from a storm-cloud. And in all the army I know of no such devotion to a general as was exhibited by the men of KEARNY'S Division."—"*The Peninsular Campaign in Virginia, etc.*," p. 42, by Rev. J. J. MARKS.

† "Yorktown was of especial interest to us, because in that place and its immediate neighborhood are found many monuments of the most interesting event in our Revolutionary history. The divisions under Generals KEARNY and HOOKER encamped on the grounds where had been spread the tents of General WASHINGTON and General LA FAYETTE. We daily looked out upon the plain where had been witnessed the combats and struggles which compelled the final surrender of Yorktown to our forces. The old lines of entrenchments and mounds of redoubts look like a chain across the field."— "*The Peninsular Campaign in Virginia, etc.*," p. 140, by Rev. J. J. MARKS.

Here "Fighting JOE" and "Fighting PHIL,"* who had won brevets "for gallant and meritorious conduct" in the Mexican war, fighting a foreign enemy to maintain the national honor, now again became associated in arms in the great American Conflict, to preserve the Nation's life, on the very spot where the shouts of triumph first proclaimed to the world the accomplished birth of our Nation.

The following was the composition of KEARNY'S Division, as furnished through the courtesy of Major-General E. D. TOWNSEND, Assistant and Acting Adjutant-General U. S. A., to whom the writer is indebted foı many similar acts of kindness:

"Brigadier-General P. KEARNY was relieved from command of the 'New Jersey Brigade' and assumed command of the 3d Division (formerly HAMILTON'S), 3d Army Corps, May 2, 1862.

"Name of Division changed to 1st Division August 13, 1862.

"FIRST BRIGADE:

"Brigadier-General CHAS. D. JAMESON, commanding until June 13, 1862; Brigadier-General J. C. ROBINSON commanding from June 14, '62, to September, 1862.

"TROOPS—First Brigade—

" 57th Pennsylvania Vols. Transferred to 2d Brigade August 12, 1862.
" 63d Pennsylvania Vols.
" 105th Pennsylvania Vols.
" 87th New York Vols. Relieved from duty with Division August 23, '62.
" 20th Indiana Vols. Joined Brigade June 10, 1862.

"SECOND BRIGADE:

"Brigadier-General D. B. BIRNEY, commanding.

"TROOPS—

" 38th New York Vols.
" 40th New York Vols.
" 101st New York Vols. Joined Brigade June 9, 1862.
" 3d Maine Vols.
" 4th Maine Vols.
" 99th Pennsylvania Vols. Joined Brigade July 5, 1862.
" 57th Pennsylvania Vols. Joined, from 1st Brigade, August 12, 1862.

* This same corps comprised as part of HOOKER'S Division the famous EXCELSIOR Brigade, commanded by another fighter, DANIEL E. SICKLES, known to his "Boys" as "Fighting DAN." It is not a little singular, in this connection, that each of this "trio" of heroes were for a long time intended for clergymen.

"THIRD BRIGADE:

"Brigadier-General HIRAM G. BERRY commanding, until August 19, 1862; Colonel O. M. POE, 2d Michigan Vols., commanding from August 20, 1862, to September, 1862.

"TROOPS—

" 2d Michigan Vols.
" 3d Michigan Vols.
" 5th Michigan Vols.
" 37th New York Vols.
" 1st New York Vols. Joined Brigade June 3, 1862

"ARTILLERY OF DIVISION:

" Company G, 2d United States Artillery. Relieved July 18, 1862.
" Company B, 1st New York Artillery. Relieved June 5, 1862.
" Company E, 1st Rhode Island Artillery.
" Company K, 3d United States Artillery. Joined July 18, 1862."

Yorktown was evacuated on the night of the 3d of May. Eleven thousand men under General MAGRUDER (who adopted here the strategem of KEARNY when approaching Manassas, and extended his little force over a distance of several miles, so as to give it the appearance of large numbers), had delayed nearly 90,000 infantry, 50 batteries of artillery, 10,000 cavalry, and a seige train of 100 guns, from the 4th day of April previous.

This fact is proof enough of the correctness of KEARNY'S opinion, both as to the injudiciousness of the route and the lack of comprehensive generalship in his commander.

On the night (3d May) Yorktown was evacuated, one of KEARNY'S new brigadiers, CHARLES D. JAMESON, "General of the Trenches," was the first to discover the fact, or, at all events, the first to enter the enemy's works, at 6 A. M. on the ensuing day. On the 4th, towards midday, STONEMAN, with the cavalry and some light batteries, got off in pursuit of the rebels; at early noon (10 A. M. ?) HOOKER moved. KEARNY did not start until 9 A. M. on the 5th. Between the Divisions of HOOKER and KEARNY strung out SUMNER'S corps of about 30,000 men.

When STONEMAN, HOOKER and SUMNER marched, on the 4th, it was a bright, sunny, or fair May day for Virginia. In HOOKER'S Division the men threw away all superfluous baggage, in consequence of the heat, and some actually dropped down from the same cause. It was not only hot, but dusty. What a contrast when KEARNY's turn to advance came on the morning of the 5th. The rain commenced falling, sprinkling, about dark, on the 4th, increasing in violence until about 11 P. M., when it set in for a regular storm. During the night it was not heavy enough to wet through the blanket covering the writer's informant, but towards morning (3 A. M.) it increased in violence.*

After daylight (5th) rain fell in torrents. The roads had become soaked with water and were perfectly horrible — ankle deep for the men, and, seemingly, bottomless to the artillery. The different commands and arms, between Yorktown and Williamsburg, between KEARNY and HOOKER, became intermingled. The confusion, worse confounded, was hourly aggravated by the weather, the mud and the muddled condition of affairs in the rear, in the direction of the movements: Witness HEINTZELMAN's statement, that he had orders from McCLELLAN himself to assume command at the front; whereas SUMNER was acting under exactly similar instructions from MARCY, Chief of Staff.

On the afternoon of the 4th, STONEMAN ran into, or overtook the rebel rear-guard, beyond WHITTAKER's house, between three and four miles this side and in sight of Williamsburg. The pursued stood at bay, turned upon and repulsed the pursuers.

Here there is as much confusion in the accounts of what followed as there was confusion reigning among the dislocated

* There is a great discrepancy, however, in the accounts of this rain-storm which exercised so great an influence on events and cost us precious time, when Time was THE element of success. It might almost be said this rain saved Richmond. It justified the remark attributed to General DIX, that, "the season was even yet too early for operations on the peninsula, since a single storm would convert its treacherous soil into a quicksand." The drizzle commenced from 11 to 12 P. M. on the 4th, and at 3 A. M., 5th, the rain came down in earnest. Twelve hours of steady down-pour was sufficient to convert the face of the country into a quagmire, in which, according to Captain CHARLES H. SCOTT, 4th New York Independent Battery, the horses sank to their knees, and another informant goes further, averring that the men, even, found the mud knee-deep. DE TROBRIAND speaks of artillery horses as "killed, or drowned in their harness" in the mud on the 5th, and of advancing "to the battle through an ocean of mire, amid wearied teams, and in the midst of an inevitable disorder, which left stragglers enough in the rear." How much does this add to the glory of KEARNY, in that he carried his men through all this into the field to save a lost battle, an achievement almost equal to that accomplished by the resolution of BLUCHER at Waterloo.

commands. About 5.30 P. M. SUMNER, with SMITH's Division, came up; but nothing seems to have been done. Darkness shut in upon the opposing forces before HOOKER got into position. Then the Union forces bivouacked in the woods and the rain, which had just commenced, and slept in the consequent mud.

It was nearly midnight when the van-guard of the Army of the Potomac sank down to rest — if such a suspense could be termed rest — under the most trying circumstances for soldiers young in active campaigning. It was a terrible initiative for the Army of the Potomac, with a battle certain at the breaking of the day. Still, they stood it nobly, and proved, as was said of other troops on other fields, "that it took an awful deal to take it out of them."

CHAPTER XXII.

THE BATTLE OF WILLIAMSBURG, MONDAY, 5TH MAY, 1862.

KEARNY AT WILLIAMSBURG.

"He (Lieutenant-General, or General of Division, the COUNT DE LORGE), gave his orders with a coolness which made it easy to see that he is the relation (nephew) of the incomparable M. DE TURENNE. (Major-General PHIL. KEARNY was nephew of the admirable Brigadier-General, Brevet Major-General, STEPHEN WATTS KEARNY.) He had a horse killed under him (this occurred to P. K. at Fair Oaks). If God had taken him from us (at the battle of Williamsburg) everything was lost." *Rousset's Histoire de Louvois*, ii., 164.

"And now, my son, let me enjoin you that *whenever you hear the names* of Generals HANCOCK and KEARNY *mentioned, respect and revere them, for never was American valor more beautifully illustrated than by these Generals on the field of Williamsburg!*" "Siege of Washington," Captain ADAMS.

"After the battle of St. Quintin (August 10, 1587) EMANUEL PHILIBERT had France at his discretion. Had his counsels been instantly followed, the Spanish army would have dictated its own terms before or within the walls of Paris. But the narrow * * * * * mind of PHILIP II frustrated the victory, and the great opportunity was lost. It is well known that when CHARLES V received the first tidings of the glorious battle, in his retirement at Yuste, he made up his mind that his son must be in full march upon Paris; and when fallen from his expectation, he sunk into one of his fits of deep gloom, and refused to open further dispatches." GALLENGA'S *History of Piedmont.*

"Seydlitz, with his conquering regiments, lay reorganized behind Zorndorf. Undaunted amidst the general alarm, he excited sixty-one squadrons to fresh exertions, by shouting—'*My children, follow me!*' 'WE FOLLOW,' answered his brave * * men with one accord. His well known voice was in their ears; his glorious example beamed before them.

"Dashing through the gaps in the Prussian line, the whole mass * * rushed upon the foe. The Russians slightly disordered, as before, by their own successes, could not withstand the onset: * * fled in confusion, and were driven in the morass under Quartschen." Capt. LAWLEY'S *Gen. Seydlitz.*

"WILLIAM (III of England) lost the fruits of his victory at the Boyne by not pressing the Irish on their retreat. Drogheda, a nominal fortress, without ramparts, bastions, or outworks, with only seven iron cannon, a garrison of twelve hundred men, and a cowardly governor, arrested his career but a single day. Three more days elapsed before his entry into Dublin, a distance of twenty-two miles only. He thus gave his enemies leisure to retreat and opportunity to reorganize. Even then, it was not too late to press and pursue with his whole force. The fortifications of Limerick had moldered to decay; he gave the Irish time to repair and add to them. He divided his forces, sending DOUGLAS with ten thousand men to besiege Athlone, while he with the remainder marched southward along the coast. Before Athlone, DOUGLAS sustained a signal defeat. WILLIAM himself did no more than take Wexford, which was betrayed, and Clonmel, which was ungarrisoned—petty conquests, interposing delay, when expedition was essential." O'CONOR'S "*Military History of the Irish Nation.*"

We *now* know that the Sikh power was completely broken by the repeated heavy blows of MUDKI, FEROZESHAH, ALIWAL and SOBRAON; but such was not then the general opinion, and there was not wanting many, even in high places, to solemnly warn the governor-general against crossing the Sutlej; as some of them said, 'only to be driven back with disgrace.' Better men declared that we had not means to lay siege to Gobindgurh and Lahore, and that, without such means it would be injudicious to cross. While thus pressed on the spot, there had been for some time as impressive suggestions from irresponsible persons elsewhere to advance and hazard all in the Punjab, before our train and ammunition had come up. The governor-general's practical common sense steered him safely between these extremes. He waited an hour beyond the arrival of the siege-train; he felt that all now depended on *Time*, on closing the war before the hot season could set in on our European troops, entailing death in a hundred shapes on all ranks, and the expenses of another campaign on the Government." SIR HENRY MONTGOMERY LAWRENCE'S *Essays, Military and Political*, written in India; London, 1859.

"Moreover, AHITHOPHEL said unto ABSALOM, 'Let me now choose out twelve thousand men, and I will arise and pursue after DAVID this night. And I will come upon him while he is weary and weak-handed, and will make him afraid, and all the people that are with him shall flee.' "—2d SAM: xvii.

"The Prince (of Wahlstadt, BLUCHER) had a very prompt and penetrating eye. If he said, 'That village there, those heights, or that copse must be taken,' or 'this or that wing, or the center must advance, in order to prevent such one or another result,' in every case the order was apposite, and perfectly practical. In such wise, alone was the battle of Laon, the key to (the capture of) Paris (in 1814) won. NAPOLEON himself exerted all his might to break the right wing and center (of BLUCHER), and get possession of the direct road to Laon. The Prince patiently observed the changes of the struggle, even until evening; at length he spoke: 'Now it is time to put an end to this business.' Then he took out his watch and gave the order accordingly, 'to make a general attack at a designated time; YORK especially shall pass from his defensive to an offensive as fierce as his force will permit; let him set fire to the adjacent village and rout the French and pursue them as fiercely and as far as circumstances will permit.' A decided victory was the result, in which YORK had the greatest share." BIESKE'S *Blucher*.

IT is very questionable if any portion of the Army of the Potomac ever fought as well — perhaps "well" is not the word — rather, ever showed more bulldog pluck than HEINTZELMAN'S corps at Williamsburg. Not that this glorious army did not fight marvelously well on other occasions; but WELLINGTON admitted that troops green to fire often face death with more reckless enthusiasm than veterans who have learned from experience the folly of exposing themselves needlessly. The "Iron Duke" spoke of the young British officers who had never been under fire before, hastening to meet death at Waterloo as gaily as if they were going to a ball. Perhaps one reason for this apparent indifference arises from the fact that men of a brave nation do not learn, before they have gone through one sharp battle, to appreciate its dangers.

Lieutenant LAMPING — so frequently quoted in the chapters relating to KEARNY in Algiers — who served with the French Foreign Legion in Africa, uses the following language in regard to his "baptism of fire:"

"This was my first battle in the open field, and I cannot say that it made much impression upon me. My imagination had pictured the terrors of the scene so vividly to me that the reality fell far short of it. I was moreover prepared for it by all manner of perils by land and by sea. I have frequently observed that men of lively imagination (and accordingly most southrons) have a greater dread of fancied than of real dangers. Before the decisive moment arrives, they have exhausted all the terrors of death and are prepared for the worst. The cold, phlegmatic northerner, on the contrary, goes with greater coolness into battle, but often finds it worse than he expected."

Marshal NEY, after explaining to General DUMAS his manœuvres at Lutren, in 1813, which decided the day, added: "I had only battalions of *conscripts* (new levies), and I have reason to congratulate myself on it; and doubt whether I could have done the same thing with the old Grenadiers of the Guard. I had before me the best of the enemy's troops, the whole of the Prussian Guards; our bravest grenadiers after having twice failed, would, perhaps, not have carried the village; but I led these *brave children five times to the charge*, and their docility, perhaps, too, their inexperience, served me better than veteran courage; the French Infantry is never too young."

It is curious to contemplate the effects of the same causes upon different individuals, and the reader will find a result similar to that at which LAMPING reached by a different process of thought, in one of the actors at Williamsburg, quoted a little furthor on. Brevet Major W. B. (then Second Lieutenant in the Fifth Excelsior) describes Williamsburgh (where he commanded his company) as the hottest fight he ever was in, Chancellorsville coming next in severity; Gettysburg, in his opinion, fell far short of both, although his brigade (Excelsior) did the hardest kind of fighting on the second day (2d July, Thursday), on the left, repulsing LONGSTREET's turning movement. The lines were closer together when they exchanged fires at Williamsburg than on any other occasion. He himself cut down and preserved a sapling, which only made a good stout cane, yet, nevertheless, had been hit by nine bullets.

Major C. S. W., First New York Artillery — who made his *debut* in this battle, served throughout the war with distinction, and was brevetted Brigadier-General at a time when brevets were indeed worth something — has often remarked that the troops, on this sombre May day, marched up under fire just as lines are represented going into battle in pictures. It is very unlikely if he exposed himself with such total disregard of self again. KEARNY often spoke of this officer's conduct on this occasion, and, highest commendation for an old soldier, said that the green volunteer behaved as well as any regular (meaning veteran) could have done.

There are many reasons why our troops should have behaved well at Williamsburg. They had been disgusted with lying in the mud throughout the previous fall and winter, blockaded, as it were, or held in check by a *phantom* enemy, whose *unreality* had been dissipated by KEARNY's sudden dash on Centreville and into Manassas. They burned to avenge Ball's Bluff; Drainville had taught them what a vigorous attempt to do something could accomplish. The inaction before Yorktown had not improved their temper; they felt their strength; they knew their capability, and they longed to measure themselves with rebels who had vanished from the battle field, which they claimed as a great Southern victory, and *was not*, and had eluded them in those fortified lines where CORNWALLIS surrendered to WASHINGTON.

Fortunately, the troops who led the Union advance up the Peninsula had been attempered into a steel lance-blade, whose point was that "Fighting Joe" who crowned a long series of desperate conflicts by the escalade of Lookout Mountain, that nonpariel "battle above the clouds."

HOOKER led his men into action and disposed of them with the calm intrepidity of a practised leader. His presence held his men up against fearful odds; and when they had to give ground (his single division had to sustain the attack of far outnumbering forces, gradually increasing to quadruple its own; we took prisoners from forty rebel regiments), he became a sort of Providence, exercising an influence of which none but the bravest of the brave are capable of; so that his troops gathered around him as a centre and a strong and unshakable tower, to make their last desperate stand. Still, even he could not have held them up to such work had not the troops felt, had not each soldier known, that the man who was coming up to relieve them was that fearless twin-spirit, who would do all that could be done to convert a momentary check into a victory. They knew that KEARNY would strain every nerve; that he valued "Fighting Joe," and that HOOKER valued "Fighting Phil." Together they had fought in Mexico; amid manifold perils they had learned to estimate each other at their full worth; and they relied upon each other with the assurance only such men can feel and inspire. Hard pressed, and aware that his troops were nearly exhausted, HOOKER felt — and so expressed himself — abandoned by those who should have been the first to support him. In anguish of spirit at his needless loss — needless had he been duly succored — he recorded his sense of this abandonment in language which, however bitter, the people feel was very near the truth: "History will not be believed when it is told that the noble officers and men of my division were permitted to carry on this unequal struggle from morning till night, unaided, in the presence of more than thirty thousand of their comrades with arms in their hands. Nevertheless it is true."

HOOKER was perfectly right, and acted in strict accordance with the principles of war, when he attacked the retreating rebels at Williamsburg. He would have violated those rules had he not done so. To press *home* a retreating foe is just what our generals always ought to have done, and just exactly as HOOKER did. The rebels also, in this fight, were true to their principles — never to shun a fight when they expected to be able to do a greater proportional damage to us than they thought we could do to them; and to reinforce their rear guard to insure its being able to make a decided stand even though they sacrificed that rear guard, as at Falling Waters, so that they saved their main army and their material. None of their generals seemed to value human life; but then they always required an equivalent for their prodigality of blood—always, except at Gettysburg. There, however, for the first time, LEE acted upon open ground, where his actions could be discerned; and there he demonstrated that he was not the general his admirers claimed him to be, and that all his reputation had been built up on the ability of his subordinates, and the errors and negligence of his opponents.

But enough of this argument. HOOKER did attack, and bravely, in the same spirit that SHERMAN, two years afterward (27th June, 1864), assaulted at Kenesaw Mountain, claiming that his daring feat "produced good fruits and demonstrated to General JOHNSTON (who commanded on the Peninsula in May, 1862) that I would assault, and that boldly." HOOKER's division seemed about to experience the fate of the assaulting column amid the Georgia Appallachians, and would have done so had he not had PHIL. KEARNY to appeal to for support, and PHIL. KEARNY to respond to his appeal and to answer promptly and efficiently the summons of HOOKER for the reinforcements necessary to preserve and maintain his soldierly honor and his division's existence.

The facts are these: Through storm and mire, and loitering after loitering regiments, brigades and divisions, HOOKER sent word back to KEARNY, furthest in the rear, to hurry forward. Other regiments intervened, but his trust was in KEARNY. "Tell HOOKER I am coming," said KEARNY, whose division was the last to leave the lines at Yorktown. These were his words to the aid who brought him HOOKER's message; and KEARNY, the last to whom such an appeal, under ordinary circumstances, would have been made, was the first to come up and save HOOKER. Yes, saved HOOKER in every sense of the word, as STEVENSON testifies in his history of the "Excelsior, or Sickles Brigade."

Captain F. E. G. wrote as follows in this connection: "I had not the honor of fighting under your illustrious relative, the lamented PHIL. KEARNY, but I did have the honor of seeing him on more than one battlefield; and especially do I remember the

MAJOR GENERAL PHILIP KEARNY AT WILLIAMSBURG,
May 5, 1862.

joy I experienced on seeing him come up the road at the battle of Williamsburg. I cheered him then, standing in mud a foot deep, with the tears trickling down my cheeks for joy. He saved *our division*, and who can tell how much more?"

"I shall never forget," said Brevet Major W. B., "the arrival of the brave General KEARNY and his troops at the battle of Williamsburg, on May 5, 1862. I at that time was a second lieutenant, in command of my company (Company I, Fifth Regiment, Excelsior Brigade). The Excelsior Brigade, except one regiment — the Second Excelsior Seventy-first New York Volunteers — together with the rest of HOOKER's division, had been engaged in the battle, and at the time of KEARNY's reaching the battle field the whole division was well fought out, as the list of killed and wounded will attest. We had been forced back a full half mile from where we had fought in the morning, and our wounded in the hospital were in great danger, not only from capture, but since the enemy's projectiles were visiting them. When General KEARNY arrived, he passed through our lines and soon retook the lost ground, and, after a short but gallant fight, he made the battle of Williamsburg a victory.

"When the Excelsior Brigade was forced back at the battle of Williamsburg, May 5, 1862, two guns were left loaded and primed, all ready to fire, by the artillery, but no artillery-man was there to fire them. A second lieutenant belonging to Company F, Fifth Regiment, Excelsior Brigade, by the name of SQUIER (a brother of Mr. SQUIER, so long connected with Frank Leslie's paper), discovered that the guns were loaded and stood by them; and when our troops had fallen to the rear of these guns, and the rebels, hard pressing them, made their appearance, he pulled the lanyards, and the rebels, not forgetting the days of masked batteries, thought it was all a Yankee trick our falling back, and they immediately retired; and before they recovered General KEARNY had arrived, and then the day was safe."

There is no question but that KEARNY fully appreciated the work before him from the outset. Brevet Brigadier-General C. S. W—— establishes this when he states that he saw KEARNY's division drawn out ready to move on the first intimation, long before any orders were issued to that effect. DE TROBRIAND says that from the start KEARNY felt that "STONEMAN had the whole rebel rear guard on his hands" on the evening of the 4th, and that HEINTZELMAN'S aid confirmed the exactitude of KEARNEY'S conjectures when, next day, about 11 A. M., this aid encountered the advancing succors, westward of the Brick Church.

Full justice has never been done, hitherto, by any historian of the war, to the battle of Williamsburg. In many of its features it was one of those conflicts which ought to be remembered in the catalogue of decisive battles. It decided one fact—that the men of the North were not the men which their detractors had pictured them; that if any people on the face of the earth would fight and stand up to their work under every disadvantage, Northerners would; that they would fight as well as Southerners, if not better, and endure as much, if not more. They were no longer QUIRITES (citizens), but MILITES (soldiers).

In this battle KEARNY showed himself also in *his true colors.* If any man doubted that he would fulfill all that report had ascribed to him, that doubt was set at rest forever. He justified the opinion of one of those generals (whose name the snarling but capable GUROWSKI declared "ought to corruscate as the purest light of patriotism for future generations; one who never fails where honor and patriotism are to be sustained"), Major-General A. A. HUMPHREYS, now Chief of Engineers—who wrote "that KEARNY'S action, by universal testimony, was magnificent." The words of BLUCHER'S biographer, BIESKE, in regard to his hero, will apply with equal force to KEARNY, an identically parallel character: "Fifteen years BLUCHER lived in his retirement very happily [KEARNY spent ten years in luxurious ease] as he declared, and yet proved (when the time came) that, with his characteristic resolution, whatever he willed to do he could accomplish."

"One memorable fact which you ought not to forget in your narrative of that fight," are HOOKER'S own words in a letter to the author, was that KEARNY'S division was the *last* to leave Yorktown, and was the *first* to come to my assistance." The reader must almost have been in such a predicament to conceive the fiery impatience of KEARNY, as he waded rather than marched forward, appreciating the due need of his friend, like Damon flying to save his Pythias, under the suspended ax. The reverberations of the battle — like the thunder of a tempest afar off — deadened into an ominous hum by the distance, the intervening forests and the pouring rain, must have inflamed his determination to press on, and have quickened his ardent thirst to make the name he knew he only required the opportunity to win, had not the necessity of straining every nerve to gain the field before it was too late to rescue HOOKER, roused his fiery nature into almost superhuman energy. Then, after he had passed the brick church, the cannon shots that almost immediately began to "lob in" from the still unseen guns, soon told their own tale. "Lob in" is an ultra English expression, but it is very significant, denoting the heavy or lazy fall into mud, distinctive of single shots at long range. These were soon succeeded by the spiteful rattling, roll and crash of the musketry nigh at hand, and then KEARNY's division, stooping upon the furious battle field, realized VOLTAIRE's description of CUMBERLAND's infantry at Fontenoy:

> "On the wings of the wind, like a storm-cloud its ranks,
> Bearing lightning and thunder and death in its flanks."

Nor was his conduct to HOOKER less generous or worthy of note. Like BOUFFLERS at Malplaquet, he would not supersede HOOKER on the field of his glory, but left him the direction, as the hero of Lille yielded the first place to VILLARS; even as OUTRAM waived his rank in favor of HAVELOCK, and allowed the latter to complete the task he had so nobly begun, of relieving Lucknow; even as NIEL, the superior of HAVELOCK, was content with being his coadjutor and with lending him all the assistance in his power in achieving the success of a cause both had so greatly and nearly at heart.

In regard to the hour when KEARNY got on the ground, there has been a great deal of discussion. KEARNY himself says 2 P. M. One of his aides-de-camp, in a letter from the battlefield, fixes 2:30 P. M. Subsequently, in conversation, the same aid stated that KEARNY ordered him to keep the time, and he did so; that the actual record was lost, but that he knew that KEARNY got up at 2:30 P. M., and that his regiments were engaged at 3 P. M. HEINTZELMAN testifies to the earlier hour of 2:30 P. M.; and the *Evening Post's* war correspondent corroborates KEARNY'S own opinion of 2 P. M. Were not this all-sufficient to establish the KEARNY side of the controversy as to time, the following method of arriving at the truth is unanswerable, because it is confirmatory evidence, unbiassed and totally disinterested—a perfectly mathematical method of demonstrating the truth like a proposition:

Major, then Lieutenant, W. B. (who distinctly remembers KEARNY'S arrival on the field, working or jerking the stump of his left arm as he was accustomed to do when excited) declares that he did not come up until 4 P. M. The major admits that the fight commenced at 7 A. M. HOOKER states 7:30 A. M., in his report; but it is well known that he brought on the fight by a daring reconnaissance with his staff as soon as it was light. It is almost certain it began at an earlier hour — about daybreak. DE TROBRIAND says that HEINTZELMAN'S aid charged with seeking reinforcements stated, when they met, that the fight had lasted over four hours. This was at the Brick Church. From this point to Fort Magruder was three miles in an air line; to the real fighting not over this distance by the road. Giving DE TROBRIAND from one hour and a half to two hours to overcome all the intervening difficulties, and become engaged, brings it down to 1 P. M. He says he had been actively engaged for about an hour, when a rapidly-developing fire on his left hand relieved his mind. This was KEARNY, at 2 P. M. Consequently, DE TROBRIAND, a disinterested witness, proves that KEARNY was not only on the field but had brought quite a large portion of his force into action by 2 P. M. As KEARNY'S reports are very detailed, it is needless to enter further into the developments of the battle, and the reader's attention is now invited to some interesting statements from the correspondence of the general and his friends. The following letter, written almost on the battlefield by one of KEARNY'S aids, will give a pretty fair general idea of the fight, and prove of interest as a contemporaneous narrative, thrown together almost by the light of the conflict:

"I am safe. You must have heard of our action by this time, though I know at first the papers did not know any thing of it. On the day of the battle (Monday, 5th), we were encamped about two miles beyond Yorktown, on the road to Williamsburg. General HEINTZELMAN, with HOOKER's division, was in advance. We were ready to start early, but did not, on account of awaiting orders. We commenced our march at about eight, and it was with great difficulty that we could get on, the roads being very bad on account of the rain which had fallen since three o'clock A. M., and continued most of the rest of the day. Just before we reached the Brick Church, orders came that we should advance as fast as possible, that HOOKER was hotly engaged. General KEARNY, after giving his orders to his generals, moved on ahead to investigate the roads. After he had gained a full knowledge he returned to the redoubt thrown up, which at one place commands the main road, though not the one which we took, which latter was a cart-road, entering the main road behind (*i. e.* turning) the redoubt.

"As soon as BERRY's division came up, the General leading, we shortly after reached General HEINTZELMAN," who, with HOOKER's assistance "was holding up the Excelsiors, who had done well in the earlier part of the day, but were disheartened by heavy loss. General HEINTZELMAN, when he saw it was useless to endeavor to get them to advance, ordered General KEARNY to advance, who was only too glad to do so. General KEARNY and General HOOKER (who, by the way, earlier in the day had a horse shot under him) led, followed by their staffs; then came General BERRY's brigadge.

"Let me now describe the country, and then the action; let me also mention that it was owing entirely to KEARNY's coming up when he did, that the day was won. The road to Williamsburg is almost entirely through the woods, except in one or two places. Where the battle (actual fighting) took place, was on the confines of the woods; here the rebels had dug rifle-pits, which they covered or protected with abatis. Behind these were works—that is, several forts.

[Here follows an original rough draft of it, drawn on the field, which was the clearest that was sent home or published.]

"Being on the staff, I saw most of the action, for my duties calling me hither and thither enabled me to observe more than one whose position was more stationary.

[The writer was engaged in his appropriate duty at the front during the fighting, and after the fray was over attending to the wounded, and collecting and bringing forward the dead, among them two comrades on the staff.]

"Just before you reach the open country, you come to a hollow, and on the left of the road a stream (emptying unto College creek, an affluent of the James.) General KEARNY rode himself up to the cannon, which, placed on a little rise, commanded the road (these guns were at the time unsupported) so as to see on what ground he was to act. He then rode to the left of the road, the bullets whizzing around us. IRVING says of WASHINGTON, that after the first fight he wrote to his brother, 'the bullets whistled around me, and really the sound was delightful.' When spoken to in after years in reference to this gasconade, he remarked that 'if he had said so, it was when he had not heard many.' Now this was the first time I had heard the bullets whistle, and I can tell you it is not delightful—not even pleasing. But though the sound does not become familiar, the thoughts getting engrossed, you forget the sound, or rather forget to hear them.

"General KEARNY ordered General BERRY to occupy the woods to the left and a little to the right, which he did. This movement retook our lost pieces, or rather some of them.

"On our right was DE TROBRIAND'S (55th N. Y. V., the LAFAYETTE Guard) and some other troops of HOOKER'S division. It appears, from what I can learn, that HOOKER kind of stumbled upon the enemy's works in the morning. Major CHARLES S. WAINWRIGHT placed his guns and silenced the battery of the enemy. The enemy's fire was very heavy upon his (C. S. W.'s) gunners, and the supporting regiment was driven from the guns, or whether HOOKER thought it better to lose the guns, so as to prevent the enemy's flanking him, I do not know.

"Well, when we came up we gained steadily on the enemy. We reached the scene of action about half-past two; the fighting ceased at six-thirty or seven; we having followed the enemy to his ramparts. At daybreak General KEARNY, leading with Brigadier-General BIRNEY's brigade, took Fort Magruder. General JAMESON, another of our brigadier-generals, marched on and entered Williamsburg, throwing out one regiment as skirmishers, supported by the rest beyond the town. At about noon we received orders to remain near Williamsburg.

"Two of our aides were killed, A. A. G. JAMES WILSON and Lieutenant BARNARD. They were killed leading an assault; the first shot through the head with the ball of a fowling rifle, most likely by a half-breed Indian. After the battle we found several dead, and the prisoners said there was a company of them used as sharpshooters. BARNARD was shot through the abdomen. He lived a little time, and was perfectly sensible.

"General KEARNY exposed himself continually. At one time he and Lieutenant MOORE and another of his aides were in advance of our guns when one of our soldiers cried 'take care, sir, they aim at you.' They had scarcely time to turn their horses when a volley whistled by. At another time he rode up to the Fire Zouaves, whose Colonel it is feared is taken prisoner, saying 'where is your Colonel, boys.' 'We don't know,' was the response. 'Well then follow me,' and he led them to a gallant charge.* Continually he exposed himself. Our men *were*

* This was substantially the reply of LYON at Wilson's creek, and it would be as just to charge him with reckless exposure as to condemn KEARNY for a similar devoted gallantry. Both felt that example was the necessity of the hour and forgot self in cause and country. "To call the deaths of LYON and BAKER 'military suicide,' as ——— has done, is a cruel aspersion upon the dead, against which they cannot defend themselves, and he has no right, sitting safely at home and knowing nothing of the circumstances, and never having seen active service, to write and publish such an article as his."

Circumstances must govern in all cases. Our men are not veterans. The fact must not be forgotten. They must be led. You cannot order them forward and expect them to go alone. You cannot station them in a heavy fire and expect them to remain without flinching, unless supported and controlled, though they be the bravest men on earth. Example is every thing; a single word, the turning of a hair may sway them, so as to make all the difference between a fight and a flight, and this is not from fickleness. They are intelligent and reasoning beings. They are not afraid to do whatever you are not afraid to lead them in yourself. But if they suspect you of flinching, there is something impossible or something going wrong, and they are like sheep without a shepherd. Thus may one firm man support a whole corps, and that one must be their leader. They absolutely lean on him, relying on his superior judgment, and thus can he control them in time of emergency, after they have learned the power of his support, and not before, They gradually learn this mesmerically, unerringly. Inexperienced troops must be led, and you all know the vital importance of their having officers reli-

brave. We had five regiments engaged contending against great odds. Our loss in killed, wounded and missing is over four hundred. The enemy's is very much greater. A commissary, a mere boy, said he wished to go into the fight. He is a crack shot, and he scarcely reached the fighting before a rebel fired, the ball grazing his hair. As the rebel was near he dropped the rifle, drew a revolver and shot him dead, saying it was a shame to use a rifle where a pistol could be used. Another boy went into the fight. Before going they tried to persuade him not to go, but he would, saying, 'I am good at a shot, and if it comes to the bayonet I shall see what I shall do.' He was found after the battle with a rebel's bayonet through him, and his through the rebel, both lying together where they had struggled."

Williamsburg, while it was one of the most glorious, was one of the most extraordinary kind of fights that was ever fought. SUMNER, the highest in rank on the field, one of the bravest and the most patriotic of men, did nothing of any consequence, and what little he did do, was rather injurious than beneficial. Impetuous to a fault, in general, on this occasion he displayed a want of energy which is almost irreconcilable with his subsequent determination at Fair Oaks. HEINTZLEMAN exhibited a magna-

---

able and equal to any emergency, who in all coolness can judge when it is necessary to be rash and when to be merely courageous, and can act accordingly.

Thus far I have spoken only of new soldiers. But even after they have learned confidence in their leaders, and still later, even after they have learned full confidence in themselves, you cannot always stay in the rear and expect your men in front to do their thorough work, however much they may feel the power of your presence to back them up. There are times when the toughest veterans will flinch and the best-drilled machines hesitate and stop, although the mighty presence of NAPOLEON himself be there to force them on! He was a model of cool courage and of caution, and knew well the necessity of guarding his own personal safety. Yet NAPOLEON in person was obliged to lead his bravest men over the bridge of Lodi, and again at Arcola and at Waterloo, in the last grand charge of the Old Guard. He felt the dire necessity of leading them himself, and he rushed to their head, but his officers seized him and forced him back. Had they left him to follow his own instinct, he might have turned the fortunes of the day.

Behind all this comes the grandest consideration of all, God guides the balls, and a man is really as safe in the front as in the rear. When his earthly mission is fulfilled, the shot will find him as quick as the bayonet. Then it is time for him to go.

All things work together for good. LYON's death was more useful than his longer life would have been, else Providence would have detained him here. Newspaper critics and some others have lost sight of this. Pages 38, 39 and 40, "*Soldiers' Letters*," by LYDIA MINTURN POST.

nimity which, while admirable as a quality, was out of place at this time in one who was not only the ranking officer, but the one placed in charge by the Commander-in-chief. The greatest part of the battle was ordered by the division-general youngest in rank, and it was not until the very close that KEARNY, HOOKER's superior, assumed his rights. Strangest of all, with two Major-Generals on the ground, and from 36,000 to 38,000, perhaps even, at the close of day, 45,000 men present, 8,000 men did all the fighting, and came near being beaten, with 30,000 who scarcely fired a shot, within a few hundred perches; who had only to have shown themselves, as determined to act, to put an end to the engagement almost as soon as it commenced. A simple strategic movement, early in the morning, such as HANCOCK made late in the afternoon, must have manœuvered the rebels out of their position with scarcely any fighting, by an effort of what DECKER would style practical-strategy. The result was, HOOKER who ought to have played only a subordinate part, and KEARNY, who ought never to have been allowed to play any part at all, became the heroes of a battle which was one of the most glorious for the Union arms, and the most obstinately contested of all in which the Army of the Potomac, in whole or in part, was engaged during the four years of the war. Williamsburg was fair stand-up fight. It was "a fight of giants," as FRANCIS I, said of Marignano, in an arena of clearing, encompassed by the primeval woods. What is grander, it was of MEN, of Americans, and amid that fearful whirlwind of battle, as was remarked by one of the bravest, KEARNY was the noblest figure in this, his first battle for freedom and nationality—"magnificent." And as he shone in this, his first, he shone in every one afterward, through all to the last, when he laid down his life for his country, feeling like HUNYADI, the Magyar hero and patriot, "It is allotted to every one once to die; it is a debt we owe to nature; but to die the death of a hero for Fatherland and Faith, it is a grace which the All-Powerful only accords to His elect. God is with us—charge!"

God was with us, indeed, at Williamsburg, only as ZIETHEN declared to FREDERICK the Great when the latter despondingly remarked, "The days of miracles were past." "Yet He, the

'Ancient of Days,' above, holds us up. He will not let us fall." He did hold us up. In this sense, the fallen at Willamsburg were only the victims on the threshold; those who fell at Five Forks the expiation at the altar. Then came triumph, freedom, a restored Constitution and country! KEARNY was to fall while the sun was rising amid clouds; WADSWORTH at his setting, amid golden glories, the promise of a halcyon morn about his crimson disk.

"Victory! Victory!
Oh. God of Battles, give us victory!"

was the cry of 1862; and in 1865 He gave it, full measure, heaped, poured out into the bosom. Alas! if only the whole nation had been as true to themselves and to Him as KEARNY and his peers!

The battle ground of Williamsburg is very peculiar, and, if strongly occupied and held and well defended, presents a better field-position than Yorktown. The head waters of College creek, which empties into the James, and those of Queen's creek, which flows into the York, were less than a mile apart, and there is actually less than two miles of available front to move upon, free from great natural obstacles.* Across the relatively unobstructed space of three miles the rebels had constructed thirteen defensive works — five, six or nine redoubts, and four to eight open works, according to different plans consulted — whose cross-fires would sweep every foot of ground by which they could be approached. About the centre stood Fort Magruder a strong bastioned fieldwork, mounting thirteen guns, situated about one mile south-east of Williamsburg, at the fork of the Yorktown and Warwick roads. In addition to this, the rebels had protected their position by heavy and extensive slashings — in fact, the forest was felled for a breadth of nearly half a mile — and moreover stood under cover of the woods; whereas our troops had to wade to the attack through mud like glue, and over a clearing six to seven hundred yards wide, advancing almost without shelter.

* The measurements, position, etc., have been taken from a map and an exquisitely executed plan, most kindly furnished the writer by Major-General A. A. Humphreys, Chief of Engineers, U. S. A., to whom also he is greatly indebted for other maps, etc.

The rebel position was indeed well adapted for the delivery of a defensive battle. It is true that it could be turned by the York river; but what did that turning amount to, when the movement was eventually made in the lukewarm way in which it was attempted? The object of the rebel Commander-in-chief was to delay General McCLELLAN. He had arrested his advance for nearly a month, before Yorktown. He had no reason to doubt he could accomplish a similar result at Williamsburg; and, judging of the future from the past, he would have done so had any general but one of the HOOKER type led the pursuit, and any general but KEARNY flown — in HOOKER-KEARNY style — to his assistance.

The effect of the victory of Williamsburg is now well known. Richmond was thrown into consternation* by the result. That victory, followed up, would have given us the rebel capital. That this crowning triumph was not achieved, was due to the only one by whom it could have been been achieved — McCLELLAN. Common sense, go-ahead leaders, like TORSTENSON or TRAUN or BLUCHER or CHANGARNIER, or any one of the French Generals who made a mark in the Algerian campaign, in which KEARNY first learned his business, would have utilized his victory, as TORSTENSON always profited by success, as TURENNE bowled the Allies out of Alsace, as TRAUN backed FREDERIC out of Bohemia, as BLUCHER swept every thing before him in 1813, 1814, and 1815, and as CHANGARNIER, when he had no cannon, gathered up his infantry and hurled them like a gigantic missile at the Arabs, exclaiming, "There is my artillery."

Almost the whole of the fighting—that is, the severe fighting—which constituted Williamsburg a battle, not a mere affair of a rear-guard, occurred in the belt of partially cleared ground in front of Fort Magruder. The hard fighting was also confined to the division of HOOKER from daylight, or 7 or 7½ A. M., to 2 or 2½ or 3 P. M., unsupported; after that time, to his own and about one brigade of KEARNY's arriving division.

* See Carleton's "Following the Flag," pp. 83, 84, etc., referring to Pollard's "Second Year of the War," p. 29, etc.; Lossing's "Civil War in America." vol. ii., p. 384, etc., and other cotemporaneous publications; "*Rebellion Record*," Vol. V; Doc., page 25 (1); GREELEY ii, 225-'6; TENNEY, 222, ¶ 1; ABBOTT, ii, 55, referring to "Report on the Conduct of the War." Ib., i, 391.

It is very doubtful if first and last the Unionists had 8,000 men actually engaged in this immediate portion of the field. On the Yorktown road — at the Adams or Whittaker House, where another road branches off to the east or right, by which Fort Magruder can be turned, and taken in rear to the right, and in the rear of HOOKER's right flank—SUMNER massed his corps. His action or inaction is unintelligible.* It is said that his dispositions were made against a supposititious line of battle in his front, and to his right, where he imagined the rebels were posted in force, manœuvering directly against him, and that he considered the attack upon HOOKER was nothing but a feint, which grew, through circumstances, into an actual engagement. SUMNER is dead. He was a true man; brave, patriotic, and whole-hearted; but, on this occasion, he could not have erred in a greater degree than he did. The true point of attack was to the right of where he stood, and against the extreme rebel left, where HANCOCK did assail HILL, and with a withering point blank volley, blew him away. Our left center and left should have menaced while being refused. It would appear that there was an impression upon the minds of HEINTZLEMAN and SUMNER, that the ground between them was an impassable swamp. Grant that. From the disposition of the ground, this was an excusable error of judgment for the moment;—but only for a moment — since a trial, a reconnoissance, out of fire, such as KEARNY made this very day, more than once under fire, would have dissipated the delusion. The whole country is very flat, and owing to heavy rains, was then covered with water; but what impediment was that to a *searching* endeavor to unite the wings of the dislocated Federal force, and act with generalship and common judgment? Let that go, however.

Had SUMNER acted differently, KEARNY would never have had this fine opportunity to display himself in all the grandeur of his complete soldiership.

As for HEINTZLEMAN, brave as steel, and generous and self-forgetting as brave; the soldiers will never forget him for

* SUMNER's conduct on this occasion, was not unlike that of SERRURIER's at Cassano, 26th April, 1799. MITCHELL's "Biographies of Eminent Soldiers." SUWAROFF, 141; BERTHEZENE's "Memoires; or SOUVENIRS Militaires," I, 33, 35; HARPER's Allison, II, 23; THIERS' History of the French Revolution, II, 432.

not forgetting them. When they were exhausted in body and despondent in spirit, before KEARNY showed himself, he felt that something must be done to cheer them. So, gathering up the scattered bands, he ordered them to play. "Play," said he, "play! it's all you're good for. Play, d—n it. Play some marching tune! Play Yankee Doodle, or any doodle you can think of; only play something." * "General HIENTZLEMAN," says private JAMES R. BURNS, in his little book, — "*The Battle of Williamsburg*" — "however, ordered several of the bands to strike up national and martial airs, and when the strains of the familiar tunes reached the ears of the wounded, as they were being carried from the field, their cheers mingled with those of the soldiers (KEARNY'S)† who were just rushing into action. The effect, too, was great on the other side, for some of the prisoners stated that when they heard the bands strike up 'Hail Columbia,' and heard our soldiers cheer, they knew that victory would be ours.

'The bands did play so merrily
Our own sweet martial airs,
And when 'Hail Columbia' was heard,
We soon forgot our cares.'"

In front of HOOKER and KEARNY it was butcher work, identical with ABERCROMBIE'S assault on the advanced works and lines of Ticonderoga, in July, 1759, in which the peerless Lord HOWE fell, and the flower of the British forces perished in vain, Lord JOHN MURRAY'S Highland regiment losing nearly one-half its privates, as well as twenty-five officers, slain on the spot, or desperately wounded. Compare this with KEARNY'S and HOOKER'S list of casualties, and it will at once be comprehended that the slaughter at Williamsburg was even more severe than at Ticonderoga; although that engagement of the past is looked upon as a marked example of desperate bush-whacking and hard fighting.‡ While this was the state of affairs on the left,

* Compare Captain BLAKE'S "*Three years in the Army of the Potomac*," page 78.

† Fortunately for his (HOOKER'S) laurels, General KEARNY, a splendid old veteran, who had seen service under the French in Algiers, came to his aid and restored the battle to the Federals. "STACKE'S *Story of the American War*." London, 1866, page 58.

‡ Out of 16,000 men (Cust. 1, 2, 279), just about the number HOOKER and KEARNY nominally had, ABERCROMBIE lost 2,000 killed and wounded (Cust. 1, 2, 282) and was defeated. Our loss on this occasion was about one-eighth heavier, and we were successful, although HOOKER and KEARNY did not have on hand over 9,000 men.

in the center or right, in front of SUMNER, there was an opportunity of displaying fine generalship.* With part of his front protected by a ravine and branch of College creek, he could have launched such a column against the ememy's left, as must have swept away opposition, swung round, taken the whole rebel line of defence in the rear, and captured a large number of prisoners.

It might have been made very much the same kind of fight as Count SCHAUMBURG LIPPE, once delivered, in 1762, when he found himself with a detachment of six hundred infantry and cavalry in the presence of 2,000 Spaniards, who suddenly issued from a wood on which he was marching. He instantly recalled to mind the fact that there was a large pond in the neighborhood, on the road by which he had come up. In front of this body of water, so as to screen it, he posted his two hundred cavalry, in a single rank; his infantry three deep, as usual at that date, constituting his other wing. The Spaniards extended their line so as to outflank him on both wings. The Count meanwhile fell back briskly on the pond, then passed his cavalry in the rear of his infantry to the opposite extremity of his line. Thus the water became a substitute for half of his front. This manœuver enabled him to outflank the enemy, to attack them (ROSBACH fashion) before they could remedy or meet the manœuver, and to roll up one wing before it could be reinforced from the other. Thus the Spaniards were completely beaten.

As to the numerical force of the rebels at Williamsburg, it is very difficult to arrive at any correct opinion. The English author of the "Battle Fields of the South" says (page 204): "LONGSTREET commanded on our side, and I *know* did not handle more than twenty-five thousand men." These words would

* A day or two after the battle, KEARNY rode up to HOOKER'S Headquarters and related as follows, in the presence of a common friend, from whose lips the statement was taken down in writing. He said "I have just seen SUMNER; SUMNER said that the battle of Williamsburg was not understood; that MCCLELLAN had considered it an affair of the heads of columns, while HOOKER claimed that the attack was made upon him (HOOKER). It was on the contrary a real pitched battle in which *I* (SUMNER) *was in command*." This KEARNY emphasized. "The attack on HOOKER was a mere feint. Their intention was to break through our centre, but I (SUMNER) frustrated their design, and had my men drawn up in five lines, 30,000 men, sir, in five lines, one line, two lines, three lines, four lines, five lines;" counting them off on his fingers; KEARNY imitating; "seeing the dispositions I had made, they did not dare to attack."

justify the question, how many did LONGSTREET have at hand, under his command, whom he did not handle? Such indirect language would lead any one to suppose that it was used on purpose to convey a false impression. Still, as he sets down the Union force at forty thousand, no great exaggeration, if any, it is fair to believe that he desired to state the exact truth. The writer has heard General HOOKER estimate the rebel strength at "from seventy to ninety thousand, but nearer the latter than the former number." Any such estimate is not borne out either by subsequent revelations or any published authority. His own opinion is that the rebels had from fifteen to forty thousand engaged, the former number, early in the morning, the latter before the action closed. Brev. Major W. B—, of HOOKER's division, had in his own hand the order regulating the retreat of the rebels. The rear-guard was to consist of six thousand men. It is most probable that STONEMAN ran into this force on the afternoon of Sunday, 4th. HOOKER encountered, first, the same troops, doubtless reinforced next day, Monday, 5th. A portion of the rebel army did march through Williamsburg, but countermarched and returned to feed the fight. As we took prisoners from forty regiments, it is equitable to suppose that at this early stage of the war, before any great battle had been fought, the rebel regiments, comfortably housed during the winter, and at home, had not been depleted sufficiently to fall below 750 each. This gives thirty thousand — CARLETON's estimate. Concede, however, that JOHNSTON or LONGSTREET did not have over twenty-five thousand men, that number in a first class intrenched position, such as they occupied, ought to have repulsed and soundly beaten back thrice if not four or five times as many, according to the rule of war applicable to such conditions. Taking their own view of the matter, every additional fact makes the Union victory more remarkable and glorious. The rebel Generals, as a rule, performed marvels in one respect—they moved their troops during an engagement, with such celerity, to menaced points, that scarcely any battle occurred in which a single one of their regiments could complain that it was not "put in," or did not have all the fighting that any reasonable body of men could desire. It is an equally difficult task to arrive at a correct estimate of the Union force which performed any service at Williamsburg. In answer to an application to HOOKER, that distinguished General replied that he had about eight thousand men; his Adjutant-General states that the morning report returned 7,300 present—and even if KEARNY had brought up his whole division, he would have had only as many more. The straggling, however, inevitable from the condition of the roads, often knee deep for men and horses, hub deep for carriages, had reduced his force greatly, and even his leading brigade (BERRY'S) had scarcely become hotly engaged when the rebel *vim* grew gradually less and less virulent; the night shut in, and the fighting ceased.

Taking HOOKER'S estimate as correct, this would not give over twelve to sixteen thousand men, without counting those under HANCOCK; but HOOKER seems to forget that in consequence of the weather and condition of the roads, the flooded flat-lands, the woods and the broken ground, the straggling must have been enormous; it is bad enough in all forced marches, even in dry weather and on dry roads. KEARNY could not have put in one-third of his men, because the same causes which must have somewhat diminished HOOKER'S effective force, contributed, in a much greater degree to decrease the numbers which KEARNY could have had in hand after such a forced march* as he had been compelled to make.

* The following is illustrative of a similar march, and worthy of comparison: "One of the worst features is the state of the weather. * * * At Weickau, that same day, (Sunday), rain began, * * * and on Monday, 19th (December, 1740), there was such a pour of rain as kept most wayfarers, though it could not the Prussian army, within doors. Rain in plunges fallen, and falling through that blessed day, making roads into mere rivers of mud. The Prussian hosts marched on all the same. * * * Rain still heavier, rain as of Noah, continued through this Tuesday. * * * This march for the rearward of the army * * * is thought to be the wettest on record. Waters all out, bridges down, the country one wild lake of eddying mud—up to the knee for many miles together; up to the middle for long spaces; sometimes even up to the chin or deeper, where your bridge was washed away. The Prussians marched through it as if they had been slate or iron. Rank and file, nobody quitted his rank, nobody looked sour in the face; they took the pouring of the skies and the red seas of terrestrial liquid as matters that must be; cheered one another with jocosities, with choral snatches (tobacco, I consider would not burn), and swashed unweariedly forward. Ten hours some of them were out, * * * ten to fifteen miles was the average distance come." CARLYLE'S '*Friedrich The Second*,' volume 3, pages 148, 149.

Consequently, after a dispassionate consideration, twelve thousand seems to be a generous estimate of our effective force "handled," to borrow a word from the statement of an opponent. Conceding that HOOKER's view is correct, and he finally had the whole rebel army on his hands, that army, according to the rebel returns, comprised fifty-three thousand effectives. As HOOKER remarks, afterward, "I have some valuable papers, relating to this fight, which I have obtained from rebel sources," it is reasonable or just to suppose that he speaks with the highest authority when he says that by the time KEARNY came up he was fighting the whole rebel army on the Peninsula, and it was that whole army that KEARNY's shock decidedly defeated.

Keeping this fact constantly in view, and another, which it would be difficult to disprove, that certainly not over ten to twelve thousand Unionists, at the utmost, fired a shot on that bloody Monday, 5th of May, 1862, Williamsburg becomes elevated into all that McCLELLAN claimed for it afterward, "a complete success." It is worthy to rank with the South Mountain battle, to the north and on our right, in Fox and Turner's Gaps — where again HOOKER commanded, KEARNY having fallen—which the writer looks upon as the finest battle of the Army of the Potomac, considering the small portion of it brought into action, the disadvantages under which it labored, and the enormous advantages of position, as at Williamsburg, enjoyed by the rebels.

A calm survey of all the circumstances must justify the decision that too much praise cannot be awarded to HOOKER for his audacity and tenacity at Williamsburg. Nor can less praise be lavished on KEARNY, since had he not brought up a portion of his division, rushed it in, disposed it, fought it, and exposed himself as he did, HOOKER must have come to grief. No wonder that McCLELLAN, at a later date, too late, however, to counteract the impression made by his previous dispatches, giving the whole credit to HANCOCK,* felt compelled to do tardy jus-

* As soon as it was discovered that the Confederates had withdrawn, a column was sent in pursuit. It came up with the retreating rear-guard at Williamsburg, now reinforced from JOHNSTON's army. LONGSTREET's division, which had already passed beyond the town, retraced its steps to aid in resisting the attack, and for *nine* hours HOOKER's division *alone* made head against the whole Confederate force. That General

tice to the real heroes of the day; that is, if honor won in the hottest fire against great odds and under tremendous difficulties, constitutes the highest glory of an officer or of a soldier. A commander-in-chief may rest his claims to the gratitude and rewards of his country on brain work, moral audacity, and able dispositions, but the subordinate general must display far different qualities, physical courage, fertility of expedient, coolness and rapidity of thought under fire, and calmness, all which united, inspire the soldier with confidence in himself and his superior, comtempt of death, and the determination to succeed or die.

At a later date, when it was too late, however, to counteract the impression made by his previous dispatches, giving the whole credit to HANCOCK, McCLELLAN wrote as follows:

CAMP, 19 MILES FROM WILLIAMSBURG,
May 11, 1862.

HON. E. M. STANTON, *Secretary of War:*

Without waiting further official reports, which have not yet reached me, I wish to bear testimony to the splendid conduct of HOOKER'S and KEARNY'S divisions, under command of General HEINTZELMAN, in the battle of Williamsburg. Their bearing was worthy of veterans. HOOKER'S division for (7) hours gallantly withstood the attack of greatly superior numbers, with very heavy loss.

KEARNY arrived in time to restore the fortunes of the day, and came most gallantly into action.

---

says, "History will not be believed when it is told that the noble officers and men of my division were permitted to carry on this unequal struggle from morning until night unaided, in the presence of more than 30,000 of their comrades, with arms in their hands; nevertheless, it is true." The entire loss during the day was 2,228, of whom 456 were killed.

General HOOKER was justified in this bitter complaint. It has been reported that he was relieved by a bayonet charge made by HANCOCK; *but there must have been an error in this assertion.* The troops by whom it was said to have been made first encountered the enemy about 4 P. M., of the preceding afternoon (Sunday, 4th May). It was a drizzly day, and the men marched forward in no small confusion, over leaves in the woods, slippery with the rain, over fallen trees, and across ravines, so that it was impossible to preserve an alignment of a company, much more of a brigade. The night came on pitch-dark; the 43d New York fired by mischance into a Pennsylvania regiment. Next day the former had to be withdrawn and another New York and Maine regiment put in its stead. All the morning (Monday, 5th May), heavy firing was heard. It was that which HOOKER was encountering. HANCOCK'S troops lay in line of battle from 1 P. M., to 4 P. M., when they receded before a front attack of a North Carolina regiment, aided by a flank attack of the Twenty-fourth Virginia. "*History of the American Civil War,*" by JOHN WILLIAM DRAPER, M. D., L.L.D., New York, 1868, vol. 2, pages 380–382.

I shall probably have occasion to call attention to other commands, and wish not to do injustice to them by mentioning them now. If I had had the full information I now have in regard to the troops above-named, when I first telegraphed they would have been specially mentioned and commended. I spoke only of what I knew at the time, and I shall rejoice to do full justice to all engaged.

GEO. B. McCLELLAN,
Major-General Commanding.

* * * * * * * * * *

General KEARNY's forces in this battle were entirely disproportionate to his success. He entered with five regiments, from all of which many men had straggled, leaving him, at the first, the sum of one thousand nine hundred men. In his correspondence he says:

"We dashed in at double-quick, our band playing, and rather reckless of myself, I located my men right, leading them off personally from the word 'go.' At the outset, seeing that time was precious, I charged back the mass of the enemy's sharp-shooters, who thought the field their own, our pieces having been abandoned by the gunners, with only two companies, barely eighty men. But I remembered that such things had been done before, and had no alternative, for my regiment had never, from morning, been allowed to close up, and so off I went, too conspicuous from my showy horse [killed under him at Fair Oaks], and for several hundred yards down the roads, with bristling abatis on each side, filled with the enemy's marksmen. This, like all other things, only succeeded because the enemy presumes them, few as they are, the precursors of crowds behind."

KEARNY wrote home on the 5th and 8th: "We had a rather unexpected and severe affair on the 5th instant, attended with a great deal of hardship afterward." He then went on to speak of his "embarrassment," which no one but himself observed, "from having been placed in command on the 2d of May, and the battle on the 5th, and the move (not his division, but STONEMAN's) from Yorktown on the 4th instant, I never had a chance to know men nor officers." Then, in his rattling way, but never intended for the public eye, he criticized the movements previous to his arrival on the field, and adds: "Still it was wonderful to think that the troops would stand fighting so long. *For ourselves, we went in as a dog takes a plunge, and swims, of course!* I must say, that the men, all (and most of the officers), were truly gallant. The wounded were not carried off the field. In one regiment I had nine officers killed and wounded in nineteen; I lost four hundred and fifty in five regiments."

"It was a source of the deepest mortification to General KEARNY that his services on this occasion seemed entirely unappreciated by his commanding officer. When the battle took place, General McCLELLAN was far in the rear. The importunity of Governor SPRAGUE prevailed on him to go to the front, and he arrived in time to witness the gallantry of HANCOCK, engaged far on the right, and who, charging with his whole brigade just at dusk, contributed, with the loss of only thirty men, to the final victory. The entire Federal loss was two thousand two hundred and twenty-eight. Two-thirds of this fell upon HOOKER, the rest upon KEARNY, demonstrating where the real fighting had been; yet, in his first bulletin, General McCLELLAN, though informed by his own aid of the facts (*so* KEARNY *says*), absolutely failed to mention either HOOKER or KEARNY, to their great and just indignation, for the success at Williamsburg evidently saved the army. Huddled in confused masses, the artillery fastened in the mud, the infantry straggling and wading through the woods, the cavalry, baggage-wagons, and all the paraphernalia of an advance confusedly edging along through miry roads, panic would have been ruin. Scarce any of the troops had ever been in action, and, had the enemy been victorious, a panic would have been almost unavoidable, and General KEARNY felt that he had prevented this by the utmost hazard of his person. He was not proud of recklessness, but he knew that there were times when exposure was essential. "It is true," he writes, "that I was fearfully exposed; for whilst the entire regiment would be sheltered by logs, I was the only officer mounted and quite in view; the only object aimed at by many hardly fifty feet from me.* I could not do otherwise, for we had the largest part of the work before us, and very few to do it. It was not useless recklessness; it saved the day."

* "With brave PHIL alone before me, leading on his men, and dashing destruction along the lines, do you know that some rebels, taken prisoners, said they and others were ordered to fire, and in every way try to kill that General with one arm, doing so much mischief?"—*E. W. L., 30th May*, 1862, *N. Y.*

McClellan reached the front just before the battle ended; and, as his attention was called exclusively to the operations of Hancock, on the extreme right, who had executed a successful flank movement, by which he had gained a position that commanded the rebel line, he received the principal commendation; while Hooker and Kearny, who, by downright hard fighting, involving the loss of twenty per cent. of their forces present and under hot fire, had first held and afterward carried the field on the left of the line, were not mentioned at all in the first bulletin of the Commanding General.

"The first time I saw Kearny in the army," writes Brevet Brigadier-General C. S. W———, "was on Saturday, May 3d, 1862, about four o'clock P. M. He had just been given Hamilton's division, and was looking for his command. I told him where it lay, and put him on the road. Watts (De Peyster, his volunteer aid) was with him at the time. The division was then the Third, of the Third Corps; but soon after, when Fitz John Porter's division was made the Third, Kearny's division was numbered the First, of the Third Corps.

"On Sunday, May 4th, when Hooker's division moved out to support the cavalry, Kearny had already broken camp, and had his division massed in the open ground beyond the saw-mill. I do not think that he had received any orders at that time, but always supposed that he moved his men, on his own responsibility, into a position where he could use them the instant orders did come.

"The hour at which Kearny's division arrived at the front at Williamsburg has always been a disputed point — he claiming to have been there at least two hours earlier than Hooker and I set his arrival.* Whatever the hour was, it was some

* "'Pray, Captain [Taylor, of Stuart's Cavalry],' said I, 'where did your men [rebels] show any superiority to ours [Union troops?]'

"'Why, I think in every battle yet fought, and now here [Savage Station], more than at Williamsburg. We fought you with our rear guard; we had no expectation of being able to do more than hold you in check until the main body of our forces were out of harm's way. But when your Generals were so easily checked, this emboldened us to hurry back reinforcements and attempt greater things, and I do believe that if we had resolved to make a final stand at Williamsburg, we could have bound you there another month, and then the heat and fever would have finished the work we began.'

"'Captain,' I replied, 'you know that the battle of Williamsburg was mainly fought

time after the enemy had captured the two batteries I had out beyond the felled timber (slashing). Our troops had recovered entire possession of the road, along-side of which I had planted another battery, and we had repelled two separate attacks of the enemy.

"The last of these had been by a column up the road, and had been broken almost solely by the fire of the Fourth New York Battery. After the attacking column was broken, detached squads from it, and single individuals, worked their way up behind the felled trees on the left of the road, until they were able to make it very hot in the battery, had any occasion arisen for opening fire. I had made two applications for some infantry, to keep these fellows quiet, but got none, our division being then about out of ammunition. On going back a third time, I found the head of KEARNY's division and KEARNY himself. On repeating my application to him, he at once gave me two companies of a Michigan regiment. *I mention this as a sample of the quickness with which he took in the state of affairs, and the promptness of his orders to meet them.*

"Before putting his men into position that day, KEARNY sent most of his staff to the right and left to examine the ground, and, leaving the remainder with his orderlies, he rode alone out on the road far beyond our skirmish line. I did not see him go out, or know that he had gone; so, on perceiving a horseman coming in, thought it must be some one from the rebels. Why he was not killed then I cannot imagine, as the rebels held the whole of the felled timber to the left of the road, but I did not see a shot fired at him.*

by one division — General HOOKER's. General KEARNY and HANCOCK rendered very essential aid, but it was almost night when they reached the field. We had not so many men in that battle as you had, and ours were all the disadvantages of position, intrenchments, and strong earthworks, and we had to debouch into the fields in your front, over a narrow neck of land. You had every advantage that men should ask — the storm was drenching and disheartening; our artillery was engulfed in the mud — yet, notwithstanding all these things, General HOOKER, with the aid of three or four regiments of General KEARNY's, held his position for five hours, until, by a flank movement of General HANCOCK, you were driven from the field. In the strength of your intrenchments, you ought to have held out against 50,000 men.' "—*Chaplain Marks*' "*Peninsula Campaign*," *page* 267.

* "As soon as possible, however, KEARNY and HEINTZELMAN pushed forward his support; and now KEARNY performed one of those brilliant feats which made him the

"When he first came up, General HEINTZELMAN asked him if he had not better let General HOOKER aid him, as he was a stranger to his command? KEARNY replied, 'General, I can make men follow me to hell.'

"Two days after the fight at Williamsburg, I saw KEARNY cross the plain in front of that town, at a time when a good part of his division was scattered over it. I have seen but one other general in our army whose presence excited so much enthusiasm among the men as was shown for KEARNY at that time, by the troops he had not been with a week. * * * *

"So far from being a hap-hazard, dash-ahead man, I saw no general who was more cautious on the march, or took more pains to know his ground before putting his men into a fight.

"This, together with the quiet working of his mind when under fire (a very rare quality with the bravest men), and his inspiriting appearance in a fight, were his most striking qualities, so far as I noticed them.

"When in the middle of a battle, his appearance certainly filled my *beau ideal* of a general better than any thing I ever saw. It made the blood thrill through one's veins, and would inspirit men, if any thing could."

When the anxiously-awaited succor, brought up by KEARNY, arrived, that General — accompanied by Major, afterward Brigadier-General, CHARLES S. WAINWRIGHT, Division Chief of Artillery to HOOKER, and ——— THOMPSON, Second Artillery, his own Division Chief of Artillery — dashed forward on the road

---

model soldier of his division. In order to disclose to his troops the concealed position of the enemy, and to exhaust (draw) their fire (like RIDGELEY, previous to MAY'S charge at Resaca de la Palma), he announced his determination to ride in front of the enemy's lines. Surrounded by his aids and officers, he dashed out into the open field, and, as if on parade, leisurely galloped along the entire front. Five thousand guns were pointed at him; the balls fell around him like hail; two of his aids dropped dead at his side; and before he reached the end he was almost alone. He secured by this hazardous exploit what he aimed to accomplish — the uncovering of the enemy's position — then riding back among his men, he shouted, 'You see, my boys, where to fire.' His forces held their own until HANCOCK, by a flank movement, compelled the retreat of the enemy within their works.

"All the soldiers and officers of this portion of the army not only spoke of HOOKER and KEARNY as displaying on that day the most brilliant soldierly qualities, but likewise commended, in the highest terms, the coolness, discrimination and courage of General HEINTZELMAN." — *Marks' "Peninsular Campaign,"* *page* 157.

leading direct to Fort Magruder, to reconnoitre the positions of the enemy. They had advanced some distance beyond their own men, when a battalion or more of rebels rose from the slashing in line of battle, and poured volley after volley upon them, as fast as they could load and fire, at a distance of not over two hundred and fifty yards. As the enemy started up, KEARNY wheeled his horse and galloped back, followed, "the devil take the hindmost," by the other two officers. Strange to say, although the bullets pattered and hissed around, like drops in a tropical storm driven by a fierce wind, not one took effect, except to gouge out a channel in the hoof of Major WAINWRIGHT's horse.

On this day, KEARNY had a third narrow escape. He spurred into a little cleared space, midway the slashing, and, looking round like an eagle in search of prey, shouted out to his own men to show themselves and drive the rebels out of their cover. Responsive to his appeal, a few Union skirmishers rose on their side of the felled timber. They had scarcely made their appearance, when a whole rebel line of marksmen jumped to their feet from their lairs, and fired simultaneously, with deliberate aim, at the "one-armed devil." It was afterward well known that in this, and subsequent engagements, the rebel officers exhorted their marksmen to take cool and careful aim at the "one-armed devil," who seemed to delight in setting them at defiance. KEARNY shook his stump at them, as he was wont to do when excited, and galloped away unscathed. Not a missile touched his person or his horse.

Thus, the battle of Williamsburg ended in establishing the character of the Army of the Potomac, but particularly of HEINTZELMAN'S (the Third) Corps; in elevating KEARNY and HOOKER to the first place in the estimation of the American free people, as generals and soldiers of the finest type, for ability, influence and gallantry; in winning the concession from MCCLELLAN that their troops had gained a complete and glorious success; but, alas! in nothing further! no trophies fell into the hands of the Union commander; no results followed the prodigal libation of blood and life. When the news arrived of the battle fought, the victory won, and the subsequent paralysis through

McClellan, the writer pronounced a judgment, recorded and attested, which events justified.* McClellan demonstrated himself a failure; the Staff which our Executive and the Nation had selected to prop the cause of the North and guide its armies, had proved a Pharaoh's reed. Witness the thousands of victims to the camp diseases, to the Chickahominy malaria, the thousands wasted in infructuose battles. Phil. Kearny had predicted all this; his predictions were, one by one, verified to the letter, in the blood and ashes of our bravest and most precious. Two months more and the Union army had been misled back — not driven back — to the James; humiliated through its chief — not conquered, or dishonored in itself. Within three months it was back whence it started, as had been foretold that it would be by more than Phil. Kearny. Let the reader who doubts this obtain Emil Schalk's "Summary of the Art of War" (J. B. Lippincott & Co., Philadelphia), of which the first edition was published about the time of the "Affair of Rivers," or Peninsula campaign was definitely resolved upon. Examine carefully "Example," pages 25, 33, particularly that wonderful map, which, had it not been prepared and issued six months before the events it prefigured, culminating in Antietam (another battle, indecisive, like Williamsburg, through the like fault of the very same supreme commander), would be almost an after-delineation, of the flow and ebb of the campaign, April — September, 1862.

That neither Hooker nor Kearny was to blame for the result, their voices, their actions, the wounds of the one and the death of the other abundantly attest.

Kearny's troops were the first to enter the abandoned works of the rebels, and detachments of Kearny's division were the first to advance on the morning after the battle of Williamsburg, and friends of the writer, who were engaged there, state that a skirmish, of greater or less magnitude, occurred. As no response has been made to published calls for information, this fact is merely mentioned to show that Kearny and his officers and men were *always on the alert, and that if he did not go ahead* it was no fault of his.

* See note *, page 63, General DePeyster's "Decisive Conflicts of the Late Civil War, or Slaveholder's Rebellion," No. 1.

HEADQUARTERS THIRD DIVISION, HEINTZELMAN'S CORPS,
WILLIAMSBURG, *May 6th*, 1862.

CAPTAIN: I have the honor to report, that, on receiving orders on the 5th instant, at nine A. M., the Division took up its line of march, and shortly after came upon the crowded columns before us.

At ten and three-quarters A. M., an order was received from General SUMNER to pass all others and proceed to the support of General HOOKER, already engaged.

With difficulty, and much loss of time, my Division at length made its way through the masses of troops and trains that encumbered the deep, muddy, single defile, until, at the "Brick Church," my route was to the left. At one and a half P. M., within three and a half miles of the battle-field, I halted my column to rest, for the first time, and to get the lengthened files in hand before committing them to action. Captain MOSES, of the General Staff, with great energy, assisted me in this effort. Almost immediately, however, on order from General HEINTZELMAN, our "knapsacks were piled," and the head of the column resumed its march, taking the "double quick," wherever the mud-holes left a footing. Arrived at one mile from the engagement, you, in person, brought me an order to detach three regiments — one from BERRY's, the leading Brigade, and two from BIRNEY's, the Second — to support EMORY's Horse, to the left of the position.

Approaching nearer the field, word was brought by an Aid-de-camp that HOOKER's cartridges were expended; and with increased rapidity we entered under fire. Having quickly consulted with General HOOKER, and received General HEINTZELMAN's orders as to the point of onset, I at once deployed BERRY's Brigade to the left of the Williamsburg road, and BIRNEY's on the right of it — taking, to cover the movement, and to support the remaining battery, that had ceased to fire, two companies of POE's Regiment.

As our troops came into action, the remnants of the brave men of HOOKER's Division were passed, and our regiments promptly commenced an unremitting, well-directed fire. However, from the lengthening of the files, the gap occasioned by the withdrawal from the column of three regiments, and the silence of this battery, I *soon* was left no alternative than to lead forward to the charge the two companies of the Second Michigan Volunteers, to bear back the enemy's skirmishers, now crowding on our pieces. This duty was performed by officers and men with superior intrepidity, and enabled Major WAINWRIGHT, of HOOKER's Division, to collect his artillerists and to re-open fire from the several pieces. A new support was then collected from the Fifth Jerseys, who, terribly decimated previously, again came forward with alacrity.

The affair was now fully and successfully engaged along our whole line, and the regiments kept steadily gaining ground — but the heavy strewn timber of the abattis defied all direct approach.

Introducing, therefore, *fresh marksmen* from POE's Regiment, I ordered Colonel HOBART WARD, with the Thirty-eighth New York Volunteers (Scott Life-Guard) to charge down the road and take the "rifle pits" (in the center of the abattis) by their flank. This duty Colonel WARD performed with great gallantry — his martial demeanor imparting all confidence in the attack. Still the wave of impulsion, though nearly successful, did not quite prevail — but with bravery, every point thus gained, was fully sustained. The *left wing* of Colonel RILEY's Regiment, the Fortieth New York Volunteers (the Mozarts), was next sent for; and the Colonel, being *valiantly* engaged in front, came up brilliantly, conducted by Captain MINDIL, Chief of General BIRNEY's Staff. These charged up to the open space, and silenced some light artillery, and gaining the enemy's *rear*, caused him to relinquish his cover. The victory was ours. About this period General JAMESON brought up the rear brigade and the detached regiments, having previously reported them in the midst of a severe fire. A second line was established, and two columns of regiments made disposable for further moves. But darkness, with the still drizzly rain, now closed, and the regiments *bivouacked* on the field they had won.

The reconnoissances during the night and the early patrols of the morning revealed the enemy retiring, and General HEINTZELMAN, in person, ordered into the enemy's works (which our pickets of the One Hundred and Fifth Pennsylvania, under Lieutenant GILBERT, were entering with General JAMESON) the Fourth Maine Regiment, to erect thereon its standard and take possession in full force.

I have to mark out for the high commendation of the General-in-Chief, Generals JAMESON, BIRNEY and BERRY, whose soldierly judgment was only equalled by their distinguished courage. I refer you to their *reports* to do justice to the names of the gallant officers and men under their immediate command. Having confined myself principally to the center, the key of the positions, I report as having conspicuously distinguished themselves, imparting victory all around, Colonels POE, of the Second Michigan Volunteers, and HOBART WARD, of the Thirty-eighth New York.

Never in any action was the influence of the Staff more perceptible. All were most efficient and defiant of danger. I especially notice Captain SMITH, A. A. General of General BERRY, and predict for him a career of usefulness and glory.

My own Staff were truly my means of vision in this battle in the woods. I have to deplore the loss of my Chief-of-Staff, Captain WILSON, who was killed putting in execution my desire for a general onset, at the period of the last charge, falling within the enemy's lines. Also, Lieutenant BARNARD, late of West Point, at the end of the engagement, after having previously lost a horse. Captain WILLIAM E. STURGES, my Aid, was brave, active and judicious. Lieutenant MOORE, another of my Aids, renewed in this field his previous distinction gained abroad. My Volunteer Aid, Mr. WATTS DE PEYSTER, bore himself handsomely in this his first action.

I have the honor to append the list of *killed* and wounded, which, though not impairing our future efficiency, was a severe loss for the few engaged.

Our batteries were on the field, but were not required, Major WAINWRIGHT (HOOKER'S Division) having, by much personal effort, resumed the fire of several pieces. But Captain THOMPSON, U. S. A., the chief of my Division artillery, in the midst of a heavy fire, gave me the benefit of his experience.

CONSOLIDATED LIST OF KILLED, WOUNDED AND MISSING, AT THE BATTLE OF WILLIAMSBURG, VA., MAY 5TH, 1862.

REGIMENT.	OFFICERS.				ENLISTED MEN.				Aggregate.
	Killed.	Wounded.	Missing.	Total.	Killed.	Wounded.	Missing.	Total.	
General KEARNY'S Staff	2	....	....	2	....	....	....	....	2
Thirty-eighth New York Volunteers	2	7	.	9	9	61	10	80	89
Fortieth New York Volunteers	....	1	....	1	5	23	....	28	29
Second Michigan Volunteers	...	3	....	3	17	35	5	57	60
Fifth Michigan Volunteers	1	5	....	6	28	110	...	138	144
Thirty-seventh New York Volunteers	2	5	....	7	21	65	2	88	95
	7	21	....	28	80	294	17	391	419

I have, sir, the honor to be,
Very respectfully,
Your obedient servant,
(Signed) P. KEARNY,
Brig.-Gen'l Commanding Third Division, Third Corps.

To CHAUNCEY MCKEEVER,
Capt. and A. A., Gen'l Heintzelman's Corps, Williamsburg.

HEADQUARTERS THIRD DIVISION, HEINTZELMAN'S CORPS,
CAMP BERRY, BARHAMSVILLE, VA., *May 10th*, 1862.

SIR: The events which crowded on us after the battle of the 5th — its stormy night — the care of the wounded — the attentions to the slain — the collection of the trophies — the moves of the next day — having prevented my report, embracing the distinguished acts of individuals, not serving in my actual presence, induced me to request that the superior authority of the commander of the corps would be employed to use, *as my own*, the separate reports of those, my brigade commanders, who so ably sustained my efforts by their gallantry; and who so amply fulfilled the high prestige which they had won as Colonels of noble regiments.

The lists of the Generals of Brigades, comprises the names of the following officers and regiments:

The right of my line consisted of the two regiments of the Second Brigade, General BIRNEY, the Thirty-eighth New York Volunteers, Colonel J. H. HOBART WARD, and the Fortieth New York, Colonel RILEY — the other two regiments of this brigade having, a mile back, been detached to join General EMORY. The Thirty-eighth New York was the regiment that, sent for by me, charged down the road, and took the pits and abattis in flank. Colonel J. H. HOBART WARD has already been noticed by me, as one of the "bravest of the brave." He reports that, "Lieutenant-Colonel STRONG certainly deserves mention for his gallantry. It would be unjust to mention any one line officer before another, when *all* behaved so well. This regiment lost one hundred and twenty-eight men on the 21st of July last, at Bull Run." This day there were nine officers killed and wounded out of nineteen in the regiment that went into action, viz.:

Thirty-eighth New York Volunteers lost —

OFFICERS KILLED:

CALVIN S. DE WITT	Captain	Company I.	
WILLIAM SHARP	Second Lieutenant	Company H.	2

OFFICERS WOUNDED:

JAMES E. STRONG	Lieutenant-Colonel.		
GEORGE W. DENNETT	Captain	Company D.	
AUGUSTUS FRINK (Funk?)	Captain	Company H.	
SAMUEL C. DWYER	Captain	Company K.	
R. J. MATSON	First Lieutenant	Company A.	
E. MILLER	Second Lieutenant	Company B.	
W. SCOTT	Second Lieutenant	Company A.	7

Total officers killed and wounded	9
Enlisted men killed	9
do do wounded	61
do do missing	10
Total loss	89

The Fortieth Regiment, Colenel RILEY, performed noble and efficient services. Colonel RILEY, with great spirit, held the right wing with half his regiment, after the Thirty-eighth and half the Fortieth had been withdrawn to act under *my personal* direction. The part of the Fortieth acting on the road against the central pits and abattis — charging down the road into the plain, passed beyond the enemy's flank, and drove off by their fire several pieces of artillery, brought *expressly against them.*

Fortune favored them. Their loss was —

OFFICERS KILLED: — (None.)

OFFICERS WOUNDED:

E. F. FLETCHER	Second Lieutenant	Company I.	1
Total officers killed and wounded			1

Enlisted men killed	5
do do wounded	23
Total loss	29

The battle on the left of the line was a series of assaults by the enemy, and repulses and outsets by ourselves — the fresh re-inforcements by the enemy, continually tending to outflank us. General BERRY was ever on the alert, and, by good arrangements and personal example, influenced the ardor of all around him. His regiments fought most desperately. Their loss attests it. It acted partly in the woods to the left of the road, and partly in carrying the abattis.

It was one of them, Colonel POE's Second Michigan, *more directly under my control*, which maintained the key point of our position.

Two of its companies led off with the first success of the day, whilst covering the artillery.

Colonel POE had already won a reputation in Western Virginia. He was a distinguished officer in the U. S. Army before taking command of this regiment.

I especially notice him for advancement. His talents, his bravery, his past services merit it. His loss was —

OFFICERS KILLED: — (None.)

OFFICERS WOUNDED:

W. R. MORSE	Captain	Company F.	
WM. B. McCRURY	Captain	Company G.	
ROBERT D. JOHNSON	Second Lieutenant	Company A.	3
Total officers killed and wounded			3
Enlisted men killed			17
do do wounded			35
do do missing			5
Total killed, wounded and missing			60

The principal loss on the left of the other two regiments (the fourth of the brigade, Third Michigan, Colonel CHAMPLAIN, having been detached with General EMORY), serving more immediately under the eye of General BERRY, was very severe. Colonel HAYMAN, commanding the Thirty-seventh New York, on the extreme left, was charged with guarding against the enemy's turning our left flank. This duty required vigilance and pertinacity. This regiment lost —

OFFICERS KILLED:

PATRICK H. HAYES	First Lieutenant	Company G.	
JEREMIAH O'LEARY	First Lieutenant	Company F.	2

OFFICERS WOUNDED:

JAMES F. MAGUIRE	Captain	Company B.	
WILLIAM H. DE LACY	Captain	Company K.	
JOHN MASSY	Second Lieutenant	Company G.	
EDWARD N. BROWN	Second Lieutenant	Company C.	
JAMES SMITH	Second Lieutenant	Company F.	5
Total officers killed and wounded			7
Enlisted men killed			21
do do wounded			65
do do missing			2
Total loss			95

Colonel TERRY, commanding the Third Michigan,* was principally engaged in carrying rifle pits (a redoubt) in the woods. His loss is the highest on the list of killed and wounded, and comprises —

	OFFICERS KILLED:		
JAMES A. GUNNING............	Second Lieutenant................	Company C.	1
	OFFICERS WOUNDED:		
HENRY D. TERRY...............	Colonel.		
SAMUEL E. BEACH..............	Lieutenant-Colonel.		
EDWARD J. SHURLOCK........	Captain...........................	Company A.	
HERBER LE FAVOUR...........	Captain...........................	Company F.	
WM. R. TILLOTSON.............	Second Lieutenant................	Company H.	5
Total officers killed and wounded			6
Enlisted men killed			28
do do wounded			110
Total loss			144

In closing this supplementary Report on the location and merits of individuals and regiments, it is proper to include, although not attached to my command, General GROVER, who, with an untiring courage, whilst most of his men, having been relieved by our arrival, were taking the merited respite after their long hours of severe fighting, still brought up into line, alongside of us, several hundred volunteers, who followed his example, encouraging them to the fight.

This report would also be incomplete did I fail to mention the meritorious services of our Medical Corps. They were everywhere, under the greatest obstacles, efficiently aiding the wounded and establishing ambulances. One of them, Dr. J. H. BAXTER, one of Acting Surgeon-General TRIPLER's Staff, Medical Inspector of Field Ambulances, assisted me greatly during the action by carrying orders.

Sir, with the trust that the division has done its duty, and fulfilled your expectations, I have the honor to be most respectfully,

Your obedient servant,

P. KEARNY,

Brigadier-General Commanding Division.

To Captain CHAUNCY MCKEEVER.

---

* LETTER OF KEARNY IN REGARD TO HIS MICHIGAN TROOPS.

HEADQUARTERS THIRD DIVISION, HEINTZLEMAN'S CORPS,
CAMP BERRY, BARKHAMSVILLE, VA., *May 10th*, 1862.

To his Excellency AUSTIN BLAIR, *Governor of Michigan:*

SIR — It gives me great pleasure to address you, in order to bring to your immediate notice the noble and brave manner with which the troops of your State, in my Division conducted themselves in the engagement before Williamsburg on the 5th instant. The Second, under Colonel POE, and the Fifth, under Colonel TERRY, behaved in the most handsome manner. I have the honor to transmit, herewith, the report of the colonels of those regiments, together with that of their general, General BERRY, commanding the brigade, and also a copy of the one sent in by myself to General Headquarters. I also send you a list of the killed and wounded. Colonel POE served more immediately under my own command, and the gallantry and soldierly qualities he displayed rendered him particularly conspicuous. Colonel TERRY's Regiment took a rifle pit of much strength, after a severe contest, and held possession until the close of the action.

Very respectfully,

PHILIP KEARNY.

CHAPTER XXIII.

EXEMPLI GRATIA.

" LET his great example stand
Colossal, * * *
And keep the soldiers firm."

Tennyson's "Ode to Wellington."

" No age hath been, since nature first began
To work Jove's wonders, but hath left behind
Some deeds of praise for mirrors unto man,
Which, more than dreadful laws, have men inclined
To tread the paths of praise, excite the mind;
Mirrors the thoughts to virtue's due respects:
Example hastens deeds to good effects."

Davenant.

" Lancelot, the flower of bravery,
* * * the chief of knights."

Tennyson's "Elaine."

" Von des Lebens Gütern allen
Ist der Ruhm das höchste doch!
Wenn der Leib in Staub zerfallen
Lebt ter grosse Name noch."

" A more fearless man probably never lived."

Abbott's "History of the Civil War in America," II, 49.

" Foresee and provide, are two words which the general should have present in his thoughts throughout every moment of his term of command."—MARSHAL BIRON, "*Ecrivains Militaires.*"

WHEN that master of logical persuasion and common-sense conception of the direct road to the human heart appealed to his recruits to remember that they were examples, one of his strongest arguments to induce them to shine as such was, that they were "compassed about with so great a cloud of witnesses." Who so surrounded by observers as the leader of an army? Every soldier, every officer must look to him, and gradually his greatness or his littleness will influence the mass. If *he is slow, want of energy leavens the whole organization*; and it is hardly unjust to say, that the lethargy of the winter of 1861–2 affected the Army of the Potomac, until GRANT and SHERIDAN came and exorcised the direst enemy to great achievements in arms. How different was it in the First Brigade and the First Division KEARNY commanded? It would be unjust to claim, and still harder to prove, that the noble spirits who emulated his example owed any of their personal rugged grandeur to him; but it is not unjust to say, and it is not difficult to believe, that, being by nature susceptible of great things, in his light, they kindled into greater brillancy.

> "Example is a living law, whose sway
> Men more than all the written laws obey."

The all-glorious sun, as it burns in heaven, does not produce rival suns; but does not its light and heat impart brilliancy and existence to creations almost as glorious and exquisite, though in other forms? And even so KEARNY'S "magnificent," "knightly," "brilliant" example of soldiership inflamed all who followed him; and in, and through the constellated radiance of his own deeds and those which had their origin in his inspiration, no wonder, as DE TROBRIAND says, he became a legendary hero, invested with a thousand memories in the bivouacs of the Army of the Potomac. "Like begets like," is a proverbial expression, and certainly those who held prominent positions under KEARNY lived and died and must always shine as types of good and gallant volunteer commanders, even as he was the "type volunteer general of the war." Nay, more, the New Jersey Brigade, which he made, to the last shone as a brilliant unit, a jewel of the first water, with the combined luster fortitude, bravery and discipline. To enter into a demonstration of this claim for his whole command, would be to block out a volume, and not a chapter. The problem can be proved by a few striking examples, as well as by many, if they all fulfill the same conditions and every requisite condition.

The reader has seen KEARNY'S promptness on more than one occasion. At the first sound of alarm, he abandoned every thing and traversed three thousand miles of sea to offer his sword to his country. Within twenty-four hours after his appointment, he was at the head of his brigade. He held the forlorn hope, or advanced post almost of our organizing great army of the war, without support, in the teeth of a victorious foe. He was the first into Mannassas, on the heels of the withdrawing rebels; and he, the rearmost in the movement, through "an ocean of mud," was the first to throw himself, like an ægis, before HOOKER, and save the first fair stand-up fight, of many hours' duration, perseveringly contested, east of the Alleghanies.

Reader, after studying his own, follow up the records of his subordinates, and consider whether such an example, never faltering or paling, but ever growing huger and brighter, must not have had its effect. "By their fruits ye shall know them."

GEORGE W. TAYLOR, of Hunterdon county, New Jersey, sailor, farmer, soldier, miner, and again soldier, commanded the Third Regiment from that State, in KEARNY'S First Brigade, and succeeded him in its command. Under the most trying circumstances — for KEARNY declared that his old Brigade was sacrificed — TAYLOR never flinched, but always, everywhere, displayed "the most indomitable courage." At Bull Run Bridge, August 27th, 1862, his brigade was made to confront the "entire corps of STONEWALL JACKSON," and, as might readily be imagined, under such circumstances, was compelled to fall back with severe loss. Himself severely wounded, in marshalling his command and setting an example of honorable leadership, he was carried back to Alexandria, and on the very day, September 1st, 1862, that KEARNY breathed his last at Chantilly, TAYLOR gave up his gallant spirit, another type volunteer general.

The Brigadier who commanded the First Brigade of KEARNY'S division was CHARLES DAVIS JAMESON, a lumberman, born in Gorham, Maine. This enterprising officer, as "General of the Trenches," showed the way into the rebel works at Yorktown. Inflamed by the example of his superior, KEARNY (at Manassas, on March 9th, 10th and 11th, 1862), at two A. M. on Sunday morning, May 4th, he led forward detachments of the Sixty-second Pennsylvania, Colonel SAM. BLACK, of the Twenty-second Massachusetts, Colonel GOVE, of the Thirteenth New York, Captain BOUGHTON, deployed as skirmishers, and clambered over the parapets of Yorktown. General JAMESON and Colonel BLACK were the first two men in, and unfurled the stars and stripes on the "great water-angle." In like manner, about an hour after midnight succeeding the battle of Williamsburg, the "eagle-eyed" JAMESON, with a picket of one hundred and twelve men of the One Hundred and Fifth Pennsylvania, one of KEARNY'S and his own regiments, took possession of Fort Magruder, and again this general was the first to enter the rebel fortifications. Continuing to display the same energy and intrepidity, JAMESON fell a victim to the Chickahominy fever. He continued in command up to June 13th, 1862, and died, in the fullness of his glory, at Oldtown, above Bangor, Maine, November 6th, 1862, another type volunteer general.

The next who claims attention in this consideration is DAVID BELL BIRNEY, born in Huntsville, Alabama, who, either as a merchant in Michigan, as a lawyer or banker, or both, in Philadelphia, certainly enjoyed none of the advantages generally supposed to be indispensable to the formation of a general. Nevertheless, he showed himself an apt scholar, and after his distinguished coming out of Williamsburg, never falsified the opinion entertained of him by KEARNY, as an extremely reliable and accomplished soldier. It has been claimed for him by his admirers, that he was the best volunteer general in the strictest sense of the word, after KEARNY, developed by the war; and, as an ear-witness (Brevet Major W—— B——) reports, WEITZEL, a capital judge, said "BIRNEY handled infantry like magic." Be this as it may, he certainly showed first-class ability throughout his career of four years; and when SICKLES — another first-rate, and a type volunteer general — lost his leg at Gettysburg, BIRNEY displayed all the attributes of a brave soldier and worthy commander, and did as much as any man could do to frustrate the efforts of LONGSTREET, and checkmate the turning plan of LEE. He continued to occupy a high position and well-earned distinction down to 1865, when, seized with typhoid, or Chickahominy fever, the same which had destroyed JAMESON, he relinquished the saddle only to return home to die. Like those previously cited, he laid down his life for his country in Philadelphia, leaving a noble record, another type volunteer general.

The next in order was HIRAM GEORGE BERRY, a native of Thomaston (now Rockland), Maine. Born a poor boy, and bred a carpenter, he worked himself up to the Mayoralty of his native city and the command of a division. Always reliable, always a grand specimen of a natural born soldier, his brigade was the first which, under KEARNY, brought relief to HOOKER. He distinguished himself in almost every battle in 1862, and fell at Chancellorsville, crowned with glory. In this battle he executed a real triumphant bayonet-charge,* one which does not merely

* "*The British Soldier*, an Anecdotal History of the British Army," by. J. H. STOCQUELER, London, Amen Corner, 1847. Bayonet Charges, pp. 132-5. "If there is one subject upon which, more than another, writers have perpetuated the *crudest* notions, and upon which the most *erroneous* ideas are still widely entertained, it is that of the BAYONET CHARGES *of lines of infantry*. The relations of modern campaigns abound, it is true, with accounts of 'splendid bayonet charges;' but did the reader ever come to a detail of the conflict — of the actuality and its material results? After the 'War of the Spanish Succession' and the Battle of Spires, the infantry of all European nations lost the taste for close conflict, and the bayonet appears everywhere more threatening than murderous. The Wars of the Eighteenth Century, with their improved fire tactics, exhibit no more the steady old practice of former days. Matters began then to terminate at the very moment which had previously been their commencement only. In the War of 1700, FOLARD says, 'it was not attempted to engage hand-to-hand, not even on the most favorable ground, although the TURENNES and the CONDÉS had never fought otherwise.' He assures us, moreover, 'that the old officers were quite beside themselves to see the decline of that good old custom.' CHARLES XII tried in vain to dissuade his Swedes from firing, and to give them a relish for falling to at once with the bayonet. MARSHAL SAXE, after describing the tactics of his day, and informing us in what manner battles were opened, suddenly inquires, 'And what happens then? Why, both sides begin to fire, which is a misery to behold. At length they advance upon each other, and, generally at fifty or sixty paces, more or less, one or the other breaks and runs. Do you call that attacking?'

"What says BERENHORST on the subject? — 'Your fabrications of military relations make it appear that all great actions are performed with the bayonet; every one is threatened with the bayonet; generals command the charge with the bayonet. But, *in petto*, it is taken for granted beforehand, that the opposite party will not wait for it.' In another place, he says: 'For him who has the right notion of this evolution, bayonet charges are mainly a figure of rhetoric, *une manière de parler*, which means nothing more than one party runs on smartly, and the other leaves the field to him.' Hear, further, JOMINI, in his 'Critical and Military History,' whose opinion is also, that bayonet attacks take place mostly in relations. The ARCH-DUKE CHARLES, no mean authority, says, in his 'Campaign of 1799': 'Physical strength decides but seldom, even in the greatest battles.' So weighty a word may be considered as expressing pretty closely the real shape of the thing; and HOYER states his conviction, that there are but few or no examples that the bayonet has been really resorted to in good earnest. It will scarcely be necessary to cite many examples in proof of the justice of the opinions of such authorities. Our own wars, in Egypt and in Spain, illustrate their truth. At Alexandria, in 1801, 'the splendid bayonet charge' of our gallant Twenty-sixth Regiment was not 'waited for' by the French, when they were seen coming down through the smoke of their last volley. In the action near Pampeluna, already referred to, the French columns refused to stop for it. At Talavera it was not 'the weight of the charge' of the first battalion, of the gallant Forty-eighth, that saved the brigade of Guards from destruction when they had advanced too far — their well-directed fire and timely advance were quite sufficient. Here and there, in a century, an *individual* instance of real crossing of bayonets wears more the character of an anomaly, or a remarkable deviation from the rule. The *tour de force*, which so much gratified the heart of the GREAT FREDERICK at Lowositz (1756), when the two battalions of BEVERN and that of BILLERBECK, denuded of cartridges, after a defense of five hours fire of the Prussian left flank, crossed bayonets with the Austrian Croats and Grenadiers, and pricked them into the town of Lowositz, found few or no subsequent imita-

demonstrate against a routed foe with cold steel, but overthrows him by it. To fire a volley at close quarters, which sweeps the field, and then run in upon a flying enemy, who suffer a few

---

tors. A solitary, but meagre attempt is seen at Gross-Beeren in 1813, when Lieutenant-General SAHR, commanding the Saxons, attached to REGNIER's Seventh French Corps, to protect the retreat of his division, led the Saxon Regiment, VON LOW, with fixed bayonets (their muskets had been spoiled by the rain), against the nearest advancing Prussian column. And how did that come off? Both parties halted suddenly, and simultaneously, at a few paces from each other — looked each other for a few moments, hesitatingly, in the face, before they would fall on, in obedience to the call of their officers. The conflict, chiefly with the butt-end of the musket, lasted but a few moments — General SAHR did receive, himself, three bayonet wounds; few others were given or received, and the Saxons broke.

"An excellant authority on the subject, not quoted in the foregoing, is the late Mr. GUTHRIE, the celebrated army surgeon, who was with the army from Rosica to Waterloo. 'A great delusion,' says Mr. GUTHRIE, 'is cherished in Great Britian on the subject of the bayonet — a sort of monomania, very gratifying to the national vanity, but not quite in accordance with matter of fact. Opposing regiments, when formed in line, and charging with fixed bayonets, never meet and struggle hand-to-hand and foot-to-foot; and this for the very best possible reason, that one side turns round and runs away as soon as the other side comes close enough to do mischief; doubtless considering that 'discretion is the better part of valor.' Small parties of men may have personal conflicts after an affair has been decided, or in the subsequent scuffle, if they cannot get out of the way fast enough. The battle of Maida is usually referred to as a remarkable instance of a bayonet fight; nevertheless, the sufferers, whether killed or wounded, French or English, suffered from bullets, not bayonets. Wounds from bayonets were not less rare in the Peninsular War. It may be, that all those who were bayoneted were killed; yet their bodies were seldom found. A certain fighting regiment had the misfortune, one very misty morning, to have a large number of men carried off by a charge of Polish Lancers, many being also killed. The commanding officer concluded they must all be killed, for his men possessed exactly the same spirit as a part of the Frence Imperial Guard at Waterloo — 'they might be killed, but they could not by any possibility be taken prisoners.' He returned them all dead, accordingly. A few days afterward they re-appeared, to the astonishment of every body, having been swept off by the cavalry, and had made their escape in the retreat of the French army through the woods. The regiment from that day obtained the ludicrous name of the 'Resurrection Men.'"

MITCHELL'S "*Fall of Napoleon*," II, 123 or 173. "It is remarkable that the only tactical regulation, or novelty, ever introduced into the French army during the warlike reign of NAPOLEON, should be dated from Düben (just before the catastrophe of Leipsic). The science of the tactics — using the word in its proper sense — had either attained to the highest perfection before his time, or he wanted the ability to improve it, even by a single step. On the 13th of the month, the Major-General is desired to circulate the following order: 'Issue a general order directing, that, from this date, the infantry are to form only two deep, his Majesty having observed that no effect is produced either by the fire or by the bayonets of the third rank,' etc. It was rather late, perhaps, to make this important tactical discovery, and it would be interesting to know when his Majesty ever saw any effects produced by the bayonets either of the first or second rank; for the world has yet to learn that these boasted military weapons were ever used in fair and manly combat. The overwhelming disaster which befel the French army in the plains of Leipsic, and of which we have now to speak, will help to show how far NAPOLEON's strategical skill exceeded his tactical knowledge."

prods and escape ("three resolute rebels who stood to receive the bayonets," says BURNS, in his *Battle of Williamsburg*, page 48, "were stricken down by the bayonet in HANCOCK's movement on our right in that conflict"), is not the grand blow which JESSUP gave the veteran British at Bridgewater, when he came up at the crisis of the day, arms port, then fired, and the two lines crossed steel, parried, thrust and slew, until RIALL's old and tried soldiers broke, sullenly retired, and yielded general, field and victory. On May 3d, 1863, when the Eleventh Corps had given way on the right of Chancellorsville, broken and driven by the furious practical strategy of STONEWALL JACKSON, HOOKER selected BERRY's division, formerly his own, to stem the seemingly irresistible flood. "Go in General," said fighting JOE, "throw your men into the breach; don't fire a shot — they can't see you — but charge *home* with the bayonet." BERRY's boys did charge home, and held, for three hours, all their bayonets so boldly won. The next day the struggle was renewed, and the brunt fell again upon BERRY, who, again and again, headed the charge of his division, and, first to meet the foe, received a bullet which ended his grand career. Thus, in the arms of victory, as far as his division was concerned, BERRY fell and died, another one of the purest and noblest of the type volunteer generals of our war — a finer West Point never has produced.

The last to whom any space can be given in this chapter is bold TOM EGAN, of New York (Brevet Major-General at the close of the war), always ready, always efficient, and always successful where the result depended on gallant leading. After KEARNY fell at Chantilly, September 1st, 1862, EGAN, with the First, Thirty-eighth and Fortieth New York, all belonging to KEARNY's division, executed a brilliant charge, which gave us the possession of the contested field, and had it been known that KEARNY had fallen (he was supposed to have been taken prisoner), he would have recovered the remains of the hero, and guarded it from desecration.

This list might be enlarged greatly, but it is an episode in a biography of KEARNY, and out of place there, except so far as it goes to show that his example found or brought out noble imitators.

Can West Point out-top six such volunteer generals in one command, generals who owed nothing to professional sway within the academic halls, or to drill upon that plain, sun-scorched in the dog-days, and wind-swept, like an Arctic steppe, in winter, trying out the weak and strengthening the strong to bear the honors and emoluments reserved to caste and graduating at the Point?

Was merchant or trader Sir WILLIAM PEPPERELL, the capturer of Louisburg, the strongest fortress in America; or Indian agent Sir WILLIAM JOHNSON, the hero of Ticonderoga and real conqueror of DIESKAU (a selection of MARSHAL COUNT SAXE), and capturer of Niagara; or surveyor and planter WASHINGTON, whose master strokes, the surprise at Trenton — "to America what Thermopylæ was to Greece" — and the blow at Trenton, which excelled it — "events sufficient," says VON BULOW, "to elevate a general to the temple of immortality" — a pupil of any military academy? No! Was gentleman-farmer SCHUYLER who paralyzed BURGOYNE and saved Fort Stanwix; or blacksmith-farmer-Quaker GREENE, the deliverer of the Southern colonies from British tyranny; or surveyor WAYNE, the capturer of Stony Point; or lawyer and militiaman SULLIVAN; or sailor and farmer "Swamp Fox" MARION, who received little education, and "made no figure" in the Congress of his State; or clerk and scrivener WILLIAMS; or SUMTER, of whom little was known until he appeared as a lieutenant-colonel of riflemen; or hold-fast MOULTRIE (like CRAWFORD, of Cedar Mountain and Gettysburg), educated a physician; or heroic MERCER, a Scotch emigrant boy, the hero-martyr of Princeton; or intrepid MORGAN, a teamster and farmer; or KNOX, or WILLET, or LAMB; — was either of these Revolutionary generals a graduate of an embryo West Point? No, no! Was lawyer and planter JACKSON, who saved New Orleans; or lawyer SCOTT, the hero of two wars; or clerk WORTH; or militiaman BROWN, the grand figure of the war of 1812 on the "Lines;" or TAYLOR, the winner of Palo Alto, Resaca de la Palma, the capturer of Monterey, and glorious conqueror of Buena Vista; or WOOL; or JESSUP; or GAINES; or HARRISON; or "light-house" artillery TOWSON; or PERSIFER F. SMITH; or STEPHEN WATTS KEARNY, the maker of our First Dragoons, as fine a regiment as ever paraded man and horse for inspection, the conqueror of New Mexico and California; or PHIL. KEARNY, "hero, patriot and martyr" — was either a graduate of West Point or any military school? No, no, no!

Would that the same pains and the immense labor which has been bestowed in collecting the statements of services performed by West Pointers had been devoted to civilian appointments to military commands since our country has had an army! The writer does not think that the people would blush at the comparative columns, had every minor duty, well done, been credited to the Volunteer as it has been to the graduate of West Point. Such a task requires health and time, which the writer has not been able to give, and cannot concede; otherwise it would have been, or be, a real labor of love, to which he has been invited by one of the most distinguished men of our country.

This chapter may be construed into a depreciation of education. Not so! Education, without bigotry, is beneficial in every profession, in some professions indispensable. But it should not be so imbued with prejudices as to constitute a bar to uneducated genius or sound judgment capable of making up, by God's especial gifts, for the want of experience and lack of technical education. The Procrustean bed of such an institute as West Point would reduce every thing to its own formulated dimensions — a process which is the hereditary foe of originality, and allows nothing not its own to be great, until compelled to do so by public opinion, or by the uncontrollable greatness of the thing itself. Several West Points, or the infusion of the military element into all our universities and colleges, with susceptibility of subsequent entry therefrom, after competition, into the regular service, would remedy the evil, since one would be jealous of the other, and thus, through this division of sentiment, outsiders would once in a while get their own — that is, the opportunity and credit due them. The abolition of all monopolies will come through time and the common sense of the people.

CHAPTER XXIV.

THE PENINSULAR CAMPAIGN.

WILLIAMSBURG TO MALVERN HILL,

(No. 1.)

SEVEN PINES AND FAIR OAKS.

" And how, in thunder, day by day,
The hot sky hanging over all
Beneath that sullen lurid pall,
The *Week of Battles* rolled away !

" Give me my legions ! so, in grief,
Like him of Rome, our father cried,
(A *Nation's Flower* lay down and died
In yon fell shade !) ah, hapless chief.

" Too late we learned *thy* Star ! o'erta'en
(Of error or of fate o'erharsh)
Like VARUS, in the fatal marsh
Where skill and valor all were vain !

" All vain—FAIR OAKS and SEVEN PINES !
A deeper hue than dying Fall
May lend is yours ! yet over all
The mild Virginian autumn shines."

BROWNELL'S " *The Battle Summers.*"

" Invasion succeeds by celerity; defence is sustained by delay."—O'CONOR'S " *Military History of the Irish Nation, page* 106."

" But though the (Anglo-Dutch) besiegers had crossed the river (Shannon), and erected a fort to secure their new position, this division of their army into two bodies, connected by a temporary bridge made their situation extremely perilous. The portion on the right bank of the river might be overwhelmed before it could receive succor from the left, and *vice versa.* A council of war on the 17th, decided that the seige should be turned into a blockade — that the resources of the garrison should be cut off, and a surrender expected from famine."—O'CONOR'S " *Military History of the Irish Nation,*" 172.

" Meantime the Carlists, made aware of his (ESPARTERO'S) inactivity, performed an exploit that deserves to rank, both in conception and execution, among the most brilliant of military achievements." * * (ESPARTERO had dislocated his command in March, 1837, retaining 40.000 men, giving 14,000 to General EVANS, of the British Legion, and 15,000 to General IRRORARREN.) " Very heavy rain fell (as at Fair Oaks) during that day and the following, rendering the ground in the Loyola very heavy for artillery and cavalry, and even difficult for infantry. The ground about Loyola is at most times swampy. * * The Carlists having thus disposed of IRROBARREN (dislocated), fell on the Legion while ESPARTERO 'remained inactive, leaving it to General EVANS and IRROBARREN to fight it out.' * * As regards the exploits of the Carlists in this affair, it is impossible to concede too much praise to them. That their opponents committed many and grave errors in no way detracts from the merit due to them. *To sieze upon an opportunity afforded by the error of your* ADVERSARY, is one of the highest attributes of generalship. To join to quickness of perception, prompptitude of decision and rapidity of execution, is given only to great leaders whose qualities of command are *inborn. These things cannot be taught in schools.*" HENDERSON'S. " *Soldier of Three Queens,*" II, I. 13-24.

"It is in time of difficulty that great men and great nations display all the energy of their character and become an object of admiration to posterity."—*Maxims of* NAPOLEON.

"Then NESTOR thus to AGAMEMNON said,
No longer must our Business be delay'd,
What JOVE hath hinted, what GOD puts us on,
Must both with Speed and Cheerfulness be done.

"It is an Old Military Maxim, * * * '*to husband Time*,' * * * no *loss* being so *costly* and irreparable as to lose an *opportunity*: whence ALEXANDER, being asked how he achieved so great things in so short a time, answered, * * * '*by not delaying*.'" OGILBY'S "*Homer's Iliad*," 1660.

——"since dangerous are Delaies."
OGILBY'S "*Homer's Odysses*," 1660.

"In military operations Time is everything."—WELLINGTON, 30th June, 1800.

IT is so difficult to treat of the Peninsula Campaign, and avoid the absolute necessity of criticisms at every step, that, beyond an analytical review, the present work will be restricted, as far as possible, to KEARNY'S Reports and Correspondence.

In order to comprehend this campaign thoroughly, an accurate map, on a large scale, is indispensable. Furnished with such a one, any reader, interested in military subjects, who will take the trouble to study the country about Richmond, and acquaint himself in regard to the geodesical features of it, will comprehend at once that McCLELLAN proved himself a very inferior general. Afterward, if he will take the additional trouble to examine and compare the campaigns in which KEARNY participated under Marshal VALEE, General SCOTT, and LOUIS NAPOLEON, he will understand at once that KEARNY, with his natural advantages and experiences, and capacity of practical application of both, must have been more fit to lead than to be led.*

If he still doubts, let him read KEARNY'S correspondence in regard to these events, and then if his mind is free from prejudice he will at once appreciate the superiority of the subordinate and the inferiority of the commander. McCLELLAN looked upon an engagement (Williamsburg) which lasted all day, as "a little matter;" when KEARNY from the first felt that HOOKER must have the whole rebel rear guard on his hands. After the battle, when glory was to be made of it for himself

* For KEARNY'S prescience before Williamsburg, see "Quatre aus de Campagnes a l'Armee du Potomac," by Major-General REGIS DE TROBRIAND, 1,193.

and friends, McClellan reported a "victory" as "a hard fought action," a "brilliant engagement" against an enemy considerably superior in force to his army.

On sound military principles, Johnston should not have fought at all at Williamsburg, because, if the expedition to West Point had been despatched and carried out with energy, the rebels would have been caught, as Frederic expressed it, "all unbuttoned," or, as Napoleon worded it, "*flagrante delicto*," in the very commission of the act of folly or crime.

It might be urged, in justification of Johnston, that he had studied and comprehended McClellan. This, however, is an after thought, for McClellan did not exhibit himself in *all* the vividness of his true colors until after Williamsburg.* There it was that he demonstrated that he had no idea of the combined or relative force of the elements indispensable to the solution of military problems. Few generals who have been called to important commands, have ever shown so little perception of the inestimable value of the most important element of success in war—Time. "In War, faults may be remedied, but not those of Time." "The only antidote to the poison of his false strategy in operating on the Peninsula at all was, rapidity of movement and dash. In this case time, therefore, was *everything*, and he maneuvered as if it was *nothing*."

---

*It was McClellan's inertia, over-cautious, over-estimate of his adversary's forces, under-estimate of his own and their capabilities; his want of comprehension of time, place and circumstances, their individual, correlative and united force, which induced the writer to predict the failure of the Peninsular Summer campaign of 1862, alluded to in the following letter. The truth of the prediction was realized within seven weeks by the result:

New York, *October* 10, 1862.

James H. Woods, Esq.:

Dear Sir—At your request I recall to mind a conversation held in your office with General J. W. de Peyster, immediately after the battle of Williamsburg on the Peninsula. In that conversation the General advanced his opinion, given in a military point of view, that, notwithstanding the successful issue of the battle, still General McClellan would be obliged to evacuate the Peninsula. Several gentlemen present, you among the number, combated the opinion, and rather ridiculed the idea. The General, on turning to go out, said, in a most decided and emphatic manner, as near as I now recall his language: "Gentlemen, you may laugh at my opinion, you may congratulate yourselves upon the victory, but, mark my words, General McClellan will be compelled to evacuate the Peninsula."

Yours truly,

R. P. S——.

[See de Peyster's "*Decisive Conflicts*, No. 1, The Maryland Campaign of September, 1862." Pages 61–4, etc.]

After the battle of Williamsburg,* all that McClellan had to do to win "panic stricken" Richmond, was to obey the precepts of Marshal Saxe, which Frederic exemplified throughout his whole career subsequent to his lesson at Mollwitz—which was to the Prussian army what Williamsburg was to the Army of the Potomac—but most notably after Leuthen or Lissa (the modern battle of which Leuctra and Mantinea were parallels in antiquity); and by Napoleon, before he became obese in body and mind; press forward, with the point of the sword in the back of the retreating foe, and enter his capital or stronghold with his "handsomely" beaten and discouraged troops. Such action would have carried our line of advance through the healthy uplands along the James, and preserved for the country, if nothing more, those tens of thousands heroic men who fell victims to the malaria of the bottom lands in which McClellan mired and stifled them and buried his own prospects.

The result demonstrated Kearny's wisdom when he desired to make Norfolk the base, and the south side of the James the line of operations after the Peninsula campaign was inevitable—and in case that McClellan was allowed to imitate (since he did not seem capable of originating) the disembarkation of the Allies in the Crimea, in 1854. McClellan's plan failed from the same lack of energy that characterized every operation which he undertook. A visit to the Crimea was all that he had ever seen of war on a large scale, and all the impression which that seems to have made upon his mind was, the scientific lethargy of the long-drawn-out engineering of the siege. It appeared as if fate had now determined that this lethargy should not only be imitated but exceeded.

On the 5th May, Kearny saved the battle of Williamsburg. From that date until the 27th, McClellan wasted twenty-two days in moving his army fifty to sixty miles—a progress of

* In regard to the account of Williamsburg, in Chapter XXII, Major-General Heintzelman wrote: "They (the pamphlets in which it originally appeared) contain the only account I ever met with of the battle, or *affair*, of Williamsburg." The veteran General added some notes, but, as this chapter was in print, they could not be inserted. This the publishers regret as much as the author. Brevet Major-General G. Mott also remarked, in a subsequent letter: "I am like General Heintzelman; the pamphlets contain the only (account) of the battle of Williamsburg I have ever seen. I was Lieut.-Col. of the 5th N. J. Vols. at that time; made Colonel of the 6th from that date."

about two miles per day—a sluggishness in May only to find its parallel in his September slackness in Maryland. Is it to be wondered at, that the wits of the army dubbed him the "Virginia Creeper?"

"And here I may point out on passing," is the remark of the PRINCE DE JOINVILLE, "a characteristic trait of the American people—that is as well in regard to the people as to an agglomeration of individuals—delay. This delay in resolving and acting, so opposed to the prompitude, the decision, the audacity to which the American, considered as an individual, had accustomed us, is an inexplicable phenomenon, which always causes me the greatest astonishment. It is the abuse of the individuals initiative that kills the collective energy," etc., etc. Attention was invited to this paragraph by a distinguished general, by no means unfriendly to McCLELLAN, with the observation, "Who could this be aimed at but the commander-in-chief? How could the Prince know the American people except through him?" A prominent cavalry commander heard the Prince make the very same remark.

Arrived in the immediate vicinity of Richmond, he posted his forces so as to violate one of the plainest rules of strategy, or grand tactics; so as absolutely to invite that attack of JOE JOHNSTON, which nearly crumbled one wing, or one-third of his army.* He acted as if totally unaware that there could be men in his front who would see quicker, think quicker, plan quicker, and act quicker than he could. There was one, however, KEARNY, in the Union army, if no more, whose quick eyes comprehended, and whose nimble pen prophesied the impending peril.

On the 28th May, KEARNY † wrote to a correspondent: "And now to our present affairs. They seem to move on tolerably,

* "The best method of defending a river, says Dumas quoting Von Bulow, xx. 196, is then to hold the army assembled at some distance from the shore and fall vigorously upon the enemy as soon as he has affected the crossing." This proposition is identical with that demonstrated by Johnston.

† The following cotemporaneous anecdotes of KEARNY from Chaplain Marks' Peninsula Campaign in Virginia are graphic and interesting. * * *

* * * * * * * *

A. M. After reaching headquarters, learned of General (Seth) WILLIAMS (Asst. Adjt.-Gen. A. of P.), that General KEARNY was upon the left wing of the army at Baltimore cross-roads, and would cross the Chickahominy at Bottom Bridge, and that I was fully

but without vitality, and with hourly signs of a want of talent and administration. We are likely to have a full battle in a very few hours. I confess myself not over sanguine with it. By mismanagement the army has lost one-third (by sickness and stragglers) since leaving Yorktown. Those brigades within my hearing only average about two thousand, instead of over three thousand; they should be four thousand. But this is not all; McClellan, most unfortunately, is putting up every three or four miles, or less, successive lines of rifle-pits, miles in length, thus too openly imparting to the soldiers his own personal distrust of them." In another letter he writes thus: "We are on the eve of a great battle, which is to decide the fate of Virginia. The enemy will fight well, although shaken by the defeat at Williamsburg. I presume that, after our lead off the other day, the rest of the army will fight well; but McClellan has been most injudicious, with his ill-organized marches and easy permission to the men to escape home, or be sent back on

---

fifteen miles from my regiment. And here I may pause for a moment to bear testimony to the uniform courtesy of this excellent officer Williams, who bore into the army and never lost the urbanity of a true gentleman and the patient kindness of a Christian.

* * * * * * *

Page 182. The following morning (25th May) I reached our encampment beyond the Chickahominy, and was gratified to learn that we were within ten miles of Richmond. I could not find the headquarters of General Kearny, and therefore reported to General Jameson the condition of the sick of our brigade left behind, and requested that he would take measures to send back nurses and hospital stores.

Very soon after General Jameson rode to the headquarters of General Kearny and reported to him my statement. In a few minutes an orderly came into our camp bearing a request from General Kearny, "that Chaplain Marks should report himself at his tent." I confess I rode to his headquarters with many misgivings, for I had not reported, as commanded, to the General himself. When I came up to his tent door, I was ushered into his presence by an orderly—his face was frowning.

"How is it, sir," said he, "that you did not report to me in person?"

"Excuse me, general," I said, "I did not think my report of sufficient consequence to authorize me to trouble you with it, and I designed, as soon as I could find your headquarters, to report to you in person; but in the meantime meeting General Jameson, I reported to him the condition of the sick in his brigade."

"Well," said he, "you reported that sick men in my division were lying in the woods and in tents, a long distance from any house without any medical attendance or nurses, and no one had looked after them since we left; is that so, sir?"

"Yes, sir."

"Why, sir, did you bring back a report so calculated to demoralize and dishearten the army?"

"I reported to none but to General Jameson, and that with the purpose of having sent back to them medicines, nurses and hospital supplies, and, if it was best, to go back myself."

the slightest pretext of sickness. McCLELLAN has been too slow; he should have annihilated the enemy in Williamsburg before they could have reached the Chickahominy. Until within three days he evidently had no fixed plan of action; since then he has done better. The battle will be on Wednesday. Unless a Bull Run, it will be full success; if a Bull Run, I expect that my division will be the only one to escape. I have my men completely in hand; they became very enthusiastic for me, but I have seen so much mismanagement that nothing will take me unawares." We did have "a full battle in a very few hours; it was the battle of Fair Oaks, called by the rebels Seven Pines."

"Well, sir, why did you not remain there, and bring in all those sick men? how did you dare to come away and leave them?"

"Sir," I replied, "I saw the last man brought in before I left; every man from the fields and woods was in the hospital."

"Well, sir," relaxing a little, "you must obey orders. Say nothing about this in camp, chaplain; everything relating to my sick men touches my heart. I'll have occasion for you again, chaplain, now go; but hereafter obey orders."

I bowed and left the tent. From that hour General KEARNY was my warmest friend, and invariably treated me with the greatest kindness.

A. M. 2—Page 185. "About this time I received the following letter from General KEARNY, which I introduce here as an illustration of his watchful interest and care for the sick of his division, expressing as it does sentiments of humanity which add to the glory of one of the bravest of our commanders.

[Copy.]

"HEADQUARTERS, THIRD DIVISION,
FAIR OAKS, June 15, 1862.

DEAR SIR: I return you my grateful acknowledgments of your noble and energetic conduct in behalf of our poor sufferers of this division.

"From long experience in the field no one appreciates more sensibly the service you thus render to humanity and to our cause.

"If there has been one point more than another, where I have hitherto laboriously, and concientiously, and successfully fulfilled my duties as an officer, it has been in my solicitude for the sick and disabled. I am thankful to find in you a strong coadjutor: and when I am a little more free to separate myself from the cares of being on the spot to command in case of attack, I will ever be found a constant visitor of the hospitals.

"Most respectfully your obedient servant,

"P. KEARNY, Brig.-Gen.

"The Rev. Dr. MARKS, *Chaplain 63d Regt. Pa. Vols.*"

Perhaps there is no greater exemplification of the incessant vigilance exercised by General KEARNY in everything which could effect the health of his troops, than the following order, which the writer picked up by accident, at the auction of the effects of a citizen of New Jersey, who, doubtless, had been one of KEARNY'S First Brigade from that State. It is very simple, and at first blush seems of little importance, but upon reflection it will speak volumes in favor of that commander who, if he seemed "*cast-iron*" and led his men to desperate ventures in the battle field, nevertheless watched over their *real* welfare with the solicitude of a *military*, and, therefore, a truly

It is well to reflect if the same volumes from which KEARNY had derived his information were not equally open to McCLELLAN.

In the history of war it is seldom that a general is found who exhibits a greater compound of caution, where that quality was the key to success, and audacity, when the opposite was the essential of the hour, than FERDINAND OF BRUNSWICK.

NAPOLEON, in his observations on FERDINAND's campaign of 1758, remarks: "The duke, no doubt, made a brilliant campaign, but his glory was so feebly contested that it would be small if he had not other and more solid titles to prove his talents and his ability.

"(1.) His passage of the Rhine was contrary to every rule. He remained several days on the left of that river separated from two-thirds of his own army. * * The plan of the duke was vicious. If CHEVERT had succeeded in getting possession of the Bridge of Rees, his army would have been lost. * * (3.) The plan of the duke, at the battle of Creveldt, was contrary to the rule: 'Never separate one wing of your army from the other, so that your enemy can thrust himself in the interval.' FERDINAND divided his line of battle into three parts, separated from each other by long intervals and defiles. He turned a whole army with a corps-in-the-air, not supported, which (this corps) ought to have been enveloped and captured."

---

considerate "father," a title often applied to generals who give an earnest attention to the bodily health and comfort of the men confided to their care, while keeping up the strictest discipline, that they might realize its benefits by enjoying "MENS SANA IN CORPORE SANO"—*i. e.* a mind perfectly attuned to their duty in noblest frames fittest to discharge it:

HEADQUARTERS, N. J. BRIGADE, Nov. 3d, 1861.

CIRCULAR,

To Commanders of Regiments:

You will be particular and see that the men of your Regiment are not kept out too long in the open air, during church service and the reading of the regulations.

By order of

Brigadier-General KEARNY.

W. E. STURGES, *A. D. C.*

It was while reflecting upon this subject, the interest felt by KEARNY in the welfare of his men, that the curious chance occurred which threw the above circular or order into the writer's way. When the season, exposure and consequent risk are considered, it is easy to perceive what an immense amount of sickness and suffering may have been prevented by this circumstance; and yet, how very, very few officers take such things into account.

Let us see if these remarks do not apply almost to the letter to McCLELLAN. In the first place he did exactly what NAPOLEON blamed the duke FERDINAND for doing. He massed more than two-thirds of his army to the north of the Chickahominy, sending one-third,* with only a single connection across that treacherous stream, for that fearful storm of the afternoon and night of 30th May—almost unprecedented in the memory of man—swept away every other means of communication.

Terrible indeed was that storm. The rain came down in tropic torrents, and the lightning descended not in flashes, but in sheets of flame, seeming from time to time to envelop the whole bivouacs in its lurid glare. An officer of the SICKLES, or "Excelsior" brigade, a truthful, matter-of-fact man, stated it was horrible to witness, and described the electric fire as running again and again along the line of stacked muskets, "tipping the points of the bayonets with flashes like jets of gas."

As soon as JOHNSTON knew of this dislocation of the Union line, he determined to attack, and coming out of Richmond, distant seven miles, he fell furiously on CASEY'S division, then partially entrenched near Fair Oaks. GREELEY is clear on the point. CASEY fought very well for a time, but he was soon flanked, and his command crumbled away into a rout, exposed as it was to a galling fire in front, flanks and rear.† KEARNY was

---

* PRINCE EUGENE owed his great victory at Zenta, 1697, to such a blunder on the part of the Turks; FREDERICK nearly lost the battle of Prague, in 1757, by leaving the PRINCE OF ANHALT DESSAU on the right bank of the Moldau, and did lose the fruits of his victory; the ARCHDUKE CHARLES could thank such an imprudence on the part of NAPOLEON for the only decided success he gained over his great adversary, at Aspern, in 1809; and at Dresden, in 1813, the great loss sustained by the Austrians was owing to their wing being separated from the rest of the Allied army by a ravine not equivalent to such a stream as the Chickahominy. McCLELLAN repeated at Antietam his fatal mistake in the Peninsula. Here, again, in September, his army was astraddle of the Maryland river as it was *a cheval* the Chickahominy in May and June. He very nearly realized the subsequent simile of LINCOLN, of the ox on, or across, the fence, who could neither use its horns to gore nor heels to kick.

† "When I reached Despatch Station I learned that a battle was then in progress. I stopped at our encampment, but found that all of General KEARNEY'S troops had been hurried up to the scene of conflict."

"I ran up the railroad towards the field of battle. It was now near three P. M.; and at Meadow Station, one mile east of Savage Station, and two and a quarter from Seven Pines, I began to meet the wounded men, who, with broken arms, shattered fingers, and fresh cuts, were wandering to the rear, without any definite purpose. They were mostly of General CASEY'S division, and being disabled, when relieved by Generals KEARNEY and HOOKER, they were at liberty to seek succor and surgical aid."—CHAPLAIN MARKS' *Peninsula Campaign*, page 187.

ordered up to re-establish the crushed line. For two hours and a half he fought gallantly against a confident enemy; convinced all the time that the true proceeding would have been to recommence the attack from a firm second line, instead of an unavailing attempt to re-establish the first. But he complained that the injustice done to him at Williamsburg, by giving to another General the praise which was due to him and others, had dampened the ardor of his men and reduced their *morale.* Nothing is so contagious among troops as the influence of apathy or lethargy, or injustice in a commander, especially when the enterprising and audacious feel that their efforts and courage are ignored and depreciated. Although unable to push the enemy, and at one time nearly surrounded, so that only one line of retreat into White Oak Swamp remained open, and thus greatly threatened, KEARNY held his own, and kept the field till the head of SUMNER'S column, having pushed across the Chickahominy Swamp, struck the enemy's line and sent him reeling in disorder from the parts of the field he had gained.

Months before, KEARNY had pronounced JOHNSTON a very slow man for the offensive, although for the defensive and offensive-defensive he displayed a masterly ability (witness his retreat before SHERMAN in 1864); and the event at Seven Pines proved the truth of this estimate. Had the furious onset made upon CASEY and continued upon COUCH, taken place at nine or ten o'clock in the day, the rout of the two corps would have been complete before reinforcements could have crossed the Chickahominy and its flooded swamps. But KEARNY was able to save the day here, as he had before at Williamsburg, by hard-hitting and stubborn holding on at a critical time.* His own account

* "Our soldiers ever spoke with the greatest admiration of the coolness and bravery of Generals HEINTZLEMAN, HOOKER, SUMNER, KEARNY and COUCH. General HOOKER on this day more than sustained the reputation he had obtained at Williamsburg, as possessed of that clear-sightedness, and courage, and prophetic prognostication of the position and movements of the enemy, which have since placed him at the head of the Army of the Potomac. General KEARNY *showed himself equal to every emergency, daring every danger, and risking his life in the most hazardous positions. His men seemed to be capable of performing anything under his eye, for their confidence in his courage and military courage was unbounded. I have often heard the men speak at the camp-fires of his unruffled coolness during both of those days.*"—CHAPLAIN MARKS' *Peninsula Campaign*, page 200.

of the battle, though only a hasty dash written on the day following, is lively and graphic:

"As the battle came off quite unexpectedly yesterday, I hasten to send you a line, knowing how anxious you will be, and to say that I thank God that the great risks (for it was again a crisis of saving a runaway people) I ran have not resulted in even a light wound. I was visiting some friends the other side of the Chickahominy, some five or six miles off, when a rattle of musketry was heard, and I instantly felt that I was concerned in it. So, mounting, I galloped back, and was just in time to lead my men some miles to the front, to save a huge corps that had run like good fellows at the first attack. This time it was an old acquaintance in Mexico, General Casey, whose men gave way most shamefully—filling the roads from the battle-field to our camp, three and a half miles, and ran away worse than at Bull Run. I am used to many strange sights, but when I saw before the race of the fugitives a whole line of wagons going full tilt, I thought that many a pretty bold man might well have his senses turned. Then came a stream of fugitives, and finally they poured in, in masses. My superior (Heintzelman) had previously ordered me to leave a brigade in the rear. He then first sent to me to send away one brigade by the railroad, quite away from my control, and then a brigade up to the battle-field. I accompanied this, ordered up, at my own responsibility, my absent brigade (Jameson's), and pushed on at a fearful pace. I got under fire, as usual, and was sent to charge, while thousands of those I came to help were left quietly to be passed by, by me, and crouch down in the rifle-pits and fortifications. We put right in, and I drove back the enemy; but McClellan's injustice has changed my men. They followed me, after a fashion, but were cold and slow; still, I won everything. When the enemy got behind us, and the troops in the rear ran like sheep, I flew to them, hurrahed at them, waved my cap, and turning them, led them into the fight again. I had hardly done this, when another large party of the enemy stole in behind my brigade, and I was nearly cut off from my own men; but rushing to a wood near by I made a stand. However, I looked back at my recent borrowed followers, and found them and all the others—some seven or eight thousand of that line (KEYES' Corps)—running like good fellows, and masses of the enemy regularly but surely, rapidly and sternly pursuing them, keeping the only reported roads of retreat. Thinks I to myself, I am cut off, me and mine.

"Most fortunately, I had that very morning examined, with a fine guide, all that secret, locked-up country of forests and swamps. I saw that they hoped to cut me off from retreat by getting between me and White Oak Swamp. By this time a regiment of mine, attracted by the firing in their rear, came along in the woods. I charged the enemy in rear, and would have gained the day but for continuous reinforcements. But I fought them long enough to enable all my intercepted regiments to retire by a secret road through the swamp; got back to my position—a very strong one, from which I should not have been taken—before the enemy arrived there, and again offered the sole barrier, when all else was confusion. Still, this was not victory. It was the first time that I had not slept on the battle-field, and but for the mismanagement as to our battle at Williamsburg, I would have been victorious here too. Still it is most infecting to be sent for to restore a fight, and see hordes of others, panic-stricken, disobedient, craven, and downcast. Anywhere it is a disagreeable sight to see the wounded being carried off the field of battle, even from a victorious one. I have again had an aid wounded, and lost a beautiful bay colt, which was shot from under me. I was not so long, but at times more exposed than ever; my colt being very fractious, kept me, while plunging, in a perfect current of cannon and rifle balls, and alone in the face of too many scamps who seemed to pick me out. It was at this time that my colt received his first wound; an hour later he was killed under me, and I mounted the horse of an adjutant who chanced to follow."

By way of illustrating the felicity of his military style, and the ringing eloquence with which he addressed his men after the smoke of battle had cleared away, two of his general orders are given, the first issued a few days after Fair Oaks, the second a short time after Malvern Hill:

HEAQUARTERS, THIRD DIVISION, THIRD CORPS,
CAMP NEAR RICHMOND, VA., June 5th, 1862.

"GENERAL ORDERS NO. 15.—Brave Regiments of the Division: you have won for us a high reputation. The country is satisfied, your friends at home are proud of you. After two battles and victories, purchased with much blood, you may be counted as veterans. I appeal, then, to your experience, to your personal observation, to your high intelligence, to put in practice on the battle-field the discipline you have acquired in camp. It will enable you to conquer with more certainty and less loss.

2. Shoulder-straps and chevrons: you are marked men, you must ever be in front. Colonels and field-officers: when it comes to the bayonet, lead the charge; at other times circulate among your men, and supervise, keep officers and men to their constituted commands, stimulate the laggard, brand the coward, direct the brave, prevent companies from "huddling up" or mixing.

3. Marksmen: never in the fight cheapen your rifles; when you fire, make sure and hit. In woods and abattis one man in three is to fire, the others reserve their loads to repel an onset, or to head a rush. It is with short rushes and this extra fire, from time to time, that much ground is gained. Each man up in first line, none delaying, share danger alike—then the peril and loss will be small.

4. Men: you brave individuals in the ranks, whose worth and daring, unknown perhaps to your superiors, but recognized by your comrades, influence more than others. I know that you exist, I have watched you in the fire; your merit is sure to have its recompense. Your comrades at the bivouac will report your deeds, and it will gladden your families; in the end you will be brought before the (your) country.

5. Color-bearers of regiments: bear them proudly in the fight, erect and defiantly in the first line. It will cast terror into the opponents to see it sustained and carried forward. Let it be the beacon-light of each regiment. The noblest inscriptions on your banner are the traces of the balls.

6. Again, noble divisions, I wish you success and new victories, until the cause of our sacred Union being triumphant, you return honored to your homes."

HEADQUARTERS, THIRD DIVISION, THIRD CORPS,
CAMP NEAR HARRISON'S LANDING, July 7th 1862.

"GENERAL ORDERS NO. 27.—Brave Comrades: As one of your Generals who has shared in your perils, so I sympathize in your cheers for victory when I pass. The name of this Division is marked. Southern records are full of you. In attack you have driven them, when assailed you have repulsed them. Be it so to the end. New regiments, we give you a name, engraft on it fresh laurels.

Comrades in battle: Let our greeting be a cry of defiance to our foe; after the fight, one greeting of victory for ourselves. This done, remember that, like yourselves, I have duties of labor, in which I must move unobserved, as a true brother in hand and heart of this our Warrior-Division-family. Success attend you."

On the same day on which he issued this order, he wrote as follows to a military friend in regard to the battle of the 31st of May, and then the affair of the following day:

"Since then (5th) we have had another severe affair at Fair Oaks Station. I whipped all before me; but 1,300 men out of 5,000; I was cut off, faced the Thirty-seventh New York, Col. HAYMAN, to their rear, attacked the second line of the enemy (from some woods) in their right rear, after their first line, having caved in our center, had occupied our line of retreat. and swept by near quarter of a mile. It was 'pull Dick, pull Devil.' I gave time to the rest of the division to retire by a 'detour,' and at one time I flattered myself that I would turn the tables on the enemy, but their admirable conduct, and the masses still in reserve, enabled them to form a strong line and nearly surround us as in a ring. It was at this time that I lost my beautiful four-year-old bay colt, a noble charger, shot in the jugular. However, as I knew from some very fortunate reconnoissances that very day (an old cavalry habit), certain blind roads through the swamp, I got off my people, and had them re-established in the camp, fortified lines from which I had been most blunderingly sent forth—after the troops in front (CASEY'S Division) had reached my position (before I started to go forward the three miles) in a most perfectly dilapidated condition. * * * As for that matter, it amused me not a little, when I arrived under fire, to find * * * whose men had proved so light-heeled, all but some less active minded, who still 'impassively' lined certain rear rifle-pits, calmly looking as if he thought it all right for his people to run. * * * With all my instinctive habit of going ahead, it did seem a little ridiculous to be sent for the whole of three miles to go in for other people, about as many hundreds of yards. A bristling abattis and dense copses, once ours, now theirs, were perfect specimens of fire-work. But my Michigan Sharpshooters soon got employed in the same way. BERRY'S Brigade, and soon after, some fine Mountain Boys from Pennsylvania, under General JAMESON, and all worked to a marvel during two hours, * * * * when the brilliant manœuvering of the Southerners, with overwhelming numbers of clock-work men (I never saw such discipline under fire, even with the French), mathematically forced our center (the residue of KEYES' Corps, etc.) to cave in, and leave poor me in the lurch. My loss had been terrific—excepting those of the Thirty-seventh New York, who helped us home—all received in victorious advance; but I at least, as the phrase goes, have the satisfaction of having counted on the field two of theirs for one of ours. Still, all this, though desperate fighting, unusual in war, unsurpassed in Europe, is conducive of no results. At Williamsburg, an unexampled success at a tremendous price, an affair that never should have been gotten into to that depth, resulted vainly, from McCLELLAN not pursuing and preventing their 'debris' (wrecks) from crossing the Chickahominy. It had been the same thing when they retreated panic-stricken from Manassas. The fight on Saturday (30th May), although, as a surprise,—it threw back a corps that never should have been so blunderingly isolated and advanced,—was not a victory for them (though a defeat for some of us), since it found my division back in my entrenched camp, prepared to defy them, and since the day following, one of my brigades and other strong detachments under SUMNER, drove back once more their advance posts, whom they had left near us, and which, if followed up, might have given forth fruit. Still it was not. It only proves that McCLELLAN * * * is utterly and absolutely unfit for his place, and is it surprising that it should be so, when one reflects that without having made any sensation in Mexico, that on a class repute for mathematics and railroad directorship in Illinois, and the most ridiculously trivial baby-fights in Western Virginia (where he never led) that he should have been lionized into a chieftainship, which he has exercised with favoritism, injustice, * * * ever keeping himself purposely in the rear in critical seasons to avoid the embarrassment of having to act and direct, when consulted. And I have only to add that we are now in a stupidly perilous condition; for, with half of the army—with which he is afraid to make the 6 ($5\frac{1}{2}$) miles to Richmond—he keeps this half of it exposed this side of the Chickahominy, with every bridge carried away by freshet, and impassable. If we escape a disaster, it is that the loss of the secessionists, the other day, was (notwithstanding their pluck) too severe to be tried twice. They must have concentrated against us on points vastly superior forces.* I am sure that I could count as before me, from sound and sight, treble my people. It is true, that McCLELLAN'S ignoring us * * has disheartened us all. *Still, if you once whip, you must always whip. It becomes a way of doing the thing, even when the heart is away.*

I have had again an aid wounded, a lieutenant MALLON. Poor WILSON and BRAINARD can never be replaced; warm in heart, devoted to me, without guile, they were talented soldiers, such as you rarely find among men."

One anecdote from a participant in that momentous struggle is worthy of insertion. On one occasion, when General McCLELLAN rode over to the left of our lines in front of Richmond, examining General HEINTZELMAN'S position, Generals KEARNY and HOOKER accompanying him, he turned to the veteran corps commander and said: "What of your position here? Can you hold it?" HEINTZELMAN, addressing his nearest subordinate, remarked: "What say you, General HOOKER?" "I can hold my position," replied HOOKER, "against one hundred thousand men." "Well, KEARNY, what say you?" "Well," rejoined

*For a comparison to Johnston's strategy at Fair Oaks, examine MIKHAILOFSKY-DANIELEFSKY'S "Campaign in France, 1814," Chapter ix, pages 192, etc.

KEARNY, "if the Rebels think they can take my position, let them come and try it." These answers are perfectly characteristic of the two men.

Before committing the criminal error of dislocating his left—NAPOLEON'S especial charge against FERDINAND OF BRUNSWICK—from whose fatal consequences MCCLELLAN was alone preserved by KEARNY'S prompt and hard fighting, and by the patriotic determination of SUMNER, whose one-man-will served as a bridge over which the corps hurried on the afternoon of the 31st of May to preserve the Union left—MCCLELLAN, meanwhile, had committed a second mistake. This is the very one to which NAPOLEON refers as the Duke's third violation of the rules of war. He projected his right wing from twelve to fourteen miles in the air on the plea of extending a hand to MCDOWELL, whose most advanced outposts were from eight to twenty miles distant on an air line to the northward.

At this time, MCDOWELL'S main army was at Fredericksburg, sixty miles distant, to which it was chained by the timidity of the government—a timidity of which MCCLELLAN was perfectly well aware from the moment he assumed command—a timidity which his own over-caution ought to have made him thoroughly appreciate—a timidity of which he again had proof April 5th, while before Yorktown—a timidity which ought to have taught him not to compromise his own army in the *hope* of receiving any re-enforcements which would leave Washington uncovered. No man of true common sense, accustomed to judge of the future from the past, would have based any project on hopes of being joined by the "Army of Virginia," as it was afterward named.

Here the observer has a right to propound the question, could PORTER have maintained himself, when so dislocated, at Hanover Court House, until MCDOWELL (that is, his army *in force*) arrived? It is true MCCLELLAN claimed for him a "glorious," a "complete victory," and dispatched to Washington a jubilant, swelling report, which LINCOLN'S common sense pricked with a single question. This glorious victory—totally destitute of result—on the right, 27th May, was succeeded on the 31st, by the surprise of the Union left, which resulted in the severe battles of Fair Oaks and Seven Pines, already dwelt on. That this surprise did not result in the destruction of our forces south of the Chickahominy, was entirely due to KEARNY's hard fighting, and tenacious holding, and "vigilant" SUMNER's resolution in crossing to the rescue. When the next day the battle was renewed and won, McCLELLAN could or would not improve it. He could have followed the "broken and dispirited" enemy into their capital, which at that time had no defense except its army — an army thoroughly "beaten and demoralized." If any proof was necessary to demonstrate in the clearest manner that the administration were correct in refusing to allow McCLELLAN to absorb McDOWELL's army, the non-improvement of Fair Oaks was all-sufficient.

REPORTS.

HEADQUARTERS THIRD DIVISION, HEINTZELMAN'S CORPS,
ENTRENCHED CAMP NEAR SAVAGE'S, June 2, 1862.

SIR: — On the 31st ultimo, at three P. M., I received an order to send a Brigade of my Division, by the railroad, to support KEYES' Corps, said to be severely engaged.

BIRNEY's Brigade was designated, and getting most promptly under arms, advanced accordingly.

Captain HUNT, Aid to General HEINTZELMAN, arriving from the field, made me aware of the discomfiture of most of CASEY'S Division. The retiring wagons, and a dense stream of disorganized fugitives, arrived nearly simultaneously. As a precaution, I ordered some picked Michigan Marksmen and a regiment to proceed and occupy the dense woods bordering on the left of our position, to take in flank any pursuers. I, however, soon received General HEINTZELMAN's directions, to order forward, by the Williamsburg road, the remaining Brigade, and to retrieve the position the enemy had driven us from. *I put myself at the head of the advanced regiment** and set forward without delay. I also sent written orders for JAMESON's Brigade, camped at our *tete-de-pont*, near Bottom's Bridge (three miles in the rear), to come up without delay. This order met with General HEINTZELMAN's approval. On arriving at the field of battle, we found certain zigzag rifle-pits sheltering crowds of men, and the enemy firing from abattis and timber in their front. General CASEY remarked to me, on coming up: "If you will regain our late camp, the day will still be ours." I had but the Third Michigan up, but they moved forward with alacrity, dashing into the felled timber, and commenced a desperate but determined contest, heedless of the shell and ball which rained upon them. This regiment, the only one of BIRNEY's Brigade not engaged at Williamsburg, at the price of a severe loss, has already out-vied all competitors. Its work this day was complete. This regiment lost: —

Third Michigan lost —

OFFICERS KILLED: — Captain S. A. JUDD, Company A,............................ 1

---

* Generals KEARNY and HOOKER did their part, and did it well, as every one will admit who saw the former dashing along the front of his line, encouraging his command to renewed exertion, and heard the latter exclaim as he emerged from the woods into the open battle-field, "*My men, follow* ME!" — (*Newspaper Slip.*)

OFFICERS WOUNDED:—Colonel S. G. CHAMPLIN; Captain S. G. LOWING, Company F; First Lieutenants:—G. E. JUDD, Company A; N. M. PELTON, Company C; G. W. DODGE, Company F; H. I. WHITNEY, Company G; S. BRENNAN, Company I; Second Lieutenants:—D. C. CRAWFORD, Company E; JOSEPEH MASON, Company I, ... 9

Total officers killed and wounded, ...	10
Enlisted men killed, ...	31
Enlisted men wounded, ...	111
Enlisted men missing, ...	14
Total loss, ...	166

One company of fifty picked marksmen lost its Captain, killed, its Lieutenant, wounded, and twenty-six men. I take pleasure in particularizing Colonel S. G. CHAMPLIN, wounded, Lieutenant-Colonel A. A. STEVENS, Major PIERIE, and Captains J. C. SMITH and E. S. PIERIE, and Lieutenant G. E. JUDD. The next regiment that came up, the Fifth Michigan, again won laurels as fresh as those due them for Williamsburg. Its loss then was one hundred and forty-four. Its loss this day:

Fifth Michigan lost—

OFFICERS KILLED:—Captain LEWIS B. QUACKENBUSH, Company H; Lieutenant and Adjutant CHARLES H. HUTCHINGS, ... 2

OFFICERS WOUNDED:—Lieutenant J. J. KNOX, Company D; Captains:—C. H. TRAVERS, Company E; WILSON, Company G; MILLER, Company K, ... 4

Total officers killed and wounded, ...	6
Enlisted men killed, ...	30
Enlisted men wounded, ...	116
Enlisted men missing, ...	7
Total loss, ...	159

Its noble officers did their duty. I directed General BERRY, with his regiment, to turn the "Slashings" and, fighting, gain the open ground on the enemy's right flank. This was perfectly accomplished. The Thirty-seventh New York was arranged in column to support the attack. Its services in the sequel proved invaluable.

In the meanwhile, my remaining Brigade, the One Hundred and Fifth and Sixty-third Pennsylvanians, came up under General JAMESON, the other two regiments having been diverted, one to BIRNEY, and one to PECK. It is believed that they did well, and most probably urgent reasons existed, *but I most respectfully submit that it is to the disadvantage of a constituted command to take men from their habitual leaders, and not to be anticipated that a brave, though weak Division can accomplish the same results, with its regiments thus allotted out to those whom they neither knew nor have fought under—at the same time that it diminishes the full legitimate sphere of the commander of the Division.* Of these regiments the One Hundred and Fifth was placed in the "Slashing," now vacated by the oblique advance of the Third Michigan, whilst eight companies of the Sixty-third Pennsylvanians, led by Lieutenant-Colonel MORGAN, and most spiritedly headed by General JAMESON, aided by his daring Chief of Staff, Captain POTTER, were pushed through the abattis (*the portions never until now occupied by us*), and nobly repelled a strong body of the enemy, who, though in a strong line, and coming up rapidly and in order, just failed to reach (to support) this position in time, but, who, nothing daunted, and with a courage worthy a united cause, halted in battle array, and poured in a constant heavy roll of musketry fire.

The One Hundred and Fifth lost—

OFFICERS KILLED:—Captain JOHN C. DOWLING, Company B; First Lieutenant J. P. R. CUMMUSKY, Company D, ... 2

OFFICERS WOUNDED: — Colonel A. A. McKNIGHT; Captains: — L. C. DUFF, Company D; J. W. GREENAWALK, Company E; R. KIRK, Company F; A. C. THOMPSON, Company K; First Lieutenants: — S. A. CRAIG, Company B; C. C. MARKLE, Company E; JAMES B. GAGGIE, Company F; Second Lieutenant A. J. SHIPLEY, Company E, ... 9

Total officers killed and wounded,	11
Enlisted men killed,	67
Enlisted men wounded,	115
Enlisted men missing,	63
Total loss,	256

Sixty-third Pennsylvania Volunteers lost—

OFFICERS KILLED: — First Lieutenant HENRY HURST, Company C, ... 1

OFFICERS WOUNDED: — Lieutenant-Colonel A. S. M. MORGAN; Adjutant GEORGE P. CORTES; Quartermaster W. N. HAYMAKER; Captain JOHN A. DEINKES, Company E; First Lieutenant T. L. MAYNARD, Company B; Second Lieutenant, L. I. MOREHEAD, Company G; Acting Second Lieutenant G. E. GROSS, Company D, ... 7

Total officers killed and wounded,	8
Enlisted men killed,	31
Enlisted men wounded,	88
Enlisted men missing,	21
Total loss,	148

This was, perhaps, near six o'clock, when our center right, defended by troops of the other divisions, with all their willingness, could no longer resist the enemy's right-central-flank attacks, pushed on with determined discipline, and with the impulsion of numerous concentrated masses. Once broken, our troops fled incontinently, and a dense body of the enemy pursuing rapidly, yet in order, occupied the Williamsburg road, the entire open ground, and penetrating deep into the woods on either side, soon interposed between my division and my line of retreat. *It was on this occasion, that, seeing myself cut off, and relying on the high discipline and determined valor of the Thirty-seventh New York Volunteers,* I faced them to the rear against the enemy, and held the ground, although so critically placed, and despite the masses that gathered on and passed us, checked the enemy in his intent of cutting us off against the White Oak Swamp.* This enabled the advanced regiments, averted by orders, and this contest in their rear, to return from their hitherto victorious career, and to retire by a remaining wood path, known to our scouts (the Saw Mill road), until they once more arrived at and regained the impregnable position we had left at noon at our own fortified division camp. The loss of the Thirty-seventh New York is severe, viz.:

Thirty-seventh New York lost—

OFFICERS KILLED: — Second Lieutenant W. J. FINNON, ... 1

OFFICERS WOUNDED: — Captains J. R. McCONNELL, A. J. DIGNAN; First Lieutenant JAMES KEELAN, Second Lieutenants JAMES H. MARKEY, WM. BIRD, WM. C. GREEN, ... 6

Total officers killed and wounded,	7
Enlisted men killed,	12
Enlisted men wounded,	66
Enlisted men missing,	2
Total loss,	87

* "General KEARNY led the charge of the Thirty-seventh New York which decided the action on Saturday (31st May) in our favor." — (*Newspaper Slip.*)

At Williamsburg its loss was 95; it there formed our extreme left. Colonel HAYMAN, its Colonel, has ever been most distinguished. He revived this day his reputation gained in Mexico. Adjutant JAMES HENRY, Captain JAMES R. O. BEIRNE, and Lieutenants W. C. GREEN and P. J. SMITH were particularly distinguished for courage and activity.

The detached brigade, under BIRNEY, had been ordered to support, by the railroad side — not to attack. It accomplished this successfully, for I understand, that it enabled General COUCH, who had been cut off with a brigade, to form a junction with the army. The Fifty-seventh Pennsylvania Volunteers (JAMESON'S Brigade) having been on fatigue, was ordered to report to General BIRNEY, and was seriously engaged. Its loss was:

Fifty-seventh Pennsylvania Volunteers lost —

OFFICERS KILLED: — Major J. CULP,	1
OFFICERS WOUNDED: — Colonel C. T. CAMPBELL; Captain S. C. SIMONTON, Company B; Captain C. S. CHASE; Lieutenant E. J. RICE, Company A,	4
Total officers killed and wounded,	5
Enlisted men killed,	17
Enlisted men wounded,	57
Enlisted men missing,	23
Total loss,	102

This brigade, again, on the following day, having been kept out in advance of the division camp, performed, under Colonel J. H. HOBART WARD, a brilliant charge. I refer you to Colonel WARD'S report.

The loss of the brigade has been:

Thirty-eighth New York Volunteers lost —

OFFICERS WOUNDED: — Lieutenant F. WALKER,	1
Enlisted men killed,	6
Enlisted men wounded,	20
Enlisted men missing,	8
Total loss,	35

Fortieth New York Volunteers lost —

OFFICERS WOUNDED: — First Lieutenant LEWIS FITZGERALD; Second Lieutenant CHAS. H. GESNER,	2
Enlisted men killed,	10
Enlisted men wounded,	51
Enlisted men prisoners,	2
Total loss,	67

Third Maine Volunteers lost —

OFFICERS WOUNDED: — Captain LAKEMAN, Company I; Captain RICHMOND, Company K; Lieutenant A. S. MERRILL, Company D; Lieutenant HASKELL, Company K,	4
Enlisted men killed,	8
Enlisted men wounded,	64
Total loss,	77

Fourth Maine Volunteers lost —

Enlisted men killed,	2
Enlisted men wounded,	8
Enlisted men missing,	1
Total loss,	11

The Second Michigan Volunteers, Colonel POE, and two companies of the Sixty-third Pennsylvania Volunteers, having been on distant pickets, were late to join in the battle, but arrived most opportunely to resist the advanced pursuers of the enemy, near our entrenched camps; and aided in giving me time to organize its defence.

The Second Michigan lost—

OFFICERS WOUNDED:—Lieutenant-Colonel A. W. WILLIAMS; Captain WM. L. WHIPPLE, ... 2

Enlisted men killed, ... 10

Enlisted men wounded, ... 42

Enlisted men missing, ... 1

Total loss, ... 55

The Eighty-seventh New York Volunteers was detached with General PECK. I refer you to him for favorable notice. Its loss was:—

Eighty-seventh New York Volunteers lost—

OFFICERS WOUNDED:—Colonel S. A. DODGE; Captain T. Y. BAKER, Company C; Captain D. O. BECKWITH, Company K: First Lieutenant D. A. FLANDREAU, Company A; First Lieutenant J. C. CLOYD, Company C; Second Lieutenant H. C. SALVAGE, Company A, ... 6

Enlisted men killed, ... 9

Enlisted men wounded, ... 62

Enlisted men missing, ... 4

Total loss 81

It is, perhaps, within the limits of my report, to mention General PECK, most distinguished, and wounded in Mexico. On the discomfiture of the right and centre, he rallied near the saw-mill several hundreds of the fugitives, and was coming with them from there again to the field, when I directed them to anticipate the enemy and man the intrenched camp. In doing this, I particularize a noble regiment, the First Long Island Legion, under Colonel ADAMS.

I have again to dwell on the exemplary conduct of the brilliant officers of the Staff. Captain POTTER, General JAMESON'S Assistant Adjutant-General, who had already attracted notice at Williamsburg, was here as conspicuously gallant as extremely useful. I have to regret the loss of Captain SMITH, A. A. General of General BERRY'S Staff—the premature fate of one whose gallantry at Williamsburg made me anticipate a career which he fulfilled again in this action. My acting Aid, Lieutenant MALLON, rendered me great service, and was wounded. My Aid, Captain STURGESS, was left to conduct General BIRNEY. Captain MOORE was sent after my Artillery, and was, as usual, active. I have again to regret that the unequalled Batteries, THOMPSON'S (2d U. S. Art.), RANDOLPH'S and REAM'S were not employed, from there being other batteries substituted.

In finishing this report, I trust that you will bring to the attention of the General-in-Chief, that masters of the lost camp, and victorious and in full career, that the fate of the centre decided our own, and that the regiments were suddenly stopped by orders despatched to them, and by hearing the fire of their support, the Thirty-seventh New York, in rear of their entire line. But undismayed, and in good order, they effected their retreat.

I have also to call to your attention, that the loss of my Regiments, only five thousand fighting men, all told, have again, within a very short period, paid the penalty of daring and success by the marked and severe loss of near thirteen hundred men. I have again to bring to notice, for conspicuous good conduct, Generals JAMESON, BERRY and BIRNEY (2d Brigade). The latter acted in an independent command. The two former led in person the advance of their men. Among numerous prisoners taken was Colonel BRATTON, Sixth South Carolina Volunteers, taken by Colonel WALKER'S Fourth Maine.

The losses of the enemy were even vastly severer than our own, and, in places, the slain were piled in confused masses.

I add, in conclusion, that the enemy's success of the afternoon did not prevent me, that very night, from pushing forward Major DILLMAN and two hundred Michigan Marksmen to the Saw-mill (one mile in advance), whence he boldly threw out reconnoissances in the vicinity, and to the left of the late battle ground.

Very respectfully, your obedient Servant,

P. KEARNY,

Brigadier General, Commanding 3d Division, 3d Corps.

To Captain CHAUNCEY MCKEEVER, A. A. G.

CONSOLIDATED LIST OF KILLED, WOUNDED AND MISSING AT THE BATTLE OF FAIR OAKS, VA., MAY 31ST, 1862.

COMMAND.	OFFICERS.				ENLISTED MEN.					Aggregate.
	Killed.	Wounded.	Missing.	Total.	Killed.	Wounded.	Missing.	Prisoners.	Total.	
General KEARNY'S Staff	......	1	......	1	....	....	....	......	....	1
General BERRY'S Staff	1	......	......	1	....	....	....	......	....	1
105th Pennsylvania Volunteers	2	9	......	11	67	115	63	......	245	256
63d Pennsylvania Volunteers	1	7	......	8	31	88	21	......	140	148
57th Pennsylvania Volunteers	1	4	......	5	17	57	23	......	97	102
87th New York Volunteers	......	6	......	6	9	62	4	......	75	81
38th New York Volunteers	......	1	......	1	6	20	8	......	34	35
40th New York Volunteers	......	2	......	2	10	51	2	2	65	67
3d Maine Volunteers	......	4	......	4	8	65	....	......	73	77
4th Maine Volunteers	......	......	......	......	2	8	1	......	11	11
37th New York Volunteers	1	6	......	7	12	66	2	......	80	87
2nd Michigan Volunteers	......	2	......	2	10	42	1	......	53	55
3d Michigan Volunteers	1	9	......	10	31	111	14	......	156	166
5th Michigan Volunteers	2	4	......	6	30	116	7	......	153	159
Total	9	55	......	64	233	801	146	2	1182	1246

HEAD-QUARTERS, THIRD DIVISION THIRD CORPS,
ENTRENCHED CAMP NEAR SAVAGE'S, June 2d, 1862.

General KEARNY'S Staff.

First Lieutenant E. MALLON, Acting A. D. C., wounded.

CONSOLIDATED LIST OF KILLED, WOUNDED AND MISSING IN THIRD DIVISION, THIRD CORPS, AT THE BATTLE OF FAIR OAKS, VA., MAY 31ST AND JUNE 1ST, 1862.

COMMAND.	OFFICERS.			ENLISTED MEN.					Aggregato.
	Killed.	Wounded.	Total.	Killed.	Wounded.	Missing.	Prisoners.	Total.	
General KEARNY'S Staff	......	1	1	....	....	....	......	....	1
General BERRY'S Staff	1	......	1	....	....	....	......	....	1
57th Pennsylvania Volunteers	1	4	5	10	44	1	......	55	60
63d Pennsylvania Volunteers	1	8	9	22	71	20	......	113	122
105 Pennsylvania Volunteers	2	9	11	39	103	8	......	150	161
87th New York Volunteers	......	4	4	11	54	6	......	71	75
38th New York Volunteers	......	1	1	1	13	3	......	17	18
40th New York Volunteers	......	2	2	12	79	....	3	94	96
3d Maine Volunteers	......	5	5	8	66	3	......	77	82
4th Maine Volunteers	......	1	1	2	7	1	......	10	11
2nd Michigan Volunteers	.. ...	2	2	10	45	....	......	55	57
3d Michigan Volunteers	1	9	10	29	115	15	......	159	169
5th Michigan Volunteers	2	5	7	29	100	19	......	148	155
37th New York Volunteers	1	6	7	11	62	2	......	75	82
Total	9	57	66	184	759	78	3	1024	1090

P. KEARNY.

Brigadier General Commanding Third Division Third Corps.

CHAPTER XXV.

THE PENINSULAR CAMPAIGN.*

FAIR OAKS TO OAK GROVE, AND ON TO MALVERN HILL.

(No 2.)

THE SEVEN DAYS' BATTLES.

The morning kiss'd each sleeping flow'r
  And woo'd each sparkling rill,
And rose the sun in haughty power
  On fated Malvern Hill.

* * * * *

It deepens !—" Forward "—" Fire again !"—
  The volley louder pours ;—
They charge our guns—" Now, steady, men,
  The day shall yet be ours."

Here dashing KEARNY leads the van,
  His eagle eye on fire ;
Alone his noble bearing can
  His weary ranks inspire.

* * * * *

The weary slept—the trumpet sound
  Had ceased, and all was still,—
And heaven was weeping o'er the ground
  Of fated " Malvern Hill."

GEORGETOWN, D. C., COURIER'S "*Battle of Malvern Hill.*"

"In this case" (if NAPOLEON abandoned Lobau, after Aspern, 1809) "it was not for a retreat upon Vienna" (a few miles—in McCLELLAN'S case the James river) "but for a retreat upon Strasburg" (the Potomac, to cover Washington) "that it behoved to prepare." THIERS, x, xxxv, 338.

"Said the General ('STONEWALL JACKSON') who is your general?" "KEARNY, as brave a man as ever drew a sword, do you know him, general?" replied the wounded Union soldier addressed? "Oh, yes, well; you are led by a good officer." MARKS, 361.

---

* Chapters xxiv and xxv were actually in print in September, 1868, and had been examined (likewise many of the preceding and subsequent ones) by an accomplished General U. S. A. That part of this, xxv, relating to Malvern Hill, was revised by a brilliant officer, who was present in the engagement. For whatever errors, here or elsewhere, may be found, the publishers are liable, as notes and references have been transposed, sometimes paragraphs, which errors it was impossible to correct, as the pages were stereotyped in some instances before a revised proof was submitted. This was excused by the plea of loss of papers in the mail. The writer supposing his work would have been published last Autumn, as agreed, allowed papers to get separated, and through the willful negligence of a trusted party his memoranda of corrections and references disappeared or was willfully destroyed to conceal a piece of negligence. This explanation is due to himself, as he is completing this work as a volunteer.

When McClellan insisted upon the movement up the Peninsula, thereby, as far as he was concerned, uncovering Washington, he had no right to suppose that the Capital would be entirely denuded of troops, and every man committed to the leadership of one who could not handle the numbers he already had or employ them to advantage. McClellan had condemned himself in the Fall of 1861, in the eyes of Kearny, and Kearny was not the only man in the country who saw through him. Was it likely that a general who allowed his army of 158,000 men to be paralyzed for eight months by 50,000 inferior troops in Manassas, would have been less benumbed with nearly that number in the presence of 100,000 better troops, occupying a more advantageous position? Now the extension of his right, and its success was an excuse; and it would seem as if McClellan was always seeking excuses for his want of enterprise.*

An apathetic lull of twelve days succeeded the victory of Fair Oaks, when McClellan's dream of action in the dim future, was broken by a sharp cavalry masterstroke, which must have been a rude awakening. This was J. E. B. Stuart's cavalry raid, which made a complete circuit of his army.† On

* After Fair Oaks, Sumner asked to be permitted to go into Richmond, and said we could go in for the Rebels were thoroughly routed. Fitz John Porter went up in a balloon, and reported that the Rebels were coming out. Thereupon McClellan expected an attack, whereas it was Rebels running out in another direction, not to attack us, but to get away from us. Hurlburt admits that the Rebels thought they were "gone in" at the time. Mag.-Gen. P. ———

"† A few hours, therefore, after the English tents had been pitched before Limerick, Sarsfield set forth, under cover of the night, with a strong body of horse and dragoons. He took the road to Killaloe, and crossed the Shannon there. * * * He learned in the evening that the detachment which guarded the English artillery had halted for the night about seven miles from William's camp; * * * that officers and men seemed to think themselves perfectly secure; that the beasts had been turned loose to graze, and that even the sentinels were dozing. When it was dark the Irish horsemen quitted their hiding place. * * The surprise was complete. Some of the English sprang to their arms and made an attempt to resist, but in vain. About sixty fell. One only was taken alive. The rest fled. The victorious Irish made a huge pile of wagons and pieces of cannon. Every gun was stuffed with powder, and fixed with its mouth in the ground, and the whole mass was blown up. * * The King guessed the design of his brave enemy, and sent five hundred horse to protect the guns. Unhappily there was some delay. * * * At one in the morning the detachment set out, but had scarcely left the camp when a blaze like lightning and a crash like thunder announced to the wide plain of the Shannon that all was over. * * * Their (Irish) spirits rose and the besiegers began to lose heart."—Macaulay's *History of England*, iii. 605–6.

"He (Boileau) sent Sarsfield with a picked body of cavalry to intercept the convoy. Sarsfield crossed the Shannon at Killaloe, twelve miles from Limerick, and the night of the 13th–14th June, this slash at his rear and communications was enough to startle any one, slow to decide and slower yet to plan. It set McClellan, doubtless, to thinking of his true base on the James, on the line indicated in the previous fall by Kearny, on the line from Williamsburg direct to Richmond. Still, like Holgar, the Dane, in the vaults of Elsinore, he only woke up to ask, "Is it time;" or like Barbarossa, in the cavern of the Thuringian Kylf-hauser Berg, awakened to ask "Whether the ravens still flew round the mountain." Ravens the general little boded were about to fly.* The reader has more than once seen Kearny's prophetic words most promptly realized. This was the case almost to the letter, before Fair Oaks. In the following communication he indicates that movement of Jackson which brought about that swift "change of base" or retreat to the James, which rendered the term almost synonymous afterwards with a flight.

Under date of 22d June, Kearny writes as follows: "I am sorry that I cannot give you interesting news. Here we are again at a dead-lock. Manassas over again; both parties entrenched up to their eyes, both waiting for something; unluckily, our adversaries gaining two to our one. Our last chance to conquer Richmond—for Dame Fortune is resentful of slighted charms—was thrown away when our great battle of Fair Oaks was thrown away. We had tempted the enemy to attack us whilst divided by the Chickahominy. Fortunately, he failed. The prestige, nearly lost to us by our inaction since Williamsburg, was once more in the ascendancy. It only required McClellan to put forth moral force and his military might, and Richmond would have been ours. But no; delay on delay; fortifications, as if we were beaten, met by stronger

marching along by-roads, surprised the escort encamped in false security, only seven miles from William's army, killed or dispersed the detachment, and having loaded the cannons to the muzzle, he buried them muzzle down in the ground, and then laid trains communicating with a match, which was fired as he retreated. All the guns burst; the explosion was terrible. Sir John Lanier had been dispatched with five hundred horsemen to prevent such a disaster, but he moved so slowly that he only arrived in sight of the detachment after the catastrophe. His efforts were in vain to intercept the return of Sarsfield's troops to Limerick."—Lamontagne's Gordon's "*Histoire d'Irlande*," ii. 479.

* For a grand description of this legend see Victor Hugo's majestic drama of "*Les Burgraves*," Part I, Scene 2, Karl speaking, pages 208–'9.

counter-fortifications, on points previously neglected; undue concentration of our troops on points already over-manned, met by a network enveloping us by them; supineness in our camps, met by daring forays by them;* the boasted influence of our reserve artillery, counterbalanced by their availing themselves of the respite to get up artillery even of greater calibre; the reliance on further troops from the north, more than met by reinforcements of two to one, by their recalling troops from the south. Indeed, every thing so betokens fear on the part of the general commanding, and the enemy show themselves so emboldened that, with the numbers crowding up around us, I am puzzled to divine the next act of the drama. *It will be either another inexplicable evacuation, or the suffocation of this army by the seizure of our communications when least expected.* The enemy wish us to attack. McClellan has proved by his fortifications that he is feeble. We are surrounded in front by a cordon of troops and forts. It is true that they will fail if they attack us; but, if they do not do that, they will leave enough troops in our front, and crossing the Chickahominy, *cut us off from our lines of communication and sustenance.*"†

With the modesty that is not often found, except with true courage, Gen. Kearny does not give, in this connection, the

---

* "Bloody conflicts, with doubtful issues, daily occurred to obtain provision, which could only be secured for either army sword in hand. A convoy, that the Imperialists were expecting from a distance, coming up under an escort of 1000 men, was pounced upon on the way by the Swedes, who, under cover of the darkness of the night, secured it for themselves; and one fine morning 12,000 cattle driven into the Nuremberg camp in despite, while 1000 wagons laden with bread were of necessity burned to save them from recapture. A more serious affair of the same kind near Altdorf also terminated to the advantage of the Swedish cavalry, who routed several Austrian regiments with the loss of about 400 men. Wallenstein, seeing these many checks and increasing difficulties, repented that he had declined to hazard a battle at the beginning; but the increased strength of the Swedish camp now rendered the thought of making an attack upon it impracticable. The king acted steadily upon his favorite axiom, "that a good general with a small army could hardly ever be obliged to fight, if he acted with due vigilance, forethought and activity."—Gen. Cust's "*Lives of the Warriors,*" 1600–1648, vol. 1, page 268.

"Nothing is done while something still remains to be done."

† But not alone as a mere strategist or military leader did Kearny shine, as extract after extract from Chaplain Mark's Peninsular Campaign, as taken in connection with other facts, abundantly testifies. For these the reader is referred to that most interesting book, as too lengthy for quotation in this work.

speech reported by an officer of HOOKER'S, a rival division, which he made to the Twentieth Indiana.

"It should be preserved," says Major W—— B——, "as a gem of battle eloquence, equal, in pith and brevity, to STARKE'S famous words at Bennington."

The enemy had come in and taken a section of a battery on the left of the position held by KEARNY, who saw at a glance the extreme importance of recovering that part of the field. Dashing up to the first regiment he saw in line, he threw himself at their head and shouted: "Twentieth Indiana, those guns must be retaken, or PHIL. KEARNY loses his other arm!" The guns were retaken.

On the 25th of June, a reconnoissance in force on the Union left brought on quite a smart engagement, in which KEARNY, originally sent to protect the left flank of the movement, participated with his usual gallantry. In half an hour after the skirmish fire began, KEARNY and HOOKER'S divisions had become quite actively engaged, and the collision gradually assumed the magnitude of what our people styled the Battle of Oak Grove,* or "The Orchard," or "The Peach Orchard," or the "Second Battle of Fair Oaks." "This," says Chaplain MARKS, "was the first of those grand and never-to-be-forgotten contests called the "Seven Days' Battles."

HEADQUARTERS THIRD DIVISION, THIRD CORPS,
CAMP NEAR SEVEN PINES, June 28th, 1862.

SIR—I have the honor to forward the reports of my three brigades for the skirmishing of the 25th instant.

During these engagements I remained at my redan, and only took personal part in the same until toward evening.

I remained at bivouac with BIRNEY'S brigade the entire night.

I have particularly to commend General ROBINSON and Colonel BROWN, Twentieth Indiana Volunteers, Colonel HAYS, Sixty-third Pennsylvania, and Lieutenant-Colonel BACHIA, Eighty-seventh New York Volunteers, but not so

---

* The attacking column consisted of Grover's, Sickles' and Robinson's brigades. General Kearny was sent to protect the left flank, and the Nineteenth Massachusetts, Colonel Hicks, was ordered to advance and protect the right." * * * * "In half an hour the skirmish extended along the entire line, and Kearny and Hooker's divisions were engaged in the liveliest action; and soon, from the arrival of fresh troops on both sides, the engagement assumed the magnitude of a battle."—Chaplain MARK'S Peninsula Campaign, page 222.

much his regiment; also, the firm, solid appearance of the First New York Volunteers, as arriving at night and taking up position.

The casualties have been principally in the Twentieth Indiana and Sixty-third Pennsylvania.

I refer you to Brigade reports.

Respectfully, your obedient servant,

(Signed) P. KEARNY,

Brigadier-General Commanding Division.

To Captain C. McKEEVER,

Chief of Staff Third Corps.

"On the very evening of 25th of June, McCLELLAN was awakened from the dream of rejoicing over what he thought the successful result of his preparations for the advance of his whole army—as inaugurated by HEINTZELMAN's gaining ground on the left—by the tidings that the right of his long straggling line of twenty miles was menaced—as KEARNY foretold four days previously would be the case—in flank and rear, by masses of the enemy; that his communications could no longer be maintained. The rebel generals seemed about to repeat the magnificent stroke of FREDERIC and of SEYDLITZ at Rosbach, by crushing the right of the Union line, some twenty miles long, rolling the whole army up, in upon itself, and 'bowling' it away to destruction."

McCLELLAN's panegyrist at a subsequent date, and accuser at this time, observes, in 1866, that McCLELLAN's project of making a counter-move, which he looked forward to on the 25th, had an illustrious precedent in TURENNE's counter to MONTECUCULI in 1674 (1675). This criticism overlooks the observations of NAPOLEON in regard thereto. If TURENNE made a brilliant move, his "position was bad," and he laid himself open to a fatal blow. Had MONTECUCULI been as enterprising as the rebels, and "employed six hours of the night in marching" direct upon the bridge which constituted TURENNE's line of retreat, that blow would have ended the campaign. The Imperial commander threw away those six hours, and his chance of success was gone. McCLELLAN was in the habit of throwing away days instead of hours, and had never profited by an opportunity. He had taken no advantage of KEARNY's brilliant move, 9th–10th March, which drove the rebels from Manassas, but turned back after a profitless fatiguing military promenade.* After Williamsburg, he had gone to sleep, as it were, and after Fair Oaks, when he might have followed the defeated rebels into Richmond, again he did nothing. He was yet to enjoy other favors of fortune, and to reject them. Forgetting "that *Fortune is a woman*, avail yourself of her favor while she is in the humor; beware that she does not change through resentment of your neglect." After the victory of Malvern Hill, as honorable to the corps commanders as Hohenlinden in 1800 to MOREAU, and, taking into consideration all its antecedents, very much the same sort of battle, he did worse than he ever had done; after South Mountain it was the same; at Antietam, worst of all.

Is it likely that a commander who left everything to his subordinates, and seemed incapable of combined action, could have conceived a plan which would have necessitated a simultaneous movement which demanded the manipulation of another army besides his own, such as he subsequently claimed was the intention of the extension of his right, which led to the engagement at Hanover Court House. The public has a right to estimate a man by his employment or abuse of opportunities. From one exemplification of character, you may judge all, says the proverb.

* OTTO HEUSINGER, in his "*Amerikanische Kriegsbilder*," furnishes some curious facts in regard to the hasty flight of the rebels from Manassas, 10th–12th March, 1862. This author served four and a half years in a German Regiment, and belonged in 1861–'2 to BLENKER's Division, which took part in MCCLELLAN's military promenade through that March mud. At page 18, he says (11th March—*Annandale*): "Here the enemy had his farthest outposts" (nearest Washington). * * "Scattered muskets and camp-equipage, or utensils bore witness to the hasty withdrawal of the enemy." Page 19 (15th March, *Fairfax Court House*), "We found plenty of first-rate gaiters, which we appropriated." "The enemy at this time were perfectly supplied with every requisite." "The enemy had withdrawn very hastily from these fearful fortifications at Centreville and Manassas." Page 21, "No one could have desired a more comfortable soldiering than the Confederates enjoyed, as testified by their rough, but well-constructed log-houses and incalculable remains of food and camp utensils, broken bottles, &c." Pages 21–22, "Burned ties, or timbers, broken and bent rails lay on the route of the advancing column; likewise railroad locomotives amid a chaos of shattered cars, while the store-houses on the railroad, partially destroyed and surrounded by stove-in, half-filled barrels of pork and rice, were the best proof of the wild flight of the Confederates." "About 4 P. M. we passed Manassas, the strong bulwark of the enemy. This hamlet, consisting of ten houses, was extremely formidably fortified; its lofty bastions seemed almost beyond capture, and we could not comprehend the flight of the Confederates out of such strong entrenchments." PHIL. KEARNY, notwithstanding, did hurry them out in his peculiar way.

To believe that McClellan calculated on utilizing a junction with McDowell was to reverse the proverb, and conceive an act of energy exceptional to a whole career, characterized by almost timid caution. One remark further presents the most extraordinary phase: McClellan was always asking for very large reinforcements, and, notwithstanding some were furnished, could not be induced to move forward decidedly; and then, when he was ordered to withdraw from Harrison's Landing, he promised that if they would only give him an additional force, small in proportion to his previous demands, he would advance on Richmond at once.

The battle of Mechanicsville, 26th — a glorious success for Reynolds and Seymour, says Carleton,* who fought it alone, repulsing double their numbers — seemed to have stunned McClellan. On the 24th, he had planned an aggressive, which was apparently inaugurated in Oak Grove on the 25th. On the 26th, this aggressive had degenerated into a pure defensive. On that night he thought of nothing but retreat. The darkness of the ensuing nights of the 27th and 28th was lighted up by the bonfire of his stores. West Point went up in flames on the night of the 28th, and it might be said, that, by their light, he commenced the withdrawal of the heavy guns and baggage, and changed his base in a manner which bore all the features of a flight.

On Friday, 27th June, the attack upon our right was renewed in the battle of Cold Harbor, as it is styled by the rebels, or Gaines' Mills (Gaines' Farm, or Ellison's Mills), as it is better known to us. In this Kearny took no part. The victory was a formal one for the rebels, but was purchased at a fearful cost. This, the third of the Seven Days' Battles, was the first of those six, styled in error, seven days' contests which was actually fighting in RETREAT.

By six A. M., 28th June, the whole Union army was on the south side of the Chickahominy. So far from this concentration being a disadvantage, if McClellan, on that day, or the

* "The united efforts of the two Hills and General Branch were not sufficient to dislodge the two brigades which held the position. Griffin, Martindale and Meade were ready to lend assistance, but were not engaged. Griffin only fired a few shots." — "*Following the Flag*," 129.

ensuing one, 29th June, had struck at Richmond, the city must have fallen in five hours.

This retreat, of which so much has been made by McClellan's admirers, was one of the simplest of military problems.

McClellan was too slow and uncertain to project and execute any plan that would be in accordance with the first principles of war. On the 27th of June his grand army was still astride the Chickahominy, and Gaines' Mill was Fair Oaks over again, the attack being this time upon the half of the army on the north bank. As at Fair Oaks, utter rout and wide disaster was prevented only by the arrival, after sundown, of fresh brigades from the other side, and by the wing of that dusky angel that has saved so many a hard pressed army—Night. "Welcome night wrapped his shattered wrecks in its preserving darkness." Under its friendly cover, the wreck of the right wing moved across that fatal swamp, and the morning of the 28th found the whole army where it should have been one month before, on the Richmond side of the Chichahominy.

But, by this time, its commander had relinquished the offensive, and was aiming, not for success, but merely laboring to keep bad enough from becoming the worst possible. In the scenes that followed, McClellan had no division commander more effective, prompt or trustworthy for a critical moment than General Kearny.*

The army had only to fall back from fifteen to twenty-five miles through a country which favored the movement. The rebels

* "In noticing the bravery of all the generals that have taken part in the late battles on the Peninsula, one of the foremost in rank is General Kearny. Words are inadequate to express the daring and bravery of this general. He is always foremost in the fray; and many times was he observed with his bridle in his teeth, while his right arm (the only one he has), with a sword at the end of it, was cutting and slashing at a furious rate among groups of the enemy. The rebels styled him the "One-armed Devil;" and, after the battle of Williamsburg, I was told by rebel prisoners, during a conversation with them, and on the night of the fight, he was closely watched by them and their officers, and that some of their most accurate sharpshooters were ordered to draw a bead on that "one-armed devil there;" yet they could not see him fall. Finally, a rebel colonel ordered his entire regiment (according to their statement) to withdraw their fire from everything else and center it upon that officer with one arm; the order was obeyed, and the entire regiment (the 5th Carolina) belched forth a volley at the one-armed officer; but he was protected by a just cause and an All-seeing Eye above, and was not seen to fall from his saddle. Such men are too precious to their country, and in the eyes of their God, to fall by a rebel's bullet." — (*Newspaper Slip.*)

had greater difficulties to overcome than the Union forces. The former were absolutely inferior in numbers, and the latter had only to protect their rear and one flank, their left. If any question of the slightest magnitude required solution, it was the saving of the artillery and trains. There are plenty of examples of vastly superior perils overcome under immeasurably greater disadvantages. A curious parallel may be recalled, which occurred during the "Thirty Years' War," when, in August, 1623, CHRISTIAN OF BRUNSWICK, with an army composed almost entirely of raw recruits, "fought almost incessantly in retreat throughout three nights and two days, over nearly thirty miles of river and marsh-intersected country." Eight times the Brunswickers reformed their lines of battle under an artillery fire, whose multiplied discharges, maintained with unusual fierceness for the epoch, "made the earth tremble, and the old walls they sought to defend quiver and shake again." All this, too, in the face of a superior veteran army led by TILLY, the best general of the day. This prolonged contest is known as the Battle of Lohn, or Stadt-Lohn.

FREDERICK's retreat in the third campaign (that in 1758), of the Seven Years' War, after he had lost all his artillery at Hochkirch, is another notable example.

The retreat of MOREAU through the Black Forest, in 1796, very much lauded at the time; that, again, of Sir JOHN MOORE, which culminated in his victory of Corunna, in 1808, greatly admired by NAPIER; that of WELLINGTON, within the lines of Torres VIEDRAS, in 1810; that of MASSENA, out of Portugal, before Wellington, in 1811, were incomparably greater.*

How much more glorious, although in miniature, CLAUSEL's retreat from his repulse at Constantine in 1836.

On Saturday, 28th June, there was an affair at Golding's Farm, in which the rebels were repulsed with so much facility that they were actually deceived for a moment as to the reality of the withdrawal of the Union army.†

* A better simile, perhaps, is the Seven Days' Battles, in Retreat, of Freiburg, 3d–9th August, 1644, which progressed and terminated very much like our own "Summer Week of Fighting," 25th June to the 1st July, 1862; STONEWALL JACKSON representing the impetuous CONDE. — CUST's "*Lives of the Warriors*," 1611–1675, I. 13.

† General KEARNY crossed the swamp one mile higher than the usual road, at Brackett's Ford, and about sundown had secured all his trains and artillery; and, after

On "the battle Sunday," 29th June, an engagement took place at Savage Station. In this KEARNY took a prominent part.

On Monday, 30th June, occurred the battle of Frazier's Farm (or Nelson's Farm, or Glendale), or New Market Cross-Roads. This resulted in a victory for the Union forces. "The rebel troops became a mob, and fled in terror toward Richmond." A mournful wail was heard from Glendale during that long dis-

---

advancing in security a short distance, his scouts fell upon the enemy's pickets, and there commenced a very brisk firing in the woods in front. The reconnoissance made it certain that the Confederate forces were near us, and that an attempt to advance along the road would be hotly contested, and might bring on a general engagement. General KEARNY drew up his men in the order of battle until after night, and then, in the darkness, sought to join the other divisions of the army. I have often heard the men and officers of the army speak of that night's march in the gloomy forest, where nothing could be seen but the flash of the fire-fly. The uncertainty of the way, the near presence of the enemy, the thunder of the battle not far from them, made this a night long to be remembered, and the most thoughtless were impressed with sad anticipations of to-morrow. * * *

To guard against the success of such a demonstration (a flank movement), strong bodies of our troops were massed at important points on the several roads. On those leading from Richmond, General HEINTZELMAN, with the divisions of Generals HOOKER, KEARNY, SEDGWICK and McCALL, were placed. Our trains and the advancing troops were to pass over the road to Turkey Bend or Malvern Hill, called Quaker Road. This road cuts at right angles the various highways running from Richmond east, and therefore is the great highway to James river from Savage Station. Along this road all the artillery troops and wagons of the army had to pass. It was the plan of the enemy, as soon as they discovered the course we were taking, to cut in twain our army, and to drive back and capture such portion as could be severed from the main body.

FRANKLIN and SUMNER held the rear, SLOCUM was on the left, and HEINTZELMAN on the right. HOOKER occupied a position on the Quaker Road; to his right, McCALL, and again KEARNY *the extreme right.* Those various divisions were thrown into these positions to protect our army, seeking its new base, and to repel the efforts of the enemy to break through our lines—a catastrophe which would have been fatal to all that portion thus cut off from the main trunk. * * *

The conduct of General KEARNY in this battle was the admiration of all his corps. He was everywhere directing in all movements, imparting, by his presence and clear-sightedness, the most determined courage to his men. Wherever the danger was greatest, there he pressed and carried with him a personal power that was equal to a reinforcement. In a pre-eminent degree, he possessed that military prescience, or anticipation of what was coming, and the point of an enemy's attack, which has characterized every great man who has risen to distinction in the art of war. * * *

General HEINTZELMAN was commander of the third army corps, all the regiments of which were engaged in this battle. For him all the officers and men had the deepest respect. He was always cool, and in danger perfectly self-possessed. A man of great kindness of heart, considerate of his men, temperate, wisely discriminating and just. There was felt in him, as a soldier, the utmost confidence; without any of those knightly and brilliant qualities which made the names of HOOKER and KEARNY the synonyms of chivalry and daring, he was brave without rashness, and life-saving without imbecility, dignified in demeanor, yet easily approached, and the friend of every soldier. —Chaplain MARKS' "Peninsula Campaign," pages 273–283.

mal night, lit up by the red glare of torches flitting to and fro as the rebels gathered up their wounded. On this occasion, KEARNY held about the center of our line.

The night before Malvern, that is, during the fierce conflict of Glendale, says Major-General B——, KEARNY had one of those escapes which must have led him to suppose that he bore a charmed life, exactly the same as occurred to him on the eve of Solferino, and cost him his life in the gloaming of Chantilly. He rode out, supposing McCall's line was a prolongation of his own to the left; McCall had not brought his men up, and KEARNY dashed directly into a body of deployed troops, firing briskly. He perceived at once that the skirmishing was after a manner different from our own, and made up his mind that he was in the midst of the rebels. Just then an officer came up, mistaking him for a rebel general, and asked what he should do now. KEARNY, looking down at him severely, answered, "Do, Sir! do as I have always directed you to do in such a case, Sir!" turned and rode quietly away, expecting every moment that the mistake would be discovered, and that he would be shot.*

During the retreat, KEARNY had relieved another division, and assumed a position for the night. With the eye of a soldier and a general, he had posted his artillery and distributed their supports, and now surveyed the approaches and his dispositions with the calm satisfaction of one who felt himself the master of the situation. Remember that this was in the midst of the turmoil and difficulties of (and such) a retreat. After this survey, he turned to an officer near by and remarked: "If they (the

* The most wonderful stories are related of the brave KEARNY, who litterally bears the character of a "*Salamander*." He was to be seen with his one arm, and holding his bridle in his teeth, everywhere during the hotest of the fight. At one time he came very near being taken at *White Oak Swamp*. He was surrounded by no fewer than thirty of the rebels, but fairly cut his way through them — turned and asking if they thought "he looked the kind of man to fall into their hands?" The men all love him for his undaunted bravery, but complain a little of his forgetting that everybody is not made of cast-iron like himself.

General HEINTZELMAL performed his duty faithfully and honestly, while the commanders of the divisions of the corps (Generals KEARNY and HOOKER) have that place in the public estimation which they have earned by many gallant and heroic actions, and which renders it unnecessary for me to do aught, except pay this tribute to the memory of one and the rising fame of the other." – (*Newspaper Slips sent to Author.*)

rebels) can drive me out of this position, they can call me a Jersey ——." The concluding word was more forcible than orthodox. It was such speeches as these, indicating imperturbable self-reliance and faith in himself and men, that gave the troops courage and confidence in times of doubt and peril.

The reader must have remarked the testimony of General WAINWRIGHT in regard to KEARNY's self-possession and power of rapid, clear and conclusive thinking to the point under the heaviest and most stinging fire. In this imperturbable active-minded physical phlegm he was only surpassed by his own fiery, headlong activity when a change of circumstances demanded a complete substitution of antagonistic characteristics. Such a combination of qualities, however strange they may appear to ordinary readers, should not be so to military students. GUSTAVUS, TURENNE, TORSTENSON, SAXE, FREDERIC, ZIETHEN, SEYDLITZ, BLUCHER (these last three should be always named together),* MASSENA, SOULT, RADETZKI, all possessed an aggressive power which was only surpassed by their resistive might when the time called for the one or the other in the superlative degree. From the earliest times, all grand types of the Anglo-Saxon, the Teutonic, or, more properly speaking, the Theotiscan race, have proved their greatness by the display of an attack like the lightning, and a resistance like a cube of granite, which was one of the emblems of the great GUSTAVUS.

In the finest specimen of the Saxon, Harold, who succumbed to fate, slain, but not vanquished, at Hastings, there is a perfect exemplification of that fiery, nervous "forward" which is ascribed to the Celt, and that stubborn, fearless, *anchored*, or rooted, steadfastness which should render immortal the Dutch infantry of Fleurus† of Almanza, in fact, throughout King William III's wars; of the English infantry of Fontenoy down to Waterloo; and of the Prussian infantry, especially the Pomeranian, of FREDERIC. If we have a real portrait of HAROLD, and not an ideal one, in him the general reader could recognize

---

* BIESKE'S BLUCHER, iii–IV.

† ROUSSET'S "LOUVOIS" IV, 408, etc., worthy examination to learn what a good infantry, when true to itself, can achieve, even amid disaster.

KEARNY; HAROLD, so mighty in his onset, as at York victorious, so unshakable in his defense at Hastings, until an arrow through the head, shot at random, ended his glorious life, just as one bullet out of a volley set free the spirit of KEARNY at Chantilly.

But it was not only on the battle-field that KEARNY displayed the superiority of his mind. He was prophetic in his common sense, and in his prescience he always found a reason and a solution of what seemed, to lesser men, temerity.

During the *six days' retreat* and the SEVEN DAYS' FIGHTING, KEARNY seems to have been the only general whose foresight is demonstrated by recorded words; who perceived that the danger arose from moral feebleness in the direction which could be only met by extra exertion and provision on the part of the subordinates. Thus, he was always on the alert to make himself perfectly acquainted with the roads, so that, if our movements were checked or choked on one, his troops could be extricated on another, just as nature turns the current of the blood by anastomosis into a new channel, when the regular one is severed or closed by accident or violence. No one knew better than he the necessity of studying the topography of a country, since a battery on a commanding knoll, or a little wood well slashed, or a gulley with an abrupt bank wisely occupied and well defended, might stop the march of a victorious column. He also knew that his men must, in such a rapid retreat (unnecessary, as it turned out, as regarded the enemy, compulsory as regarded their general-in-chief), must carry with them and upon them the means to feed themselves and to feed the fight. Thus, when he fell back from his original position on the railroad, his last care was to see that each man of his division had upon him not only the regular quantity of ammunition, but one hundred extra cartridges per man stowed away upon his person. What was the result? KEARNY never was *driven*, and, when in the White Oak Swamp, everything depended upon a continuous, well-sustained, heavy fire, his lines were able to respond to the exigencies of the crisis, *not* out of their cartridge-boxes, *not* out of their ordinary supply, but *out of the extra quantity with which the prescience of* KEARNY *had loaded their pockets and their haversacks.* An officer of wonderfully tenacious memory, who was in HEINTZELMAN'S corps, says that nothing saved the Union army in the White Oak Swamp but those hundred rounds of cartridges per man, insisted upon and seen to by KEARNY.

Tuesday, 1st July, our "Boys in Blue" were drawn up on the pleasant estate of Dr. CARTER, known as Malvern Hill, and there the Army of the Potomac won a Hohenlinden victory which, under any other general, would have been improved, and resulted in the capture of Richmond. Here PORTER'S corps constituted the extreme left of our line, whose shape resembled that of a bill-hook. Next to PORTER'S came the division of COUCH, then KEARNY, then HOOKER; to the right of these, SUMNER'S corps, then SMITH, then SLOCUM.

The posting of our troops on that day was intrusted to one, of whom a friend — who served under him for many years — writes thus, confirming the report of every one who knew him: "General A. A. HUMPHREYS was once Assistant in charge of the Coast Survey office, and his survey and report of the Mississippi river placed him, scientifically, at the apex of his corps and of the army, and, strange to say, after he got command of a fighting column, his courage and energy were equal to his mental attainments."

The following is worthy of incorporation, as the facts are from the pen of one who greatly admired KEARNY, and spoke of him in the warmest terms — more particularly as it furnishes a complete account of the posting of our troops at Malvern Hill:

General A. A. HUMPHREYS* posted the army at Malvern, with the exception of PORTER'S corps (the Fifth), and COUCH'S division of the Third Corps, which were already in position when he arrived on the ground. The Head-Quarters of the army were at Haxall's Landing. About two o'clock A. M., General McCLELLAN sent for General HUMPHREYS, to inform him that SUMNER'S and HEINTZELMAN'S corps were at Malvern, but not in position — (FRANKLIN, an hour or so later, came in toward Haxall's with his corps; KEYES' corps was already there) — and requested HUMPHREYS to proceed thither at daylight, and post the troops

* See Maj.-Gen. BARNARD'S "*Peninsula Campaign*," Note 21, page 91.

as massively as he could. General HUMPHREYS had been over Malvern the day before, and over the ground to the right of it. This he did, sending up some of KEYES' troops that he found coming toward Haxall's. He saw General PORTER, and, accompanied by General HUNT, commanding the Artillery Reserve of the Army, rode at once to COUCH'S Division, on the right of the Fifth Corps. The Fifth Corps was well posted; whether trenched or not was not observed. Then HUMPHREYS saw General COUCH, and discussed with him the position as they rode over the ground. Some part of COUCH'S ground was slightly trenched.

At his right, extending down toward the enemy a considerable distance, was a thick grove. This HUMPHREYS endeavored to have slashed, as he believed the enemy would use it as a cover in attack, which they did. The force he sent for, to have it slashed, was otherwise occupied, and, as the next best thing, the woods were occupied by COUCH as well as it could be. From COUCH'S position, he rode along the ground and selected the position for HEINTZELMAN'S and SUMNER'S Corps to occupy. By this remark, it is not intended to convey the idea that he went into the details of the ground; that, of course, was left to the commanders of troops. He sent the directions by aids to KEARNY and HOOKER, as HEINTZELMAN was not on the ground, but had gone to see General MCCLELLAN, as had also SUMNER. It would appear that neither HEINTZELMAN'S nor SUMNER'S ground was trenched, except a small part of the right of the latter. General BARNARD joined General HUMPHREYS in the course of the ride, and went over that part of the ground with him which KEARNY'S and HOOKER'S Divisions occupied. They parted, and General BARNARD joined General MCCLELLAN about half-past eight A. M., as General MCCLELLAN rode through the ground which KEARNY afterward occupied. General BARNARD continued with General MCCLELLAN to the Head-Quarters camp; and General HUMPHREYS, with General HUNT, continued selecting the ground for the line of battle, advising with HUNT for the artillery positions.

They finally reached a point where it was necessary to descend from the hill of Malvern, where the position or country was open, and enter low wooded ground. Here General HUNT left General HUMPHREYS, and returned to his Reserve Artillery; and the latter sent word to PORTER, or SUMNER, or to the latter's division commanders, designating the ground they were to occupy. General McCLELLAN passed General HUMPHREYS on the hill, at the distance of two hundred or three hundred yards, so that he did not speak to him. He appeared to be conversing at one time with SUMNER and HEINTZELMAN about the ground, as they stopped and pointed in different directions. It was not until General HUMPHREYS had reached the vicinity of Haxall's that he had determined what grounds ought to be occupied between Malvern and the river. At Haxall's he saw General McCLELLAN, told him what he had done, and what he proposed to do. He also saw General FRANKLIN, and had some conversation as to how his corps should be posted; then passed to the corps, and saw General W. F. SMITH; pointed out a mill-dam where his right could rest, and gave him the compass direction by which to extend to his left through low wooded ground so as to unite with the troops on the hill; General SLOCUM's left (if memory serves) joined SMITH's right, and the latter division closed in on the river, on the extreme Union right. PECK's division, of KEYES' Corps, supported on the right. He then rode rapidly up to Malvern, the artillery fire having begun, and went to see about connecting SMITH's troops with SUMNER's. With some difficulty he (HUMPHREYS) got SUMNER (after taking him over the ground) to extend his right to meet SMITH. HUMPHREYS rode with SUMNER's *extending troops, and, as they entered a field on one side from the woods*, SMITH'S *troops entered it on the other, from the same woods, the two lines of troops being as exactly identical in direction as if they had been moving on a line marked out by instruments.* HUMPHREYS had not ridden over the line before, though he had examined the ground in the vicinity closely.

The exact coincidence was, of course, accidental, but it was somewhat remarkable.* Now, all the line through this wooded

* Such remarkable accuracy of direction and time constitutes, it is said, the chief excellence of the Prussian Infantry. Precision and punctuality were the principal causes of the success of the followers of the Black Eagle during the "Seven Weeks'

ground, from the brow of the hill to the right, on the river, was trenched, and near the river the ground was open, and SLOCUM's front was, probably, not at all trenched, or not entirely. HUMPHREYS did not give it his attention, but sent Major DUANE, of the Engineers, with his battalion, to slash in front of the mill-pond on SMITH's right, as a main road, entered at this point from the crossing of White-Oak-Swamp-Creek, the road by which FRANKLIN's troops came in. Having completed the line, HUMPHREYS returned to Malvern Hill, where the cannonading was going on, but no infantry fire had as yet begun. He remained on the fronts of HEINTZELMAN and SUMNER during the greater part of the rest of the day, as there were indications of an attack on SUMNER's right and SMITH's left, a weak part of the line. Near this weak position, however, stood three of the hardest fighting men of the army, a trio, known as "Fighting PHIL," "Fighting JOE" and "Fighting DAN," lions at bay, the first since "dead on the field of honor;" the second, afterward severely wounded, holding his ground under a like desperate attack at Antietam; the third losing his leg, a year and a day subsequently, stemming the fearful onset of LONGSTREET and saving the position at Gettysburg. When the infantry fire began to be sharp, or rather when the skirmishing began to be heavy, on COUCH's front, he concluded that the battle was about to begin in earnest. This was about three and a half or four, not later than four and a half P. M. From certain indications during the morning, he inferred that the fight would not begin until the afternoon, and had so expressed himself to General McCLELLAN, to whom HUMPHREYS now sent a brief dispatch, stating that he believed the fight was about commencing in earnest, and rode to PORTER's position to meet him. McCLELLAN came up there shortly afterward, receiv-

War" in 1866. Brev. Brig.-Gen. W. P. W——, who commanded the 76th N. Y. V. in 1862–3, and studied his profession as a soldier in Prussia, often related his astonishment at the precision of the movements during the grand military manœuvres around Berlin. He said that he believed that, if a Prussian line of battle encountered an obstacle in their advance, and had to break to pass it, although the two wings continued on, separated and out of sight of each other for the distance of a mile, they would come together with as much accuracy as if the line had remained unbroken, with the flanks in contact throughout the whole interval. This (if remembrance is correct) shows the reliability of the Prussian drill.

ing his note just before reaching that point where COUCH had his fight.

On the 1st July, at Malvern Hill, the Army of the Potomac won a Hohenlinden victory. This furious conflict, so destructive to the assailants, did not cease until about nine P. M., having lasted over five hours after it grew into the magnitude of a grand battle. The rebels were finally "driven to the shelter of ravines, and woods, and swamps, utterly broken and despairing."

The worst of the story now remains to be told. After the Army of the Potomac had won such a victory, and the exulting troops looked forward to harvesting the fruits of their bloody toils, orders were given to retreat to Harrison's Landing. Then, and not till then, the bonds of discipline seemed to be unloosed, and a disorderly rush ensued, which justified the remark that, "in the storm and darkness, the Union Army fled from a victory as though it had been a rout." *

That night a circumstance occurred which recalled an incident connected with the defeat of the French army at Oudenarde, in 1708. PRINCE EUGENE says: "The darkness of the night prevented our pursuit, and enabled me to execute a scheme for increasing the number of our prisoners. I sent out drummers in different directions, with orders to beat the retreat after the French manner, and posted my French Refugee officers, with directions to shout on all sides: — *Here Picardy! Here Champagne! Here Piedmont!* The French soldiers flocked in, and

---

* "On the evening of Saturday, the 24th November, the King (James II) called a council of war" (in his camp at Salisbury, when in the presence of the PRINCE OF ORANGE and the tenure of the English crown depended on the result, just as the fate of Richmond hung on McClellan's decision on the eve of Malvern). "FEVERSHAM, the Royal Commander-in-Chief, expressed his opinion that it was expedient for his Majesty to fall back. DUNDEE earnestly upheld a contrary opinion, and entreated JAMES to allow him to march at once and attack the PRINCE OF ORANGE.

"Then out spoke gallant Claverhouse,
And his soul thrill'd wild and high,
And he show'd the King his subjects,
And he pray'd him not to fly."

The King decided for a retreat. The camp broke up at Salisbury, with all the confusion of a flight." The result was, JAMES lost his throne, and WILLIAM, Prince of Orange, became King of England.—General Hon. SIR EDWARD CUST'S "*Lives of the Warriors*," 2d Series, vol. I, page 239.

I made a good harvest of them; we took in all about seven thousand." *

In our own case, after Malvern, the troops were intermingled to such a degree that an eye witness, an officer of HOOKER's division, states that corps, division, brigade and regimental staff officers were stationed at certain points to disentangle the snarled skein and reassemble under their proper commanders, in designated localities, the armed and uniformed flood which was flowing multitudinously and incoherently to shelter itself under the broadsides of the gunboats.†

* As to condition of roads and line of retreat, "*one narrow pass*" (Major W—— B——'s gate), etc., see SUMNER's Testimony; "*Report of Committee on the Conduct of the War*," part 1, 1,365; Compare GREELEY II, 167, Text and Notes; Prof. JOHN WILLIAM DRAPER's "*Civil War in America*," II. 414 and 415, quoting very strong language from the "*Report of the Committee on the Conduct of the War;*" BLAKE's "*Three Years in the Army*," 113, etc.; – DE TROBRIAND, 1,276, says well: "There (on Harrison's Plantation) the Army rallied itself like a *shipwrecked crew;* this army which had accomplished its own salvation of itself and despite of every obstacle;" Chaplain MARK's "*Peninsula Campaign*," 294; Chaplain CUDWORTH's "*First Massachusetts*," 233; HARPER's "*History of the Great Rebellion*," 377 (1), etc.; COOKE's "STONEWALL JACKSON, a *Military Biography*," 257, etc.; Major-General BARNARD's "*Peninsular Campaign*," Note 22 (to page 47), page 97, ¶ 3, etc., etc.

† "The great battle of Malvern Hill was fought just to the right of us, and I can safely say that I have never yet heard any thing like the thunder of the artillery on that day; it was one long, incessant roll; *when we left the place, the regiments were leaving in a panic; wagons, sick and wounded, artillery, all in one jumble.* 'Colonel HIRAM' (DURYEA) *would not take us into such a disorganized mass, and we waited for the road to clear; he said he would rather face the whole Southern Confederacy than take his regiment into that rabble:* and he backed his word by marching us down the road toward the rebel position, and there we were obliged to stay until the road was clear enough to march on and keep our order. We experienced that day the hardest marching we have yet seen; in mud knee deep, fording streams to our middle, raining in torrents, and no place to sit down, unless we could sit in slush a foot deep; and, to add to our misfortunes, there was a hard slippery bottom under the layer of slush, which made it as difficult to walk as if we were on ice, and we were continually falling down. Everybody and everything was wet through, and all tired out and half dead with the continued fatigue we had gone through."—Soldiers' Letters, edited by LYDIA MINTURN POST, pages 145, 146.

"The battle was followed by a dark and stormy night, hiding the agony of thousands who lay on the blood-stained slopes of Malvern Hill, and in the copses and woodlands beyond. The rain came down in torrents. Neither Jackson, nor Longstreet, nor A. P. Hill, had taken part in this attack. It was made by D. H. Hill and Magruder. Some of their men slept through the tempestuous night within one hundred yards of the national batteries. With inexpressible astonishment, when day broke, they cast their eyes on the hill from which they had been so fearfully repulsed. Their enemy had vanished—the volcano was silent. Among the Confederates, everything was in the most dreadful confusion. One of their Generals says: "The next morning by dawn I went to ask for orders, when I found the whole army in the utmost disorder; thousands of straggling men were asking every passer-by for their regiments; ambulances, wagons

"On the fleeing columns of the enemy," is the language of Chaplain MARKS, "our batteries and gunboats continued to fire until ten o'clock at night, throwing the shells into the forest; for hours not a gun replied, and not even a courier dared to show himself in the open field.

---

and artillery obstructing every road, and all together in a drenching rain presenting a scene of the most woeful and heart-rending confusion."

"Seventh Day, Wednesday, July 2d.—The retreat to Harrison's Landing, not even in the awful night that followed this awful battle, was not allotted to the national army. In less than two hours after the roar of the conflict had ceased, orders were given to resume the retreat and march to Harrison's Landing. *At midnight the utterly exhausted soldiers were groping their staggering way, along a road described as desperate, in all the confusion of a fleeing and routed army.* There was but one narrow pass through which the army could retreat, and, though the distance was only seven miles, it was not until the middle of the next day that Harrison's Landing was reached. The mud was actually ankle deep all over the ground. The last of the wagons did not reach the selected site until after dark on the 3d of July. The rear guard then moved into their camp, and everything was secure. The paralyzed Confederates made a feeble pursuit, and, on the 8th, went back to Richmond. Not without profound reluctance was the order to continue the retreat to Harrison's Landing obeyed. General KEARNY, than whom there was not a more noble soldier in the whole army, exclaimed, in a group of indignant officers: "I, PHILIP KEARNY, an old soldier, enter my solemn protest against this order to retreat. We ought, instead of retreating, to follow up the enemy and take Richmond. And, in full view of all the responsibility of such a declaration, I say to you all that such an order can only be prompted by cowardice or treason." The French princes left the army early the next morning; its condition was to all appearances desperate. They went on board a steamer, and soon after departed for the north. The Committee of Congress on the Conduct of the War, referring to these events, declare "The retreat of the army from Malvern to Harrison's Bar was very precipitate. The troops, upon their arrival there, were huddled together in great confusion, the entire army being collected within a space of about three miles along the river. No orders were given the first day for occupying the heights which commanded the position, nor were troops so placed as to be able to resist an attack in force by the enemy, and nothing but a heavy rain, thereby preventing the enemy from bringing up their artillery, saved the army from destruction." There had been sent to the Peninsula about one hundred and sixty thousand men (159,500). On the 3d of July, after this great army had reached the protection of the gunboats at Harrison's Landing, MCCLELLAN telegraphed to the Secretary of War, that he presumed he had not "over 50,000 men left with their colors." Hereupon President LINCOLN (July 7th) went to Harrison's Landing, and found that there were about 86,000 men there. * * * Thus ended the great, the ill-starred, the melancholy Peninsula expedition. It had no presiding genius, no controlling mind. There was an incredible sluggishness in the advance; it actually gave the Confederates time to pass their Conscription Law and bring their conscripts into the field. The magnificent army, which had been organized with so much pageantry at Washington, and moved down Chesapeake Bay with so much pomp, had sickened in the dismal trenches of Yorktown, and left thousands upon thousands in the dark glades and gloomy marshes of the blood-stained Chickahominy. It is the testimony of the corps commanders that they were left as best they might to conduct the fatal retreat. The General was importunately demanding of the government more troops, never using all that he had. Countless millions of money had been wasted; tens of thousands of men had been destroyed. From the inception of the campaign to its end, military audacity was pitted against military timidity, promptness

"The battle was over, but the cannonading still continued, and shells and balls of every kind tore through the woods in a ceaseless whirlwind of fury. In the mean time, thousands of Confederates fled in the wildest disorder from the scene, and hid themselves in swamps and hollows; soldiers without guns, horsemen without caps and swords, came to the hospitals in the battle field of Glendale, 'two and a half miles from Malvern,' and reported that 'their regiments and brigades were swept away, and that they alone were escaped to tell the tale.' It is one of the strangest things, in this week of disasters, that General McClellan ordered a retreat to Harrison's Landing, six miles down the James river, after we had gained so decided a victory. When this order was received by the impatient and eager

---

against procrastination, and the result could not be other than it was. The Confederates at Centreville, in inferior numbers, and in contemptible works, held McClellan at bay. They did the same at Yorktown, though he had much more than ten times their strength.—Prof. Draper's "*Civil War in America*," vol. II, page 413, etc.

"The country in the vicinity of Harrison's Landing has been aptly termed the "Eden of Virginia;" but, when the army of McClellan gathered itself together the morning after the terrible battle of Malvern Hill, and moved toward the Landing, the ripening fields of wheat and corn, in all their golden luxuriance, were trampled under foot, and the beautiful picture of plenty and peace passed like a mirage from the view, and, before the night of that day, the scene that presented itself defies description. It was a desolate sight to behold the remnant of that once splendid Army of the Potomac huddled together under the pelting storm, without shelter, without food, knee-deep in mud, weary and exhausted, vainly seeking a dry spot whereon to stretch their sore and tired limbs. In spite of the discomforts of that day, one could scarce forbear smiling as he beheld the soldiers plodding their way through the mud. A step, and down they would go, leaving shoes and boots behind them with placid resignation, knowing that it was useless to struggle, and finally sinking from sheer exhaustion. Millions' worth of property was destroyed upon the route. In the fields, wagons and commissary stores of all kinds were piled together and burned, to prevent them from falling into the hands of the enemy. Barrels of sugar, coffee, pork, rice, beans, and boxes of bread, were recklessly flung into the road, or piled in masses and set fire to. Public and private stores shared the same fate. The luxuries of the general were flung into the same blaze that consumed the coarse necessaries of the soldier; no distinctions were made; destruction was the order of the day, and everything that could not be transported was given over to the destroying element.

When the soldiers witnessed this dire destruction, they could no longer doubt the magnitude of their misfortune. Those burning piles were significant of defeat, and they turned their eyes, sad and dispirited, in the direction of the Landing, where were gathered the transports that were soon, they supposed, to take them from the scenes of their great disasters.

The rebel army were, however, in a far worse condition than ourselves. They were actually starving, and, fortunately for us, in the language of the Prussian officer, Colonel Estvan, "they had no army with which to pursue us." Officers of every grade were down at the Landing, having no commands, and waiting for an opportunity to get aboard the transports.—McNamara's "*Irish Ninth Massachusetts*," vol. I, page 109, etc.

army, consternation and amazement overwhelmed our patriotic and ardent host. Some refused to obey the command. General MARTINDALE shed tears of shame. Even (GREELEY 11, 167, [43]) FITZ JOHN PORTER's devotion to his chief was temporarily shaken by this order, which elicited his most indignant protest."

After the final clinch on the bloody slope of Malvern Hill, when the enemy recoiled, bleeding and crushed, from the unbroken and defiant Union line, KEARNY felt, through every fibre of his spirit, that a swift advance would have crushed the exhausted rebel force, and, by the seizure of its capital, dealt the Rebel Government a death blow. The failure to seize any of these opportunities extorted from "the brave and chivalrous KEARNY" the memorable words attributed to him in more than one popular history, which were uttered in the presence of several officers: "I, PHILIP KEARNY, an old soldier, enter my solemn protest against this order for retreat. We ought, instead of retreating, to follow up the enemy and take Richmond; and, in full view of all the responsibility of such a declaration, I say to you all, such an order can only be prompted by cowardice or treason." *

And, with all, hopelessness and despair succeeded the flush of triumph. In silence and gloom our victorious army commenced retiring from an enemy utterly broken, scattered and panic stricken.

And, when there was not a foe within miles of us, we left our wounded behind to perish, and any one witnessing the wild eagerness of our retreat would have supposed that we were in the greatest peril from a vigilant and triumphant enemy.

Up to the time when this chapter was actually in hand, many seriously doubted if that excellent man, Chaplain MARKS, had recorded the exact language used by KEARNY, and the writer, in a previous brief biography of KEARNY, expressed the following opinion:† "During the remainder of that ill-starred and mis-

* [LOSSING II, 435 (2); quoting GREELEY II, 167 (43, 45); Dr. MARKS' Peninsula Campaign, 294; GUROWSKI, 1, 236–8; SYPHER's Pennsylvania Reserves, 305–6.]

† If any reader believes that the author is actuated by any prejudice against McCLELLAN, he does the author injustice. The opinions herein expressed are founded on careful examination and comparison of facts. McCLELLAN was not up to his part in the work in hand, just as SAINT ARNAUD was wanting if KINGSLAKE is correct after the

managed campaign (2d–25th June), General KEARNY did his duty, and more than his duty, on all occasions; but his spirit was fettered, and his hopes damped, by a growing disbelief, at first in the capacity, and at length in the loyalty, of the commanding general. By loyalty, KEARNY could not have intended to convey the idea that McCLELLAN was false to the Union; for, if he had done so, he would have been found, like too many others, in the ranks of the rebels in the field, or their abettors at home; nor could he, as he is reputed (erroneously, I believe), to have in any way reflected on the personal courage of his commander; but, as an officer remarked, on reading the charge reported by MARKS and SYPHER, and quoted elsewhere, he did not seem morally brave enough to 'go in' like GRANT, and SHERMAN, and THOMAS, and ROSECRANS, and SHERIDAN, and 'fight the thing out' then and there, being deluded with the idea of the possibility of conciliating the rebels. He was, too, infected with the genius of what NAPOLEON styled *mezzo-termine* (half measures), by FREDERIC, 'haggling' to fight and drive them to the wall, which was the only fighting susceptible, then or ever, of securing speedy and assured victory."

Since then, however, an officer of high rank in the regular army stated he was by at the time, and that KEARNY made use of the same language attributed to him by Chaplain MARKS. When the order was brought to KEARNY, he became so excited that "he went on like a wild man" at the idea of a victorious

Alma (*Invasion of the Crimea*, II. 32, 40, 44, etc.; Major-General (B. A.) GEORGE BELL'S "*Rough Notes of an Old Soldier*," II, 183–184, etc.); or the Archduke CHARLES after Aspern: or CHARLES ALBERT after his successes at the opening of the Campaign of 1848 in Italy; or the Carlist General GOMEZ when he forebore to enter Madrid, in 1837 (HENDERSON'S "*Soldier of Three Queens*," VI. 42); or any other general — and there have been hundreds equally guilty — who let "I dare not wait upon, I would." (Compare KINGSLAKE II. 156; TODLEBEN I. 257; KINGSLAKE II. 173–189, etc.) The successful generals of history are those who wooed Fortune as the experienced Lovelace skilled in the wiles and daring of conquest, and by audacity and even pitiless aggression convert defeat — as did SANTA ANNA his crowning victory over the Spaniards — into victory. It is not physical courage that wins the great prizes of glory, but that moral power (KINGSLAKE II. 587), which by marvelous triumphs over physical prostration, by omnipotent will and skill, like the fearless surgeon, cut to within a hairbreadth of deadly peril and wrest life and the future, as it were, from death. (KINGSLAKE II. 413.) The over-cautious operater deals like McCLELLAN; the responsibility-assuming MOTT or CARNOCHAN, like KEARNY, THOMAS, GRANT, SHERIDAN, BLUCHER, SEYDLITZ, FREDERIC and other godlike parallels, examples or imitators.

army abandoning the field to a flying foe, and, in spite of every effort to restrain him, he gave vent to his indignation in sentences, of which the one quoted was the most severe. Reference to his letters would lead to the just conclusion that KEARNY never meant cowardice, as it is generally understood, but that mental quality which ruined Archduke CHARLES, and often springs from a mistaken view of policy or unwillingness to assume responsibility. Those who object to the forcible elocution of passion, excited by wrong, not to self, but to country, should recollect that even the cold temper of WASHINGTON was roused to violent invective by the conduct of LEE at Monmouth.

The following order shows KEARNY did not think *himself* beaten:

HEADQUARTERS, THIRD DIVISION, THIRD CORPS,
CAMP NEAR HARRISON'S LANDING, July 7th, 1862.

GENERAL ORDERS No. 27.—Brave comrades, as one of your generals, who has shared in your perils, so I sympathize in your cheers for victory when I pass. The name of this division is marked. Southern records are full of you. In attack you have driven them; when assailed you have repulsed them. Be it so to the end. New regiments: we give you a name; engraft on it fresh laurels.

Comrades in battle, let our greeting be a cry of defiance to our foe; after the fight, one greeting of victory for ourselves. This done, remember that, like yourselves, I have my duties of labor, in which I must move unobserved, as a true brother in hand and heart of this our Warrior Division family. Success attend you.

Few officers had more skill than General KEARNY in developing high *esprit de corps* among men, so that every one in his command felt the honor of the division to be a personal trust committed to him. At first, his men wore a red patch; afterward, a device in the form of a Greek cross, called the KEARNY cross. Such was the spirit, pride and discipline of his troops, that a KEARNY cross became a sign of good character and a badge of honor, and every wearer of it seemed imbued with the spirit of their general's motto:

"DULCE ET DECORUM EST PRO PATRIA MORI."

HEADQUARTERS THIRD DIVISION, THIRD CORPS,
July 6, 1862.

SIR—I have the honor to report, in continuation, that, at the close of the battle on the New Market Road (Glendale Nelson's Farm, or Frazier's farm, 30th June), our men remained in position until midnight, when orders were brought from General HEINTZEL-

MAN to effect a retreat, as General FRANKLIN had already abandoned his position. This move was again effected quietly and rapidly, but at some sacrifice from the want of transportation. By dawn we were in a new and strong position.

It was toward noon when the battle was again renewed.

THE BATTLE OF MALVERN HILLS.

In this battle, while all our regiments were on the alert and under artillery fire, and all, more or less, lost from the enemy's shelling and grape-shot, none but our artillery and skirmishers were immediately engaged. Captain THOMPSON managed his battery with the full genius of that arm, while Captain RANDOLPH, with his Parrot guns, persecuted all that attacked him, silencing, several times, batteries that were sweeping our front, or covering their columns of attack on General COUCH to our left. The Fourth Maine particularly distinguished itself for its coolness in holding the ravine in our front, and daringly engaged the skirmishers of the enemy's attacking columns. Their loss was considerable.

The brigades of Generals ROBINSON and BERRY were principally in reserve, but were constantly sent forward in support as the battle swerved to and fro on our left. The first line was held by General BIRNEY with coolness and firmness, and the regiments, even under fire, erected for themselves well-arranged rifle-pits. Had the next day witnessed a renewal of the battle, success was sure.

Our loss has been nine hundred and fifty-one in the several engagements.

It was at midnight that we were again called on to move in retreat, and, tired as were all our command, it was again executed with much regularity, and we arrived by ten A. M. (2d) at Harrison's Landing.

I am, Sir, very respectfully,
Your obedient servant,
(Signed) P. KEARNY,
Brigadier-General Commanding Division.

To Captain C. MCKEEVER,
Assistant Adjutant-General, Third Corps.

CONSOLIDATED TABULAR STATEMENT OF THE KILLED, WOUNDED AND MISSING IN THE THIRD (KEARNY'S) DIVISION, THIRD CORPS, SINCE THE BATTLE OF FAIR OAKS, MAY 31, 1862.

COMMAND.	OFFICERS.				MEN.				Aggregate.
	Killed.	Wounded.	Missing.	Total.	Killed.	Wounded.	Missing.	Total.	
Co. G, 2d U. S. Artillery	......	......	......	......	1	13	2	16	16
Co. E, 1st R. I. "	......	......	......	......	1	3	3	7	7
1st Brigade (ROBINSON'S)									
57th Pennsylvania Volunteers	1	2	......	3	8	38	12	58	61
63d " "	2	5	......	7	12	74	23	109	116
105th " "	......	2	......	2	8	56	67	131	133
87th New York "	......	......	......	......	7	34	34	75	75
20th Indiana "	1	2	2	6	15	80	77	172	178
2d Brigade (BIRNEY'S)	......	1	......	1	......	......	......	......	1
38th New York Volunteers	......	......	......	......	......	4	24	28	28
40th " "	......	......	......	......	4	24	51	79	79
101st " "	......	......	......	......	5	15	27	47	47
3d Maine "	......	......	......	......	1	5	22	28	28
4th " "	......	1	......	1	1	8	23	32	33
3d Brigade (BERRY'S)									
2d Michigan Volunteers	......	......	......	......	2	24	18	44	44
3d " "	......	......	......	......	1	8	31	40	40
5th " "	1	5	......	6	1	29	20	50	56
1st New York "	3	5	......	8	28	118	53	199	207
37th " "	......	......	......	......	1	40	48	89	89
Total	8	24	2	34	96	573	535	1204	1238

(Signed) P. KEARNY,
Brigadier-General Commanding Third Corps, Third Division.

MEMORANDUM OF LOSS IN THE LATE BATTLES — SINCE JUNE 26TH, 1862 — IN KEARNY'S DIVISION.

PRESENT EFFECTIVE.	Officers.	Enlisted Men.	KILLED.		WOUNDED		MISSING.	
			Officers.	Enlisted Men.	Officers.	Enlisted Men.	Officers.	Enlisted Men.
1st Brigade	73	1644	4	29	8	213	1	82
2d "	117	2253	....	7	2	43	....	184
3d "	84	2124	3	33	10	197	....	167
Co. G, 2d U. S. Artillery	4	96	....	1	....	13	....	2
Co. E, 1st Rhode Island Artillery	5	125	....	1	....	3	....	3
Total	283	6242	7	71	20	469	1	438

The missing include many killed and wounded.

(Signed) P. KEARNY,

July 5th. *Brigadier-General Commanding Division.*

HEADQUARTERS, THIRD DIVISION, THIRD CORPS,
July 6, 1862.

CONSOLIDATED REPORT OF KILLED, WOUNDED AND MISSING, IN ENGAGEMENTS OF JUNE 30TH AND JULY 1ST, 1862.

	OFFICERS.			ENLISTED MEN.				
	Killed.	Wounded.	Total.	Killed.	Wounded.	Missing.	Total.	Aggregate
Co. G, U. S. Artillery	......	......	......	1	13	2	16	16
Co. I [E?], 1st Rhode Island Artillery	......	......	......	1	3	3	7	7
1ST BRIGADE.								
57th Pennsylvania Volunteers	1	2	3	8	38	10	56	59
63d " "	1	6	7	10	89	23	122	129
105th " "	......	......	......	10	56	25	91	91
87th New York "	......	......	......	1	2	....	3	3
20th Indiana "	2	......	2	......	28	22	50	52
2D BRIGADE.								
38th New York Volunteers	......	......	......	......	4	33	37	37
40th " "	......	......	......	3	18	38	59	59
3d Maine "	......	......	......	1	6	27	34	34
4th " "	......	1	1	1	6	21	28	29
101st New York "	......	......	......	2	10	13	25	25
3D BRIGADE.								
37th New York Volunteers	......	......	......	......	39	39	78	78
2d Michigan "	......	......	......	2	12	....	14	14
3d " "	......	......	......	1	3	28	32	32
5th " "	1	5	6	2	27	21	50	56
1st New York "	2	6	7	28	116	79	223	230
Total	7	19	26	71	470	384	925	951

HEADQUARTERS, THIRD DIVISION, THIRD CORPS,
HARRISON'S LANDING, July 6, 1862.

SIR — I have the honor to report as follows on the moves and battle of the last week :

On the twenty-eighth of June, at midnight, I received orders to prepare to retire from Fair Oaks. This was executed at six A. M., regularly and without annoyance, the enemy appearing with distrust as we left, without pressure. My division then took up its position in the very strongly fortified camp near Savage's. In the afternoon we received orders again to retire across the White Oak Swamp. This I executed by the back (the Mill) road. Some artillery and my Twentieth Indiana Marksmen held this place for several hours, after the retreat commenced, and manned the works on the right of the road, for the purpose of preventing the enemy from hurrying us. Colonel BROWN, Twentieth Indiana Volunteers, greatly distinguished himself. His regiment lost some killed and wounded, as the enemy shelled the works toward the last, and parties of his advance and our rear guard became engaged.

Fearing lest the roads to the White Oak Swamp bridge and Beckett's Ford might be unduly clogged with troops, I proposed crossing at Jordan's Ford, three miles below my camp. I had reconnoitered it in the morning, and found that the enemy was in force on the Central road, but not on the Charles City road, and did not then seem to be on the lookout. General ROBINSON was to cover my retreat, and was cautioned against the enemy's troops arriving from across the Williamsburg road. General BIRNEY, with his brigade, was to lead the march; General BERRY to follow.

It was found, after crossing the double arm of the Swamp at Jordan, that our moves had been expected, and it being problematical whether the relative position of the lines of retreat justified a full engagement, after a successful skirmish of the advanced pickets; and, on learning that the road to Brackett's was then free, I withdrew the troops and proceeded by that ford. General BERRY's brigade, however, finding Fisher's Ford unobstructed, passed by that route.

This same night, by ten P. M., the whole division was encamped on and near the Charles City road, at a point subsequently during the battle occupied by General SLOCUM.

In the morning of the 30th June I drew up in a very strong position on the Charles City road. Subsequently, I was assigned to guard the New Market road and country thence to the Charles City road, a space of near two and a half miles.

In taking up my line of battle, General ROBINSON, with the First Brigade, was posted on the left; his left on the New Market road supporting THOMPSON's Battery. General BIRNEY divided the distance with him to the Charles City road. General BERRY was in reserve. General SLOCUM was to the right of my line of battle; General McCALL to its left.

The enemy's attack commenced on General McCALL at about two P. M.; at about three P. M. it seemed to be fully developed; but, as I rode over to visit it, it did not seem to me to be unduly threatening, further than from the shape of his line—its left greatly refused—it had disadvantages for myself, although advantages for those to whom the enemy must present its flank in making an attack on him.

At four P. M. the attack commenced on my line, with a determination and vigor, and in such masses, as I had never witnessed. THOMPSON's battery, directed with great skill, literally swept the slightly falling open space with the completest execution, and mowing them down by ranks, would cause the survivors a momentary halt; but almost instantly after increased masses came up, and the wave bore on. These masses coming up with a rapid run, covering the entire breadth of the open ground, some two hundred paces, would alone be checked in their career by the gaps of the fallen. Still no retreat; and again a fresh mass would carry on the approaching line still nearer. If there was one man in this attack, there must have been ten thousand; and their loss by artillery, although borne with such fortitude, must have been unusal. It was by scores. With the irrepressibility of numbers, on they persisted. The artillery, destructive as it was, ceased to be a calculation. It was then that Colonel HAYS, with the Sixty-third Pennsylvania* and half the Thirty-seventh New York Volunteers, was moved forward to the line of the guns.

---

* General KEARNY uniformly spoke of the conduct of the Sixty-third Pennsylvania at Glendale in terms of the highest praise. He returned to the regiment his thanks for their glorious deeds on that day. It was detailed to support THOMPSON's battery, the men lying on their faces in front of the guns. Four several times the Confederates came out of their forests and charged to take them. The serving of this battery was most admirable, and its sweep of grape and shell frightfully destructive. With desperate courage, in four lines of battle, one pressing on the other, the enemy came forward to take it at all hazards; they were met by a terrific storm of grape, canister and shrapnell, and wide lines were opened in their ranks, and men fell as grass before the mower. But still the tremor was only for a moment; on they pressed, closing their broken files as they ran; another terrific burst of flame would dash scorching streams into their very faces; but still on the broken fragments pressed, until almost to the muzzle of the cannon; then up sprang the protecting regiments, the firing of the artillery ceased, and musket and bayonet were left to decide

I have here to call the attention of my superior Chiefs to this most heroic action on the part of Colonel HAYS and his regiment. The Sixty-third has won for Pennsylvania the laurels of fame. That which grape and canister failed in effecting was now accomplished by the determined charge and rapid volleys of this foot. The enemy, at the muzzles of our guns, for the first time, sulkily retired, fighting. Subsequently, ground having been gained, the Sixty-third Pennsylvania was ordered to "lie low," and the battery once more reopened its ceaseless work of destruction.

This battle saw renewed three ontsets as above, with similar vicissitudes, when finally the enemy betokened his efforts as passed, by converting his charges into an ordinary line fight of musketry, embracing the whole front of the brigade, for, by this period, he was enabled to do so, from THOMPSON'S pieces having left the field after expending their grape and becoming tired of the futility of round shot.

It may have been then half-past seven P. M., full day-light remained, and anticipating that the enemy, foiled in the attempt to carry the New Market road and adjacent open ground, would next hazard an attack toward the Charles City road, or intermediate woods, that my attention was called there. I therefore left everything progressing steadily on the left, and visited the entire line to the right, notwithstanding that the line was long, and that no reserves (excepting the weak Third Michigan) existed. The cheerful manner and solid look of BIRNEY'S brigade gave assurance of their readiness to be measured with the foe, and they met my warning of the coming storm with loud cheers of exultation.

Half an hour or forty minutes may have been thus passed. I then returned to the extreme left of my line. Arriving there, I found that Colonel HAYS had been relieved by Colonel BARLOW, of the Sixty-first New York Volunteers, the head of General CALDWELL'S brigade, sent to me from SUMNER'S Corps, and which had reported to General ROBINSON.

Almost in the commencement of the action, within the first half hour, as I had plainly foreseen and warned my superior, General HEINTZELMAN, and General HUMPHREYS, Engineers, who most kindly had gone over my position with me, every man was engaged, or in position or in close support. The Eighty-seventh New York Volunteers had been ordered by General HEINTZELMAN to Brackett's Ford, and the First New York Volunteers was diverted from me by a misapprehension of Colonel DYCKMAN. This fact I announced to General HEINTZELMAN, without asking reinforcements, since I did not conceive them necessary, nor would they have been but for the diverting of my First New York Volunteers, a very strong regiment, to General MCCALL.

The Sixty-first New York Volunteers, under its most intrepid leader, Colonel BARLOW, had vied with the brave regiment he had relieved, and charging the enemy, borne off as a trophy one of his colors. It had subsequently taken up its position to the left of the One Hundred and Fifth Pennsylvania, and itself been subsequently retired, but none appointed to take its place, that breastwork being unoccupied. It was at this conjuncture that I arrived from my right. I found MCCALL'S position abandoned, although not occupied by the enemy. I placed in it the First New Jersey Brigade, General TAYLOR. I then knew it to be in true hands. I observed that whilst the enemy were amusing my entire front with an ordinary musket fire, that strong parties of rebel skirmishers, in the gloom of the evening, rendered denser by the murky fogs of the smoke, were feeling their way slowly and distrustfully to the unoccupied parapet. Galloping back to find the nearest troops, I met General CALDWELL, who, under General MCCALL'S supervision, was putting two or more of his regiments into line to the right of the road (a quarter of a mile in rear of the breastworks) to move up in order. Circumstances denied this delay; accordingly I directed General CALDWELL to lead a wing of a regiment at double [quick] up the road to open on these rebel skirmishers. This was done promptly, but, from their being foreigners, not with a full comprehension, and darkness embarrassed them, they fired at the rebels, but in direction of others of my line, and thus, while the enemy were swept off the arena, it left, for some little time, our troops firing at each other. To increase this confusion, the residue of the Brigade, who had not filed into the woods and formed on the road,

---

the contest. The enemy could not stand the heavy stroke of the moment, but broke and fled: rallying three several times with fresh reinforcements, they ventured out into the open ground, and each time they were repelled with even greater slaughter than before, until great heaps of their dead were lying like mounds on the field.—Chaplain MARKS' "*Peninsula Campaign*," page 284.

opened on us all who were in the front. It is my impression that General McCALL (taken prisoner) must have been killed by this fire.

The errors of cross-firing having at last subsided, my Fifth Michigan gallantly crossed the parapets and pursued the retiring enemy. The Eighty-first Pennsylvania then nobly responding to my orders, gallently led by Lieutenant-Colonel CONNER, and Captain MILES, of General CALDWELL'S staff, dashed over the parapet, pursued, charged, and with a few vigorous volleys finished the battle at half-past nine at night.

I remained much longer on the field, and reported in person to General HEINTZELMAN at his quarters.*

In concluding my report of this battle, one of the most desperate of the war, the one most fatal, if lost, I am proud to give my thanks, and to include in the glory of my own Division the first New Jersey Brigade, General TAYLOR, who held McCALL'S deserted ground, and General CALDWELL whose personal gallantry and the bravery of whose regiments not only entitle them to share in the credit of our victory, but also ever after engender full sympathies between the two corps.

In this engagement the coolness and judicious arrangements of General BIRNEY influenced his whole command to feel invincible in a very weak position. General BERRY, as usual, was active. The fearful losses which his noble regiments have sustained, reducing them to scarce two hundred to a regiment, oblige me to preserve such heroes for the decisive moments. Still, they will not be repressed, and the Fifth Michigan, under Major FAIRBANKS, was the first to pursue the enemy. I regret, for ourselves, that he, almost the last of our noble distinguished at Williamsburg and Fair Oaks. and the forced advance of the 25th of June (second battle of Fair Oaks or of Oak Grove), is dangerously wounded. I have to state that this Division has been extremely used. This has prematurely reduced to nothing regiments of the highest mark.

I have reserved General ROBINSON for the last. To him this day is due — above all others in this Division — the honors of this battle. The attack was on his wing. Everywhere present, by personal supervision and noble example, he secured for us the honor of the victory.

For the names of officers distinguished in their regiments, I, for the present, refer you to the brigade and regimental reports.

As to the action of my artillery (Battery G, Second United States Artillery), it has never been equaled for rapidity and precision of fire, and coolness amidst great loss of men and horses. The gallantry of its commander, Captain THOMPSON, identifies him with its distinction.

Our loss has been severe, and when it is remembered that this occurs to mere skeletons of regiments, there is but one observation to be made — that previous military history presents no such parallel

Very respectfully,
Your obedient servant,
(Signed) P. KEARNY,
Brigadier-General Commanding Third Division.

To CAPTAIN C. McKEEVER,
Assistant Adjutant-General Third Corps.

---

* Under a tree at the junction of the Quaker and Charles City Roads.
(Signed) S. P. H. (SAMUEL P. HEINTZELMAN.)

CHAPTER XXVI.

COMPANION AND SUPPLEMENTARY.

A PARTIAL REVIEW OF THE PENINSULA OPERATIONS ON THE LEFT — POPULAR PRONENESS TO EXAGGERATION — KEARNY'S PRACTICAL FORESIGHT AND ABILITY — THE KEARNY PATCH, DIAMOND AND CRÔSS, AND BADGE OR MEDAL.

I saw the ground on which * * the opposing armies had gazed on each other: the Confederates on the ridge of the valley to the south, guarding Richmond, the Federals on that to the north. The valley is nearly a mile wide. Muddy and sluggish was the stream (Chickahominy) in August (1862), winding through reedy meadows and swamps. * * * Rev. WM. WYNDHAM MALET'S "*Errand to the South in the Summer of* 1862," pages 165–'6.

"The (battle) ground (of Seven Pines) was very unfavorable for operations on either side — a *broad wooded flat*, intersected with morasses and open spaces; and the roads were bad and marshy beyond description, owing to the late violent rains." — *31st May*, 1862. VON BORCKE'S "*Memoirs*," chap. ii, page 17.

"A general should understand his opponents' character." — PRINCE EUGENE; Maj.-Gen. MITCHELL'S "*Biographies of Eminent Soldiers*," page 253.

"The Commonwealth is sick of her own choice:
Her over greedy Love is surfeited."

SHAKESPEARE'S "*Henry IV.*"

"'Tis drilling that makes him (a soldier), *skill* and SENSE —
Perception — thought — INTELLIGENCE."

SCHILLER'S "*Wallenstein's Lager*."

It is one of the fine, high-sounding axioms of the moral throng: "Man shall do what is good only because it is good." The philosopher, however, likewise the close observer of human nature, knows that there is another motive which influences men in a higher degree: "Honorable recognition by his fellow-men." * * Under these considerations, is there a more sensible recognition, a more disinterested reward than by means of a simple ribbon, a cross, a star, in short, some badge of honor, whose entire value is its moral effect? And yet, the whole history of the world demonstrates what wonderful effects have been produced by such ribbons, crosses, stars and badges * * in developing grand conceptions, lofty ideas; in causing valorous and glorious actions; in reaching the loftiest attaining aims, believed to be beyond the reach of man. So it has been throughout all times. The mural crown and the laurel wreath had the same effect upon the ancient Romans as the Golden Fleece upon the knights of the middle ages, and as the cross or badge of honor exercises among soldiers at the present day. — "*Das Buch der Ritterorden und Ehrenzeichen, Vorwort.*"

"The history of WAR MEDALS is not well known. Many are believed to exist, that were struck by order of QUEEN ELIZABETH and JAMES I; but *the first of which there is any authentic account was worn as a military decoration*, and was granted by CHARLES I, in 1642, for such as distinguished themselves in *forlorn hopes*. The name of ROBERT WALSH is recorded as the *first* recipient. He gained it at Edge Hill." — General CUST'S "*Lives of the Warriors*," 1611-1675. Vol. 11, 572, OLIVER CROMWELL.

AFTER MALVERN.

Although this work appears late in the autumn of 1869, it was written in the summer of 1868, and the preceding chapters were in print soon after. Had it been prepared at a later date, many of the views presented would have been much modified, but not in favor of the Commander-in-Chief who threw away his chances with as prodigal and reckless a defiance of Fortune as if the goddess had been inextricably chained to his chariot wheels, or as subservient to his will as Ariel to Prospero. When this work was finally passing through the press, May, 1869, the writer visited Richmond for no other purpose than to examine the battle-fields around that city, where the Union leader of 1861–'2 seemed desirous of surpassing the "Host Waster" of the Thirty Years' War and elevate the worst miscarriage of the Slaveholders' Rebellion to a par with the failure before St. Jean de Losne in 1636.

One of the party was an officer who served meritoriously in the Peninsular Campaign of 1862, and recognized these battle grounds as familiar scenes. All agreed that however a critic might have condemned McClellan from official documents, nothing could have made that general's weaknesses so apparent as a visit to his line of positions along the Chickahominy. Or as one said, who had predicted his miscarriage, "he had never been so satisfied of McClellan's insufficiency* as to-day."

Any one who will start out from Richmond on the Mechanicsville pike, and make a circuit of the positions assumed by the disposer of the Army of the Potomac in May–July, 1862, any one, whether he be tyro or expert, laic or initiate, will return into the Rebel capital overwhelmed with the conviction that the plan of swinging into Richmond with the Union right, was to "take the bull by the horns," while, on the other hand, to "swing in" on the left was the correct and only course justified by every conclusion, military, sanatory or practical, since

* That this epithet is not applied without authority, the reader is referred to The *Times'* "Review of McClellan: His Military Career Reviewed and Exposed," by William Swinton, afterwards author of the "Campaigns of the Army of the Potomac;" Major-General J. G. Barnard's (U. S. A.) "Peninsular Campaign;" Denslow's "Fremont and McClellan: Their Political and Military Careers Reviewed;" and a number of cotemporary and subsequent publications in regard to the mournful Peninsular failure.

"strategy is nothing more than common sense applied to war." HOOKER, grand on any field which he could supervise; KEARNY, tried and true on so many different fields, perfect soldier, admirable commander and excellent general; HEINTZELMAN, honest, loyal, spirited, a capital soldier, brim-full of common sense; and even "worthy" SUMNER, all indicated the left as the point of vantage, and begged to be permitted to push in on that wing. Then, in May, up to the middle of June, there were no defensive works of any consequence, if any, on that front, and the natural disposition of the ground favors an assailant from the southeast and south of Richmond. This was admitted to the writer in that city. After advancing over a flat, certainly as advantageous for an aggressive as a defensive, the country becomes more open and subsides, in rolls, down into the suburbs of the Rebel capital, which lies uncovered at the mercy of batteries on a high hill just south of it. From this hill the Union troops could have shelled the city with ease. Along the Williamsburg road, indeed, there are comparatively fair open fields to fight over, although in some directions, it is true, it is almost a wilderness up to within three miles of the city limits, and, if those limits were correctly indicated by the driver, even nearer on the east-southeast, where the largest of the five National Cemeteries is located (that which contains the victims of LEE's cold, apathetic, and DAVIS' concentrated barbarism, at Belle Isle and the Richmond city prisons), there is sheer fighting ground. This is two miles from the Rebel capital, and near the Turnpike Gate and Oak-Grove-Family-Store (1869). In this direction, and within this circle, the ground is broken, often favorable and never unfavorable to an assailant.

When HEINTZELMAN's Corps, KEARNY's and HOOKER's Divisions, advanced on the 25th June and fought the "AFFAIR OF THE PEACH ORCHARD,"* MCCLELLAN† said, these troops "are

* This affair is mis-named by several writers the "Battle of Oak Grove." By the senior General present, HEINTZELMAN, it was entitled the Affair of the "Orchards." He said he applied the name because there were some peach trees hereabouts, but particularly to distinguish it from the battle of Seven Pines and Fair Oaks on the preceding 31st May—1st June, with which it was often confounded. All these "*high-for-Newton*" titles, however, are humbugs, as much as the god-like attributes of the Rebel and the Napoleonic gifts of the Union Commander. There are plenty of scrub oaks in this locality, but such a thing as a holt of noble oak trees there is not. In fact, there are no FAIR Oaks, no Oak GROVE, no SEVEN Pines!

† MCCLELLAN's "*Report*," Second Period, June 25, 1862, pages 236–238; particularly 237.

where I want them." At that time KEARNY and HOOKER were pushing ahead gallantly down the Williamsburg road, and the latter went within four miles of Richmond. And KEARNY, properly supported by the troops in that quarter, could have gone in with ease had the Commander-in-Chief so willed it.

And here, before turning from this quarter, where every thing invited success, the reader may desire to know what is the aspect of this portion of the country east and southeast of Richmond. To the New Yorker, as a rule, it appears to be a wilderness of scrub and jungle springing up from whitish or red sand or loam, recalling Eastern Long Island before industry and judgment took hold of its "barrens" and converted them into prolific fields.

In the neighborhood of the "Cool Arbors," or "Cold Harbors," "New" and "Old," between which there is a National Cemetery, it seems a desolate, poverty-stricken, almost uninhabited district. In May, 1869, one very extensive watermelon patch looked like a large field of white sea-sand blown into little ridges or ripples by the wind. With the exception that the hills were crested with sparse sprouts instead of marine wire grass, it resembled one of those flats lying just *within* the Dunes along the Long Island coast of the Atlantic.

Through this wilderness, bare or tangled, and a deep and wide depression filled with rank vegetation, amid much lofty timber mingled with lowland trees, such as swamp oak, willow and black gum — a tree with a leaf like the maple and a bark like the cork or rock-oak — steals the CHICKAHOMINY. Like a venomous and treacherous reptile it serpentines, along the marshy flat, almost unobservable within the dense foliage which screens its subtle course. In its rage it suddenly swells like the deadly Cobra snake, hisses and lifts its augmented volume filling the bottom land. And then, shrinking back into its channel, or rather its lair, it leaves its borders covered with a poisonous slime for the sun to convert into the deadliest effluvia, augmented by the decay of a rank vegetation fed by the muddy overflowing of the river — a miasma almost as fatal as the blast which smote the army of the Assyrian — a miasma which stung the Army of the Potomac and consigned so many of our thousands to graves along its dark shores, or left them infected to suffer on for years, or to fill at home the unnoticed graves for which their bodies had been prepared by needless exposure.

Such was the fearful obstacle — the Chickahominy and its swamps — which McClellan interposed between his army and its objective, through his willful adherence to a plan which Lincoln's telegram of the 4th April should have demonstrated was no longer feasible. Thereupon a clearsighted man would have comprehended that he must depend, or at all events base, his calculations upon the means which he had on hand and upon himself.

On the 5th May, the victory of Williamsburg opened the direct road to Richmond; on the 11th the self-immolation of the Merrimac cleared the direct route by water to that city and permitted the army to have a base, *following* it, upon the James, whither, after all, McClellan was compelled, or deemed that he was necessitated, to fall back. That McClellan did not perceive his true line of advance, was either because he could not or would not see things as they were, and seemed to be persistently determined to base his plans on things as he would or did see them, and as no one else did or could see them. His continual over-estimate of the Rebel force in his front is one great proof of this fact, among many other attestations.

A fair deduction from the consideration of the Peninsular Campaign from different stand-points is, that the commanding general was not up to the time or to his people. In that people's over-estimate of men they were alone false to their superiority to every other people of the present or past time.

The proneness to exaggeration of which the human mind is susceptible, is generally displayed in the greatest degree by the estimate put upon the military ability or prowess of an individual, or a nation, after a great success or a victory. This was particularly so in regard to the French after their Revolutionary successes. It amounted to almost a superstitious awe, which it was deemed in vain to combat.* It was

* De Quincey's "*Confessions of an Opium Eater*," Routledge & Son's Edition, p. 100.

not until the Old Blucher toppled over several of these traditional heroes and traversed the plans of even Napoleon, wiping out his "Army of the Bober," that men began to obtain again anything like "level heads" as to the fabulous French invincibility. So it was likewise in the Thirty Years' War in regard to the Old Corporal Tilly and his Veteran Tercios. It required a battle at Leipsic, and the still more wonderful passage of the Lech, to dispel the illusion, and the Swedes rose to fill the place relinquished by the beaten Imperialists and Bavarians. And thus, in like manner, nothing but a Jena could have shaken the faith of Europe in the armies which Frederic "the Nonparœil" had evoked and embattled. This truth holds good more particularly as to McClellan, who soared to greatness on a fictitious fame for West Virginia "baby fights," in which the real hero Rosecrans, to whom they were due, was ignored. That the first reverse at Bull Run did not depress our people more than it did, is one of the best proofs of the calm equipoise of Northern courage. Any other people would have been overawed by the victory attributed to Southern valor, and, as such, trumpeted forth by prejudice as an evidence of Southern superiority. That the North shook off the incubus sought to be imposed upon it, demonstrates that a Free and Educated people are insensible to the superstitious influences of the Old World, even as our American children are insensible to the fear of bogies and ghosts so terrible to the early life of other days and lands.

On the other hand, there are abundant indications in almost everything he said, wrote or did, that Kearny was ahead of his surroundings and alive to the exigencies of the hour. Take, for instance, his conception of the necessity or influence of a distinctive badge, the "Kearny Cross," or, more properly speaking, the Kearny Patch. The Cross was an afterthought of Birney, whereas the original Patch, or Diamond, from first to last, designated the Third Corps, whether while it remained a unit or afterward became a fragment, since the two divisions of this corps were first consolidated, in 1864, into one, which, while still retaining the distinctive badge of the Third Corps, became the third Division of the Second Corps, and, as such, continued up to the end under the command of Major-General Mott.

This matter of the Kearny Patch may seem to one of little consequence, but it is almost impossible to estimate its moral effect. At the battle of Bristow Station, Warren acknowledges that numbers of stragglers who had been forced to fall out by reason of physical incapacity to keep up — not moral weakness from unwillingness to "go in"—joined themselves to his command, and did their duty faithfully. Estimating from causes and effects, according to the ordinary rule of judgment, Warren was indebted to Kearny for the assistance which he received on that occasion by those who wore that *patch.*

According to officers of the Third Corps on the Peninsula, Kearny, about the time of the battle of Fair Oaks, directed his officers to wear a *red patch* or diamond as a distinguishing mark. As there were no red goods on hand for this purpose, Kearny gave up his own red blanket as material for these patches. Soon after, the men, of their own accord, cut pieces of the red lining out of their overcoats to make similar distinguishing marks for themselves. Simultaneously with the idea of the *patch* for the officers, Kearny adopted a plain red flag to indicate his Division Headquarters; and soon afterwards Hooker assumed a simple blue flag for his, the second Division of the Third Corps. Although application has been made to different parties who served with or beside Kearny for more definite particulars, none but the following has been received. Neither did advertisements inserted in the newspapers inviting coöperation meet with a more satisfactory result. That the idea of the Patch or Corps Badge originated with General Kearny, no one disputes or even doubts. The writer either received a letter from General Birney to this effect, in the Fall of 1862, or else some other friend transmitted to him a newspaper slip, both of which have either been lost, stolen or mislaid. If spared, they lie amid a mass of similar documents and papers whose arrangement was intrusted to an incompetent clerk, who made confusion worse confounded.

At all events, the idea of a division or corps badge which first suggested itself to the practiced and practical mind of KEARNY, although it owes its simple introduction to him, its after development is equally due to Major-General BUTTERFIELD, when he became Chief-of-Staff of the Army of the Potomac, in the Spring of 1863. His plan was finally perfected and introduced by Major-General HOOKER while in command of that glorious army.* This last distinguished officer deserves far more credit than he has ever received for many improvements of the highest utility in almost every branch of the service, but particularly the staff, cavalry and artillery. In fact, the cavalry may be said to owe to him its first impulse in the rapid advance to that organization and efficiency, which soon afterward, under that

---

* *Editor of the Soldiers' Friend:*

CORPS BADGES.—It has been the subject of much argument and interrogation, when were corps badges adopted, and by whom? * * *

When General HOOKER assumed command of the Army of the Potomac, January 26th 1863, he found that its *morale* had never been so bad. The army had become despondent through repeated reverses and the incapacity of its leaders. Upon assuming command, General HOOKER at once addressed himself to the task of elevating the character of the army. None knew it better than he. All through the bloody Peninsula, from the fierce and sanguinary conflict at Williamsburg, where his division held the enemy at bay all day, until the voluntary assistance of the lamented KEARNY relieved him; at Fair Oaks; the Seven Days' Battles—those days of bloodshed and sacrifices—through all the sanguinary campaigns which filled Virginia with cemeteries, and brought sorrow and desolation to many a fireside. Truly did General HOOKER know the character of that army, and what could be brought out of that chaos. He had not fought with them in the past, and seen their elasticity, faith and bravery, to forget them now.

It is conceded now, that General HOOKER has had too little credit for the great work he accomplished; the many valuable reformations he caused; and, what proved ultimately so valuable, the consolidation of the cavalry into one corps, which rendered them an efficient and valuable arm of the service, which they had never been before. The grand divisions were done away with, and the army divided into seven corps. It was at this time the corps badge was introduced—a badge which afterward became an emblem of honor, and to-day is worn with pride and affection. General HOOKER saw the value of some such corps designation, and adopted it.

To the First Corps, he gave the circle: Second Corps, trefoil; Third Corps, diamond; Fifth Corps, Maltese cross; Sixth Corps, Grecian cross; Eleventh Corps, crescent; and Twelfth Corps, star.—(See LOSSING'S "*Civil War in America*," iii, 20 [1], note and illustrations.) The division was designated by colors—red, white and blue respectively. Through the eventful future these badges were to be worn, emblems of his thoughtfulness and love. Before the end of the war, this idea was carried out through all the army. General KEARNY, as your correspondent suggests, adopted a badge for his division—a red diamond made out of flannel. General HOOKER permitted the division to retain this emblem when the reorganization took place. Many did not find out the value or appreciate the badge until it had been baptized under fire, and honors had gathered around it. Chancellorsville was its glory, and only the crescent came out of the conflict marred with dishonor.

Yours truly,

JOHN N. COYNE,

Brevet Colonel U. S. Vols.

model cavalry officer, Major-General ALFRED PLEASONTON, rendered it so far superior to the boasted mounted troops of the South and finally a model of the practical serviceableness so admirably brought to bear by the able and gallant SHERIDAN.

When this work was nearly half completed, the writer received a letter from Major GEORGE H. HICKMAN (who, as Adjutant of the 99th Pennsylvania Volunteers, performed good service in BIRNEY'S Brigade, under KEARNY):

"During the 'seven days' fight' before Richmond, General KEARNY saw the necessity of having some distinction mark by which the officers and men of his division could be recognized. Consequently, after the arrival of the division at Harrison's Landing, General KEARNY issued an order, July 4th, 1862, illustrative of his design. Officers were directed to wear a red patch in shape of a diamond on the crown or left side of their cap, while enlisted men were to wear theirs in front of the cap. The order was eagerly and readily complied with.

"Upon the death of General KEARNY, and Brigadier-General DAVID B. BIRNEY assuming command of the division, he issued an order September 3d, 1862, announcing, in appropriate terms, the death of our General, and directing the diamond red patch still to be worn. Without any official order, or concert of action on part of officers or men, the red patches were seen draped in mourning. It was a noted fact, and the subject of remark in orders, that during the retreat from Harrison's Landing, and the several marches and campaigns, ending with that of Fredericksburg, a diamond patch was a rarity among the stragglers.

"It is related that Colonel MCKNIGHT, One Hundred and Fifth Pennsylvania Volunteers (No. 9 on the roll of officers who received KEARNY badges), who was killed in action at Chancellorsville, on May 3d, 1863, and whose body fell into the hands of the enemy, being observed to have on his KEARNY medal, was, by order of the enemy's officers, buried with due respect."

In this connection, the following paragraph clipped from a paper and entitled "The KEARNY 'Red Patch,'" seems pertinent:

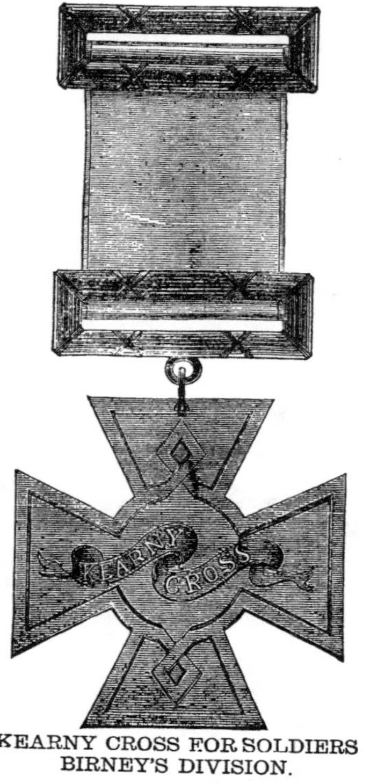

KEARNY CROSS FOR SOLDIERS
BIRNEY'S DIVISION.

KEARNY BADGE OR MEDAL,
From the original of KEARNY'S Aid de Camp.

"A correspondent with the Army of the Rappahannock learns from reliable authority, that whenever our men are discovered by the rebels, and they are found to have upon them the KEARNY 'Red Patch,' if wounded, they are kindly cared for, and if dead, they are buried with all the honors of war; their graves so marked as to be readily recognized. (Colonel McKNIGHT, of the One Hundred and Fifth Pennsylvania, was so buried, his body followed to the grave with a guard of honor, many officers being present. A band played a funeral dirge, while over his remains was fired the usual salute due to an officer of his rank.)"

"The diamond red patch became very popular, and the men felt proud in wearing it. The contagion spread throughout the army, and in January, 1863, when HOOKER took command, and BUTTERFIELD became his chief-of-staff, the general system of designating was adopted throughout the army.

"Our division being the First Division of the Third Corps, General BUTTERFIELD, in his orders, directed that the color of the corps marks of the First Division should be red; Second Division, white; Third Division, blue. In thus making the selection, he allowed our division to retain its color, and thus made, in that respect, all the others subservient to it."*

After KEARNY fell at Chantilly, his successor and imitator in the command of his division adopted what has been styled the "KEARNY Cross." KEARNY's own "battle-flag," presented by BIRNEY, is still preserved among the "Memorials of the War," in the collection of the Philadelphia Loyal League Club. It is folded in such a manner that no one can discover whether it is plain or bears any distinguishing mark in the centre. †

* "The KEARNY patch was a diamond or lozenge, and the Third Division received the lozenge in BUTTERFIELD's or HOOKER's distribution of corps badges; so that KEARNY's (then BIRNEY's) division continued to wear throughout the war the identical patch, shape and color of the originator.

"KEARNY, according to the statement of Major W—— B——, was also the first to use a division headquarters flag, which bore the cross (red) that subsequently received his name, which flag was cherished by the division commanders who succeeded him, and was displayed at division headquarters alongside of that bearing the lozenge directed in HOOKER's orders."

† LA PIERRE HOUSE, PHILADELPHIA, July 17, 1869.

General DE PEYSTER:

Dear sir—"The Union League of Philadelphia are the custodians of the KEARNY Battle Flag, placed there by the officers of KEARNY's division. It is made of plain red bunting,

After McClellan had fallen from his pride of place, and his successor, Burnside, had led the Army of the Potomac down to Fredericksburg (to attempt the overland route, which was one of those suggested by Kearny,* and actually followed by Grant), a number of the officers surviving, representing the regiments which had served under Major-General Philip Kearny, met at the headquarters of the Third Brigade, First Division, Third Corps, in the camp near Falmouth, Virginia, on the 29th November, 1862. At this meeting a series of resolutions were adopted, expressive of the admiration felt by those present for their deceased commander. And it was determined to procure a medal or badge, the famous Kearny Cross, of which a representation is herein presented, and means were carefully devised to prevent any one from obtaining or wearing this badge who was not entitled to display it in consequence of actual service in battle under the eyes or leading of the hero whose motto was to be emblazoned thereon. As an evidence of the care which has attended their issue to the proper parties, only three hundred and twenty-five officers had received them up to the date when this chapter was prepared. These names, a roll of honor, have been published in a very neat pamphlet, issued by Ball, Black & Co., the sole manufacturers of the "Kearny Medal."

In the meanwhile, Major-General Birney had likewise procured, at his own expense, a bronze cross,† to be worn by his

nearly square, seventy and a half inches long by fifty-six and a half inches wide, somewhat riddled by shot, and is now tacked on to a piece of white muslin (of the same size as the flag itself), in order to preserve it as much as possible from further destruction. It is without device of any kind. The facts stated were obtained from Mr. Whipple, the Secretary of the League."

* Compare Articles, "*Errors of the Campaign*," New York Times, Sunday, 19 Oct., 1862; "*Mr. Russell on the Fredericksburg Route to Richmond*," New York Times, 20th Dec., 1862; New York Times, 1st page, Thursday, 12th May, 1864; and "*Observations on the Military Operations in Virginia, in 1864*," by Brig.-Gen. Israel Vogdes, U. S. A., N. Y. Historical Magazine, May, 1869, pages 309–313.

† Rewards for Brave Men.—Brigadier-General Birney, while recently in Philadelphia, on a visit home, ordered a thousand crosses of honor, to present to such of his command as might distinguish themselves by deeds of valor. The design is that of a Maltese Cross, inscribed "The Kearny Cross," appended to an ornament attaching it to a ribbon. Mr. George Bullock, of Philadelphia, learning that such an order had been given, called upon the manufacturers, directed them to double the amount of labor expended upon the decorations, and assumed the expense of the entire affair. The obverse of the decorations bears the names of the battles in which the soldiers have participated.

own division, previously that of KEARNY, of which a *fac simile* has been presented to the publishers. The obverse, in a scroll, bears the words "KEARNY CROSS," the reverse, "BIRNEY'S DIVISION."

In July, 1863, the lamented BIRNEY sent one to the writer,* from which the accompanying representation was prepared, while that of the KEARNY medal, badge or cross, for officers, was photographed from that worn by KEARNY'S cousin and volunteer aid-de-camp on the Peninsula.

Few simple practical ideas have ever been productive of so much effective good as the KEARNY PATCH. Its introduction developed an amount of emulation which was productive of the most glorious results. Nor was BIRNEY'S liberality less remunerative in its incentive to discipline and valor. Those who were fortunate enough to be entitled to the more beautiful and costly KEARNY medal, display them with a pride which is sufficient testimony of the love and veneration entertained for the brave and able soldier, in whose memory they were adopted and are worn.

Five men fell while bearing the brigade flag, but five others sprang into their places, and kept it waving during the continuance of the memorable fight at Fredericksburg. The Color Sergeant (Brigade Orderly ?) had three horses shot down under him. It is such men as these that General BIRNEY desires to reward. Five hundred crosses will be distributed, through Mr. BULLOCK, forthwith; the other five hundred will be reserved for future disposal.—*Newspaper slip sent to the author — no name, place or date.*

* CAMP NEAR WARRENTON, VIRGINIA, July 28, 1863.

My dear General:

I am in receipt of your kind favor, enclosing the additional photographs of the General (KEARNY) and also of FREDERIC THE GREAT. I am very much obliged, as I appreciate such beautiful specimens of art. The KEARNY likeness is admirable and his seat is perfectly given. (The wood cut on the TITLE PAGE is taken from this photograph, by GURNEY, from the grand equestrian portrait by BOLLES, in the possession of the author.)

I send you the Medal, a very simple affair; but in giving a thousand at my own expense I had to be governed by economical views, to a certain extent. However, I trust that it will please you and his family.

Our old Division is sadly thinned out; 3,400 men for duty, although some ten regiments have been added since KEARNY'S death. Fredericksburg, Chancellorsville and Gettysburg sent thousands of my gallant fellows to another world. I lost in those three battles, killed and wounded, over 5,200 — and the men never flinched. They are very proud of KEARNY, and you would be satisfied with their enthusiasm. I must confess, too, participating fully in their feelings. * * * *

Yours truly,

(Signed) D. B. BIRNEY, *Major-General.*

General DE PEYSTER.

CHAPTER XXVII.

HARRISON'S LANDING.

CHAFING ON THE BIT.

"Harrison's Bar (Landing) is simply a long wharf, extending into the river, close by the famous mansion where WILLIAM HENRY HARRISON, a President of the United States, was born." — "*Campaigns of a Non-combatant*," 209.

This one's (MASSENA'S) heroism saved the retreating army (French) from destruction (after Aspern, 1809). "He, himself (NAPOLEON), made haste to get away from the Lobau, in a fisherman's skiff, over to the Castle of Kaiserebersdorf, where he sank into a slumber of thirty-three hours, which resembled the sleep of death." — SCHERR'S "*Bluchcr*," II, 306.

"The campaign was ended; the Spaniards (pursuers) saw all their plans baffled, and, in spite of tremendous losses, had accomplished nothing except to exhaust their own strength."—SCHMALZ'S "*Schaumburg Lippc*," 33.

"What are we to do next?" "Hunt red-legged partridges, I suppose." (WELLINGTON'S remark after the Convention of Cintra, 1808.) — GLEIG'S "*Wellington*," 78.

"He (ACHILLES) doth rely on none;
But carries on the stream of his dispose,
Without observance or respect of any,
In will peculiar" —

SHAKESPEARE'S "*Troilus and Cressida*, II, iii.

His "words were half battles." They have "the true ring in them."—OLINS' "*Renee of France.*"

"Arouse ye, my comrades, to horse!
To horse!
To the field and to freedom we ride!
For there a man feels the pride of his force,
And there is the heart of him tried!"

SCHILLER'S "*Wallenstein's Lager.*"

If ever the striking truth embodied in BYRON'S lines was ever realized in a human being, that —

"Quiet to quick bosoms is a hell,"

it was so in the case of General KEARNY. Never in the whole course of his checkered career can it be said that he enjoyed tranquillity of mind. It was as impossible for him to be physically quiet as it is for the ocean to cease to heave, or to be mentally at rest as it is for the air to pause in its circulation. His was a nature which was ever acting upon others and reacting upon itself. His thirst for excitement was no sooner gratified than he was possessed with a hunger for some other form of activity to work off the tremendous stimulus which rendered him so nervous that it became an utter impossibility to enjoy anything like repose of mind or body. Then it was that he would throw himself into the saddle and ride, like the Wild Huntsman, clearing the turnpike gates or highest fences, like Dick Turpin, to the outrageous disgust of bilked toll-takers or furious farmers, indignant at the trespass. With him it was a word and a blow. Only, as the old family nurse used to say, the blow generally came first. Indeed, it was under such accesses he would seize his pen and dash off those caustic letters which often grieved his friends as much as they irritated the objects of his sarcasm, striking off word or pen-pictures, which embodied startling truths while they were invested with an exaggeration of bitterness which was the offspring of the same wild genius that characterized GUSTAVE DORÉS' greatest work, his illustrations of the career of the "Wandering Jew." Nevertheless, with all this, KEARNY felt a perfect adoration for the beauties of nature, and even while chafing under the inaction of Harrison's Landing, with our forces "boxed up like herrings," his letters demonstrate that he was susceptible to the charms of the surrounding scenery, and in his communications to relatives and friends at home his enthusiastic love of the beautiful found its expression in that talent which he so eminently possessed of writing descriptions of what he saw, almost as vivid as pictures which present the object to the eye. His health suffered greatly at this time, and he never seemed to enjoy perfect health except in the saddle, and, in the saddle, every ride that he took through the camps was a perfect ovation, such an ovation as that which proved to be the military symphony that preceded the last scene of his glorious military drama. So constantly did these occur that he was compelled, in orders, to endeavor to restrain these testimonials of admiration and affection, the cheers and hurrahs with which the soldiers greeted the "Fighting General" of the army whenever he appeared.*

---

* HEADQUARTERS, THIRD DIVISION, THIRD CORPS,
CAMP NEAR HARRISON'S LANDING, July 7, 1862.

General Orders, No. 27. — Brave comrades: As one of your Generals who has shared in your perils, so I sympathize in your cheers for victory when I pass. The name of this Division is marked. Southern records are full of you. In attack, you have driven them;

Dismounted, his complaints returned upon him with increased weight, almost as soon as his feet quitted the stirrups, and with them a depression of spirits, augmented by inaction. Then it was that the "Fighting PHIL. KEARNY," the "indomitable," the "ubiquitous," the "heroic," became the prey of feelings engendered by his personal disappointments; by the unsuccessful consequences of such a fearful waste of life and of resultless battles; by the utter failure in his commanding general; by the apparent want of appreciation of himself; and by what he thought himself compelled to believe, a semi-treasonable political creed; by a haughty disgust of the "small men of small motives," who managed this great war. He was bitterly chagrined at their incompetency to discriminate between capable and incapable men. This last misapprehension led him to think seriously that he should no longer consent to be their puppet. Above all this, however, an acute grief was gnawing at his heart, on account of the losses and almost ruin of his pet Jersey Brigade, the first from that State, which he had made, whose career of glory, infructuous, though so fearfully bloody, he had watched with the same anxiety that a parent accords to a son whom he has educated himself, and sent forth to prove to the world the stuff which is in him, developed by the careful training of the best of masters.

Nor would this work be complete did it fail to present some portions of General KEARNY's correspondence, which are dated

---

when assailed, you have repulsed them. Be it so to the end. New regiments, we give you a name; engraft on it fresh laurels.

Comrades in battle, let our greeting be a cry of defiance to the foe; after the fight, one greeting of victory for ourselves. This done, remember that, like yourselves, I have my duties of labor in which I must move unobserved, as a true brother in hand and heart of this, our Warrior-Division-Family. Success attend you.

By command of Brig.-General KEARNY, commanding Third Division.

(Signed) ALEX. MOORE, *A. A. A. G.*

HEADQUARTERS THIRD DIVISION, THIRD ARMY CORPS, July 7, 1862.

Orders No. 97. — The Brigadier-General commanding Division takes great pleasure in the kind receptions given him whenever he presents himself among the men of his command, but prefers, in ordinary times, to be allowed to pass quietly and unobserved. Immediately after a battle, he has no objection to a few hearty cheers.

Commanders of regiments will please inform the men of the General's request.

(Signed) ALEX. MOORE, *A. A. A. G.*

How many generals have had to request their men NOT *to cheer them!?! Let veracious historians answer.*

at Harrison's Landing. These letters, better than any other medium, will make the reader acquainted with the military character of the individual who dashed them off. Several are due to the preserving interest of CORTLANDT PARKER, Esq., to whom all who honor KEARNY must feel grateful, for the care he has evinced in collecting so many valuable records of the best soldier of the period.

"It will be more interesting, and more in accordance with our present purpose, to resume again the correspondence of General KEARNY, and thence derive our acquaintance with his military character. A letter of anxious inquiry has been written to him respecting the fate of Major RYERSON,* of Sussex, reported at first to have fallen. Under date of the 10th of July, from Harrison's Landing, he writes as follow: 'Your request as to Major RYERSON's effects shall be attended to; but I am glad to have it from reliable sources that he is a prisoner, and not dangerously though badly wounded. The siege of Richmond was raised, and here we are drifting down the stream. How curious all this verification of prognostications I so correctly read, and yet feared to translate; so strangely correct have been my instincts in this war as in previous ones. In Italy, in 1859, it was the same thing, and made my betters sometimes wonder; but this war is plain to those who, with experience, will take pains to look danger in the face, to leave little to mere hope, and remember that a Southern army can not afford to be idle. Our coming here has been a most cowardly and unwise alternative. The battles on the left bank of the Chickahominy were mismanaged. I had been over there several days before, and observed to all around how we would be strategically † and tactically whipped; attacked from an inland

* Afterward killed at the "Wilderness."

† "In the course of the seventeenth century, and until near the close of it (second and third decade), the principles of offensive war had not been settled into that code which we now call STRATEGY (the word itself is not in JOHNSON'S *Dictionary*). War was the mere trial of strength between individual warriors until the time of the Barons, when it advanced into becoming a struggle of bodies of men, either behind stone walls or some inaccessible natural defences. The object sought to be obtained by leaders of armies was just the mastery for the moment, without much combination or any previously considered plans, which form the science of a campaign."—General CUST'S "*Lives of the Warriors*," 1611—1675, vol. ii., 455.

point not provided against, and be thrown down-hill, and then have to work up again, and be thus crippled and destroyed. It occurred so precisely. Then comes the fearful error of McClellan's want of nerve. Instead of *instanter* reducing his line of defense to a certain intrenched *tête-de-pont* on the right bank, merely covering Bottom's Bridge and the Railroad bridge, and beyond which he never should have made a *serious* advance short of adopting an attack and rushing into Richmond by that side — a *tête-de-pont* fully fortified and strong; and crossing the night of the first, or certainly the second battle, when he could no longer have been deceived, *all his troops*, except the 10,000 men requisite for the *tête-de-pont*, to the left bank, there to defy and give a general battle — and the ground was admirable for us; then, in case of victory, recrossing and rushing into Richmond; in case of defeat, retiring, as other beaten armies do, back along his line of communications, to his basis of operations, be it to White House, be it to Williamsburg, be it to Yorktown; thus always firm, always secure, always covering his own supply, always embarrassing his enemy by drawing them on when they have no transportation to follow, when they dare not leave Richmond too far. Instead of all this, as simple as the pursuit of the panic-stricken army running from Manassas, he loses head and heart, throws himself back on the shipping, and gulls the silly public with a hard name, namely, that he had changed his base of operations. This is false, and by this time he knows it. We have no basis whatever to act on. As to ascending the James, when, after the successful fight at Malvern Hill, he yielded the strongest battle-field that we have yet had, he gave to the enemy a fearfully strong position which debars our future advance. As to crossing the James river, that is out of the question. It would result in nothing, but only the more endanger Washington. And now I distinctly assure you that there are ninety-nine chances in a hundred of Washington's being taken in less than fifteen days. But the falsity of the James river being a base of operations is this, that it is quietly known that, if there were full peace, the James river has been so effectively obstructed that it could not be cleared under many weeks; besides, gunboats are overrated. The enemy fought very cowardly in the West, hence their success. In this region the rebels face full batteries on the open ground, hurling grape at them, and come up to the muzzles of the guns. This was the case on the 30th ult., on the New-Market road, where nothing but my so-called personal rashness in heading the Sixty-third Pennsylvania and a part of the Thirty-seventh New York, in leading them to the charge, saved my pieces. To me the most cruel thing of this war is the unhandsome attempt of crushing my military mastery of my profession under the decrying epithets of rashness.* My best results of head would often fail but for the stimulus of my lead. No; very far from having a base to act on, General McClellan has *boxed* us. You will soon hear of the James river being rendered impassable for our supplies, and then, like drowned rats, we must soon come out of our holes. But it will be done with more awful sacrifices of useless because avoidable battles. We are fortifying here again, unnecessarily so. It breaks the hearts of the soldiers, gives them the idea that they can not win fields, and yet, in a few days, sooner or later, we will have to burst through the network that the enemy are preparing around us, and, if we do not look out for Washington, that city will go. They will crush Pope, by leaving McClellan in ignorance of their departure, then for a foreign alliance, and good-night to the North. Even now McClellan's defeat will be likely to produce this. His 'change of base' may cheat the American newspapers and fool the American people; but the ignominious retreat, the abandonment of the sick and wounded, the abandonment of stores, and loss of strategical supremacy can not be concealed from the military eyes of France, England, nor elsewhere. So much for McClellan and the politicians.

"'P. S. — One curious fact: knowing the case of carrying off my sick and wounded from Fair Oaks (I sent them off early), I was ordered to unload them and abandon them; but I did not,

---

* Lord Napier, of Magdala, said in one of his recent speeches in London that the "way to defeat an Asiatic enemy is by going straight to their heads on every occasion." The hero of Abyssinia was loudly cheered at this remark; but we suspect it *contains the first principle of successful war everywhere.* — Capt. P—— (one of the finest military writers in this country, during the years 1863-'5 military Editor of the Army and Navy Journal). — *N. Y. Times.*

and carried them off, but, although I had twenty empty wagons, was prevented taking off those of another hospital. Fortunately, they, too, principally got clear.'

"I will not apologize," is the remark of CORTLANDT PARKER, in his sketch of PHILIP KEARNY, Soldier and Patriot, "for extracting this long letter. There is much in it to exhibit the peculiarities of General KEARNY'S character. Next to his sense of the disgrace inflicted upon the army at large, and the country, by the retreat which he so severely denounced, was his grief at the losses and almost ruin of his pet Jersey Brigade, upon whose fate he ever looked with parental anxiety. 'I am sickened,' he writes in a letter of July 24th, 'by the falseness of the times, and the gratuitous sacrifice of the Jersey Brigade, is enough to make me so. Why did not their division general go to command in person? It was his own part of the division (* *). It was half of his own provisional corps, and surely why not place it in the fight, even if he did no more? There is some awful secret history to this * * division at Friday's fight. You will learn it in the end; the battle which had been won, was lost by imbecility.' July 31st, he writes: 'Major RYERSON is home to tell his own story, and more have escaped than we counted on. I am much affected by two circumstances, the loss of the colors of the Second regiment, and the surrender of the Fourth, with scarcely a man hurt, all of which only proves the want of confidence incident on a want of military management on the part of the noblest troops on the earth, my old brigade, in that disastrous battle of the 27th of June, on the Chickahominy. General TAYLOR tells a sad story of it; the brave HEXAMER, of the battery even worse; and yet McCLELLAN screens PORTER, and Congress brevets him. As to their commanding general, I cannot understand how a general like him, with his legitimate division, one half of his command committed to fight under his own eye, in his very presence, and that he should have never taken charge of their welfare. At Williamsburg, I engaged the enemy with but five regiments, and at Fair Oaks with but one brigade, and yet this is set down as rashness of my own person. I dislike to think of this, the noblest brigade in the army, frittered to shreds in a moment. How truly and honestly would I have served under General Cook, had Jersey but united her soldiers for us.

"'Our great anniversary is hardly past, recalling most painfully the uprising of the North at this epoch last year, till then much treachery, but not a reverse of arms. How vividly do I recall, in an oration I heard that day, the truthful tribute to General Scott, as the only man who could have impressed with certain victory the mass of his countrymen, who, had he been left in general control, would have mesmerized us with his own unrivaled conviction of success. But where are we now? Whither has gone the dignity of the finest army ever raised in the hemisphere, if I may not say the world? All disappeared, as if wilted by the touch of some evil genius's wand. An army victorious in retreat, even brilliantly so in the advance, and even in the false position into which it had been exposed, more lavish of blood than aught history presents on record; and yet all this timorously placed in a *cul-de-sac* of which the enemy holds the strings.

"I am glad," he proceeds, "to hear you boldly mention the principle of drafts. Believe me, without it, not only is the Union imperiled, but I will not answer for the existence of the North. The Southerners have long years proclaimed that they could of all people the best sustain a war. Is the North to shut her eyes to the past, and forget Sparta and the Helots, a fighting aristocracy, and the cultivator a slave? The slothfulness of the North, the schisms of its politicians, the trifling of all — in fine, this crisis, dictated by small men of small motives, has developed in the South confidence, and increased venom and the activity of hopefulness, even more than the spasmodic action of despair. They have boldly launched into the experiment which Washington dared not, even for our sacred Revolution; and they have invented the conscription, in which they have succeeded by terrorism, or as likely because, from our temporizing, the South is united to a man; and thus from being weak, comparatively, in population, it is they who outnumber us at present, and will do so the more each succeeding day. Do not be deceived by big words; we have been blinded by them too long. Do not believe that you can starve them by intercepting railroads. In the first place, the position of any railroad argues an unlimited concentration against the assailant, a speedy return to another quarter. But that apart, do not let us fancy that if, for thirty years, all Germany was overrun by armies, living as they went; if that same country was more recently the theatre of war for twenty years of the vast forces of Napoleonic times, and with armies that moved with hardly a provision train, there is any starving an army in the heart of Virginia, where, cut what roads you may, you still have manifold branches near at hand. Besides, look out! the war will be carried into Egypt, and our own purse-strings will be unfastened with a vengeance.

"Why we hesitate, I cannot imagine. It is fearful infatuation to wait. The people are ripe for it, as you remark. Of course they are. First, they are earnest as patriots; and next, they have an instinct of the storm brewing in the horizon. Why the enemy leave us as long alone really embarrasses me; not but that it is very certain that their tremendous, unparalleled daring in facing our artillery has been attended with unparalleled loss. Though successful on the Chickahominy against PORTER; unsuccessful on the 30th of June, on the New-Market road; by the spirited advance of the Sixty-third Pennsylvania and half the Thirty-seventh New York, which I led up against ten times our number, who, unchecked by the ceaseless discharge of six pieces firing grape, nearly reached the muzzles as soon as ourselves; again unsuccessful at Malvern Heights, from its amphitheatre shape, permitting a concentration of our over-numerous artillery (the only battle where it has come well into play), the result of all which was, for the moment, that they could no longer force their men to an immediate repetition. I myself think that they can never repeat it, for it is unusual in war; it is against the axioms of Napoleon as to the capabilities of human courage. Still, their losses, though surpassing ours, are more than made good."

The same letter contains General KEARNY's views on a question then much mooted — the employment of negroes in aid of the Union cause.* He says: "But besides drafting, it is time for us to deprive the enemy of their extraneous engines of war. There is no more Southern man at heart than myself. I am so from education, association, and from being a purely unprejudiced lover of the Union. But this is now no longer time for hesitation. As the blacks are the rural military force of the South, so should they indiscriminately be received, if not seized and sent off. I would not arm them, but I would use them to spare our whites, needed with their colors; needed to drill, that first source of discipline — that first utility in battle. But in furtherance of this, instead of the usual twenty pioneers per regiment, I would select fifty stalwart blacks; give them the ax, the pick and the spade. But give them high military organization. We want bands — give twenty blacks — again military organization. So, too, cooks for the companies, teamsters — even artillery drivers. Do not stop there — and always *without arms* — organize engineer regiments of blacks for the fortifications, pontoon regiments of blacks, black hospital corps of nurses. Put this in practice, and the day that, from European interference, we have to look *bitterness* nearly in the face, *then*, and not till then, awaken to the conviction that you have an army of over fifty thousand *highly* disciplined soldiery — superior to double the number of our ordinary run of badly disciplined, badly officered, unreliable regiments now intrusted with the fortunes of the North. I would seek French officers for them, from their peculiar gift over 'natives.' In their own service they easily beat the Arabs — and then officer them and

---

* EMPLOYING THE CONTRABANDS. – Brig.-General BIRNEY lately wrote to Maj.-General KEARNY for instructions as to the employment of blacks. The following is General KEARNY's reply:

HEADQUARTERS FIRST DIVISION, THIRD CORPS,
CAMP NEAR HARRISON'S LANDING, August 5, 1862.

General—Your communication of this date relative to contrabands is received. The Southerners employ blacks as a military unarmed element, viz.: ruralists. I am of opinion that we should employ them, unarmed, in like manner, for any thing in which they can render service, and thus enable the whites to carry the musket. Therefore, I fully advise their being employed as teamsters, pioneers (unarmed), and as cooks in the regiments. Lieut. Col. INGALLS will furnish them.

Respectfully,
(Signed) P. KEARNY.

To Brig.-General BIRNEY.

In accordance with these instructions, it is understood that Gen. BIRNEY has ordered each regiment in his command, to obtain twenty cooks, ten teamsters and twenty pioneers, making three hundred contrabands employed in the brigade.

surpass their own troops in desperate valor. Also, I should advise some Jamaica sergeants of the black regiments. As for the women, employ them in hospitals, and in making cartridges, etc. I know the Southern character intimately. It is not truly brave. It is at times desperate, invincible if successful — most dispirited if the reverse — is intimidated at a distant idea, which they would encounter, if suddenly brought to them, face to face. This idea of black adjuncts to the military awakens nothing inhuman. It but prevents the slave, run away or abandoned to us, from becoming a moneyed pressure upon us. It eventually would prepare them for freedom; for surely we do not intend to give them to their rebel masters. In fine, why have we even now many old soldiers on the frontier garrisons? Send there a black regiment on trial — not at once, but gradually — by the process I named above. Do this, and besides acquiring a strong provisional army, you magnify your present one by over fifty thousand men."*

Again, on the 17th of July, he addressed his tried friend, O. S. HALSTEAD, Jr., of New Jersey, better known, in the political world, as "PET HALSTEAD." "Is it not strange, here is an army nearly strong enough to go to Richmond. It was *quite so* when it arrived, but has lost the half of its numbers by sickness and *imbecile* administration of a commonplace, unmilitary * * * a weak-kneed General; and also its losses in useless, but *terribly severe battles, are beyond all European previous experience.* In honor to the Southerners I must say, that theirs has been even severer. THEY face *grapeshot*, as Napoleon laid it down as an *axiom* to be IMPOSSIBLE. They are noble fellows. But our men have displayed *just as much courage*, but have not yet been led against batteries. In their doing this, as a friend, though I say it, who should not, I beg you to make all remember, that it was by *my* personal influence going into the first line of fire, precisely as the French Generals have ever done,

* The three preceding letters are from PARKER'S "KEARNY, Soldier and Patriot." KEARNY'S idea of organizing, militarily, the blacks was ahead of any thing originating in the Army of the Potomac, but not in advance of the common friend of KEARNY and his cousin, Brig.-General J. W. PHELPS, U. S. V., of Vermont, nor of the writer, who, in the public prints, advocated — in case of hostilities between the North and South — organizing colored regiments under white officers; and of arming the blacks in the ensuing year when a long war had become a mournful fixed fact.

* * * that FIRST gave this impulse of fighting to the army of McCLELLAN. *In return* there is silence to my powers of administration, my talents for high discipline, my perfect, *business-like* management of all my quotas on a field of battle, and the stupid crowds take up the words prompted to them by the emissaries of the envious and others, my enemies, and say—"Ah! there is a worthless General, he exposes himself." "He is rash." "He must be an ignoramus." Our poor Jersey brigade was cut up, to pieces, from mismanagement (I refer you to General TAYLOR) in PORTER'S fight. The only *battle* which we have yet lost—and this entirely owing to PORTER'S *want of head.* The country permitted an impregnable field, it was not developed. He used regiments and brigades with no concerted action, and lost all * * * and yet McCLELLAN, *in the face of the* President, gives [him] * * a *provisional* corps—and then the President gives him an advanced rank. Whilst *I*, the like unknown before in history—a successful division commander, am left * * * without recognition. Be sure if this army was in the hands of a man likely to save it (it is in a bad fix), I would *pitch* my *commission* to the winds and serve my country otherwise."*

Ten days afterward he addressed the following characteristic epistle to a young cousin, a New Yorker by birth, who had just been appointed a Captain in the Eleventh New Jersey Volunteers. This gallant young man was mortally wounded at Gettysburg and died, aged only twenty-one years, on the 9th of August, 1863, in St. Luke's Hospital, New York city, in consequence of the amputation of his leg, too long deferred for his fragile constitution:

"I am glad to find you in arms. I am truly sensible to the kindness of Gen. STOCKTON and Col. SCRANTON, as well as to his Excellency the Governor. I must confess, that I would have preferred you to have commenced as a Lieutenant, for a Captaincy involves fearful responsibility—and *I have*

---

* Other letters of KEARNY, very interesting and able productions they are, might have been added in this chapter, but it is not just to the dead to publish what he would not have desired or suffered to be made public had he lived. As remarked in a previous chapter, many of his ebullitions were the result of pain acting on a nervous temperament. KEARNY was a magnanimous man, and such men do not utter injustices in their cool moments, or desire to have them remembered if spoken or uttered under irritation or suffering, mental or physical.

the weight of our military name on my shoulders. But I do not say this to discourage you. I am proud that you are in the service. *If you display courage it will gracefully cover a multitude of short-comings.* You must have learned something of the nature of men, as to controlling them with *decision but little harshness; with discipline but justice; but above all with a careful watchfulness of their rights and comforts—they are very grateful, far more so than the little one may do for them deserves.* As to perfecting yourself in your new position, never let it pass from your mind in what a false position a gentleman is, *who assumes to be that which he is not.* That you necessarily must be so for a while is not your fault but that of the volunteer system, that takes new (men) instead of doing justice to those who have served. In telling you all this, my dear cousin, it is only to stimulate you to a high energy. Adopt a military carriage, and perfect yourself in the tactics and in army regulations. Study them constantly. Add to this an investigation of military law, and your course will be right, and a battle or so dashingly carried through, will secure to you my warm sympathies and any assistance I can render you. We are still (within) about five and a half miles of Richmond. Continued alarms, now a shell booming in the air, now a brisk picket fight, now a foray by the enemy, and then again some grey-coats brought in from the other side. In our two battles of Willamsburg and Fair Oaks, my division is the only one that has been engaged (here some words apparently were omitted) in the two battles. These two battles looked more like the picture books than any thing I had ever before seen, except one small point in the battle field of Solferino. The slain were actually piled up in heaps. My *Michigan Marksmen* are fearful with their rifles. I have also some Pennsylvania Mountain Men who are brave fellows, and some *Maine Woodmen,* who seem at home anywhere in the woods, whether balls are whizzing by them or not. My *New York regiments* include the celebrated HOBART WARD Thirty-eighth and the MOZART. On the whole it is a very exciting life, but I never get over the feeling that after every battle I am as fearful of hearing of friends being killed in the opposite army as in our own."

If his detention at Harrison's Landing was a short period of comparative rest and recuperation to General KEARNY, it was destined to be but a short interval of repose. Within two weeks he was again in motion and on his march to join POPE. He left the banks of the James with alacrity, for to take the field again was to him a renewal of life. It is true, that he was no longer buoyed up with those brilliant hopes of success which animated him when he first took the field, still, his spirit was nevertheless elate with the prospect of once more participating in an active campaign, which promised, even if it held forth no other incentives, a certainty of again meeting the enemies of his country and the traitorous foes to right and progress; a certainty of fair stricken fields, where brilliant examples, stern intrepidity, and able generalship might undo, by hard fighting to the purpose, what had already been ill done by the sheerest incompetency — an inability to harvest by decision what had already been reaped in blood.

Here the reader must leave KEARNY for a few pages in order to consider what had occurred in the "Army of Virginia" between the date when the "Army of the Potomac" was compelled by its commander, not by the rebel foe, to commence its rapid retreat to the James, and the date when KEARNY was enabled to bring up his division to the assistance of POPE. While KEARNY lay in enforced inaction at Harrison's Landing, stirring events had been occurring in another quarter, whither the rebels had been permitted to direct those forces which should have been fully occupied, if not destroyed by McCLELLAN.

Then, if ever, was justified that indignant outburst which Shakespeare places in the mouth of the hunchbacked but lion-hearted RICHARD III. LINCOLN, when he learned of the breaking forth of LEE, might have addressed to McCLELLAN the very words which the indomitable PLANTAGANET addressed to STANLEY:

KING RICHARD — "Where is thy power, then, to beat him back?
Where be thy tenants and thy followers?
Are they not now upon the western shore,
Safe-conducting the rebels from their ships?"
STANLEY — "No, my good lord, my friends are in the north."
KING RICHARD — "Cold friends to me; what do they in the north,
When they should serve their sovereign in the west?"

CHAPTER XXVIII.

POPE AND THE "ARMY OF VIRGINIA."

(No. 1.)

FROM THE RAPIDAN TO WARRENTON.

"SOLDIERS: We have had our last retreat. We have seen our last defeat. You stand by me and I will stand by you, and henceforth victory will crown our efforts."—MCCLELLAN, September 10th, 1861.—"*Rebellion Record*" *Diary of Events*, Vol. III., 22 (2).

"Very grievous was the disappointment of the loyal people when they knew that the Grand Army of the Potomac had been driven from the front of Richmond, had abandoned the siege, and had intrenched itself in a defensive position in the malarious region of the James River."—LOSSING'S *Civil War in America*, II., XVII, 441.

"POPE, on taking the field, issued an address to his army, censuring, by implication, the course of MCCLELLAN, and breathing a spirit of confidence which belied the forebodings which he felt."—HARPER'S *History of the Great Rebellion*, 382, and note 3.

"What is an army in which the commander is at the mercy of his subordinates?"—MASSENA TO NAPOLEON; MITCHELL'S *Biographies of Eminent Soldiers*, 188.

"I am clear that one of two courses should be adopted:

"First. To concentrate all our available forces to open communication with POPE.

"Second. To leave POPE to get out of his scrape, and at once use all our means to make the Capital perfectly safe."—MCCLELLAN TO LINCOLN, August 29th, 1862.

"POPE now repeated with greater earnestness his request, made before he took the field, to be relieved of the command of the Army of Virginia, and allowed to return to the West."—LOSSING'S *Civil War in America*, II., 462.

"Money is precious, human life is precious, but TIME is the most precious of all."—Field Marshal SUWAROW to General BELGRADE, 1799.

"This Cabinet order deranges all my plans. . . . Every individual general addresses himself to the Aulic Council, not only about his own particular affairs, but about general affairs also; and has thus a right to intrigues, for his own pleasure and advantage, which gives the Council power to direct and to bind him. If the Aulic Council would only leave me alone, then one or two campaigns would not cost me more than so many months; but with their hyper-strategy and generalship, one month of their operations will extend over entire campaigns."—SUWAROW to ROSUMOWSKY, Russian Ambassador at Vienna, 1799.

"Your Excellency knows that my functions are confined to transmitting the King's orders, and reporting all events to your Excellency. I believe I have fulfilled my duties with care and exactness. If I had supposed it was the Emperor's intention to invest me with more extensive functions, I should have begged to be excused; first, because the supreme direction of affairs in Spain is much beyond my ability; and, secondly, because it is necessary to success in war, that a chief should have under his orders officers of inferior rank who will obey him; not comrades, who think their merits superior to his."—Marshal JOURDAIN to the French Minister of War, June, 1809.

"It is true, that, in the absence of the Crown Prince [HALLECK], the chief command of the troops was entrusted to the Duke of WIEMAR [POPE], . . . but, in point of fact, his authority was very limited, or, to speak more accurately, imaginary; and this for two reasons. In the first, because the Emperor Alexander [LINCOLN] had written to the Duke [POPE], to act in all things conformably to the arrangements of the Crown Prince [HALLECK], who was at a distance from the theatre of war; and, secondly, because orders were forwarded directly from the headquarters . . . to WINTZENGERODE and BULOW [PORTER and others], who, of course, acted as if they were not under the command of the Duke [POPE]."—General DANILEFFSKY, *Campaign in France*, 1814, 29.

Although it does not come within the scope of this work, to enter into any detailed historical review of the operations of the "Army of Virginia," it is, nevertheless, absolutely necessary to present a statement of its operations after General POPE assumed the personal direction of it at Warrenton, July 29th, 1862. He received the command "with grave forebodings of the result," but with the assurance that the enemy would never detach from Richmond any considerable force for an advance upon Washington, so long as the "Army of the Potomac" remained at Harrison's Landing, since as long as it lay *there* the rebel capital was in imminent danger.

Any military student who has examined accurate and detailed maps of the country between the Potomac, east, the Rapidan, south, and the Bull Run mountains, west, will see what an extremely difficult task was assigned to POPE. The rebels were advancing along those mountains, using them partially as a screen, and yet POPE was compelled to cover Fredericksburg from twenty to thirty miles to the east, and entirely out of the line of their march.* The authorities in Washington and McCLELLAN must bear the greater share of the blame originally laid upon POPE. Indeed they, and not he, are responsible for his want of success. Considering all the difficulties front and rear with which POPE had to contend, the only wonder is that he accomplished as much as he did. The latter should have clung to the rear of LEE, or at least have made a diversion, if he did no more. LEE manœuvred as if he deemed that the army at Harrison's Landing was deprived of all power of aggressive injury.

Was he not right? was he not justified in his conclusions by the result? for McCLELLAN's whole action, correspondence and dispositions from the day when he landed on the Peninsula, place him in the same category with those French generals who, abounding in troops, but wanting in themselves, limited themselves almost entirely to demonstrations on the western frontier of Prussia, during the "Seven Years' War."

Imagine such a general as McCLELLAN had proved himself,

* See EMIL SCHALK's "Campaign of 1862 and 1863." "Of what use was or could be the occupation of Fredericksburg? *None.*" Page 187.

especially in his retreat to the James, in Pope's place. Would he have held at bay one hundred thousand men flushed with success, with forty to fifty thousand, and have checked them for two weeks, disputing every inch of ground from Culpeper to Fairfax, fifty miles, holding back Lee's whole army on a line of from thirty to forty miles in extent of front? Compare Pope's action with that of McClellan in the Peninsula. The latter retreated precipitately twenty-five or thirty miles which interposed between Mechanicsville and Harrison's Landing, although he had numbers equal, if not very greatly superior, to the rebels, and his lieutenants held their own gloriously in every encounter. McClellan had better troops than Pope; better executive generals than Pope, until he was joined by Reno and Kearny; better means of supply, and heartier co-operation. Whatever may have been Kearny's personal feelings toward McClellan, he never flinched from his duty to him as his superior. The following may be cited as a specimen of his style of expressing his sentiments in the field:

"The conduct of General Kearny in this battle (Glendale) was the admiration of all his corps. He was everywhere directing all movements, imparting, by his presence and clearsightedness, the most determined courage to his men; wherever the danger was greatest, there he pressed and carried with him a personal power that was equal to a reinforcement. In a pre-eminent degree he possessed that military prescience, or anticipation of what was coming and the point of an enemy's attack, which has characterized every great man who has risen to distinction in the art of war." (Chaplain Marks' "Peninsular Campaign," pages 282, 283.)

*Justice has never been done to Pope.** The merits of the general

---

* "Justice has not been rendered to General Pope for his conduct in this campaign." [The writer penned his sentiment in the *summer* of 1868, having always previously maintained that view of the case. He did not know Professor Draper was engaged in his grand work until the ensuing winter, and never heard or read this judgment until the *winter* of 1868-1869.] "He had a most difficult task to accomplish, and had to depend on very unreliable means. Though there never was purer patriotism than that which animated the soldiers of the Army of the Potomac, that army had been brought, through the influence of officers who surrounded General McClellan, into a most dangerous condition — dangerous to the best interests of the nation — of having a wish of its own, and that wish in opposition to the convictions of the government. In armies it is but a very short step from the possession of a wish to the expression of a will. Perhaps at no period of the war were thoughtful men more deeply alarmed for the future of the nation than when they heard of the restoration of McClellan to the command, and recognized the unmis-

have been lost sight of in the demerits of the individual, if demerits is a proper term for unconciliatory manners and rough deportment. McClellan, as wisely observed by Chaplain Marks, won his popularity by demeanor more than by any thing else. "Much of the devotion of the army to General McClellan was owing to the fact, as he rode through the ranks, he always looked upon the men kindly; and when he had to press a soldier out of his way, it was never with rudeness or insult."

Pope, on the other hand, was undoubtedly sometimes, if not often, the exact reverse of this, if prejudice has not influenced

---

takable constraint under which the government had acted. It was in vain for well meaning persons to affirm that the general had never been relieved, and that what had now taken place was no more than an ordinary proceeding. The Peninsular disaster was too recent, the complaints and asseverations of Pope of disobedience to his orders, among the higher officers, too loud for the real state of affairs to be concealed.

"'Leave Pope to get out of his scrape!' What had Pope done to merit inevitable destruction? He had gone down to the Rapidan in obedience to orders to compel the enemy to release his hold on the army in the Peninsula. He was keeping at bay in the best manner he could—nay, more, he was desperately assailing—Lee's ablest lieutenants. For more than a fortnight he was fighting battle after battle against overwhelming forces, first to prevent the junction of his antagonists and then to resist their whole mass. He might have been indiscreet in his reflections on the generalship of his predecessor, but had he been ten times more so, this was not the moment for retaliation for such offenses. *Was he not now the soldier of the republic, at the head of her forlorn hope, in the very breach?* When, from the midst of the fire converging upon him, he cried out for more ammunition to enable him to keep his foothold, how was he answered? 'I know nothing of the calibres of Pope's artillery!'

"The operations of Pope with the army of Virginia were based entirely on the expected junction of reinforcements from the Army of the Potomac. Not without indignation does he say in his report, '25,000 men were all of the 91,000 veteran troops from Harrison's Landing, who ever drew trigger under my command, or in any way took part in this campaign. The complete overthrow of Lee's army, or at least the entire frustration of his movement toward the Potomac, was defeated by the failure of the Army of the Potomac to effect a junction in time with the army of Virginia on the line of the Rappahannock, or even so far back as the line of Bull Run.'

"From the tenor of Pope's complaint, the reader cannot fail to discern that the national government was, at this time, passing through a serious crisis. The triumphant confederate army threatening Washington, was by no means the only formidable object before the republic. Individual grievances are of little moment in the eye of history, save when they are connected with national interests; they become of supreme importance when they presage public perils. Enough has been said to enable the reader to perceive that at this momentous period the government was acting under constraint. . . . Military critics will, doubtless, point out professional mistakes in Pope's campaign. In justice, however, they must bear in mind his disappointed expectations of support. Well might Lincoln, who, notwithstanding his general buoyancy, was subject to paroxysms of deep depression, almost despair, when he saw so much gallantry wasted—well might his heart sink within him, when he was now sardonically told in allusion to his former solicitude for the seat of government at the outset of the Peninsular campaign, 'at once to use all due means to make the capital perfectly safe.'" Professor John William Draper's *History of the American Civil War*, vol. 2, p. 444.

the pen-portrait of the man. A friend and relative of the writer was present "at an interview just in the rear of the latter's (KEARNY's) division, on a slight eminence, at nightfall, about 9 P. M., August 29, 1862, the first day of the Second Battle of Bull Run. KEARNY asked to have his troops — whom he said had sustained hard fighting and were worn out — relieved by fresh ones." Such a request from such a man as KEARNY, should have been met with sympathetic courtesy and consideration, even if the exigencies of the service prevented POPE from acceding to it. Nevertheless, "the request was refused in rough terms," so much so as to leave the most painful impression upon the mind of the narrator, an officer of high rank and position, who dwelt upon the interview with admiration, "in describing KEARNY's magnificent presence during the whole scene."

Nevertheless, it would be highly unjust and untrue not to express the conviction that POPE's tenacity saved Washington, imperiled by the practical incapacity of HALLECK, and the languor or procrastination of McCLELLAN, aided in either case by the vacillation, feebleness, and utter want of comprehensive ideas and of strategic penetration among those who controlled events at the Capital. All, however, could have been remedied by will and alacrity on the part of McCLELLAN, and more than one of his generals. Results distinctly demonstrated that these were wanting. Those who cannot, or will not judge by results, will, perhaps, pay as little attention to the following extract from the letter of an honest man, who served in a most responsible position on the staff of the Army of the Potomac for over three years, which throws strong light upon the subject:

"On September 2d (this morning), General POPE, while on Centerville Heights, pointing toward four different encampments, directed me to carry orders to Major-Generals HEINTZELMAN, SIGEL, RENO and PORTER. I found neither of these generals at the encampments indicated; in fact, I was so misled by this indication by General POPE as to make it three or four hours before all the orders were delivered.

"I rode up to one headquarter tent, and meeting General FRANKLIN, asked him the whereabouts of these generals; he told me that there were other generals in the tent who, perhaps, might inform me. I found five generals in consultation, one of whom immediately replied to my inquiries by saying that they did not know anything about General POPE, or his generals."*

SUCHET, on the Var, in April and May, 1800, occupied an analogous position to that of POPE, in August, 1862. Defeated by ELSNITZ, but disputing every inch of ground, he clung so tenaciously to the Austrians, and occupied their attention so thoroughly, that his diversion exercised a most important influence upon the event of Marengo, and NAPOLEON acknowledged it. MASSENA's defence of Genoa operated in a similar and almost equal degree, although he was forced to capitulate. Both, by their obstinate resistance, gained TIME, the most

---

*"The operations of the English army (1595, in Ireland) were retarded and counteracted by disunion. RUSSELL, the Deputy, envied the glory of NORRIS, and NORRIS, the General, was jealous of the interference of Russell."—O'CONOR's *Military Memoirs of the Irish Nation*, 9.

"ST. RUTH (the French general sent over to command the Irish in 1691) did not reach Athlone until the siege of the Irish town had commenced. Dissensions are said to have arisen between him and Sarsfield. Possibly, upon his arrival at the camp, he may have reproached Sarsfield with the unnecessary and hopeless defence of Ballymore, and of the English town of Athlone, where so many of the best soldiers of the army had been sacrificed in posts which were notoriously untenable. That discord prevailed, most prejudicial to the service, is certain, but whether excited by these reproaches, or by the jealousies too frequently attendant on camps, is a speculation now enveloped in obscurity."—O'CONOR's *Military History of the Irish Nation*, p. 139.

"The day is (1643) reported to have been intensely hot, and this oppressed the soldiers; many of the Cavaliers of note, moreover, had fallen before the rebel artillery, which had been advantageously posted and well served. * * * At all events, when the day broke, ESSEX found the way open; and marching through Newbury, unopposed, he pursued his way to London by way of Reading and Windsor. Here he found Sir WILLIAM WALLER, with about 4,000 horse and foot, *apparently quite unconcerned about his safety at Newbury, which was not above twenty miles distant!*"—*Lives of the Warriors of the Civil Wars of France and England*, by General the Hon. Sir EDWARD CUST, DCL. London, JOHN MURRAY, Albemarle street, 1611-1675; 1867, Vol. I., 292.

"It is very curious, but the history of the Great Civil War of England, like our own 'Slaveholders' Rebellion,' a contest between an aristocratic faction and the People, was prolific in examples of the pernicious effects of the jealousies between rival commanders and their favorites or adherents. The same was the case in the Civil Wars of the French Monarchy, although the French *Republican* armies were wonderfully free of such exhibitions. The Austrian military records are full of similar cases, and, strange to say, it is insinuated that the successes of both the Bonapartes, Emperors, in Italy, were owing to the facility with which they could bribe some of the Imperial commanders. Still, in justice, it must be added that, two of the chiefs, over whom he gained the greatest advantages, were 'above suspicion,' 'but some of the subordinate officers, especially of the staff, in that and the subsequent wars, have not come off so clear.' Names have been mentioned, and charges distinctly made. In the *Recit de la Campagne en Italie*, BONAPARTE is reported to have said, at Milan, after the war was over, in allusion to an article in a German newspaper—the 'Ratisbon Mercury'—which insinuated that he had bribed the Austrian generals: 'It is true that I have spent much money, but not to win over the generals. I thought it better for my purpose to try the staff, and I have had no reason to regret it.'"—Vol. 1, pp. 91, 92; VIEUSSEUX's *Napoleon Bonaparte: his Sayings and his Deeds*.

important element in military success; POPE, likewise, gained time of *inestimable* value. He held in check for ten days the army which McCLELLAN had permitted to escape, and thus was let loose upon Washington. He saved the National Capital, and from the buckler which he interposed, LEE glanced off to Frederick. This gave ten days more. Then the "Army of the Potomac," having absorbed the "Army of Virginia," threw back the rebels across the Potomac.

The Army of Virginia, in July, consisted of about 34,000 infantry and artillery, and about 5,000 cavalry, of which a considerable part was in bad condition.

This force was stretched out along a front of forty miles, with its left resting on Sperryville, and its right on Fredericksburg. On July 14th, General HATCH had been directed to occupy Gordonsville, which, with Charlotteville, KEARNY had indicated from the very first as strategic key-points to any overland advance upon, or operations against, Richmond.* HATCH failed to execute this order, which would have enabled him to destroy the railroads which connect at Gordonsville, and was superseded in the command of the cavalry by the model commander of that arm, glorious JOHN BUFORD.

On the 13th July, JACKSON, with his own division, and that of EWELL, had been ordered to Gordonsville, where he was joined on the 27th by A. P. HILL. This accession augmented the forces in the presence of the Army of Virginia, on the 7th of August, to 35,000 men. POPE concentrated his infantry along the road from Sperryville to Culpepper; his cavalry being thrown ten miles forward. On the 9th, occurred the battle of Cedar or Slaughter Mountain, or Cedar Run, whose results so alarmed the Federal authorities, that General HALLECK tele-

---

* The English author of the *Battle-Fields of the South*—quite a fair book for a rebel work—remarks, page 424, in this connection: "BANKS, with a strong force of New England troops, was stationed within a short distance of Culpepper Court-House, while strong detachments of cavalry and artillery had penetrated even so far southward as Gordonsville, but did not retain possession of that all-important point. They were merely feeling their way to its ultimate occupation. This was perfectly well known to us, and the value of Gordonsville fully appreciated: for the only two routes to Richmond and the South united there, and if once strongly garrisoned by the enemy, they would circumscribe all our operations, and cause the fall of Richmond without the absolute necessity of losing a man." If this was anywhere near true in the summer of 1862, how perfectly correct in the fall of 1861!

graphed at once to McClellan to send forward General Burnside with his corps—which had been brought from North Carolina to Fortress Monroe, and was lying there—to reinforce Pope through Fredericksburg. Five days previous to this bloody and indecisive conflict, on the 4th,* McClellan had been ordered to withdraw from the Peninsula, whereupon he became very bold, and made the abortive movement under Hooker to Malvern Hill. This apparent initiative occasioned the remark by Kearny, who supposed that this was the first of a renewed advance upon Richmond, "that Hooker got all the good chances, and none fell to his share." As long as McClellan lay at Harrison's Landing, in his very strong and fortified position, Lee, with the main body of the rebel forces, remained in Richmond, to watch him and protect the rebel capital.

Indiscretion or treason in the Northern ranks revealed to Moseby,† passing through the fleet of transports at Fortress Monroe, as a prisoner, that the troops assembled at that point were not to join McClellan, but were destined, in fact were on their way, to reinforce Pope. Feeling satisfied, from his knowledge of its commander, that there was no danger to be apprehended from the Army of the Potomac, wasting most precious time at Harrison's Landing, Lee, as soon as Moseby made his report, began to move northward. This was on the 13th of August. In the meanwhile Pope, who foresaw the coming storm, was losing reputation daily, through his strict observance of the orders of that general who had already given him a very unfavorable character before the people, by fathering upon him a report which Pope declares that he never made. This report was the one in regard to the capture of 10,000 prisoners during Halleck's own operations against Corinth, June 12th, 1862. Such a report Pope declares never emanated from him, and with some reason, since he says he was confined to his tent by sickness at the time.

Pope did well in Virginia, considering the forces at his disposition, and all his reverses were due to his honest endeavors

---

* "*Annals of the Sixth Pennsylvania Cavalry*," 5th August, p. 83.

† John Esten Cooke's *Military Biography of Stonewall Jackson*, pp. 255, 256.

to obey the orders daily transmitted from Washington, and the positive assurances that he would receive cordial support and adequate reinforcements. The first was not given, and the second did not arrive either in the force promised or at the time stated.

On the 14th of August, the Army of Virginia was reinforced with 8,000 men of BURNSIDE's Corps, under the gallant and reliable RENO, from Falmouth, four days after HALLECK telegraphed that the enemy was crossing the Rapidan in large force. POPE, thereupon, was making preparations to push forward, when, on August 16th, his cavalry captured J. E. B. STUART's Adjutant-General, on whom was taken an autograph letter of General LEE, dated Gordonsville, August 15th, which revealed the rebel intention and LEE's plan to overwhelm the Army of Virginia before it could be reinforced by any portion of the Army of the Potomac. This left Pope no other option than to fall back upon a stronger position, and await the arrival of the expected support. Even the British Colonel FLETCHER, in his *History of the American War*, virtually admits that POPE did well; that he accomplished his retreat in good order behind the Rappahannock; and, during the 20th, 21st and 22d of August, foiled every attempt of the rebels to pass that stream, although they tested every ford. The "English Combatant," author of the *Battle-Fields of the South* (page 425), speaking of the retiring of the Union forces back toward the Rapidan, or Rapid-Anna, does justice to the movements in these words: "This was generalship." Captain NOYES, an eye-witness, whose peculiar duties gave him opportunities of seeing everything, confirms this in his "*Bivouac and Battle-Field.*"

Three precious days had thus been gained, since every day that LEE's advance was delayed was of incalculable value to the country. Finding that he could not force the passage of the river Rappahannock—which rose seven feet,* in consequence

* Men often talk of parallels and coincidences in war, and such there are infinite and curious. At the battle of Fornova the Italians attacked the French and were repulsed, as at Cedar Mountain. At the same time the Italian Stradiotti cut around and plundered the French camp. When, the next morning, CHARLES VIII had completed his preparation to attack the Italians, he found that a torrent which interposed had been so swollen by a sudden storm (such as occurred at Oriskany 1777, at Solferino in 1859, and did after-

of a heavy rain on the night of August 22 — LEE determined to throw JACKSON round POPE's right, the movement being screened by the Bull Run mountains.

During that terrible night of the 22d — "the darkest night he ever knew," according to Brevet-Col. PAINE — occurred that raid of 1,500 cavalry under Stuart, who stole around POPE's flank, just as the same leader had made the circuit of McCLELLAN two months previous in the Peninsula, and captured POPE's headquarter wagons, at Catlett's Station. This exploit made a great noise at the time, and augmented the causeless ridicule heaped upon the Union commander, because his uniform coat was captured. Even had his whole personal baggage from his undershirt to his overcoat, even had his whole camp become the prey of the enemy, such a misfortune need not have had any effect on the campaign. At Jankau, March 6, 1645, in one respect the decisive battle of the Thirty Years' War, the imperial light cavalry got possession of the Swedish camp, without affecting the military or political result* in the slightest degree. After the Swedes had won the victory, their cavalry cut down the marauders and re-captured their booty. At Mollwitz, 10th April, 1741, the Austrian Horse renounced charging, and "the Hussar part did something of plunder to rearward," at a moment when every bayonet and sabre was needed in the opposite quarter. At Chotusitz, May 17, 1742, and again at Soor, September 30, 1745, the Austrian light troops made themselves masters of the Prussian camp. But this undue diversion of so many cavalry doubtless gave FREDERICK the victory, which he deemed cheaply purchased by the loss sustained through the plundering of the Croats, Pandours and such like.

At Arbela, B. C. (October 1), 331, the Persians who had broken or permitted to traverse the Grecian line, could have

---

wards occur at Chantilly), that the river had risen seven feet, and was no longer fordable. Exactly such was the case with POPE on the 25th August, 1862, when he intended to cross the Rappahannock and attack the rebels, at the same time that STUART was making his raid round upon his rear. A peculiarly heavy rain, which set in on the 24th, so raised the river that the bridges were carried away. Before the water subsided the opportunity had passed, JACKSON had thrown himself in POPE's rear, and the whole aspect of the campaign had changed.

* GEIJER's *History of the Swedes*, 326 (6). COMBE's "Histoire Generale de la Diplomatie Europeene," Sec. 2, pages 211-215.

overwhelmed the left wing under PARMENIO, already hard pressed, had they not amused themselves with the pillage of ALEXANDER'S camp. When the rest of the array of DARIUS had been dissipated, PARMENIO cut up the marauders, and, despite the temporary occupation of his camp, ALEXANDER triumphed and became master of Asia.

At Fornova, or the battle of the Taro, 6th July, 1495, the Stradriots or Albanian light cavalry gave the victory to the French by turning aside to pillage their camp.

Unfortunately, however, among STUART'S spoils were the maps and memoranda of the Topographical Staff, and worst of all POPE'S dispatch-book. This revealed to LEE not only the plans of the Union general, but the disposition of his forces and their comparative feebleness. Well may the historian, GUERNSEY, remark, "When that unnamed negro, accidentally encountered in the darkness, guided the Sixth Virginia cavalry to POPE'S tent, he was potentially fighting the battles of Groveton and Antietam."

This was one of those interventions of Providence which men style accidents,* such as decided Aughrim and the fate of Ireland, 1691, by the hand of an outraged husband, a pedlar; Denain and the fate of France, 1712, through the casual stroll of a "priest and civic functionary;" Mollwitz, 1741, through the meeting in the snow of the Prussian Aid, SALDERN, with a farm laborer sent in search of a clean shirt for an Austrian trooper; Catholisch-Hennersdorf, 1745, by the guidance of a miller's boy; Vittoria, 1813, through the information of "a brave peasant;" Waterloo, through the piloting of a shepherd's lad. But a still more apposite parallel is that pilotage of "an humble and unknown individual," "a Piedmontese peasant," who found the French army of FRANCIS I. pounded in the passes of the Alps, and by his guidance rendered the defeat of the Swiss at Marignano or San Donato, September 13–14th, 1575, possible, and the conquest of Italy an accomplished fact.

On that night of darkness and storm, Major-General PHILIP KEARNY'S Division, which had landed at Alexandria 1:30 P.

* "In war sometimes accidents happen, accidents above human power to prevent, they are like the interfering of Providence." SCHALK'S "*Campaigns of 1862 and 1863*," page 251.

M., 21st, was at Burke's Station, having left Harrison's Landing on the 15th of August, and marched thence, via Jones' (Soan's) Bridge (August 15th), "which we (the 3d Corps) were to hold till the troops had all started from our old camp at Harrison's Bar." On the 16th, via Diascund Bridge, KEARNY fell back to Barhamsville, and Williamsburg (17th), to Yorktown (20th), sailing thence August 21st.* KEARNY's division and MEADE's Pennsylvania Reserves were the first troops from the Army of the Potomac to reinforce—that is, *effectively*, in the face of the enemy—the Army of Virginia.

The disclosures of POPE's dispatch-book developed at once to LEE the practicability of turning the right of the Army of Virginia, getting in its rear, capturing its supplies and cutting it off from Washington. The execution of this hazardous stroke of generalship was confided to the audacious and ever-ready JACKSON. It was nevertheless fraught with peril, and had POPE been reinforced, as he expected to be and should have been, the biter would have been bit, like the Saxons at Kesseldorf, in 1745; like the Russians at Austerlitz, in 1805; and like the French at Haynau and at Culm, in 1813; and like CHARLES ALBERT at Novara, in 1849. Had the Army of the Potomac, *as a unit*, supported the Army of Virginia, as did the divisions of RENO, KEARNY, HOOKER and MEADE, the star of STONEWALL JACKSON would have set on the same field where it rose and gave him a name.†

On the 22-23d of August, while POPE was revolving in his mind a good plan to overwhelm JACKSON, and making prepara-

---

* HEINTZELMAN'S Report (POPE'S Report), page 54: "*Life of Maj.-Gen.* DAVID BELL BIRNEY," pages 60-61.

† "He (POPE) had labored hard under many difficulties, and he bitterly complained of a lack of co-operation with him in his later struggles by MCCLELLAN and some of his subordinates." "It is clear to the comprehension of the writer, after a careful analysis of reports and dispatches, that had these corps and Porter's been allowed to give timely assistance to POPE, as they could have done, LEE'S army might have been captured or dispersed, and perhaps a death-blow given to the rebellion. In view of all the testimony and especially of that given in MCCLELLAN'S Report, it does not seem to be a harsh judgment to believe that the Commander of the Army of the Potomac and his friends were willing to see POPE defeated. 'POPE'S appointment to the command, and his address to his army on opening the campaign,' says a careful writer, 'had been understood by them as reflecting on the strategy of the Peninsular campaign; and this was their mode of resenting the indignity.'"—LOSSING'S *Civil War in America*, II., 462, Text and Note, 4, pages 462-3.

tions to carry it out effectively, another general as prompt, bold, and expeditious as the greatest of rebel lieutenants, the dashing KEARNY, was already at Warrenton Junction, and had placed sufficient guards all along the railroad in his rear.

At midnight, on the 25th, STONEWALL JACKSON was at Salem, at the western issue of Thoroughfare Gap, having operated under cover of the Bull Run Mountains; just as TRAUN moved to and fro, like a shuttle, under the blind of the Range of the Spessart, in 1745, when, by practical-strategy and without the necessity of a battle, he compelled the French to retire precipitately beyond the Rhine; just as LEE was about to throw back, by a series of battles, the Union armies beyond the Potomac.

Those who observed attentively the operations of the "Seven Weeks' War," in 1866, will perceive that the Bull Run Mountains occupied identically the same relation to POPE's line of supply and retreat, that the Giant Mountains and the ranges which constitute their prolongation toward the south-east, bore to the line of supply and retreat of BENEDEK—the slopes of Silesia representing the Shenandoah Valley. The possession of the passes through these rugged barriers and of the fortresses which secured them, enabled the Prussians to flank the Austrian army, and, throughout, menace the communications on which it was completely dependent. It was this fact forbade BENEDEK's selecting a more advanced battle-field than that of Sadowa, where he was nipped and crushed as was POPE in the second battle of Manassas Plains or Bull Run.

The authorities at the National Capital, always extremely timid, never seemed to feel that they were safe, not even for a moment, without keeping a considerable army in front of the defenses of Washington, when the circle of forts and works around that city ought, if they had been properly manned and commanded—backed by a sufficient central reserve, ready to move to any over-matched or mastered point—in itself to have been sufficient to render them secure. They appeared to be desirous of realizing the truth of the old Swedish proverb, that "they defended not their men with walls, but their walls with their men"—when Swedes fought, as FREDERICK intimates, "Swedes did fight," rendering the proud assurance, however, in any thing but the grand though boasting spirit of the original. Moreover, even when they had selected a general, they were unwilling to concede any independent action to the man of their choice. POPE was, in reality, nothing more—as a Major-General (who ought to have known) expressed it—than a sort of Adjutant-General, to promulgate and see to the execution, views and orders of a sort of Aulic Council or Cabal, presided over by the Commander-in-Chief, of which the President was, *ex officio*, a member, and yet, through his right of patronage, the ruling spirit. These pulled POPE here, and ordered him there, until they made themselves responsible for all his shortcomings. The only wonder is, that, under the circumstances, POPE accomplished as much as he did. A patriot martyr, whose word could be implicitly relied on, reported these facts, as well as the admission of Mr. LINCOLN, who was honest enough to confess that "POPE went all right enough, until one day we *geed* him, when we ought to have *hawed* him, and then all went wrong!" This, doubtless, referred to HALLECK, or his council, insisting upon POPE "geeing" in his retreat, to cover Fredericksburg as a place of disembarkation for reinforcements from the Army of the Potomac, when POPE wanted to mass to the right, and stop the gaps through the Bull Run Mountains; at the same time receiving reinforcements through Alexandria.

POPE has never received full or even justice at the hands of any writer who has as yet prepared a history of the great American conflict.* A military history of the war has not yet been written. In that, if the pen is not dipped in prejudice, the commander of the "Army of Virginia" during its last campaign will receive more credit than has hitherto been accorded to him. The writer is no particular admirer of POPE, but he is a believer in truth and justice in history, and a worshipper of good old fashioned honesty in thought, word and deed. The author who has been most severe on POPE seems

* Since this was written the second volume of Prof. JOHN WILLIAM DRAPER'S *Civil War in America* has appeared, which does justice to POPE. It is somewhat curious, but the learned and distinguished professor writing in his study in Westchester county, and the author of this work in his library in Dutchess county, unknown to each other, were taking identically the same views of POPE and his operations, and using in one or two sentences the very same words and in many expressing exactly similar ideas.

always to have written like "Planchette," submissive to a superior directing will, and the brilliancy of his paragraphs has often misled the reader into accepting his prejudices for unquestionable narrative.

POPE apparently experienced about the same treatment at the hands of McCLELLAN, or whoever regulated that general's movements, as many of the French generals, during the Seven Years' War, received from their government in Paris, but more especially from their associates or colleagues in command, and just about as much support as the Austrians afforded to the Russians at that period, or the Russians accorded in turn to them. Had they pulled together, FREDERICK must inevitably have succumbed.* The assistance given to POPE was something equivalent to that of Lord GEORGE SACKVILLE to FERDINAND, of Brunswick, at the battle of Minden, in 1759, because the Englishman was "too proud to submit to the control of a German prince," or, perhaps, more akin to that which LANGERON, the Russian subordinate, lent to BLUCHER until events compelled entire submission. If any reader does not comprehend this, let him examine the secret history of these events and he will be astonished when he learns to what lengths jealousy or worse will carry military leaders. This was exemplified by BERNADOTTE'S conduct toward DAVOUST at the period of Auerstadt, in 1806, when THIERS states that he refused to support DAVOUST and left him alone in the presence of the Prussian army, subsquently exhibited in regard to BULOW, TAUENZEIN, BORSTELL and even BLUCHER, in 1813, in fact toward all his colleagues and the general cause throughout the German and French campaigns of 1813, 1814.† The inner history of the

---

* SUWAROFF, at the head of the Austro-Russian army, cleared Italy (Genoa and Riviera excepted) of the Republicans; the ARCHDUKE CHARLES defeated JOURDAIN, and drove him back across the Rhine and obliged MASSENA to abandon Zurich, and retire behind the Aar; while, at the same time, an Anglo-Russian army landed in Holland. But JEALOUSIES and an ignorance of the simplest principles of strategy ruined this fair commencement. Gen. MITCHELL'S "*Biographies of Eminent Soldiers*," page 177.

The DUKE OF WELLINGTON and BLUCHER got on admirably together during their short campaign (1815); but the imbecile arrogance so constantly displayed by the Spanish commanders rendered it impossible for English officers to act in concert with them. *Ibid.*, page 235.

† The reader will pardon a few further remarks in regard to the pernicious influence upon public affairs of jealousies — nay, even rivalries — between generals; the more dangerous in this country, a republic, than in a monarchy, because here every cunning man —

Italian war of 1859, and of the Seven Weeks' War in 1866, might disclose some such deafness as affected DAUN when he left LAUDOHN to take care of himself at Liegnitz. Upon this occasion "neither the Marshal (DAUN) nor LASCY

---

through the press, or political affiliations — makes himself the representative of a party or the available weapon of a "ring."

As a striking evidence of what difficulties and complications arise from such jealousies between generals of equal rank and reputation, even in absolute monarchies, take the case of GNEISENAU, in the Waterloo campaign of 1815. His abilities were conceded by all. Like NAPOLEON'S idea of the French republic, they needed no acknowledgment. They were as clearly visible as the sun; the blind could appreciate them. Throughout the campaigns of 1813-'14 (after the untimely fall of SCHARNHORST at Lutzen, or Gross Gorschen), he had mixed the pills which BLUCHER administered. Nevertheless, the four senior Prussian generals considered "it a point of honor not to allow themselves to be put under the command of a junior in commission." TAUENZEIN founded his claims on his storm of Wittingberg; YORK on his success (subordinate to the direction of BLUCHER, and according to the plans of GNEISENAU) at Wurtemburg, from which he derived his title, and to his patriotic course at TAUROGGEN, which committed Prussia to the War of Liberation for Germany; BULOW for his undoubtedly glorious conduct at Gross Beeren and Dennewitz, and KLEIST to his equally conceded decisive gallantry at Culm. What was the result? BLUCHER was indispensable; and if BLUCHER had command, GNEISENAU was indispensable to him, and, as chief of his staff, and cognizant of his plans, must succeed to the supreme command in case of BLUCHER'S fall or illness. The result was, TAUENZEIN and YORK were honorably shelved with peace commands in war time; KLEIST received the command of the "army of reserve," which BLUCHER and GNEISENAU, by their conduct of affairs, rendered unnecessary; and BULOW was placed at the head of another reserve corps, not expected to be brought into action. He was not at Ligny, and was somewhat blamed for dilatoriness at that period of the campaign; and as he could not object to serve under BLUCHER, and as BLUCHER kept the saddle, he was pushed forward into Waterloo. That victory settled the matter in regard to the obedience of Prussian generals, in 1815, as the victory of the Katsbach crushed out all such bickerings in the Russian lieutenants of BLUCHER in 1813. Still, if such things can occur in absolute monarchies, how much more likely are they to do so in republics, and the more reason to provide against them by instant removals and subsequent severe punishments in case of any display of lukewarm co-operation on the part of any corps or division commander. Such jealousies would have ruined NAPOLEON'S cause in Spain under the most favorable auspices; they did ruin it, and speedily, under existing circumstances. King JOSEPH, nominally commander-in-chief, could do nothing with the arrogant lieutenants, French marshals sent him by NAPOLEON and JOURDAIN, his chief of staff (whom the Emperor acknowledged to be a true patriot, yet disliked him because he had gained what NAPOLEON had not — a battle (Fleurus) which saved France — a victory as influential, if not more so, than any of his own), threw up his hands in despair at the insubordination of those on whose cheerful co-operation success inevitably depended. The culmination of the row was Vittoria, and ended the French career in Spain. MASSENA previously had had to send NEY home for positive disobedience; and WELLINGTON owed more than one escape from the closing vice because one jaw, a French marshal (who, according to LANNES' idea, was better than a king) would not work evenly, or make his moves subservient to another marshal after such moves were indispensable to success.

SOULT, in 1814, implored SUCHET to join him for the battle of Thoulouse, offering to cede the chief command to him and fill a second part if he would do so. SUCHET, playing the despotic king in Catalonia, liked that duty better than propping a lost cause under another; and taking the hint of Marshal CLARKE, Duke of Feltre, the French Minister of War, who knew "the thing was played out," "could not see it" — that is, the force of SOULT'S disinterested patriotism; and so SOULT came to grief, and WELLINGTON beat him and captured Thoulouse. POPE was exactly in the same plight as GNEISENAU, JOURDAIN and MASSENA.

(his lieutenant) heard the firing of the artillery, behind Pfaffendorf, at the distance of half a mile (2 miles English), although there were two hundred cannon playing in the two armies," and heavy cannon at that. There is a similar story told of GORGEY, when he left the First Corps, under NAGY SHANDOR, exposed on the 2d August, 1849, to the attack of the whole Russian army, under PASKIEWITCH. The evening before he said to his staff, "To-morrow, NAGY SHANDOR will get a dressing;" and yet he, the superior, took no measures to protect his subordinate from the licking (Wicks, German) he was sure to receive. Our own military records are not free from such antagonisms. The New England troops would not support SCHUYLER against BURGOYNE; even STARKE held back, and LEE ruined himself by such conduct at Monmouth. Unfortunately, history swarms with such exemplifications of the country subordinated to self, and at Solferino there was considerable ill-feeling evinced at the non-co-operation of one never before so reproached, whose corps, says BOSSOLI, was nicknamed by its comrades, "La Providence des familles."

KEARNY seemed to feel none of that unwillingness to serve under POPE which actuated so many of his rank in the army of the Potomac. He appeared to comprehend the whole case.

"How do they expect POPE," he wrote, under date of August 4th, 1862, "to beat, with a very inferior force, the veterans of EWELL and JACKSON? Get me and my 'fighting division' with POPE," and in the same letter, "with POPE's army I would breathe again."

Little did he dream, when he wrote thus, that within three weeks he would "breathe freely again," as he desired, and, alas! in another week, breathe no more the breath of this life. With what eagerness he looked forward to being relieved from what, to him, was the crushing weight of irresolute mediocrity, superior in rank, inferior in capacity, vacillating in purpose and weak in execution, and of a following (*Gefolge*) as devoted to the interests of their chief, or, rather, through him to their own interests, as the Homeric Myrmidons to Achilles, or the *Leichtach*, or foster-brethren-life-guard, to a Highland chief.

KEARNY's breathing again was very much like the rally or

flow of spirits in a man about to perish, which the Scotch called "fey." His prayer was granted, and Shicksal—the best word for Fate, since it signifies something sent by a higher power which a mortal cannot shun—relieved him and placed him where there was no Laodicean controller of events to fetter his ardent soul or trouble his spirit more.

CHAPTER XXIX.

POPE AND THE "ARMY OF VIRGINIA."

(No. 2.)

THE SECOND BATTLE AT MANASSAS.*

GAINSVILLE, GROVETON, BULL RUN SECOND.

"See, her generous troops,
Whose pay was glory, and their best reward
Free for their country and for me to die."
THOMSON'S "*Liberty.*"

"The retreat (after GROVETON) was conducted in good order across Bull Run. General STAHL'S brigade was the last to cross Stone Bridge, which was accomplished at midnight, without molestation from LEE, who was too much exhausted to make the attempt to rout the forty thousand men who had resisted the attack of all his troops—the same army which had compelled General McCLELLAN, commanding an army of a hundred thousand, to move from the Chickahominy to the James.

* * * * * * * * * * * * * *

"The battle of GROVETON was, therefore, one of the most bravely fought and obstinate contests of the war;—fought by General POPE under adverse circumstances,—great inferiority of numbers, with a subordinate commander who disobeyed orders; with other officers who manifested no hearty co-operation. It will be for the future historian to do full justice to the brave men who made so noble a fight, who, had they been supported as they should have been, would doubtless have won a glorious victory."—CARLETON'S "*Following the Flag,*" pages 180, 181.

"This latter (JACKSON) meets the army of General POPE on the very battle-field of Bull-Run; this time there is no panic, but a dreadful effusion of blood that lasts two days." —"*The United States during the War.*" By AUGUSTE LAUGEL, pages 2-5.

"KING'S Division of our corps had encountered, near Groveton, JACKSON'S forces, *whom KEARNY had in the afternoon driven out of Centreville, and who were retreating towards Thoroughfare Gap* to form a junction with the main army. About the same time RICKETT'S Division became engaged with LONGSTREET'S Corps, near Thoroughfare Gap, about eight miles further west. Both actions were severe, but not decisive for either side."—WOODWARD'S "*Our Campaigns,*" page 176.

"Our loss during the day was estimated by General POPE at from six to eight thousand killed and wounded and Generals HOOKER and KEARNY, who had been over the whole field, separately estimated the loss of the enemy at *from two to one* and from *three to one* of their own."—WOODWARD'S "*Our Campaigns,*" page 181.

---

* In the examination of this campaign, the writer has received the greatest assistance from army maps and an exquisite series of plans of POPE'S battles, furnished to him by Major-General A. A. HUMPHREYS, Chief-of-Engineers, U. S. A., whose kindness in similar respects, has been previously noticed. The plan of the battle-field of Chantilly was drawn for the writer by Brevet Colonel W. H. PAINE, Topographical Staff. The writer cannot refrain from expressing his obligations to these gentlemen; also to the latter for most valuable information which enabled him to form his judgment.

THE IMPETUOSITY OF KEARNY AND HOOKER'S ATTACK AT BRISTOW AND BULL RUN 2D. —"On Wednesday last, 27th August, KEARNY and HOOKER attacked the enemy about one and a-half miles beyond *Bristow;* the enemy at that point being commanded by General EWELL. Our forces attacked the rebels with such impetuosity, that they fell back in some confusion at least two miles. Night came on, which saved the enemy from *total rout.* Yesterday (Saturday, 30th August), at daybreak, Generals KEARNY and HOOKER opened the ball, the enemy falling back toward Centreville. At this point our forces came up with them, when a severe engagement ensued, which lasted until dark, with heavy losses on both sides. The enemy fought with great desperation, and the shades of night again caused a cessation of hostilities." —*New York Herald*, Sunday, Aug. 31st, 1862, p. 5, col. 1.

"General HOOKER, as at Williamsburg, bore the brunt of the battle on Thursday (28th August), and as he fought the rebel General JOHNSTON at Williamsburg and defeated him, so he fought the rebel General JACKSON and utterly routed him. On Friday (29th August) he was reinforced by General KEARNY'S Division, as at Williamsburg, and so these two divisions, forming HEINTZELMAN'S Corps, *drove the enemy to the wall.* HOOKER'S and KEARNY'S Divisions *have done more fighting than any others in the Army of the Potomac,* and their ranks are terribly decimated." —*New York Herald*, Sept. 2d, 1862, p. 1, col. 3.

On the night of the 22d of August occurred the "camisado," or surprise, of Catlett's Station, by STUART. Contrary to the opinion generally received as correct, STUART'S Chief-of-Staff, VON BORCKE, in his "Memoirs of the Confederate War," demonstrates that all our troops did not behave badly; and that some of the Union infantry, despite the surprise, storm and fearful darkness, stood up to their work like true Northern men. On the 23d, LEE was in possession of POPE'S secrets; on the 24th, his movements, based on their discovery, were matured; and on the 25th, JACKSON was off on that daring flank march which did result so disastrously to us, but should have ended so ruinously to him.

The very night of STUART'S "onfall," PHIL. KEARNY, ever foremost — as in front of Alexandria, July, 1861; as into Centreville, Manassas, 9-11th March, 1862; as up to Williamsburg, 5th May, and at Fair Oaks, 31st May, 1862 — was at Burke's Station, and on the morning of August 25th, when JACKSON moved, at Warrenton. Thus the first, the very first division of the "Army of the Potomac," which effectually in its place in the line, re-enforced the "Army of Virginia" was KEARNY'S, brought up by the same energy which carried it ahead of, and by, all others, for HOOKER'S salvation, in the first battle of the Peninsula.

POPE had not been surprised, in the true sense of the term, by LEE. He was aware of the flanking movement of JACKSON; but, even in this critical emergency, he was crippled by the intermeddling of the Washington War-Junta. This must have been the time to which LINCOLN alluded, when he said they *gee'd* him when they ought to have *haw'd* him. They tied his left to Fredericksburg, when he ought to have been allowed to cut loose and move to the right. Assurances of speedy re-enforcements were so precise and definite, that he felt warranted in holding his position. He was assured that 30,000 would reach him by the 25th, but on the evening of that day only 7,000 or 8,000 had come up.

On the 26th, LONGSTREET, who had kept up a show of force in front of POPE, yet all the while creeping away to his right, commenced his march to unite with JACKSON, who, having left Salem at daybreak, was passing through Thoroughfare Gap. POPE then abandoned the line of the Rappahannock, and undertook to throw his whole force in the direction of Gainsville and Manassas Junction. On the morning of the 27th he had 54,000 infantry, made up of his own "Army of Virginia" and the re-enforcements which had reached him from BURNSIDE's Corps and the Army of the Potomac. He had also nominally 4,000 cavalry, but their horses were so broken down that hardly 500 were fit for service. * * *

Those who most admire NAPOLEON's efforts in 1814 seem to belong to the same class with those who are the loudest in their condemnation of POPE, and yet, although they might not be willing to admit it, there is a closer resemblance between the plans of NAPOLEON and those which POPE now sought to execute than would appear without critical examination.

POPE was blamed for setting out with the idea that all-absorbing attention to bases and lines of supply were not indispensable to success. More than one general, renowned in war, attained his object for the very reason that he set iron-clad rules at defiance, and substituted the lights of genius for the laws of blind theory. MARLBOROUGH achieved his greatest triumph, Blenheim, in 1704, by cutting loose from his base and plunging forward with audacity into the very midst of the enemy. Prince EUGENE, in 1706, saved Turin, and compelled the French to evacuate Italy by a manœuvre — as a rule, universally condemned — a flank march in the presence of an enemy, after cutting entirely loose from his base. Another wonderful instance of a triumphant flank march and turning movement-in-attack, is that of STONEWALL JACKSON the evening before he fell. It will be cited to his credit as long as military history is written, and will rank with any on record.* NAPOLEON himself violated, again and again, acknowledged principles, and achieved the most brilliant results when he did so. FREDERICK THE GREAT, in like manner, ignored what routine generals seek to consecrate as principle to cloak their own limited capacity or utter incapacity to improvise. IBRAHIM PASHA, by a flank march, in 1839, on a very small scale in comparison, but still similar to that of Prince EUGENE, in 1706, turned the Turkish position, almost, if not in sight of his antagonist, possessed of equal if not superior light cavalry, at Nezib, and ended the campaign by destroying the Sultan's army. It is true that it does not do for little men to play the big game; but POPE was not a little man. If mere flashes of genius constitute greatness, he was as much better a general than McCLELLAN, as the latter was better than the commander at Big Bethel. The day will come when his campaign of August, 1862, will redound as much to his credit as McCLELLAN's whole career will be condemned for want of every element of true or brilliant generalship.

What is more, if LEE had been the great general which blind admiration insists that he was, he could have gone to Philadelphia, and heaven only knows how much farther in 1863, if he had imitated MARLBOROUGH in 1704; Prince EUGENE in 1706; NAPOLEON in 1796–'7, in 1805, in 1806, in 1814; and even IBRAHIM PASHA in 1839. This is susceptible of proof, and Major-General PHILIP KEARNY, overestimating LEE, seems to have feared such a result.† It was a fortunate thing for the

---

* The secret of the Rebel success at Chancellorsville was the sentiment which filled the breasts of the French Republican soldiery of 1792–'7, which enabled them to perform such undisciplined miracles against disciplined odds. (Witness CARNOT's famous Report of the 4th March, 1795, inserted in J. TALMA's "Chronological Account * * of the French Revolution, 1789—1795.") In 1813, the same idea permeated BLUCHER's "Army of Silesia, as attested by its effects upon the Russian general OSTEN SACHEN's reply to firm old Marshal FORWARDS, when on the 26th August, 1813, he received the orders to "go in." "Tell the general," he replied, "Hurra!" — "*Adams (Co., Penn.) Sentinel*," 1st December, 1813.

† See WILKES' "*Spirit of the Times*," Vol. VII, No. 25, Oct., 1862, page 118, KEARNY's Letter of 4th August, 1862.

North that STONEWALL JACKSON was effectually disposed of on that bright moonlight night, 2d May, 1863, and did not survive, as the "right hand," to execute the plans with which his active, acute brain inspired LEE, when the latter invaded Pennsylvania in June, 1863.

After the battle of Cedar Mountain, August 9th, 1862, analogous, under some aspects, to that of Brienne, February 1st and 2d, 1814, LEE made a forward movement on Washington very much akin to that of BLUCHER toward Paris. On the 9th of February, 1814, the Army of Silesia was dislocated and strung out on the arc of a circle, from the Marne to Montmirail, fifty miles from front to rear, very much as the Army of Northern Virginia was extended on the 25th and 26th of August, 1862, over about the same distance from the Rappahannock to Salem and the Thoroughfare Gap. NAPOLEON at Sezanne occupied very much the same position relative to BLUCHER, and with the same intentions, as POPE at Rappahannock Station, and then Warrenton, to LEE. By a series of actions, attacks in flank, by bringing his forces almost as a unit against fractions of his enemy, in eight days NAPOLEON inflicted such a succession of defeats upon the Russo-Prussians, as would have settled any other antagonist but BLUCHER.* POPE's efforts lasted almost exactly the same time — eight days, August 25th to September 2d; but, badly supported, if not abandoned, with intentions and ideas as clear as those of the French Emperor, he failed where NAPOLEON succeeded. Nevertheless, POPE so crippled LEE, that had SHERIDAN or THOMAS commanded the "Army of the Potomac," the career of the "Army of Northern Virginia" would have ended at Antietam, just as "fiery PHIL." disposed of EARLY in the Shenandoah Valley, in the autumn of 1864, or bull-dog THOMAS rubbed out HOOD between the Cumberland and Tennessee, in December of the same year. What is more, POPE's problem involved natural difficulties, which were absent from that of NAPOLEON. The Bull Run Mountains presented

* "That old devil (BLUCHER) always attacked me with the same vigor. If he was worsted the next moment he demonstrated that he was ready to renew the fight." — NAPOLEON'S "complimentary tribute to the bull-dog tenacity of BLUCHER," addressed to Major-General SIR NIEL CAMPBELL in 1814. — LITTELL'S *Living Age*, 1302, 15th May, 1869, p. 447 (2)

a screen to LEE's operations, which were entirely wanting to those of BLUCHER. On the other hand, NAPOLEON exercised despotic authority, and the supersedure of VICTOR demonstrated how little attention he paid to the rank or feelings of a subordinate, who did not come to time or answer his expectations. NAPOLEON was ably supported, whereas POPE, to use the language of the coadjutor on whom everything depended, was "left to get out of his scrape" as best he could. Viewed in the light of truth and weighed in the scale of justice, POPE's eight days in August, 1862, will not compare unfavorably, when existing circumstances, human difficulties and natural obstacles are taken into account, to NAPOLEON's eight days, 9th to 17th of February, 1814.

On the morning of the 26th, JACKSON rushed through the Thoroughfare Gap with the same fiery energy with which MONTROSE, in 1645, swooped down upon Argyle. At sundown, he was at Bristow Station, on the Orange and Alexandria railroad, which constituted POPE's principal line of supply, directly in POPE's rear. TRIMBLE, with two regiments of infantry, about 500 men, and STUART, with his two brigades of cavalry, pressed on, hot foot, through the darkness, to Manassas Junction, where they captured a vast amount of stores: in fact, this was the only grand depot short of Washington. With the exception of little above what was about sufficient to feed JACKSON's hungry followers for a single day, everything was destroyed. The rebels swept on along the line of the railroad, to Burke's Station, within twelve miles of Alexandria.

Here Brigadier-General TAYLOR, who succeeded KEARNY in the command of the latter's glorious FIRST NEW JERSEY BRIGADE — KEARNY's own, which grew from a pygmy into a giant under his fostering care — 1,000 men, was hurled upon EWELL. On the 26th August, at Bull Run Bridge, it was called upon to confront "the entire corps of STONEWALL JACKSON," comprising, according to GREELEY (II, 181 [1]), "ten brigades and twelve batteries." As may be imagined, it was obliged to fall back, having lost, in killed, wounded, prisoners and missing, 283, over a quarter of the number which were engaged. Its commander, mortally wounded, lingered to die on the very same day that

KEARNY fell, 1st September, 1862. FOSTER records that STONEWALL JACKSON "said that he had rarely seen a body of men who stood up so gallantly in the face of overwhelming odds as did the Jersey troops on this occasion." KEARNY's teaching and example had not been lost with the troops he had made. KEARNY's spirit was with them and in them to the last.

To any one of common sense, this must show clearly the utter want of foresight which compelled POPE to cling so long to Fredericksburg. It was a complete illustration of the invariable tactics of the Austrian Aulic Council, always desirous of holding everything, even the unimportant to the neglect of the essential, and thereby losing everything. When will men learn? When will common sense rule? Will humanity ever profit by the lessons of the past? Alas! it is to be feared never, if civilians, or politicians, or pedants are to exercise the chief command, and men like KEARNY be shoved, like a plug, into the gap to lose their lives in stopping the torrent let in by incapacity and worse.

POPE and LEE were now in situations equally dangerous, in some respects. It is true that POPE's communications were cut and the enemy was in his rear; still POPE's re-enforcements were coming up in that very quarter, and with ordinary energy could sweep away the audacious foe — with a little alacrity, annihilate him. The rebel generals, on the other hand, had so dislocated their forces that two days' march intervened between their right and left. FREDERICK, under such circumstances, would have exclaimed, like CROMWELL at Dunbar, that the Lord had delivered the enemy into his hand; NAPOLEON would have declared, as on the 18th Brumaire, that the god of war and the god of victory was on his side; BLUCHER would have sworn a thousand honest oaths, tossed his pipe into the air like DOLF at Haynau, or SEYDLITZ at Rosbach, and cut in.

POPE had ability enough to appreciate his opportunity, but he was clogged with the half-heartedness of those with whom he had to operate. Fortunately he had a few stalwart and true subordinates. On the 27th of August he hurled HOOKER upon EWELL, who was driven back with a loss of a part of his baggage. On the 28th, he launched "the prompt" KEARNY against

JACKSON. KEARNY, like the DOUGLASS, "ever faithful and true," drove JACKSON's rear guard out of Centerville, late in the afternoon of the 28th, and the main body of the Confederates fled by the way of the Sudley Springs Road and Warrenton Turnpike, destroying the bridges over the little streams behind them. PORTER, who was to have supported KEARNY, "failed utterly to obey the orders which were sent to him, giving as an excuse that his men were tired, although his corps was by far the freshest in the whole army."* Thus the blow by which

*"Had BARCLAY DE TOLLY (after Dresden, 1813) obeyed the order and joined OSTERMANN's corps on the Pirna road, the force in that direction would have been strong enough to make head, both against VANDAMME and the French Guards; but the Russian commander, conceiving that he might be placed in great peril if the French pushed rapidly along the Pirna road, that he might even be cut off and encompassed by the principal part of their army,—which, had they followed the pursuit vigorously, was very possible,—took upon himself to disobey the order of the Field-Marshal, and, to save his own corps, endangered that of the whole army.—" *The Fall of Napoleon.*" "*The Rising of the Nations*,' by Maj.-Gen. J. MITCHELL, vol. ii. pages 67 and 68.

"All night Austrian and Russian troops continued to pour into the plain; and orders were sent to General KLEIST, directing him to hasten the march of his Prussians, and arrive in time to share the honors of tho battle. The officer who carried this order found the road so completely encumbered with artillery and wagons of every description, that he was forced to dismount and make his way on foot; *but these obstacles damped not the zeal of the Prussian commander, who declared that he would cross the summit of the mountains rather than fail the cause in danger's hour, a resolution as bravely acted upon as it had been formed.*"—"*The Fall of Napoleon.*" "*The Rising of the Nations*," by Maj.-Gen. J. MITCHELL, vol. ii. page 74.

"The battle of Dennewitz was fought and gained by 47,000 Prussians, contending against more than 60,000 French, that actually came into fire, and reflects as much credit on the gallantry of the troops as on the skill, zeal and energy of the commanders. The conduct of BULOW, brother of the author of the 'Modern System of War,' and who confessed that he derived all his military knowledge from the works of that unfortunate writer, is spoken of as above all praise; and even PELET admits that the Prussian generals manœuvered with the greatest ability.

"French historians, anxious at all price to uphold the infallibility of NAPOLEON, had ascribed the defeat at Dennewitz, and the failure of the expedition against Berlin, to the *tardy arrival* of Marshal OUDINOT, who, with the twelfth corps, only reached the battle-field at two o'clock in the afternoon. The *charge of tardiness* brought against the marshal *may not be without foundation, and his defense is far from satisfactory;* but the writers who lay so much stress on the late arrival of a single French corps, forgot the non-arrival of more than half the allied army who ought to have been present in the field; and on the absence of which neither NAPOLEON nor any general projecting a plan of attack on Berlin could ever have calculated. If OUDINOT was discontented, as it is usual to assert, *what can be said of Napoleon, who left that officer to serve in a subordinate capacity* in the very army from the chief command of which he had just been removed, in a manner that might almost be termed insulting. Could any one, possessing the slightest knowledge of human character, have committed such an error at such a moment? The world has been stunned with the praise heaped on NAPOLEON's pretended skill in appreciating individuals; and yet how vastly inferior, in tact and judgment, was his conduct here to that of SCHWARZENBERG placing the disobedient BARCLAY DE TOLLY in command of the troops certain to conquer at Culm, and of BLUCHER's reclaiming the envious LANGERON by treating his misconduct as an oversight of orders." "*The Fall of Napoleon.*" "*The Rising of the Nations*," by Maj.-Gen. J. MITCHELL, vol. ii. page 95.

POPE justly calculated to bag JACKSON, or destroy him, failed through the non-coöperation of MCCLELLAN's favorite corps commander.*

On the same afternoon that KEARNY drove JACKSON out of Centreville, LONGSTREET fought his way through Thorougfare Gap, to the relief of his hard-pressed rebel associates.

The wedge which POPE had fashioned and pointed with the steel of a KEARNY and a HOOKER, to split asunder LEE's army, had failed because the beetle of the reserve would not give force to the blow. POPE, however, "instead of being ground to powder, had manœuvred so admirably," that, had he been supported by all his subordinates as he had been by KEARNY and HOOKER, JACKSON, instead of himself, would have crumbled beneath the upper and nether millstone. Nevertheless, the grand opportunity had not been improved. *The probability* had sunk into *a possibility.*

"The morning of the 29th of August dawned calm, clear and beautiful."† It was the dawn of the first day's battle of Bull Run Second, generally known as the Battle of Groveton. "KEARNY and HOOKER were astir at daylight," to quote the language of an eye-witness. "They crossed the stream at the Stone Bridge, swung out into the fields, and moved north toward Sudley Springs, forcing JACKSON back on LONGSTREET, who was resting after his hard march; his men eating a hearty meal from the stores captured at Manassas. He was in no condition to fight at that early hour.

"Time slipped away — precious hours! MCDOWELL had not come, PORTER had not been heard from. 'LONGSTREET is getting ready,' was the report of the scouts.

"Noon passed; one o'clock came around. 'LONGSTREET is joining JACKSON,' was the word from the pickets.

"The attack must be made at once, if ever. It began at two o'clock by HOOKER and KEARNY on the right, pushing through

* "The rebels came on and swept everything before them, completely turning the left wing of the army. There was no support whatever behind us, and somebody was evidently to blame; it looked to me as if it was left so on purpose to defeat POPE — the old corps commanders of the Army of the Potomac being jealous of him, and not willing to co-operate with him." — Page 152, *Soldiers' Letters*, edited by LYDIA MINTURN POST.

† These are the words of CARLETON (an eye-witness of much that he records), in his "*Following the Flag*," chap. x, page 169, etc.

the woods and across the fields between DOGAN's house and Sudley Church.

"The veterans of the Peninsula move upon an enemy whom they have met before. JACKSON has made the line of a half-finished railroad his defense, and his men are behind the embankment and in the excavations. It is a long, desperate conflict. There are charges upon the enemy's lines and repulses. Three — four — five o'clock, and PORTER has not come. McDOWELL, who should have marched north-west to Groveton, to meet LONGSTREET, has, through some mistake, marched east of that place, and joined the line where KEARNY *and* HOOKER *are driving* JACKSON.

"At this hour, sunset on August 29th, KEARNY, HOOKER and RENO are pushing west, north of the turnpike, close upon the heels of JACKSON. KING's Division, of McDOWELL's Corps, is moving west along the turnpike, past DOGAN's house, to attack what has been JACKSON's right centre, but which is now the left centre of the united forces of JACKSON and LONGSTREET. SIGEL's brigades have been shattered, and are merely holding their ground south of the turnpike. Oh! if PORTER, with his 12,000 fresh troops, was only there to fall on JACKSON's right flank! But he is not in sight. Nothing has been heard from him. He has had all day to march five miles over an unobstructed road. He has had his imperative orders — has heard the roar of battle. He is an officer in the regular service, and knows that it is the first requisite of an officer or a soldier to obey orders.

"LONGSTREET is too late upon the ground to make an attack with his whole force. The sun goes down and darkness comes on. The contest for the day is over. JACKSON has been driven on his right, and HEINTZELMAN's Corps holds the ground. Both armies sleep on their arms. The auspicious moment for crushing JACKSON has passed."

Let us see how McCLELLAN views* things on this momentous day (at 2:45 P. M., August 29th, 1862), while the battle of Bull Run Second was raging, and when the fate of the National

* "BERTHIER's hatred of JOMINI drove the latter out of French service and cost NAPOLEAN Dennewitz, since the same talent won Friedland." — LITTELL, 1301, 8, 5, 69, 378.

Capital was trembling in the balance. He takes a mathematical view of the situation, tabulates it, and telegraphs to the President:

" * * * I am clear that one of two courses should be adopted: first, to concentrate all our available forces to open communication with POPE; second, to leave POPE to get out of his scrape, and at once use all our means to make the Capital perfectly safe. No middle ground will now answer."

This was philosophic, if not patriotic.

It is related that " when President LINCOLN read the despatch cited above, he was so horror-stricken, he fell back in his chair." This despatch alone, perhaps, might have been explained, but it must be taken in connection with McCLELLAN's action in regard to ammunition and provisions.* To the demand for the one, the reply is, "I know nothing of the calibres of POPE's artillery;" for the other, he required POPE to furnish a cavalry escort, when POPE's cavalry were so completely used up " that there were not five horses to the company that could be forced to the trot." And then, when the officer in command of re-enforcements, which could have saved everything, and have retrieved all that had been lost, when he delayed so that he was not present when most needed, McCLELLAN telegraphs, "I am responsible," etc.†

* " He (POPE) had sent to Alexandria for provisions. General McCLELLAN was there. The Army of the Potomac, when it arrived there, was in the department commanded by General POPE, and was, therefore, subject to his orders, which left McCLELLAN without a command. FRANKLIN and SUMNER, with thirty thousand men, were moving out and could guard the trains. At daylight, while General POPE was forming his lines, endeavoring to hold at bay the army before which McCLELLAN had retired to the Chickahominy, Savage Station, Glendale and Malvern, General McCLELLAN informed General POPE that the supplies would be loaded into cars and wagons as soon as POPE would send in a cavalry escort to guard the trains!

" 'Such a letter,' says General POPE, 'when we were fighting the enemy, and Alexandria swarming with troops, needs no comment. Bad as was the situation of the cavalry, I was in no situation to spare troops from the front, nor could they have gone to Alexandria and returned within a time by which we must have had provisions or have fallen back in the direction of Washington. Nor did I see what service cavalry could give in guarding railroad trains. It was not till I received this letter that I began to feel discouraged and nearly hopeless of any successful issue to the operations with which I was charged.' "— CARLETON'S " *Following the Flag*," pp. 175–'6.

† Without comment or endorsement or opinion, the following is inserted for what it may be worth.

General VON VEGESACK, the Swedish officer who served for several years in the "Army of the Potomac," says in his recent work on the American war, that one of the most

On the 28th and 29th, KEARNY's Division formed the extreme right, and right well it did its duty. Did KEARNY ever do it otherwise? On the 28th, POPE had the opportunity to put in practice the golden rule of tactics, to bring his force as a unit to bear upon a fraction of the enemy's force. On the morning of the 29th, there was still a chance. On that night, the chance was with LEE.

The morning of the 30th dawned as calm, clear and beautiful as on the preceding day of slaughter. It was as beautiful a Sabbath morning as that on which the first great conflict of the war was fought, on the same ground, but under what different auspices! as lovely as that Sabbath morning when the same troops, under trusty RENO and honest HOOKER, forced the principal pass of the South Mountain, defended by the same bitter but earnest D. H. HILL and the same able LONGSTREET, who encountered them on the plains of Manassas.

The night was to witness a reverse as terrible in the imaginations of the Northern people as that of July 21st, 1861, but not attributable to the like cause, as might be shown could the grave or the ashes of burnt war archives reveal their secrets.

The Army of Virginia, notwithstanding its re-enforcements, had dwindled again, through privation, sickness, fatigue and casualties in battle, to forty thousand men. LEE had sixty to eighty thousand; perhaps, could the real facts be come at, even more. If ever the rebels displayed audacious — which in most cases is true — generalship, it was in the campaign from the Rapidan to Antietam. They seemed to adapt their lines to the ground in the most masterly manner. KEARNY was the only one who equalled them in this respect. His success on the 29th was due to his topographical explorations during the previous spring. On the 29th, the rebel line of battle was a perfect exemplification of engineering, as applied to tactics. It was something between a (and an L. The left, or perpendicular, under JACKSON, rested on Sudley Springs, and it extended thence to Warrenton pike, about a mile and a-half west of

grievous mistakes which President LINCOLN committed during the early part of the war, was that he did not order General MCCLELLAN to be court-martialed after the disastrous campaign on the Peninsula, as he was urged to do by several generals and by the Secretary of War."—"*Soldiers' Friend*," 27th February, 1869.

Groveton. Then there was an interval comparatively unoccupied; but in this interval there was a high knoll or ridge of land, which commanded two-thirds of LEE's front. Behind the crest of this ridge stood forty-eight pieces of artillery, with nothing but their muzzles visible.* The rebel right, constituting the horizontal of the L, bent round to the south-east across the Manassas Gap railroad. Any one who has made such matters a study, must regard these dispositions of men and guns very much as an artist views a gem in painting or sculpture. These forty-eight pieces of artillery could be trained to sweep the whole ground in front of both of the rebel wings. Their concentrated mass resembled a gigantic pistol — to use one of the expressions attributed to NAPOLEON, which he kept in reserve to aim at the vulnerable point or heart of his adversary. KEARNY refers to these guns in his report, where he states that he "suffered in the morning from an enfilading fire of the enemy's batteries."

POPE's forty thousand men were crowded within the horns of this crescent. HOOKER was on his extreme right, KEARNY next, then RENO. It is said that LEE and POPE had both resolved to attack with their right. LEE certainly did, and it was his move to cut POPE off from his supplies of all kinds. HOOKER, KEARNY and RENO held their ground, and actually drove the superior masses of the enemy; but the rebels had the best upon the other wing, which was outflanked and overpowered. The battle lasted until it was put an end to by the darkness. Then KEARNY, and those who had borne the brunt of the fighting on so many fields, covered the retreat.

"I served with the same army corps as KEARNY," are the words of a friend directed to the writer, "during the Peninsular campaign, under HEINTZELMAN, and need not recapitulate to you its story. The last time I saw him was on the second day of the battle of Manassas, August 30th, 1862, in the forenoon. He was then much excited and mortified at the result of the failure to support the attack he had been directed to make from

* "A similar concentration of fifty-eight guns tore to pieces the rebels under BRECKENRIDGE, at Stone River." — *The Story of a Regiment*, Sixth Ohio Vols., G. HANNAFORD, page 400.

our right, on the day previous, on the enemy's left, and criticized POPE severely, as was, in fact, just, for such blundering I never witnessed. I said to him: 'PHIL., this is the day which is to decide this battle, is it not?' 'No,' said he. 'Don't say so to any one else, but *the chance of success was thrown away on yesterday*. Had POPE supported my flank attack by a vigorous charge on the enemy's front, we must have overwhelmed JACKSON's inferior force. It is too bad, for I lost many fine fellows in gaining the ground we can now never recover.'" (This was not POPE's fault, however, though it seemed to be so at the time. The blame lay with those who did not execute POPE's orders or work in together to carry out his plans. One received his deserts according to the decision of his peers; how many did not receive theirs, Heaven alone knows.) "'But,' said I, 'we are still superior in point of numbers, and may decide the fight in our favor to-day.' He hesitated, evidently unwilling to speak out, and then said: 'We must all do our best; but I sincerely hope LEE and LONGSTREET will not be here to-day.' This was about noon, and our short interview was suddenly cut off by the sound of cannon on our left announcing the arrival of the worthies he spoke of on the field. He rode to a battery in our front, and I lost sight of him. The battle had begun, and we were soon all busy again as we had been the day before. I was wounded that afternoon and sent to the rear, and the next day, September 3d, learned the fate of our poor PHIL. KEARNY. He died at an inopportune moment, for he would have had command of the Army of the Potomac, and, had he been untrammeled in that position, the war would have ended two years sooner than it did, for he was the best general and the most thorough soldier in the country. This ending, however, was not in the programme."

"The forces of POPE were now in sad condition. Defeated, disheartened, lacking food, and wearied with continual watching, fighting and marching, thousands had straggled from their commands, and those that remained fought with little hope. The truth was, they lacked confidence in their commander. Their instinct was not very incorrect. They followed McCLELLAN more readily than POPE, but even he had not fully their hearts. * * * Such of the troops as were led by KEARNY, HOOKER and RENO were ever ready—dispirited at last, indeed, but always ready when their generals led.

"With this half-despairing army, POPE, nevertheless, determined again to fight the victorious rebels. Better, perhaps, to have retired upon McCLELLAN, since he and his corps commanders seemed resolved not to advance to him. The disposition of the troops was as follows: HEINTZELMAN, whose corps contained HOOKER and KEARNY, held the right of our lines, McDOWELL the left, while FITZ-JOHN PORTER, SIGEL and RENO held the centre. By one of those accidents which sometimes occur in war, LEE and POPE had each determined to attack his adversary's left. So, when POPE pushed forward for that purpose, he found no troops, and hence it was concluded that LEE was retreating up the Warrenton turnpike toward Gainesville. So, McDOWELL was ordered, with three corps, PORTER's in advance, to follow up the enemy, and press him vigorously the whole day. But this provoked a heavy fire from the Confederate artillery, and, while the advance was checked, clouds of dust on the left showed that the enemy was moving to turn our extreme left. Immediately McDOWELL detached REYNOLDS from PORTER's left, and directed him on a position south of the Warrenton turnpike, so as to check this menace. This position was a hill, called Bald Hill, situate west of another hill, on which the Henry house stands, between them being a brook or creek. While it was judicious in McDOWELL to occupy this point, the detachment of REYNOLDS for that purpose exposed the key-point of PORTER's line. The enemy saw this, and poured in a destructive fire of artillery, and PORTER's troops, about five o'clock P. M., gave way and retired from the field. The Confederate line then advanced to cut off the retreat of the Union forces; Bald Hill was carried; it became doubtful whether even the "Henry House Hill" could be maintained so as to cover our retreat over Bull Run, for LONGSTREET had thrown around his right so as to menace that position. What I have said will enable us better to understand the further report of KEARNY.

"'We took no part,' he says, 'in the fight of the morning,

although we lost men by the enfilading fire of the enemy's batteries. A sudden and unaccountable evacuation of the field by the left and centre occurring about five o'clock P. M., on order from General POPE, I massed my troops at the indicated point, but soon re-occupied, with BIRNEY'S Brigade, supported by ROBINSON, a very advanced block of woods. The key-point of this new line rested on the Brown house toward the creek. This was held by regiments of other brigades. Soon, however, themselves attacked, they ceded ground, and retired without warning us. I maintained my position till ten o'clock P. M., when, in connection with General RENO and General GIBBON, assigned to the rear-guard, I retired my brigade. My command arrived at Centerville, in good order, at two o'clock this morning, and encamped in front of the Centerville forts. My loss, in killed and wounded, is over 750 — about one in three — none taken prisoners, except my engineer officer,* who returned to the house supposed to be held by the troops alluded to.'

---

* On August 31st, an incident occurred which is worth narrating. General KEARNY had on his staff at that time Second Lieutenant J. C. BRISCOE, a tall, soldierly-looking Irishman, who, after graduating as a civil engineer at Dublin University, came to America to seek his fortune, without friends, without influence, and without money * * *

During the fall (1861) General MANSFIELD procured his promotion to the rank of Second Lieutenant. In the spring of 1862, his regiment was put into the brigade of General HAMILTON, and during the Peninsular Campaign was part of General KEARNY'S division. On May 30th, 1862, Lieutenant BRISCOE was superintending the digging of rifle-pits, and his overcoat concealed his shoulder-straps. General KEARNY riding up criticised in rather severe terms the plan of the works, and inquired for the officer in charge. Lieutenant BRISCOE answered, and gave his reasons for constructing the works as he had. General KEARNY at once admitted that he was wrong, and apologized, addressing BRISCOE as Colonel.

"I am not a Colonel," said BRISCOE.

"Well, then, Major."

"I am not a Major."

"What the d—l are you?" asked KEARNY.

"A Second Lieutenant, sir."

"Do you want to go on my staff as Engineer Officer?" said the General.

"Yes," said BRISCOE, "I should like it very much."

When Briscoe returned to camp he found the order for the detail on the staff of General KEARNY, where he remained until August 31st, 1862, when he went to Libby Prison. * *

The incident of August 31, 1862, to which reference has been made, illustrates BRISCOE'S coolness, without which no soldier can gain the admiration of his comrades. About noon he had been sent by General KEARNY to carry an order to a remote part of the lines. When returning, about four o'clock, he met the General riding with General BIRNEY. After hearing BRISCOE'S report, KEARNY directed him to accompany him to a house at some distance from the point where they were standing, which he had selected as his headquarters for the night. Briscoe replied, "That house, General, is in possession of the enemy: when I rode by it I narrowly escaped being taken prisoner."

"Nonsense," said KEARNY, "you are timid, Lieutenant, come ahead."

"Translated, this report shows the state of the case. It was HEINTZELMAN — namely, KEARNY and HOOKER — who was to make the attack and open the battle. The enemy having massed to the other side of the line, they remained in position. When all was lost, KEARNY remained and covered the retreat. He was ever in the post of danger, for he was always reliable and never to be defeated.

"Arrived at Centerville, where were the corps of FRANKLIN and SUMNER, POPE remained there during all the 31st of August. And then KEARNY penned the report from which I have quoted, the last he ever wrote."*

Amid all the misrepresentations in regard to the second day of the battle of Bull Run Second, one fair man has lifted up his voice in defense of the maligned POPE and calumniated Army of Virginia: "The army retreated in order. It had suffered a defeat; but there was no disgraceful panic, like that which had marked the close of the battle fought a year before almost on the same ground."

When the reader reflects that POPE, "gee'd and haw'd" from Washington, with forty thousand troops, gathered from where-ever lay-timidity had previously bedropped them, held in check, for ten days, LEE, with his hundred thousand victorious, first-class soldiers, all as perfectly in hand as a four or six-horse team under a good driver, who gathers up his reins and distributes them between the proper fingers, it is very hard to excuse the general, who, with over one hundred thousand picked troops, acting on his own plans, for not ruining an army inferior in number and quality, under JOHNSON, after Williamsburg and Fair Oaks, or LEE, after Gaines' Mills, Glendale and Malvern, as well as at various intermediate points and moments,

---

"Well, sir," rejoined BRISCOE, "if you think I am mistaken, let me ride in advance; if our men hold the house, I will fire my pistol; if I do not return, you may know I am a prisoner."

"All right," replied KEARNY, and BRISCOE rode forward into the rebel lines, was taken prisoner and sent to Libby Prison, of which he had the honor of being one of the first inmates. He thus saved KEARNY and BIRNEY from capture, for the same rashness which would have impelled KEARNY to have gone to the house which he proposed, led him forward the next day within the lines of the enemy, where he fell mortally wounded. — *Life of* DAVID BELL BIRNEY, *Major General United States Volunteers: Philadelphia, King & Baird,* 607 *Sansom street; New York, Sheldon & Co.,* 400 *Broadway,* 1867; *pages* 64-68.

* "PHILIP KEARNY, *Soldier and Patriot,*" by CORTLANDT PARKER, pp. 35-38.

when a feline or leonine spring, in the manner of FREDERICK or NAPOLEON, or RADETSKY, or VON MOLTKE, would have carried the Army of the Potomac triumphantly into the rebel capital.

There is one thing certain — that is, whatever may have been POPE's faults and mistakes, shunning exposure and responsibility on the battle-field was not one of them. It cannot be said of him, as was charged against his rival, of "even keeping himself purposely in the rear in critical seasons" (mark! there is *no* charge here of want of manliness), "to avoid the embarassment of having to act and direct when consulted." Of POPE, an officer, able, brave and experienced, often quoted, remarked: "He was the first general, in chief command, I had ever seen present on the battle-field under fire."

Shame to those who, to screen the guilty in high places and popular illusions, dip their pens in gall and vilify their own people and their own section! Our army had suffered terribly — probably eleven thousand would scarcely cover the total loss; but the simple possession of the battle-field had cost the rebels between eight and nine thousand men. Had the troops with which Alexandria was swarming been up to support their outnumbered brethren — the foot fasting, foot-sore and worn out; the cavalry fagged out and almost destitute of serviceable horses; or had McCLELLAN sent forward supplies, a glorious victory would have rewarded the valor of the Army of Virginia.

August 31st was a day of rest and recuperation, as far as the terrible storm which set in would permit. The rebels, under JACKSON, attempted to repeat their flanking movement on our right; but the tempest delayed their march, so that there was no collision.

During this twenty-four hours of partial respite, KEARNY prepared his last report, which he never lived to sign. It was found among his papers, and is an evidence of that astonishing energy and application, whenever duty demanded an exertion, which characterized PHIL. KEARNY. This is the report from which the preceding sentences are quoted.

"Thence, too" (at Centerville), "he wrote a letter in pencil,* among the treasures of his family a striking exhibition of his wonderful elasticity, his positive enjoyment of conflict."

"I am permitted," says PARKER, in his eloquent address, "to use this relic. 'I wrote you yesterday morning. Since then there has been a sort of Bull Run episode to the first day's fight. * * * It is dangerous work to fight in this army; you have to fight ten times your share, and expose yourself, to prevent the demoralizing effect of almost cowardice in others. HOOKER'S Division is almost the only exception. This army ran like sheep, all but a General RENO and a General GIBBON. As for myself, I was abandoned shamefully. My only salvation depended on holding a certain hill and house in the rear adjoining me. In the darkness of twilight, the enemy came, fired a few trifling shots, and STEVENS' people ran, we alongside never dreaming of it. The worst was, * * * * * never informed me. I had a staff-officer taken prisoner, and I was only a few yards behind him. It was perfectly ridiculous; but he was so unsuspicious that I could not help him, as scouts were stealing in all around me. He was so surprised; it was very funny. I will tell you some other time. My regiments behaved like perfect loves — so beautifully steady. I stayed for more than three hours after all the Americans but RENO and STEVENS had left, and RENO was as much to the left as I was to the right, behaving very handsomely. My friend, General TOWERS, was wounded.

"'*This disaster is not* POPE'S *fault, but rather* HALLECK'S *and* McCLELLAN'S, *high generals in places they are not fit for.*

"'It is tiresome to have one's victories ignored, as at Sangster's Station, and Williamsburg, and on the Newmarket road, and to be confounded, though fighting hard and successfully, and exposing myself, as my nature unfortunately is, in other people's defeats. Yesterday would have been extremely amusing, from its ridiculousness, if not so sad for our cause. Our

* This was supposed to have been his last letter; but Brigadier-General V—— told the writer last June that he had received a disinterested communication, dictated by the most generous impulses, which from the date and attending circumstances must have been penned by KEARNY only a few hours before his movement to the field on which he fell. General V—— would have forwarded a copy, but he had loaned or given it away.

men would not fight one bit; it was amusing to watch them. I foresaw it all three hours before it took place. But I am sorry for the cause.' "

DOCUMENTS, REPORTS, ETC.

HEADQUARTERS, FIRST DIVISION, THIRD CORPS, OF THE ARMY OF THE POTOMAC, CENTREVILLE, VIRGINIA, August 31, 1862.

Colonel GEORGE D. RUGGLES,
Chief of Staff to Major-General JOHN POPE:

COLONEL: — I report the part taken by my division in the battles of the two previous days.

On the twenty-ninth, on my arrival, I was assigned to the holding of the right wing — my left on the Leesburg road. I posted Colonel POE, with BERRY'S Brigade, in first line, General ROBINSON, First Brigade, on his right, partly in line and partly in support, and BIRNEY'S most disciplined regiments reserved and ready for emergencies. Towards noon I was obliged to occupy a quarter of a mile additional on left of said road from SCHURTZ' troops being taken elsewhere.

During the first hours of combat, General BIRNEY, on tired regiments in the centre falling back, of his own accord rapidly pushed across to give them a hand to raise themselves to renewed fight.

In early afternoon General POPE'S order, per General ROBERTS, was to send a pretty strong force diagonally to the front to relieve the centre, in the woods, from pressure. Accordingly, I detached on that purpose General ROBINSON with his Brigade, the Sixty-third Pennsylvania Volunteers, Colonel HAYS, the One Hundred and Fifth Pennsylvania Volunteers, Captain CRAIG, the Twentieth Indiana, Colonel BROWN, and additionally the Michigan Marksmen under Colonel CHAMPLIN. Gen. ROBINSON drove forward for several hundred yards, but the centre of the main battle being shortly after driven back and out of the woods, my detachment thus exposed so considerably in front of all others, both flanks in air, was obliged to cease to advance, and confine themselves to holding their own. At five o'clock, thinking — though at the risk of exposing my fighting line to being enfiladed — that I might drive the enemy by an unexpected attack through the woods, I brought up additionally the most of BIRNEY'S regiments, the Fourth Maine, Colonel WALKER and Lieutenant-Colonel CARVER, the Fortieth New York, Colonel EGAN, First New York, Major BURT, and One Hundred and First New York, Lieutenant Colonel GESNER, and changed front to the left, to sweep with a rush the first line of the enemy. This was most successful. The enemy rolled up on his own right; it presaged a victory for us all; still our force was too light. The enemy brought up rapidly heavy reserves, so that our further progress was impeded. General STEVENS came up gallantly in action to support us, but did not have the numbers.

On the morning of the thirtieth, General RICKETTS, with two brigades, relieved me of my extra charge of the left of the road, and I again concentrated my command. We took no part in the fighting of the morning, although we lost men by an enfilading fire of the enemy's batteries. A sudden and unaccountable evacuation of the field, by the left and centre, occurring about five P. M., on orders from General POPE, I massed my troops at the indicated point, but soon re-occupied with BIRNEY'S Brigade, supported by ROBINSON'S, a very advanced block of woods. The key point of this new line rested on the Brown house towards the creek; this was held by regiments of other brigades; soon, however, themselves attacked, they ceded ground and retired without warning us. I maintained my position until ten P. M., when, in connection with General RENO and General GIBBON — assigned to the rear guard — I retired my brigades.

My command arrived at Centreville in good order at two A. M. this morning, and encamped in front of the Centerville forts. My loss in killed and wounded is over seven hundred and fifty, about one in three, in some regiments engaged a great deal severer; in the Third Michigan, one hundred and forty out of two hundred and sixty; none taken prisoner, except my engineer officer, who returned to the house supposed to be held by the troops alluded to.

It makes me proud to dwell on the renewed efforts of my Generals of Brigade, BIRNEY and ROBINSON. My regiments all did well, and the remiss in camp seemed as brightest in the field. Besides my old tried regiments, who have been previously noted in former actions and maintained their prestige, I have to mark the One Hundred and First New York Volunteers and Fifty-seventh Pennsylvania Volunteers, as equalling all that their comrades have done before; their commanders, Lieuteuant-Colonel GESNER, with the One Hundred and First New York Volunteers, and Major BIRNEY, with the Fifty-seventh Pennsylvania Volunteers, have imparted to them the stamp of their own high character. The Sixty-third Pennsylvania and Fortieth New York Volunteers, under the brave Colonel EGAN, suffered the most. The gallant HAYES is badly wounded. The loss of officers has been great; that of Colonel BROWN can hardly be replaced. Brave, skillful, a disciplinarian, full of energy and a charming gentleman, his Twentieth Indiana must miss him. The country loses in him one who promised to fill worthily high trust. The Third Michigan, ever faithful to their name, under Colonel CHAMPLIN and Major PIERCE, lose one hundred and forty out of two hundred and sixty combatants. Colonel CHAMPLIN is again disabled. The staunch Fourth Maine, under WALKER, true men of a rare type, drove on through the stream of battle irresistibly. The One Hundred and Fifth Pennsylvania Volunteers was not wanting. They are Pennsylvania's Mountain Men; again have they been fearfully decimated. The desperate charge of these regiments sustain the past history of this division.

The lists of killed and wounded, and reports of brigades and regiments, will be shortly furnished.

RANDOLPH'S Battery of Light Twelves was worked with boldness and address. Though narrowly watched by three long-reaching enfilading batteries of the enemy, it constantly silenced one of theirs in its front, and shelled and ricocheted its shot into the reinforcements moving from the enemy's heights down into the woods. On the 27th, with two sections and ROBINSON'S First Brigade, Captain RANDOLPH had powerfully contributed to General HOOKER'S success at Bristow Station.

Captain GRAHAM, First United States Artillery, put at General SIGEL'S disposition, as repeatedly drove the enemy back into the woods, as the giving way of that infantry left the front unobstructed. This practice was beautifully correct, and proved irresistible. On the 31st, Captain GRAHAM, not being required on the right, was sent to the extreme left, and rendered important service with General RENO, firing until late in the night.

Lieutenant ———, a German officer of distinction, put at my disposal by General SIGEL, with two long-range Parrots, covered our right flank and drove off an enemy's battery and regiments. I name these gentlemen as ornaments to their branch of the service.

I must refer to General HOOKER to render justice to the part taken by my First Brigade under General ROBINSON, and RANDOLPH'S Battery, in the affair of the 27th at Bristow Station.

Again am I called on to name the efficiency of my staff. Captain MINDIL, often cited brave and intelligent, was the only military aid present to assist me; but Dr. PANCOAST Division-Surgeon-General, not only insured the promptness of his department, but, with heroism and aptitude, carried, for me, my orders.

Very respectfully,
Your obedient servant,

———————,
Commanding Division.

Lieutenant-Colonel C. MCKEEVER,
Chief-of-Staff, Third Army Corps.

INDORSEMENT ON THE FOREGOING.

HEADQUARTERS, FIRST DIVISION, THIRD CORPS,
ARMY OF THE POTOMAC,
FORT LYON, September 4, 1862.

Respectfully forwarded as the official report drawn up by the late Major-General PHILIP KEARNY, and intended to have been signed by him the day of his death.

(Signed) D. B. BIRNEY,
Brigadier-General Commanding Division.

Official:
Lieutenant-Colonel C. MCKEEVER,
Assistant Adjutant-General, Third Army Corps.

LETTER FROM PHIL. KEARNY'S BUGLER.

The following artless letter, by PHIL. KEARNY'S "Little Bugler," as he was universally styled, is too characteristic and interesting to be omitted. It speaks equally well in favor of the General who could inspire a lad of twelve years with such sentiments of admiration and devotion, and of the drummer boy who, at the age of sixteen, could indite such a grateful and agreeable memorial of his old commander. PHIL. KEARNY to him, indeed, was the "Legendary hero of the Bivouacs of the Army of the Potomac," and every one who can lay a claim to service under the "Bayard of that Army," glories in the fact, and clings to it as the chief honor of his military career. To follow KEARNY, was to tread the path of duty and of valor; to honor him with unimpaired respect, to testify an appreciation of his manliness, and to cherish his memory, as PHIL. KEARNY'S memory is cherished by his "braves," is to possess a portion of those patriotic virtues which made him an example, a type and a guiding light.

> "Far through the tempest-horrors of the night,
> The seaman marks the distant gleam of light
> Which points the course to haven and to home,
> The guiding star with hope and safety dight."

Yes, KEARNY was a guiding star, and if it pointed out, as it often did, to death, the grave which received the fallen was the honored bed of repose for the Warrior who fell in the path of glory, the Patriot who died for Faith and Fatherland.

NEW YORK, July 23, 1868.

I will try and detail, in the smallest possible compass, as far back as I can recollect, my experience with General KEARNY. In the first place, I will begin with my enlistment. In the early part of 1861, I was drumming recruits in Chatham Square, New York city, for the Forty-second Regiment Volunteers (Tammany), for a couple of months, when my father enlisted in the Fortieth N. Y. Volunteers (Mozart) at Yonkers. When the Forty-second, not treating me well, I left them, not being mustered in, and tried to join the Fortieth; but its commander, Colonel RILEY, would not take me, on account of my being too small, and also too young, being only eleven years old. As soon as the Colonel said "No," I began to cry, and turned away from the tent; but my father went and spoke to him, when he called me back and made me take a drum and beat. All the men commenced to laugh, because the drum was nearly as big as myself; but nevertheless, the Colonel said I would do. So I was mustered in on the 26th June, 1861, and discharged on the 26th June 1864. Our regiment was guarding the railroad during the first battle of Bull Run. I was with the regiment from the Battle of Williamsburg, our first fight, until we came to Harrison's Landing, when a Corporal BROWN, clerk at General KEARNY'S headquarters, and also a member of our regiment, came to me one day, stating that General KEARNY ordered him to get him a drummer from our regiment to serve as an orderly for one day, as General MCCLLELAN was to review the army the next day. I reported myself the next day. I reported myself next morning early. He received me kindly, gave me his gray horse (Baby), one that he brought from Mexico. During the review, the General had occasion to jump a very large ditch. I jumped it with him, but a great many of the officers had to cross further up. I think my jumping this ditch brought me favorably to his notice. Accordingly, when I reported myself in the evening, after the review, so as to return to my regiment, he said, "No; but go and bring my baggage over to headquarters, and consider yourself my Orderly in the future." From that day until his death, I was always with him. It was his habit to ride outside of the picket-guard every day at Harrison Landing, only taking me with him. Many a time I would have to ride on top of the horse, lengthwise, so as not to knock my legs against the trees. He would go so fast through them, one time my hat was knocked off; the General never stopping, so by the time I was in the saddle again, there was no General to be seen, but I gave "Baby" his own way, when in less than five minutes he brought me up to him. I have known that same horse to kick at him as he went in the gate. The General would then "damn" me for not holding the horse tight; but for all that, the General always treated me the same as my own father would have done, and no one mourned his untimely death more than I did. The first affair of any note in which I was with the General, was the skirmish near Black River, or Water. The rebel cavalry made a charge on our skirmishers, but we gave them one volley, when they retreated, but came very near making a prisoner of General D. B. BIRNEY, near the skirmishers at the time. He managed to kill one with his pistol, and flung it in the face of another. Nothing of note took place on our march from Harrison's Landing to Alexandria, except at the second battle of Bull Run, when during the engagement the General had occasion to write orders, which he did on his knee, while I steadied the paper with my fingers. When noticing that I trembled some he asked me "what was the matter." I replied, "nothing, only I was a little frightened." He said, "I must never get frightened at any thing;" any other man but him, would have acted just the same as I did, for the way the rebels were throwing shell and minie-ball in that particular spot was a caution. During another part of the fight, several officers had congregated in a group—a few Generals and aides-de-camp—when one of the enemy's batteries fired a piece of railroad iron at us, and struck on my left, the General said "it was aimed at him," but did no harm except scattering dirt and gravel all around us. That place, getting a little too hot to hold us, we moved further on. At another time, he went outside the line of battle—the men all having lain down—to view the enemy, which went within an inch of costing him his life, for we had no sooner got outside when their sharpshooters commenced making a target of us. Some of the men called him in, but he took his time, until he saw all he could see, when he condescended to turn his horse's head, and show the enemy his rear. After we retreated to Centerville, early on the morning of the 31st of August, 1862, he called me into his room; he was then quartered in a small cottage. I found him in bed; he gave me some official documents, and a letter directed to Mrs. KEARNY, which I believe was the last letter he ever wrote home, and three or four golden dollars and some silver, to defray my expenses, and told me to post them in Alexandria. This was the last time I ever saw the General alive or dead. Inclosed you will find the pass he gave, which you will return after you have examined it. I proceeded to Alexandria, but came near being cut off by the enemy, who were then trying to surround us, which, I think, led to the battle of Chantilly.

Having obeyed orders I commenced to retire, the afternoon of September 1st. Understanding from some stragglers that our troops were engaged — this was in the evening — I proceeded as far front as I dared, not knowing the position our men occupied, and remained there, in there in the road, under as heavy a shower as it has ever been my misfortune to be in, until next morning, when I moved on, and inquired for the General's headquarters, when I was told that he was either dead or a prisoner. I found out all that I could about it, which was, that the previous evening General KEARNY had asked General * * * to reconnoiter a certain gap which was left unguarded, but General * * * advised him not to go; he said "he would go any how," which he did, and that was the last that was ever seen of him alive. A great many seem to think that the General rode a gray horse at the time; but the one he rode was a coal black. I never saw the General's body after it was sent into our lines, and conveyed to Alexandria in an ambulance. I then reported to General BIRNEY, was with him some time, when General STONEMAN, taking command of the Third Army Corps, I went with him, and was with him in the battle of Fredericksburg, when he being ordered to the command of the Cavalry of the Army of the Potomac, General SICKLES then had the command, and I was under him in the battle of Gettysburg, which was the last engagement I was in — making ten battles in all, and never received a scratch. A little while after General SICKLES was convalescent (after the loss of his leg at Gettysburg), I was sent on to school at New York city to educate myself for West Point, as President LINCOLN said he would send me there. But President LINCOLN's untimely death blew my prospects to the wind. The gentleman who was to have taken care of my mother (my father having died from effect of disease contracted during the first year of the war), went away from me, and consequently I had to leave school and go to work. My stopping at the White House you know, so I will not speak of that. My only hope of going to West Point is the election of General GRANT as President, which General SICKLES promised me, if he became President. I also received the Maltese (KEARNY) Cross from General BIRNEY. Hoping that the little information I have been enabled to give you will assist the gentleman (the author), you spoke to me of,

I remain, your obedient servant,

GUSTAVE A. SCHURMANN.

CHAPTER XXX.*

CHANTILLY.

ONE OF JACKSON'S FAMOUS FLANK MARCHES OR TURNING MOVEMENTS, OR DIVERSIONS, DEFEATED BY THE FIGHTING DIVISIONS OF THE ARMY OF THE POTOMAC.

"Ein Mann soll steller Grosse."

SCHMALZ'S "*Denkwurdigkeiten des Grafen* WILHELM'S *zu* SCHAUMBURG LIPPE."

" War is honorable
In those who do their native rights maintain;
In those whose swords an iron barrier are
Between the lawless spoiler and the weak."

THOMSON'S "*Liberty.*"

" A power is passing from the earth." — WADSWORTH.

" How sleep the brave who sink to rest,
By all their country's wishes blessed!"

WILLIAM COLLINS.

" —— Who'er amidst the sons
Of reason, valor, liberty and virtue,
Displays distinguished merit, is a noble
Of nature's own creating."

THOMSON.

" A heart to resolve, a head to contrive, and a hand to execute." — EDWARD GIBBON.

" Heart to conceive, the understanding to direct, and the hand to execute." — JUNIUS.

" You talk always of my person, of my dangers. Need I tell you, it is not necessary that I live, but it is that I do my duty, and fight for my country to save it if possible." — FREDERIC THE GREAT to MARQUIS D'ARGENS, 18th September, 1760, Guttmansdorf, day after his march athwart a fearful Austrian cannonade.

" To fight, Æmilius,
In a just cause, and for our country's glory,
Is the best office of the best men."

HARVARD'S "*Regulus.*"

" Death! thou fell tyrant, hast no fears for me,
A hero's Fame is Immortality."
" NON MORITUR CUGUS FAMA VIVIT."

---

* After having prepared a synopsis of the August campaign of the " Army of Virginia,' with authorities and notes, the writer was notified by the publishers that he must restrict himself within a certain number of pages. This compelled the excision of all POPE'S movements not immediately connected with KEARNY, and even contracted KEARNY within limits insufficient to do him justice. This change in the plan was contrary to agreement; but as the author considers himself absolved by such changes, errors and delays, from all responsibility, he finishes the work, as far as he is permitted, simply that an immense amount of labor may not be lost; labor involving the collection of a vast amount of information, whose publication is due to the gentlemen and friends who kindly united in assisting him.

"The officers vigorously exerted themselves to restore the broken ranks, but in the midst of their efforts the right center column, led by the good and gallant Lord HOWE, was suddenly fronted by the body of the enemy who had gone astray in the forest. They joined in bitter strife, almost hand to hand, in the swamps, or from tree to tree on the hill-side. * * At the first shock many of HOWE'S light infantry went down, he himself, hurrying to the front, was struck by a musket ball in the breast and instantly expired. His men, infuriated by the loss of their beloved leader, swarmed on through the woods and finally overpowered or destroyed the enemy. * * *

"That night the victors occupied the field of battle; to this their advantage was confined, for the disorganization of the troops had frightfully increased during the unpropitious march, in the hard fought skirmish, and by the *loss of their best and most trusted chief. The vigor and spirit of* ABERCROMBIE'S *army seemed to pass away with* Lord HOWE. This gallant man, from the time he had landed in America, had wisely instructed his regiments for the peculiar service of that difficult country. No useless incumbrance of baggage was allowed; he himself set the example, and encountered privation and fatigue in the same chivalrous spirit with which he faced the foe; graceful and kind in his manners, and considerate to the humblest under his charge, his officers and soldiers heartily *obeyed the chief because they loved the man.* At the fatal moment when he was lost to England her glory and welfare most needed his aid. *He lived long enough for his own honor, but not for that of his country.*"—Major WARBURTON'S "*Conquest of Canada,*" page 184.

"Among the dead were two generals, one of whom was the famous warrior PHIL. KEARNY."—VON BORCKE.

"—— The darkest day,
Live till to-morrow, will have passed away."

COWPER.

"Now Night her course began, and over Heaven
Inducing darkness, grateful truce, impos'd
Her silence on the odious din of war;
Under her cloudy covert both retir'd,
Victor and vanquish'd."

MILTON'S "*Paradise Lost,*" B. 6.

"Yet, Freedom! yet thy banner, torn, but flying,
Streams like the thunder-storm against the wind:
Thy trumpet voice, though broken now and dying,
The loudest still the tempest leaves behind;
Thy tree has lost its blossoms, and the rind,
Chopped by the axe, looks rough and little worth.
But the sap lasts,—and still the seed we find
Sown deep, even in the bosom of the NORTH;
So shall a better spring less bitter fruit bring forth."

BYRON'S "*Childe Harold.*"

"I never heard the old song of PERCY (STONEWALL JACKSON) and DOUGLAS (PHIL KEARNY), that I found not my heart moved more than with a trumpet."—SIR PHILIP SIDNEY.

"This battle (Chantilly) was especially unfortunate to the North, and deprived it of the life of General KEARNY, whose services on many fields had rendered his name distinguished."—*Life of* STONEWALL JACKSON, 1866.

"There was a fight at Chantilly, where the brave and impetuous KEARNY was killed, and the enemy fell back." * * * —CARLETON.

"Fortunately for his (HOOKER'S) laurels, General KEARNY, a splendid old veteran, who had seen service under the French in Algeria, came to his aid, and restored the battle (Williamsburg) to the Federals."—STACKE'S (London, 1866) "*Story of the American War.*"

"General PHILIP KEARNY was also killed. * * * His loss is deeply deplored by the whole army. He was considered one of the bravest generals in the service, and the enemy made repeated efforts to kill, wound or capture him. His dashing and fearless bearing and his conspicuous figure, with but one arm, made him an easily distinguished and coveted aim. Up to the night of his death, he was on every occasion to be found in the thickest of the fight, and seemed to lead a charmed life. The Union Army has not lost an officer who will be as much regretted as General KEARNY." — *Leaves from the Diary of* (Dr. ELLIS) *an Army Surgeon.*

"From this time (July 20th, 1861, at Harrison's Landing) I had no personal intercourse with General KEARNY until the fatal day of Chantilly. While the army was yet at Centreville, I entered his room to obtain permission to visit the wounded at Fairfax Station. This, without a moment's hesitation, he granted, and urged me to remain with him a few minutes; during the course of our conversation, he spoke of the causes which led to the disastrous defeat of the previous Saturday, and then of the spirit which animated the South. For the first time in our intercourse he spoke on the subject of religion. He regretted that it had been so little his study, but said his knowledge of the world and experience taught him that the only hope of the future was in the Gospel of our Lord, and that everything else would signally fail in producing peace on earth and good-will among men. He said the scenes in which we were living more deeply impressed him with the value of the teachings of the Bible.

"We parted, and in the sanguinary struggle of the evening General KEARNY fell, and with him a thousand hopes for the country and the army. He was a man of far more talent than many have been willing to concede to him. While ardent and impulsive, he was capable of the most wily caution; while often stern and withering in rebuke, he was generous and forgiving; though ambitious he was above all low, mean jealousies. No officer in the army was more laborious and sleepless; his keen eye was everywhere, and with an energy that never faltered, he corrected every abuse, and fully investigated everything that pertained to the discipline and well-being of his division. If he had lived, his brilliant and chivalrous qualities would have won for him a very high place in the admiration and gratitude of his country." — MARKS' "*Peninsula Campaign.*"

"It having been ascertained that the enemy were attempting to turn our right, and cut off our communications with Washington by moving a large force on the Little River or Aldie turnpike toward Fairfax Court House, our army was stretched along the Warrenton and Alexandria pike, from Centreville to beyond the Court House. At noon we moved off down the pike, marching on the fields along the sides of the road, which was filled with continuous strings of wagons, moving both ways. A little before sunset, just as our division had passed in front of Chantilly, an attack was made by the enemy on the troops in our rear, and we were put in position in a large open field in reserve. The battle raged furiously for some time, the shot and shell falling amongst us, but doing little damage to our division. In the midst of it a terrific thunder storm occurred, and it appeared as if heaven and earth were contending for the mastery. But the darkness of night terminated the conflict, the enemy was driven entirely back from our front, but the gallant Generals KEARNY and STEVENS fell.—WOODWARD'S "*Our Campaigns*," pp. 189, 190.

"The army mourned the national loss of Major-General KEARNY, who was killed at Chantilly, and his memory will be cherished as long as exalted patriotism, inspiring courage, and justice toward men are revered by mankind. *Qualified to be the head of the army*, he accepted the command of a brigade. Leaving the comforts which his large wealth afforded, he welcomed the most trying hardships of the service. In another zone, the enemies of his country had taken his arm; but his zeal triumphed over the disability, and he fought until hé had sacrificed his life. Placing the reins between his teeth and grasping in his single hand the two-edged sword, he led his men in the charge that was never checked. Humane to those who were his inferiors, the orderlies were directed to bring water in canteens to the soldiers when the exigencies of the hour required that all should remain in the ranks at the front. Impetuous in thought and action as the flash of his fiery eye, he censured with the same vehemence the misconduct of the private or the general of the highest rank in the Union forces. Beloved by his division, the RED BADGE which he instituted was always worn by the officers and men with the same proud feeling with which the heroic commander displayed the Legion of Honor, which never enrolled a nobler chevalier. Bravely performing his public tasks, the death of this puro patriot and consummate soldier was a fitting conclusion of his eventful life."—"*Three Years in the Army of the Potomac*," by Captain HENRY N. BLAKE, pp. 140-1.

"The day passed on with no signs of the enemy, and about 4 P. M. our brigade was ordered off as a protection to Fairfax Station, a new disposition of the troops being now required. Shortly after we had marched through Fairfax Court House we were met by a most drenching storm. *The rain laughed to scorn our rubber cloaks, filled our top-boots to the brim, trickled in rivulets between our shoulders, while the wind fairly swayed our horses before its fury. The road speedily became a lake*, and our brigade became a sorry figure indeed, as, with muskets reversed, they waded through the mud, staggering against the blinding storm. In the midst of this fury of the elements, heavily and continually the sound of cannonading upon our right broke upon our ears, seeming almost a horrid mockery, and once more Treason and Loyalty fought to the death at Chantilly. In this battle KEARNY and STEVENS, *two of our very best generals*, met their fate. Many a brave fellow was killed or wounded, but the *victory was ours, and the enemy's attack was repulsed with great slaughter*." —"*The Bivouac and the Battle-Field, or Campaign Sketches in Virginia and Maryland.*" By GEO. F. NOYES, Captain U. S. Volunteers, page 145.

"At 5:50 firing commenced by General RENO on the enemy, between the Little river and Warrenton turnpikes. The enemy were within half a mile of the latter when they attacked him. A portion of General RENO'S troops gave way, but General BIRNEY'S Brigade of General KEARNY'S Division gallantly supported them. General KEARNY rode forward alone to reconnoitre, in his usual gallant, not to say reckless, manner, and came upon a rebel regiment. In attempting to escape, he was killed. The country has to mourn one of her most gallant defenders. At the close of the seige of Yorktown, he relieved General HAMILTON in command of the Division, and led it in the various battles on the Peninsula, commencing with Williamsburg. His name is identified with its glory." —Extract from General HEINTZELMAN'S official report of the Battle of Bull Run, dated Oct. 21st, 1862.

"During that engagement (Chantilly) we lost two of our best, and one of our most distinguished officers, Major-General KEARNY and Brigadier-General STEVENS. * * * * Words cannot express my sense of the zeal, the gallantry and the sympathy of that most earnest and accomplished soldier, Major-General KEARNY. In him the country has suffered a loss which it will be difficult, if not impossible, to repair. He died as he could have wished to die, and as became his heroic character." —*Report of Major-General* POPE.

The second battle of Manassas, or Bull Run, which terminated on the evening of 30th August, was the closing scene of a series of reverses, redeemed, however, by the unflagging energy and desperate courage of the majority of the Union troops engaged in them. When these combats are dispassionately studied out and commented on, justice will concede that, although apparently abandoned and sacrificed, the Army of Virginia and its reinforcements in line of battle from the Army of the Potomac were fought to pieces, not wasted by diseases, disorganized by inaction or humiliated by needless withdrawals from fields of victory abandoned to defeated antagonists. While thus fought to pieces, it inflicted such terrific losses upon the rebels that the future operations of LEE were so crippled, and his fighting aggressive so depleted,* and followed up by an

---

* *Compare* Chapter XVI, pages 277—286, Vol. I, Histoire de la Guerre Civile Americaine, 1860-1865, par Mm. L. CORTAMBERT et F. DE TRANALTOS, Paris, Amyot Editeur, 8 Rue de la Paix, 1867; also pages 128-'9, "*Die innern Kampfe der Nordamerikanischen Union*, von HEINRICH BLANKENBURG, Leipzig, F. A. BROCKHAUS, 1869, etc., etc.

The reader would be astonished if he knew the number of foreign and native works on

able general, the Army of Northern Virginia would have disappeared in the first half of the month of September, 1862, between the Catoctin and the Potomac, as if the mountains had toppled over and buried it, or the earth had gaped and swallowed it up.

COOKE, in his "Life of STONEWALL JACKSON," draws a doleful picture of the condition of the rebel forces and of the dismal landscape which environed them. The same state of affairs existed on our side, as borne witness to by a friend, an officer of HOOKER's Division. The rebels, however, had enjoyed some full meals out of our plundered stores at Manassas, a piece of good fortune denied to our poor fellows.

"The scene at this moment was interesting. The men of the STONEWALL Brigade and their comrades were lying on the side of the road hungry and exhausted. They had not seen their wagons since they had left the Rappahannock, and the rations secured at Manassas were long since exhausted. Green corn and unripe apples had for some days been their sustenance, and now they were in a country that did not afford even these. The hungry men saw on every side bleak fields and forests, with scarce a roof visible in the entire landscape; and thus famished and worn out they were lying down awaiting the order to advance and attack." HENSINGER, referring to the desolation which brooded over this district, observes, "a solemn or mysterious silence reigned over this wide, desolate flat, the plains of Manassas."

The attempt to cut our communication, and intercept our retreat upon the defenses of Washington was resumed by LEE on the 1st of September; but the deluge of rain, unusually cold for the season, presented obstacles almost as difficult to overcome as the resistance of men. All day long LEE's heavy columns moved along the Little River pike toward Fairfax. The enemy's objects developed themselves so clearly on the

---

this war which have been examined in connection with this biography. Only a few of them have been cited, because very often they have merely served to confirm or justify an opinion. Not that the writer considers that an honest opinion needs justification, but the world is so constituted that it often requires the testimony of many who are actual humbugs with high titles to establish a fact, when the judgment of a single expert, or hard student and unprejudiced man, is worth the whole of their pedantic *dicta* following in one track like a flock of sheep led by a cosset with a bell.

afternoon of this day, September 1st, and it was so evident that they intended to try and turn POPE's right, by Fairfax Court House, that the Army of Virginia was disposed so as to receive or give battle, between the Little River pike and the road from Centreville to Fairfax Court House. Early in the afternoon, HOOKER was directed to assemble all the troops in his vicinity and push forward to Germantown, about a mile and a half west of the Court House. His own division constituted the right of our line, which was formed upon a range of heights (Ox Hill), between the Warrenton and Little River pike. This line nearly bisected the angle formed by their junction. McDOWELL was on his left; next FRANKLIN, somewhat in the rear; next RENO, with KEARNY in his rear, in reserve; next PORTER, behind whom POPE posted himself; SUMNER held the extreme left of the Union line, near the house of J. MILAN (or MILLEN), about three miles due west of Germantown.

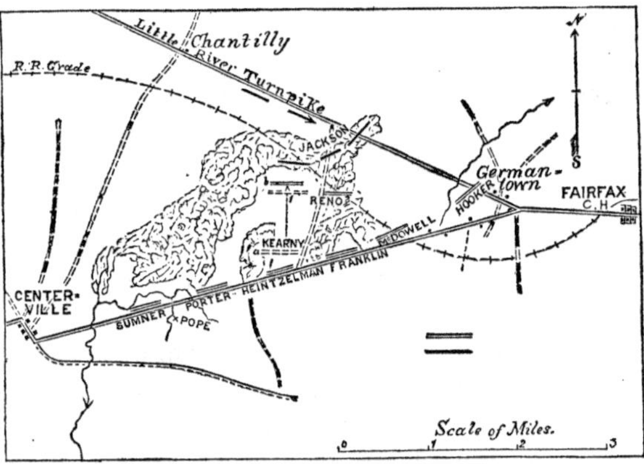

PLAN OF THE BATTLE-FIELD OF CHANTILLY, OR OF OX HILL, OR GERMANTOWN, 1ST SEPTEMBER, 1862.

Such were the dispositions made by POPE for a collision which deserves a far more prominent place among the conflicts of the war than it has ever yet received. The Battle of CHANTILLY — or, as it is more appropriately but less euphoniously named by the rebels, OX HILL, from the elevation or range on which it was fought, or Germantown, near which the hardest fighting occurred (Chantilly is more than three miles from the stage of action, to the northeast and in rear of the rebel forces) — belongs to the same class of fights as Oriskany (1777) at the North, and King's Mountain (1780) at the South, during our first great revolutionary struggle; or the "Cannonade of Valmy," which last has been placed by CREASY among his "Twelve Decisive Battles of the World." Any one who will turn to a good map of the region will perceive that the locality in which the troops collided was a very important one strategically considered. The battles of Gainesville and Groveton, or Second Bull Run, had been fought on the line of the Warrenton turnpike, which passing through Centreville west by north, is intersected at Fairfax Court House by the Little River pike, from Aldie, running northwest and southeast. The Union line of retreat lay along the Little River pike, which, about a mile and a half beyond Annandale, bifurcates — the left-hand branch, the Columbia turnpike, leading across the Long bridge into Washington — the right-hand road into Alexandria. Consequently, if JACKSON could get possession of the turnpike at Fairfax Court House, and the Orange and Alexandria Railroad near Burke's Station, only three miles to the south, POPE was entirely cut off; Washington was uncovered; and the rebel problem, as to advantage of position, solved. The battle which ensued to prevent this turning of our right — or rather, cutting our line of retreat and supply — was very short, very sharp and very decisive. The intentions of the rebels were completely frustrated, their attack repulsed, and the Union troops retained possession of the field. Chantilly was an undoubted victory, and from it, as a buckler, the rebel attack glanced off. No other blow was delivered in this direction. The result proves that, as HALLECK mildly expressed it, "had the Army of the Potomac arrived a few days earlier, the rebel army could have been easily defeated and perhaps destroyed." And in another place, "some of the corps moved with becoming activity — [he might in justice have indicated KEARNY's, HOOKER's and RENO's commands] — but the delays of others were neither creditable nor excusable."

The theatre and time of action were as gloomy as the Northern people deemed our fortunes in front of the National Capital, to become still more gloomy through the fall of two of our most eminently patriotic generals. STONEWALL JACKSON was in command of the rebels and pressed the attack, supported by the fire of his artillery on an eminence to the left and north of the Little River pike. His troops, as usual with the rebels, were disposed in the woods to the right and east of it; JACKSON'S own division was on the left of his line; EWELL'S, under LAWTON, "who ably sustained its reputation," in the centre, and HILL'S on the right. The struggle which ensued, ending as it did, almost justified HOOKER in saying that he never met JACKSON without whipping him; and proves that it required to beat JACKSON, not the kind of men who encountered him at Chancellorsville on our right, but such as met him and drove him back at Chantilly.

Just before sunset a terrific thunder storm, similar to one which actually, for a time, palsied the fight at Oriskany, in 1777, and Solferino, in 1859 — a storm cold and pitiless as the rebels themselves — burst over the field; and amid the convulsions of the elemental warfare and the drenching rain, the blaze of battle rivaled the fierce lightning. It was a fearful hour. A distinguished staff officer, little given to emotional feeling, describes it as the worst he encountered in his term of service, which lasted throughout the war and enabled him to participate in the grandest triumphs as well as the greatest reverses of the Army of the Potomac. The day became suddenly almost converted into night, and, amid the darkness and tropical down-pour of water, the heads of the rebel and Union columns came in contact at Ox Hill, near Chantilly. A number of the hardest fighting men of the two armies — RENO, STEVENS, HOOKER and KEARNY; JACKSON, EARLY and HILL — encountered amid this churm of battle and of nature. EWELL had lost a leg through a wound received in the previous battle and was not present, although his division took part under LAWTON, a very able and valiant officer. The rain was so furious that ammunition could scarcely be kept serviceable, and the thunder so loud that the roar of the artillery was utterly unheard at Centreville, three miles distant. The action began about five P. M., near Chantilly. At first the rebels gave way before the stern aggressive of

RENO, then, re-enforced, drove back STEVENS' division, and STEVENS, "bearing aloft the colors of one of his regiments, cheering on his men, fell fatally wounded by a minie-ball through his head." Confused and out of ammunition, the dying general saw his troops compelled to give way. "To repair this break," says an elegant writer but prejudiced historian, for once kindled into due appreciation of this "Type Volunteer General," "KEARNY, with the promptitude that marked him, sent forward BIRNEY's brigade, of his own division; and presently, all aglow with zeal, brought up a battery which he placed in position. But there still remained a gap on BIRNEY's right, caused by the retirement of STEVENS' division. This BIRNEY pointed out to KEARNY, and that gallant soldier, dashing forward to reconnoitre the ground, unwittingly rode into the enemy's lines and was killed.* In his death, the army lost the living ideal of a soldier — a *preux chevalier*, in whom there were mixed the qualities of chivalry and gallantry as strong as ever beat beneath the mailed coat of an old knight. Like DESAIX, whom NAPOLEON characterized as 'the man most worthy to be his lieutenant,' KEARNY died opposing a heroic breast to disaster."†

---

* "On Monday evening following the disastrous battle of Bull Run, a severe engagement with the enemy took place at Chantilly, two miles north of Fairfax Court House, between a portion of our army and JACKSON's forces. Our loss was very heavy, including General STEVENS, who was shot in the head while he was leading his brigade into action, bearing the colors, the color-sergeant having been previously shot. His son, also, who was acting on his staff, was wounded. General PHILIP KEARNY was also killed the same evening. He was shot through the back while wheeling his horse around to cheer on his men. His loss is deeply deplored by the whole army. He was considered one of the bravest generals in the service, and the enemy made repeated efforts to kill, wound or capture him. His dashing and fearless bearing and his conspicuous figure, with but one arm, made him an easily-distinguished and coveted aim. Up to the night of his death he was on every occasion to be found in the thickest of the fight, and seemed to lead a charmed life. The Union Army has not lost an officer who will be as much regretted as General KEARNY. The operations of the contending armies on the south side of the Potomac completely absorb the attention and interest of every body — citizens and soldiers. The excitement which would naturally be awakened by the knowledge of the fact that bloody battles were being fought within cannon sound of the national capital was considerably increased, because no full and authentic information respecting the results, or losses, had been received from the scene of action."—"*Leaves from the Diary of an Army Surgeon*," p. 209.

† "Among the reports, true or false, which were repeated to me during this sad night (1st September, 1862), there was one whose mournful impression has never been effaced. 'KEARNY had been killed the previous evening.' It was not only a source of mourning for his friends, it was a great loss for the army and the country.

"PHILIP KEARNY belonged to a family of high consideration, which had already furnished a general to the United States. No one possessed in a higher degree the tastes and the qualities of a professional soldier. To these natural gifts and military education, * * he added, besides, an experience which very few officers in our army possessed. For example,

It would seem as if the demon of civil war had demanded the most precious jewels of the nation to pay for the security

---

despatched on a mission to France to study, there, particularly cavalry organization, instead of being content with the information afforded by the War Department and examination of the regiments in garrison at Paris, he had applied himself resolutely, manfully to all the exercises of the School at Saumur, where he remained two years. He afterwards visited Algeria, where he obtained permission to accompany the Duke of Orleans as honorary Aide-de-Camp in the campaign of the 'Iron Gates.'

"There he obtained the only distinction within his reach, the Cross of the Legion of Honor. After this it was optional with him to enter the French service by accepting a command in the Foreign Legion, which was offered to him; but he preferred to return to America, where the Mexican War soon furnished him an opportunity of distinguishing himself. After having signalized himself in many engagements, he lost an arm and won the rank of (BREVET) MAJOR in the attack on Mexico.

"In the Peninsula he commanded a division which shone among all the rest, by its bearing, its discipline, its dash in the attack, and its tenacity in the defense. KEARNY'S spirit permeated it even to the end, after it had lost the commander, whose memory always survived as a living principle in its ranks.

"KEARNY was created Major-General at Harrison's Landing. This promotion, merited rather twice than once, lost much of its value in his eyes by being included in one baking, without discernment, on the occurrence of the 4th July, the anniversary of the National Independence. All the Brigadier-Generals who, during the campaign, had commanded a division, whether well or ill, were promoted, even as he was, and all the Colonels, who accidently happened to have a brigade, received, without distinction, the Single Star, denoting Brigadier-General. Deplorable system, which contributed not a little to prolong the period of our reverses. KEARNY played an active and brilliant part in the series of combats which POPE had to sustain. At Manassas he fell so vigorously upon the enemy's left that he threw it across the railroad which it covered. This partial success should have been made the stepping-stone to victory. Indeed, PORTER should have attacked the left of the Confederates, coincident with the attack of KEARNY. PORTER did not move up into line, and left the enemy full liberty to despatch reinforcements to the wing assailed. Thus overwhelmed, KEARNY was forced to abandon the ground which he had won, and Fortune turned against us.

"On the 1st September, LEE, following up our retreating forces, collided with our right near *Chantilly*. General STEVENS having been killed, his Division, through want of ammunition, fell back in disorder. KEARNY hastened to send forward BIRNEY'S Brigade to maintain our line, and supported it with a battery of artillery, which he posted himself. A breach, notwithstanding, still remained unfilled. To reconnoitre the extent of this gap, he dashed forward alone in this direction, taking with him neither his staff-officers nor his orderlies, so as not to attract attention. These awaited his return in vain; he never came back. Carried away by his ardor, he had penetrated, without perceiving it, within the line of the enemy's skirmishers, concealed in the skirts of a wood. When he was within a few paces of them, the nearest hailed him to surrender. For sole reply, he wheeled his horse, and, crouching upon the neck of the animal, set off at a gallop. The balls flew faster than he did. One of them struck him below the haunch and traversed his body. He fell, and died in a few minutes.

"The Confederate Generals, whose comrade and associate he had been before he became one of their most fearful (or redoubtable) adversaries, took this occasion to testify their high esteem for him. By order of General LEE, KEARNY'S corpse, his horse, his equipments and his arms were restored to us. * * *

"Ardent head (head full of zealous enthusiasm) and noble heart, he thus inspired the enemies with sympathy and admiration whom he fought hand to hand. His fatal death made me recall the last words which he had addressed to me in my tent, whither he came from time to time to chat of France, of Paris, of friends common to both in New York, and of the thousand things which were always interesting to him, the man of the world amid the duties of the man at arms. When I drew his attention to the fact that he was now launched upon a voyage which would bear him to any height of success,—

of the Nation's capital — patriots pure and unselfish in their devotion. Pre-eminently such was KEARNY. If any man, like CURTIUS,* would have spurred his horse into the gaping chasm to save the republic, he would have done it. The sacrifice, if the crisis demanded such a precious offering, was accepted. The career of the rebel was stayed. Instead of following up his success, he turned aside from the reality to grasp at the phantom of evoking an armed insurrection in the North, of firing the hearts of rebels in Maryland and liberating her imaginary oppressed, and of conquering the recognition of an Oligarchy founded on Slavery, under the Banner of Democracy, among the "heaven-kissing mountains" of the free North. Then was realized the prediction of KEARNY, that the North deceived itself if it hoped to beat back the determination of the South without exhibiting an energy and determination — a physical force backed by a moral force — as intensely earnest

---

"'Bah!' said he, 'it is wrong to exaggerate. Without doubt, I believe I could command an army-corps, but a higher responsibility would probably surpass my ability, and I do not think that I ever aimed at a command-in-chief — such a one shines in the second rank; you understand. Moreover, I have not the ambition which my friends may conceive for me. Let the war finish one way or another, I shall return at once and resume my home-life in Paris, satisfied with having done my duty, and with having nothing to reproach myself for.'

"Such is man! He had not taken into his calculations the death which awaited him within twenty days.

"The mourning for him was public (not private), especially at New York, where they accorded him magnificent obsequies. But nowhere was his loss felt so profoundly as in the Army of the Potomac, of which he had been one of the first (greatest) glories, and in which the thousand narratives of the bivouac finished by investing his memory with the proportions of a legendary hero."

[DE TROBRIAND is very much mistaken as to General KEARNY's ambition. He was exceedingly ambitious, and in one of his own letters, so far from underrating his powers to command the largest body of troops, he speaks of being "able to handle the 'Army of the Potomac' with as much facility as his own division."] — "*Quatre Ans de Campagnes a Armee du Potomac.*'" By Major-General REGIS DE TROBRIAND, i, 290, 293.

* "CURTIUS MARCUS, a Roman hero who lived about the middle of the fourth century B. C., and who is said to have sacrificed himself for the good of his country. The legend which relates this event is in substance as follows: An earthquake once happened at Rome, a large portion of the area of the forum sank down, and a vast chasm appeared there. All attempts to fill it up were vain and the city was smitten with consternation, especially as the haruspices had declared that it could only be filled by casting into it that on which the greatness of Rome depended. While every one was hesitating and doubting as to the meaning of the haruspicial declaration, the heroic MARCUS presented himself, and proclaiming that *Rome contained nothing more indispensable to her greatness than a valiant citizen fully accoutred for battle*, he offered himself as a victim, and, having arrayed himself in complete armor and mounted his war-horse, he galloped into the abyss. Then the earth closed, the chasm vanished, and the forum resumed its wonted aspect." — APPLETON'S "*New American Cyclopædia*," Part XVI., p. 156.

as that of the Slavocracy, with their free Spartans to fight and their slave Helots to dig and delve and feed their phalanxes in the field. The very month in which KEARNY died witnessed the inauguration of those measures which finally ended the Slaveholders' Rebellion and whetted the sword of Justice, which fell heavily even while it seemed to spare, upon those most guilty in the eyes of men.

Then, too, was realized that marvelous prediction of SCHALK, not only described, but actually mapped out in the previous winter and printed before McCLELLAN started on that expedition whose failure the German officer prophesied. He not only marked out the marches and retreats and battle-fields of the Army of the Potomac, but placed his red blocks and green blocks, representing the opposing Unionists and Rebels, in the identical locality where the first decisive battle (decisive in any respect worthy to entitle it to the term) of the war at the East — Antietam — overthrew the proud projects of the Slavocrats, and put the seal to the Proclamation of Emancipation: where the first decided repulse of the latter occurred — a drawn battle as regarded the Union commander, but a victory for his troops.

Strange to say, KEARNY lost his life, so precious to his country, almost upon the very spot where he witnessed a similar but more youthful and inexperienced hero lay down his life on the 9th of the preceding March. This was during KEARNY'S carefully and intentionally ignored swoop upon Manassas, when, had he been let loose, he would have clutched the Rebel rear, and very likely have caught or measured swords with the greatest of the Rebel generals at the East, JOE JOHNSTON. Thus his circle of intrepid action commenced and ended amid the same scenes. Its initiative was full of the promise of glory and success; the conclusion, of gloom and sorrow. Even a stranger to KEARNY (LOSSING, in his "Civil War in America," ii, 358 and 454 [2],) has referred to this curious reflux of the careers of the Army of the Potomac and of KEARNY to the vicinity of Manassas.

With the disappearance of KEARNY from the scene forever, wrapt from us in the fiery gloom of tempest and of battle, his mantle fell on a disciple, who, on this field as on other fields, demonstrated that he had grown into the lustre of generalship in the exceeding brightness of KEARNY's example. This was Pennsylvania's patriotic son, DAVID BELL BIRNEY, who, like the friend he revered, the commander he imitated, gave up his life for his country two years and seventeen days later — October 18, 1864 — exclaiming, with his last breath, "Boys, keep your eyes on that flag!" Noble BIRNEY! true in life and death to KEARNY.

The command of KEARNY's division devolved on General BIRNEY, who promptly, KEARNY fashion, ordered a bayonet-charge* (according to the popular preference for the word — in reality, a forward rush) by his own brigade, consisting of the First, Thirty-eighth and Fortieth Regiments of Volunteers from KEARNY's native State, New York. This order was executed with great gallantry by Colonel, now Major-General, TOM EGAN, likewise of New York, and the Rebel advance driven and repulsed so that BIRNEY retained possession of the field of battle during the night, burying our dead and removing our wounded. This, according to the military code of the Romans — in the art of war, the masters of the world and of all times — constituted KEARNY's Division the victors at Chantilly. "It was ever a glorious sign of victory," says the famous critic, VON KAUSLER, in his "*Treffen bei Mantinea*," 1543, "when the conqueror not only bore off and buried his own dead, but granted to the enemy permission to recover their dead also, under a suspension of arms accorded for that very purpose."

And if the spirit of its former leader (KEARNY) could have looked upon that ensanguined stage, it must have rejoiced in the proud consciousness that his influence had survived him, and rendered the men he had disciplined triumphant; that, like the DOUGLAS — the blood of whose breed of men flowed in the veins of KEARNY — like DOUGLAS dead, his name had won the field; or better, perhaps, like HENRY the Upright, slain in the Battle of Wablstadt, 1241, dying, he had preserved the land of civilization from the barbaric wave of slavery.

---

* JOMINI, in his large experience of war, notices one remarkable fact often asserted by other military writers, that "he had seen positions carried by troops with shouldered arms, but that in the line of battle he never saw a conflict with the bayonet."—LITTELL's "*Living Age*," 1301, 8th May 1869, p. 380 (2).

BIRNEY'S REPORT OF CHANTILLY.

HEADQUARTERS FIRST DIVISION, THIRD CORPS,
FORT LYON, VA., Sept. 4th, 1862.

Colonel:—

I have the honor to report the part taken by this division in the battle at Chantilly between Centreville and Fairfax Court House, on Monday, September 1st. The division reached Chantilly at about five o'clock, P. M., under orders from General HEINTZELMAN to support General RENO, and found him actually engaged with the enemy. Under orders from General KEARNY I reported my brigade to General RENO, and by him was ordered to the front. On reaching that point, I found the division of General STEVENS retiring in some disorder before the enemy; the officers in command of regiments stating that their ammunition had been exhausted. I immediately ordered forward the Fourth Maine Volunteers, which gradually advanced and was soon in active conflict, and successfully took forward the One Hundred and Forty-first New York, Third Maine, Fortieth New York, and First New York Regiments. (See KEARNY's letters following Report in regard to his Maine and New York Troops.) These held the enemy, and sustained unflinchingly the most murderous fire.

At this juncture, General KEARNY reached the hill with RANDOLPH'S Battery, and, placing it in position, aided my brigade by a well-directed fire. I then pointed out to the General a gap on my right, caused by the retreat of STEVENS' Division, and asked for BERRY's Brigade to fill it. He rode forward to examine the ground, and, dashing past our lines into those of the enemy, fell a victim to his gallant daring.

I sent forward the Thirty-eighth New York and Fifty-seventh Pennsylvania to complete our victory. They advanced gallantly, and when night closed, my brigade was in full possession of the battle-field on which it was engaged.

General KEARNY not returning, and supposing that he had been taken prisoner, I assumed command of the Division; and ordering forward ROBINSON'S and BERRY's Brigades, relieved my tired regiments and held the battle-ground until three o'clock A. M., at which time the Division followed the Corps of General RENO to Fairfax Court House.

During the night we removed our wounded. Our loss has been heavy.

I was ably supported by the commanding officers of my regiments, all of whom sustained the high character accorded by our late, lamented commander, in his report of Friday's engagement. Lieutenants LEE and PHILLIPS, of my staff, deserve especial mention for their untiring efforts in carrying my orders to all parts of the field. I have mentioned these in previous reports for gallantry. ROBINSON'S Brigade had been placed on the left of my Brigade, by General KEARNY, to support GRAHAM'S Battery. It was not, unfortunately, called upon to engage the enemy, but assisted greatly, with BERRY'S Brigade, during the night, in holding the field in face of a vastly superior force of the enemy. I was much indebted to General ROBINSON and to Colonel POE, commanding BERRY's Brigade, for their prompt assistance and the gallant bearing of their tired commands.

I am, very respectfully,
Your obedient servant,
D. B. BIRNEY.
Brigadier-General Commanding Division.

Lieutenant-Colonel McKEEVER,
Assistant Adjutant-General, Third Army Corps.

LETTER OF KEARNY IN REGARD TO HIS NEW YORK REGIMENTS.*

HEADQUARTERS, THIRD DIVISION,
HEINTZELMAN'S CORPS,
CAMP BERRY, BARHAMSVILLE, *May 10th*, 1862.

To his Excellency Governor MORGAN:

SIR—It is with great satisfaction that I have the honor of bringing to your notice the *distinguished* conduct of Officers and Regiments of the State of New York comprised in

---

* This note and the following should have followed KEARNY's Report of Williamsburg, but they are too important and characteristic to be omitted.

my Division, and as particularly illustrated in the late severe, but victorious engagement of the fifth instant in front of Williamsburg. These were the Thirty-seventh, Colonel HAYMAN; the Thirty-eight, Colonel J. H. HOBART WARD; and Fortieth, Colonel RILEY. *New York will ever hold her place as* EMPIRE STATE *as long as she has such sons to represent her!*

If, your Excellency, I do not particularize individual officers, it is that I could not, where all was zeal, distinguish one without injustice to the other. The Colonels are of the same opinion as myself. Colonels of two of them, stop before the difficulty of a selection; another, Colonel HAYMAN, includes his entire list.

The services of these regiments were most necessary. Each of the three bore the full brunt of the battle. The Thirty-seventh, Colonel HAYMAN, constituted our extreme left, part of General BERRY's brigade. The Thirty-eighth and Fortieth Regiments served on the right flank. During the action the Thirty-eighth, Colonel WARD, and a wing of the Fortieth regiment, were marshaled for the desperate work of piercing the enemy's left centre and carrying the rifle-pits in the nearly impassable abattis; a desperate undertaking. But I knew their reputation, and I was sure of their success. Colonel HOBART WARD lost nine officers out of the nineteen that went into action. Two of them were prisoners and were rescued.

Your Excellency, I particularly name to you these Colonels as most meritorious and gallant officers, and trust that their State will ever be mindful of them as her proud representatives.

Your Excellency, in making you this, my first official communication, I am happy to embrace the occasion to assure you how sensible I have ever been of your having recommended me, originally, as one of the Generals within your nomination.

I enclose the list of killed and wounded of these three New York regiments.

Most respectfully,

Your obedient servant,

P. KEARNY,

Brig.-Gen. Commanding Third Division, HEINTZELMAN'S *Corps.*

(Reb. Rec., V, Doc., page 18 [2].)

LETTER OF KEARNY IN REGARD TO HIS MAINE TROOPS.

HEADQUARTERS, THIRD DIVISION,
HEINTZELMAN'S CORPS,
CAMP BERRY, BARHAMSVILLE, VA., *May 10th*, 1862.

To his Excellency, ISRAEL WASHBURN, JR., *Governor of Maine:*

SIR — As Commanding General of this Division, of which two of the generals commanding brigades (General JAMESON and General BERRY), as well as two regiments, the Third Maine, Colonel STAPLES, and the Fourth, Colonel WALKER, form a part, I take this opportunity of calling to your notice their meritorious conduct in the late fight, and to display the fact that, although these regiments were not sufferers in the late engagement at Williamsburg — having been detached by General HEINTZELMAN to guard the left flank — by their steady and imposing attitude they contributed to the success of those more immediately engaged. And I assure you, sir, that with such material, commanded by such sterling officers, nothing but success can crown our efforts when the occasion requires. I have the honor to enclose the report of General D. B. BIRNEY, who commanded the noble brigade of which these two regiments form a part. General BIRNEY commands two New York and two Maine regiments.

It is peculiarly appropriate, after having rendered justice to the Regiments and Colonels, to bring Generals JAMESON and BERRY to the especial attention of yourself and citizens at home, who look to them for noble deeds to illustrate their annals, and I am proud to state that they have amply filled the full meed of anticipated distinction.

General BERRY, charged with the left wing of our line of battle, evinced a courage that might have been expected of him (when, as Colonel of the Fourth regiment of Maine Volunteers, he nearly saved the day at Bull Run), and also a genius for war and a pertinacity in the fight, that proved him fit for high command — for he was most severely assailed on the left, and had most difficult rifle-pits and abattis to face and carry.

General JAMESON, who commands the First Brigade (One Hundred and Second, Sixty-third and Fifty-seventh Pennsylvania Volunteers, and Eighty-seventh New York), forming the rear of the column, on the march from camp on the fifth instant, used vigor in bringing up his men under every difficulty, and was with me, under severe fire, where he arrived and gave guarantee of a resolution that promised success in case, daylight remaining to us, he had been advanced to the attack of Fort Magruder and those works which the enemy evacuated to us during the night, and *which he was the first to enter at daylight.*

I have the honor, sirs, to be

Your obedient servant,

P. KEARNY,

Brigadier-General Commanding Third Division, HEINTZELMAN'S *Corps.*

(Reb. Rec., V, Doc., pages 18 [2], 19 [1].)

KEARNY PATCH.

AFTER THE BATTLE OF CHANTILLY the army retired to the defenses of Washington. General BIRNEY retained the command of the First Division of the Third Army Corps, which had devolved upon him, on the death of General KEARNY, by right of seniority. General KEARNY, before his death, had issued an order requiring the officers and men under his command to wear a BADGE or *Mark*, by which they would be known wherever met. This *Badge* was a *piece of scarlet cloth*, worn on the cap or hat, so as to be visible at all times. This was the first attempt to designate officers or men in our army by any distinctive mark or badge. The evident object of this order was to *individualize* the members of this division, and to designate the officers and men, should they lag on the march, or straggle in action.

General BIRNEY and his men reached the defenses of Washington, after a tedious march, on the 3d of September, 1862. On the next day he issued the following order:

HEADQUARTERS KEARNY'S DIVISION,
FORT LYON, VA., September 4, 1862.

[GENERAL ORDERS, No. 49.]

The Brigadier-General commanding this division announces with deep sorrow the death of Major-General KEARNY, its gallant commander. He died on the battle-field of Chantilly as his division was driving the enemy before it.

The entire country will mourn the loss of this chivalric soldier, and officers and men of this division will ever hold dear his memory.

Let us show our regard for him by always sustaining the name which, in his love for the division, he gave it, viz., the "FIGHTING DIVISION."

As a token of respect for his memory, all the officers of this division will wear crape on the left arm for thirty days, and the colors and drums of regiments and batteries will be placed in mourning for sixty days. To still further show our regard, and to distinguish his officers as he wished, each officer will continue to wear, on his cap, a piece of scarlet cloth, or have the top or crown piece of the cap made of scarlet cloth.

By command of

Brigadier-General D. B. BIRNEY.

J. B. BROWN,

Acting Assistant Adjutant-General.

The *Scarlet Patch* referred to in the foregoing order was soon converted into a piece of red cloth or flannel, cut in the form of a DIAMOND, and this for some time was known as the KEARNY PATCH.—*Life of* DAVID BELL BIRNEY, *Major-General U. S. Volunteers* (Philadelphia, King & Baird, 607 Sansom St.; New York, Sheldon & Co., 400 Broadway, 1867), page 73.

CHAPTER XXXI.

DEATH AND OBSEQUIES OF MAJOR-GENERAL PHILIP KEARNY.

"THE END CROWNS ALL." — *Shakespeare.*

"A gentle knight was pricking on the plain." — SPENSER.

"Be bold. Be bold, and everywhere be bold." — SPENSER.

"High erected thoughts seated in the heart of courtesy." — *Sir* PHILIP SIDNEY.

"That chastity of honor which felt a stain like a wound." — WORDSWORTH

"BOLD as thou in the fight,
Blithe as thou in the hall,
Shone the noon of my might,
Ere the night of my fall.

"How humble is death,
And how haughty is life;
And how fleeting the breath
Between slumber and strife!"

HAROLD.

"Three hundred brave men lay down to sleep upon the sod, which sod, within three days, they were to sleep beneath." — BACHE'S DUMAS' "*Tales of Algeria.*"

"Triumph for freedom's battle-cry
Shall give us courage new;
Our country shall stand fixedly
While Northern hearts are true;
Then, countrymen, we'll hand in hand
To honor's fight away;
And free shall be our Fatherland
Until the Judgment-day."

Siegeslied nach der Schlacht bei Leipzig.

"False flew the shaft, though pointed well,
The rebel lived, the hero fell!
Yet marked the Peri where he lay,
And when the rush of war was past,
Swiftly descending on a ray
Of morning light, she caught the last —
Last glorious drop his heart had shed,
Before its freeborn spirit fled.
'Be this,' she cried, as she winged her flight,
'My welcome gift at the Gates of Light:
Though foul are the drops that oft distil
On the field of warfare, blood like this,
For Liberty shed, so holy is,
It would not stain the purest rill
That sparkles among the bowers of bliss!
Oh! if there be on this earthly sphere
A boon, an offering Heaven holds dear,
'Tis the last libation Liberty draws
From the heart that bleeds and breaks in her cause!'"

MOORE'S "*Lalla Rookh.*"

"Good fortune," says POLYBIUS, "is equally open to every one; but they are only Generals endued with prudence, discrimination and fortitude, whom we must consider as cherished by the gods. When any persons, from weakness of intellect, want of knowledge and experience, or through inattention, fail to perceive the various principles and tendencies of an action, they commonly ascribe to the immediate interposition of Heaven, or the favor of Fortune, the success which was owing to the united result of wisdom and sagacity."

" And Ardennes waves above them her green leaves,
Dewy with nature's tear-drops as they pass,
Grieving, if aught inanimate e'er grieves,
Over the unreturning brave. Alas!
Ere evening, to be trodden like the grass,
Which now beneath them, but above shall grow
In its next verdure, when this fiery mass
Of living valor, rolling on the foe,
And burning with high hope, shall moulder cold and low."
BYRON'S " *Childe Harold*," iii, 27.

" Let the tide of the world wax or wane as it will," MORTON thought, as he looked around him, " enough will be found to fill the places which chance renders vacant; and, in the usual occupations and amusements of life, human beings will succeed each other, as leaves upon the same tree, with the same individual difference, and the same general resemblance." OLD MORTALITY, II, 277—'8.

" RESPLENDET GLORIA MARTIS
ARMATI REFERAM VIRES."
CLAUDIAN *de Laud: Stil.*

" Brothers-in-arms, attend my prayer:
When I in battle die,
To my native 'State' my body bear,
In my native 'State' to lie."
The Grenadiers.

" By fairy hands their knell is rung;
By forms unseen their dirge is sung;
There Honor comes, a pilgrim gray,
To bless the turf that wraps their clay
And Freedom shall a while repair,
To dwell a weeping hermit there."
WILLIAM COLLINS.

' That life is better life, past fearing death,
Than that which lives to fear."
" *Measure for Measure.*"

" Noblest of men woo't die?
* * * * * * *
O, withered is the garland of the war,
The soldiers' pole is fallen."
SHAKESPEARE'S " *Anthony and Cleopatra*," Act iv, scene 13.

" Oh! happy the man around whose brows, he (Death) wreaths the bloody laurels in the glitter of victory." — GOETHE'S " *Faust*."

" Now let us all for the PERCY praye
To Jesu most of myght.
To bring his sowle to the blysse of heven,
For he was a gentyll knight."
Ancient Ballad.

" Hail, Rome, victorious in thy mourning weeds!
* * * * *
Thou great defender of this Capital,
Stand gracious to the rites that we intend! —
* * * * *

Behold the poor remains alive and dead!
These that survive let Rome reward and love;
These that I bring unto their *latest* home
With burial amongst their ancestors:
* * * * *
Make way to lay them by their brethren.
(*They open the tomb.*)
These greet in silence as the dead are wont,
And sleep in peace, slain in your country's wars!
O, sacred receptacle of my joys,
Sweet cell of virtue and nobility" ——

SHAKESPEARE'S "*Titus Andronicus.*"

"Lo, the leader in these glorious wars
Now to glorious burial slowly borne —
. . . .
Lead out the pageant, sad and slow,
. . . .
Let the long, long procession go,
And let the sorrowing crowd about it grow."

TENNYSON.

KEARNY had fallen, one of those men to whom a country could look for saving service in the crisis of a nation. A man who, at the same time, realized CHAUCER's idea —

"That he is gentil that doth gentil dedis" —

as well as that of Sir WALTER SCOTT, as expressed by the loss of his hero, ROLAND GRÆME: —

"He who fights well must have fame in life or honor in death" —

one of those men MONTGOMERY had in his eye when he wrote —

"Gashed with honorable scars,
Low in glory's lap they lie,
Though they fell, they fell like stars,
Streaming splendor through the sky."

Like CROMWELL and NAPOLEON, and many other great soldiers, his spirit passed away amid the turmoil of the tempest; in his case a tempest of the elements as well as of men, as if nature, in convulsion, sympathized with the conflict of human passion.

At the very moment that he died, he seemed to stand upon the threshold of a grand future, for no part which a man can be called upon to play, is so grand as that of a great general, to whom Heaven accords the glory of preserving his country, and maintaining the rights of the people; for, says DECKER, the most practical and concisely comprehensive of all military writers, "A great captain is the greatest gift which God can vouchsafe to a nation." It does not always require the explicit language of official commission to designate the man to whom the leading staff will be intrusted when a catyclism occurs;

when a man is found whose whole life has been consistent, resplendent, indicative of combined energy, ability and intrepidity. In the words of a world-wide known writer, words applied to HAROLD, the great, popular Saxon King of England, "The final greatness of a fortunate man is rarely made by any violent effort of his own. He has sown the seed in the time foregone, and the ripe time brings up the harvest. His fate seems taken out of his own control; and greatness seems thrust upon him. He has made himself, as it were, a want to the nation, a thing necessary to it; he has identified himself with his age, and in the wreath of the crown on his brow, the age itself seems to put forth its flower." How eminently true, however, in its highest signification, is this applicable to GRANT, whose greatness KEARNY dimly foresaw or estimated while his star was just rising above the horizon of the mass of military appointments, and how fully realized in his election to the Presidency, exactly as HAROLD was elected Basileus (King) of England.

Rarely an event occurs of general importance which does not confirm the adage that "coming events cast their shadows before," and public opinion — like those rumors which often fill the air, yet are not susceptible of being traced to any particular source — seem gradually to have embraced the conviction that the man best fitted to command THE Army of the Republic, the "Army of the Potomac," was that one-armed PHILIP KEARNY, who combined in a very great degree the indomitable constancy or will of U. S. GRANT; the fiery energy and dash of PHILIP SHERIDAN; the personal courage and winning manners of HOOKER; the practical strategy and foresight of WILLIAM STARKE ROSECRANS; and the cultivated mind and military information of MEADE. According to the testimony of intimate friends, one the principal adviser of General KEARNY — one who had the best opportunity of knowing every fact connected with the last twelve months of PHILIP KEARNY'S career — the command of the Army of the Potomac would have been given to KEARNY had he survived a few days longer to assume that responsible position; to which it was deemed that POPE had proved himself unequal, and to which the supreme authority was most unwilling to restore McClellan; yes, was almost humiliated in being compelled to restore McClellan.* Pope could not retain the command since, weighed in the balance of prejudice — unjustly weighed — he had been found wanting, sacrificed in a measure as another patriot was subsequently sacrificed — in the opinion of another general as personally brave as General Kearny, betrayed as well as sacrificed — his failure was attributed not to those who had been the active or passive causes of it, but to himself.

Kearny died impressed with the false idea that he was the object of neglect and injustice on the part of those in whose opinion he stood the highest; in the estimate of the people, and in the judgment of those who represented the people. Never was a man more greatly self-deceived. Chafing under the wrongs of little minds, tempororarily invested with power to wound his sensitive nature, he did not look abroad beyond the narrow circle which hemmed him in with its unintelligent lethargy — harder to bear than open animosity — to the great mind of the great people, who, in Abraham Lincoln, had its rugged, truthful, apt expression.

At the very moment when that fatal single shot or volley struck down the "bravest of the brave, and the most perfect soldier," a letter was lying in the War Department, signed by the Assistant Secretary, ready for transmission, and which was forwarded after his death, of which the following is a copy:

---

* "McClellan should never have received the command again, because, to use the language of one of the ablest and most philosophical historians of the 'Slaveholders' Rebellion': 'Though there never was purer patriotism than that which animated the soldiers of the Army of the Potomac, that army had been brought, through the influence of officers who surrounded General McClellan, into a most dangerous condition — dangerous to the best interests of the nation — of having a wish of its own, and that wish in opposition to the conviction of the government. *In armies it is but a very short step from the possession of a wish to the expression of a will.* Perhaps at no period of the war were thoughtful men more deeply alarmed for the future of the nation than when they heard of the restoration of McClellan to the command, and recognized the unmistakable constraint under which the government had acted. It was in vain for well meaning persons to affirm that the General had never been relieved, and that what had now taken place was no more than an ordinary proceeding; the Peninsula disaster was too recent, the complaints and asseverations of Pope of disobedience to his orders, among the higher officers, too loud for the real state of affairs to be concealed.'" — John W. Draper's "*Civil War in America*," 11, 444-'5.

"WAR DEPARTMENT,
"WASHINGTON, *September 1st*, 1862.

"SIR — The Secretary of War directs me to acknowledge the receipt of your note of August 23d, warmly urging that Major-General KEARNY be assigned to one of the corps d'armee, to be formed from the new levies. In reply, the Secretary instructs me to say that he knows no one more capable and worthy of command than Major-General KEARNY, and that, on the re-organization of the army, he will endeavor to assign him a position commesurate with his eminent merits and distinguished services."

"I have no warrant to state," continues CORTLANDT PARKER, Esq., KEARNY's counsel, friend and biographer, "and yet there is satisfactory ground for believing that even a higher position than that alluded to, namely, the command of the 'Army of the Potomac,' would have been his, had he lived long enough to take POPE's place. Mr. STANTON had ceased to have respect for the ability of General McCLELLAN. With that great man

* * * * * * * * *

halting aud timorous hesitation and procrastination had no favor, while bravery, skill and constant success like KEARNY's had overcome original prejudice and detraction, and converted him into admiration and confidence. In a letter under his own hand to Mrs. KEARNY, he says: 'His devoted patriotism, heroic courage, and distinguished military skill, had secured to him the confidence and admiration of the government, and endeared him to the people of the United States, who mourn his loss.' *

---

* But language will vainly endeavor to describe the grief, either of the army or the people, at this sad event. Both had long been intelligent observers of his career — the army, through daily opportunity, the people, in spite of his contempt of newspaper fame, and of the fulsome efforts made by so many officers, or their friends, to extol their merits while ignoring those of others. They knew him to be the savior of the Army of the Potomac, and consequently of the country, on various occasions — at Williamsburg, by rushing on the field at the moment of almost complete defeat, after jamming his way for hours through miles of encumbering masses, and by his skill, rapidity, and personal exposure, snatching splendid victory out of the very jaws of defeat; at Fair Oaks,* by stopping the demoralized retreat of the divisions

---

* FAIR OAKS.— SEDGWICK came, HOOKER and KEARNY came — HOOKER with the 2d New Hampshire and the 1st and 11th Massachusetts; KEARNY *with the life blood of New Jersey, brave men, all of them.* They rallied for a *desperate* charge — one which has determination in it; *when every man feels that he stands at the gateway of centuries, as* LEONIDAS *stood at Thermopylæ.* Twenty-four cannon, additional, were brought up. The united divisions, firm and unyielding as the granite of their native mountains, moved to the charge — onward, right onward, unheeding death or life! They came upon the enemy like a thunderbolt — bore down the living masses in front as if they were automatons — sent them flying over the field, and captured twelve pieces of artillery; one brigade, including three regiments; also Col. PENDLETON, of the Louisiana battalion, and Ex-Congressman LAMAN, of the 1st Georgia regiment. It was the finale. The enemy was defeated at last. He had come on with high hopes; he retired discomfitted. It was a brilliant victory. It inspirited our troops.

And, again: 'His high appreciation by this Department was shown by the rank he had won by long services and many gallant deeds, which would have been acknowledged by still higher command, if he had not fallen on the field of Chantilly.'

At first it was supposed and generally believed that KEARNY had been taken prisoner. The hope of the soldiery had been father to the thought. A few short hours, however, dissipated the doubt. His body,* on the morning of September 2d, was

of COUCH and CASEY, withstanding the exultant rebels pressing on to the destruction of all the troops then on the Richmond side of the Chickahominy, until the arrival of SUMNER restored the equality of numbers, and enabled us to gain the victory of the next day; on the New Market road, by again rushing in at the critical moment and beating back the triumphant masses of the pursuing rebels; they now saw him at the Second Manassas, on the first day, checking the enemy after all others had tried without success, almost driving them back, and sustaining the unequal contest with their heavy reserves till night closed the combat; on the second day, standing till 10 P. M., the rear guard of our retreat, covering it, and at last himself retiring to take his place in camp, in front of the advancing Confederates; and finally, at Chantilly, after passing from front to rear (that is, from opposing the enemy in front, to opposing the same enemy in the opposite direction), losing his inestimable life in driving off the untiring JACKSON from cutting our communications—a task which his lieutenant, BIRNEY, whose whole experience in war had been under him, performed. So that to KEARNY'S division again was due the safety of the discomfited army. They saw elsewhere, from MCCLELLAN down, personal jealousies and personal views interfering with and restraining the energy of officers who should have known nothing but their duty and the enemy, while KEARNY was always reliable, and, when danger was greatest was always there. And so they mourned for him, not with grief only, but with fear. For where, where was there then such another? HOOKER had his bravery, but not his skill. Besides these two, what generals at that time, in that army, were famous either for military skill or self sacrifice? And the exulting were more successful than ever! The North lay, to all appearance, at their mercy. (CORTLANDT PARKER'S "PHILIP KEARNY, Soldier and Patriot," pp. 40-41.)

*"The remains of General KEARNY were brought into Washington on the morning of the 3d of September, 1862, under charge of Capt. G. W. MINDIL, Assistant Adjutant-General for General KEARNY, and Captain FITZHUGH BIRNEY, Assistant Adjutant-General to General BIRNEY. They were embalmed by Drs. BROWN and ALEXANDER. The Secretary of War granted a furlough, which he wrote with his own hands, to Captains M—— and B—— for five days, to enable them to carry the remains to New York. If I remember correctly, the New York *Herald* of the 5th or 6th of September, '62 (perhaps 7th or 8th), gives an accurate account of the ceremonies.

"Captain MINDIL afterward became Colonel of (the 27th and 33d) New Jersey Regiments, and Brigadier-General and Brevet Major-General U. S. V. He was a highly distinguished officer. The Adjutant-General of New Jersey could inform you of his whereabouts. I feel assured he could give you some valuable information.

Captain BIRNEY, a noble officer and a martyr to the duties of his office, died at Georgetown, D. C., in July, 1864, from sickness incurred in the Wilderness fight, etc."—Major G. H. HECKMAN.

sent in to the Union lines, his horse, saddle and sword were likewise subsequently returned,* but his person had been rifled and no doubt of articles of value, for it appears to be an acknowledged fact, that KEARNY usually carried large sums of money upon him; money which he always used with lavish generosity to relieve the wants of our own soldiers, and had often been expended in alleviating the necessities of rebels and enemies.

General HOOKER has often alluded to the fact that ROBERT E. LEE sent in KEARNY'S body and effects to *him*, as an act of intentional courtesy. If so, the choice of HOOKER was most appropriate, for of all his brethren in arms, there was not one who was more highly appreciated, or was more greatly esteemed by the fallen hero. They had fought side by side, they had borne the heaviest burden and the hottest heat of the day together, and, in one of the hardest, if not the hardest, conflict they had passed through, HOOKER, almost in extremity, had sent forth a despairing cry for succor, addressed not to those most near, not to those most able to give it, but to that man, the farthest from him, whom he knew, that, if manhood and

---

* While it must be conceded, that, according to received opinion, KEARNY'S remains were treated with the highest respect by those into whose hands they fell, and that ROBERT E. LEE evinced a generous conduct in this regard, the following quotation is entitled to a place. It is an extract from "Field and Camp," "by an officer," and published in *Scott's Monthly* (a Georgia) *Magazine*, transmitted from Kentucky to the writer:—

"Just before dark, an ambulance came up and deposited a dead man in a house near by. He proved to be Major-General PHIL. KEARNY, U. S. A. During the fight, he had accidentally ridden on one of our regiments, when the men called out to him to surrender. Disregarding this, he suddenly wheeled his horse about and attempted to gallop off, when he was shot, and died almost immediately. He had lost an arm in Mexico — was a large handsome man, and, as he lay there buttoned up in his uniform, presented a splendid specimen of physical strength. Our men, of course, crowded around to see a Yankee general. One poor, ragged, barefooted fellow, cast a longing look at the fine cavalry boots he had on, remarking, as he did so: 'Number nines—just fit me,' and turned away, no doubt thinking it a great hardship that he was not permitted to appropriate them to his own use."

The following paragraph from the same article would lead the reader to suppose that the treatment of our dead at this time depended on individuals, rather than on the spirit which animated some of the enemy:—

"I was very tired, and as all was quiet, laid still. Presently I heard one of the men remark to another, 'Do you believe a hog would eat a dead Yankee?' 'No, I don't,' said the other. 'Well, look there,' was the reply. I looked also. There were two dead Yankees lying close to the fence. They had been killed by shells, and were badly blown to pieces. One had his breast torn open, and the greater portion of the liver was hanging out. Two or three hogs were at work on it, tearing it to pieces, and eating away with great satisfaction."

Does this need comment?

soldiership could save him, would overcome every obstacle, and be in time to do so. HOOKER has often reverted, with great feeling, to the fact that KEARNY's corpse was consigned to his friendly hands, and the writer records the fact with the greater pleasure, since the last person to whom he was introduced by his lamented cousin was JOSEPH HOOKER, whose "Battle above the Clouds," the capture of the formidable positions on the summit of Lookout Mountain, as extraordinary an exploit as the theatre of the action was extraordinary, has invested his achievement with a romantic interest of which scarcely any other event of the war is susceptible.

"That glorious chief, to whom was given
The right to scale the clouds of heaven,
And bear the starry flag on high,
Back to its native regions in the sky,
Behold our General on the rocky height!
A stately statue in a dome of light, —
With all the Rebel army put to rout,
Our 'fighting' HOOKER takes a long Look Out."

There is nothing which makes so deep an impression upon those who have loved and lost, as the fact that it matters not who disappears from the ranks of the living, no matter how high in intellect, or exalted in position, or extensive in influence, nature evinces no knowledge of the accident, and no sympathy with the event. Poets and historians have endeavorod to connect convulsions of nature with the fall of great men, but it is doubtful if any can be authenticated, since the "Prince of life yielded up the ghost," and the "Light of the world," as far as regarded the garb of humanity, was extinguished. Still curious coincidences do occur, and one of these distinguished the hour when KEARNY fell. Everything was invested with the deepest gloom. A fearful storm burst upon the field with unusual violence and unseasonable rigor, bringing in premature darkness. As DUMAS says of Preuss-Eylau, "sudden night" set in. The fortune of the country seemed enshrouded in gloom and at its lowest ebb; the popular military idol had proved himself unworthy of confidence; the wiliest politician, grown gray in studying the expressions of human inconsistencies, had uttered the falsest prophecies and the most delusive hopes. The shepherds and watch-dogs were both at fault, and events had proved that the solution of the problem was not with them, nor within the scope of their control or comprehension. Thenceforward the question was to rest with the *People.* It was the crisis of the fate of the Nation. Almost in despair, men, thoughtful men, began to look alone to God as the arbiter. They began to feel that eternal justice must be propitiated before we could hope for success. LINCOLN, never leading, but always being propelled by the people, saw this. Slavery was the curse of our nation, and the origin of all our difficulties. Then the nation bowed to His will, who alone can "give us help from trouble; for vain is the help of man." Emancipation was the solution. The people, moved by the Spirit of God, which is Liberty, willed it: LINCOLN decreed it. Then was realized the promise, that "through God we shall do valiantly; for He it is that shall tread down our enemies." Then night fled, and morning broke.

At this crisis, the darkest hour, that darkest hour which always precedes the dawn of a new day, KEARNY fell. The sun of his day, on that dismal first evening of the autumn of 1862, sank shrouded in gloom, as if the great light of the universe veiled its face from the fall of such lights as STEVENS and KEARNY, and the kindred spirits who perished at the climax, sacrifices to redeem their country. On the morning of September 2d, the sun rose again unclouded, as if the propitiation had been accepted, and shone in all its splendor, while the honored remains of the hero were restored to his mourning friends.

Four days later they lay in state, in his residence at Bell Grove, opposite Newark, filled with the gems of art with which the taste of the living man had surrounded himself. But the most glorious object there, amid that profusion of precious things, was the body of the slain warrior, with his remaining arm pressing to his bosom that exquisite sword* which he had won at the price of the absent limb.

---

* In connection with this "exquisite sword," the reader's attention is invited to three documents following this chapter. The *first*, "Sword Presentation for KEARNY's Services in Mexico," was kindly furnished by Mr. THOMAS S. TOWNSEND, who deserves to become famous for his compilation of a stupendous Cyclopedia of newspaper articles in connection with the "Slaveholders' Rebellion," which, in itself, is equal to a large library on that subject. It should constitute a portion of Chapter XII, and precede the concluding para-

His funeral can never be forgotten by an eye-witness. Words cannot do justice to it, for it was sublime in the spontaneous exhibition of the grief, respect, and love exhibited by the population of a huge city. It was a marvel, not in what was ordered, but in what was not decreed. His obsequies were those which in Europe are only accorded to a king and a conqueror. Let the relative be silent; let the faithful friend tell the rest. He has indeed told the truth, and tears almost start in the eyes at the perusal of his pages, linked with the recollection of those mourning drops upon the cheeks of tens of thousands, whose honest tears accompanied and followed the corpse of New Jersey's most brilliant soldier, the son of her adoption, but the son of her deepest love.

"It is impossible to forget his funeral, or to refrain from recalling here its striking circumstances. Intended to be simple and quiet in the extreme, the people willed it to be an occasion of most solemn grief, and would not be restrained from the privilege of being mourners. Crowds daily thronged his mansion, while the dead hero lay awaiting burial, his bronzed features seeming to smile defiance even of the last conqueror. The city authorities of Newark almost compelled the procession to cross the Passaic, and traverse the streets of the city; while deep bells tolled, and wailing music thrilled the air. And, most affecting of all, from the entrance of the cortege into the city till it reached the point of departure from it, spontaneously, irrepressibly, in solemn silence, except for the tears and sobs of many, came forth a crowd of people, of all ages and each sex, reverently baring their heads in presence of the dead for which they had stood hours in waiting, as orderly and as carefully placed as if under military directions, yet entirely unregulated

graph on page 153. It was not received, however, until six months after that chapter was *in print*. The *second*, "KEARNY'S CHARGE IN MEXICO," should have been incorporated in Chapter XI, and refers partly to an incident alluded to on pages 138 and 149, but principally to the grand charge which is the main subject of the chapter. This highly interesting letter from a participater in the glorious achievement did not come to hand until nearly a year after this chapter was in print. The *third* document, "REMINISCENCES OF KEARNY," is from the pen of Brevet-Major U. S. V. and Colonel N. Y. V. CLIFFORD THOMPSON. It relates to KEARNY's first association with any military organization in connection with our Great Civil War. This, too, was not sent to the author until about ten months after the Chapters XVI., XVII., XVIII., XIX., to which it refers, were in the hands of the printer.

by authority — an army of mourners testifying thus the depth of their grief, and their appreciation of their hero's services. On no occasion, except the funeral of LINCOLN, was such regard, within my knowledge, manifested. And so he was borne to the venerable yard where his father and his dead, darling boy lay. The magnificent service of its cathedral church was chanted over his remains. The final salute echoed through the great city, startling the speculations of its busy exchange. There he lies, not mouldering, but embalmed, while his memory is embalmed in the hearts of his countrymen."

"Four days later" — is the corroborative language of an eloquent writer and acute observer — "all Newark was in tears as the long funeral cortege filed slowly through the streets, bearing to his honored burial her most brilliant son; nay, the bravest, the ablest and most accomplished soldier that had as yet poured out his life-blood on any battle-field of the great war. Trinity church, in the metropolis, was opened. The coffin, with the sword and trappings of the deceased, was placed in the main aisle; the service was read, and then the choir poured over the vast assembly those sublime words of MENDELSSOHN's 'St. Paul:' 'Happy and blessed are they which have endured; yea, blessed and happy are they.'

"The massive portal of the family tomb was opened, the coffin and its load of sacred dust laid away for its perpetual rest beside a soldier kindred in blood and qualities; while the wails of martial music and the thrice-repeated volleys showed that no mark of respect, no sign of woe, was wanting in the funeral ceremony.

> "'Such honors Ilium to her hero paid,
> Then peaceful slept the mighty Hector's shade.'

"General KEARNY fell in the dimmest and gloomiest hour of the great struggle. Two weeks more of life and he would have seen a noble stroke falling full on the rebel crest" at South Mountain, and three days after that again, had HOOKER been supported as KEARNY had ever supported HOOKER, such soldiership and leadership as the former ever evinced would have made Antietam what it should have been, what it must have been with any effort of true generalship — the decisive battle of the war at the East, a Gettysburg, with consequences as awful to the rebels as the discomfiture of their hopes, their plans and their efforts had been complete. "Impetuous, fiery, sanguine, and brave almost to recklessness, it was his misfortune to be commanded, during the year of his service in our war, and the last of his military career, by men for whose military ability he seemed to feel only a mutilated respect. Though at no time permitted to engage in a decisive battle, and generally leading a forlorn hope or fighting against time till reënforcements came, or called to restore a shattered front, or to make a retreat sullen and dangerous, General KEARNY in no instance failed to execute the precise duty which the commanding general expected of him. At Williamsburg he was ordered to hasten to the front and support HOOKER. He reached the front by exertions the most strenuous, and he did more than merely support HOOKER, 'he saved HOOKER.' At Fair Oaks, after CASEY's division had crumbled under the impact of the rebel force, he arrested the rout, stayed the enemy's advance, fell back in order when sorely pressed, and held the field till the heavy reënforcing column from the north bank could reach the scene and retake the ground. In the Seven Days' retreat he was vigilant, firm and defiant, protesting at every step of retrograde and making the enemy pay dear for every advantage gained. At Groveton, his fighting and the ground he twice wrested from the clinch of STONEWALL JACKSON is the one brilliant jewel on the sackcloth of disaster. Chantilly is redeemed from obscurity and made fascinating, though not emblazoned with positive victory, by the story of his spirited defense, the brave front he opposed to disaster, and the uncalculating courage with which, in that lowering night-fall, he dashed out through the unknown forest, resolved to master the situation though the reconnoissance might cost him his life — as it did.

"PHILIP KEARNY's place in the Army of the Potomac was never made good. His mantle fell on no man's shoulders. Brave men and brilliant men rose after him, and fought well and died well. The face of the country was made historical by great battles, from the Susquehanna to the Appomattox. But no such figure as his careered with knightly grace in front of the serried battle-line; no voice like his to ring above the roar of the cannon; no spirit so potent as his, whether to sustain men through disaster or cheer them on to victory!"

Consigned to the family vault in Trinity churchyard, his remains were deposited by the side of two of his relatives, who, like him, had held commissions from their country in a previous war; one of whom was a cavalry officer, with a record almost as resplendent as his (KEARNY's) own, one who had preceded him as an aid on the staff of Major-General SCOTT. At the same time, a staff officer in one of the regiments which had occupied the ground around Arlington House, up to the time that KEARNY assumed the command of his famous New Jersey First Brigade, and now formed part of the funeral escort, was another cousin who had won his warm regard, and received the highest approbation of his superior for gallant service at the First Bull Run, a brother of KEARNY's Volunteer Aid at Williamsburg.

One, however, was wanting at his funeral whom the dead warrior held in the highest respect and regarded as the first general of his time. This was Lieutenant-General WINFIELD SCOTT. The veteran commander's letter, however, sufficiently explains the reason of his absence. Brief as it is, the concluding sentence is such a glorious testimonial to the worth of the deceased, that it might be selected almost without the change of a word as the most appropriate inscription for a monument to KEARNY.

In the opinion of the American people, Lieutenant-General SCOTT must always occupy a place in the first rank of their military leaders — between Lieutenant-General or General (it is questionable if the latter title was ever actually conferred) WASHINGTON, and Lieutenant-General, afterward General, GRANT. Neither the services of the Father of his Country, in establishing the nation, nor those of GRANT, in preserving it, can lessen the glory of the "hero of two wars," who maintained the national honor amid so many doubtful issues on our northern frontiers, and carried "Old Glory" through obstacles apparently insurmountable, to a consummate triumph in Mexico. No one was capable of forming a juster estimate of KEARNY

JOHN WATTS' FAMILY VAULT, TRINITY CHURCH YARD,

NEW YORK CITY.

Burial place of Major Gen. Philip Kearny, U. S. V., and of Lieut. George Watts, U. S. A.

This gentleman is Brevet-Colonel W. H. PAINE, of the Topographical Staff of the Army of the Potomac. He describes the afternoon and evening of the 1st September, 1862, as the worst he remembered, during his term of service. The storm

---

the army occupies. He must take surveys, question contrabands, deserters and prisoners in regard to roads, bridges and fords, draw maps, and consult, oftener even than corps-commanders, with the 'Major-General Commanding.' In a word, the army is often dependent upon the judgment of this one captain. A fortnight ago, at Spottsylvania, he partly discovered and partly made a road, where four miles were saved in moving troops from right to left of line. That night, amid the darkness and rain, he piloted over this road the Second and Sixth Corps, and next morning, by attack and surprise, we captured twenty guns and 7,000 prisoners. But for the discovery of a blind bridle-path, which fifty pioneers in two hours' time widened and improved to the capacity of a road fit for artillery, the attack which resulted so successfully would not have been thought practicable. VICTOR HUGO attributes the timely arrival of BLUCHER at Waterloo to a happy choice by a subordinate (a country lad) of the right road, which was but a half-defined path—so much do battles hinge on apparent trivialties. The officer I have been talking of—a modest man, who will be startled beyond composure should he ever see this—is Captain W. H. PAINE, of the Topographical Engineers, an appointee from civil life." In 1675, ROUSSET (at page 172, vol. ii.) of his "Life of LOUVOIS," the great war-minister of LOUIS XIV (in whom we had a feeble parallel in STANTON as to capacity, but exact in energy and despotic prejudices), represents the PRINCE OF CONDE as begging "that *one* CHAMLAY may be sent to comfort or assist him, as he knows exactly how to do so." "This CHAMLAY, ROUSSET remarks, deserves to hold a much higher rank or consideration in the military history of LOUIS XIV, than is generally conceded to him. He discharged the duties of *Marechal General des Logis de l'Armee*, which is translated in technical dictionaries "Quartermaster-General." This does not by any means express his peculiar functions. The duties of this office consisted in reconnoitering the routes which the troops were to follow, the encampments which they were to occupy, and, on occasion, the ground on which they were to fight. These are the very services which are now discharged by officers of the general staff, or, with us, are more peculiarly those of the Topographical Engineers. CHAMLAY possessed the genius of military topography. In April, 1672, when LOUVOIS was having the routes studied out by which the armies of LOUIS XIV were to advance to attack the forces and strong places of Holland, the DUKE OF LUXEMBURG wrote to him: "This, sir, is a report whose preparation I have assigned to SIEUR DE CHAMLAY. I do not know him, but, perhaps, he is the most proper person who can be found for such a duty. *The man is a living map*, and he can make an exact map of any ground, even if he has only seen it once." What is more, CHAMLAY was an honest man and a capable one outside of his profession, but withal, so modest that he did not seek to obtain what he deserved. His merit naturally compelled its recognition and impressed capable judges. TURENNE and CONDE quarreled to get him. He soon won the confidence of LOUVOIS, and under him became a second minister of war. After the death of LOUVOIS, LOUIS XIV wished to make him, CHAMLAY, titular minister of war. CHAMLAY refused. Having been the friend of the father, he did not wish to supercede the son, or rather he would only accept the burthensome portion of the inheritance; the business, the cares, the work; leaving to BARBEZIEUX the honor of the success, the distinction of the ministerial office, and the enjoyment of the power. CHAMLAY, like VAUBAN, like CATINAT, was one of those men so rarely found, at once full of intelligence and integrity, whom any one can praise without distrust (or discount) because the cynical SAINT SIMON has praised him; one whose constant and sincere friendship, after being an endorsement for LOUVOIS, living, continues as an honor for his memory, and in case of necessity, a shield (or justification)." If such a character applies to any one man more than another in the armies of the United States, evoked for the suppression of the "Slaveholders' Rebellion," it belongs to the civilian-appointment, originally a surveyor, Titular Captain, Additional Aid-de-Camp Guide and Topographical Engineer, Brevet Colonel U. S. V., W. H. PAINE.

was so violent that, then and there, for the first time, he found it impossible to make any observations or take any notes.

It was during this fearful storm, through which the battle continued to rage until the enemy were repulsed and their attempt to flank us frustrated, that he met General KEARNY. The following is his statement of that interview, intensely interesting because he or General BIRNEY were the last with whom KEARNY conversed upon earth:

DEAR GENERAL: In accordance with your request, I will mention such circumstances as occurred under my own observation, just previous to the death of the brave and gallant General PHILIP KEARNY upon the field of battle, knowing that any incident, however trivial in itself, which tends to throw any additional ray of light upon the events of the last hour of one whose memory all delight to honor, will be appreciated, and by none more than by yourself.

The rebel General JACKSON'S troops were moving on the 1st of September, two days after the battle of Groveton, down the Little River turnpike, with a flank well extended and protected, while the Union army was moving upon and holding the road leading from Centreville and intersecting the Little River turnpike, about one and a half miles west of Fairfax Court House.

General RENO'S Corps was moving down between these two roads, and, becoming engaged with the enemy, formed in line of battle facing the north. It soon became very stormy and dark, but still the battle raged, and, as it progressed, General RENO'S forces moved further to the right, vacating the ground previously held by his left.

On riding from this point, I found General KEARNY, with his command, about to advance from the rear toward this vacated position, and informed him that it was vacated, and that his own left and front were uncovered by the movement of General RENO'S troops. He expressed surprise, and said that, from the instructions he had received, he thought there was a force there which he was to support, if necessary. After replying to his particular inquiries as to who I was, and my means of information, he added that it conflicted both with his instructions and other information received; but if true, was very important for him to know. I then left him. I learned, subsequently, that he went forward immediately, and came soon upon the enemy, by whom he was shot.

We all know of his personal bravery and courage, and are not surprised at the idea of his braving the danger of a personal reconnoissance to ascertain the relative position of the enemy to our own troops, when that point was in doubt and the knowledge of vital importance.

KEARNY could scarcely have parted from PAINE when he

encountered BIRNEY. The particulars were thus given by General BIRNEY,* his valuable subordinate, afterward himself

* "On reaching the field, near the village of Chantilly, General BIRNEY, by orders from General KEARNY, reported to General RENO, and was ordered to the front. When he arrived, a portion of the division of General STEVENS was retiring in disorder, the officers of the regiments stating that their ammunition was exhausted. BIRNEY ordered forward the 4th Maine, and then took forward the 101st New York, 3d Maine, 40th and 1st New York. These regiments engaged and drove back the enemy, though greatly inferior in numbers. As the regiments were going forward, General KEARNY came up with RANDOLPH'S Battery, which was at once put in position to sustain the brigade. General BIRNEY pointed out to General KEARNY a gap on his right, caused by the retiring of STEVENS' men, and asked that BERRY'S Brigade be ordered up to fill it. KEARNY insisted that it was impossible for such a gap to exist, and said he would ride forward to see what troops were there. BIRNEY warned him, and urged him to remain, saying he would ride into the enemy's lines, but KEARNY retorted a jesting remark about BIRNEY'S caution, and dashed ahead. This was the last BIRNEY ever saw of his friend. In the words of General HEINTZELMAN, he pressed 'forward' to reconnoitre in his usual gallant, not to say reckless, manner, and came upon a rebel regiment. In attempting to escape he was killed. The country has to mourn one of its most gallant defenders. At the close of the siege of Yorktown he relieved General HAMILTON in the command of the division, and led it in the various battles on the Peninsula, commencing with Williamsburg. His name is indentified with its glory.

"As General KEARNY did not return, General BIRNEY supposed he had been taken prisoner, and assumed command of the division, being the ranking brigade commander on the field. Though a violent thunder-storm was raging, our men fought desperately, and *the enemy were driven from our front.* Their retreat was hastened by the Thirty-eighth New York and Fifty-seventh Pennsylvania, which BIRNEY ordered up 'to complete the victory.' Afterwards ROBINSON'S and BERRY'S brigades were ordered forward to relieve the tired and decimated regiments, and BIRNEY remained in possession of the field until 3 A. M., the next day, when he followed, with the division, the corps of General RENO to Fairfax Court House.

"During the night (1st September) our men were busy in removing the wounded and burying the dead. About 10 P. M., the officer in command of the enemy's lines sent a flag to General BIRNEY and made himself known as a former correspondent of BIRNEY'S, at Columbia, South Carolina. He said he had within his lines the body of General KEARNY, and would forward it if General BIRNEY wished him to do so. Of course General BIRNEY requested that the mangled body be sent him, and when the troops moved they carried with them the remains of their beloved and gallant general. That midnight march was a sad one for officers and men. They had gained a victory, and an important one, but their brave leader had fallen, and his death caused grief which prevented any exultation over their success. BIRNEY was not the least of the mourners. Though for months he had been in the midst of carnage and slaughter, he could not restrain his feelings, and had the enemy, during the darkness, made an attack upon those lion-hearted men, who a few hours before had won a victory at the point of the bayonet, they would have found them unmanned and almost incapable of resistance.

"The success of our arms at Chantilly was of great importance to our army. General POPE, disheartened by the want of co-operation on the part of some corps commanders, was on the retreat towards Washington with exhausted troops, who had become dispirited by frequent reverses. The rebel commander, with troops flushed with success, attempted to out-flank General POPE. Had this movement been a success, such of our men as succeeded in ragaining Washington would have entered it as a disorganized mob and not as an army. Besides this, the wounded and sick were suffering for want of care and medicine. One large train of medical stores had been captured, and the movement which Chantilly had frustrated would have resulted in the loss of the second train, which was then on its way to General POPE'S Army. General POPE, in his official report, on pages 18 to 27, gives to the success of Chantilly its real importance. He says (page 27), 'The main body of our forces was so much broken down and so completely exhausted, that

a martyr to his country's cause: "During the battle of Chantilly, my brigade was actively engaged. I noticed that STEVEN's Division had * * retreated, leaving a gap of half a mile on my right. I asked General KEARNY for BERRY's Brigade, to fill it; he stated that he had ordered the colonel commanding to report to me, and was indignant at his delay. But he said it was impossible that General RENO could have permitted *such* a gap; that I must be mistaken; that there certainly were troops there of ours. I assured him that there was not. At this time it was raining, and the smoke from the batteries hung low. I galloped down to send in a regiment to my left. He accompanied me, and as we leaped a ditch his horse shied, and he remarked how disagreeable that a horse should behave so in a battle. He then galloped to the right, and I saw him no more." From Colonel, now General MEDILL (MINDIL ?), then his Aid, I fill out the history. General KEARNY was on a black horse, and covered with an india-rubber cloak. It was late in the evening — dark with clouds, the drizzly rain, and the shade of the woods. He determined to see for himself if such a danger existed as such a gap in the Union line. Bidding Colonel MEDILL stay behind, he dashed forward to inspect. POLLARD says: "General KEARNY met his death in a singular manner. He was out reconnoitering, when he suddenly came upon a Georgia regiment. Perceiving danger, he shouted, 'Dont fire — I'm a friend' — but instantly wheeled his horse around, and, lying flat upon the animal, had escaped many bullets when one struck him at the bottom of the spine, and, ranging upwards, killed him almost instantly."

---

they were in no condition, even on the 1st of September, for any active operations against the enemy, but I determined to attack at daylight on the 2d of September in front of Chantilly. The movement of the enemy had become so developed * * * * and was so evidently directed to Fairfax Court House, with a view of turning my right, that I made the necessary disposition to fight a battle on the road from Centreville to Fairfax Court House.

"RENO was to push forward to the north of the road in the direction of Chantilly. HEINTZELMAN's Corps was directed to take post immediately in the rear of RENO. * * Just before sunset on the first, the enemy attacked us on our right, but was met by a counter attack by HOOKER, MCDOWELL, RENO and KEARNY's Division, of HEINTZLEMAN's Corps. A very severe action occurred in the midst of a terrific thunder storm, and was terminated shortly after dark. The enemy was driven back entirely from our front.'"— "*Life of* DAVID BELL BIRNEY, *Major-General United States Volunteers*" (Philadelphia, King, Baird & Co., 7 Sansom St.; New York, Sheldon & Co., 400 Broadway, 1867), p. 69, etc.

Doubtless this is very near the truth, and tallies almost exactly with the story related to the writer at the time, substituting a Louisiana for a Georgia regiment. Had KEARNY enjoyed the use of two arms he would have escaped, since he could have thrown himself completely out of the saddle, Indian fashion, thus interposing his animal as a shield. An inch more depression would have saved him, for the angle of incidence was such that in the latter case the ball would have been deflected *outward*, occasioning a mere superficial wound, whereas it glanced *inward*, with mortal effect.*

After KEARNY left BIRNEY, he was next seen by Brevet Lieutenant-Colonel SAMUEL N. BENJAMIN, Second U. S. Artillery, whose account is as follows: "After the action at Chantilly had been over for more than an hour, troops from my left began marching past my position going toward the turnpike. I was on our right, and a country road, or a farm road, ran past my left and then went up an opening toward our left flank. After a number of troops had passed and the road was clear, I saw General KEARNY ride past at a swift gallop, entirely alone, and turn down the road toward our left, in the direction the troops had come from. It was dark (probably between 8 and 9 P. M., I am uncertain as to time), but he passed within twenty feet of me, and in the full light of my fire. I called to him to warn him that the troops there had been partially or entirely withdrawn, but he did not hear. I called one of my officers to send after him, but the General was well out of sight for some minutes before he came, and we thought it was useless to look for

* WASHINGTON, *Sept. 5th*, 1862. — "Having discovered a prevailing error in regard to the wounds upon the body of Major-General PHILIP KEARNY, created, no doubt, by the mere surmises of various newspaper correspondents, we, as the embalmers of the body, feel it a duty we owe to the public, and the family of the deceased, to give a true statement of the facts. Major-General KEARNY met his death by the reception of a Minie rifle-ball of large calibre, which entered his body through the gluteus muscles, at a point a little back of the articulation of the left hip joint. The ball, impinging on the bones of the pelvis, penetrated the os-innominata, whence it directed its course through the abdominal viscera, to the integument just above the umbilicus, sliding up between the skin and the sternum, where it lodged, forming a distinct and discolored tumor just above the centre of the breast. We cut the ball out, which was much flattened and abraded by the resistance it met in passing through bones. We placed the missile in the hands of Captain W. C. MORFORD, Quartermaster of General KEARNY'S staff, to be by him delivered over to the disconsolate family, who will no doubt keep it as the most valuable relic bequeathed to them by the "bravest of the brave."

(Signed) DRS. BROWN & ALEXANDER,
Embalmers of the Dead.

him in the dark (I was lame and could not rise from the ground without assistance), although we both felt uneasy about him. Fifteen or twenty minutes later, I heard in that direction two musket shots, followed by a straggling volley of perhaps thirty shots, or less. It was the firing which sealed his fate. I was in the same place until 2 A. M. of the same morning, and heard no other firing.

"A Captain HALL, who was one of BURNSIDE'S Quartermasters when in Pleasant Valley, Maryland, during October, 1862, gave me an account of his death, which he got from a rebel officer, then a prisoner. I am not sure whether it was direct or not, but I think the officer either claimed to have been present or to have got it from one present with the party who killed the General. I loved and admired General KEARNY, and am glad his record is to be placed before his countrymen." *

The news of KEARNY'S fall shocked the whole nation. KEARNY had enjoyed so many miraculous escapes and passed through so many perils, that the people had almost come to believe, with the old officer of the Huguenot wars, that "a gallant and all-daring heart is a buckler which neither steel nor lead can penetrate." Nay, KEARNY almost seemed to realize the superstition of the Thirty Years' War, and of the "Iron Age" of Sir JAMES TURNER, that there were men, "*Gefroren*

---

* This note is inserted that every account may be presented, but the author places the most implicit confidence in Col. BENJAMIN'S story.

"We are informed by a prominent lawyer of this city, that, while sojourning in Amboy last night, he passed a pleasant hour in company with a former rebel officer, who was attached to STONEWALL JACKSON'S division of the Confederate army during the war, and who related an interesting reminiscence of the death of General KEARNY, of which sad event he was an eye-witness: 'The gallant KEARNY,' he said, 'received his death wound from a private soldier under my command, and, when he fell from his horse, I hastened, with many others, to the point where he lay, not supposing that his wound was a mortal one. Just as we reached his body, however, his limbs gave one convulsive quiver, and then all was over. Seeing that he was a major-general, word was sent to headquarters to that effect, and General Jackson, coming to the spot, immediately gave one glance at the dead officer's features, and exclaimed, "My God, boys, do you know who you have killed? You have shot the most gallant officer in the United States army. This is PHIL. KEARNY, who lost his arm in the Mexican war." He then involuntarily lifted his hat, every officer of the group following his example, and for a moment a reverential silence was observed by all. Subsequently, the body of the dead soldier was placed upon two boards, and, when being removed to headquarters, was followed by General JACKSON, General EWELL, and other officers, while a regimental band preceded it, playing a dead march.'" — *West Virginia News* (quoting *Newark* [N. J.] *Courier*), Ravenswood, W. Va., April 8th, 1869, forwarded by Col. F. R. HASSLER.

as the soldiers termed it," that it is rendered impervious, by magic arts, to steel or to bullet. CLAVERHOUSE, Viscount of Dundee, was looked upon by foe and friend as one of these charmed men. He was a leader much like KEARNY, killed like the latter in the moment of success, at Killiekrankie, whom WORDSWORTH commemorated in the verse —

> "O, for a single hour of that Dundee,
> Who on that day the word of onset gave." —

whom Sir WALTER SCOTT selected as one of his prominent heroes; whose history has employed so many and such able pens.

The very fact that it was so unexpected, rendered KEARNY's death the more shocking. His fall was looked upon as a national calamity. For a prominent and magnificent figure to fall from its pride of place is always a startling event; but immeasurably more so, when that figure is being elevated to the highest position, and is shattered at the moment when it is about to be set up on the very pinnacle of the temple.

When the certain news of his death came home to those scenes which he admired most, and where, as late as in 1855, he intended to locate himself for life, a young officer, a cousin, who had been with him at Williamsburg, and won KEARNY's handsome mention for his deportment there, lay stricken with James River fever, battling for life with that fell disease. When the news of his beloved cousin and commander's death was communicated to him, no one was aware how deeply gratitude for almost fatherly kindness, mingled with the warmest affection, had rooted itself in the young man's heart. Raising his enfeebled head, he exclaimed: "My cousin Phil. killed?" "Yes." The young officer sunk back upon his pillow, lay silent for a moment, as if almost unable to credit that the warrior he had witnessed defying death triumphantly, had indeed fallen. Then suddenly, as if the full realization of the sad truth had flashed upon his fevered mind, he burst into a passion of tears, turned his face to the wall, and scarcely spoke for two days. Many who evinced less visible emotion than the sick soldier, felt almost as deeply as he did, and were almost tempted to exclaim, that the glory had departed, that a planet had been stricken from its orbit.

When KEARNY joined the "Army of Virginia," dispirited by the treatment he had experienced; disheartened at the prospects; disgusted at the intermeddling of politicians with things beyond their sphere, he looked forward with a soldier's anxiety to the immediate future of our arms; but like a true, patriotic, and brave American, he "never despaired of the commonwealth," or the restoration of the Union.

No officer in the army of the Potomac had knit himself so deeply into the respect of all true soldiers in it. The *masses* might hurrah for McCLELLAN, but the FIGHTING MEN cheered for KEARNY. How he stood with those who had borne the burden and heat of the day, from Yorktown to Richmond, from the Chickahominy to Malvern Hill, from Warrenton to Fairfax Court House, was demonstrated to him that day, with whose sun "his own glorious light went out." KEARNY who had covered the retreat on the night of the 30th of August, with HOOKER (stricken down severely wounded, in the hour of success at Antietam), with RENO (slain at South Mountain), (both of these within three weeks, subsequently), with STEVENS (killed almost at his side), was again summoned to assume the post of danger and of honor. He rode forward like a triumphal conqueror.

Regiment after regiment, as his erect and martial form, like a stately apparition, passed by through the hurtling storm, "hailed him with cheers upon cheers," and followed his shining locks (grown prematurely gray with cares for his men) with their shouts of admiration. This is the picture drawn by one who watched his career with unflagging interest.

An eye witness, who had fought by his side, from the beginning of the campaign, within hearing of his guns, and in sight of their flashes, in every engagement in which he participated, corroborates this statement in these words: "On the afternoon of the 1st of September, HEINTZELMAN'S (Third) Corps was ordered to move towards Chantilly, where General STEVENS was contending with the rebels for the road on which our trains were retiring. The Second Division (General HOOKER'S) was in line and about to march; the First Division (General KEARNY'S) had already moved, and General KEARNY, seeing the rear of his division well on the way, spurred his horse to hasten forward so that he might reach the head of his command, for it is well known that KEARNY was always restless when not at that post. As he passed along the line of the Second Division he received such a salvo of cheers from that command — each regiment taking up the cheer in succession, and all swelling into acclamations which rung again — as proved to all within miles that a favorite and appreciated General was passing. This was a compliment indeed, doubly so when it came, as it did, from a rival division, and that division a body of troops which had fought for months by the side of the gallant 'Fighting Phil' KEARNY's especial command, and had been led by General HOOKER ('Fighting Joe'). KEARNY testified how much he appreciated the compliment intended, for, letting drop the reins, he took his little military cap in his hand, and bowing low, even to the saddle bow, with head uncovered, his horse galloping at the top of his speed, he acknowledged this truly heartfelt demonstration in his favor." This we have from an eye witness, W. B. And thus, as was said of Rienzi — when the wing of the death angel cast a shadow over his proudest moment of triumph, so that the Popular Tribune seemed by one step to descend from the pinnacle of glory into the grave — even so "the Bayard of our Host," crowned with the applause of those best able to judge of his merit, spurred, as it were, invested with the blaze of acknowledged pre-eminent soldiership, into a grave which is all aglow with his never contested or even questioned fame, a very Phœnix to *his* Pyre. "I can, indeed, sympathize with you, my dear O. S. H ——," are the words (12th of September, 1862, Washington) of a letter from a common friend (D. de K——) to one of KEARNY's original staff officers, "in the loss of the noble and chivalric KEARNY. I rode with him an hour before his death as he passed along the lines, and received the cheers and plaudits of every regiment he passed, not only his own, but troops of other corps. Two days before, in a long talk with him, he said, "Ah, well! when this war is over, after a quiet sojourn at my Jersey home, I will go to Paris and lead a happy life, and make up for all this discomfort which surrounds me here." Glorious KEARNY. *He fell, and his men, by his spirit, won the fight and saved the Army of Virginia.* And, alas that it should be so! he was there obliged to die by the jealousies and lukewarmness of other Generals (more of this anon). Truly you say that we can not replace him. His brilliant daring made timid Generals brave, his fame and name made others emulous." It is scarcely worth while to accumulate evidence of the exalted opinion entertained of KEARNY by all who knew or watched his "course of light." Still the following incident, whether it be wholly true or not, proves what a hold KEARNY had won upon all who had come in contact with him. After the war the writer encountered on the Upper Potomac an Irishman, in 1862 an employee of the quartermaster's department, who served with the Army of Virginia. Upon learning the relationship existing between the person addressing him and KEARNY, he became very communicative and enthusiastic, and spoke long and loud in praise of the dead hero. He said he well remembered that fearful night at Chantilly, for on that occasion he was in charge of a corrall of 1,500 horses, and had his hands full restraining the animals, frenzied by the lightning and the blaze of the conflict. When he had almost succeeded in making them secure, news came that KEARNY was killed. "By ——," said he, with an awful oath, "when I heard *that*, I thought it was all up, and I let the 1,500 horses go." Doubtless, the man's nerve-force, had become almost exhausted, and it is easy to conceive that the tidings of the death of such a favorite as KEARNY, generally supposed to bear a charmed life, made him feel all was lost, completely unnerved him and paralyzed his energy and strength.

A writer herein before referred to, who never did justice to KEARNY while living, relents over his corpse, and pays him an elegant but deserved tribute of admiration. "A firm front was maintained at Chantilly by RENO, HOOKER, a part of MCDOWELL and KEARNY, until STEVENS' division of RENO's corps, owing to the exhaustion of its ammunition and the death of its General, was forced back in disorder. To repair this break, KEARNY, with a promptitude that marked him, sent forward BIRNEY's brigade of his own division; and presently, all aglow with zeal, brought up a battery which he placed in position. But there still remained a gap on BIRNEY'S right, caused by the retirement of STEVENS' division. This BIRNEY pointed out to KEARNY, and that gallant soldier, dashing forward to reconnoiter the ground, unwittingly rode into the enemy's lines, and was killed. In his death the army lost the living ideal of a soldier — a *preux chevalier*, in whom there were mixed up the qualities of chivalry and gallantry as strong as ever beat beneath the mailed coat of an olden knight. Like DESAIX, whom NAPOLEON characterized as 'the man most worthy to be his lieutenant,' KEARNY died opposing a heroic breast to disaster."

The simile, however beautiful, is not exactly apposite. DESAIX fell in a victorious advance, which decided triumphantly, for his superior, one of the most momentous battles of modern times — a battle which changed the whole face of Europe for fourteen years, which established a new dynasty on one of the oldest thrones in Europe, and has still its effect, after sixty-eight years, upon the world.

A better comparison in some respects — as regards regrets and admiration — would be the idolized MARCEAU, killed by a rifle-ball at Altenkirchen, on the last day of the fourth year of the French Republic, 20th September, 1796. This ornament to his profession, of whom it was said that his monument required no inscriptions since his name was enough, was charged, like KEARNY, with the duty of covering the retreat of the French army. Like KEARNY in this also, he determined to check the enemy by a vigorous offensive-defensive. A wood was held by a body of Tyrolese riflemen. MARCEAU advanced, exactly as KEARNY did, to *reconnoiter* the ground, when a ball entered his left side, traversed the body and lodged under the lower rib, and caused his death. Of him, as of KEARNY, it is recorded, "France (America) adored, and her enemies (rebels) admired; both wept over him."

"By Coblentz, on a rise of gentle ground,
There is a small and simple pyramid,
Crowning the summit of the verdant mound;
Beneath its base are hero's ashes hid,
Our enemy's — but let not that forbid

Honor to MARCEÁU! o'er whose early tomb
Tears, big tears, gush'd from the rough soldier's lid,
Lamenting and yet envying such a doom,
Falling for France, whose rights he battled to resume.

"Brief, brave and glorious was his young career—
His mourners were two hosts, his friends and foes;
And fitly may the stranger lingering here
Pray for his gallant spirit's bright repose;
For he was Freedom's champion, one of those,
The few in number, who had not o'erstept
The charter to chastise which she bestows
On such as wield her weapons; he had kept
The whiteness of his soul, and thus man o'er him wept.'

CHILDE HAROLD, III, LVI, LVII.

In other respects, however, the fate of Field Marshal KEITH, the friend and subordinate of FREDERICK THE GREAT, is a very apt parallel, who fell, exactly like New York's brightest warrior son, in the darkest hour of the war which his deeds illustrated. On the night of the 13th of October, 1758, Marshal DAUN surprised the Prussian army. At the first sound of the cannon, KEITH put himself at the head of a few battalions to retrieve the disaster, and in this supreme act of duty, fell. General LACY, whose father had served with KEITH in the Russian army and himself with him on other fields, but now against the gallant Scot, recognized the dead body, and burst into tears. Like KEARNY and MARCEAU, KEITH was equally admired in both armies. All three fell endeavoring to retrieve a disaster; not like DESAIX, in a victorious advance.

The comparison, however, between KEARNY and DESAIX is a just one in some regards, and is strikingly appropriate in more than one respect, never contemplated in the quotation referred to. Those who concede the justice of the parallel are not aware, as a rule, that by the admission they pay the highest possible compliment, under every consideration, to KEARNY. Desciples of West Point, who consider NAPOLEON an oracle who can not err, should remember that the Emperor spoke of his death as "an irreparable loss," and declared throughout life, that in losing him "France has lost one of her most able defenders, and I my best friend. No one has ever known how much goodness there was in DESAIX's heart, and how much genius in his head.' "My brave DESAIX," he added, with tears in his eyes " always wished to die thus, but death should not have been so ready to execute his wish. Not the slightest stain blemishes his beautiful life." NAPOLEON accorded him the highest esteem, not only for talents but for virtues; and in assigning the summit of the Alps as his burial place to DESAIX, he contemplated "a homage such as no man ever received, a homage due to transcendent virtue and heroism." Those who prefer home authorities will defer to the opinion of General SCOTT. He remarked: "For scientific war no one has exceeded DESAIX. He also excelled in the handling of troops." This is incontestibly true of KEARNY. There are other points of resemblance between KEARNY and DESAIX, which were equally marked, which are as curious as those which are strictly military. Such as ancestry, education, bravery, generosity, and a combination of fiery enthusiasm with perfectly cool judgment under fire. Both were the souls of honor, and to both glory was as the very breath of their nostrils. In the manner of their death they were so far alike that both fell at a crisis. DESAIX, however, died with the assurance that his blood had not flowed in vain, that he had brought up victory with him. KEARNY died in the midst of disaster, without the consolation of knowing that the tide was about to turn, nay, that the event actually hinged upon his death.

One of the leading New York journals, commenting on his fall, observes: "A Washington dispatch has the following: 'The following Major-Generals, who were killed in battle, were confirmed to-day: MANSFIELD, STEVENS, KEARNY,* RICHARDSON, and

* ADJUTANT-GENERAL'S OFFICE, WASHINGTON, Nov. 5, 1868.

MY DEAR SIR: In reply to your note of the 2d instant, I have had the records examined, and find the following answers for your questions in relation to General KEARNY:

1. When General KEARNY was appointed Major-General of Volunteers, he stood number *six* on the list of Brigadier-Generals.

2. His commission as Brigadier-General of Vols. was dated 7 Aug., 1861, to rank from 17 May, 1861.

3. He was appointed, during the recess of the Senate, Major-General of Vols.; the letter of appointment was dated July 25, 1862, to rank from July 4, 1862. His *commission*, prepared after his death, bears date of March 13, 1863. The records do not show that the services, on account of which the rank of Major-General was conferred were stated in either the letter of appointment or the commission.

4. At the date of his death, he stood number thirty on the list of Major-Generals of Vols.

GEN'L DEPEYSTER, Tivoli, N. Y. Very truly yours, E. D. TOWNSEND,
then Asst. Adjt.-General, now Adjt.-General U. S. A.

PHILIP KEARNY was not confirmed as Major-General of Volunteers until March 9th, 1863, nor was the order, says Brevet-Maj. G. E. H——, announcing his promotion as Major-General, received by his old, then BIRNEY'S division, until November, 1862.

Reno.' There is something inexpressibly yet heroically mournful, in the brief paragraph above quoted. These noble men who went down amid the storm of battle when dark days were upon the land, who saw not the brightness of coming dawn making golden the horizon of promise — lying in the cold tomb all unconscious of the barren honor thus paid their names, made 'Major-Generals' months after the sods of the valley have closed over their silent clay!

"And yet there is appropriateness in this act. These iron-soldiers of our war for liberty, though dead, 'still live,' as, in the days of the Empire, when a hero of the 'Old Guard' was killed, his comrades at roll-call would answer to his name, '*Mort, sur le Champ d'Honneur.*' So we would have our dead Kearny, bravest of the brave, a 'Major-General' among our generals, speaking to them with dumb, yet eloquent life; interfusing among them somewhat of the fiery force, the calm, the cool yet impetuous courage, the rare genius to create, and the ready hand to execute, and, above all, the pure, unselfish, superb patriotism which distinguished the dead New Jersey General.

"Brave Phil. Kearny! Our best beloved, our peerless leader, we hail thee, though dead, with thy hard won title — To the memory of Major General Philip Kearny!" And again, "Army officers here think this the greatest loss we have sustained during the war, and freely acknowledge that we had no abler General in the service. General McClellan wept bitterly at the sight of his (Kearny's) dead body here to-night."

The *Times*, commenting upon his fall, remarked: "The doubt as to the death of General Philip Kearny seems to be set at rest. In the contest of Monday, that gallant officer, always forgetful of his own safety, fell mortally wounded while leading his men into action; and the country has to deplore the loss of one of its most accomplished, experienced, and enterprising officers. General Kearny was peculiarly a professional soldier. To a thorough elementary training in the art of war, he had added careful studies of all the great military authorities, with reference to every department of the profession. These studies had been the business of his life; and to give them experimental value, he served throughout the Mexican war, it is needless to say with the highest honor and distinction, having previously participated in the Algerian campaign, and yet more recently in the war of Italian liberation. From the leading French Generals of the time, he received testimonials of the most flattering description, attesting his intrepidity and skill. Had his bravery been attempered with the slightest dash of personal prudence, a career so splendid and so promising would not have been so untimely ended." GREELEY fell into the same error and ascribed his fall to reckless or imprudent exposure. This is a great error, an unjust, though unintentionally unjust, judgment. The last sentence of the *Times* is eminently unjust. The identical manner in which KEARNY rushed upon his fate showed not the slightest want of prudence or discretion; such has been the end of many of the greatest Generals who have filled the world with their fame, and ranked the highest in the military annals of their respective countries. Many distinguished Generals have perished reconnoitering, and many more have been severely wounded in this service, one which, when circumstances demand it, is no reckless exposure on the part of a commander, but an absolute duty. WASHINGTON owed his life, on a similar occasion, to the generosity of that marksman of marksmen, Bull-dog Ferguson, who fell himself by the bullet of a sharpshooter, at King's Mountain, 1780; FREDERICK THE GREAT, to the awful reverence of a Croat; Stonewall JACKSON lost his life in the performance of this duty, at Chancellorsville; REYNOLDS, at Gettysburg; LONGSTREET was severely wounded under similar circumstances, and SEDGWICK killed in the Wilderness campaign; RANTZAU, 1569; TURENNE, 1675; the Duke of Berwick, 1734; BESSIERES, 1813; and MOREAU, 1813, lost their lives by cannon shots while reconnoitering; RICHARD CŒUR DE LION, by a crossbow bolt, 1799; DE LA MOTT, 1595, by a bullet; WARD, the Americo-Chinese Commander-in-Chief, by a jingall ball. GUSTAVUS ADOLPHUS was again and again wounded observing the enemy before he made his own dispositions; FREDERICK would see with his own eyes, because he could not in a crisis trust the eyes of others, and escaped on more than one occasion as if by a miracle. This list might be swelled into pages.

Another notable instance most apposite to this occasion, is

that of General HOTZE, who, at the battle of Zurich, 25th September, 1799, "finding affairs becoming serious, and desirous of reconnoitering the force and position of the enemy, fell in the discharge of a duty which is considered one of those few occasions in which a General is justified in the reckless exposure of his life." This officer was so especially esteemed, that while his troops continued to do their duty bravely, they lost that energy, which alone can give effect to courage.

A stranger, not conversant with the feelings of the army and our people, might under-estimate the loss sustained in the death of KEARNY, after reading the eulogies lavished upon so many of our fallen Generals. In the case of KEARNY, however, there is an accumulation of testimony which becomes mournfully impressive when taken as a whole and compared with that in regard to others. All the histories of the war, loyal or rebel, all the poetry, all the newspaper notices, all the official reports, all private correspondence and oral testimony are in accord. The whole constitute a magnificent memorial, a national martial symphony, whose keynote was struck by DE TROBRIAND when he wrote the concluding sentence of his biographical notice of the division commander he so greatly admired. "Such is man. He (KEARNY) had made his calculations for the future without taking into account the death which awaited him twenty days after our last conversation. It occasioned something equivalent to a public mourning, at New York especially, where the people accorded him magnificent obsequies. But nowhere was his loss so profoundly felt as in the Army of the Potomac, of which he had been one of the first glories, and wherein the thousand stories of the bivouac finished by investing his memory with the proportions of a legendary hero."

KEARNY's career of generalship was crowded into the space of thirteen months, his career as a military power into four months; but what enormous proofs did he give of his capacity and his courage in that short space of time, of his ability not only to make troops, but use them. As an organizer he emulated the instinctive efforts of disciplinarians whose names have become synonymous for systematic and energetic action. In the field his chivalric gallantry displayed a brilliancy equivalent to that of the CID, and an indomitable tenacity up to a level with that which ELLIOTT in Gibraltar, and MASSENA in Genoa, have made proverbial. Condemned to waste eight months in the mud in front of Washington, he utilized every moment, and then, the very minute when the opportunity occurred — to use his own words on another occasion — "he led off personally from the word 'GO.'" Thenceforward with him, GO was the spirit of his every-day life. Had the Russians of 1812–'13 served with him they would have saluted him with the same endearing epithet with which they hailed the master-spirit of the War of Liberation in those years, "the little Suwarrow," the highest honor conceivable in their opinion, and have ennobled him with a title derived from the imperative of a Russian verb, which has no present, since it designates action complete. "Pascholl!" "Go ahead," "Forwards."

This epithet of the "American BAYARD" was applicable to PHIL. KEARNY in more than one respect, and even appropriate in the manner of his death. The typical French hero is said to have been disgusted with the gradual introduction of firearms, because their general use was a death blow to every thing that was glorious in chivalry. KEARNY, like BAYARD, was killed by a single shot while striving to avert disaster as far as possible by personal courage and exposure, and in the fall of both of these brave men it might be said that France and America lost the greatest treasure a country can possess — a citizen who, to devoted patriotism, united the powers of a General and a soldier fully possessed of the capacity to influence, electrify and lead.

In reflecting upon PHIL KEARNY's untimely fall, the lines of HERMAN MELVILLE's "Battle Pieces" (Chattanooga, 92) must recur to the mind of whoever has read them:

"Near and more near; till now the flags
Run like a catching flame;
And one flares highest, to peril nighest —
He means to make a name;
Salvos! they give him his fame!
* * * * *
"But some who gained the envied Alp,
And — eager, ardent, earnest there —
Dropped into Death's wide-open arms,
Quelled on the wing like eagles struck in air.
* * * * *
"The smile upon them as they died;
Their end attained, that end a height:
Life was to those a dream fulfilled,
And death a starry night!"

As an echo to the spirit of these lines and their apposite appropriateness, drifts back from the far distant past the kindred idea embodied in the words addressed by EPAMINONDAS to his surrounding and lamenting soldiery. "This is not the end of life, my fellow-soldiers — it is now your General is born!" Born indeed — born to Immortality, whether as regards Existence or Fame!

DOCUMENT No. 1.

THE SWORD PRESENTATION TO GENERAL KEARNY AFTER HIS RETURN FROM MEXICO.

It will be remembered that a sword was presented to General (then Major) KEARNY by the UNION CLUB after his campaign in Mexico. The following is the address of the CLUB, with the reply of the GENERAL in full:

To Major KEARNY *of the 1st Regiment, United States Dragoons:*

On your return from the war in Mexico, where, in a gallant and successful charge at the very gates of the Capital, you lost an arm in your country's service, your friends and fellow townsmen. members of the Union Club, felt desirous to testify their sense of your deserts, by offering you an appropriate testimonial in honor of your noble bearing in that arduous campaign. Too national in our feelings not to proffer a general tribute of admiration where all employed on the service have deserved so high a meed of praise, we are still free to confess that, as New Yorkers, we feel a special pride when our city's sons are enabled to contribute to our country's fame.

You followed the career of arms as one leading to honorable distinction, and you have liberally applied your means and zealously devoted your energies to the profession of your choice.

When called to the field a soldier inquires not into the causes of the war, but looks to the issue of the contest, being mindful only of the honor of his country's flag. You and your companions in arms planted our National banner in a foreign soil; it there became the symbol of our glorious Union, the type and emblem of home, of country and of fame. On every field it waved defiance to the foe, in every conflict it proved the harbinger of victory. Let this sword, which I have the honor of being charged to present for your acceptance, when it reminds you of a war in which you shared alike the glories and the sufferings, be not valued the less since peace has followed in the train of victory; nor yet let the weapon rust in its scabbard during a night of repose, lest another day should again summon you to the battle. We ask of you, for our sake, to regard the sword as a trophy that you both sought and won. Wear it in peace as in war, as a token of our admiration and (your) modest merit. Accept it as a testimonial from the friends whose esteem you possessed in the relations of peace, and who now acknowledge with pride your conduct in war.

NEW YORK, 3d *November*, 1848.

GENERAL KEARNY'S REPLY.

NEW YORK — *November*, 1848.

SIR — The sword of honor which I have this day received at the hands of my fellow-townsmen, members of the Union Club, is an overwhelming mark of distinction. It has been conferred by you in language, the kindness of which renders the gift doubly interesting. You bid me to consider this sword in the light of a distinction — of a trophy. Indeed, sir, such I most sensibly feel it. I behold in it the mark of regard of gentlemen whose esteem is not the "vivat" of the mere enthusiast, but the approval of men calmly weighing actions as they pass before them in the moving panorama of life. Yet could I scarcely in due modesty admit to myself this full meaning of so honorary an emblem, but that silence might be interpreted into insensibility. I am also aided in this avowal by the consideration, as you, sir, have so happily expressed it, that the insignia with which I am this day endowed are given to me as your townsman, sharer amidst others far more prominent, who, forming part of our late army, planted our country's banner in Mexico, and now receive its ennobling tribute of admiration — a host whom our country sent forth to exemplify in the eyes of all nations those qualities which every individual of the United States is ready to bring forward as an offering when the public welfare may require.

For myself, sir, when on returning from Mexico, with other crippled remnants of the victorious army, I shared, in the hospitable city of New Orleans, those distinguished marks of attention which none knew better how to bestow than the generous Southerner, whose whole being vibrates in unison at the touch of honor, I was rewarded.

When, on arriving in my native city, I felt the pulse of sympathy beat high, and was received with cordiality by gentlemen whom I realize the honor of calling my friends and associates in the Union Club, my heart was touched.

This day, on being presented with a sword of honor, I confess that my cup of ambition is filled to the brim and overwhelming, and that most amply am I repaid, whatever of peril and suffering I have encountered.

In presenting me with this sword, sir, you charged me not to value the gift less, that "peace has followed in the train of victory." In our country, where military ardor is dangerous unless controlled, the soldier may well prefer the sword, no longer 'baton' in marshalling to the fight, now trophy of victories passed, emblem of a successful war achieved. Still, with the predilections of a youth spent in my present profession, must I ever as strongly bear in mind that a republic particularly applies the motto "*dulce et decorum est pro patria mori.*" With a tear to the memory of cherished comrades, who, having already fulfilled the noble role, have passed from a death-bed of fame to a still more glorious rest, and with a profession of readiness, if at any future period my services be needed, joyfully once again to follow our country's banner on the war-path, I have the honor to conclude my thanks to you as Chairman of the Committee of Presentation.

But, sir, the associations connected with this day have no conclusion; they will extend, with this sword, which you have put in my power, after proudly wearing during my own life, to bequeath, a sparkling memento, to a succeeding generation of republican soldiers

(Signed) KEARNY.

[Document No. 2.]

KEARNY'S CHARGE IN MEXICO.

GRAND RAPIDS, MICHIGAN, July 12th, 1869.

General DE PEYSTER:

MY DEAR SIR — Your favor of the 24th ultimo (informing me that you contemplated writing a life of your cousin, the late Maj. Gen. PHILIP KEARNY, killed at Chantilly, and requesting me to give you particulars of his charge at the San Antonio Gate, City of Mexico, in which I participated, and any other incident of interest connected with him that might occur to me), reached me by due course of mail. * * * When the army. under the command of Lieut. Gen. SCOTT, reached Puebla (Mexico), where we remained some four weeks for the purpose of reorganizing and awaiting reinforcements previous to entering on the campaign of the valley, having for its objective point the City of Mexico; an order issued from headquarters detaching Captain KEARNY and myself, with our troop, from our respective regiments, the 1st and 3d dragoons, and attaching us to headquarters in squadron organization, as escort or body guard to the General-in-Chief (Captain KEARNY being the senior and I the junior captain), which position our squadron occupied during the campaign of the Valley and until our flag floated in triumph over the Halls of the Montezumas, and the Conqueror of Mexico was relieved from the command of an army that by his matchless military genius he had immortalized. Although attached to headquarters, yet such was the impulsive ardor and heroic daring of the lamented KEARNY, that no opportunity was lost by him where dragoons could operate against the enemy; this, too, with the sanction of our chief, and our adventures in that direction were frequent and successful. I well remember, that on the morning of the 19th of August, 1847, and previous to the battle of Contreras of that day, our squadron, together with three companies of infantry, under the command of Major (Lt. Col. WM. MONTROSE) GRAHAM, I think, of the (11th U. S.) infantry, was detailed to accompany Captain ROBERT E. LEE, then of the headquarters staff (the Lieut. Gen. LEE of the Confederate Army), who had been ordered by Gen. SCOTT to reconnoitre the enemy's works at Contreras, for the purpose of ascertaining their strength and position. ("*Official account of the Mexican War,*" *Ex. Doc. No.* 1, 304). Gen. VALENCIA, in command of the Mexicans, anticipating the object of our movement, sent a force of five hundred lancers to drive us back. They moved by a circuitous route, and, undiscovered by us, until they reached a position on our right flank under cover of a prominence. Our dragoons were in the advance; our infantry, not keeping pace with us, were a a short distance in our rear. When we approached within range the Mexicans opened fire upon us, when KEARNY, whose keen military eye was quick to see an opportunity and prompt to embrace it, without waiting for our infantry, promptly gave proper form to our squadron and ordered a charge, when the enemy, as promptly, retreated to a point where the ground was broken and covered with *pedregal* or lava, the result of an eruption of the earth, where they fancied our dragoons could not conveniently operate. But KEARNY, ever equal to an emergency, immediately ordered our dragoons to dismount, and advancing on foot, killed, wounded and captured quite a number, and drove the remainder to flight. The infantry-major, in command of our detachment, was quite indignant that KEARNY should have acted without his orders and thus bear off the laurels that, of right, belonged to him; he being the senior in command: but KEARNY never stood on the order of his going; when opportunity offered he always "went." The great conflict of the day (the battle of Contreras) followed. The struggle was terrific, and when night closed upon the gloomy scene the victory was with neither army; but, at the dawn of the following morning, by a desperate and sanguinary charge upon the enemy's strong works they were car ried in triumph, and nearly the entire force of VALENTIA either killed or captured. The slaughter was terrible; little did we then dream, that within a few hours we should be again engaged in the *crowning battle of the war — the battle of* CHURUBUSCO — distant some three or four miles from Contreras. There, General SANTA ANNA, with his entire available army, were in strong position, evidently anticipating the utter annihilation of our noble little army, and well he might, when the great strength of his position and his superiority of numbers, at least four to one, is considered. This battle was a surprise, as the first inti mation we had of his presence in that immediate vicinity, was a furious and destructive fire opened on our advance. Then it was, that the military genius of "the great Captain of the age" was again invoked, and after a conflict of nearly four hours duration, as sanguinary and bloody as ever had taken place on the American Continent, *the last stronghold* of the Mexicans, *the great Tete-de-pont* — was stormed by our noble army and the battle won. At this opportune moment, our *squadron was in the right place*, and as the Mexicans retreated on the causeway that led to the City of Mexico, distant about two miles, with SANTA ANNA at their head, the gallant KEARNY saw his opportunity and made the charge that terminated at the base of the battery that covered the San Antonio Gate, and that is fathfully described in the newspaper article that I send you; which, after diligent search among my papers, is the only one I could find that gives particulars: and, being a participant, I prefer that others than myself should speak. Disclaiming, however, for myself, any other merit than that of following my gallant leader, as to him all the credit of the movement belongs, I write with less diffidence. I would here remind you of the impression the charge made on the mind of SANTA ANNA, when in his report to his congress, exculpatory of his fresh disasters, he said, "*what might we expect when a mere handful of the enemy's dragoons had the temerity to mount the* VERY RAMPART *of our defences;*" and, again, when on the occasion of a large assembly of officers at Willard's Hotel in Washington city, congratulatory to Gen. SCOTT, at the close of the Mexican war, I chanced to be of the number; the General, in introducing me to Gen. DEARBORN, of Massachusetts, stated that I had participated in KEARNY's charge at the gates of Mexico, and in his emphatic manner added: "*Sir, it was the boldest charge I have ever seen or read of.*" Maj. Gen. PILLOW made an official report of the charge, in which I remember he pictured it in glowing colors. I did not preserve it, but presume it will doubtless be found in the War Department at Washington.

It was my fortune to be again associated with Gen. KEARNY in the early days of the late rebellion. Indeed, I was present when President LINCOLN conferred upon him his first commission as Brigadier-General. A committee of gentlemen from New Jersey, of whom Governor NEWELL was one, was sent to Washington for the purpose of securing the

* Lieut. EWELL, named in the article as having participated in the charge on the Garita San Antonio, who was First Lieutenant in our squadron and a brave and gallant soldier, is Lieut. Gen. EWELL of the Confederate Army, and strange to relate was in command of the Confederate troops in our immediate front, when KEARNY and I lay at Alexandria, Va., in 1861 and 1862. It is my fervent prayer that our country may never again be the scene of an incident so unnatural. (Signed) A. T. McR.

appointment of Brigadier-General of the 1st New Jersey Brigade for Gen. KEARNY. I was then in the city and was invited by them to accompany them and state to the President what I knew of General KEARNY's military qualities. I gladly consented; indeed, it was a labor of love as well as duty, and I had the pleasure of hearing the President grant their request; and during that fall and winter (1861 and 1862) we were organized in the same division (FRANKLIN'S), with our quarters adjoining each other near the Alexandria Seminary, Va.; during which time our intercourse was daily and of the most intimate and friendly character, and so continued during the war and until he fell, nobly defending the flag of his country that he loved so well. *He was the soul of chivalry, generosity and hospitality: well may it be said of him that he was "bravest of the brave" and generous as he was brave.* I knew him well, and here permit me to seek to correct a somewhat popular error in reference to his qualities as a soldier. *To the casual observer he seemed to be recklessly impulsive in his movements,* and such was the impression of many. *This,* in my humble judgment, *is a grave mistake. In military movements his perceptive faculties were intensely acute, he saw quickly, reached conclusions rapidly, and under the inspiration of the military genius with which he was by nature endowed and a Spartan heroism that never failed him, executed promptly and vigorously.* Thus it was, that movements that were the result of rapid deliberations (if I may be permitted the expression) were by some deemed to be reckless and without aim. *In my humble judgment neither army, during the rebellion, produced his superior in all the qualities that constitute the true and accomplished soldier, and had his life been spared and the opportunity given him, none would have eclipsed him in the brilliancy of his achievements.* * * * * * *

(Signed) ALEX. T. McREYNOLDS.*

[Document No. 3.]

THE IRISH IN THE AMERICAN ARMY.

[New York True Sun, Thursday morning, June 22d, 1848.]

One of the most interesting incidents of the meeting at the Tabernacle, on Tuesday evening (20 | 6 | 48), was the introduction of Captain McREYNOLDS, of the U. S. Dragoons, one of the heroes of *Churubusco.* The eloquent, off-hand speech which he made on the occasion was the subject of much admiration, and has caused a general desire among those who heard him to know something more of the eloquent Irish soldier who stood before the meeting, a monument of the zeal and devotion which Irishmen have always exhibited in warmly expousing the cause of their adopted country on the field of battle. Captain McREYNOLDS came to this country when a youth of eighteen, and has, we believe, since then resided in *Detroit,* in Michigan. To the Legislature of that State he has been several times elected, and in it he has occupied a high, honorable position. He was a member of the Michigan Senate when the war with Mexico broke out, and immediately tendered his services to the government. The President promptly gave him a captain's commission in the Dragoons, and the gallant discharge of his duties in that position has won for him enduring honors. The assault of KEARNY'S and McREYNOLD'S Dragoons, on the bloody field of Churubusco, was one of the most daring and brilliant deeds of heroism among the many proud instances of valor which have shed such undying lustre on the American arms in the history of the Mexican war.

In casting our eye over a number of the *Dublin Freemans' Journal,* we met with the following paragraphs relating to this battle, which will no doubt be interesting to many of our readers. The gallant KEARNY, who bore a conspicuous part in this heroic exploit is a (native) resident of (and buried in 1862-'4) in our city (of New York):

---

* "ANDREW T. McREYNOLDS (Michigan), Captain 3d dragoons, 9th of March, 1847: Brevet Major for gallant and meritorious conduct in battles of Contreras and Churubusco, 20th of August, 1847, (Aug. 18, 1848); where he was severely wounded in a charge of dragoons at San Antonio Gate; disbanded 31st of July, 1848." (*Dictionary of the Army of the United States,* GARDNER'S 2d Edition, page 305). Major McREYNOLDS afterwards commanded 1st New York Volunteer (LINCOLN) cavalry, to whose conmand he was invited at the suggestion of Major-General PHILIP KEARNY. In regard to the facts connected with this command, see Document No. 4.

"The following appears in the *N. O. Picayune:* 'The charge of dragoons referred to was made by two troops—one led by Captain KEARNY, the other by MCREYNOLDS. The name KEARNY sounds rather Irish, but of the birth or descent of that gallant soldier we are unable to speak. We are happy, however, to be able to claim Captain MCREYNOLDS as Irish-born, and no one will believe him to be a whit the less a true American on that account. Captain MCREYNOLDS is a native of *Dungannon*, in the county of *Tyrone*.' The *Detroit Free Press*, in quoting from the New Orleans *Picayune* the passage which we subjoin, speaks thus:

"'It was in this charge that Captain MCREYNOLDS, of this city, received his serious wound, his troop,—all *Michigan* boys—together with KEARNY'S, participating. It was undoubtedly one of the boldest and most desperate charges on record. The commanding General of the division thus speaks of the charge and Captain MCREYNOLDS and his bold dragoons: 'Captain MCREYNOLDS' 3d Dragoons nobly sustained the daring movements of his squadron commander, and was wounded in his left arm."

Both of these fine companies sustained severe losses, in their ranks and file also (very sad casualities). We are informed that the enemy numbered, by their own report, five thousand infantry and one thousand cavalry,* while our dragoons did not exceed one hundred. This small force drove the Mexicans upwards of two miles and ceased not until they were *within the battery* that *covered the gate of the city*. In this charge the dragoons cut down more than their entire number of the enemy. When we consider the extraordinary disparity in point of numbers, and the raking position of the enemy's battery, into the very mouth of which our brave dragoons fearlessly threw themselves, we think we may safely say *it has* NO *parallel in modern warfare.*

The following is the passage from the *Picagune:*

"CAPT. KEARNY'S CHARGE.

"The charge of KEARNY'S Dragoons, upon the flying masses of the Mexicans, in the battle of Churubusco, is *one of the most brilliant and decisive feats* which have occurred during the war. As soon as our troops had carried the formidable *tete-de-pont*, by which the avenue leading to the city was laid open to the cavalry, Captain KEARNY'S Dragoons rushed upon the yielding masses of the Mexicans with an impetuosity and fury which made amends for the scantiness of their numbers, and bore them back in confusion upon the causeway, a force in cavalry four fold that of ours, but the narrowness of the avenue prevented him from availing himself of this superiority, and reduced the conflict to those single handed issues in which Mexicans must ever yield to our prowess. The audacity of the onset of KEARNY'S troops struck dismay to the hosts which fled before them. The retreat became a confused rout, and the causeway was blocked up by the entangled masses of the enemy. But *even through this obstacle* the triumphant dragoons forced their way, trampling down those who escaped their relentless sabers.

"Scattering their foe before them, the dragoons came at last within reach of the formidable batteries which defended the gates of the city, and a murderous fire was opened upon them, which was even more terrible to the fugitive Mexicans than the dragoons.

"The latter continued their pursuit up to the very gates of the city, and were shot down or made prisoners upon the very parapets of its defenses. This was the moment, if ever, that General SCOTT might have entered the city, had the instant possession of it conformed to his preconceived designs. Already had the inhabitants of the town set up the cry that 'the Americans were upon them,' and the whole population was stricken defenseless by panic terrors. But the dragoons were recalled from the pursuit and the survivors of that desperate charge withdrew, covered with wounds and with honor."

In every narration of the events of *Churubusco* we have seen this charge and pursuit by KEARNY'S Dragoons commemorated and applauded; but it appears to have impressed the Mexicans far more than the popular mind of our own countrymen. In various letters we have seen written by them from the capital, *they speak of the audacity of the dragoons as terrible and almost supernatural.*

---

* The statement of the New Orleans *Picayune*, as to the numbers of the Mexicans, is evidently a blunder, as the estimate of their numbers at the time was about 5,000.—A. T. MCREYNOLDS, on margin of "Sun."

[Document No. 4.]

REMINISCENCES OF MAJOR-GENERAL PHILIP KEARNY.

"The regiment which was known throughout the war as the 1st N. Y. (LINCOLN) Cavalry, was organized immediately after President LINCOLN issued his first call for volunteers (the call of April 15, 1861). The day following the one upon which that call was made public, a notice appeared in the New York papers calling for young men of dash and energy to meet for the purpose of forming the regiment. This brought together a number of the first young men of the city, possessing wealth and a high social position. They set to work earnestly, and in a brief space of time had twelve companies organized with full ranks. Col. BAYARD CLARK, of New York, was chosen as their Colonel, and he used every endeavor to have the regiment accepted by the authorities in Washington, but without success. Gen. SCOTT was then (acting) Secretary of War, and he decided that the rebellion could be crushed out in a short time by the Regular Army. He was willing to accept a few Volunteers, infantry regiments for garrison duty, but the Regular Army was to have the honor and glory of crushing the rebellious "anaconda." At least he would have no cavalry. Colonel CLARK became disgusted at his non-success and withdrew from the organization."

"Gen. KEARNY, who had then freshly arrived from Europe, having hastened home on the first announcement of threatened hostilities, was then tendered the command of the 1st N. Y. Cavalry. Being informed of the fruitless efforts made by Col. CLARK to get the regiment accepted, he consented, conditionally, to assume command. He reopened communication with Gen. SCOTT, urging the acceptance of the regiment, and when this was refused, he proceeded to Washington, and in person endeavored to effect his object. But even his brilliant record as a cavalry officer and his experience of actual war were treated with contempt and he returned in despair. He urged the continuance of the organization, predicting that their services would be needed, but as New Jersey, at that time, tendered him a full Brigade of Infantry, he withdrew from the New York regiment and accepted the brigade."

On leaving, he recommended the officers to invite Brev. Maj. ALEX. T. MCREYNOLDS, to replace him. This officer had been his Junior Captain in the squadron with which KEARNY made his famous charge in Mexico. At the very San Antonio gate, MCREYNOLDS, like KEARNY, was severely wounded in the left arm. The former refused to submit to the amputation, to which KEARNY consented, and saved his limb with an anchylotic joint or stiff elbow. MCREYNOLDS came on from his home in Michigan and took the command of the 1st N. Y. (LINCOLN) Vol. Cavalry, and lay all winter with his regiment along side of KEARNY near Alexandria. A squadron (Companies A and H: See pages 233-4 and 243—244 and 249 *supra*) of this regiment was attached to KEARNY's Brigade when he advanced to Manassas, March 9th and 10th, 1862. "He (KEARNY) frequently declared, however, that he would prefer being a Colonel of cavalry to a Brigadier-General of infantry. He was by education and instinct essentially a cavalry commander, and it was always a matter of regret to him, that he was not assigned to that arm of the service." *

"The early commanders of the Army of the Potomac were too cautious to entrust to one so skillful and daring that arm of the service where daring, not to say recklessness, was predominant."

"The 1st N. Y. Cavalry subsequently came to have an actual existence. Gen. SCOTT was contented with his infantry till Bull Run occurred, when the mythical "Black Horse Cavalry" of the Rebels struck terror to his heart and forced him to accept all the cavalry he could get. The 1st N. Y. (then known as the LINCOLN Cavalry) was summoned forthwith to Washington, was speedily armed and equipped, and in a few weeks was serving in the same division with that intrepid and able soldier whom they had once chosen as their leader—General PHIL. KEARNY."

INCIDENTS.

"Gen. KEARNY in camp was a *martinet*, and before his fighting qualities made him famous throughout the world and beloved by every soldier, was looked upon with aversion by all Volunteers. His own brigade and the 1st N. Y. cavalry were encamped together during

---

*This is an error of memory, or Gen. KEARNY must have altered his opinions; such, at all events, is the view of the author of this book.

the winter of 1861 and 1862, near Fairfax (Alexandria) Seminary. The men of these commands were a frolicksome and mischevious lot of young fellows who had been used to rather better fare than was furnished by the Quartermaster, and consequently soon acquired an unenviable reputation for "accumulating" things. The 4th N. J. and the 1st N. Y., were frequently complained of to Gen. KEARNY, not only by the residents in the vicinity (to whom eggs, butter, milk and poultry, soon became *unknown* quantities), but by neighboring commands who made up (unwillingly) all the losses sustained by these two regiments in the way of pistols and equipments generally. On one occasion when complaints had come in rather more freely than usual Gen. KEARNY indulging in considerable profanity, wound up by declaring, that he believed the shortest way to capture Richmond, was "to put a rail fence on the other side and the 4th New Jersey and Lincoln thieves would charge through h—l to get it."

* * * * *

"At a subsequent period the Lieutenant (one who incurred KEARNY's displeasure at an earlier date) so conducted himself in the field under the General's immediate eye as to win from that officer the highest compliments."

Indeed the same occurred with the whole 1st N. Y. regiment, and one of the finest monuments in Greenwood Cemetery—that of Lieut. HARRY HIDDEN—bears witness to the General's opinion of the fighting qualities of those whom he formerly spoke of as "the Lincoln thieves."

"If a *martinet* in camp, he was the reverse in the field, and would censure an officer for exacting from his men those little matters of etiquette and routine duty, which he so strenuously insisted upon in camp. On one occasion while on a campaign the General rode up to one of his pickets and was formally met by the reserve, who had been summoned from their sleep to receive him. Returning their salute, he commanded "break ranks," and turning to the officer in command said, "let us have no more of this d—d nonsense on this campaign, it's well enough when there's nothing else to do; now we're out here to fight, and when we can't fight, let your men sleep. Feed them well, give them plenty of sleep, and they'll fight like h—l."

"A corporal of cavalry on one of KEARNY's campaigns had gallantly led a small squad of men against some rebel infantry, routing them and capturing some prisoners. That night the General rode to the camp of the cavalry, called the corporal out in front of his comrades, complimented him highly for his bravery and promised him promotion. In two weeks the young corporal was a Second Lieutenant, sustaining the position with credit and winning still further promotion."

CHAPTER XXXII.

THE EPILOGUE.

A SUMMING UP OF THE CHARACTERISTICS OF MAJOR-GENERAL PHILIP KEARNY, WITH INTERESTING ANECDOTES THROUGHOUT HIS CAREER.*

"When Erin cites her heart's delights,
The men of her right hand,
'Mid statesmen, priests, and bards and knights,
'Tis SARSFIELD leads the band —
Who, haloed with the battle's lights,
Where Erin's foes oppose him, fights
And falls for Fatherland!"

"*Le Vraie Guidon d'Honneur* (BAYARD):
The true Ensign (or Standard) of Honor."

"BON was he (BAYARD) in Generosity and Justice;
SANS-PEUR, in that he never knew Fear:
SANS REPROCHE, since he was never wanting to Duty!"

Ideas from Old Life of BAYARD.

"NO OFFICER LIVING," said WILLIAM III (the great Dutch King of England — one of the best judges of human character and military merit who ever lived), "WHO HAS SEEN SO LITTLE SERVICE AS MY LORD MARLBOROUGH (the first of English generals), IS SO FIT FOR GREAT COMMANDS." — MACAULAY'S "*History of England,*" iii, 616–17.

Perhaps no equal number of words could be selected to express more justly PHIL. KEARNY'S capabilities as a Commander.

"Tell me (NAPOLEON to DUMAS), what do you think of NARBONNE, whom I have sent to command at Raab?" "Sire," I replied, "I think he is a man whose capacity is fit for everything; he has an elevated heart, and I believe he has all sorts of courage." "Good! but he has never seen a gun fired." "*Sire, I do not believe that he needs any apprenticeship.*" — "*Memoirs of his own time; including the Revolution, the Empire, and the Restoration.*" By Lieut.-Gen. Count MATHIEU DUMAS, in two volumes, vol. II, pp. 317–18.

---

* In presenting this work to the public, the author begs its indulgence. Stimulated by no ambition of applause, nor yet actuated by any pecuniary inducement, he commenced the Life of PHILIP KEARNY as a labor of love, and now offers it as a memento of almost fraternal regard and respect — a rough but honest monument of the worth, patriotism and ability of a relative, deeply regretted by the whole nation, and who was as a brother to the writer, and a father to the writer's son, serving, at one time, with him in the field. If this work exhibits imperfections, he will none the less be fully compensated by the reflection that he was willing to hazard everything, in order to place in a proper position the man to whom this nation is so much indebted. The book has been written during intervals, from pressing business pursuits, and, indeed, the author never was sure that it would be published. The greater part was written and stereotyped in the summer of 1868; but its publication has been neglected up to the present time. Such as it is, we offer with all due humility, only regretting that our ability is not equal to the grandeur of our subject.

"Though a strict disciplinarian, (Prince) EUGENE (of Savoy) was a Friend of the Soldier; and, owing to his kindness of disposition and easy affability of manners, greatly beloved by officers as well as privates. His exertions to secure regular supplies of provisions for the troops were constant and unremitting; and many of his letters, written on this important point, bear the strongest possible affinity to those by the Duke of Wellington on the same subject." — "*Biographies of Eminent Soldiers of the last Four Centuries.*" By Major-General JOHN MITCHELL, page 247.

"Fond man
* * yet take this truth from me,
Virtue* alone is true nobility." JUVENAL.

"The fav'ring gods the brave consign
E'en in their death to song divine." PINDAR.

"Hier lyes SIR JOHN THE GRAHAME wight and wise,
Ane of the Chief *reskewit* Scotland *thrise*,
Ane Better Knight not to the worlde was lent,
Nor was guid GRAHAM, of Truth and Hardiment.
Sir JOHN was slain by the Englishe
22d July, 1298."

Epitaph in Falkirk Church Yard, Scotland.

"Ay, man is manly. Here you see
The warrior-carriage of the head,
And brave dilation of the frame;
And lighting all the soul that led
In (Williamsburg's hot) charge to victory,
Which justifies his fame.

'A cheering picture. It is good
To look upon a Chief like this,
In whom the spirit moulds the form,
Where favoring nature, oft remiss,
With eagle mien expressive has endued
A man to kindle strains that warm.

"Trace back his lineage, and his sires,
Yeoman or noble, you shall find
Enrolled with men of Agincourt,
Heroes who shared great HARRY's mind,
Down to us come the knightly Norman fires,
And front the Templars bore.

"Nothing can lift the heart of man
Like manhood in a fellow-man.
The thought of heaven's great King afar
But humbles us — too weak to scan;
But manly greatness men can span,
And feel the bonds that draw."

"*Battle-pieces and Aspects of the War.*" By HERMAN MELVILLE.

"It has been remarked, and no doubt with truth, by those who best knew Sir RALPH (ABERCROMBY), that the circumstances attending his death were nearly such as he would have chosen for himself. The same sentiment has been thus beautifully expressed by one who did not personally know him: '*Over* Sir RALPH ABERCROMBY *I do not much lament; full of years and full of honor, he seems, with his own hands, to have erected a monument of glory, and then calmly entered it. When death must come, it never comes better than disguised as glory. Such as his should rather be revered than deplored.*'

"Sir RALPH, who always regarded unhesitating devotion to the public service as the first duty of a soldier, could not review his own career during the war without a conscious feeling that neither unlooked for disappointment nor ultimate failure, which might have

---

* VIRTUS, "Manhood, the sum of all the corporeal or mental excellencies of man."
ANDREWS.

weighed with less elevated minds, had relaxed his untiring zeal and ardor in the cause of his country. He must have felt that he possessed in full measure the respect, the confidence and the warmest attachment of the officers and soldiers under his command. He must have dwelt with unmingled satisfaction on the promptitude, precision and good order with which all the movements of the troops had been conducted by the officers and men; the legitimate result of the just and rigid discipline which he had constantly enforced. Anticipated difficulties and serious deficiencies had been overcome, and the character of the * * Army for discipline and valor had been raised and confirmed by three actions, which had been fought and won against a brave enemy, * * animated by the recollection of the splendid victories in which they had shared. Such are some of the reflections which must have soothed and cheered the dying moments of the veteran commander.

"Sir RALPH died too soon to know the full extent of the service he had rendered to his country. He did not live to know that the battle of the 21st March virtually decided the fate of Egypt." * * — *Lieut.-Gen.* ABERCROMBY, K. B., 1793—1801. A Memoir by his son JAMES LORD DUNFERMLINE, pp. 301-'2.

To sum up the character of Major-General PHILIP KEARNY, so as to present a word-portrait which will be satisfactory at once to the author and to the reader, is a task of no small difficulty. CORTLANDT PARKER, Esq., of New Jersey, has done so with great ability; but it is rather of the Man than the Soldier. KEARNY has been compared to DESAIX, and to BAYARD, and to RUPERT, and to CLAVERHOUSE, and to ZIETHEN, and to SEYDLITZ, a twin spirit. Popular opinion assigns all these to one and the same class, although they differed, the one from the other, in many particulars, as much as days differ, or twilight from morning; yes, even moonlight from sunlight. KEARNY had more reckless dash than DESAIX, more ambition than BAYARD, more patriotism than CLAVERHOUSE, more judgment than RUPERT, and yet he possessed elements in common with them all, even as each was akin to the other in certain marked characteristics. Reflection has led to the conviction that PHIL. KEARNY, taken altogether, bore the most striking resemblance to the great Prussian hero, GEBHARD LEBERECHT BLUCHER, in his tastes, habits, tactics and texture of mind, in a word, in his "*direct* and daring genius," not only as a soldier, but as an individual. BLUCHER, for a long time, was misunderstood and under-estimated, until results demonstrated that the popular hero was the real hero. So was KEARNY. NAPOLEON used to call BLUCHER the "Dragoon"; the old military high-caste, "Yunkerthum," nicknamed him "Slash-sabre," and the world believed that these epithets were just, until he arrived at the position where he could display his wonderful common sense. Experts then discovered that the dash and the cut and the stab of the cavalry officer, or "Old Trooper," were subordinate to mental faculties which only required certain circumstances for their display in all their intense brightness. Was not this emphatically so with KEARNY — cruelly depreciated by McCLELLAN — until, being dead, he no longer stood in the way of either chief or favorites? If McCLELLAN did shed tears over his dead body, as was reported, were they the tears of regret for the great soldier lost to his country, or of remorse, which recognized, when too late, injustice done, fidelity unrewarded and services ignored? BLUCHER is almost better known as Marshal "Forwards" than by any other title. This term, first applied to him by the Russian contingent serving under his orders, was at once adopted by the Prussians, immediately after by the whole of Germany, by England, and throughout the vast forces of the Allies. Yet few Generals ever retreated oftener than BLUCHER, but then his retreats were masterpieces. His circuitous retreat to Lubeck, in 1806, doubling like a fox, was wonderful in its fierce obstinacy; his falling back before NEY, to the Bober, in 1813, during which the affair of Haynau occurred, cost NAPOLEON a division, without any adequate return. By his alternate advancing and retiring, in September, 1813, he exasperated and depressed NAPOLEON, who saw the illusion of French glory passing away. This systematic plan of avoiding a battle, irritated the Emperor even more than the loss of contemporaneous battles, and occasioned the French greater suffering and casualties than could have resulted from a general engagement. In 1814, BLUCHER never retreated but to return again with redoubled vigor, doubly dangerous. How beautifully Norvins expresses this when NAPOLEON, hoping (22d February, 1814) to catch SCHWARTZENBURG alone, "learns with the greatest surprise that the corps (in his front) is that of SACKEN, belonging to that *eternal army of* BLUCHER, *which, everywhere, reproduced itself and seemed to be born again from its ruins.*" Was it not even so with KEARNY and his division, "fought to pieces through the incapacity of superiors?" Again, CUST remarks of that same army of BLUCHER: "He (NAPOLEON) forgot that five victories were not a campaign, and that the wave (BLUCHER) which he had forced back, would at length return in *pristine* power to engulf him." Did not the gallant remains of KEARNY's division win and hold the field of Chantilly, on which he himself breathed forth his glorious life?

Who, but BLUCHER, could have brought up an army from lost Ligny to victoriously-annihilating Waterloo? Was it not even so with KEARNY? His prompt advance to Manassas,* his hurrying on to Williamsburg, bearing with him succor, safety and success, was not near as grand as his tenacity before Richmond in the retreat to the James, and during the gradual falling back from Warrenton to Fairfax. The very fact that he restrained the pursuit at Fair Oaks, as represented by HEINTZELMAN, shows that the fiery ardor of the soldier was tempered by the sound discretion of the General.

Here another of the many close resemblances to BAYARD presents itself. After the battle of Ravenna, fought on Easter Sunday, 10th April, 1512, the remnant of the defeated Spaniards were retiring slowly, but in good order, upon the fastness of Ravenna. Bayard, returning from the pursuit in another direction, descried this still unbroken force, and prepared to charge it. Thereupon a single Spaniard left the ranks, and accosted him gravely thus: "Senor, you must perceive that you have not men enough with you to charge us to advantage (or to effect any thing). You have won the battle; be satisfied, and let us go; for if we get off safe, it is God's will." The veteran BAYARD

---

* In the New York TIMES of 6th September, 1869, is an allusion to the Report of KEARNY as to this advance on Manassas, which proves (as that Report is quoted) that the statement of its suppression is true. The article referred to is on the second page, entitled, "A DAY IN GREENWOOD," and the quotation occurs in the last paragraph (2d column of it,) in the section:

"LIEUTENANT HIDDEN.

"Turning away from these ponderous dwellings of the dead, cross to the modest granite column which rises on the grassy slope beyond. It is the monument of Lieutenant HENRY B. HIDDEN, who fell in a gallant charge in 1862. In the beginning of the war when a very general desire prevailed among the regular army officers to make the cavalry arm of the service illustrate the dashing heroism associated with it in all countries from time immemorial, but which, owing to the nature of the country through which the struggle was fought out had never been realized, the dashing heroism of Lieutenant HIDDEN was memorialized as an example to that arm of the service. (See Chapter XIX and accompanying Documents.) Beneath the bronze figure of the dead soldier is the following inscription:

"'Lieutenant HENRY B. HIDDEN: Born in New Kork: Killed at Sangster's Station, Va., March 9, 1862, at the age of 23 years, in a gallant and successful charge with 14 dragoons upon 150 rebel infantry.'

"HE ILL, TRATED THE CAVALRY SERVICE AND OPENED FOR IT A NEW ERA." — *Vide* Major-General PHIL. KEARNY's Report.

silently acknowledged the justice of the warning, even though uttered by an enemy. His men and horses were both fought out, he had no supports or reserves, the enemy was falling back on his intrenchments; the judgment of the cool and experienced leader regulated the ardor of the knightly swordsman. He held in his men.

A short time afterward, the French General-in-chief, Gaston de Foix, incrusted, from plume to spur, with blood, came galloping up with a body of cavalry, upon the rear of the same force of Spaniards. "Who goes there?" he demanded of his officers. "The Spaniards whom we have beaten." "Charge them!" and the French horse spurred upon the Spanish pikes. Thereupon the defeated but undaunted musketeers poured out a murderous volley. Down went Gaston, and the French were repulsed. Then the Spanish infantry rushed upon him with their pikes and halberts (the bayonets of that era), hamstrung his horse, and despatched him with a hundred stabs. He had fifteen wounds in the face alone.

At Fair Oaks, if Heintzelman is correct, Kearny acted like the sagacious Bayard, not like the impetuous Gaston.

Nevertheless, when the hour was propitious, no one was prompter to say "On." "He has heart and courage," was his highest commendation of an officer, but he also said "judgment and experience." Misjudged Kearny — grand soldier, but consummate General!

Superficial writers have styled Phil. Kearny "the Bayard of our army," because Bayard's name is universally considered as synonymous with gallantry. But, carry out the comparison in all its bearings, and it will hold equally good. This parallel between Kearny and Bayard commences with the careers of both men — the "bravest of the brave" — and holds good in almost every detail. Both were consummate riders in early youth; the latter distinguishing himself as such at thirteen. Charles VIII, of France, no mean horseman himself, nicknamed him "*Piquet*," from his furious spurring — "*pique!* pique!" ("spur! spur!"). Kearny's crossing the Pedregal in Mexico by night, as a feat, will pair off with Bayard's charge at Agnadello, through water up to his horse's belly; and the former dashing on in 1847, to the attack of the San Antonio gate of Mexico, with the latter's equally audacious charge into the streets of Milan in 1500. Both believed in the doctrine never to despise an enemy, and like ROHAN, a master spirit in war, considered that too much money could not be thrown away on good spies, who had proved they were to be trusted. BAYARD paid his spies so well that they would rather have died than betray him, and he never slept before any affair of importance, passing the previous night in preparation. KEARNY was in an equal degree wisely lavish and presciently vigilant. KEARNY as richly deserved the motto ascribed to his valor as BAYARD: "*Vires agminis unus habet.*" Nor was the chevalier son of warlike Dauphiny more generous to captured foes than the knightly son of New York.

Lieutenant R. L——, aid to Major-General D. B——, relates an anecdote of KEARNY to demonstrate his sympathy and generosity toward the sick of our army. L—— was on board the Knickerbocker steamer prostrate with Chickahominy fever, and the vessel was filled with victims to the same terrible disease, due to the long inaction and severe labors of our army in that pestiferous region. He says that KEARNY came on board to visit the sick and cheer them up by this evidence that they had the warm and active sympathy of their superior. KEARNY went through that large boat — that floating lazar-house — with a kind word, a pleasant smile, a grasp of his single hand and some soothing or inspiriting remark for every one. Nor was his sympathy confined to words and smiles alone. Wherever he thought that money was needed he did not wait till it was asked. L—— saw him put a twenty dollar gold piece into the hands of more than one, and thinks he must have bestowed several hundreds of dollars in this glorious exhibition of manly feeling on that occasion. Is there any record of McCLELLAN's having done any thing like this?

Nor was KEARNY's generosity confined to our own men, to our sick and our wounded. On more than one occasion he supplied Rebel officers who had been taken prisoners with means not only sufficient to meet the exigencies of the moment but to enable them to get along until they could receive remittances from home. KEARNEY's generous liberality, although frequent and munificent, was of that sterling kind, which has the commendation of scripture, done in secret, not even letting the left hand know what the right hand had done.

KEARNY never forgot the gallant STUART, who was mortally wounded by his side in the engagement with the Rogue River Indians, 17th June, 1851, and died on the following day. After the campaign was over and KEARNY had returned to California, he wrote to his friend RUFUS INGALLS — then Captain and Assistant Quartermaster, now Colonel, Chief Quartermaster, New York city, and Brevet Major-General U. S. A., the distinguished Quartermaster-in-Chief of the Army of the Potomac — and requested him to send a detachment from Fort Vancouver, Washington Territory, and obtain the body of Captain STUART, which had been buried on the field, where, nobly discharging his duty, he had been shot down. KEARNY likewise forwarded a fine metal case for the remains, and continued to display his interest in the matter by letters even after he reached the Sandwich Islands and China, remitting a draft for the expenses incurred, and paying this last tribute of respect to a deceased brother in arms, a man after his own heart.

Captain INGALLS faithfully complied with his wishes and the body was restored to STUART's relations and native State, South Carolina, which voted a sword to the captain's eldest brother as a token of the peculiar pride and affection with which it cherished the memory of its dead son and soldier.

How many more instances of this, KEARNY's disinterested liberality, might be related.

No man understood better than KEARNY the meaning of "military arithmetic," as NAPOLEON styled "his meting out death by the hour."

Both our own and France's "knightly," "electric" and electrifying BAYARDS bore themselves with knightly courtesy to the vanquished. Both may be said to have possessed three excellent qualities of a great General, "assault of the ram (the Roman aries, or ram, battered down every thing before it), the defense of the wild-boar (an animal famous for its fierce resistance) and the flight of the wolf" (most dangerous if close pressed). Both left behind them the reputation of fearing neither the vicissitudes of the seasons, the tempests of life, nor the violence of men — ever wise and bravely loyal. When we think of how KEARNY's deeds tallied with the promise of his few but earnest words in relation to the duty of a citizen and a soldier, at the crisis of the nation, words uttered while a boy at school; words repeated in his letter accepting the magnificent sword presented after his return from Mexico; words always borne in mind and lived up to by him; words totally misunderstood by too many of our own people, and which could not have been felt by those who were —

> * * "mere foreigners of much renown,
> Of various nations, and all Volunteers;
> Not fighting for the country or its crown,
> But wishing to be one day brigadiers;"

it seems as if no praise which has been accorded to him is too flattering. He relinquished all that made life desirable, like another son of our Empire State, the honest, fearless WADSWORTH, and like him, to use LINCOLN's words, which can never die while our language lives, both "gave (for the Union) the last full measure of devotion," and on their biers fell fast and freely the tears* of the people, in whose cause they died.

It has been justly remarked that no fine, manly character can exist which does not possess, and present, many traits of the womanly. This was eminently the case of PHIL. KEARNY,

---

* "He was the best General in the army; *his loss will never be made up;* every man in the division adored him. Many a poor fellow was seen on the road, *crying for his loss* — and I, too, do not blush for my manhood, when I acknowledge that I shed tears." — *N. Y. Times*, Saturday, September 13th, 1862.

"His death has cast a feeling of gloom over the city. All the flags are at half-mast, and the deepest regret is everywhere manifested for the death of this brave, gallant, fearless and accomplished soldier." — *Newark paper*, 4th September, 1862.

"Early the next morning (2d September), however, a flag of truce came in from General LEE, with word that KEARNY's body had been found. * * General HEINTZELMAN at once detailed Major BIRNEY, * * to receive it; * * but before reaching the outposts he met a party having the remains in charge. They had been informally delivered up to our men, without waiting for the usual escort to come up. *The body had been rifled of sword, pistol, watch, diamond brooch, finger-rings, and the pocket-book, in which the General always kept a large amount of money.*

"Among the visitors to-day, to see the remains, was the colored servant of General KEARNY, who burst into an agony of grief on taking a parting look at the body of his dead master." — *Atlas and Argus* (Correspondence), Monday, September 5th, 1862.

[For the sentiments of general gloom felt by all classes, see JOHN Y. FOSTER's "*New Jersey and the Rebellion*," pages 815, 816 and 817, which there is no room to insert.]

and was expressed in a hundred ways, but never more touchingly so than in his watchful care of his men. In a letter to his cousin, PHILIP JOHN KEARNY, Major of the Eleventh New Jersey Volunteers, a victim, at the age of twenty-one, to a mortal wound received at Gettysburg, he writes: "You must have learnt something of the nature of men, as to controlling them with decision, but little harshness; with discipline, but justice; but, above all, with careful watchfulness of their rights and comforts. *Men are very grateful; far more so than the little one may do for them deserves.* As to perfecting yourself in your new position (as an officer) never let it pass from your mind in what *a false position a gentleman is, who assumes to be what he is not.*" Previously he had remarked as a sequence to the foregoing advice: "*If you display courage, it will gracefully cover a multitude of shortcomings.*" Was not this nobleness and gentleness combined, justifying the words of an aid-de-camp in referring to the letters of his deceased General: "To you (the author) they will serve to recall that charming trait in his noble character, thoughtfulness of others, and the desire to reward whom he admired, and condemn whom he despised. Had he lived, his sword would have been his history." No wonder this aid remembered KEARNY's words of cheer when severely wounded: "I regret extremely the pain you must suffer, and yet it is the high insignia of distinction." What a balm such language to the young and brave aspirant for military honors, to whom he added, "Join me as soon as you can," and then, "knowing your ardent military spirit, I caution you not to retard your cure by over anxiety. And yet, I trust to having you shortly, permanently installed as one of my staff." Could man have written more comforting words to a gallant soldier, burning to join his beloved commander, words with promise of fresh opportunities of acquiring glory in the light of an example such as KEARNY's, and breathing a compassionate interest, such as never exists but in the heart of a hero.*

* The following letters were forwarded, for insertion, just eleven months ago, but were mislaid through the inexcusable delay in prosecuting the publication of this book. They contain some sentences which induced the author to lay them aside at the time, for the same reason that he rejected a number of others. Nor would they now be inserted were it not to *prove* the warm-hearted interest which KEARNY — in the midst of his own disheartening difficulties — took in the career of a young friend and youthful soldier.

"No. 1, BARCLAY ST., NEW YORK, *Sept. 14th*, 1868.

"DEAR GENERAL — Your favor of the 5th came duly to hand. Thanks for your kind remembrance of me. I enclose four letters from General KEARNY to me, written to me when I was suffering intense agony from wounds received at Fair Oaks and he suffering as much from the blundering on the Peninsula. These letters, I fear, on looking over them again, will not prove of much interest to the public, but for me they shed a bright halo over that otherwise wretched portion of my military experience. To you, they will serve to recall that charming trait in his noble character, 'thoughtfulness for others,' and the desire to reward where he admired, and condemn where he despised. Had he lived his sword would have been his history. His death leaves to you the honorable task — may God speed you in it is the wish of

"Your friend,

"FITZGERALD."

"HEADQUARTERS THIRD DIVISION,
"FAIR OAKS, *8th July*, 1862.

"MY DEAR LIEUTENANT — I regret extremely the pain you must suffer, and yet it is the high insignia of distinction. I regret extremely that you are not here, for I shall miss you in the coming fight. I now propose to you what I had always contemplated, making you my Aid, if it meets your pleasure. At the same time you are proposed for a captaincy in your regiment. * *

"Ever sincerely yours,

"P. KEARNY,

"*Brig.-Gen. Commanding 3d Division.*"

"HEADQUARTERS, THIRD DIVISION,
"HARRISON'S LANDING *5th July*, 1862.

"MY DEAR CAPTAIN — I was very happy to receive yours of the 25th June. I am sorry that your wound is still troublesome. However, join me as soon as you can — and there will be plenty of office work, until you can mount.

"We have had several desperate engagements and fearful losses, but strange to say, the pique and jealousy of ———, from his ignorance, or of MCCLELLAN, from sundry old reasons and new ones — the principal one that I made an outcry at his intrigues to have General SCOTT driven out of service by '*slights and disgusts*;* more recently that, from before the enemy's leaving Manassas, I criticised his * * * (plans) have proven a prophet. There is not an action, not a position, not a retreat that I did not point out three weeks since.

"Whilst I sincerely sympathise with the pleasure you must afford those at your home, and join most heartily in the ovations your noble courage entitles you to, I do hope that you will not delay your arival. My letter is sufficient authority for you as of a full order.

* * * * * * * * * * * *

"Very sincerely yours,

"P. KEARNY,

Brig.-Gen. Commanding Division.

"Capt. LOUIS FITZGERALD, *40th N. Y. Vols.*

"Whilst I study in my Staff the ornamental, remember that I unite with it immense exertion, such as I have already found in you. K'Y.

"Our command is small in numbers, but in very high spirits * * *

"HEADQUARTERS, THIRD DIVISION, THIRD CORPS,
"HARRISON'S LANDING, *17th July*.

"MY DEAR FITZGERALD — I have just received a letter from Mr. E. L. LYNCH stating that, although recovered from your wound, you are suffering from typhoid.

"Knowing your ardent military spirit, I must caution you not to retard your cure by over-anxiety. And yet, I trust to having you shortly permanently installed as one of my Staff.

---

* "Genéral SCOTT's partisans complain that MCCLELLAN is very disrespectful in his dealings with General SCOTT," etc. — GUROWSKI's "*Diary*," vol. I, page 103. [This note is not added to justify the opinion, but excuse it.]

"We are resting here most lazily and ignobly. McCLELLAN always has a *hibernation* after every fight. He has talents, perhaps, military, none — nor nerve.

"Yours very truly, etc.,

"P. KEARNY.

"To Captain LOUIS FITZGERALD, *40th N. Y. Vols.*"

[In regard to what has been styled the "KEARNY CORRESPONDENCE," the reader, who is curious, is referred to other sources of information; for instance, the New York Herald of 13th and 21st September, 19th October, 8th November, 1862, etc.; likewise other periodicals. The author has had many letters at his disposal, but has inserted only such as he believed the dead soldier would have no objection to appearing, had he lived. As stated elsewhere, General KEARNY, throughout his life, corresponded regularly with a relative since dead, of whom the writer was heir and executor. During her last illness she destroyed everything from his pen. From what she said, KEARNY's letters must have been intensely interesting.]

Like BLUCHER, like SEYDLITZ, and all natural born soldiers, KEARNY could not live without excitement. He was fond of wine, as a gentleman, a real gentleman, should be, in moderation; of good cheer; of good company; of the society of the accomplished of the opposite sex, and speculation, which in him represented BLUCHER's addiction to games of hazard. In speculation he was eminently successful, for his judgment, despite the vivacity of his temperament, was excellent. Like BLUCHER, also, he was passionately fond of horses, rode like a Centaur and like the wind.* His appearance at middle age was very deceptive. Ordinary observers would have set him down as a light weight, and as slightly built. This was, in reality, the case in 1846–'7, in Mexico (when, at 32, he looked like a youth, with his long flowing hair crowned with a taking cap, and lithe figure set off by his graceful shell-jacket), but not so in 1861–'2. On the contrary, he was a powerfully built man, weighing about one hundred and sixty pounds, and about five feet ten inches in height. His make was perfection for a trooper, his chest massive, his legs sinewy columns. He lay on the embalming-table a perfect specimen of manly strength. He was as striking in his carriage as in his character; his step was as elastic as an Indian's, and in his movements he was lithe and

* Indeed KEARNY often made the exact remark that Captain LAWLEY, the Biographer of SEYDLITZ, attributes to his hero, that "he would never cross a heavy underbred horse again;" selecting always such as had "strong loins and hindquarters, and were fit for galloping, leaping, or any violent exercise." (Pages 82, 83, "General SEYDLITZ, *a Military Biography*." by Captain Hon. ROBERT NEVILLE LAWLER, 2nd Life Guards, London, *printed for private circulation only*, 1852.)

As for BLUCHER, whatever might be shabby or out of order about him, owing to the exigencies of the service, he was always magnificently mounted, and, despite his seventy years, he rode with all the grace, ease and stability of an A 1 horseman in the prime of life active as a panther; in fact, he was as spry as a cat, despite the loss of an arm. Few men were more winning in their address, although he seemed somewhat haughty in his manners. His conversation, always agreeable, at times was perfectly brilliant. To know him was to be won by him. His very vices would have been virtues in cold men. All he did wrong came from a mistaken sense of the highest, or rather, perhaps, the most sensitive honor. On horseback, KEARNY was in his element. On his famous white, or flea-bitten gray (almost white), charger, Moscow — the handsomest horse, perhaps, the writer ever saw — he looked the picture of a cavalier, and was a modern ALEXANDER. In battle he generally rode a smaller, but extremely active black, on which he was killed, and sometimes, on parade, a heavier brown. His magnificent bay colt, conspicuous for its beauty and action even in an engagement, and so remarkable as to attract the fire of the enemy's sharp-shooters at Williamsburg, was killed under KEARNY at Fair Oaks.

Even after he lost his bridle-arm, he continued to be the same fearless rider as before. One-armed, he would dash through the woods or leap walls, ditches and obstructions in such a manner as to astonish the boldest riders, who had the use of all their members; and yet, strange to say, although the loss of his arm did not interfere with his movements while on his feet, when visiting the writer in 1853, he always had to fix a pillow under his left shoulder at night for fear of suffocating if he rolled over on his left side, since from its shortness, or some other difficulty connected with his stump, he could not, then, turn over readily in bed without assistance. Such was his reckless riding that he had several fearful falls, with — not from — horses, since, having but one arm, he could not save himself or even break his fall. Once, in Paris, his horse fell over backward upon him and he struck the back of his head a fearful blow on the pavement. Another time his horse tumbled with him through a bridge, in St Lawrence county, N. Y., and smashed him up generally.

He could swim like a fish, and would undress, plunge in, disport amid the waves, come out and dress himself far better and quicker than most active and adroit men with a whole complement of limbs.

In disposition General KEARNY was most peculiar. His very bravery was of a peculiar stamp. General SCOTT, who knew him well, and had ample opportunities for judging, said: "PHIL. KEARNY was the bravest man I ever knew, and the most perfect soldier." At Williamsburg he dashed alone into the slashing or abatis, which the rebels had cut down for their protection, and called out to his own skirmishers, concealed among the fallen timber, to drive the enemy — using an epithet toward these by no means complimentary — out of their cover. As soon as a few of our men showed themselves, a whole rebel regiment rose on the further edge of the slashing and fired at him deliberately. Notwithstanding their proximity and numbers, neither himself, his clothes, nor his horse was touched.

It has often been asked whether KEARNY cared for the private. Yes! He believed with CHANGARNIER, with whom he had received his baptism of fire in the Atlas, "To eat well and to sleep well are the two most important things in war." Or, to use his own language, to a subordinate on the Peninsula, "Let us have no more of this d——d nonsense (referring to some useless parade). It's well enough when there's nothing else to do; now we are out here to fight, and, when we can't fight, let your men sleep. Feed 'em well, give 'em plenty of sleep, and they'll fight like h—l!" Even in camp his iron discipline was ever subordinated to sanitary considerations. Witness his Circular (dated 3d November, 1861) to commanders of regiments, directing them to be particular and see that their men were not kept out, standing exposed, on the damp ground, to the rigor of the season, on such occasions as were, after all, mere matters form, and intended not for war-time and bivouacs, but peace-times and sheltered quarters. After a combat he was sure to visit and inspect the hospitals of his command to see that the wounded were properly, nay, thoroughly, cared for. He was constantly about his camps, supervising the cooking — an important military art, much neglected and misunderstood in our army — and cleanliness. He was only careless of the lives and blood of his men when great objects were to be accomplished, and the soldier's safety was subordinate to the importance of the event, which depended on the expenditure of men.

Few who read this would believe that KEARNY was a politic man; but he was eminently so. This was doubtless due to the canny Scotch element in him, which he derived from his purest of pure Saxon blood, for in no country is there to be found the truer Saxon than in the lowland shires of Scotland. In fact, strange as it is, there is an immense amount of astuteness in the most royal of animals, which are synonyms for courage and ferocity, even as there was in the boldest of all prime ministers, Cardinal RICHELIEU, and in the most powerful of all the famous Spartan Generals, LYSANDER (died B. C. 395), both of whom knew how, upon occasion, to eke out the lion's skin with that of the fox. And we find in the old Norse, or Berseker (Vikinger), the "world-ravager," and in his descendant, the Norman, the universal conqueror when the mediæval was merging into the modern, an adroit policy which, in a less courageous blood, would have been deemed foreign to a bold nature.

Two anecdotes will demonstrate how utterly devoid of fear KEARNY was, and even as he rose above the infirmities of the flesh, he deemed it to be the duty of every man to tread under foot physical debility, when the need of the hour required moral fortitude. The first was furnished by a gallant young man, Colonel R. TYLDEN AUCHMUTY, the descendant, like KEARNY, of a race of fine soldiers, one of whom took the Cape of Good Hope in 1800, Montevideo in 1807 and Java in 1811, three resplendent exploits in as many different quarters of the globe.

"The following anecdote illustrates General KEARNY's peculiar indifference to death," are the words of this officer, belonging to the staff of the First Division, Fifth Army Corps:

"About noon, during the battle of Malvern Hill, while the troops were lying on the ground for concealment and for protection from the enemy's artillery and sharpshooters, General KEARNY appeared riding slowly along our lines, mounted on his light-gray, almost white, horse. He stopped on the highest point of ground in front of the house used, during the engagement, as division-headquarters, and gazed quietly on the scene. At length he saw me sitting, with the other officers of the staff, on the lawn, and calling me, he remarked that all was quiet on his end of the line, and he had come to see how things were managed in the Fifth Corps. He then proceeded to ask some gossiping questions about affairs in New York, oblivious, to all appearance, that he had become a target for the rebel sharp-shooters posted in the trees and among the holly bushes on our front. I stood perfectly sheltered, the General's horse being between me and the enemy, curious to see how long he would stand the fire without flinching. He chatted on, giving no sign, either in look or manner, that he was aware of the danger, until, remembering that a valuable life was in peril, I remarked, presuming on an old acquaintance, that, were I a superior officer, I should order him back to his command. The General laughed and rode away, not taking a sheltered road in the rear, running parallel with the front, but as he came, along the crest of the hill, between the line of battle and the skirmish-line. Such needless exposure would have been regarded in most men as foolhardy; but no thought of applause or reputation probably for a moment entered General KEARNY's head. He seemed to have learned one of the great lessons of life,

'To dread
The grave as little as his bed.' "

That this is no exaggerated picture is attested by the conviction of his soldiers, and those who served with him. "Be gorra," said a wounded Irish soldier in the field-hospital, "we heard a great many Generals and officers say that they would rather be in a fight than ate their breakfast, but the only one that I ever saw at his ase there, was that one-armed divil of a PHIL. KEARNY; but, then, faith, he seems to think himself made of cast-iron, and from the way he gets us knocked about, be dad, he thinks all the rest of us are of the same matarial." And yet, with all this apparent neck-or-nothing way of "seeking the bubble reputation in the cannon's mouth," there was an awful deal of method in PHIL. KEARNY's madness.

The second was related by a brave staff officer, who served throughout the war, and, in 1862, fought alongside of KEARNY and in sight of him, in HOOKER's division:

"An officer rode up to KEARNY just before Malvern Hill and asked to be relieved on account of illness. 'Sir,' said KEARNY, this is no time for well men to get sick; these are the times, for sick men to get well, sir.'"

"I wish I had seen more of your heroic cousin KEARNY in the field," are the words of a letter written by Major-General A. A. HUMPHREYS, U. S. A., himself of acknowledged ability, of capacity of the highest grade, and for intrepidity among the very bravest of the brave; "I only met him occasionally, and never, to my regret, saw him in action, *where, by universal testimony, he was magnificent.*"

A brevet general officer, C. S. W——, who held a high artillery command at the battle of Williamsburg, and won great commendation for his energy and bravery in that engagement, made a very striking remark in regard to KEARNY. "There were twenty thousand men," said he, "in the army of the Potomac as brave as PHIL. KEARNY, but of all that twenty thousand there was not one whose bravery shone like his upon the battle-field, and told like his upon the men. He seemed to stoop upon the battle-field like an eagle, and his glances to kindle a kindred fire in the faces of all he looked upon, and all who looked upon him." He became at once the cynosure of every eye, the "electric commander," and his confident chivalric bearing diffused a kindred courage; and then his voice, heard amid the roar of battle, was like the note of the Abysinian war-trumpet, known as the "Cry of the Eagle," whose peculiar and exciting tone will rouse the native warrior into vigorous action whenever and wherever it is heard. Even in the time of profound peace let its shrill and startling notes be blown, and the wild soldiery will start up from their repose, brandish and clash their weapons, each limb and feature quivering and kindled at the summons, instant for death or glory. As was said of the great FREDERIC's great SEYDLITZ, such was KEARNY's "upright and proud carriage on horseback" (particularly alluded to by his disciple BIRNEY), "that his figure alone, without the spirit which animated it, would have led a line of cavalry against an enemy."

Then again, KEARNY knew how to appeal to the little peculiarities of the soldier. His dress was taking, and he wore it jauntily. Man, horse, seat, uniform, gesture, tone, all — all were in keeping. He liked to see his Staff and Orderlies dashing, or, as he expressed it, "elegant" and in accordance with his own natty appearance. By the way, he never wore heavy boots coming up above the knees, as he is usually represented, but laced bootees, which were more manageable with his one arm. He insisted that the equipments, in fact, every thing connected with his military family, should always be kept in apple-pie order. Boots and leather had to be well blacked, and brass and steel shine like gold and silver. Moreover, his experience in foreign war enabled him to pay more attention to his creature comforts than our other generals, either of old or new creation. On the Peninsula his *fourgon* (provision cart or wagon) was always up in place in time, and could furnish an appetizing meal when improvident or unacclimated officers were almost starving. His was almost the exceptional case at the beginning of the war, although some of our generals lived and learned, towards the end, how to do it. Nevertheless, KEARNY never allowed his peculiar "impedimenta" to interfere with those of the army proper. He had the knack of making everything work in together nicely like a well adjusted piece of machinery. Thus, in Mexico, he kept a light wagon which followed his movements, not for his own luxurious ease, but for occasion. On the march its seat was usually filled by a sick or wounded soldier, with whom, not malingerers, he was always willing to share his last crust. It was this manly or generous sympathy which redeemed his iron-clad severity and, together with his acknowledged bravery, made him the most popular general in the army, among real soldiers, and the fact that all old soldiers claim to have served with or under him somewhere, or at some time or another, in some kind of a way, proves the truth of the opinion on which the writer started and which induced the preparation of this book, that PHIL. KEARNY was the *beau ideal* of a soldier. He had a Bugler-Boy mounted on a pony of appropriate size. After KEARNY'S death, SICKLES took him. At the latter's headquarters a purse was made up and a beautiful uniform purchased for KEARNY'S little Bugler. He was TAD LIN-

COLN's companion when the President reviewed HOOKER's army. On that occasion TAD rode his pony, and afterward took its ordinary rider back with him to the White House. Subsequently SICKLES' purveyor sent him to school to prepare him for West Point; but, with the assassination of the President, the little Bugler's prospects clouded, and he disappeared in the general gloom.*

To sum up KEARNY's military character — for in that phase of the man alone posterity will know and honor him, as, indeed, any of the great generals of our great civil war — he was what General SCOTT said of him, a "perfect soldier." He had the coolness to plan and the energetic ardor to execute, the fortitude to suffer, and the intrepidity to bear until the moment arrived to pass from inaction to activity as prompt, as vigorous, as well-timed and well-aimed as the leap of the tiger. He comprehended in its full force, the motto of the Algerian army, with which his fighting career begun, "to fight and to suffer." He was wonderful for his conception of the relative value of positions, the importance of reconnoitering, his knowledge of topography and the use he made of it. He filled every position to which he was assigned equally well, and of him might be said, as GRANT is reported to have observed of SHERIDAN: "Give him one man, and with him he will do all that can be done with one man; reinforce him with one hundred thousand, and he will do with them well, all that such a force is capable of accomplishing." Fate denied him a great command and a grand theater, but, judging from his past, he would have risen with responsibility, with duties and with augmented forces and powers.

There is something very curious in regard to the manner of KEARNY's death. The reader will remember that his unhappy fall at Chantilly had nearly occurred to him in the glooming of Glendale and on the night before Solferino.† It was only one

* See letter from PHIL. KEARNY's Little Bugler, pp. 425–'6.

† KEARNY's fearless zeal more than once so involved him in the enemy's lines that he was supposed to be killed or wounded. The occasion referred to in the following notice must have been after Glendale or Malvern. Could it have been at the time when he lost the scabbard of his sword (referred to on a subsequent page, 503–'4), which he is said to have regarded as ominous?

"It is rumored that General KEARNY is killed. Another statement says he is wounded and a prisoner. It is hard to tell, just now, the true state of our missing· but quite a number reported killed and wounded have since turned up all right." — *New York Herald*, Monday, July 7th, 1862, page 1, col. 6.

more of those fearless personal exposures which, under different circumstances, lost him his arm, but won him immortal renown, at the gates of Mexico in 1847, and earned the decoration of the Legion of Honor on the Atlas in 1840,* or on the plains of Lom-

---

* The following note presents to the reader the opening paragraphs — all that relates to military service, proper — of one of the missing Reports of General (then Lieutenant) KEARNY. After a long search, founded on the indications of Major-General GEORGE W. CULLUM, U. S. A., it was discovered in one of the pigeon-holes of the United States Ordnance Department and a copy furnished through the kindness of one, to whom the writer owes many thanks for similar courtesies, Major-General E. D. TOWNSEND, U. S. A. Unfortunately, it was not found until nearly six months after nearly half the book had been stereotyped and some time after the stereotype plates had been actually revised. It is presented in this Summing-up chapter, as a Note, because it is not the Military Report or Statement — so often sought and alluded to — which entered into the details of all that KEARNY witnessed while serving with the French Troops in Africa. Major-General DIX took some steps to obtain information for the writer while he was United States Minister to France, but without result. Two gentlemen, abroad, are now endeavoring to unravel KEARNY's participation in the Algerian and Solferino campaigns; and an Agent has been employed to try and obtain certain works which are supposed to treat of the subject. If any new facts are traced out they will be embodied in a second edition of this Biography:

" ALGIERS, *July 1st*, 1840.

" *To Honorable* J. R. POINSETT, *Secretary of War:*

" SIR — I have the honor to inform you that I am just returned from the late expedition to *Milianah* in the province of *Algiers*, Africa, with the French Army, under the orders of Marshal VALEE.

" As I previously informed you, in a letter of May 8th, 1840, difficulties presented themselves on my first arrival in Africa, from the want of a proper authorization from the French Government, and also from the communication with the army, then in the field, being cut off by the number of Arabs in the plain of the Metidja. This prevented my taking part with the *first* expedition, in May, under the command of the Marshal and with which the DUC D'ORLEANS was also present, as Lieutenant-General commanding a Division. My time, however, was fully occupied in visiting the camps and advanced stations of this province, and in accompanying General ROSTOLAN with a detachment of 1,500 men, sent to Mansajah in charge of a convoy. The 23d of May the army of Marshal VALEE re-entered Algiers, but as the principal objects proposed in their expedition, the taking of *Milianah* and the occupation of the plain of *Cheliff*, had not been achieved, from a want of provisionment for a sufficient time, a second was immediately again set on foot, which opened on the 1st of June with an army of 12,000 men. This, through the intervention of General SCHRAMM, Chief-of-Staff of the Army of Africa, and late Minister of War, I obtained permission to join, and was attached, accordingly, to a Regiment of Cavalry, the 1st Chasseurs d'Afrique. The considerations which first urged my going to Africa promised the study of the cavalry, that, by personal observation, I might assure myself of the manner in which it was conducted in campaigns, as a component part of an entire army; the tactics it generally employed in its movements; and the various details by which a regiment regulated its system of interior police. This last was a study particularly interesting for us, since our cavalry being of but a few years' formation, however perfect might be our practice, there was an incertitude from the short period of our experience: and, if other inducements mingled with the above, it was the expectation in a war of the French with the Arabs, *from the resemblance that must ever exist between all wars with uncivilized nations, of finding something in the service generally that might be of utility to us in our Indian Wars.* Moreover, from the view in which I have looked on the selection of young officers for the mission abroad, I have ever considered that their individual instruction was even more the solicitude of government than the actual improvements they might introduce, and certainly no military information can be so generally instructive as that derived from being with a large army in the field, where large bodies of different Corps are united and wielded for the purposes of war, and where,

bardy in 1859. When he was a youth, he often used to say, that when his hour should come he wanted to die alone; that he wanted to get away in the woods and die in solitude. And exactly so he died. Some invidious person might misinterpret this; but in KEARNY it was in the highest expression of manliness. The moment of death is almost invariably that of physical weakness, and he did not wish to be seen when mind could no longer control matter. The idea was the offspring of a feeling akin to that which animated BEORN, Earl of Northumberland, "Clothe me in my mail, let me die standing, not lying, as a cow dies." Or, like the fever-stricken MAURICE of Saxony, at Zara: "Buckle on my armor, give me my sword, hold me up; let me die standing." Men are not permitted so to die in these prosaic days, and therefore KEARNY, if he could not die in battle, willed to die alone, unwatched, alone with his own thoughts. And so he was permitted to die.

A great many persons have been curious to learn something in regard to KEARNY's religious opinions. All that the writer can say, in reply, is to repeat the General's own answer to a similar question: "Responsibilities," said he, "increase with the development of our knowledge. As for myself, I can answer with the veteran HUGH BRADY, my knapsack is always packed and I hold myself ever ready for the order 'to march.'"* Still,

---

by personal observation, one learns to appreciate and understand those nameless and many wants, the necessities of troops in campaign, which with an army cannot be dispensed with, and which, though not mingling immediately in the combat, tell the most in the general operations of the field, and yet can never be learned by mere theory or study.

"That the utility of this measure of sending officers into Africa is recognized by other governments, is proved by the number of foreign officers who have been here previously, and that there are sixteen Belgian and two Danish officers present at this moment. * * *

"Your obedient servant,

"P. KEARNY, Junior,

"*Lieutenant 1st Regiment Dragoons, U. S. Army.*"

* In religious matters the parallel between KEARNY and BLUCHER and SEYDLITZ holds particularly good; LAWLEY remarks: "In relating the peculiarities of our hero, we omitted to mention one of them, which, contradictory as it may seem, was an esteem of piety, and of the customs of the Church; an esteem which he maintained through the wild years of his youth, and the stormy time of his manhood. Though his own passions were never mastered by these influences, and he may never have had recourse to religion for that purpose, yet he nourished a devoted adoration of the Supreme Being, and during the Seven Years' War invariably caused his horsemen to be encouraged to perseverance and valor, before every engagement, by the field-preacher, who was also commanded to administer spiritual consolation and the holy communion to the wounded and dying.

"He was once during the war riding near the King (FREDERIC THE GREAT), when a regiment of dragoons came forward singing a hymn as they marched. 'They appear to

whatever may have been KEARNY's earlier expressions of opinion as to *his* and THE future, there is little doubt but that his feelings had undergone a great change during the few months — some say weeks — of active service which preceded his death. Chaplain MARKS, who, upon the Peninsula, came to the conclusion that he dreamed that he was a "soldier of destiny," found him in a far different state of mind on the fatal day of Chantilly. Then, for the first time in their intercourse, he spoke on the subject of religion. It has always been the writer's opinion that KEARNY at this time was what the Scotch term *fey*, that is, like many other brave men before him, he had the presentiment of approaching death upon him. This idea has been gathered from remarks of relatives, one a distinguished physician, since dead. The loss of the scabbard of his sword, which he had caused to be prepared for him in Paris, before he sailed for America, impressed him as an omen, foreboding evil. The weight of metal in this sword had been distributed in such a way that it balanced in the hand, so that he could manage both weapons and reins with one arm. When the scabbard was lost, or shot away from his side, he is reported to have remarked (or rather so ran the story), that if it had been picked up and carried into Richmond as a trophy he would follow it thither, as a prisoner; if lost and left upon the battle-field, his body, in like manner, would be found among the dead. If this be true, the

me to be poltroons of horsemen who sing there,' said the King; but SEYDLITZ, although not in the habit of singing, defended the men, and remarked that General VON ZIETEN was accustomed to sing; upon which the King remained silent.

"With the field-preacher of his regiment, who lived as pastor in Ohlau until the year 1791, SEYDLITZ was on friendly terms, and honored him publicly on every occasion. Nor would he permit the younger officers to speak lightly or jocosely against religion and its ministers, although he otherwise cared but little about this faith or practice."

BIESKE, BLUCHER's body-surgeon, declared that "the Prince (BLUCHER) was very religious," and SCHERR corroborates this. It was a wild kind of religion, but far more honest than the majority of the cultivated formalisms, more highly esteemed among men.

KEARNY, again, was very much like BLUCHER in that both men were exceedingly whimsical and given to presentiments. BLUCHER never believed that he would be killed or mortally wounded, and KEARNY held the same idea; certainly down to the period of the POPE campaign. One of KEARNY's forecastings came true in a most extraordinary manner. When he went to Mexico, he said he was certain he would escape with his life but lose his left arm. This was the case. The bravest of men are often subject to these vagaries. Thus STEEDMAN (whom our great GEORGE H. THOMAS declared the best volunteer general he had met), before the Battle of Chickamauga, became impressed that he was going to lose his right leg in that battle. (SHANKS, 285–'6.) Even when his horse was shot under him and he escaped, he did not get over the feeling. Having mounted another a bullet cut his *right*-stirrup-leather, without injuring that leg. Then he considered the risk had occurred, and Fate had been satisfied.

idea must have originated in one of those inexplicable fits of depression of spirits which, at times, come over the bravest of men of strong nervous temperament. KEARNY was peculiarly so. He slept badly. His cousin and Aid said that the General often called him up at night to make coffee for him and amuse him with his conversation. Sometimes KEARNY would listen for hours in silence, and then again, at other times, he would chat away gaily of balls and parties, and the thousand trifling incidents of fashionable life in New York; particularly of fair and agreeable women whom he had met, and gay scenes in which both had participated. Even if the morning found him still awake, he was on the alert and in the saddle as usual, for personal suffering with him was no excuse for neglect of duty. His iron constitution could stand the strain. Often sick, often depressed in spirits, there was a spring of recuperative force in him which enabled him to cry and feel with the brave PLANTAGENET, who fell at Bosworth, "Richard's himself again!" Like the bent bow, he straightened himself out as soon as the constricting cord was loosed.

During the Seven Days' Fight KEARNY seemed to be imbued with the idea that he and his division, in consequence of their fighting properties, their intrepid alacrity, their rugged endurance, would be sacrificed to make up for the shortcomings of others. On one occasion, during the retreat to the James, after a hard fight and harder march, he had returned to his quarters, ordered a repast and a bath, and was prepared to take the latter, when a pressing or peremptory order was delivered, commanding him to return to the front, as regarded the fighting, or rather, rear, for he was protecting the retrograde. Without hesitation, he left the inviting bath and needed food unenjoyed and untasted, but as he swung himself into the saddle he exclaimed, in bitterness of spirit, "My poor, decimated division! my poor, decimated division!"

The death of his idolized and beautiful boy, to whose deathbed he was recalled from the front, in the preceding spring, cast a deep gloom over this otherwise iron-man.* His cousin,

* It was observed by one or another of a small circle terribly abridged, since the General himself fell, by death and sickness, that it sometimes appeared as if PHIL. did not greatly care to live after the death of lovely little "ARCHIE." In some respects, the world was "leer" to KEARNY as it seemed to THEKLA after her MAX PICCOLOMINI plunged headlong on the embattled pikes, and, like a hero, died upon their points.

Dr. ROBERT WATTS, since deceased, the attending physician, says that when he arrived from the army and rushed up stairs, his affliction and the nervousness consequent upon it had taken such possession of him that he acted like a crazy man. He seized the Doctor, with that powerful single right-arm of his, and actually shook him in the violence of his emotion. "You must save him," he cried; "you will save him?" he added, with despairing entreaty. Then, sternly, as if the issues of life and death were as much in his hands as the movements of his division, "You shall save him!" When the fatal bolt fell, and his noble child-boy ARCHIBALD — for he was a grand specimen of childish beauty and strength — died, KEARNY was broken-hearted. Then the iron-man, the man whom the outer world judged unsusceptible of tender feelings, testified what a mine of gentle sympathy lay hidden beneath the rugged exterior of the stern soldier. He crushed down the grief which was rending his own soul. He vailed it from the eyes of the world, and the lion-heart grew tender at the thought of the bereaved mother, * * * at home, without any distraction for her sorrow, while duty, vigilance and activity gave him, from time to time, partial oblivion of the great loss which rushed in upon his unoccupied moments.

* * * * * * * * *

KEARNY was a BAYARD in generosity, in generous sentiments, in patriotic devotion, in his comprehension of the requisites of command and of soldierly duty. On how many occasions, in his short career of generalship, did it occur that to him fell the hard task of retrieving what others had lost or jeopardized. When an incapable BONNIVET had been compelled to place the fate of his army in the hands of BAYARD, that worthy example for all time exclaimed: "It is very late, this confidence, but it matters not; my soul belongs to God, my life to my country. I promise to (do all I can to) save the army at the expense of my remaining days." Was not this exactly the case with KEARNY? Did he not express in language and action all that BAYARD set forth in his words and deeds? "*Dulce et decorum est pro patria mori*," KEARNY wrote home to his friends, and he soon after proved how grand and glorious it was thus to die for the Fatherland. Like QUINTUS CURTIUS, he solved the haruspicial riddle, and leaped full-armed into the gulf to save the State, an example, if equalled, not surpassed throughout the war. Let those who search through ancient and foreign history for examples of patriotic self-sacrifice, learn that our own annals present as notable instances as any in the past or present in other lands. No ARNOLD of Winkelreid was a truer patriot; no BAYARD a more fearless knight; no LEONIDAS a more devoted leader; no HOFER a warmer lover of his country, than that one-armed New Yorker, who sleeps under the shadow of old Trinity's trees, near the original monument of one inspired with kindred ideas, LAWRENCE, famous forever for his dying exhortation, "Don't give up the ship." Not even his warmest eulogist would say PHIL. KEARNY had no equals; but they could justly say he had no superior in our army as a soldier.

Major KEARNY, as a youth, had a rather feminine face, as has been the case with a great many distinguished captains; for instance, Sir CHARLES NAPIER, the conqueror of Scinde; MONTROSE, the flower of loyalty; CLAVERHOUSE, the light of chivalry, and BAYARD, the knight without fear or reproach. With years, his traits seemed attempered into steel through the heat of battle and the cold of resolution and fortitude. Pre-eminently a cavalry leader, he grew to prefer a combined command to that of a grand division of troopers, but he carried into his new sphere, all the fire and decision peculiar to his original training and experience. In this, indeed, he resembled BLUCHER, more than any man in this war, that grand exemplar of old Berseker ardor, just as our FARRAGUT is a perfect antitype of the mediæval Vikinger resolution. An attack of varioloid, as severe in its effects as the more fearful disease of which it is generally considered a milder phase, marked KEARNY deeply. Thenceforward he could not be considered handsome, but, like MIRABEAU, when he spoke, and like CROMWELL, when he acted, there was a manly grandeur, something leonine, which rendered the expression of his face heroic. The fire of battle lit up his eye, and the "cannon fever," as GOETHE expressed it, in the description of his own feelings at Valmy, flushed his cheeks, making his whole face radiant, so that, amid the conflict, KEARNY appeared like a spirit in its element.

His taste in pictures, in statuary, in every thing pertaining to the fine arts, was remarkable, and showed itself in the collection with which he adorned his mansion at Belle Grove, and the patronage he gave to artists.

A lady, who knew General KEARNY intimately when he was a young man, remarked, while this chapter was in the printer's hands: "Well do I remember that his taste in pictures was even then remarkable. There was not a painting of note in his native city, or which was brought to it, that he did not know all about its history and its merits." He was also very curious on statuary and every kind of carved work. He may be said to have had a positive passion for every thing connected with art. This he derived in a measure from an intimate friend (C——D L——N) who died early, but a great deal was natural.

This fondness for the beautiful extended throughout every branch, and manifested itself after he inherited his fortune in his choice of exquisite saddle and driving horses, harness, equipages and every thing connected with a gentleman's establishment.

He wrote fluently and clearly, often as brilliantly as he talked. Some of his letters are perfect specimens of style and different styles. Gathered and edited with judgment, his correspondence, in itself, would furnish a portrait of the man, of his character, of his life, just as MICHELET produced the best biography of LUTHER, simply by culling and arranging his letters on different subjects — arranging them systematically and chronologically with tact and sympathetic feeling. His letters demonstrate that KEARNY had in him not only the powers of a great General, but all that instinctive comprehension of men and things which go so far to produce a statesman, far abler and more fitted to grapple with the astute diplomacy of the old world, than the great majority of those who have directed and controlled the affairs of this, our country.

In a differently constituted man, KEARNY's errors or faults would have been virtues. In this he was a perfect Celt,* and

* After the Mexican war, KEARNY's opinion of the different nationalities which filled our ranks was very much that of Captain DUGALD DALGETTY: "The Irish are pretty fel-

true to his lineage. Irish on his father's side, even his cold, calculating lowland Scotch, pure Saxon blood, scarcely tempered his impetuousness. As in WILLIAM the Conqueror of England, the astuteness which comes from common sense, had been whetted and pointed by the intermixture of Celtic, until it became even more wily than the original. The Norman, with all his Northern phlegm, was the wiliest of men. It was an element of the very Berseker. "In him — HAROLD HARDRADA, poet and warrior, the giant king of Norway, slain by HAROLD, the Great Saxon king of England — we see the race from which the Norman sprung." With all his acknowledged bravery — for he united the courage of the Northman, or Teuto-Scandinavian, with that of the Frank or Teuto-Saxon (not French) — the Norman could plot and scheme with the wiliest. Dissimulation was one of his powers, and guile or craft his wisdom. "He exulted in mastering them (the Welsh, or Outlander) in their own wily statesmanship." Yet a braver race or better soldiers, for their era, never lived. The Saxon was a braver and better man, but it was hard to train him to the *business* of soldiering, since the military service was foreign

---

lows — very pretty fellows — I desire to see none better in the field. I once saw a brigade of Irish, at the taking of Frankfort upon the Oder stand to it with sword and pike until they beat off the Blue and Yellow Swedish brigade, esteemed as stout as any that fought under the immortal GUSTAVUS. And although stout HEPBURN, valiant LUMSDALE, courageous MONROE, with myself and other cavaliers, made entry elsewhere at point of pike, yet, had we all met with such opposition, we had returned with great loss and little profit. Wherefore, these valiant Irishes, being all put to the sword, as is usual in such cases, did nevertheless gain immortal praise and honor; so that, for their sakes, I have always loved and honored those of that nation next to my own country of Scotland."

These were just the ideas of KEARNY. He said he had never seen braver troops than the Irish. When asked where he placed the Americans, then, he answered, "First," and his explanation of this apparent paradox was this: "The Irish," said he, "were as brave as any, but the highest phase of their bravery was a reckless rollicking bravery, without judgment — a perfect practical illustration of their *Faugh-a-ballagh*, 'bludgeon fighting,' as WELLINGTON called it on more than one occasion. American bravery is equal to the Irish as far as a proper contempt or disregard of danger is concerned, but it is rendered more telling by a common sense instinct which teaches our people, where exposure is needless, how to take care of themselves without shirking their work. Order an Irish regiment to charge and it would make the attack brilliantly" — "brilliant" and "elegant" were great words with KEARNY — "but do it in such a manner as to suffer all that could be suffered. Order a regiment of Americans to perform the same work, and they will do it just as thoroughly, but they will do it in such a manner as to inflict all the loss possible upon the enemy and suffer as little as possible themselves. In open ground the only difference would be, that the Americans would take things the most coolly. With regard to the Germans, he exactly agreed with the opinion of GEORGE ALFRED TOWNSEND, as expressed in the "*Campaigns of a Non-combatant*" (p. 233): "The Germans, as a rule, lacked the dash of the Irish troops and the tact of the Americans." TOWNSEND may have heard KEARNY utter these very significant words.

to his nature. Yet necessity made him the *best* soldier the world has ever seen.

Like a great many other distinguished men, PHIL. KEARNY's life had a dawn that did not promise any more than an ordinary day. In early boyhood, his characteristics did not give promise of what he became. Even in youth, they were not more decided in him than in many others who never made any mark. His instincts, it is true, were such that they might be compared to the first streaks of that peculiar light, or to those clouds by which meteorologists or accurate observers of nature are enabled at daybreak to predict the course of the day.

"Fighting JOE" and "Fighting PHIL.," however loudly and bitterly they railed against McCLELLAN, never failed to do their duty, and even more than their whole duty, in carrying out McCLELLAN's plans on the battle-field.

What a contrast, in this respect, is presented by the conduct of more than one of McCLELLAN's favorites or friends, when a similar promptness, energy and patriotism would have saved POPE, and prevented the disasters which clustered "thick as leaves in Vallombrosa," around the second Bull Run battle-field; yes, he would have converted defeat into victory. But it was not to be so. The nation had to pass through this as well as other vicissitudes to ripen the public mind for ideas which came with time, and then the end came. God willed it to be so.

Like BAYARD,* KEARNY died in the forty-eighth year of his

* HENRY THE FOURTH, King of France, decreed that a sum of six hundred dollars, equal to ten times that amount at the present day, should be assigned for the erection of a monument to BAYARD; and the city of Grenoble—about a mile and a-half beyond whose walls he lies buried—voted a fund of two hundred dollars with the same object. As in the case of our glorious New Yorker—HARKEIMER—and a number of other heroes of the Revolution, this project had no further result than the fact that the edict was engrossed. No authentic bust, portrait, or likeness exists of the great soldier, who is one of the chief military glories of a country which takes especial pride in warlike achievements. The first to honor BAYARD, by a monument, was a stranger, neither a relation nor a connection, whose name deserves to be commemorated. At his own expense he placed a memorial tablet over his grave, surmounted by a bust which like the head of ETHAN ALLEN's statue, under the portico of the Vermont State Capitol, at Montpelier, was modelled from traditionary features, not any reliable traits. This patriot's name was SCIPIO DE POLAND, Siegneur * * (illegible.)

This epitaph is prefaced with the truism:

"This stone excels the grave, not the name it bears. Wherever the greatest hero is buried, he constitutes, for himself, the grandest sepulchral monument."

It concludes with another axiom:

"This monument is susceptible of decay, but the ashes it covers live immortal in fame."

In many respects BAYARD and KEARNY closely resembled each other, and, what is strange

age.* "France little knows," said the Constable DE BOURBON, the General of the enemy, when BAYARD's death was announced to him, "how great is the loss she sustains to-day." LEE, an arch-rebel, like BOURBON, like him leading an army against his own country, to which he owed his military education and his elevation, acted as if he felt this, if he did not say it. BAYARD's body, like KEARNY's fell into the hands of the foe, and by them was delivered up with all honor to his own army. Both were embalmed, and their bodies were treated with the utmost respect that could possibly be paid to mortal remains in every locality through which they passed on their way to rest with their fathers. No monument marks the tomb of either,† nor is any needed. Their proudest monument is the

their similarities were those of DESAIX. In youth, as has been said, all three were rather effeminate in appearance, but the deceptive externals concealed a soul of fire, a will of iron, magnanimity, detestation of flattery, horror of humbug, perfect calmness under the most perilous circumstances, ardent valor in the onset, indomitable fortitude in defense, exact obedience in inferior positions and the grandest capacity for superior command. "I have but one master above," said BAYARD, "and he is God in Heaven; I have but one master on earth and he is the King of France;" which, according to the ideas of the day, signified France, that is, his country. Like BAYARD and DESAIX, KEARNY was ever faithful to duty and, like BAYARD, exemplified the latter's proverb in regard to money, that "what the guantlet wins the gorget spends or squanders." especially where comrades, necessitous, sick or wounded soldiers were concerned. All three of these great captains were capable of extricating themselves from almost any danger controllable or resistible by head-work or hand-work, yet all three perished by the shot of a miserable friquenelle or musket, which BAYARD held in especial disgust, as something unworthy of heroic war.—"*Histoire de* PIERRE DU TERRAIL, *dit* LE CHEVALIER BAYARD, *Sans Peur et sans Reproche, par* M. SUGARD DE BERVILLE."

* The plate on his coffin set forth 47 years, 2 months and 30 days.

† Since this was written the writer has learned that a monument has been erected to BAYARD at Grenoble, but none marks his birth or burial place. The same will be exactly the case with KEARNY. New Jersey seems anxious to do him every honor, whereas New York has not taken a single step to perpetuate the memory of a man who did more as a marvellous soldier and military genius to honor his native State and city than any one to whom, as yet, either State or city have ever set up a memorial or raised a monument. The following shows the intention of New Jersey; time can prove if they will advance beyond mere joint resolutions on paper like those in the case of other worthies:

NUMBER ONE.—Joint Resolution relative to appropriation for procuring statues of STOCKTON and KEARNY.

Whereas, By concurrent resolutions of the Senate and General Assembly of the State of New Jersey, unanimously passed on the thirtieth day of January, one thousand eight hundred and sixty-eight, RICHARD STOCKTON, one of the signers of the Declaration of Independence and Major-General PHILIP KEARNY, late of the United States Volunteer Army were designated as the illustrious Jerseymen eminently worthy of national commemoration, whose statues in bronze or marble shall occupy the places reserved for New Jersey in the national statuary hall in Washington.

1. Be it *resolved*, by the Senate and General Assembly of the State of New Jersey, That the treasurer of the State be authorized and directed to pay, under the direction of the committee hereinafter selected, or a majority of them, the sum of ten thousand dollars ($10,000), or so much thereof as may be required to procure the statues above indicated, the civilian marble, the soldier bronze.

place they occupy in the hearts of their countrymen. Both will live in the affections of the American people as long as they have a flag and a country.

Like the Suabian, or German hero, *the* Infantry General of the first half of the sixteenth century, FREUNDSBERG, or GEORGE of Fronsperger — the "Alp-passer" — most famous, perhaps, for his exhortation to LUTHER* — and many other eminent soldiers, among these CHARLES XII, of Sweden, BAYARD had a great detestation of fire-arms, as if, according to one of his biographers, he felt a presentiment he was to owe his death as he did, to a bullet: one cut his back-bone in two. It was a shame, he said, that a brave man should be exposed to die by a miserable pop-gun ("*friquenelle*"), against the effect of which he cannot defend himself.† When bullets came in, the number of victims to cowardly snap-shots, or deliberate, murderous sharpshooting only augmented, and leaders experienced the same fate which had previously been distributed more

---

2. And be it *resolved*, That a joint committee of three from the Senate and five from the House of Assembly (to be appointed by the presiding officer of each house), and of which the President of the Senate and Speaker of the House shall be one, be appointed to carry out the object above contemplated.

3. And be it *resolved*, That the committee or a majority of them, shall make report in writing of their proceedings in the premises at the meeting of the next Legislature.

Approved April 18th, 1868.

NUMBER SIX. — Joint Resolution, directing the payment of three hundred dollars for the portrait of the late Major-General PHILIP KEARNY.

1. Be it *resolved*, by the Senate and General Assembly of the State of New Jersey, That the Treasurer of this State be directed to pay upon the warrant of the Comptroller, to WILLIAM J. ROBERTS, three hundred dollars, in payment for his portrait of the late Major-General PHILIP KEARNY, which has been purchased by order of the House of Assembly and placed in the Assembly Chamber.

Approved April 3, 1868.

* Little monk! little monk!" said he, patting LUTHER on the shoulder as he was about to appear before the Diet at Worms, "thou goest now upon the way to make such a stand as neither I and many other colonels (veteran commanders) have not made, even in our most desperate dispositions for battles."

† A bullet, it is true, was a very mean way of finishing a hero: nevertheless, a tile or stone, out of a sling, or an arrow, or a javelin, or a cross-bow bolt, was only another primitive form of the same kind of missile; and yet, so died ACHILLES, ABIMILECH, GOLIATH, PYRRHUS, EPAMINONDAS, RICHARD the lion-hearted, BOURBON, MONTMORENCI, NELSON, ROSS, and a thousand other demi-gods of sacred and profane, ancient and mediæval story. This remark of BAYARD recalls that of the Fop, in SHAKESPEARE (I. HENRY IV, 1, 3), which so excited PERCY's indignation, when he declared

"That it was a great pity, so it was,
That villainous saltpeter should be digg'd
Out of the bowels of the harmless earth,
Which many a good, tall fellow had destroy'd
So cowardly; and, but for these vile guns,
He would himself have been a soldier."

liberally among the led. Now-a-days — when bullets are whistling and screaming by, unseen, in myriads — it takes a much bolder man "to adventure" in the forefront of battle, and perform deeds of "high emprise," like KEARNY did, than of old when arrows could be stopped by leather shield or steel harbergeon, or when javelin could be turned aside by jack or dodged or cleft in twain by a battle-ax or falchion.

If valor could have availed against a Minie-ball, KEARNY would have been invulnerable. His reputation as "the bravest of the brave" is inexpugnable. The motto on the memorial of SEYDLITZ, in the Church at Ohlau, KEARNY'S patriotic ardor made his own —

"Unsterblichkeit ist dein Eigenthum."
"IMMORTALITY IS THY PREROGATIVE."

No death on the battle-field inspired more real poetry than KEARNY'S. Truly was it sung:

As man may, he fought his fight,
Proved his truth by his endeavor;
Let him sleep in solemn night,
Sleep forever and forever.
Lay him low!

Low, indeed, the head to plan and hand to execute, but high the memory of his deeds, glorious the light of his example — high as the highest as a soldier, bright as the brightest as a patriotic man.

"Hush, the Dead March wails in the people's ears;
The dark crowd moves, and there are sobs and tears;
The black earth yawns, the mortal disappears."

"But speak no more of his renown,
Lay your earthly fancies down,
And in the vast cathedral leave him,
GOD ACCEPT HIM, CHRIST RECEIVE HIM."

www.ingramcontent.com/pod-product-compliance
Lightning Source LLC
LaVergne TN
LVHW021304110826
845150LV00003B/481
9781425559649